A Comprehensive Russian Grammar

Blackwell Reference Grammars

General Editor: Glanville Price

The *Blackwell Reference Grammars* are essential companions for students of modern languages at senior secondary school and undergraduate level. The volumes provide a comprehensive survey of the grammar of each language and include plentiful examples. The series will cover the major European languages, including French, German, Spanish, Portuguese, and Russian.

Already published

A Comprehensive French Grammar, Fifth Edition
Glanville Price

A Comprehensive Russian Grammar, Second Edition
Terence Wade
Advisory Editor: Michael J. de K. Holman

A Comprehensive Spanish Grammar
Jacques de Bruyne
Adapted, with additional material, by Christopher J. Pountain

A Comprehensive Welsh Grammar
David A. Thorne

Colloquial French Grammar: A Practical Guide
Rodney Ball

In preparation

A Comprehensive German Grammar
Jonathan West

A Comprehensive Portugese Grammar
Steven Parkinson

A Comprehensive Ancient Greek Grammar
David Langslow

A Comprehensive Latin Grammar
Jonathan Powell

Grammar Workbooks

A Russian Grammar Workbook
Terence Wade

A French Grammar Workbook
Dulcie Engel, George Evans, and Valerie Howells

A Spanish Grammar Workbook
Esther Santamaría Iglesias

A Comprehensive Russian Grammar

Second Edition, revised and expanded

Terence Wade

Edited by Michael J. de K. Holman

Blackwell
Publishing

© 1992, 2000 by T. L. B. Wade

BLACKWELL PUBLISHING
350 Main Street, Malden, MA 02148-5020, USA
9600 Garsington Road, Oxford OX4 2DQ, UK
550 Swanston Street, Carlton, Victoria 3053, Australia

The right of T.L.B. Wade to be identified as the Author of this Work has been
asserted in accordance with the UK Copyright, Designs, and Patents Act 1988.

First published 1992
Second edition published 2000

9   2007

Library of Congress Cataloging-in-Publication Data

Wade, Terence Leslie Brian.
    A comprehensive Russian grammar / Terence Wade; edited by Michael J. de K.
Holman. — 2nd ed.
        p.   cm. — (Blackwell reference grammars)
    Includes bibliographical references and index.
    ISBN 0-631-21891-2 (alk. paper) — ISBN 0-631-20757-0 (pbk.: alk. paper)
    1. Russian language—Grammar.   I. Holman, Michael (Michael J. de K.)
II. Title.   III. Series.

PG2106.W33   2000
491.782'421—dc21   99–047633

ISBN-13: 978-0-631-21891-3 (alk. paper) — ISBN-13: 978-0-631-20757-3 (pbk.:
alk. paper)

A catalogue record for this title is available from the British Library.

Set in 10 on 10.5 pt Times
by Open World Data Ltd
Printed and bound in Singapore
by Fabulous Printers Pte Ltd

The publisher's policy is to use permanent paper from mills that operate a
sustainable forestry policy, and which has been manufactured from pulp processed
using acid-free and elementary chlorine-free practices. Furthermore, the publisher
ensures that the text paper and cover board used have met acceptable environmental
accreditation standards.

For further information on
Blackwell Publishing, visit our website:
www.blackwellpublishing.com

Contents

Introduction

Pronunciation

The Noun

Declension

The Pronoun

The Adjective

The Long Form of the Adjective

The Superlative Degree of the Adjective

The Numeral

Cardinal, Collective and Indefinite Numerals

Ordinal Numerals

Special Functions of Numerals

The Verb

Conjugation

Reflexive Verbs

Impersonal Constructions

Participles

Spatial Prepositions

*Prepositions that Denote the Position of an Object in Relation to
Another Object (Behind, in Front of, Below, on Top of etc.), or
Movement to or from that Position*

*Prepositions that Denote Spatial Closeness to an Object, Movement
Towards or Away from an Object, or Distance from an Object*

Prepositions that Denote Along, Across, Through a Spatial Area

Prepositions that Denote Spatial Limit

Temporal Prepositions

The Use of Prepositions to Denote Action in Relation to Various Time Limits

Other Meanings

The Conjunction

The Particle

Word Order

To May

Preface

The *Comprehensive Russian Grammar* is meant for English-speaking pupils and students of Russian at the post-introductory stage. It is also a reference aid for teachers, translators and interpreters and others who use the language in a professional capacity.

The first new reference grammar of Russian to have been published in the United Kingdom since the 1950s, it is based on personal research and observation, long experience of teaching Russian at all levels from beginners up to the Honours Degree and the Civil Service Interpretership, and on a close study of reference materials by Russian, British and American linguists.

The approach is descriptive throughout, and rules of usage are constantly measured against current practice as reflected in contemporary journalistic and literary sources. It is entirely practical in conception and design and has no pretensions to theoretical disquisition. Particular emphasis is laid on problems which are of especial difficulty for the English speaker.

The grammar provides comprehensive guidance to usage, with exhaustive tabulated material and succinct explanations. It is presented in 484 sections which are further subdivided to take account of finer points of usage. It provides mainstream rules for quick reference, as well as access to the subtleties of the language for those who need more detailed information.

The intention is to provide the essential facts of the language and to tackle perennial problems such as adverbs and pronouns in -то and -нибудь, agreement, animacy, conjugation, declension, gerunds, long and short adjectives, numerals, participles, the partitive genitive, verbs of motion, and so on, as well as problems which have often received less attention: the gender of acronyms, alphabetisms, soft-sign nouns, the differences between в/на and other key prepositions, and between тóже and тáкже, the use of capital letters, particles, the principles of word order etc. Treatment of verbal aspect differentiates usage in the past, future, imperative and infinitive, thus throwing the rules into sharper relief. Special emphasis is given to stress patterns.

Ease of reference is assured by comprehensive indexing of subject headings and Russian words, and by general adherence to the alphabetic principle throughout.

Preface to the Second Edition

A Comprehensive Russian Grammar was first published in 1992, since when the book has been reprinted eight times, on most occasions with minor amendments. The present, second, edition of the *Grammar* takes account of the very considerable changes, both social and linguistic, that have taken place in the post-Soviet period.

The transliteration system of the Library of Congress has been added to those enumerated in section **1**, but that of the British Standards Institute continues to be used throughout the *Grammar*.

Amendments have been made to sections dealing with all parts of speech, with pronunciation, the noun, the adjective, the verb and the preposition most affected.

There are three entirely new, substantial sections on word formation in the Russian noun. These comprise sections **27** (general), **28** (prefixation) and **29** (suffixation), the sections that formerly bore these numbers having been conflated with earlier sections to make room for the new material. These sections have not been curtailed in any way.

Some sections on pronunciation have been amplified by additional examples, sometimes involving new lexis, e.g. при́нтер 'printer', Интерне́т 'Internet' and экстрасе́нс 'psychic' in section **7**. Changes have also been made to sections **12**, **13**, and **15** (on the pronunciation of -чн-, consonants omitted in pronunciation, and stress, respectively).

Section **17** (on the use of capital and small letters in titles and names) has been completely rewritten in the light of changes that have occurred over the past few years. Many of the changes involve new names such as Росси́йская Федера́ция 'Russian Federation' and Сове́т Федера́ции

'Council of the Federation', but historicisms such as Советский Союз 'Soviet Union' will clearly remain current for some time to come and have been retained. Other changes result from new official attitudes, affecting, for example, the spelling of the names of deities.

Other amended sections on the noun take account of recent neologisms, e.g. флоппи 'floppy disk', папарацци 'paparazzi' (section **36**), ВИЧ 'HIV', СКВ 'freely-convertible currency' (section **40**), забастком 'strike committee' (section **42**), etc. Most amendments have grammatical implications, e.g. the genitive plurals байт 'byte' and бит 'bit' (section **56**), the plurals технологии 'technologies' and экономики 'economies' (section **48**), the use of the accusative case in заказал вино 'ordered some wine' (section **83**), and so on, others reflect name changes of the past decade (e.g. the replacement of the former place name Киров 'Kirov', section **71**).

Amendments to the sections on adjectives also reflect changes in nomenclature, e.g. думский 'Duma' (adj.), or amplify extant categories, e.g. лизинговый 'leasing' (adj.) (both section **148**).

Changes to the sections on the verb include an increase in the number of biaspectuals with alternative perfectives (e.g. профинансировать 'to finance', section **237**), and the amplification of other sections.

Section **404** on the buffer vowel -o in prepositions has been expanded, as has section **424** on через and по in the meaning 'across', and section **451** on по with nouns that denote means of communication (по мобильному 'on a mobile', по факсу 'by fax'), including variant usage in conjunction with телевидение 'television'. The preposition порядка in the meaning 'approximation' has been added to section **445**.

The bibliography has been expanded to include new dictionaries, grammars and other works of the mid- to late 1990s, especially those specifically describing the language at the end of the twentieth century (Comrie, Stone and Polinsky, Dulichenko, Karaulov, Kostomarov, Offord, Rakhmanova and Suzdal'tseva, Ryazanova-Clarke and Wade, Shaposhnikov and Zemskaya), as well as new journals, newspapers, magazines and prose works.

A glossary of grammatical terms has also been included in the new edition. The table of contents and indexes have been revised to take account of new material and revised pagination.

TW, Glasgow 2000

Acknowledgements

I wish to thank the following for advising on aspects of the book: Natalya Bogoslavskaya (University of Leeds), Sheelagh Graham (University of Strathclyde), Larissa Ryazanova (Edinburgh University), who also read the page proofs, Professor Dennis Ward (University of Edinburgh), Nijole White (University of Strathclyde); also Dr Marina Kozyreva (Moscow and Leeds Universities) for reading through a late draft and writing a helpful report. I am particularly grateful to my specialist readers, Dr R. Bivon (University of Essex, formerly of the University of East Anglia) and Dr Svetlana Miloslavskaya (Pushkin Institute, Moscow) for writing detailed reports at an early stage, thus enabling me to make substantial improvements. I also valued a lengthy consultation with Svetlana Miloslavskaya which allowed me to make amendments to the final draft. My editor, Professor Michael Holman (University of Leeds), supplied helpful and detailed critical analyses of each chapter during the writing of the grammar and I am most grateful to him for his support and encouragement and for the many insights that he provided. I should also like to thank Professor Glanville Price (University College of Wales), general editor of Blackwell's series of grammars of European languages, for his comments on some early chapters, particularly that on verbs. Any errors are, of course, entirely the responsibility of the author.

I wish to thank my late mother, who first encouraged me to learn Russian.

The book is dedicated to my wife, May, who bore with me throughout the thousands of hours and nine drafts that went into this grammar.

Finally, I would like to express my appreciation to the publishers of the books I was able to consult (see bibliography): Akademiya nauk, Birmingham University, Collets International, CUP, Dover Publications,

Durham University, Harcourt Brace Jovanovich, Hutchinson, Kniga, MGU, Nauka, Oliver and Boyd, OUP, Pan Books, Pergamon, Progress Publishers, Prosveshchenie, Russkii yazyk, Sovetskaya entsiklopediya, University of East Anglia, University of London Press, Vysshaya shkola.

TW

Acknowledgements to the Second Edition

I am grateful to Russian colleagues who have helped with the new edition, particularly Professor V. G. Kostomarov, Rector of the Pushkin Institute, Moscow, for allowing me to carry out research at the Institute on a number of occasions.

I wish to thank Professor G. Corbett (University of Surrey) and Professor B. Scherr (Dartmouth College) for their valuable comments on the first edition of the *Grammar* and suggestions for improving the second.

I also wish to express my thanks to Mrs Nijole White, my colleague at the University of Strathclyde, who read the sections on word formation in the Russian noun and gave valuable advice on presentation.

I should also like to thank editorial and production staff at Blackwell: Tessa Harvey, Louise Spencely, Lorna Berrett, Brian Johnson, Helen Rappaport, and proof reader Penny Dole for their work in producing this second edition of the book.

Above all I am again indebted to my editor, Professor Michael Holman, of the University of Leeds, who has supplied unstinting supportive and professional assistance throughout, especially in preparing the new sections on word formation in the Russian noun.

Abbreviations

The following abbreviations are used:

acc.	accusative
adj.	adjective
cf.	compare
dat.	dative
f.	feminine
fig.	figurative
gen.	genitive
imper.	imperative
impf.	imperfective
infin.	infinitive
instr.	instrumental
lit.	literally
m.	masculine
n.	neuter
nom.	nominative
part.	participle
pf.	perfective
pl.	plural
prep.	prepositional
sing.	singular
theatr.	theatrical
trans.	transitive

Introduction

1   The Cyrillic alphabet

(1) The Russian Cyrillic alphabet contains 33 letters, including 20 consonants, 10 vowels, a semi-consonant/semi-vowel (**й**), a hard sign (**ъ**) and a soft sign (**ь**).

(2) There are a number of different systems for transliterating the Cyrillic alphabet. Three of these, that of the International Organization for Standardization (ISO), that of the British Standards Institution (BSI) (whose system is used throughout this *Grammar*), and that of the Library of Congress (LC) are listed alongside the Cyrillic alphabet, as well as the Russian names of the individual letters:

Cyrillic letters	Letter name	ISO	BSI	LC
Аа	[a]	a	a	a
Бб	[бэ]	b	b	b
Вв	[вэ]	v	v	v
Гг	[гэ]	g	g	g
Дд	[дэ]	d	d	d
Ее	[e]	e	e	e
Ёё	[ё]	ë	ë	ë
Жж	[жэ]	ž	zh	zh
Зз	[зэ]	z	z	z
Ии	[и]	i	i	i
Йй	[и кра́ткое]	j	ĭ	ĭ
Кк	[ка]	k	k	k
Лл	[эль]	l	l	l

Cyrillic letters	Letter name	ISO	BSI	LC
Мм	[эм]	m	m	m
Нн	[эн]	n	n	n
Оо	[о]	o	o	o
Пп	[пэ]	p	p	p
Рр	[эр]	r	r	r
Сс	[эс]	s	s	s
Тт	[тэ]	t	t	t
Уу	[у]	u	u	u
Фф	[эф]	f	f	f
Хх	[ха]	h/ch	kh	kh
Цц	[цэ]	c	ts	t͡s
Чч	[че]	č	ch	ch
Шш	[ша]	š	sh	sh
Щщ	[ща]	šč	shch	shch
Ъъ	[твёрдый знак]	”	”	”
Ыы	[ы]	y	ȳ	y
Ьь	[мя́гкий знак]	’	’	’
Ээ	[э оборо́тное]	ě	é	ė
Юю	[ю]	ju	yu	i͡u
Яя	[я]	ja	ya	i͡a

Note

(a) Certain letters with diacritics and accents which appear in the standard BSI system (ё for ё, ĭ for й, é for э, ȳ for ы) are used without diacritics and accents here.

(b) The ligatures used over certain combinations of letters in the standard LC system (t͡s, i͡u i͡a) are often omitted by other users.

(c) An apostrophe (’) for the soft sign (ь) is used only in the bibliography.

(d) The endings -ый/ -ий are rendered as -y in names.

2   The international phonetic alphabet (IPA)

The following symbols from the IPA are used in the Introduction for the phonetic transcription of Russian words.

Vowels

i   as in ил   [il]
ɨ   as in пыл   [pɨl]
ɪ   as the first vowel in игла́ [ɪˈgla]
ɪ̵   as the first vowel in дыра́ [dɪ̵ˈra]

ɛ	as in лес	[l̦ɛs]
e	as in весь	[ve̦ș]
a	as in рад	[rat]
æ	as in пять	[p̦æț]
ʌ	as the first vowel in оди́н	[ʌˈd̦in]
ə	as the first vowel in хорошо́	[xərʌˈʃo]
o	as in мох	[mox]
ö	as in тётя	[ˈțöțə]
u	as in бук	[buk]
ü	as in ключ	[kl̦üțʃ]

Semi-consonant/semi-vowel

j	as in бой	[boj]

Consonants

p	as in пол	[pol]
p̦	as in пёс	[p̦os]
b	as in бак	[bak]
b̦	as in бел	[b̦ɛl]
t	as in том	[tom]
ț	as in тем	[țɛm]
d	as in дом	[dom]
d̦	as in день	[d̦en̦]
k	as in как	[kak]
k̦	as in кем	[k̦ɛm]
g	as in гол	[gol]
ɡ	as in гид	[ɡit]
f	as in фло́ра	[ˈflorə]
f̦	as in фен	[f̦ɛn]
v	as in вот	[vot]
v̦	as in вино́	[v̦ɪˈno]
s	as in сам	[sam]
ș	as in сев	[șɛf]
z	as in зуб	[zup]
z̦	as in зе́бра	[ˈz̦ɛbrə]
ʃ	as in шум	[ʃum]
ʒ	as in жук	[ʒuk]
x	as in хам	[xam]
x̦	as in хи́мик	[ˈx̦im̦ɪk]
ʃʃ	as in щека́	[ʃʃɪˈka]
ts	as in цех	[tsɛx]

tʃ	as in чин	[tʃin]
m	as in мол	[mol]
m̥	as in мел	[m̥ɛl]
n	as in нос	[nos]
n̥	as in нет	[n̥ɛt]
l	as in лак	[lak]
l̥	as in ляг	[l̥ak]
r	as in рак	[rak]
r̥	as in река́	[r̥ɪ'ka]
j	as in я́ма	['jamə]

Pronunciation

3   Stressed vowels

Russian has ten vowel letters:

а	э	ы	о	у
я	е	и	ё	ю

(1) **А** is pronounced with the mouth opened a little wider than in the pronunciation of 'a' in English 'father', e.g. зал [zal] 'hall'.

(2) **Э** is pronounced like 'e' in 'end', but the mouth is opened a little wider and the tongue is further from the palate than in articulating English 'e' in 'end', e.g. э́то ['ɛtə] 'this is'.

(3) **У** is pronounced with the tongue drawn back and the lips rounded and protruding. The sound is similar to but shorter than the vowel in 'school', e.g. бук [buk] 'beech'.

(4) **О** is also pronounced with rounded and protruding lips, but to a lesser extent than in the pronunciation of **у**. The sound is similar to the vowel in English 'bought', e.g. бок [bok] 'side'.

(5) The vowel **ы** is pronounced with the tongue drawn back as in the pronunciation of **у,** but with the lips spread, not rounded or protruding, e.g. сын [sɨn] 'son'.

(6) The vowels **я** [ja], **е** [jɛ], **ё** [jo] and **ю** [ju] are 'iotated' variants of a, э, o and y (i.e. they are pronounced like those vowels preceded by the sound [j]). The vowel **и** resembles 'ea' in English 'cheap', but is a 'closer' sound, that is, the centre of the tongue is nearer to the hard palate in articulation, e.g. мир [m̥ir] 'world, peace'. After a preposition

or other word ending in a hard consonant, however, stressed initial **и** is pronounced [ɨ]: от Игоря [ʌ't ɨɡəɾə], cf. also **4** (4) note.

Note
Vowels can be classified as:

(a) **back** vowels (pronounced with the back part of the tongue raised towards the back of the palate): **у/ю, о/ё;**

(b) **central** vowels (pronounced with the central part of the tongue raised towards the central part of the palate): **ы, а/я;**

(c) **front** vowels (pronounced with the central part of the tongue raised towards the front of the palate: **и, э/е.**

4   Unstressed vowels

(1) Unstressed у, ю, и and ы

The sound of unstressed **у/ю** is similar to that of English 'u' in 'put': дугá [du'ɡa] 'arc', юлá [ju'la] 'top'. Unstressed **и** and **ы** are shorter and pronounced in a more 'relaxed' fashion than their stressed equivalents: игрá [ɪ'ɡra] 'game', былá [bɨ'la] 'was'. **Ё** does not appear in unstressed position. The other vowels are 'reduced' in unstressed position.

(2) Reduction of o and a

(i) The vowels **o** and **a** are pronounced as [o] and [a] only when they appear in stressed position: дом [dom], зал [zal]. In unstressed position they are reduced, **o** being the vowel most affected by various forms of reduction resulting from its position in relation to the stress.
(ii) In pre-tonic position or as the unstressed initial letter in a word **o** and **a** are pronounced [ʌ]: потóм [pʌ'tom] 'afterwards', одúн [ʌ'd̡in] 'one', парóм [pʌ'rom] 'ferry', акýла [ʌ'kulə] 'shark'. This also applies to pre-tonic prepositions: под мóрем [pʌ'd̡ m oɾum] 'under the sea', над дóмом [nʌ'd̡ doməm] 'above the house'. The combinations **aa, ao, oa, oo** are pronounced [ʌʌ], e.g. сообразúть [sʌʌbrʌ'z̡it̡] 'to comprehend'.

(iii) In pre-pre-tonic position (except as initial letters, see (ii)) or in post-tonic position both vowels are pronounced [ə]: thus парохóд [pərʌ'xot] 'steamer', молодóй [məlʌ'doj] 'young', рáно ['ranə] 'early', вúлка ['vilkə] 'fork'. This also applies to prepositions (под водóй [pəd vʌ'doj] 'under water', над головóй [nəd ɡəlʌ'voj] 'overhead') and to the initial letters of words governed by prepositions (в огорóде [v əɡʌ'rod̡ɪ] 'in the market garden' (cf. огорóд [ʌɡʌ'rot] 'market garden')).

Note

(a) Unstressed **o** is pronounced [o] in a number of words of foreign origin (кака́о 'cocoa', ра́дио 'radio', ха́ос 'chaos'), with an optional [o] in ве́то 'veto', досье́ 'dossier', шоссе́ 'highway' and some other words. In certain cases, pronunciation is differentiated stylistically. The pronunciation [ʌ] in words such as поэ́т 'poet' and шоссе́ 'highway', said to be the more colloquial variant, has gained ground in educated speech and is found even in the pronunciation of foreign names such as Шопе́н [ʃʌ'pɛn]/[ʃo'pɛn] 'Chopin', especially where these have gained common currency (e.g. Тольятти 'Togliatti'). However, [o] is retained in words where it follows another vowel: три́о 'trio'.

(b) The vowel **a** is pronounced [ɪ] in pre-tonic position after **ч** and **щ**: thus часы́ [tʃɪ'sɨ] 'clock', щади́ть [ʃʃɪ'ditʲ] 'to spare'. The pronunciation of unstressed **a** as [ɨ] after **ж, ш** is now limited for many speakers to жале́ть [ʒɨ'letʲ] 'to regret', к сожале́нию [k̂ sɐʒɨ'lenʲju] 'unfortunately' and end-stressed plural oblique cases of ло́шадь 'horse', e.g. gen. pl. лошаде́й [lɐʃɨ'dej]. **Ца** is pronounced [tsɨ] in the oblique cases of some numerals: двадцати́ [dvɐtsɨ'tʲi] 'twenty' (gen.).

(3) Reduction of e and я

(i) In pre-tonic position both **e** and **я** are pronounced [(j)ɪ]: язы́к [jɪ'zɨk] 'language', перево́д [pʲɪrɪ'vot] 'translation'. Thus, разреди́ть 'to thin out' and разряди́ть 'to unload' have the same pronunciation.

(ii) In post-tonic position **e** is pronounced [ɪ] (по́ле ['polʲɪ] 'field'), while **я** is usually pronounced [ə] (ды́ня ['dɨɲə] 'melon'). However, post-tonic **я** is pronounced [ɪ] before a soft consonant (па́мять ['pamʲɪtʲ] 'memory') and in non-final post-tonic position (вы́глянул ['vɨɡlʲɪnul] 'looked out').

(4) Reduction of э

Э is pronounced [ɪ] in unstressed position (эта́п [ɪ'tap] 'stage').

Note

Unstressed initial **и** and **э** and conjunction **и** are pronounced [ɨ] after a preposition or other word ending in a hard consonant (see 3 (6)): в Ита́лию [v ɨ'talʲju] 'to Italy', брат идёт к Ива́ну [brat ɨ'dot k̂ ɨ'vanu] 'my brother is on his way to see Ivan', над эква́тором [nəd ɨ'kvatərəm] 'above the equator'. **И** is also pronounced [ɨ] in certain stump compounds, e.g. Госизда́т [ɡosɨ'zdat] 'State Publishing House'.

5   Hard and soft consonants

With the exception of **ж, ц** and **ш**, which are invariably hard, and **ч** and **щ**, which are invariably soft, all Russian consonants can be pronounced hard or soft.

(1) Hard consonants

(i) A hard consonant is a consonant which appears at the end of a word (e.g. the **м** in дом [dom] 'house', the **т** in вот [vot] 'here is') or is followed by **а, ы, о** or **у** (**э** appears only as an *initial* letter, except in acronyms such as нэп 'NEP' (New Economic Policy) and rare words such as сэр 'sir'). Thus, the consonants in the words голова́ [gəlʌ'va] 'head', мы́ло ['mɨlə] 'soap' and ду́ма ['dumə] 'thought' are all hard.

(ii) Most hard consonants, e.g. **б, в, г, з, к, м, п, с, ф,** are pronounced in similar fashion to their English counterparts, i.e. 'b' in 'bone', 'v' in 'van', 'g' in 'gone', 'z' in 'zone', 'c' in 'come', 'm' in 'money', 'p' in 'pun', 's' in 'sun', 'f' in 'fun'. However, **к** and **п** (and **т**; see (iii)) lack the slight aspiration of 'k', 'p' and 't'.

(iii) In pronouncing the dentals **д** [d], **т** [t] and **н** [n], the tip of the tongue is pressed against the back of the upper teeth in the angle between teeth and gums.

(iv) **Р** is a moderately 'trilled' [r]. **Л** is pronounced with the tip of the tongue in the angle between the upper teeth and the gum, and the middle of the tongue curved downwards. The 'l' sound in English 'bubble' is a good starting-point for the pronunciation of this letter.

(v) **X** sounds as 'ch' in 'loch' or German 'acht', but is formed a little further forward in the mouth.

(vi) Unlike other consonants, **ж, ц** and **ш** are always pronounced hard (see, however, note (b), below). This means in practice that the vowels **е** and **и** are pronounced as **э** and **ы** after **ж, ц** and **ш** (жест [ʒɛst] 'gesture', жир [ʒɨr] 'fat', цех [tsɛx] 'workshop', цирк [tsɨrk] 'circus', шест [ʃɛst] 'pole', маши́на [mʌ'ʃɨnə] 'car') while **ё** is pronounced as **о** after **ж** and **ш** (жёлоб ['ʒoləp] 'groove', шёлк [ʃolk] 'silk'). A soft sign (as in рожь [roʃ] 'rye') has no softening effect on the pronunciation of **ж** or **ш**.

Note
(a)   Neither a soft sign nor the vowel **ё** can be written after **ц**.

(b) **Ш** is sounded hard in the loan words парашют [pərʌˈʃut] 'parachute' and брошюра [brʌˈʃurə] 'brochure', while **ж** is pronounced soft in жюри [ʒüˈr̡i] 'jury'.

(2) Soft consonants

(i) A soft consonant is a consonant (other than **ж, ц** or **ш**) followed by a soft sign, e.g. **ль** in сталь 'steel', or by **я, е, и, ё** or **ю**. Thus, the initial consonants in мята [ˈm̡atə] 'mint', лес [l̡ɛs] 'forest', пил [p̡il] 'was drinking', нёбо [ˈn̡obə] 'palate' and дюна [ˈd̡unə] 'dune' are all soft.

(ii) Soft consonants are pronounced with the centre of the tongue raised towards the hard palate, as in articulating **и,** for example. Correct rendering of the vowels **я** [ja], **е** [jɛ], **и** [i], **ё** [jo] and **ю** [ju] will assist in the articulation of the preceding soft consonants. Soft [l̡] as in только 'only' is similar to 'll' in 'million', with the tip of the tongue against the teeth-ridge and the front of the tongue pressed against the hard palate.

(iii) Soft consonants may also appear at the end of words, e.g. **пь** and **ть** in топь [top̡] 'swamp' and мать [mat̡] 'mother'; the final sounds in these words are similar to those of the initial consonants in 'pure' and 'tune' (standard British English 'Received Pronunciation').

(iv) Unlike other consonants, **ч** and **щ** are always pronounced soft. In practice this means that the vowels **a, o** and **y** are pronounced as [ja], [jo] and [ju] following these consonants (час 'hour', чопорный 'prim', чугун 'cast iron', пощада 'mercy', щука 'pike').

(v) The consonant **щ** is pronounced as a long soft **ш** [ʃʃ] (e.g. защищать [zəʃʃɪˈʃʃæt̡] 'to defend'); the pronunciation [ʃtʃ] is falling into disuse.

(vi) The double consonants **жч** (мужчина 'man'), **зч** (заказчик 'client'), **сч** (подписчик 'subscriber') are pronounced like **щ** [ʃʃ]. The pronunciation [ʃtʃ], however, is preferred in prefixed forms such as бесчисленный 'innumerable', расчленить 'to dismember'.

(vii) **Жж** and **зж** may be pronounced either as a double soft **ж** (with the front of the tongue raised towards the hard palate) in words such as вожжи [ˈvoʒʒ̡ɪ] 'reins', дрожжи 'yeast', жжёт 'burns', жужжать 'to buzz', брызжет 'sprays', визжать 'to scream', езжу 'I travel', поезжай! 'go!', позже 'later', especially in the speech of the older generation, as well as in that of actors and professionally trained announcers, or alternatively as a double hard **ж** [ˈvoʒʒɨ], a pronunciation preferred by very many younger speakers. Зж is invariably pronounced as hard [ʒʒ] across the boundary between prefix and stem: изжить 'to eradicate'. The cluster жд in дождя́ 'of rain' etc. is pronounced as soft жж by some speakers and as [ʒd̩] by others.

(3) Use of hard and soft consonants to differentiate meaning

Hard and soft consonants may be used to differentiate meaning, cf. лук [luk] 'onions' and люк [l̩uk] 'hatch', мат [mat] 'checkmate' and мать [mat̩] 'mother' etc.

6   Double palatalization

Some words contain two adjacent soft consonants, a phenomenon known as 'double palatalization' or 'regressive softening'. The following combinations of letters are involved:

(1) [d̩], [t̩] and [n̩] followed by other soft dentals or by [ş], [z̩], [tʃ], [ʃʃ] or [l̩]: о́ттепель ['ot̩t̩ɪp̩l̩] 'thaw', дни [d̩n̩i] 'days', ко́нчик ['kon̩tʃɪk] 'tip', го́нщик ['gon̩ʃʃɪk] 'racer', пя́тница ['p̩æt̩n̩ɪtsə] 'Friday', пе́нсия ['p̩en̩şɪjə] 'pension'.

(2) [ş] or [z̩] followed by a soft dental, [ş], [z̩] or [l̩]: возни́к [vʌ'z̩n̩ik] 'arose', разде́л [rʌ'z̩d̩ɛl] 'partition', здесь [z̩d̩eş] 'here', снег [şn̩ɛk] 'snow', стена́ [şt̩'na] 'wall', вме́сте ['vm̩eşt̩ɪ] 'together'.

Note
In some words, single or double palatalization is possible: две [dvɛ] or [d̩vɛ] 'two', дверь [dv̩er̩] or [d̩v̩er̩] 'door', зверь [zv̩er̩] or [z̩v̩er̩] 'wild animal', пе́тля ['p̩etl̩ə] or ['p̩et̩l̩ə] 'loop', свет [s v̩ɛt] or [şv̩ɛt] 'light', след [sl̩ɛt] or [şl̩ɛt] 'trace', че́тверть ['tʃetv̩ɪrt̩] or ['tʃet̩v̩ɪrt̩] 'quarter'.

7   Non-palatalization of consonants in some loan words

(1) The consonants т and д are pronounced hard before e in certain loan words and foreign names (те́рмос ['tɛrməs] 'thermos flask', анте́нна 'aerial', апарте́йд 'apartheid', ателье́ 'workshop', бифште́кс 'beef-steak', бутербро́д 'sandwich', оте́ль 'hotel', парте́р 'stalls', при́нтер 'printer', стенд 'stand'), in words with the prefix интер- (Интерне́т 'Internet'), ко́декс 'legal code', моде́ль 'model' стюарде́сса 'stewardess' and in many words with the prefix де- (деграда́ция 'degradation').

(2) Hard **з** has been retained in безе́ 'meringue'; hard **м** in консоме́ 'consommé', резюме́ 'résumé'; hard **н** in кашне́ 'scarf', би́знес 'business', киберне́тика 'cybernetics', тонне́ль 'tunnel', турне́ 'tour', фоне́тика 'phonetics', эне́ргия 'power'; hard **п** in купе́ 'compartment'; hard **р** in кабаре́ 'cabaret', реле́ 'relay'; hard **с** in шоссе́ 'highway', экстрасе́нс 'a psychic'; and hard **ф** in кафе́ 'cafe'.

Note
A hard consonant is more likely to be retained in foreign loan words immediately preceding the stressed vowel (e.g. те́ннис 'tennis'). Dental consonants (**д, т, н**) are more likely to remain hard than labials (**б, п, м**).

8   Hard sign and soft sign

(1) The hard sign appears only between a hard consonant — usually at the end of a prefix — and a stem beginning **я, е, ё** or **ю**: отъе́зд [ʌˈtjɛst] 'departure', объясня́ть 'to explain'.

(2) A soft sign appearing between a consonant and **я, е, ё** or **ю** indicates that the consonant is soft and that the sound **й** [j] intervenes between consonant and vowel: семья́ [ʂɪˈm̩ja] 'family'. See also **5** (2) (i) and (iii).

9   The reflexive suffix -с ь/-с я

(1) The pronunciation of **сь** as [ʂ] is widespread: бою́сь [bʌˈjuʂ] 'I fear', боя́сь [bʌˈjaʂ] 'fearing' etc.

(2) The suffix **-ся** is usually pronounced [sə] in the infinitive (мы́ться 'to wash') and the present tense (мо́ется 'he washes'), though an alternative soft pronunciation [ʂə] is also found in the second-person singular and first-person plural.

(3) [ʂə] is preferred in participles (смею́щийся [ʂə] 'laughing'), the imperative (не сме́йся 'don't laugh') and the past tense (он смея́лся 'he was laughing') — except for forms in **-сся** or **-зся** (па́сся [ˈpassə] 'was grazing').

10   Effect of a soft consonant on a vowel in the preceding syllable

(1) **Э** and **е** are pronounced [ɛ] and [jɛ] in stressed position when followed by a hard consonant (e.g. э́то [ˈɛtə] 'this is', лес [l̡ɛs] 'forest'),

but as [e] and [je] (similar to French 'e acute' [é]) when followed by a soft consonant (e.g. э́ти ['eţi] 'these', весь [veʂ] 'all').

(2) **Я** is pronounced as [æ], **ё** as [ö] and **ю** as [ü] preceding a soft consonant: мяч [m̩ætʃ] 'ball', тётя ['ţöţə] 'aunt', ключ [kḽütʃ] 'key'.

(3) **А, о** and **ы** are also affected as the tongue is raised closer to the palate in anticipation of a following soft consonant (e.g. мать 'mother', ночь 'night', пыль 'dust', where **а, о** and **ы** are pronounced as if followed by a much-reduced **и** sound).

11   Voiced and unvoiced consonants

(1) Some consonants are pronounced with vibration of the vocal cords ('voiced' consonants), and others without such vibration ('unvoiced' consonants).

(2) There are six pairs of voiced and unvoiced equivalents:

Voiced	Unvoiced
б	п
г	к
з	с
д	т
в	ф
ж	ш

The eight other consonants include the unvoiced **ц, х, ч, щ** and the voiced sonants **л, р, м, н**.

(3) **Б, г, з, д, в, ж** are pronounced as their unvoiced counterparts when they appear in final position or before a final soft sign.

ло**б** 'forehead'	is pronounced [lop]
лу**г** 'meadow'	is pronounced [luk]
ра**з** 'time'	is pronounced [ras]
са**д** 'garden'	is pronounced [sat]
ле**в** 'lion'	is pronounced [ḽɛf]
му**ж** 'husband'	is pronounced [muʃ]

(4) When a voiced and an unvoiced consonant appear side by side, the first assimilates to the second. Thus, voiced consonant + unvoiced

consonant are both pronounced unvoiced, while unvoiced consonant + voiced consonant are both pronounced voiced.

(i) Voiced + unvoiced (both pronounced unvoiced)

гу́бка	'sponge'	is pronounced ['gupkə]
загс	'registry office'	is pronounced [zaks]
ре́зко	'sharply'	is pronounced ['r̥ɛskə]
ло́дка	'boat'	is pronounced ['lotkə]
вхо́дит	'goes in'	is pronounced ['fxod̥ɪt]
ло́жка	'spoon'	is pronounced ['loʃkə]

Note

(a) Devoicing also takes place on the boundary between preposition and noun or adjective: в ко́мнате [ˈf͡ komnəţɪ] 'in the room', под столо́м [pət st͡ʌˈlom] 'under the table'.

(b) The devoicing of a final consonant may in turn cause the devoicing of the consonant which precedes it: визг [visk] 'scream', дрозд [drost] 'thrush'.

(c) **Г** is pronounced as [x] in лёгкий 'light, easy', ле́гче 'easier', мя́гкий 'soft' and мя́гче 'softer', as well as in Бог 'God' (only in the singular nominative case, however). The initial consonant in Го́споди! 'Lord!' is now usually pronounced as [g], though [h] is still heard. The noun бухга́лтер 'book-keeper' is the only word in which **хг** is pronounced as [h].

(ii) Unvoiced + voiced (both pronounced voiced)

футбо́л	'football'	is pronounced [fuˈdbol]
к до́му	'towards the house'	is pronounced [ˈg͡ domu]
про́сьба	'request'	is pronounced [ˈprozʲbə]
та́кже	'also'	is pronounced [ˈtagʒɨ]
мàшбюро́	'typing pool'	is pronounced [maʒbʲuˈro]

Note

(a) The voicing of consonants also occurs at the boundary between words, especially when the second word is a particle or other unstressed form: Я спас бы его́ [ˈspaz͡ bɨ] 'I would have saved him'. **Ц** is voiced as [dz] in such circumstances (Оте́ц был до́ма [ʌˈţɛdz bɨl] 'Father was in') and **ч** as [dʒ] (дочь была́ [dod͡ʒ bɨˈla] 'the daughter was').

(b) **В** has no voicing effect on a preceding unvoiced consonant, e.g. твой [tvoj] 'your'.

12   The pronunciation of -чн-

(1) -чн- is pronounced [ʃn] in certain words (конечно [kʌˈn̪ɛʃnə] 'of course', нарочно 'on purpose', очечник 'spectacle case', прачечная 'laundry', скучно 'boring', яичница 'fried eggs'), as well as in the patronymics Ильинична 'Ilinichna', Саввична 'Savvichna' and Никитична 'Nikitichna'.

(2) However, the pronunciation [tʃn] is used in more 'learned' words such as алчный [ˈaltʃntj] 'greedy', античный 'ancient' добавочный 'additional', and конечный 'ultimate'.

(3) -чн- is pronounced either as [ʃn] or [tʃn] in булочная 'bakery' and молочная 'dairy'. Коричневый 'brown' is pronounced with [tʃn].

Note
Ч is also pronounced [ʃ] in что 'that' and чтобы 'in order to'.

13   Consonants omitted in pronunciation

In some groups of three or more consonants one is omitted in pronunciation. Thus, the first в is not pronounced in здравствуйте! 'hallo!', чувство 'feeling' (however, it **is** pronounced in девственный 'virgin' and нравственный 'moral'), д is not pronounced in звёздный 'starry', ландшафт 'landscape' поздно 'late', праздник 'festival' or сердце 'heart' (however, it **is** pronounced in бездна 'abyss'), л is not pronounced in солнце 'sun' (however, it **is** pronounced in солнечный 'solar') and т is not pronounced in грустный 'sad', известный 'well-known', лестный 'flattering', местный 'local', окрестность 'vicinity', частный 'private' and счастливый 'happy' (however, the first т in постлать 'to spread' **is** pronounced).

14   The pronunciation of double consonants

Double consonants are pronounced as two letters across the boundary between prefix and stem, e.g. оттащить [tt] 'to drag away'. When a double consonant appears within a stem, practice varies, cf. грамматика [m] 'grammar', группа [pp *or* p] 'group'. A single consonant is pronounced in final position: грамм [m] 'gram', грипп [p] 'influenza'.

15   Stress

(1) Stress in Russian is 'free', that is, in some words it falls on the initial syllable (до́лго 'for a long time'), in others on a medial syllable (доро́га 'road') and in others on the final syllable (каранда́ш 'pencil'). The vowel **ё** is *always* stressed.

(2) A change in stress may indicate a change in meaning: о́рган 'organ of the body', орга́н 'organ' (musical instrument). A few words have alternative stress without a change in meaning: творо́г (the commoner form)/тво́рог 'cottage cheese'.

(3) For stress patterns in individual parts of speech see nouns (**57, 60, 62, 63** (4)), adjectives (**164, 165**), verbs (**219, 223, 228, 232, 341, 343, 345, 350, 369**) and prepositions (**405**).

(4) Secondary stress (a weaker stress marked here with a grave accent [`]) is found in some compounds, e.g. машѝнострое́ние 'engineering' (in fast speech, however, the word is pronounced with one full stress only: машинострое́ние). Secondary stress is particularly common in words with foreign prefixes (àнтикоммуни́зм 'anti-communism', кòнтрме́ры 'counter-measures', трàнсатланти́ческий 'transatlantic', у̀льтракоро́ткий 'ultra-short' (also in words with the prefix сверх-: свèрхуро́чные 'overtime'), in technical terms (морòзоусто́йчивый 'frost-proof'), in compounds where there is a polysyllabic gap between the natural stresses in the components (врèмяпрепровожде́ние 'pastime') and in compounds consisting of a truncated word and a full word (гòсбюдже́т (= госуда́рственный бюдже́т) 'state budget'). The use of secondary stresses is sometimes optional, varying with speaker and speech mode. Generally speaking, the newer a compound word is, the more likely a secondary stress (e.g. кѝносцена́рий 'film script'). Tertiary stresses are found in some compounds: àвтомòтоклу́б 'car and motor-cycle club'.

(5) Some primary-stressed adverbs take secondary stress when used as prepositions: внутри́/внутрѝ 'inside', во́зле/вòзле 'near', вокру́г/вокру̀г 'around', ми́мо/мѝмо 'past', о́коло/òколо 'close (to)', по́сле/пòсле 'after'.

Note
Stresses are marked in a Russian text only:

(a)   to resolve ambiguity, cf. Я зна́ю, что он говори́т 'I know that he is speaking' and Я зна́ю, что́ он говори́т 'I know what he is saying', больша́я часть 'a large part', бо́льшая часть 'a larger part';

(b) to denote archaic pronunciations (e.g. библио́тека for contemporary библиоте́ка 'library');

(c) in rendering certain professional words, non-Russian words, dialect and slang words;

(d) in verse, where normal stress is sometimes distorted in the interests of rhythm.

Orthography

16   Spelling rules

Spelling rule 1

ы is replaced by **и**, **я** by **а** and **ю** by **у** after **ж, ч, ш, щ** and **г, к, х**:

> нога́, 'leg', gen. sing. ноги́
>
> молча́ть, 'to be silent', first-person sing. молчу́, third-person pl. молча́т

Note
Exceptions are found in some non-Russian words and names: брошю́ра 'brochure', Кызылку́м 'Kyzylkum Desert', Кя́хта 'Kyakhta'.

Spelling rule 2

o is replaced by **e** in unstressed position after **ж, ч, ш, щ, ц**:

> не́мец 'German', instr. sing. не́мцем, gen. pl. не́мцев

Spelling rule 3

Initial **и** is replaced by **ы** following a prefix ending in a consonant:

> impf. игра́ть/pf. сыгра́ть 'to play'
> небезынтере́сный 'not uninteresting'
> (for exceptions see **28**(3)(c))

Spelling rule 4

The prefixes **без-/бес-; вз-, воз-/вс-, вос-; из-/ис-; раз-/рас-** are spelt with **з** before voiced consonants, voiced sonants or vowels and with **с** before unvoiced consonants: **беззу́бый** 'toothless' but **бесконе́чный** 'infinite'; **взлета́ть** 'to take off' but **всходи́ть** 'to rise'; **избить** 'to beat up' but **испи́ть** 'to sup'; **разобра́ть** 'to dismantle' but **расцепи́ть** 'to uncouple'.

Spelling rule 5

Prefixes ending in a consonant (e.g. **под-**, **от-**, **раз-**, **с-**) are spelt **подо-**, **ото-**, **разо-**, **со-**:

(i) In compounds of **-йти** (**подойти** 'to approach', **подошёл** 'I approached' etc.) (see **333** (2)).

(ii) Before consonant + **ь** (**сошью** 'I shall sew') (see **234** (5)).

(iii) Before certain consonant clusters (**разогна́ть** 'to disperse') (see **234** (1–4)).

Note
For spelling rules relating to prepositions see **404**.

17   Use of capital and small letters in titles and names

(1) In the names or titles of most posts, institutions, organizations, books, newspapers and journals, wars, festivals etc., *only the first word* is spelt with a capital letter: Всеми́рная федера́ция профсою́зов 'World Federation of Trade Unions', Европе́йский сою́з 'European Union', Министе́рство тра́нспорта 'Ministry of Transport', Моско́вский госуда́рственный университе́т 'Moscow State University', Политехни́ческий музе́й 'Polytechnical Museum', Росси́йская акаде́мия нау́к 'Russian Academy of Sciences', Тверско́й муниципа́льный суд 'Tver Municipal Court', Худо́жественный теа́тр 'Arts Theatre', «*Война́ и мир*» '*War and Peace*', *Нью-Йо́рк таймс* '*New York Times*', Семиле́тняя война́ 'Seven Years' War' (but Вели́кая Оте́чественная война́ 'Great Patriotic War'), Но́вый год 'New Year', Пе́рвое ма́я 'May Day', Но́белевская пре́мия 'Nobel Prize'.

Note
Any word spelt with a capital letter in its own right retains the capital in extended titles: Госуда́рственный академи́ческий **Большо́й** теа́тр 'The State Academic Bolshoi Theatre'.

(2) In geographical names, the names of administrative areas, local features and so on, the generic terms are spelt with a *small* letter and the descriptive words with a *capital*: о́зеро Байка́л 'Lake Baikal', Бе́лое мо́ре 'the White Sea', пусты́ня Го́би 'the Gobi Desert', мыс До́брой Наде́жды 'the Cape of Good Hope', тро́пик Ра́ка 'the Tropic of Cancer', Се́верный Ледови́тый океа́н 'the Arctic Ocean', полуо́стров

Таймы́р 'the Taimyr Peninsula', Ю́жный по́люс 'the South Pole', Тверска́я у́лица 'Tverskaya Street', Зи́мний дворе́ц 'the Winter Palace', Исаа́киевский собо́р 'St Isaac's Cathedral', Кра́сная пло́щадь 'Red Square', Ми́нский автомоби́льный заво́д 'Minsk Car Factory'.

Note

Generic terms are spelt with a *capital* letter, however, if used in a non-literal sense: Золото́й Рог 'the Golden Horn' (a bay), О́гненная Земля́ 'Tierra del Fuego' (an archipelago).

(3) Some titles consist of words, all of which have *capital* letters. These include the names of exalted governmental institutions and organizations, as well as a number of international bodies (and certain geographical names, e.g. Бе́лый Нил 'the White Nile', Да́льний Восто́к 'the Far East', Но́вая Земля́ 'Novaya Zemlya'): Генера́льная Ассамбле́я ООН 'the General Assembly of the UNO', Междунаро́дный Кра́сный Крест 'the International Red Cross', Сове́т Федера́ции 'the Council of the Federation', including, as a rule, the names of states: Объединённые Ара́бские Эмира́ты 'the United Arab Emirates', Респу́блика Татарста́н 'the Republic of Tatarstan', Росси́йская Федера́ция 'the Russian Federation', Сове́тский Сою́з 'the Soviet Union', Соединённое Короле́вство 'the United Kingdom', Соединённые Шта́ты Аме́рики 'the United States of America'.

Note

(a) Госуда́рственная ду́ма *or* Госуда́рственная Ду́ма 'the State Duma'

(b) Па́ртия 'party' is not usually spelt with a capital letter: Коммунисти́ческая па́ртия Росси́йской Федера́ции [КПРФ] 'Communist Party of the Russian Federation', Либера́льно-демократи́ческая па́ртия Росси́и [ЛДПР] 'the Russian Liberal Democratic Party'.

(4) Unofficial titles, the names of foreign parliaments and some other titles consist of words, all of which are spelt with a *small* letter: моско́вский аэропо́рт 'Moscow Airport' (cf. official titles, now also used colloquially, e.g. аэропо́рт Вну́ково 'Vnukovo Airport'), па́ртия большевико́в 'the Bolshevik Party' (cf. official Росси́йская социа́л-демократи́ческая рабо́чая па́ртия (большевико́в) 'Russian Social Democratic Workers' Party (of Bolsheviks)'), пала́та о́бщин 'House of Commons', бундеста́г 'the Bundestag', сейм 'the Sejm'.

(5) Nouns denoting nationality, town of origin etc., are also spelt with a *small* letter (англича́нин 'Englishman', москви́ч 'Muscovite'), as are

corresponding adjectives (англи́йский 'English', моско́вский
;cow'), except where they form part of a title (Англи́йский банк
Bank of England', Моско́вский цирк 'Moscow Circus'). This
ciple is also applied to the names of months, thus март 'March',
;брь 'October', октя́брьский 'October' (adj.), but 8 Ма́рта '8
ch' (International Women's Day), Октя́брь/Октя́брьская рево-
ция 'the October Revolution'; and to days of the week, thus пя́тница
day', but Страстна́я Пя́тница 'Good Friday'.

The words земля́ 'land', луна́ 'moon', со́лнце 'sun' are spelt with
itals when they denote heavenly bodies: Земля́ 'the Earth', Луна́
: Moon', Со́лнце 'the Sun'.

(i) Names of deities are spelt with capital letters: Алла́х 'Allah', Бог
od', Бра́хма 'Brahma', Ши́ва 'Shiva'.

te
' heathen gods, one of a number of gods, or figuratively, бог is spelt
th a *small* letter: бог Аполло́н 'the god Apollo', бо́же мой! 'my
od!' In certain contexts, however, a capital is possible:

"Как хорошо́ – сказа́ла жена́, ме́дленно натя́гивая на себя́
шёлковое одея́ло. – Сла́ва **Бо́гу**, сла́ва **Бо́гу** . . ." (Nabokov)
'That is good', said his wife, slowly drawing a silken blanket about
her. 'Thank God, thank God . . .'

ii) Capitals are also used for religious festivals: Па́сха 'Easter',
'ождество́ 'Christmas', holders of exalted ecclesiastical offices:
Звяте́йший Патриа́рх Моско́вский и всея́ Руси́ 'His Holiness the
Patriarch of Moscow and all Russia', Па́па Ри́мский 'The Pope', and
;acred texts: Би́блия 'the Bible', Кора́н 'the Koran', То́ра 'the Torah',
Галму́д 'the Talmud', Ве́ды 'the Vedas'.

Division of Words

18   Division into syllables

(1) Each syllable in a Russian word contains a vowel and, in most cases,
consonants peripheral to it, e.g. па́-спорт.

(2) Russian distinguishes 'open' syllables, which end in a vowel (го-ло-
ва́) from 'closed' syllables, which end in a consonant (нос).

(3) The principles of syllabic division are different in English and Russian, cf. E doc-tor/R до́-ктор, E her-o/R ге-ро́й. Russian non-initial syllables are formed on the basis of an ascending level of 'sonority', vowels being the most sonorous letters, the voiced sonants (**р, л, м, н**) the next most sonorous and noise-consonants (the other sixteen consonants) the least sonorous.

(4) In practice, this means that the **syllable boundary** occurs either:

(i) **between a vowel and a following consonant**: со-ло́-ма, сте-пно́й, ка́-ска, ко-стю́м, ста-ле-ва́р, стра-на́, о-тбро́-сить, вра-жда́ etc.;

or:

(ii) **between a sonant and a following consonant** (including another sonant): су́м-ка, кон-ве́рт, боль-шо́й, ка́р-та, вол-на́, чёр-ный, кар-ма́н.

Note
Non-initial syllables cannot begin with the sequence sonant + noise-consonant (this sequence is possible, however, in an *initial* syllable, e.g. **мши́**-стый). Note, however, the sequences sonant + sonant (во́-**льн**ый), consonant + consonant (ме́-**ст**о) and noise-consonant + sonant (ме-**тл**а́). The syllabic boundary may occur *before* or *between* two sonants (ка-**рм**а́н ог ка**р**-**м**а́н, во-**лн**а́ ог во**л**-**н**а́).

Syllabic division in a text

Я встал и на-де́л паль-то́. Же-на́ ре-ши́-ла, что я по-шёл за си-га-ре́-та-ми, и ве-ле́-ла не су-ту́-ли-ться при хо-дьбе́. О-на́ ска-за́-ла, что ко-гда́ я хо-жу́, то ны-ря́-ю вниз го-ло-во́й, как при-стя-жна́-я ло́-шадь. Е-щё о-на́ ска-за́-ла, что я всё вре́-мя смо-трю́ вниз, бу́-дто хо-чу́ най-ти́ на а-сфа́ль-те мо-не́-тку (Tokareva).

19   Splitting a word at the end of a line

(1) Two basic criteria are observed in splitting a word at the end of a line:

(i) Syllabic division: **го-лова́** ог **голо-ва́**.

(ii) Word structure: it is desirable, for example, not to disrupt monosyllabic prefixes etc. (**под-бежа́ть, со-гла́сен**) (cf. **пе-ревод** and note that the rule does not apply when a prefix is no longer perceived as such: **ра́-зум, разо-ря́ть**).

(2) A word is normally split **after a vowel:** го́-род, го́-лоден or го́ло-ден, ребя́-та or ре-бя́та. Sometimes this involves splitting a two-vowel sequence: **чита́-ете.**

(3) A sequence of **two or more consonants** may also be split: ме́д-ленно, ро́д-ственники, проб-ле́ма, и́стин-ный etc.

(4) Other conventions include the following:

(i) A hard or soft sign must not be separated from the preceding consonant (**подъ-е́зд, боль-шо́й**) and **й** must not be separated from the preceding vowel (**вой-на́**).

(ii) A single vowel should not appear at the end of a line or be carried over onto the next: **аги-та́ция** (*not* *а-гита́ция or *агита́ци-я).

(iii) Two identical consonants appearing between vowels should be split: **жуж-жа́ть, ма́с-са, ко́н-ный.**

(iv) A monosyllabic component of a stump compound should not be split (**спѐцоде́жда**); nor should abbreviations (**ОО́Н, и т.д.**).

(5) Some words can be split in different ways, e.g. **се-стра́, сес-тра́** or **сест-ра́.**

Punctuation

20   Introductory comments

Rules of punctuation are, in general, more rigorously applied in Russian than in English. Differences of usage between the two languages relate in particular to the comma (especially in separating principal from subordinate clauses), the dash and the punctuation of direct speech.

21   The full stop, exclamation mark and question mark

Usage of the full stop, exclamation mark and question mark is comparable in the two languages:

Лю́ди и́щут сча́стья в любви́.	People seek happiness in love.
Кака́я прекра́сная пого́да!	What magnificent weather!
Куда́ вы идёте?	Where are you going?

Note

(a)   There is a tendency to use exclamation marks more frequently in Russian than in English.

(b)   An exclamation mark may appear in the middle of a sentence: Так мне бы́ло пло́хо, **так го́рько и посты́ло!** — ху́же вся́кой боле́зни (Rasputin) 'I felt so bad, so bitter and wretched! — it was worse than any illness'.

(c)   Exclamation marks are also used in commands expressed other than by a grammatical imperative: **Молча́ть!** 'Shut up!', **За мной!** 'Follow me!', **Вста́ли!** 'On your feet!'.

(d)   An exclamation mark enclosed in parentheses (!) may be used to indicate irony or indignation.

(e)   Exclamation and question marks may appear together for special emphasis: **Да что же э́то тако́е?!** 'Now what's all this?!'.

22   The comma: introductory comments

The comma is more frequently used in Russian than in English. In extreme examples a series of commas in a Russian sentence may have no English equivalents at all:

Мака́ренко пи́шет, что де́ти, кото́рые уме́ют труди́ться, уважа́ют труд други́х люде́й, стремя́тся прийти́ на по́мощь тем, кто в э́той по́мощи нужда́ется (Belyakova)

Makarenko writes that children who know how to work respect the labour of other people and strive to come to the assistance of those who need it

23   Uses of the comma

Correspondence with English usage

Commas are used, in Russian *and* English, to perform the following functions:

(1) To separate

(i) **two or more adjectives** which define one noun:

Он шёл по **тёмной, гря́зной, шу́мной** у́лице
He was walking down the dark, dirty, noisy street

(ii) **two or more adverbs** qualifying one verb:

Ме́дленно, мучи́тельно он встал с посте́ли
Slowly, painfully he rose from the bed

(2) To separate **items in a list**:

Пла́та за **кварти́ру, электри́чество, газ** составля́ет о̀коло 20 рубле́й (Belyakova)
The rent, electricity and gas bills amount to about 20 roubles

(3) To mark off words and phrases which stand **in apposition**:

Валенти́на Терешко́ва, рабо́чая девчо́нка из стари́нного текти́льного городка́, ста́ла пе́рвой же́нщиной-космона́втом
Valentina Tereshkova, a working girl from an ancient textile town, became the first woman in space

(4) To mark off words which serve to **define and specify**:

Зда́ние де́тского са́да двухэта́жное, **с больши́ми све́тлыми о́кнами, с вера́ндами для дневно́го сна** (Belyakova)
The building of the kindergarten is two-storey, with large light windows and verandas for a daytime nap

(5) After **да** 'yes' and **нет** 'no':

Да, я согла́сен с ва́ми/**Нет,** я не согла́сен
Yes, I agree with you/No, I don't agree

(6) In **addressing people**:

Здра́вствуйте, Ива́н Ива́нович!
Hallo, Ivan Ivanovich!

(7) After **interjections**:

— **Ой,** как неуда́чно. Вчера́ упа́л йли сего́дня? (Rasputin)
'Oh, what bad luck. Did you fall over yesterday or today?'

(8) Between **repeated words**:

Ничего́, ничего́, утеша́л он себя́, са́мое тру́дное позади́ (Abramov)
Never mind, never mind, he consoled himself, the worst is over

(9) To mark off **participial phrases**:

По равни́не, **освещённой по́здним со́лнцем,** скака́л табу́н ди́ких лошаде́й
Over the plain, (which was) illuminated by the late sun, galloped a herd of wild horses

(10) To mark off **gerundial phrases:**

Я молча́л, **не зна́я,** что де́лать (Rasputin)
I was silent, not knowing what to do

Note
In English, 'and' is often used as an alternative to a comma before the final element in enumerations and when two or more adjectives qualify a single noun or two adverbs a single verb (cf. (1) and (2) above).

Differences in usage between Russian and English

Russian *requires* the use of a comma in the following contexts, where usage in English is optional or inconsistent:

(1) Between clauses linked by **co-ordinating conjunctions** (see **454** (2) (i) and **455–457**):

О́ля зна́ет бу́квы, **но** я пока́ помога́ю ей чита́ть (Belyakova)
Olya knows the letters, but for the time being I help her to read

Note
(a)   While a comma *always* appears before **но** (except when it is the first word in a sentence), the insertion of a comma before English 'but' depends largely on the length of the pause required by the context, cf. 'He is young but experienced' and 'He is young, but everyone trusts him'.
(b)   A comma is used between clauses linked by **и** if the clauses have different subjects (Но волк был мёртв, **и** его́ сейча́с никто́ не боя́лся (Abramov) 'But the wolf was dead, and no one was afraid of him any more'), but not if they have the same subject (Разожгли́ костёр **и** свари́ли грибно́й суп (Belyakova) 'They lit a fire and made mushroom soup'). In such contexts **и** may be replaced by a comma: Два дня он **не пил, не ел** (= не пил и не ел) (Abramov) 'For two days he did not drink or eat'.

(2) Between clauses linked by the conjunctions **и . . . и** 'both . . . and', **ни . . . ни** 'neither . . . nor', **и́ли . . . и́ли** 'either . . . or', **то . . . то** 'now . . . now':

На ве́чере выступа́ли **и** ма́льчики, **и** де́вочки
Both boys and girls performed at the party

Нельзя́ **ни** споко́йно почита́ть, **ни** сосредото́читься (Belyakova)
You can neither do a little quiet reading, nor concentrate

Э́то **и́ли** соба́ка, **и́ли** волк
That is either a dog or a wolf

Она́ **то** смеётся, **то** пла́чет
Now she laughs, now she weeps

(3) Between **a principal and a subordinate clause** (see **458–467**):

Я зна́ю, **что** коне́ц бу́дет не ско́ро
I know the end is still some way off

Мы не отдава́ли дете́й в я́сли, **хотя́** така́я возмо́жность была́ (Belyakova)
We didn't put the children into a day-nursery, even though we had the opportunity to do so

Дени́с стал с нетерпе́нием ждать ле́та, **что́бы** пое́хать с ба́бушкой к Чёрному мо́рю
Denis waited impatiently for the summer, in order to go with his grandmother to the Black Sea

Он рабо́тал бы, **е́сли бы** мог
He would work if he could

Она́ ухо́дит, **потому́ что** она́ опа́здывает
She is leaving because she is late

Note
The appearance of a comma between **потому́** and **что** in Мы победи́м потому́, что мы сильне́е throws the element of cause into sharper relief: 'We shall win because we are stronger' (i.e. and for no other reason). This effect can be intensified by distancing потому́ from что (**Потому́** мы победи́м, **что** мы сильне́е), or by the addition of **лишь, то́лько** or other intensifying words before **потому́**.

(4) To separate **main from relative clauses** (see **123**):

Я посеща́л го́род, **в кото́ром (где)** провёл де́тство
I was visiting the town in which (where) I had spent my childhood

Note
English distinguishes *relative* clauses (which are marked off by commas) — 'Cats (i.e. *all* cats), who have excellent night vision, are nocturnal predators' — from *adjective* clauses (which are *not* marked off by commas): 'Cats (i.e. only *those* cats) who have no tails are called Manx cats'. In Russian, however, both types of clause are marked off with commas.

(5) To mark off **parenthetical words:**

во-пе́рвых/во-вторы́х in the first place/in the second place
допу́стим   let us assume   наприме́р   for example

ка́жется	it seems	пожа́луйста	please
коне́чно	of course	по-мо́ему	in my opinion
к сожале́нию	unfortunately	ска́жем	let us say
мѐжду про́чим	incidentally	с одно́й, друго́й	on the one, the
мо́жет быть	perhaps	стороны́	other hand
наве́рное	probably		

Он, **должно́ быть,** ушёл
He must have left

Нам, **коне́чно,** удо́бнее, что де́ти сидя́т ти́хо (Belyakova)
Of course, it's more convenient for us if the children are sitting quietly

Не спорь, **пожа́луйста,** со мной, я зна́ю (Rasputin)
Please don't argue with me, I know best

Он сказа́л, что, **к сожале́нию,** нам придётся идти́ без него́
He said that unfortunately we would have to go without him

(6) In **comparisons:**

Он ла́зит по дере́вьям, **как обезья́на**
He scrambles about in the trees like a monkey

Кто́-то научи́л своего́ малыша́ пла́вать **ра́ньше, чем** тот стал ходи́ть (Belyakova)
Someone taught his baby to swim before he could walk

Он спал беспробу́дным сном, **бу́дто** его́ ничто́ не трево́жило
He was sound asleep, as though without a care in the world

24   The colon. The semicolon. The dash

The colon.

The colon is used to perform the following functions:

(1) To **introduce a list,** in which case the colon is usually preceded by a generic term:

Моя́ семья́ состои́т из четырёх челове́к: **мой муж Ви́ктор, дво́е детей и я** (Belyakova)
My family consists of four people: my husband Victor, the two children and myself

(2) To introduce a statement which **elaborates on, supplements or indicates the cause** of the statement which precedes the colon:

И тут их ожида́ла но́вая беда́: **оте́ц пропа́л** (Abramov)
And now a new misfortune awaited them: father had disappeared

В нау́ке всегда́ должна́ быть то́чность: **ка́ждому нау́чному те́рмину должно́ соотве́тствовать одно́ поня́тие** (Vvedenskaya)
There should always be accuracy in science: a single concept should correspond to each scientific term

У́тром я со стра́хом смотре́л на себя́ в зе́ркало: **нос вспух, под ле́вым гла́зом синя́к** (Rasputin)
In the morning I gazed at myself in the mirror in horror: my nose had swollen up, there was a bruise under my left eye

(3) To **introduce direct speech, thought or other communication:**

В кинофи́льме *«Доживём до понеде́льника»* подро́сток пи́шет: **«Сча́стье — э́то когда́ тебя́ понима́ют!»** (Kovaleva)
In the film *We'll survive till Monday* a teenager writes, 'Happiness is when people understand you!'

(4) To introduce a **quotation:**

По́мните, в *«Евге́нии Оне́гине»*:
Привы́чка свы́ше нам дана́:
Заме́на сча́стию она́
Do you remember, in *Evgenii Onegin*:
Habit is granted us from on high:
It is a substitute for happiness

The semicolon

The semicolon is used to **separate extensive clauses** which are **not linked by conjunctions,** especially if each clause is itself broken up by commas:

В Ленингра́де все хотя́т посмотре́ть на легенда́рную «Авро́ру», побыва́ть в пу́шкинских места́х, в многочи́сленных дворца́х; в Улья́новске познако́миться с места́ми, где жил и учи́лся В. И. Ле́нин; в На́бережных Челна́х прое́хать по огро́мному молодо́му го́роду, посмотре́ть КамА́З (Vvedenskaya)
In Leningrad everyone wants to see the legendary 'Aurora', visit places associated with Pushkin, the numerous palaces; in Ulyanovsk to get to know the places where V. I. Lenin lived and worked; and in

Naberezhnye Chelny to drive through the enormous new town, see the Kamaz truck factory

Note

In 1991 Ленингра́д 'Leningrad' reverted to Санкт-Петербу́рг 'St Petersburg' and Улья́новск 'Ulyanovsk' to Симби́рск 'Simbirsk'.

The dash

The dash is extremely widespread in Russian. It not only has a number of specific uses of its own but in some contexts substitutes for other punctuation marks, in particular the comma, the colon and parentheses.

(1) Specific uses of the dash.

(i) It separates **subject noun** from **predicate noun**, replacing the verb 'to be':

Мой оте́ц — преподава́тель ву́за, а ма́ма — врач (Belyakova)
My father is a college lecturer, and my mother is a doctor

Са́мое глубо́кое о́зеро ми́ра — э́то пресново́дный краса́вец Байка́л (Vvedenskaya)
The deepest lake in the world is the beautiful fresh-water Lake Baikal

Note

(a)   The subject may sometimes be an **infinitive:**

Са́мое тяжёлое при проща́нии — **не огля́дываться** (*Ogonek*)
The hardest thing on parting is not to look back

(b)   The dash is not normally used to replace the verb 'to be' when the subject is a pronoun: Он водола́з 'He is a diver'.

(ii) In elliptical statements it replaces a word, usually a verb, which is 'understood':

Студе́нт смотре́л на профе́ссора, профе́ссор — на студе́нта (Shukshin)
The student was looking at the professor, and the professor (was looking) at the student

(2) The dash is also used as a substitute for:

(i) The comma (when, for example, introducing an unexpected turn of events or sharp contrast):

Она́ сде́лала ещё попы́тку посади́ть меня́ за стол — **напра́сно (=, но напра́сно)** (Rasputin)
She made another attempt to seat me at the table, but in vain

Note
Generally speaking, the dash indicates a *more pronounced pause* than the comma, for example, in expressing apposition: Со мной был грузи́нский чай — моё еди́нственное удово́льствие (=, моё еди́нственное удово́льствие) 'I had with me some Georgian tea, my only pleasure'.

(ii) The colon:

(a) in introducing an **enumeration,** following a generic term:

Иногда́ клуб приглаша́ет госте́й — **учёных, педаго́гов, враче́й** (Belyakova)
Sometimes the club invites guests — scientists, teachers and doctors

(b) in **elucidating** a statement:

У Соколо́вых ещё не спа́ли — **в избе́ мига́л огонёк**
The Sokolovs were still up — a light was flickering in the hut (cf. ещё не спа́ли: в избе́ мига́л огонёк)

(iii) Parentheses:

На террито́рии Росси́йской Федера́ции — **не забыва́йте о том, что она́ занима́ет одну́ седьму́ю часть всей су́ши Земли́!** — ты́сячи рек и речу́шек
On the territory of the Russian Federation (do not forget that it occupies one-seventh of the Earth's surface!) there are thousands of rivers and streams

25   The punctuation of direct speech

(1) If the introductory verb *precedes* the direct speech, the verb is followed by a *colon*, and the direct speech *either*

(i) appears on a new line, preceded by a *dash*:

Я промя́млил:
— **Пра́вда** (Rasputin)
'It is true', I mumbled

(ii) *or* runs on after the colon and is enclosed in *guillemets* (« »):

Сам хозя́ин ра́за два крича́л с крыльца́: «Эй, кто там?»
The master himself shouted a couple of times from the porch,
'Hey, who's there?'

(2) If, however, the verb *follows* the direct speech, the latter is flanked
by *dashes*:

— Усну́л, — услу́жливо отве́тила Си́ма (Rasputin)
'He's fallen asleep', answered Sima obligingly

(3) A **conversation** may be rendered as follows:

— И сего́дня уже́ ссо́рились? — спра́шивала их сотру́дница
за́гса.
— Коне́чно!
— Ну из-за чего́ сего́дня?
— Из-за чего́? . . . Я уже́ забы́ла . . . (Belyakova)
'And have you quarrelled today too?', asked the registry office
official.
'Of course!'
'And what have you been quarrelling about today?'
'What have we been quarrelling about today? . . . I forget . . .'

Note
(a) A full stop, comma, semicolon or dash *follow* inverted commas.
(b) Quotes within quotes may be distinguished as follows:
«Кре́йсер "Авро́ра" стоя́л на я́коре» 'The cruiser "Aurora" lay at
anchor'.
(c) In cursive script, inverted commas are rendered as follows:
«*Приве́т!*» 'Greetings!'

26   Suspension points (многото́чие)

Suspension points (. . .) indicate one of the following.

(1) **Hesitation:**

— Про́игрываешь, наве́рное?
— Нет, **вы . . . вы́игрываю** (Rasputin)
'I suppose you lose?'
'No, I – I win'

(2) An **unfinished statement:**

Знать бы нам, чем э́то всё ко́нчится . . . (Rasputin)
Had we but known how it would all end . . .

The Noun

Word Formation

27   Word formation in the noun I: general

(1) Nouns in Russian may be basic irreducible stems (e.g. **лес** 'forest') or form the basis of compound nouns (e.g. **лесору́б** 'wood cutter'). Compounding takes a number of different forms, involving *initial* components which may be the stems of:

(i) nouns: **ледоко́л** 'ice-breaker' (**лёд** 'ice', коло́ть 'to split')

(ii) adjectives: **черно**зём 'black earth' (**чёрный** 'black', земля́ 'earth')

(iii) numerals: **дву**́окись 'dioxide' (**дву-** 'two', о́кись 'oxide')

(iv) adverbs: **гро̀мко**говори́тель 'loud speaker' (**гро́мко** 'loudly', говори́ть 'to speak');

and *second* components which may be:

(i) nouns: тяжело**ве́с** 'heavy weight' (тяжёлый 'heavy', **вес** 'weight')

(ii) of verbal origin: сено**ко́с** 'haymaking' (се́но 'hay', **коси́ть** 'to mow').

Note
(a)   Compounds may also be based on phrases: **инопланетя́нин** 'extra-terrestrial' (cf. ина́я плане́та 'another planet'), **одно-фами́лец** 'namesake' (cf. одна́ фами́лия 'the same name');

(b) The components of a compound are usually linked by the infixes **-о-**: снегопа́д 'snow fall', маши́нопись 'typing', самолёт 'aeroplane', or (where the stem of the first component ends in a soft consonant or in **ж, ч, ш, щ** or **ц**) **-e-**: общежи́тие 'hostel', овцево́д 'sheep-breeder', пулемёт 'machinegun' (cf. пу́ля 'bullet'), сталева́р 'steel founder' (cf. сталь 'steel'), пешехо́д 'pedestrian'. However, **-о-** sometimes appears as an 'illogical' link-vowel when the stem of the first component of a compound ends in soft **в** (e.g. кровообраще́ние 'circulation of the blood', cf. кровь 'blood'), soft **н** (e.g. баснопи́сец 'fabulist', cf. ба́сня 'fable'), soft **р** (зверолов 'trapper', cf. зверь 'animal'), or soft **т** (честолю́бие 'ambition', cf. честь 'honour').

(2) A group of compounds with second components that denote persons or places is particularly common. Some of the elements are indigenous: **-вед**, as in **литературове́д** 'literature specialist', **-вод**, as in **скотово́д** 'stock-breeder', others international: **-граф**, as in **гео́граф** 'geographer', **-дром**, as in **дельтадро́м** 'hang-glider launch site', **-лог**, as in **био́лог** 'biologist', **-ман**, as in **балетома́н** 'balletomane', **-тека**, as in **фоноте́ка** 'sound library', **-фил**, as in **славянофи́л** 'Slavophile', **-фоб**, as in **англофо́б** 'Anglophobe'.

(3) While most second components in compounds tend to be truncated forms: водопа́д 'waterfall', парово́з 'steam engine', пчелово́д 'apiarist', etc., some are suffixed: монеторазме́нник 'change machine', пивова́рня 'brewery', работоспосо́бность 'efficiency', судостро́ение 'ship-building'.

(4) The relationships between initial and second components may be as follows:

(i) the first component may denote the object of the second: **бензово́з** 'petrol tanker' (cf. вози́ть бензи́н 'to transport petrol'), **книголю́б** 'book lover', **нефтепрово́д** 'oil pipeline', **пылесо́с** 'vacuum cleaner';

(ii) the second component may denote an object designed for the first: **бензоба́к** 'petrol tank' (cf. бак для бензи́на 'tank for petrol'), **дѐтса́д** 'kindergarten';

(iii) the action denoted by the second component may be performed in or over the area designated by the first: **вездехо́д** 'cross country vehicle' (cf. ходи́ть везде́ 'to go everywhere'), **домосе́д** 'stay-at-home', **морепла́ватель** 'seafarer';

(iv) the first component may qualify the second: **новостройка** 'new building' (cf. **новая стройка** 'new building'), **общежитие** 'hostel', **пятиборье** 'pentathlon';

(v) the first component may denote the means by which the second is accomplished: **вертолёт** 'helicopter' (cf. **вертеть(ся)** 'to rotate', лёт 'flight'), **газосварщик** 'gas welder', **пароход** 'steamer'.

Note
For the formation of compound *abbreviations*, see **39** (acronyms), **40** (alphabetisms), **41** (stump compounds), **42** (compound hyphenated nouns).

28   Word formation in the noun II: prefixation

(1) Prefixes, while fewer in number than suffixes, effect more radical change than suffixes are capable of. Thus, in the word **бесконфликтность** 'absence of conflict' the suffix **-ость** merely denotes the abstract nature of the noun, while the prefix **бес-** fufils a semantic role in denoting the absence of the quality denoted by the root noun (**конфликт** 'conflict').

(2) The following prefixes used with nouns are also commonly used with verbs (for the full range of their meanings, see sections **254** and **331**; for spelling rules see **16,** rules 3–5):

в- 'into':	**вложение** 'investment'
вз-/вс- 'upwards':	**взлёт** 'take-off'
воз-/вос- (i) 'upwards':	**восход солнца** 'sun-rise'
(ii) 're-':	**воссоединение** 'reunification'
вы- 'outwards':	**выпуск** 'output'
до- 'addition':	**дополнение** 'supplementation'
за- (i) 'beyond':	**зарубежье** 'foreign countries'
(ii) 'closing':	**закрытие** 'closure'
из-/ис- 'ex-, out':	**исключение** 'expulsion'
на- (i) 'on, onto':	**наушник** 'earphone'
(ii) 'quantity':	**надой** 'milk yield'
над- 'above':	**надсмотрщик** 'supervisor'
недо- 'shortfall':	**недооценка** 'underestimate'
о-/об- (i) 'encompassing':	**охват** 'scope, range'
(ii) 'avoidance':	**объезд** 'detour'
от- 'away from':	**отъезд** 'departure'
пере- (i) 'across':	**переход** 'crossing'

(ii) 'repeat':	переигро́вка 'replay'
под- (i) 'support':	подсве́чник 'candle-stick'
(ii) 'sham':	подде́лка 'forgery'
пре- (i) 'trans-':	преобразова́ние 'transformation'
(ii) 'excess':	преувеличе́ние 'exaggeration'
пред- 'pre-':	предысто́рия 'pre-history'
при- (i) 'arrival, joining':	приземле́ние 'landing'
(ii) 'attachment':	приложе́ние 'magazine supplement'
про- 'through, past':	про́пуск 'pass'
раз-/рас- (i) 'spread':	распростране́ние 'dissemination'
(ii) 'reversal':	разря́дка '*détente*'
с- (i) 'together':	съезд 'congress'
(ii) 'down':	спуск 'descent'
у- 'away':	увольне́ние 'dismissal'.

(3) A further set of prefixes are used mainly with nouns, in some cases adjectives, and a few also with verbs (e.g. **без-/бес-, дѐ-, дис-, рѐ-**). Many are loan prefixes and combine mostly with foreign roots, while some (**без-, между-, не-, по-, под-, пра-, пред-, само-, свѐрх-, после-, противо-, чрез-/чрес-**) are indigenous.

а- 'devoid of':	алоги́чность 'illogicality'
а̀нти- 'opposed to':	антиры́ночник 'opponent of a market economy'
а̀рхи- 'extreme':	архиплу́т 'arch villain'
без-/бес- 'deprived of:	бессо́нница 'insomnia'
вѝце- 'deputizing for':	вѝцепредседа́тель 'vice-chairman'
гѝпер- 'extreme':	гѝперинфля́ция 'hyper-inflation'
дѐ- 'reversal':	децентрализа́ция 'decentralization'
дѐз- 'removal':	дезодора́нт 'deodorant'
дис- 'deprived of':	дисквалифика́ция 'disqualification'
ѝнтер- 'international':	интерде́вочка 'hard-currency prostitute'
ква̀зи- 'quasi-':	ква̀зидемокра́тия 'quasi-democracy'
ко̀нтр- 'counter to':	ко̀ нтрразве́дка 'counter-espionage'
между- 'intermediate':	междуца́рствие 'interregnum'
мѝкро- 'small':	мѝкрооргани́зм 'micro-organism'
не- 'negation of':	неприсоедине́ние 'non-alignment'
нѐо- 'revived':	нѐокапитали́зм 'neo-capitalism'
по- 'along':	погра́ни́чник 'frontier guard'
под (i) 'subordinate to':	подви́д 'sub-species'
(ii) 'proximity':	Подмоско́вье 'Moscow region'
после- 'following':	послесло́вие 'epilogue'
по̀ст- 'subsequent':	по̀стмодерни́зм 'post-Modernism'

пра- 'great' (in relationships)	**праба́бушка**: 'great-grandmother'
преди- 'preceding':	**предисло́вие** 'foreword'
про- (i) 'supportive of':	**проамерика́нец** 'pro-American'
(ii) 'deputizing for':	**проре́ктор** 'vice-principal'
противо- 'opposed to':	**противоре́чие** 'contradiction'
псѐвдо- 'sham':	**псѐвдодемокра́тия** 'pseudo-democracy'
рѐ- 're-':	**рѐинтегра́ция** 'reintegration'
само- 'self':	**самообслу́живание** 'self-service'
свѐрх- 'extreme':	**свѐрхдержа́ва** 'super-power'
су̀б- 'subordinate':	**су̀бподря́д** 'subcontract'
су̀пер- 'extreme':	**су̀перзвезда́** 'super-star'
у̀льтра- 'extreme':	**у̀льтрареакционе́р** 'ultrareactionary'
чрез-/чрес- 'excessive':	**чрезме́рность** 'excessiveness'
экс- 'former':	**экс-премье́р** 'the former premier'
экстра- 'beyond':	**экстрасе́нс** 'psychic'.

Note

(a) A number of prefixes fall into definable categories:

(i) excess (**а̀рхи-, гѝпер-, свѐрх-, су̀пер-, чрез-**);

(ii) negation (**а-, без-, дѐ-, дѐз-, дис-, не-**);

(iii) time (**нѐо-, после-, по̀ст-, преди-, рѐ-, экс-**);

(iv) opposition/support (**а̀нти-, ко̀нтр-, про-, противо-**);

(v) sham (**квѐзи-, псѐвдо-**).

(b) in some cases a prefixed word has been borrowed virtually in its entirety (e.g. **анеми́я** 'anaemia') and should thus be regarded as a non-derivative stem in Russian.

(c) spelling rule **16** (3), in accordance with which initial **и** is replaced by **ы** following a prefix ending in a consonant, does not apply to the loan prefixes **гѝпер-, дѐз-, по̀ст-, су̀б-, су̀пер-** (thus **дезинформа́ция** 'misinformation', etc.).

29   Word formation in the noun III: suffixation.

Introductory remarks

(i) Noun suffixes number over one hundred and play a fundamental role in the creation of nouns. Suffixed nouns may derive from verbs:

стрельба́ 'shooting' from стреля́ть 'to shoot'; adjectives: малы́ш 'child, small boy' from ма́лый 'small'; other nouns: рыба́к 'fisherman' from ры́ба 'fish'; prepositions: пре́док 'ancestor' from перед/пред 'before'; numerals: тро́йка 'troika' from тро́е 'three'; adverbs: почему́чка 'inquisitive child' from почему́? 'why?'.

(ii) While little or no guidance can be offered on the selection of suffixes to convey particular meanings, familiarity with the range of suffixes available within each field of meaning can be beneficial.

(iii) Many loan suffixes are components of nouns that have been borrowed virtually in their entirety:

-аж as in тонна́ж 'tonnage'
-ант as in дилетта́нт 'dilettante'
-арий as in планета́рий 'planetarium'
-ат as in электора́т 'electorate'
-ент as in аге́нт 'agent',
-ер as in тре́нер 'trainer'
-есса as in поэте́сса 'poetess'
-иада as in олимпиа́да 'Olympiad'
-изм as in социали́зм 'socialism'
-ик as in диабе́тик 'diabetic'
-ир as in банки́р 'banker'
-иса as in актри́са 'actress'
-ист as in коммуни́ст 'communist'
-ит as in артри́т 'arthritis'
-итет as in приорите́т 'priority'
-ор as in агре́ссор 'aggressor'.
-тор as in авиа́тор 'aviator'

Note
Some of the compounds are based on Russian stems: ельцини́ст 'Yeltsin supporter', трудоголи́зм 'workaholism', in which case the suffixes (here, -ист, -изм) can be identified as separate formants.

(iv) Other suffixes cover broad categories of meaning (the most characteristic suffixes are listed here for each category; a full list appears under (vi), below, which enumerates fifty-two suffixes with their meanings):

(a) Abstract meanings (attitudes, feelings, qualities):
-ба, -ие/-ье, -изм, -ость/-есть, -ота, -ствие, -ство, -сть.

(b) Actions (verbal nouns):

-ация/-изация, -ка, -ние, -ок, -ство, -тие.

(c) Animate beings (agents of actions, nationals, inhabitants, members of organizations, etc.):
-ак/-як, -анин/-янин, -арь, -ач, -ец, -ик, -ист, -ник, -ок, -тель, -ун, -щик/-чик.

(d) Collectives:
-ство, -ура.

(e) Objects/implements:
-ик, -ка, -ло, -ник, -ок, -тель, -щик/-чик.

(f) Places:
-ище, -ня, -ье.

(g) Quantity, dimension:
-ина, -ство.

Note
(a) Some suffixes have certain very specific meanings: **-ёнок/-онок** (young of animals), **-ика** (berries), **-ина** (types of meat), **-ки** (remnants), **-ница** (containers), **-ович/-(ь)евич/-ич** (patronymics), **-от** (sounds), **-ота** and **-уха** (medical conditions);
(b) The commonest feminine suffixes (in addition to **-есса, -иса**, which are listed under (iii)) are: **-иня/-ыня, -иха, -ица, -ка, -ница, -ша, -щица/-чица, -ья.**

(v) Most consonant changes in suffixed nouns affect the velar consonants. The following changes occur: **г: ж, к: ч** and **х: ш** before the suffixes: **-ество** (e.g. мона́х 'monk': мона́шество 'monks'), **-ие** (вели́кий 'great': вели́чие 'greatness'), **-ина** (горо́х 'peas': горо́шина 'pea'), **-инка** (снег 'snow': снежи́нка 'snow-flake'), **-ист** (шпа́га 'sword': шпажи́ст 'fencer' [but танк 'tank': танки́ст 'tank-driver']), **-иха** (ме́льник 'miller': ме́льничиха 'miller's wife'), **-ица** (волк 'wolf': волчи́ца 'she-wolf'), **-ник** (молоко́ 'milk': моло́чник 'milk-jug'), **-ница** (спи́чка 'match': спи́чечница 'matchbox stand'), **-ня** ([in names of places] ко́нюх 'groom': коню́шня 'stable'), **-ок** (пры́гать 'to jump': прыжо́к 'jump'), **-онок** (волк 'wolf': волчо́нок 'wolf-cub'), **-ье** (бе́рег 'shore': побере́жье 'coastline'.

Note
Nouns in **-онок** also undergo the mutations **д: ж** (медве́дь 'bear': медвежо́нок 'bear-cub') and **ц: ч** (за́яц 'hare': зайчо́нок 'leveret'), those in **-ество** — **т: ч** (студе́нт 'student': студе́нчество 'student body'), those in **-ина** — **ск: щ** (тре́скаться 'to crack': тре́щина

'crack') and **ст**: **щ** (**тóлстый** 'thick': **толщинá** 'thickness'), those in **-иха** and **-ница** – **ц**: **ч** (**пловéц** 'swimmer': **пловчúха** 'female swimmer', **пéрец** 'pepper': **пéречница** 'pepper-pot'). For consonant change in the verbal noun, see section on **-(е)ние** (28) (ii), below and for consonant change in nouns in **-анин**, see (2), below.

(vi) *Noun suffixes*

(1) -ак/-як (-чак after -ль)

Persons

(a) with particular physical characteristics or personality traits (based on adjs.):
бедня́к 'poor person', **весельча́к** 'jolly person', **пошля́к** 'vulgar person', **смельча́к** 'daredevil', **толстя́к** 'fat person'.

(b) practitioners (from nouns):
горня́к 'miner', **моря́к** 'sailor', **рыба́к** 'fisherman'.

(c) nationalities, inhabitants of certain ancient towns and cities:
пермя́к 'inhabitant of Perm', **поля́к** 'Pole', **слова́к** 'Slovak', **твержя́к** 'inhabitant of Tver'.

Note
сибиря́к 'Siberian'.

(2) -анин/-чанин/-янин

(i) nationals, inhabitants, members of social, religious and other groups:
армяни́н 'Armenian', **граждани́н** 'citizen' (from **град** 'town'), **крестья́нин** 'peasant', **мусульма́нин** 'Moslem', **парижа́нин** 'Parisian', **рижа́нин** 'inhabitant of Riga' (from **Ри́га** 'Riga'), **северя́нин** 'northerner', **славяни́н** 'Slav', **христиани́н** 'Christian', **южа́нин** 'southerner' (from **юг** 'south').

Note
Derivative **-чанин** (with infix **-ч-**) appears after **и** in **англича́нин** (but **россия́нин** 'inhabitant of Russia'), **в** in **ростовча́нин** 'inhabitant of Rostov', **харьковча́нин** 'inhabitant of Kharkov' (but **варшавя́нин** 'inhabitant of Warsaw', **киевля́нин** 'Kievan'), **ль** in **сельча́нин** 'villager', **м** in **сумча́нин** 'inhabitant of Sumy' (but **ри́млянин** 'Roman'), **н** in **клинча́нин** 'inhabitant of Klin', **т** in **датча́нин** 'Dane' (but **египтя́нин** 'Egyptian', **израильтя́нин** 'Israeli'), and replaces **ск** in **братча́нин** 'inhabitant of Bratsk', **минча́нин** 'inhabitant of Minsk', **норильча́нин** 'inhabitant of Norilsk'.

(3) -анка/-янка/-енка

Female nationals (from zero-suffixed m. forms and some in **-ец**):

гречáнка 'Greek woman' (cf. грек 'Greek'), индиáнка 'Indian woman' (cf. индúец 'Indian', индéец 'North American Indian'), китаáнка 'Chinese woman' (cf. китáец 'Chinese'), турчáнка 'Turkish woman' (cf. тýрок 'Turk'), француúженка 'Frenchwoman' (cf. францýз 'Frenchman').

(4) -арь

(i) Practitioners:

(a) from nouns:
    аптéкарь 'chemist', библиотéкарь 'librarian', вратáрь 'goalkeeper'.

(b) from verbs:
    звонáрь 'bell-ringer', пéкарь 'baker', тóкарь 'turner'.

(ii) Objects (from nouns or adjs.):
    буквáрь 'primer', словáрь 'dictionary', сухáрь 'rusk'.

(5) -ация/-изация/-фикация

Verbal nouns (from verbs in **-овать/-(из)ировать/-фицировать**):
    демонстрáция 'demonstration', классификáция 'classification', приватизáция 'privatization', рекомендáция 'recommendation' роботизáция 'robotization'.

Note
(a)   **-яция** after **л**: вентиляáция 'ventilation'.

(b)   some nouns in **-фикация** denote provision of facilities: кинофикáция 'supplying with cinemas', электрификáция 'electrification'.

(6) -ач

Persons:
(i) with particular characteristics:

(a) from adjs.:
    богáч 'rich man', лихáч 'reckless driver', ловкáч 'dodger'.

(b) from nouns:
    бородáч 'bearded man', силáч 'strong man', усáч 'man with large moustache'.

(ii) practitioners (from verbs or nouns):
    врач 'doctor', скрипáч 'violinist', трубáч 'trumpeter', ткач 'weaver'.

(7) -ба

Verbal nouns (from impf. verbs):
   борьба́ 'struggle', **жени́тьба** 'marriage', **про́сьба** 'request', **слу́жба** 'service', **стрельба́** 'shooting', **ходьба́** 'walking'.

(8) -ёж

Verbal nouns in **-ёж** derive from verbs in **-ить:**
   грабёж 'robbery', **кутёж** 'carousing', **платёж** 'payment'.

Note
   галдёж 'din', from галде́ть 'to make a din'.

(9) -ёнок/-онок

The young of animals and birds:
   медвежо́нок 'bear-cub', **львёнок** 'lion-cub', **орлёнок** 'young eagle', **тигрёнок** 'tiger-cub', **утёнок** 'duckling'.

(10) -ец

Persons:
(i) with personality traits (from adjs.):
   горде́ц 'arrogant man', **мудре́ц** 'wise man', **счастли́вец** 'happy person', **хитре́ц** 'cunning devil'.

(ii) agents of actions (from verbs):
   боре́ц 'wrestler', **гребе́ц** 'oarsman', **певе́ц** 'singer', **продаве́ц** 'salesman'.

Note
In **-лец: владе́лец** 'owner', **корми́лец** 'bread-winner' and from verbal nouns in **-ение: переселе́нец** 'settler', **снабже́нец** 'supplier'.

(iii) many nationals:
   америка́нец 'American', **испа́нец** 'Spaniard', **италья́нец** 'Italian', **кана́дец** 'Canadian', **не́мец** 'German', **норве́жец** 'Norwegian', **украи́нец** 'Ukrainian'.

(iv) most inhabitants:
   европе́ец 'European', **кавка́зец** 'Caucasian', **ло́ндонец** 'Londoner', **новгоро́дец** 'inhabitant of Novgorod', **петербу́ржец** 'inhabitant of St Petersburg'.

Note
Infix **-ов-** in **донба́ссовец** 'inhabitant of Donbass', etc.

(v) members of organizations, including acronyms and indeclinable nouns (often with infix -ов-):

ву́зовец 'higher education student' (from **вуз** 'institution of higher education'), **дина́мовец** 'member of Dynamo', **неде́лец** 'employee of *Nedelya*', **омо́новец** 'member of OMON' (special police force), **оо́новец** 'UNO official'.

(11) -знь

States (based on verbs):

боле́знь 'illness', **боя́знь** 'fear', **жизнь** 'life', **неприя́знь** 'hostility'.

(12) -ие/-ье

Qualities (based on adjs.):

вели́чие 'greatness', **весе́лье** 'gaiety', **здоро́вье** 'health'.

Note

Usage in compound words: **долголе́тие** 'longevity', **остроу́мие** 'wit', **равноду́шие** 'indifference'.

(13) -изм

Policies, attitudes:

брежневи́зм 'Brezhnevism', **вещи́зм** 'acquisitiveness', **наплеви́зм** 'couldn't-care-less attitude', **плюрали́зм** 'pluralism'.

(14) -изна

Qualities (based on adjs.):

белизна́ 'whiteness', **дешеви́зна** 'cheapness', **крутизна́** 'steepness', **новизна́** 'newness'.

Note:

Infix **-ов-** in **дорогови́зна** 'expensiveness'.

(15) -ик

(i) Persons:

(a) (based on adjs. in -н-):

вече́рник 'evening-class student' (cf. вече́рний 'evening'), **вино́вник** 'culprit', **шко́льник** 'schoolboy'.

Note

Some forms are based on adjs. in **-нный: тамо́женник** 'customs officer', adjs. in **-ственный: обще́ственник** 'public figure', or verbs in **-ствовать: путеше́ственник** 'traveller'.

(b) practitioners, based on adjs. in:

-в-: **биржеви́к** 'stockbroker' (cf. биржево́й 'stock-exchange' [adj.]), **кроссови́к** 'cross-country runner', **оптови́к** 'wholesaler', **планови́к** 'planner'.

-н-: **глазни́к** 'oculist' (cf. глазно́й 'eye' [adj.]), **железнодоро́жник** 'railway worker', **пожа́рник** 'firefighter', **сезо́нник** 'seasonal worker'.

(ii) Objects based on adjs. in:

-в-: **белови́к** 'fair copy' (cf. белово́й 'fair' [adj.]), **броневи́к** 'armoured car', **грузови́к** 'lorry', **чернови́к** 'rough copy'.

-н-: **купа́льник** 'bathing costume' (cf. купа́льный 'bathing' [adj.]), **па́мятник** 'monument'.

(16) -ика

Berries:

брусни́ка 'red whortleberry', **голуби́ка** 'bilberry', **земляни́ка** 'wild strawberries'.

(17) -ин

Nationals:

болга́рин 'Bulgarian', **грузи́н** 'Georgian', **осети́н** 'Ossetian', **тата́рин** 'Tatar'.

(18) -ина

(i) dimensions:

глубина́ 'depth', **длина́** 'length', **толщина́** 'thickness', **ширина́** 'width'.

(ii) the results of actions or processes (based on verbs):

впа́дина 'hollow', **морщи́на** 'wrinkle', **ржа́вчина** 'rust', **тре́щина** 'crack', **цара́пина** 'scratch'.

(iii) types of meat:

бара́нина 'mutton', **говя́дина** 'beef', **осетри́на** 'sturgeon', **свини́на** 'pork'.

Note

Derivative **-атина/-ятина,** based on the plural of young animals: **медвежа́тина** 'bear meat', **теля́тина** 'veal'.

(iv) Singulatives:

бу́сина (from бу́сы 'beads') 'bead', **виногра́дина** 'grape', **горо́шина** 'pea', **соло́мина** 'straw'.

Note

Forms in **-инка:** **снежи́нка** 'snowflake', **ча́йнка** 'tea-leaf'.

(19) -иня/-ыня

Feminine counterparts of zero-suffixed and some other nouns:
ба́рыня 'lady' (from **ба́рин** 'lord'), **герои́ня** 'heroine', **мона́хиня**
'nun'.

(20) -ист

Persons (based on nouns):

(a) musicians:
арфи́ст 'harpist', **виолончели́ст** 'cellist', **гитари́ст** 'guitarist',
пиани́ст 'pianist'.

(b) sportsmen:
волейболи́ст 'volleyball player', **тенниси́ст** 'tennis-player',
футболи́ст 'footballer', **хоккеи́ст** 'ice-hockey player', **шахмати́ст**
'chess-player'.

(c) drivers:
такси́ст taxi driver, **танки́ст** 'tank driver', **тракори́ст** 'tractor
driver'.

(21) -иха

Feminine ending (based on m. counterparts):

(a) women with particular characteristics:
труси́ха 'cowardly woman', **щеголи́ха** 'showy dresser'.

(b) practitioners:
пловчи́ха 'female swimmer', **повари́ха** 'cook', **портни́ха** 'dress-
maker', **ткачи́ха** 'weaver'.

(c) wives:
купчи́ха 'merchant's wife', **ме́льничиха** 'miller's wife', **полко́в-
ничиха** 'colonel's wife'.

(d) animals:
зайчи́ха 'doe', **лоси́ха** 'female elk', **осли́ха** 'female ass', **слони́ха**
'cow elephant'.

(22) -ица

Feminine ending:

(a) counterparts of zero-suffixed m. nouns:
фельдшери́ца 'female surgeon's assistant', **цари́ца** 'tsarina'.

(b) counterparts of nouns in -ец:

> **ревни́вица** 'jealous woman', **сослужи́вица** 'female colleague', **счастли́вица** 'happy woman'.

(c) animals and birds:

> **волчи́ца** 'she-wolf', **льви́ца** 'lioness', **медве́дица** 'she-bear', **орли́ца** 'female eagle'.

(23) -ич

Inhabitants of certain ancient towns and cities:

> **вя́тич** 'inhabitant of Vyatka', **костроми́ч** 'inhabitant of Kostroma', **москви́ч** 'Muscovite', **о́мич** 'inhabitant of Omsk', **пско́вич** 'inhabitant of Pskov'.

(24) -ище

(i) places (from nouns or – particularly those in -лище – verbs):

> **вмести́лище** 'receptacle', **жили́ще** 'dwelling', **кла́дбище** 'cemetery', **стре́льбище** 'firing range', **убе́жище** 'refuge'.

(ii) handles:

> **ножеви́ще** 'knife-handle', **кнутови́ще** 'whip-handle', **топори́ще** 'axe-handle'.

(25) -ка

(i) verbal noun:

The suffix appears after vowel + consonant combinations, and derives from:

(a) some 2nd-conjugation verbs in **-ить**: **запра́вка** 'refuelling' (from запра́вить(ся) 'to refuel'), **перево́зка** 'transportation', **чи́стка** 'cleaning'.

Note

> **Гла́жка** 'ironing' from гла́дить 'to iron', **слёжка** 'tracking' from следи́ть 'to track', and derivative **-ёжка/-овка** after vowel + *two* consonants: **бомбёжка** 'bombing' (from бомби́ть 'to bomb'), **сверло́вка** 'drilling'.

(b) from some verbs in **-ать**: **заде́ржка** 'delay' (from задержа́ть 'to delay'), **обрабо́тка** 'processing'.

Note

> **-овка** after vowel + *two* consonants: **переигро́вка** 'replay' from переигра́ть 'to replay'.

(c) from many verbs in **-овать**:**стыко́вка** 'docking' from стыкова́ть-ся 'to dock'; and **-ировать**: **меблиро́вка** 'furnishing' from меблирова́ть 'to furnish'.

Note

Some verbs in **-ировать** have alternative verbal nouns in **-ка** and **-ние**, e.g., **регулиро́вка/регули́рование** 'regulation' from регули́ровать 'to regulate'.

(d) from some verbs in **-оть**, e.g. **ко́лка** 'chopping' (from коло́ть 'to chop').

(e) from a number of other verbs: **мо́йка** 'washing' (from мыть 'to wash'), **по́имка** 'capture' (from пойма́ть 'to catch'), **стри́жка** 'hair-cutting' (from стричь 'to cut').

(ii) feminine suffix (from many zero-suffixed m. nouns and many m. nouns in **-ент, -ец, -ин, -ист, -ич**):

грузи́нка 'Georgian woman', **конькобе́жка** 'skater', **москви́чка** 'Muscovite', **студе́нтка** 'student', **трактори́стка** 'female tractor driver'.

(iii) contracted forms (from adj. + noun phrases):

вечёрка 'evening paper', **Ле́нинка** 'Lenin Library', **откры́тка** 'postcard', **со́тка** 'mobile phone', **электри́чка** 'suburban commuter train'.

Note

Some nouns in **-лка** denote rooms, e.g. **раздева́лка** 'changing room'.

(iv) objects (in **-лка**, from impf. verbs):

ве́шалка 'stand', **гре́лка** 'hot-water bottle', **зажига́лка** 'lighter', **открыва́лка** 'bottle-opener', **точи́лка** 'pencil sharpener'.

(26) **-ки**

Remnants:

объе́дки 'scraps', **опи́лки** 'sawdust', **очи́стки** 'peelings', **подо́нки** 'dregs'.

(27) **-ло**

Implements, agents of action (from impf. verbs):

крыло́ 'wing', **мы́ло** 'soap', **сверло́** 'drill', **точи́ло** 'grind-stone', **ши́ло** 'awl'.

Note

N. pl. counterparts **черни́ла** 'ink', **удила́** 'bit'.

(28) **-ние** (**-ание**/**-ение**)

Verbal nouns:

(i) in -ание/-яние (from many verbs in -ать/-ять):

вяза́ние 'knitting' (from **вяза́ть** 'to knit'), **пая́ние** 'soldering' (from **пая́ть** 'to solder'), including verbs in:

-овать/-евать (**рисова́ние** 'drawing', **завоева́ние** 'conquering');
-ствовать (**бо́дрствование** 'keeping awake');
-ировать (**клони́рование** 'cloning').

(ii) in -ение, from:

(a) many 2nd-conjugation verbs in **-ить**: **куре́ние** 'smoking' (from **кури́ть** 'to smoke'), **сохране́ние** 'preservation';

(b) verbs in **-еть**, of either conjugation:

старе́ние 'ageing' (from **старе́ть** 'to age'), **горе́ние** 'burning' (from **горе́ть** 'to burn')

Note

Consonant change applies to the following stem consonants:

б: **бл** **употребле́ние** 'use' (from **употреби́ть** 'to use');
в: **вл** **выздоровле́ние** 'convalescence' (from **вы́здороветь** 'to convalesce');
д: **ж** **броже́ние** 'fermentation' (from **броди́ть** 'to ferment');
д: **жд** **освобожде́ние** 'liberation' (from **освободи́ть** 'to liberate');
з: **ж** **отраже́ние** 'reflection' (from **отрази́ть** 'to reflect');
м: **мл** **оформле́ние** 'lay-out' (from **офо́рмить** 'to lay out');
п: **пл** **подкрепле́ние** 'reinforcement' (from **подкрепи́ть** 'to reinforce');
с: **ш** **приглаше́ние** 'invitation' (from **пригласи́ть** 'to invite');
ст: **щ** **упроще́ние** 'simplification' (from **упрости́ть** 'to simplify');
т: **ч** **кипяче́ние** 'boiling' (from **кипяти́ть** 'to boil');
т: **щ** **посеще́ние** 'visit' (from **посети́ть** 'to visit');
ф: **фл** **графле́ние** 'ruling of lines' (from **графи́ть** 'to rule lines').

(c) Verbs in **-сть**, **-чь** and **-ти** (with present-future stem consonant in verbal noun):

нападе́ние 'attack', from **напа́сть** 'to attack' (cf. 3rd person sing. нападёт)

прочте́ние 'reading', from **прочéсть** 'to read' (cf. 3rd person sing. прочтёт)

извлече́ние 'extraction', from **извлéчь** 'to extract' (cf. 3rd person sing. извлечёт)

пренебреже́ние 'disdain', from **пренебрéчь** 'to scorn' (cf. 3rd person sing. пренебрежёт)

введе́ние 'introduction', from **ввести́** 'to introduce' (cf. 3rd person sing. введёт)

спасе́ние 'salvation', from **спасти́** 'to save' (cf. 3rd person sing. спасёт)

погребе́ние 'burial', from **погрести́** 'to bury' (cf. 3rd person sing. погребёт).

Note

Derivative **-овение** (mainly from pf. verbs in **-нуть(ся)**): **возникнове́ние** 'rise', **исчезнове́ние** 'disappearance', **столкнове́ние** 'collision'.

(29) -ник

(i) Animate nouns:

(a) agent nouns (many based on verbs):
защи́тник 'defender', **изме́нник** 'traitor', **охо́тник** 'hunter', **рабо́тник** 'worker'.

(b) practitioners (based on nouns):
дво́рник 'yardman', **мясни́к** 'butcher', **пло́тник** 'carpenter'.

Note

Some nouns in **-ник** denote animate beings *and* inanimate objects:
проводни́к (a) 'guard on train' (b) 'electrical conductor'.

(c) nouns based on passive parts, (with retention of passive meaning):
воспи́танник 'pupil', **избра́нник** 'chosen one', **ста́вленник** 'protégé'.

Note

Some forms in **-еник** are active, others passive: **му́ченик** 'martyr', **тру́женик** 'worker', **учени́к** 'pupil'.

(ii) Inanimate nouns (based on nouns):

(a) groups of plants and trees:
е́льник 'fir plantation', **крапи́вник** 'clump of nettles', **мали́нник** 'raspberry bushes', **оси́нник** 'aspen copse'.

(b) printed materials:
зада́чник 'book of problems', **разгово́рник** 'conversation manual', **сбо́рник** 'collection', **сло́вник** 'glossary'.

(c) other objects:

бага́жник 'boot', **гра́дусник** 'thermometer', **моло́чник** 'milk-jug', **спу́тник** 'satellite', **ча́йник** 'teapot'.

Note
Objects in **-льник** take penultimate stress and derive from verbs:
   буди́льник 'alarm clock', **холоди́льник** 'refrigerator'.

(d) animal housing:
   коро́вник 'cow shed', **куря́тник** 'hen coop', **пче́льник** 'apiary'.

Note
Forms in **-атник/-ятник** are based on the names of young animals:
гуся́тник 'goose-run', **крольча́тник** 'rabbit-hutch', **теля́тник** 'calf shed'.

(30) -ница

(i) Feminine suffix:
   шко́льница 'school-girl', **уча́стница** 'participant', **учи́тельница** 'female teacher'.

(ii) Names of receptacles:
   мы́льница 'soap-dish', **пе́пельница** 'ash-tray', **пе́речница** 'pepper pot', **са́харница** 'sugar-bowl'.

(31) -ня

(i) verbal nouns (denoting energetic, protracted, sometimes irritating, activity):
   беготня́ 'rushing around', **болтовня́** 'chatter', **возня́** 'romping around', **суетня́** 'fuss, bustle'.

(ii) animate groups:
   ребятня́ 'kids', **родня́** 'relatives', **солдатня́** 'soldiery'.

(iii) places (based on nouns):
   колоко́льня 'belfry', **пека́рня** 'bakery', **тамо́жня** 'customs house'.

Note
(a)   Some nouns denote housing for birds: **голубя́тня** 'dovecote', etc.

(b)   Forms in **-льня** derive from verbs: **купа́льня** 'bathing-place' (from купа́ться 'to bathe'), **спа́льня** 'bedroom', **чита́льня** 'reading room'.

Note
Also **ба́ня** 'bath-house', **бо́йня** 'slaughter-house', **ку́хня** 'kitchen'.

(32) -ович/-(ь)евич

The suffixes **-ович/-(ь)евич** are used to form masculine patronymics, **-ович** for first names ending in a consonant: **Алекса́ндрович** 'Aleksandrovich', **-евич** for names in **-ай/-ей**:**Андре́евич** 'Andreevich', **Никола́евич** 'Nikolaevich', **-ьевич** for names in **-ий**: **Васи́-льевич** 'Vasilevich', (but **Дми́триевич** 'Dmitrievich' from **Дми́трий** 'Dmitrii').

Note
(a) f. equivalents: **Алекса́ндровна** 'Aleksandrovna', **Андре́евна** 'Andreevna', **Васи́льевна** 'Vasilevna'.

(b) m. patronymics in **-ич** from first names in **-а/-я**: **Ильи́ч** 'Ilich' (from **Илья́** 'Ilya'), **Кузьми́ч** 'Kuzmich' (from **Кузьма́** 'Kuzma'), with f. in **-инична**: **Ильи́нична** 'Ilinichna', **Кузьми́нична** 'Kuzminichna'.

(33) -ок

(i) Agents of actions (based on verbs):
ездо́к 'rider', **знато́к** 'expert', **игро́к** 'player', **стрело́к** 'marksman'.

(ii) Verbal nouns (individual physical actions, based on unprefixed verbs):
бросо́к 'a throw', **глото́к** 'a swallow', **зево́к** 'a yawn', **звоно́к** 'a phone call', **прыжо́к** 'a jump', **свисто́к** 'a whistle', **скачо́к** 'a leap'.

(iii) Objects (mostly based on prefixed verbs):
набро́сок 'sketch', **обло́мок** 'fragment', **оку́рок** 'cigarette end', **оско́лок** 'splinter', **пода́рок** 'gift'.

*Note: Un*prefixed **кипято́к** 'boiling water'.

(34) -ость/-есть

(i) Qualities (based on adjs. in -ый/-ий):
ве́жливость 'politeness', **го́рдость** 'pride', **гру́бость** 'coarseness', **све́жесть** 'freshness', **хра́брость** 'bravery'.

Note
Some are based on passive parts: **сде́ржанность** 'restraint', **терпи́мость** 'tolerance'.

(ii) Feelings:
жа́лость 'pity', **не́жность** 'tenderness', **ра́дость** 'joy', **ре́вность** 'jealousy'.

(iii) States, based on passive parts.:

(a) in -мость:
   невесо́мость 'weightlessness', **незави́симость** 'independence', **совмести́мость** 'compatibility'.

(b) in -нность:
   ангажи́рованность 'partisanship', **влюблённость** 'infatuation', **вседозво́ленность** 'permissiveness'.

(iv) ratio or rate (based on passive parts.):
   разводи́мость 'divorce rate', **рожда́емость** 'birth rate', **успева́емость** 'academic progress'.

Note
Сме́ртность 'death rate'.

(35) -от

Sounds (based on verbs):
   гро́хот 'din', **ро́пот** 'murmur', **то́пот** 'clatter', **шёпот** 'whisper'.

(36) -ота

(i) Qualities (based on adjs. in -ый/-ой):
   доброта́ 'kindness', **красота́** 'beauty', **простота́** 'simplicity', **чистота́** 'cleanliness'.

(ii) States (based on adjs.):

(a) general:
   беднота́ 'poverty', **теснота́** 'cramped conditions', **пустота́** 'emptiness', **теплота́** 'warmth'.

(b) disabilities and ailments (based on adjs. in -ой):
   глухота́ 'deafness', **немота́** 'dumbness', **слепота́** 'blindness', **хромота́** 'lameness'.

Note
Based on *verbs*, in -ота: **дремо́та** 'drowsiness' (from дрема́ть 'to doze'), **зево́та** 'fit of yawning', **ико́та** 'hiccuping'.

(37) -ствие

(i) Abstract states:
   бе́дствие 'disaster', **споко́йствие** 'tranquillity', **сумасше́ствие** 'madness'.

(ii) Verbal nouns (from verbs in **-ствовать**):
   путеше́ствие 'journey', **соде́йствие** 'cooperation', **соотве́тствие** 'accordance'.

(38) -ство

(i) Qualities (mostly from adjs. in **-ый**):
безу́мство 'foolhardiness', **досто́инство** 'dignity', **лука́вство** 'craftiness', **постоя́нство** 'constancy', **упо́рство** 'stubbornness'.

Note
Some nouns in **-ничество** correlate with verbs in **-ничать:** **ло́дырничество** 'skiving' (cf. ло́дырничать 'to skive'), **скря́жничест-во** 'miserliness'.

(ii) States (based on nouns or adjs.):
а́вторство 'authorship', **бога́тство** 'wealth', **матери́нство** 'mo-therhood', **одино́чество** 'solitude', **пья́нство** 'drunkenness'.

Note
Some nouns in **-ничество** correlate with verbs in **-ничать:** **бродя́жничество** 'vagrancy' (cf. бродя́жничать 'to be a tramp').

(iii) Verbal nouns:
бе́гство 'escape', **воровство́** 'thieving', **дежу́рство** 'being on duty', **уби́йство** 'murder'.

Note
(a) Infix **-ов-** in **мотовство́** 'extravagance' (from мота́ть 'to squander'), **сватовство́** 'match-making', **хвастовство́** 'boasting'.

(iv) Collectives (national, social, administrative or other groups):
госуда́рство 'state', **министе́рство** 'ministry', **о́бщество** 'society', **прави́тельство** 'government', **студе́нчество** 'student body', **чело-ве́чество** 'mankind'.

(v) Quantity (based on adverbs):
большинство́ 'majority', **коли́чество** 'quantity', **меньшинство́** 'minority', **мно́жество** 'multitude'.

(39) -сть

Feelings
за́висть 'envy', **не́нависть** 'hatred', **страсть** 'passion'.

(40) -тель

(i) Agents of actions (mainly based on verbs):

(a) -атель (stress as in infinitive):
избира́тель 'voter', **покупа́тель** 'customer', **по́льзователь** 'user', **слу́шатель** 'listener', **чита́тель** 'reader'.

(b) -итель (stress on -и-):

граби́тель 'robber', **жи́тель** 'inhabitant', **зри́тель** 'viewer', **мысли́тель** 'thinker'.

(ii) Practitioners:

води́тель 'driver', **писа́тель** 'writer', **строи́тель** 'builder', **учи́тель** 'teacher'.

(iii) Objects (many from transitive verbs):

выключа́тель 'switch', **дви́гатель** 'engine', **загрязни́тель** 'pollutant', **истреби́тель** 'fighter plane'.

(41) -тие

Verbal nouns, from verbs, mainly transitive and prefixed, based on:

-бить (e.g. **разби́тие** 'smashing')
-быть (e.g. **прибы́тие** 'arrival', but **добы́ча** 'extraction')
-вить (e.g. **разви́тие** 'development')
-дуть (e.g. **разду́тие** 'inflating')
-жать (e.g. **сжа́тие** 'compression')
-клясть (e.g. **прокля́тие** 'damnation')
-крыть (e.g. **закры́тие** 'closure')
-лить (e.g. **кровопроли́тие** 'bloodshed'
-плыть (e.g. **отплы́тие** 'departure')
-пять (e.g. **распя́тие** 'crucifixion')
-чать (e.g. **зача́тие** 'conception')
-(н)ять (e.g. **приня́тие** 'taking').
Also **взя́тие** 'capture' (from взять 'to take').

Note
Correlation with perfective passive participles in **-т-** (e.g. **взя́тый** 'taken', **взя́тие** 'taking', etc. See **357–358**).

(42) -ун

Agents of actions (from unprefixed impf. verbs):

бегу́н 'runner', **лгун** 'liar', **несу́н** 'pilferer', **опеку́н** 'guardian', **плясу́н** 'dancer'.

Note
-ун in the names of some animals: **грызу́н** 'rodent', **скаку́н** 'racer'.

(43) -ура

Collectives:

адвокату́ра 'the Bar', **клиенту́ра** 'clientele', **номенклату́ра** '*nomenklatura*' (Soviet élite), **прокурату́ра** 'staff of procurator's office'.

(44) -уха

(i) Medical conditions (based on colour adjs.):
желту́ха 'jaundice', золоту́ха 'scrofula', красну́ха 'German measles'.

(ii) Contracted forms (usually with pejorative meaning):
группову́ха 'gang crime', показу́ха 'sham, façade', порну́ха 'pornography', черну́ха 'denigration'.

(45) -ча

Verbal nouns (from compounds of **-дать** and some others, e.g. по́рча 'spoiling', from по́ртить 'to spoil'):
вы́дача 'issue', переда́ча 'transmission', разда́ча 'distribution', сда́ча 'handing over'.

Note
(a) Some verbs in -дать have verbal nouns in **-дание** (e.g. изда́ние 'publishing'), прода́ть 'to sell' has прода́жа 'sale'.
(b) Добы́ча 'mining' from добы́ть 'to mine' (some verbs in -быть have verbal nouns in -тие, e.g. прибы́тие 'arrival').

(46) -ша

Feminine suffix (especially from nouns in -р/-рь, colloquial):

(a) practitioners:
ба́рменша 'barmaid', библиоте́карша 'librarian', касси́рша 'cashier'.

(b) wives:
генера́льша 'general's wife', министе́рша 'minister's wife', профе́ссорша 'professor's wife'.

(47) -щик (-чик after д, ж, з, с, т):

(i) Persons:

(a) general (from nouns or transitive verbs, often with a pejorative meaning):
обма́нщик 'deceiver', отмы́вщик де́нег 'money-launderer', попу́тчик 'fellow-traveller', уго́нщик 'vehicle thief'.

(b) practitioners:
а́томщик 'atomic scientist', дальнобо́йщик 'long-distance lorry-driver', лётчик 'pilot', перево́дчик 'interpreter', часовщи́к 'watch-maker'.

Note

Some denote persons *and* implements: **счётчик** 'census-taker', 'meter'.

Forms in derivative **-льщик** (with penultimate stress) derive from impf. verbs: **боле́льщик** 'fan', **чисти́льщик** 'cleaner'.

(ii) objects:

автоотве́тчик 'answerphone', **бомбардиро́вщик** 'bomber', **переда́тчик** 'transmitter', **погру́зчик** 'loader', **тра́льщик** 'trawler'.

(48) -щина (-чина after д and т),

Attitudes and trends (from adjs. and nouns, especially surnames, usually pejorative):

вое́нщина 'military attitude', **обло́мовщина** 'Oblomovism', **ста́линщина** 'Stalinism'.

Note

-ов- infix in **дедовщи́на** 'army brutality' (from дед 'senior soldier'), **митинго́вщина** 'megaphone diplomacy'.

(49) -щица

Feminine counterparts to nouns in -щик/-чик:

буфе́тчица 'bar-maid', **крановщи́ца** 'crane-driver'.

(50) -ыш

Non-adults and some others (sometimes expressing sympathy or condescension, from adjs.):

коротьı́ш 'short person', **крепы́ш** 'sturdy child', **малы́ш** 'child, little boy'.

(51) -ье

Districts, areas, surroundings:

верхо́вье 'upper reaches', **низо́вье** 'lower reaches', **побере́жье** 'coastline', **предго́рье** 'foothills', **Подмоско́вье** 'Moscow region'.

(52) -ья

Feminine counterparts to nouns in -ун:

бегу́нья 'runner', **лгу́нья** 'liar', **плясу́нья** 'dancer'.

Note

For diminutive suffixes, see **105** 1–4 and **106** 1–2, for augmentative suffixes, **109** 1–2, for gender differentiation through suffixes, **43**.

Gender

30   Masculine, feminine and neuter gender

(1) Adjectives, pronouns and the past-tense forms of verbs have the same gender as the noun they qualify or stand for:

хоро́ший муж	a good husband
хоро́шая жена́	a good wife
хоро́шее де́ло	a good cause

Оте́ц **дово́лен**	Father is pleased
Мать **дово́льна**	Mother is pleased

Где **стол**? Вот **он**	Where is the table? There it is
Где **ка́рта**? Вот **она́**	Where is the map? There it is
Где **окно́**? Вот **оно́**	Where is the window? There it is

Дом стоя́л в це́нтре го́рода
The house stood in the city centre

Ёлка стоя́ла в це́нтре го́рода
The Christmas tree stood in the city centre

Зда́ние стоя́ло в це́нтре го́рода
The building stood in the city centre

Note

(a) There is no equivalent in Russian of the articles 'a' and 'the'. Thus, for example, **дом** means 'a house' and 'the house', the difference being resolved by context or word order (see **476** (1) note (b), as well as **126** (2) (i), **128** (2) note, **138** (1) (iii) (b), **143** (2) (i), **193** (4) (iii)). Note that such forms as **э́тот** 'this', **тот са́мый** 'the very', **вы́ше упомя́нутый** 'the above-mentioned' etc. are sometimes used where an article would be used in English.

(b) When the predicate precedes the subject and the subject consists of a number of nouns, agreement may be with the first noun only: **Ну́жно** терпе́ние, понима́ние, взаи́мная откры́тость и доброжела́тельность (*Komsomolskaya pravda*) 'Patience, understanding, mutual openness and benevolence are necessary' (pl. **нужны́** would also be possible, however).

(2) Grammatical gender (the assignment of gender to a noun in accordance with its ending) is distinguished from **natural** gender (the

assignment of gender in accordance with the sex of the being denoted by the noun, e.g. **мать** 'mother' (feminine), **дядя** 'uncle' (masculine)). Some nouns which can denote persons of either sex have **common** gender, that is, their gender varies in accordance with the sex of the person concerned (e.g. **сирота́** 'orphan' (masculine or feminine) see **35**).

(3) Gender affects only the **singular** of nouns; **plural** forms do not exhibit gender characteristics. The same adjectival endings, for example, are used for the plurals of nouns of *all* genders, cf.:

Singular	Plural
хоро́ший муж a good husband	**хоро́шие** мужья́ good husbands
хоро́шая жена́ a good wife	**хоро́шие** жёны good wives
хоро́шее де́ло a good cause	**хоро́шие** дела́ good causes

Note

Gender may, however, be revealed in, for example, a subordinate clause: хоро́шие мужья́, **ка́ждый** (masculine singular relative pronoun) из кото́рых помога́л по до́му 'good husbands, each of whom helped around the house'.

31   Masculine nouns

The following categories of noun are masculine:

(1) All nouns ending in a hard consonant, e.g. **заво́д** 'factory'

(2) All nouns ending in **-й**, e.g. **музе́й** 'museum'

(3) 'Natural' masculines in **-а/-я**. These include:

(i) Nouns which by definition denote males:

де́душка	grandfather
дя́дя	uncle
мужчи́на	man
па́па	Dad
слуга́	male servant
ю́ноша	youth, young man

including a few obsolescent nouns, e.g. **воево́да** 'commander'.

(ii) Some masculine first names:

Илья́	Ilya
Ники́та	Nikita
Фома́	Foma

(iii) The familiar forms of many masculine first names:

Ва́ня	Vanya (short for Ива́н)
Воло́дя	Volodya (short for Влади́мир)
Са́ша	Sasha (short for Алекса́ндр (*or* for feminine Алекса́ндра)) etc.

(4) Diminutives and augmentatives based on masculine nouns:

| **доми́шко** (from дом 'house') | little house |
| **доми́на, доми́ще** (also from дом) | enormous house |

(5) **Подмасте́рье** 'apprentice'.

(6) Many nouns ending in a soft sign (see **33**).

32   Feminine nouns

Categories of feminine noun include the following.

(1) Most nouns in **-a/-я** (see, however, **31** (3) and **34** (4)).

(2) Many nouns which end in a soft sign (see **33**).

33   Soft-sign nouns

Some soft-sign nouns are feminine (approximately three-quarters of the total); the rest are masculine. It is possible to give guidelines for determining the gender of many soft-sign nouns.

(1) Feminine soft-sign nouns

(i) 'Natural' feminines: **дочь** 'daughter' (see also (ii)), **лань** 'doe', **мать** 'mother', **не́тель** 'heifer', **свекро́вь** 'mother-in-law' (husband's mother).

(ii) All nouns in **-жь, -чь, -шь, -щь, -знь, -мь, -пь, -фь.**

(iii) All nouns in **-сть**, except for masculine **гость** 'guest', **не́христь** 'infidel, rogue' and **тесть** 'father-in-law' (wife's father).

(iv) All nouns in

-бь except for masculine **го́лубь** 'dove'

-вь except for masculine **червь** 'worm'

-дь except for masculine **вождь** 'leader', **гвоздь** 'nail', **Господь** 'Lord', **груздь** 'milk-agaric', **дождь** 'rain', **жёлудь** 'acorn', **лебедь** 'swan', **медведь** 'bear' and a few historicisms

-зь except for masculine **князь** 'prince', **ферзь** 'queen' (chess), **язь** 'ide' (fish of the carp family) and a few archaisms such as **витязь** 'knight'

-сь except for masculine **гусь** 'goose', **карась** 'Crucian carp', **лосось/лосось** 'salmon', **лось** 'elk'

-ть except for natural masculines (see (2) (i) below) and masculine **дёготь** 'tar', **коготь** 'claw', **лапоть** 'bast shoe', **локоть** 'elbow', **ломоть** 'slice', **ноготь** 'finger-nail', **путь** 'way', **тать** 'thief', **ять** 'the letter *yat*'

(v) Nouns derived through deaffixation from adjectives: **высь** 'heights' (cf. **высокий** 'high'), **гладь** 'smooth surface', **глубь** 'depth', **глушь** 'backwoods', **даль** 'distance', **зелень** 'greenery', **лень** 'laziness', **мель** shallows', **новь** 'virgin soil', **тишь** 'quiet', **удаль** 'daring', **ширь** 'expanse', **явь** 'reality'.

(vi) Nouns derived through deaffixation from verbs: **гарь** 'burning' (cf. **гореть** 'to burn'), **мазь** 'ointment', **насыпь** 'embankment', **подпись** 'signature', **связь** 'connection', **смесь** 'mixture', **тварь** 'creature'.

(vii) Deverbal nouns in **-ель**, e.g. **гибель** 'ruin' (cf. **гибнуть** 'to perish'), **колыбель** 'cradle', **метель** 'snow storm'.

(2) Masculine soft-sign nouns

(i) 'Natural' masculines: **гость** 'guest', **деверь** 'brother-in-law' (husband's brother), **зять** 'son-in-law/brother-in-law', **князь** 'prince', **кобель** 'male dog', **король** 'king', **парень** 'lad', **селезень** 'drake', **тесть** 'father-in-law' (wife's father), **царь** 'tsar'.

(ii) Deverbal agent nouns (animate and inanimate) in **-тель** (**создатель** 'creator', **выключатель** 'light-switch') or **-итель** (**учитель** 'teacher', **краситель** 'dye').

(iii) Nouns in **-арь** derived from verbs (**пекарь** 'baker'), nouns (**вратарь** 'goal-keeper') or adjectives (**дикарь** 'savage').

(iv) The names of **months** ending in a soft sign.

(v) All names of birds ending in a soft sign except for feminine **выпь** 'bittern' and **неясыть** 'tawny owl'; all names of insects ending in a soft sign except for feminine **моль** 'moth'.

The gender of other soft-sign nouns has to be learnt individually.

34   Neuter nouns

Categories of neuter noun include the following.

(1) Nouns in **-o** (see, however, **31** (4)).

(2) Nouns in **-e**. However, **кóфе** 'coffee' is masculine (neuter in substandard registers only; see **36** (1) note (a)). See also **31** (4).

(3) Nouns in **-ё**.

(4) Nouns in **-мя: врéмя** 'time', **и́мя** 'first name etc. See **64**.

(5) Other parts of speech functioning as nouns: **грóмкое** «урá» 'a loud "hurrah"'.

35   Common gender

A number of nouns in **-a** and **-я** have common gender. They can denote males or females, adjectival, pronominal and verb agreement varying with the sex of the person denoted by the noun, e.g. **гóрький** пья́ница 'confirmed drunkard' (male), **гóрькая** пья́ница 'confirmed drunkard' (female). Among the commonest of the nouns are бродя́га 'tramp', главá 'head, chief', калéка 'cripple', коллéга 'colleague', левшá 'left-handed person', малю́тка 'baby', невéжда 'ignoramus', неря́ха 'litter-bug', обжóра 'glutton', одинóчка 'lone person', пья́ница 'drunkard', сиротá 'orphan' (кру́глый/кру́глая сиротá 'person who has lost both parents'), уби́йца 'murderer', у́мница 'clever person':

> Говори́те со мной, как с **кру́глым** невéждой (Grekova)
> Speak to me as to a complete ignoramus

36   Indeclinable nouns of foreign origin

(1) Most indeclinable loan-words in **-ao, -ay, -e, -и, -o, -оа, -оу -у, -уа, -ю, -э** are neuter: какáо 'cocoa'; нóу-хáу 'know how'; ательé 'workshop', желé 'jelly', кабарé 'cabaret', кафé 'café', кашнé 'scarf', коммюникé 'communiqué', купé 'compartment', портмонé 'purse', резюмé 'résumé', тирé 'dash', фойé 'foyer', шоссé 'highway'; ви́ски 'whisky', жюри́ 'jury', пари́ 'bet', пенáльти 'penalty' (also masculine), рáлли 'rally', такси́ 'taxi', шасси́ 'undercarriage'; бистрó 'bistro', бюрó 'office', депó 'depot', кинó 'cinema', метрó 'underground railway', пальтó 'overcoat', пиани́но 'piano', рáдио 'radio'; боá 'boa'

(but боа́ 'boa-constrictor' is masculine); шо́у 'show'; рагу́ 'ragout'; амплуа́ 'role'; интервью́ 'interview', меню́ 'menu', ревю́ 'review'; карата́ 'karate'.

Note

(a) **Ко́фе** 'coffee' is masculine: Ля́ля спроси́ла, не сде́лать ли **кре́пкий** ко́фе (Trifonov) 'Lyalya asked if she should not make some strong coffee', and масс-ме́диа, 'mass media' is feminine.

(b) Only context can show the number (singular or plural) of an indeclinable noun: thus В шкафу́ **виси́т но́вое** пальто́/**вися́т но́вые** пальто́ 'A new coat is hanging/new coats are hanging in the cupboard'; **одно́** пальто́ 'one coat', **де́сять** пальто́ 'ten coats'.

(2) Some indeclinables assume the gender of the central or 'generic' noun. Thus, **торна́до** 'tornado' is masculine (cf. ве́тер 'wind'), likewise **пушту́** 'Pushtu', **урду́** 'Urdu', **хи́нди** 'Hindi' (cf. язы́к 'language') and **фло́ппи** (cf. фло́ппи-диск) 'floppy disk'. **Авеню́** 'avenue' is feminine (cf. у́лица 'street'), as are **саля́ми** 'salami' (cf. колбаса́ 'sausage'), **цеце́** 'tsetse fly' (cf. му́ха 'fly') and **цуна́ми** 'tsunami' (alternatively neuter) (cf. волна́ 'wave'):

Цуна́ми **унесла́** его́ в океа́н (Gagarin)
The giant wave carried him out to sea

(3) The gender of many indeclinable nouns which denote human beings follows the principle of natural gender. Thus, буржуа́ 'bourgeois', крупье́ 'croupier', мафио́зо/мафио́зи 'mafioso', маэ́стро 'maestro' and ре́фери/рефери́ 'referee' are masculine, while ле́ди 'lady' and мада́м 'madam' are feminine. Some nouns have common gender (визави́ 'counterpart', '*vis-à-vis*', протеже́ 'protégé(e)', хи́ппи 'hippy'), whereas атташе́ 'attaché', инко́гнито 'person who is incognito' and конферансье́ 'compère' are masculine and папара́цци 'paparazzi' is plural only.

(4) Indeclinable names of animals also have common gender: гну 'gnu', кенгуру́ 'kangaroo', шимпанзе́ 'chimpanzee' etc. Nouns are treated as masculine when the sex of the animal is irrelevant (**ра́неный** гну 'a wounded gnu'), but feminine gender is assigned in 'female' contexts:

Шимпанзе́ **корми́ла** детёныша
The chimpanzee was feeding her baby

(5) The names of some birds are masculine (какаду́ 'cockatoo', марабу́ 'marabou', флами́нго 'flamingo') while коли́бри 'humming-bird' is masculine or feminine.

37   Indeclinable place names

Indeclinable place names take the gender of the central ('generic') noun. Names of towns and islands are masculine (cf. го́род 'town' and о́стров 'island'): Баку́ 'Baku', Гла́зго 'Glasgow', Кале́ 'Calais', О́сло 'Oslo', Ско́пье/Ско́пле 'Skopje', Со́чи 'Sochi' (also plural: ста́рые Со́чи 'old Sochi'), Тбили́си 'Tbilisi', То́кио 'Tokyo'; Ка́при 'Capri', Таи́ти 'Tahiti'. Similarly, the names of rivers are feminine (cf. река́ 'river'): споко́йная Миссиси́пи 'the calm Mississippi'. Ю́нгфрау 'the Jungfrau' is feminine (cf. гора́ 'mountain'). Э́ри 'Lake Erie' is neuter (cf. о́зеро 'lake'). Мали́ 'Mali' has alternative feminine and neuter gender (cf. страна́ 'country' and госуда́рство 'state'). Despite exceptions to the rule, the 'generic' principle is the norm.

38   Titles of books etc.

The generic principle is usually applied in assigning gender to titles which are indeclinable: **турге́невская** «*Муму́*» 'Turgenev's *Mumu*' (cf. по́весть (f.) 'tale'), **ло́ндонская** «*Таймс*» 'the London *Times*' (cf. газе́та 'newspaper'). A title based on an oblique case may observe the generic principle (**го́рьковская** «*На дне*» 'Gorky's *Lower Depths*' (cf. пье́са 'play')) or take a neuter adjective (**го́рьковское** «*На дне*»).
Otherwise, gender is determined by the gender and number of the title: **пу́шкинский** «*Евге́ний Оне́гин*» 'Pushkin's *Eugene Onegin*', турге́невское «*Дворя́нское гнездо́*» 'Turgenev's *Nest of Noblemen*', **савра́совские** «*Грачи́ прилете́ли*» 'Savrasov's (painting) *The rooks have arrived*'.

Note
In order to avoid possible incongruence, a genre word may be introduced: **рома́н** Толсто́го «*А́нна Каре́нина*» 'Tolstoy's novel *Anna Karenina*'.

39   Acronyms

The gender of acronyms is usually determined by their ending. Thus, бомж (from без определённого ме́ста жи́тельства 'without a definite place of residence') 'homeless person', **вуз** (from вы́сшее уче́бное заведе́ние 'higher teaching establishment'), **загс** (from отде́л за́писи а́ктов гражда́нского состоя́ния 'registry office') are masculine. However, the gender of the central noun may sometimes prove decisive.

Thus, **роно́** (from райо́нный отде́л наро́дного образова́ния 'local education authority') was originally neuter but is now usually treated as masculine.

Note
Loan acronyms such as ла́зер, from English 'laser' (light amplification by stimulated emission of radiation).

40   Alphabetisms

Alphabetisms consist of initial *capital* letters, many being pronounced as letters rather than words, and most are indeclinable, though there are exceptions among those assigned masculine gender (see **73**). In terms of gender assignment, alphabetisms subdivide as follows:

(1) Those which retain the gender of the central noun:

(i) Masculine: **ВИЧ** [вич] (ви́рус имму̀нодефици́та челове́ка) 'human immunodeficiency virus', 'HIV', **МГУ** [эм-гэ-у́] (Моско́вский госуда́рственный университе́т) 'Moscow State University', **МХАТ** [мхат] (Моско́вский худо́жественный академи́ческий теа́тр) 'Moscow Art Theatre', **НИИ** [ний] (Нау́чно-иссле́довательский институ́т) 'Scientific Research Institute', **ОВИР** [ови́р] (Отде́л виз и регистра́ция иностра́нных гра́ждан) 'Visa Department and Registration of Foreign Nationals', **СКА** [эс-ка́ or ска] (спорти́вный клуб а́рмии) 'Army Sports Club'.

(ii) Feminine: **АТС** [а-тэ-э́с] (автомати́ческая телефо́нная ста́нция) 'automatic telephone exchange', **ГАИ** [гай] (Госуда́рственная автомоби́льная инспе́кция) 'State Vehicle Inspectorate' (see page 596), **ГЭС** [гэс] (гѝдроэлектри́ческая ста́нция/гѝдроэлектроста́нция) 'hydroelectric power station', **ООН** [оон] (Организа́ция Объед-инённых На́ций) 'United Nations Organization', **СКВ** [эс-ка-ве́] (свобо́дно конверти́руемая валю́та) 'freely-convertible currency', **ТЭЦ** [тэц] (теплова́я элѐктроцентра́ль) 'thermal power station':

> Здесь **рабо́тала** мо́щная ГЭС (*Sputnik*)
> A mighty power station was in operation here

(iii) Neuter: **СНГ** [эс-эн-гэ́] (Содру́жество незави́симых госуда́рств) 'Commonwealth of Independent States', 'CIS', **СП** [эс-пэ́] (совме́ст-ное предприя́тие) 'joint venture', **ТЯО** [тя́о] (такти́ческое я́дерное ору́жие) 'tactical nuclear weapons'.

(iv) Plural: **ЯКВ** [я-ка-ве́] (я́дерные косми́ческие вооруже́ния) 'nuclear space armaments'.

(2) Some much-used alphabetisms acquire the gender implied by the ending. Thus, **БАМ** [бам] (Байка́ло-Аму́рская магистра́ль 'Baikal–Amur Railway') is masculine, despite feminine магистра́ль, **ДОСААФ** [доса́ф] (Доброво́льное о́бщество соде́йствия а́рмии, авиа́ции и фло́ту 'Voluntary Association for Cooperation with the Army, Air Force and Navy') is masculine, despite neuter о́бщество, **МИД** [мид] (Министе́рство иностра́нных дел 'Ministry of Foreign Affairs'), which was once neuter, is now masculine, **НЭП** [нэп] (но́вая экономи́ческая поли́тика 'New Economic Policy'), which was once feminine, is now masculine and **ТАСС** [тасс] (Телегра́фное аге́нтство Сове́тского Сою́за 'Telegraphic Agency of the Soviet Union'), (now replaced by **ИТА́Р-ТАСС:** Информацио́нное телегра́фное аге́нтство Росси́и – Телегра́фное аге́нтство суверéнных стран 'Information and Telegraphic Agency of Russia – Telegraphic Agency of the Sovereign Countries'), once neuter, also acquired masculine gender:

> БАМ **был объя́влен** всесою́зной стро́йкой (*Sputnik*)
> The Baikal-Amur Railway was declared a national construction zone

(3) Some alphabetisms differentiate gender stylistically. Thus, **ЖЭК** [жэк] (жили́щно-эксплуатацио́нная конто́ра 'housing office'), initially feminine in written styles (cf. конто́ра), is commonly assigned masculine gender in everyday speech.

(4) Those based on the initials of *foreign* words tend to acquire gender in accordance with the ending. Thus, **ФИАТ** [фиа́т] (Fabbrica Italiana Automobili Torino) is masculine, **ФИФА** [фифа́] (Fédération Internationale de Football Association) is feminine and **НАТО** [на́то] (North Atlantic Treaty Organization) is neuter. **США** [сша/сэ-ше-а́] (Соединённые Шта́ты Аме́рики 'United States of America') is plural.

Note
Alphabetisms may be rendered phonetically, particularly in dialogue:

> Ва́шу **эн-тэ-э́р** (НТР – нау́чно-техни́ческая револю́ция)
> я ви́дел (Grekova)
> I have seen your scientific-technical revolution

> Е́сли не в реме́сленное, то в **фе-зе-о́** (ФЗО – фабри́чно-заводско́е обуче́ние), мо́жет быть, возьму́т, сказа́л он. (Panova)
> 'If I don't get into trade school', he said, 'I might get accepted for factory apprentice training'.

41   Stump compounds

'Stump compounds' incorporate the truncated forms of one or more words: **забастком** (from забастовочный комитет) 'strike committee', **колхо́з** (from коллекти́вное хозя́йство) 'collective farm', **ликбе́з** (from ликвида́ция безгра́мотности) 'elimination of illiteracy', **собе́с** (from социа́льное обеспе́чение) 'social security' (all masculine). Most nouns in this productive category take their gender from the ending of the stump compound. Those which denote people may have common gender, e.g. **управдо́м** (from управля́ющий/-ая до́мом) 'house manager' (управдо́м **сказа́л**, что **дово́лен** 'the house manager said he was pleased', управдо́м **сказа́ла**, что **дово́льна** 'the house manager said she was pleased') and similarly **за̀вка́федрой** (from заве́дующий/ -ая ка́федрой) 'head of university department'. **Са́мбо** (from само-оборо́на без ору́жия) 'unarmed combat' is neuter, **стѐнгазе́та** (from стенна́я газе́та) 'wall newspaper' is feminine.

Note
The full title заве́дующий ка́федрой 'head of department' is preferred to за̀вка́федрой in official contexts, referring to persons of either sex, and in contexts where the sex of the person is irrelevant, заве́дующая being confined to colloquial registers or references to a particular person, cf.:

Собесе́дник называ́ет Евге́нию Ива́новну Ду́рову, **заве́дующую** гру́ппой биохими́ческих иссле́дований (*Pravda*)
The person I am speaking to mentions Evgeniya Ivanovna Durova, head of the biochemical research group

42   Compound hyphenated nouns

The gender of compound hyphenated nouns is determined by the gender of the central noun, which often precedes the qualifier: **га́лстук-ба́бочка** (m.) 'bow-tie', **дива́н-крова́ть** (m.) 'divan-bed', **кре́сло-кача́лка** (n.) 'rocking chair', **раке́та-носи́тель** (f.) 'carrier-rocket', **шко́ла-интерна́т** (f.) 'boarding school'. However, in some compounds the qualifier precedes the central noun: **автома́т-заку́сочная** (f.) 'vending machine', **штаб-кварти́ра** (f.) 'headquarters':

Автома́т-заку́сочная **отремонти́рована**
The vending machine has been repaired

13 июля на ста́ртовом по́ле **появи́лась** дубли́рующая раке́та-носи́тель (*Russia Today*)

A reserve carrier-rocket appeared on the launch pad on 13 July

43   Differentiation of gender through suffixes

(1) Suffixes are used to distinguish male and female representatives of various occupations, professions, organizations, functions, nationalities etc. See also **29**.

Male	Female	
армяни́н	армя́нка	Armenian
бегу́н	бегу́нья	runner
большеви́к	большеви́чка	Bolshevik
корми́лец	корми́лица	breadwinner
крановщи́к	крановщи́ца	crane operator
лётчик	лётчица	pilot
не́мец	не́мка	German
поэ́т	поэте́сса	poet
сто́рож	сторожи́ха	guard
супру́г	супру́га	spouse
учени́к	учени́ца	pupil
учи́тель	учи́тельница	teacher

Note also стари́к 'old man', стару́ха 'old woman'.

(2) The masculine form may, however, be used for persons of either sex:

(i) Where gender differentiation is of no significance in a particular occupation. Thus, библиоте́карь 'librarian', води́тель 'driver', касси́р 'cashier', кондӯ́ктор '(bus-) conductor' etc. can be used of men *and* women. The feminine suffix -ша (as in библиоте́карша, касси́рша, конду́кторша) has in any case been devalued by its earlier use in designating a woman in terms of her husband's occupation: генера́льша 'general's wife' (cf. купчи́ха 'merchant's wife'). In modern Russian -ша is reserved for some occupations practised predominantly by women (e.g. маникю́рша 'manicurist' (маникю́р means 'manicure')) or denotes a lower-prestige occupation (cf. секрета́рша 'shorthand typist' and секрета́рь 'secretary' (of, for example, a party committee)). See also **29** (46).

Note

Учи́тель tends to sound more prestigious than **учи́тельница** and may refer to a female as well as to a male teacher, especially where the subject is specified: Она́ **учи́тель** матема́тики 'She is a mathematics teacher'. Compare Онá наилýчший **учи́тель** в шкóле 'She is the best teacher in the school' (i.e. of all the teachers, male and female) and Онá наилýчшая **учи́тельница** в шкóле 'She is the best woman-teacher in the school'.

(ii) In cases where a plural covers male and female practitioners: профсою́з **рабóтников** трáнспорта 'transport workers' union'.

(3) Gender differentiation is retained, however, when male and female practitioners fulfil different functions: thus **актёр**, **актри́са** 'actor, actress' (playing, respectively, male and female roles). This also applies in most sports (where men and women compete against others of their own sex, not against each other): thus **конькобéжец/конькобéжка** 'skater', **пловéц/пловчи́ха** 'swimmer', **чемпиóн/чемпиóнка** 'champion' (note, however, that only the more prestigious-sounding **чемпиóн** is used in official titles).

(4) In cases where men take up a 'female' occupation, a male equivalent of the name of the profession may be created, e.g. **дои́р**, cf. дои́рка 'milkmaid' (however, both have been superseded in mechanized dairies by **опера́тор** or **ма́стер маши́нного доéния** 'milking-machine operator'), **перепи́счик на маши́нке**, cf. **машини́стка** 'typist' (машини́ст 'engine-driver'). Note also **медици́нский брат** (or **санита́р**) 'male nurse' (cf. медици́нская сестра́ 'nurse'). The male equivalent of балери́на 'ballerina' is **арти́ст балéта**. However, there are seemingly no masculine equivalents for **моди́стка** 'milliner' and **швея́-мотори́стка** 'sewing-machine operator'.

44   Professions

(1) Where professions which were almost exclusively male dominated before the Revolution are now also practised by women, the same designation is used for either sex. This applies to all professions in -**вед**, -**граф**, -**лог** (языковéд 'linguist', биóлог 'biologist', топóграф 'topographer' etc.) and to а́втор 'author', архитéктор 'architect', ветерина́р 'veterinary surgeon', врач 'doctor' (же́нщина-врач 'woman doctor' is no longer appropriate in a society where most doctors *are* women; cf., however, **же́нщина-космона́вт** 'space-woman' and **же́нщина-офицéр** 'woman officer'), ди́ктор 'announcer', дирéктор 'director', дóктор 'doctor', инженéр 'engineer', композитор 'composer', мини́стр 'minister', парикма́хер 'hairdresser', пóвар 'cook', почтальóн 'postman', председа́тель 'chairman', продавéц 'sales assistant', профéссор 'professor', строи́тель 'builder', судья́ 'judge',

счетово́д 'accountant', тре́нер 'trainer', шеф 'boss, head', экскурсово́д 'guide' etc.

Note

(a) Though some of the above have feminine equivalents which are also in use (e.g. **продавщи́ца** 'sales-girl'), all *can* be used to designate either men or women. Masculine and feminine forms may, however, be distinguished stylistically, with masculine (**продаве́ц** 'sales assistant', **секрета́рь** 'secretary' etc.) preferred in official contexts and feminine in conversation (Она́ рабо́тает **продавщи́цей** 'She works as a shop assistant').

(b) The sex of an individual may be indicated by context: В клу́бе с роди́телями не раз **встреча́лась** профе́ссор **А. А. Любли́нская**, специали́ст по де́тской психоло́гии (*Rabotnitsa*) 'Professor A. A. Lyublinskaya, a specialist in child psychology, met parents in the club on more than one occasion'.

(c) In colloquial Russian, **истори́чка** refers to a female history teacher (cf. исто́рик 'historian, history teacher'). **Электри́чка** (cf. эле́ктрик 'electrician') and **техни́чка** (cf. те́хник 'technician') mean respectively 'suburban commuter train' and 'cleaning lady'.

(d) Male and female also share ranks in the services: **Рядово́й** Ве́ра Захаре́нко награждена́ о́рденом Оте́чественной войны́ (*Rabotnitsa*) 'Private Vera Zakharenko has been awarded the Patriotic War Medal'.

(2) The nouns are qualified by *masculine* attributive adjectives irrespective of sex:

Он хоро́ший врач	He is a good doctor
Она́ хоро́ший врач	She is a good doctor

Note

The use of feminine adjectives in such cases (e.g. **молода́я** экскурсово́д 'a young guide') is characteristic of 'relaxed' speech. **Молодо́й** экскурсово́д is preferred for persons of either sex. In oblique cases masculine agreement is mandatory: Он подошёл к на́шему экскурсово́ду Ивано́вой 'He approached Ivanova, our guide'. Since there are some professions with which feminine adjectives may not combine (**агроно́м** 'agronomist', **учи́тель** 'teacher', **хиру́рг** 'surgeon'), feminine agreement is best avoided altogether.

(3) The gender of **predicative** adjectives and past verb forms depends on the sex of the individual:

Врач **бо́лен**	The doctor (male) is sick

Врач **больна́**   The doctor (female) is sick

Касси́р о́чень ве́жливо и о́чень про́сто всё **объясни́ла** (*Izvestiya*)

The cashier explained everything very politely and very simply

Библиоте́карь **доба́вила**: У нас 12 000 томо́в (Nosov)

The librarian added 'We have 12,000 volumes'

45   Animals

(1) Most nouns denoting animals, birds, insects etc. refer to the species in general: **ёж** 'hedgehog', **жура́вль** (m.) 'crane', **кит** 'whale', **кры́са** 'rat', **мышь** (f.) 'mouse' and so on. Thus, there is no indication of the sex of the animal or bird in Ёж скры́лся в лесу́ 'The hedgehog disappeared into the forest', Ла́сточка вила́ гнездо́ 'The swallow was building a nest'. Male and female can be differentiated where necessary by using the words **саме́ц** 'male' and **са́мка** 'female' followed by the genitive case of the name of the animal: саме́ц/са́мка ежа́ 'male/female (of the) hedgehog' etc.

(2) Some animal names, however, do distinguish male and female: волк/волчи́ца 'wolf', за́яц/зайчи́ха 'hare', лев/льви́ца 'lion/lioness', слон/слони́ха 'elephant', тигр/тигри́ца 'tiger/tigress'. The male form also denotes the species in general (except for **кот/ко́шка** 'cat', where the female form **ко́шка** denotes the species in general).

(3) Male and female are differentiated in the names of farm animals: бара́н/овца́ 'ram/sheep', бо́ров/свинья́ 'boar/sow', бык/коро́ва 'bull/cow', козёл/коза́ 'billy-/nanny-goat', пету́х/ку́рица 'cockerel/hen', се́лезень/у́тка 'drake/duck'.

(4) A few species have three names denoting (a) the species in general, (b) male and (c) female: гусь (m.) 'goose', гуса́к 'gander', гусы́ня 'goose'; ло́шадь (f.) 'horse', жеребе́ц 'stallion', кобы́ла 'mare'; соба́ка 'dog', кобе́ль (m.) 'male dog', су́ка 'bitch'.

Declension

46   Introduction

(1) Nouns decline according to one of three declension patterns. Most

masculine and neuter nouns belong to the first declension and most feminine nouns to the second, except for feminine soft-sign nouns, which belong to the third declension (see **63**).

(2) The first and second declensions contain both hard-ending nouns (e.g. first-declension **дом** 'house', **окно́** 'window', second-declension **ка́рта** 'map') and soft-ending nouns (e.g. first-declension **музе́й** 'museum', **гость** 'guest', **мо́ре** 'sea', second-declension **ку́хня** 'kitchen'). All nouns in the third declension are feminine and end in a soft sign.

(3) Some declension endings are affected by the rules of spelling (see **16** (1) and (2)).

(4) For *stress* changes in all three declensions, see **57**, **60**, **62**, **63** (4).

47   Animacy

(1) The accusative case of an animate **masculine** singular noun is identical with the genitive, (see **(51)**) cf.

дом **бра́та** (genitive) 'my brother's house'
ви́жу **бра́та** (accusative) 'I see my brother'

Note
The differentiation of animate subject and animate object is important in a language where either may precede the other with virtually no change in meaning, cf. Оте́ц лю́бит сы́на 'The father loves the son' and Сы́на лю́бит оте́ц 'The father loves the son' (or 'It is the father who loves the son', see **475** (2)). The need to avoid ambiguity determines the accusative/genitive rule in animate masculine nouns.

(2) The following types of masculine singular noun are affected:

(i) Human beings: Оте́ц лю́бит **сы́на** 'The father loves the son'.

(ii) Animals: Я ви́жу **быка́** 'I see the bull'.

(iii) Common nouns used figuratively to denote human beings: болва́н 'blockhead', дуб 'dunce', куми́р 'idol', тип 'type' etc.:

Я ре́дко встреча́л **тако́го болва́на/тако́го заба́вного ти́па**
I have seldom met such a blockhead/such a funny character

Note
(a)   Я вёл «Москвича́» 'I was driving a "Moskvich"' (car) is more colloquial than Я вёл «Москви́ч».

(b) Usage with póбот: cf. Инженéр конструи́рует **póбот** 'The engineer is designing a robot' (i.e. an automaton), and figurative usage in превращáть человéка в **póбота** 'to turn a man into a robot'. However, the animate accusative/genitive is now normal in non-figurative contexts also:

Компáния «Мацуси́ма» ужé испытáла póбота (*Nedelya*)
The 'Matsushima' company has already tested a robot

(iv) Some folk dances, e.g. пляса́ть **трепака́, гопака́** 'to dance the trepak, the gopak'; animate beings in book titles, e.g. Держáл в рукáх «**Чапáева**» 'In his hands he held *Chapaev*' (a novel); playing cards, e.g. сбрóсить **валéта**, снять **туза́**, 'to discard a knave, cut an ace'; billiards and snooker balls, e.g. положи́ть **зелёного** (шара́) в лýзу 'to pocket the green'; chess pieces, e.g. взять **слона́, короля́, ферзя́** 'to take a bishop, the king, the queen'; the words **змей** 'kite' and **развéдчик** 'reconnaissance aircraft' (cf. animate connotations ('serpent' and 'reconnaissance agent' respectively)), e.g. пускáть **змéя** 'to fly a kite', сбить **развéдчика** 'to shoot down a reconnaissance aircraft'. Analogous usage such as сбить **истреби́теля** 'to shoot down a fighter' and постáвить **двóрника** 'to fit a windscreen wiper' characterizes professional colloquial speech but is otherwise regarded as substandard for usage with standard inanimate accusatives истреби́тель and двóрник.

Note
(a) Collective nouns (e.g. нарóд 'people', полк 'regiment', скот 'cattle') are *not* treated as animate:

Вначáле тигр напада́ет на **скот** (*Russia Today*)
First a tiger attacks the cattle

(b) The nouns мертвéц 'dead person' and покóйник 'deceased' are treated as animate, while труп 'corpse' is not, cf.

Он взял **мертвеца́** за плечó и повернýл нá спину (Nagibin)
He took the dead person by the shoulder and turned him on his back

and

Он рассказáл, как он обнарýжил **труп** (Nagibin)
He told how he had discovered the corpse

(3) The following types of **plural** noun are affected by the rule.

(i) Human beings and animals of *all* genders: (see **51**, **61**, **158** (6) (iv))

Онá кóрмит **мáльчиков** и **дéвочек**
She is feeding the boys and girls

Он ко́рмит **осло́в и ове́ц**
He is feeding the donkeys and the sheep

Он ви́дит **живо́тных**
He sees the animals

Note

Лови́ть **ома́ров** 'to catch (live, i.e. animate) lobsters', but есть, покупа́ть **ома́ры** 'to eat, buy (dead, i.e. inanimate) lobsters'. The distinction applies mainly to crustaceans, but is not consistently observed.

(ii) Toys fashioned in human form:

Там де́лают **матрёшек**	Nesting dolls are made there
Де́вочка одева́ет **ку́кол**	The little girl is dressing the dolls

Note

Марионе́тка 'puppet' also belongs in this category.

(iii) Plural equivalents of the singular categories listed above: чита́ть «***Бра́тьев Карама́зовых***» 'to read *The Brothers Karamazov*' (see (2) (iii) and (iv) above).

Note

(a)   Бакте́рия 'bacterium', баци́лла 'bacillus', ви́рус 'virus', заро́дыш 'foetus', микро́б 'microbe' are treated as inanimate: Челове́к убива́ет **баци́ллы** и **бакте́рии** 'Man kills bacilli and bacteria'. Use of the accusative/genitive in such cases is regarded as somewhat old-fashioned but may be encountered in books on biology and medicine: Изуча́ть **бакте́рий, ви́русов, микро́бов** 'To study bacteria, viruses, microbes'.

(b)   **Войска́** (pl.) 'troops' is treated as inanimate and has accusative войска́.

(c)   The animate accusative genitive rule also applies to adjectives, pronouns and certain numerals (see **193** (1 note (c)), **196** (2) and **200**).

48   Nouns which are used only in the singular

Some nouns have singular form only. They include nouns which denote:

(1) **Qualities, sensations:** хра́брость 'bravery', грусть 'sadness'.

(2) **Collectives:** бельё 'linen', листва́ 'foliage' etc.

(3) **Substances, foods, cereals:** де́рево 'wood', овёс 'oats' and so on. Note, however, that the plurals of some nouns in these categories are encountered in the meaning 'brands', 'large quantities': жиры́ 'fats'. This also applies to certain **natural phenomena** normally found in the singular only: дожди́ 'persistent rain', моро́зы 'persistent heavy frost', снега́ 'heavy snow'. The names of some **vegetables and fruits** are also used in the singular only (виногра́д 'grapes', горо́х 'peas', изю́м 'raisins', капу́ста 'cabbage', карто́фель 'potatoes', лук 'onions', морко́вь 'carrots'), a different word being used to denote 'one onion' (лу́ковица/голо́вка лу́ка or лу́ку): cf. виногра́дина 'a grape', горо́шина 'a pea', изю́мина 'a raisin', карто́фелина/клу́бень карто́феля 'a potato', коча́н капу́сты 'a cabbage', морко́вка 'a carrot'. Compare also соло́ма 'straw', соло́мина 'a straw'; шокола́д 'chocolate', шокола́дка 'a chocolate'.

(4) 'Singulatives' are also used to create plural forms from abstracts and collectives which have no plural of their own: долг 'duty' (**обя́занности** 'duties' (note that долг in the meaning 'debt' *has* a plural: долги́)), ложь 'lie' (**вы́думки** 'fabrications, lies'), ору́жие 'weapons' (pl. **ви́ды** ору́жия), поли́тика 'policy, politics' (полити́ческие **направле́ния** 'policies'), промы́шленность 'industry' (**о́трасли** промы́шленности 'industries'), спорт 'sport' (**ви́ды** спо́рта 'sports, events'). Note also that разли́чия can be used as the plural of ра́зница (which has no plural of its own).

(5) The names of animals, trees etc. may denote a whole species:

В на́шем лесу́ растёт то́лько **сосна́**
Only pine trees grow in our forest

Здесь ло́вят то́лько **леща́**
Only bream is caught here

(6) Names of professions and some other words can also be used collectively: День **шахтёра** 'Miners' Day', Дом **кни́ги** 'book shop', Дом **учи́теля** 'Teachers' Club'.

Note
A number of nouns, once used only in the singular, have acquired plurals: риск 'risk', pl. ри́ски, техноло́гия 'technology', pl. техноло́гии, эконо́мика 'economy', pl. эконо́мики, etc.

49   Nouns which have a plural form only

(1) Many plural-only nouns denote objects comprising two or more essential components: **брю́ки** 'trousers', **но́жницы** 'scissors'. Others denote complex processes (**ро́ды** 'childbirth'), games (**пря́тки** 'hide and seek') etc.

(2) Morphologically, the nouns subdivide as follows.

(i) Plurals in **-ы/-и/-á**, genitive **-ов**:

>**аплодисме́нты** 'applause'   gen. **аплодисме́нтов**

Similarly бегá 'trotting races', весы́ 'scales', вы́боры 'election', дебáты 'debate', джи́нсы 'jeans', духи́ 'perfume', зáморозки 'light frosts', консе́рвы 'preserves', мемуáры 'memoirs', остáнки 'human remains', очки́ 'spectacles', переговóры 'negotiations', подóнки 'dregs', припáсы 'stores', рóды 'childbirth', счёты 'abacus', трóпики 'tropics', тру́сики/трусы́ 'shorts', штаны́ 'trousers', щипцы́ 'pincers, tongs'.

Note
Nouns ending in two vowels or unstressed -цы have gen. **-ев:** обóи, **обóев** 'wallpaper' (likewise побóи 'beating', помóи 'slops'), плоско-гу́бцы, **плоскогу́бцев** 'pliers'.

(ii) Plurals in **-ы/-и** with zero genitive ending:

>**ви́лы** 'pitchfork'   gen. **вил**

Similarly Афи́ны 'Athens', брю́ки 'trousers', де́ньги (gen. **де́нег**) 'money', имени́ны 'name-day', кальсóны 'pants', кани́кулы 'holidays', носи́лки (gen. **носи́лок**) 'stretcher', нóжницы 'scissors', нóжны (gen. **нóжен**) 'sheath', опи́лки (gen. **опи́лок**) 'sawdust', панталóны 'knickers', плáвки (gen. **плáвок**) 'swimming trunks', пóхороны (gen. **похорóн**) 'funeral', салáзки (gen. **салáзок**) 'toboggan', сáнки (gen. **сáнок**) 'sledge', сли́вки (gen. **сли́вок**) 'cream', су́мерки (gen. **су́мерек**) 'dusk', су́тки (gen. **су́ток**) '24-hour period', у́зы 'bonds', хлóпоты (gen. **хлопóт**) 'trouble', шáхматы 'chess', шóры 'blinkers'.

(iii) Plurals in **-a** with zero genitive ending:

>**ворóта** 'gate'   gen. **ворóт**

Similarly дровá 'firewood', кружевá 'lace' (also sing. **кру́жево**), не́дра 'bowels of the earth', пери́ла 'railing', черни́ла 'ink'.

(iv) Nouns in **-и,** genitive **-ей:**

качéли 'swing'   gen. **качéлей**

Similarly бýдни 'weekdays' (gen. also **бýден**), вóжжи (gen. **вожжéй**) 'reins', грáбли 'rake' (gen. also **грáбель**), джýнгли 'jungle', дрóжжи (gen. **дрожжéй**) 'yeast', клéщи (gen. **клещéй**) 'pincers', кýдри (gen. **кудрéй**) 'curls', пóмочи (gen. **помочéй**) 'braces', сáни (gen. **санéй**) 'sledge', щи 'cabbage soup'.

Note
(a) Прéния, gen. **прéний** 'debate', свéдения, gen. **свéдений** 'information'.
(b) Countable nouns in the series, e.g. **сáни** 'sledge', can denote one object ('sledge') or a number of objects ('sledges'). Meaning is determined by context: Из санéй вы́скочил **солдáт** 'A soldier jumped from the **sledge**'; Из санéй вы́скочил **цéлый взвод солдáт** 'A whole platoon of soldiers jumped from the **sledges**'.

50   Declension chart

The following chart shows, in simplified form, the declension pattern in all three declensions.

		Singular				Plural		
		m	n	f		m	n	f
	N	cons. -й -ь	-о -е -ё	-а/-я	-ь	-ы/-и	-а/-я	-ы/-и
A	INAN	= N	= N	-у/-ю	-ь	= N		
	ANIM	= G				= G		
	G	-а/-я		-ы/-и	-и	-ов/-ев/-ей	zero/ей	
	D	-у/-ю	-е	-и		-ам/-ям		
	I	-ом/	unstr. ем str. ём	-ой/	-ей -ёй	-ью	-ами/-ями	
	P	-е		-и		-ах/-ях		

51   First declension: masculine nouns

(1) Hard-ending nouns

Declension of **завóд** 'factory' (inanimate) and **студéнт** 'student' (animate):

	Singular		Plural	
Nom.	завóд	студéнт	завóд-**ы**	студéнт-**ы**
Acc.	завóд (=nom.)	студéнт-**а** (=gen.)	завóд-**ы**	студéнт-**ов**
Gen.	завóд-**а**	студéнт-**а**	завóд-**ов**	студéнт-**ов**
Dat.	завóд-**у**	студéнт-**у**	завóд-**ам**	студéнт-**ам**
Instr.	завóд-**ом**	студéнт-**ом**	завóд-**ами**	студéнт-**ами**
Prep.	о завóд-**е**	о студéнт-**е**	о завóд-**ах**	о студéнт-**ах**

Note

(a) Nouns in **г, к, х/ж, ч, ш, щ** have nominative and inanimate accusative plural **-и:** урóк 'lesson', **урóки;** нож 'knife', **ножи́** (see **16** (1)).

(b) Nouns ending in **ж, ч, ш, щ, ц** and with stem stress in declension have instrumental singular -**ем:** душ 'shower', **ду́шем;** мéсяц 'month', **мéсяцем** (see **16** (2)).

(c) Nouns ending in **ж, ч, ш, щ** have genitive plural -**ей:** нож 'knife', gen. pl. **ножéй.**

(d) Nouns ending in -**ц** with stem stress in declension have genitive plural -**ев:** шприц 'syringe', gen. pl. **шпри́цев** (see **16** (2)).

(e) The genitive plural of some nouns is identical with the nominative singular (see **56**).

(f) **Год** 'year' has genitive plural **лет** (**годóв** in denoting decades: мóды **50-х годóв** 'the fashions of the fifties'); cf. dative, instrumental, prepositional plural **годáм, годáми, о годáх.**

(2) Soft-ending nouns

(i) Nouns in -**й**

Declension of **музéй** 'museum' and **герóй** 'hero':

	Singular		Plural	
Nom.	музéй	герóй	музé-**и**	герó-**и**
Acc.	музéй (=nom.)	герó-**я** (=gen.)	музé-**и**	герó-**ев**
Gen.	музé-**я**	герó-**я**	музé-**ев**	герó-**ев**
Dat.	музé-**ю**	герó-**ю**	музé-**ям**	герó-**ям**

Instr.	музé-**ем**	герó-**ем**	музé-**ями**	герó-**ями**
Prep.	о музé-**е**	о герó-**е**	о музé-**ях**	о герó-**ях**

Note

(a) Nouns in **-ий** have prepositional singular **-ии**: гéний 'genius', о **гéнии**.

(b) **Воробéй** 'sparrow' is declined as follows: acc./gen. воробья́, dat. воробью́, instr. воробьём, prep. о воробьé; nom. pl. воробьи́, acc./gen. воробьёв, dat. воробья́м, instr. воробья́ми, prep. о воробья́х. Similarly, муравéй 'ant', соловéй 'nightingale' and inanimate (acc. = nom.) репéй 'burdock', ручéй 'stream' and stem-stressed у́лей 'bee-hive'.

(ii) Soft-sign nouns

Declension of **портфéль** 'briefcase' and **тесть** 'father-in-law':

	Singular		*Plural*	
Nom.	портфéль	тесть	портфéл-**и**	тéст-**и**
Acc.	портфéль (=nom.)	тéст-**я** (=gen.)	портфéл-**и**	тéст-**ей**
Gen.	портфéл-**я**	тéст-**я**	портфéл-**ей**	тéст-**ей**
Dat.	портфéл-**ю**	тéст-**ю**	портфéл-**ям**	тéст-**ям**
Instr.	портфéл-**ем**	тéст-**ем**	портфéл-**ями**	тéст-**ями**
Prep.	о портфéл-**е**	о тéст-**е**	о портфéл-**ях**	о тéст-**ях**

52   The fleeting vowel

The vowel in the final syllable of many nouns which end in a hard consonant or soft sign does *not* appear in oblique cases. Vowels affected include the following:

(1) 'o': ры́нок 'market'

	Nom./Acc.	Gen.	Dat.	Instr.	Prep.
Singular	ры́нок	ры́нка	ры́нку	ры́нком	о ры́нке
Plural	ры́нки	ры́нков	ры́нкам	ры́нками	о ры́нках

Most nouns in **-ок** are similarly declined. Exceptions include **знатóк** 'connoisseur' (gen. **знатоќа**), **игрóк** 'player', **урóк** 'lesson'.

Note

Some other nouns also contain a fleeting **-o-**:

(a) Hard-ending nouns: лоб 'forehead', gen. **лба**; мох 'moss'; посóл 'ambassador'; рот 'mouth'; сон 'sleep'; у́гол 'corner'; шов 'seam'.

(b)   Soft-sign nouns: дёготь, gen. **дёгтя** 'tar'; ко́готь 'claw'; ломо́ть 'slice'; но́готь 'nail'; ого́нь 'fire'; у́голь 'coal', gen. **угля́/у́гля**.

(2) 'e': коне́ц 'end'

	Nom./Acc.	Gen.	Dat.	Instr.	Prep.
Singular	коне́ц	конца́	концу́	концо́м	о конце́
Plural	концы́	концо́в	конца́м	конца́ми	о конца́х

Most nouns in -ец are similarly declined. However, stressed -е́- is retained when preceded by a double consonant: близне́ц 'twin', gen. **близнеца́**; кузне́ц 'blacksmith', gen. **кузнеца́**.

Note

(a)   See **51** (1) notes (b) and (d) for the instrumental singular and genitive plural of stem-stressed nouns in -ц.

(b)   -ле- becomes -ль- in oblique cases: па́лец 'finger', gen. **па́льца**.

(c)   A fleeting vowel preceded by another vowel is replaced by -й- in oblique cases: бельги́ец 'Belgian', gen. **бельги́йца**; кита́ец 'Chinese', gen. **кита́йца**. Cf. заём 'loan', gen. **за́йма**; за́яц 'hare', gen. **за́йца**.

Other hard and soft nouns with a fleeting -e- include ве́тер 'wind' (gen. **ве́тра**), за́мысел 'project', у́зел 'knot' (gen. **узла́**), хребе́т 'range of hills'; день 'day' (gen. **дня**), ка́мень 'stone', ка́шель 'cough', ко́рень 'root', ли́вень 'downpour', па́рень 'fellow', пень 'stump', реме́нь 'strap', сте́бель 'stalk'.

(3) 'ё': ковёр 'carpet'

Nouns with a fleeting ё include ковёр 'carpet' (gen. **ковра́**), козёл 'goat', костёр 'bonfire', котёл 'boiler'. Note that in some words ё is replaced by a soft sign following л, н or р: лёд 'ice' (gen. **льда**), конёк 'skate' (gen. **конька́**), хорёк 'ferret' (gen. **хорька́**).

53   Partitive genitive in -у/-ю

Some hard-ending masculine nouns and a few nouns in -й have an alternative genitive singular in -у/-ю. The nouns all denote measurable quantities, e.g. виногра́д 'grapes' (gen. **виногра́да/виногра́ду**), чай 'tea' (gen. **ча́я/ча́ю**). Other nouns with a partitive genitive in -у/-ю include:

жир	fat	**са́хар**	sugar

квас	kvass	**снег**	snow
клей	glue	**суп**	soup
лук	onions	**сыр**	cheese
мёд	honey	**табáк**	tobacco
мел	chalk	**творóг**	cottage cheese
мех	fur	**чеснóк**	garlic
нарóд	people	**шёлк**	silk
песóк	sand, castor sugar	**шоколáд**	chocolate
рис	rice		

Most genitives in **-у/-ю** appear only in quantitative expressions: кусóк **сы́ру** 'piece of cheese', чáшка **чáю** 'cup of tea'. See also **84**.

Owing to the colloquial nature of the genitives in **-у**, they are not found with nouns denoting rarer substances such as, for example, **молибдéн** 'molybdenum'.

54   Prepositional/locative singular in -ý/-ю́

(1) Locative in -ý

Some nouns have an alternative prepositional singular in stressed **-ý**; it is used with the prepositions **в** and **на** to denote location, but not with other prepositions that take the prepositional case (о, по, при); cf. в портý 'in the port' and **о пóрте** 'about the port':

аэропóрт	airport
бал	ball, dance
бéрег	shore, bank
бок	side
бор	coniferous forest
борт	side (of a ship, etc.)
	на бортý 'on board'
верх	top, summit
глаз	eye
Дон	the Don
Клин	Klin
Крым	the Crimea
лёд	ice
	(**на льдý** 'on the ice')
лес	forest
лоб	forehead
	(**на лбý** 'on the forehead')

луг	meadow
мост	bridge
мох	moss
	(**во мху** 'in the moss')
нос	nose, prow
плот	raft
пол	floor
полк	regiment
порт	port
пост	post
	(**на посту́** 'at one's post')
пруд	pond
рот	mouth
	(**во рту** 'in the mouth')
сад	garden, orchard
снег	snow
тыл	the rear
у́гол	corner
	(**в/на углу́** 'in/at the corner')
шкаф	cupboard

Note

(a)   Some phrases denote state: **в бреду́** 'in a delirium', **в быту́** 'in everyday life', **в жару́** 'in a fever', **в плену́** 'in captivity'.

(b)   Where **в** or **на** have non-locational meanings, the noun takes the ending -**е**: знать толк **в** ле́се 'to understand the forest'.

(c)   The ending -**е** is also used in the names of books: **в** «*Вишнёвом са́де*» Че́хова 'in Chekhov's *Cherry Orchard*'.

(d)   Sometimes both -**е** and -**ý** are possible, the form in -**ý** being the more colloquial variant: **в о́тпуске/отпуску́** 'on holiday', **в це́хе/цеху́** 'in the workshop'.

(e)   The endings -**е** and -**ý** may be differentiated semantically and phraseologically, cf. в XX **ве́ке** 'in the twentieth century' and Мно́го ви́дел я люде́й на своём **веку́** 'I have seen a lot of people in my time'; **в ви́де** исключе́ния 'by way of an exception' and име́ть **в виду́** 'to bear in mind'; в **до́ме** 'in the house' and на **дому́** 'on the premises'; в спаса́тельном **кру́ге** 'in a lifebelt' and в семе́йном **кругу́** 'in the family circle'; труди́ться в **по́те** лица́ 'to labour by the sweat of one's brow' and весь в **поту́** 'bathed in sweat'; в **ря́де** слу́чаев 'in a number of cases' and в пе́рвом **ряду́** 'in the front row'; умере́ть во **цве́те** лет 'to die in one's prime'

and дере́вья в по́лном **цвету́** 'the trees are in full bloom'; в **ча́се**
лёта от Москвы́ 'an hour's flight from Moscow' and во второ́м
часу́ 'between one and two o'clock'.

(f)   Note also жить в **ладу́** 'to live in harmony', ку́ртка **на меху́** 'fur-
lined jacket', **на ка́ждом шагу́** 'at every step'.

(2) Locative in -ю́

A few nouns in -**й** and -**ь** have a locative singular in -**ю́: бой** 'battle', в
бою́ 'in battle' (but о бо́е 'about the battle'). Similarly рай 'paradise',
строй (стоя́ть **в строю́** 'to stand in line'). Cf. на **краю́** 'on the edge', в
родно́м **краю́** 'on one's native soil', but в Краснода́рском **кра́е** 'in
Krasnodar Territory', на пере́днем **кра́е** оборо́ны 'in the front line of
defence', from край 'edge, territory, front line'. Хмель (a) 'hops' (b)
'inebriation' has a locative in -ю́ in meaning (b): во хмелю́ 'in his
cups', cf. о хме́ле 'about hops'.

55   Special masculine plural forms

Some first-declension masculine nouns have special plural forms.

(1) Nominative plural in -á/я́

(i) Some hard-ending nouns have a nominative plural in stressed -á:
а́дрес 'address', pl. **адреса́**. Similarly:

бе́рег	shore	**но́мер**	number, issue
бок	side	**обшла́г**	cuff
борт	side of ship	**о́круг**	district
бу́фер	buffer	**о́рдер**	warrant
ве́ер	fan	**о́стров**	island
век	age, century	**па́рус**	sail
ве́чер	evening	**па́спорт**	passport
глаз	eye	**пе́репел**	quail
го́лос	voice, vote	**по́езд**	train
го́род	town	**по́яс**	belt
дире́ктор	director	**профе́ссор**	professor
до́ктор	doctor	**рог**	horn
дом	house	**рука́в**	sleeve
ко́локол	bell	**сорт**	brand
лес	forest	**сто́рож**	watchman
луг	meadow	**том**	volume
ма́стер	craftsman	**че́реп**	skull

Note

(a) Some plurals in -**a** and -**ы**/-**и** are differentiated semantically: кондуктора́ 'bus-conductors', конду́кторы 'electrical conductors'; корпуса́ 'corps, buildings', ко́рпусы 'torsos'; меха́ 'furs', мехи́ 'bellows'; образа́ 'icons', о́бразы 'forms'; ордена́ 'orders, decorations', о́рдены 'monastic orders'; провода́ 'electric wires', про́воды 'send-off' (no sing.); счета́ 'accounts', счёты 'abacus' (no sing.); тона́ 'colour shades', то́ны (musical) 'tones'; тормоза́ 'brakes', то́рмозы 'hindrances'; хлеба́ 'cereals', хле́бы 'loaves'; цвета́ 'colours', цветы́ 'flowers' (sing. цвето́к).

(b) Some plurals in -**ы**/-**и** are used in written styles, and their counterparts in -**á** in colloquial or technical contexts: год 'year', инспе́ктор 'inspector', инстру́ктор 'instructor', корре́ктор 'proof-reader', кре́йсер 'cruiser', реда́ктор 'editor', цех 'workshop'.

(ii) A few nouns ending in -**й** or -**ь** have nominative plural -**я́**: край 'edge', pl. **края́** (gen. pl. **краёв**); ве́ксель 'bill of exchange', pl. **векселя́**. Likewise ла́герь 'camp' (but ла́гери 'political camps'), то́поль 'poplar', учи́тель 'teacher' (but pl. учи́тели in the meaning 'teachers of a doctrine', e.g. учи́тели коммуни́зма 'the teachers of communism'), шта́бель 'stack', штемпель 'stamp', я́корь 'anchor'.

Note
Пе́карь 'baker', сле́сарь 'metal worker' and то́карь 'turner' have standard plurals in -**и** and alternative, colloquial plurals in -**я** (also used in professional parlance).

(2) Nominative plural in -ья

(i) Stem-stressed: **стул** 'chair' (inanimate), **брат** 'brother' (animate).

Plural	Nom.	Acc.	Gen.	Dat.	Instr.	Prep.
	сту́лья	сту́лья	сту́льев	сту́льям	сту́льями	о сту́льях
	бра́тья	бра́тьев	бра́тьев	бра́тьям	бра́тьями	о бра́тьях

Similarly (all inanimate): брус 'beam', зуб 'cog' (cf. зуб 'tooth', pl. зу́бы, зубо́в), клин 'wedge', клок 'shred' (pl. **кло́чья, кло́чьев** 'tatters'), кол 'stake', ко́лос 'ear of corn' (pl. **коло́сья**), ком 'lump', лист 'leaf' (cf. лист 'sheet of paper', pl. **листы́, листо́в**), лоску́т 'scrap' (pl. **лоску́тья** 'rags', cf. **лоскуты́** 'scraps of paper'), о́бод 'rim' (pl. **обо́дья**), по́вод 'rein' (pl. **пово́дья**, cf. **по́воды** 'causes'), по́лоз 'runner' (pl. **поло́зья**, cf. **по́лозы** 'grass-snakes'), прут 'twig', струп 'scab', сук 'bough' (pl. **су́чья, су́чьев** or **суки́, суко́в**). Note also the plural-only form **хло́пья** 'flakes'.

(ii) End-stressed in plural.

(a) **Де́верь** 'brother-in-law', **друг** 'friend', **муж** 'husband', **сын** 'son':

Plural	Nom.	Acc./Gen.	Dat.	Instr.	Prep.
	деверья́	деверёй	деверья́м	деверья́ми	о деверья́х
	друзья́	друзе́й	друзья́м	друзья́ми	о друзья́х
	мужья́	муже́й	мужья́м	мужья́ми	о мужья́х
	сыновья́	сынове́й	сыновья́м	сыновья́ми	о сыновья́х

(*But* мужи́ нау́ки 'men of science', сыны́ ро́дины 'sons of the fatherland'.)

(b) **зять** 'son-in-law, brother-in-law', **кум** 'godfather':

Plural	Nom.	Acc./Gen.	Dat.	Instr.	Prep.
	зятья́	зятьёв	зятья́м	зятья́ми	о зятья́х
	кумовья́	кумовьёв	кумовья́м	кумовья́ми	о кумовья́х

(3) Plural of nouns in -анин/-янин, e.g. англича́нин 'Englishman'

Plural	Nom.	Acc./Gen.	Dat.	Instr.	Prep.
	англича́не	англича́н	англича́нам	англича́нами	об англича́нах

Note the stress change in **граждани́н** 'citizen', pl. **гра́ждане**, **гра́ждан**.

(4) Plural of ба́рин, болга́рин, тата́рин, цыга́н

The plural of **болга́рин** 'Bulgarian' is: nom. болга́ры, acc./gen. болга́р, dat. болга́рам, instr. болга́рами, prep. о болга́рах. Similarly ба́рин 'landowner' (nom. pl. (demotic) ба́ры/ба́ре), тата́рин 'Tatar', цыга́н 'gipsy' (nom. pl. цыга́не).

(5) Plural of nouns in -ёнок/-онок

Nouns in **-ёнок/-онок** have plurals in **-ята/-ата: котёнок** 'kitten'.

Plural	Nom.	Acc./Gen.	Dat.	Instr.	Prep.
	котя́та	котя́т	котя́там	котя́тами	о котя́тах

Similarly **волчо́нок** 'wolf-cub', pl. **волча́та, волча́т** etc.

Note
(a) Щено́к 'puppy' has alternative plurals **щеня́та, щеня́т/щенки́, щенко́в**.
(b) Ребёнок 'child' has plural **де́ти** 'children', acc./gen. **дете́й**, dat. **де́тям**, instr. **детьми́**, prep. **о де́тях**. Colloquially, **ребя́та** is also used as a plural of ребёнок. **Ребя́та** can also mean 'the lads', cf. **девча́та** 'the girls' (also де́вушки и ребя́та 'young men and girls').

(6) Plural of сосе́д and чёрт

Сосе́д 'neighbour' and чёрт 'devil' have hard endings in the singular, soft endings in the plural: **сосе́ди, сосе́дей, сосе́дям; че́рти, черте́й, чертя́м**.

(7) Plural of господи́н and хозя́ин

Господи́н 'master' and хозя́ин 'owner, host' have nominative plural -**a**:

Plural	Nom.	Acc./Gen.	Dat.	Instr.	Prep.
	господа́	госпо́д	господа́м	господа́ми	о господа́х
	хозя́ева	хозя́ев	хозя́евам	хозя́евами	о хозя́евах

56 Nouns whose genitive plural is identical with the nominative singular

The genitive plural of some masculine nouns is the same as the nominative singular: глаз 'eye', пого́н 'epaulette', раз 'time', челове́к 'person' (after numerals: пять **челове́к** 'five people', cf. нет **люде́й** 'there are no people'). Note the stress difference in во́лос 'a hair', gen. pl. **воло́с**. Categories also include:

(1) Footwear: боти́нок 'shoe', ва́ленок 'felt boot', носо́к 'sock' (gen. pl. also **носко́в**), сапо́г 'boot', чуло́к 'stocking'.

(2) Nationalities (including some minorities in the former USSR): башки́р 'Bashkir', буря́т 'Buryat', грузи́н 'Georgian', мадья́р 'Magyar', осети́н 'Ossetian', румы́н 'Romanian', ту́рок 'Turk'.

(3) The military: партиза́н 'partisan', солда́т 'soldier' and others.

(4) Measurements: ампе́р 'ampere', байт 'byte', бит 'bit', ватт 'watt', вольт 'volt', герц 'cycle', грамм 'gram',媒дециб́ел 'decibel' (10 **ампе́р** '10 amperes', 100 **ватт** '100 watts', 5 **вольт** '5 volts'). The zero genitive plural is used in technical and scientific contexts, especially after numerals, and in colloquial speech, while -**ов** is normal in literary styles with some measurements, especially **грамм** 'gram' (Вы́пили сто **гра́ммов** тёплой во́дки (Vanshenkin) 'They drank 100 grams of warm vodka'), though here too the zero ending is making headway.

(5) Fruits (colloquial speech only): абрико́с 'apricot', апельси́н 'orange', баклажа́н 'aubergine', помидо́р 'tomato'. In written Russian, however, the genitive plural -**ов** is preferred for these nouns.

57   Stress patterns in first-declension masculine nouns

There are three basic types of stress pattern in declension.

(1) Fixed stem stress

Стул 'chair', **герой** 'hero', **автомобиль** 'car' etc.

Note
(a)   With few exceptions (e.g. дире́ктор 'manager', pl. директора́), nouns with medial stress have fixed stem stress in declension.
(b)   Most nouns of three or more syllables have fixed stem stress throughout declension (парохо́д 'steamer' etc.).
(c)   All masculine nouns with unstressed prefixes or suffixes have fixed stem stress throughout declension (**разгово́р** 'conversation', **ма́льчик** 'boy' etc.).
(d)   Only a limited number of monosyllabic masculine nouns have fixed stem stress throughout declension (e.g. **звук** 'sound').

(2) Fixed end-stress

(i) Hard ending:

	Nom./Acc.	Gen.	Dat.	Instr.	Prep.
Singular	стол	стол-а́	стол-у́	стол-о́м	о стол-е́
Plural	стол-ы́	стол-о́в	стол-а́м	стол-а́ми	о стол-а́х

(ii) Soft ending:

	Nom./Acc.	Gen.	Dat.	Instr.	Prep.
Singular	рубль	рубл-я́	рубл-ю́	рубл-ём	о рубл-е́
Plural	рубл-и́	рубл-е́й	рубл-я́м	рубл-я́ми	о рубл-я́х

Note
(a)   This category includes many hard-ending nouns, including almost all those with the stressed suffixes: -а́к/-я́к, -а́ч, -ёж, -ёж, -и́к, -и́ч, -у́н, -у́х: бегу́н 'runner', моря́к 'sailor', платёж 'payment', рубе́ж 'boundary', скрипа́ч 'violinist', стари́к 'old man' etc.
(b)   Soft-ending nouns include богаты́рь 'hero', вождь 'leader', врата́рь 'goalkeeper', дождь 'rain', жура́вль 'crane' (bird), календа́рь 'calendar', кора́бль 'ship', кремль 'kremlin', ломо́ть 'slice', ноль/нуль 'nought', реме́нь 'strap', секрета́рь 'secretary', слова́рь 'dictionary' etc.

(3) Mobile stress

(i) Stem stress in the **singular**, end stress in the **plural**: дуб 'oak', **бой** 'battle'.

	Nom./Acc.	Gen.	Dat.	Instr.	Prep.
Singular	ду́б	ду́б-а	ду́б-у	ду́б-ом	о ду́б-е
Plural	дуб-ы́	дуб-о́в	дуб-а́м	дуб-а́ми	о дуб-а́х
Singular	бой	бо́-я	бо́-ю	бо́-ем	о бо́-е
Plural	бо-и́	бо-ёв	бо-я́м	бо-я́ми	о бо-я́х

Note

(a)   Many nouns in the category have a prepositional-locative in -у́/-ю́:
бой 'battle', **круг** 'circle', **мост** 'bridge', **ряд** 'row', **сад** 'garden'
etc. (see **54**).

(b)   Other nouns in the category include many with plurals in -ья (see
55 (2) (ii)) and in -а́/-я́ (see **55** (1)).

(ii) End stress in **oblique** cases of the **plural**: порт 'port', жёлудь
'acorn'.

	Nom./Acc.	Gen.	Dat.	Instr.	Prep.
Singular	порт	по́рт-а	по́рт-у	по́рт-ом	о по́рт-е
Plural	по́рт-ы	порт-о́в	порт-а́м	порт-а́ми	о порт-а́х
Singular	жёлудь	жёлуд-я	жёлуд-ю	жёлуд-ем	о жёлуд-е
Plural	жёлуд-и	жёлуд-е́й	жёлуд-я́м	жёлуд-я́ми	о жёлуд-я́х

Note

This group comprises mainly soft-sign nouns: го́лубь 'dove', гость
'guest', гусь 'goose', зверь 'wild animal', ка́мень 'stone', ко́готь
'claw', ко́рень 'root', ло́коть 'elbow', но́готь 'fingernail', па́рень 'lad',
сте́бель 'stalk' (gen. pl. also **сте́блей**). Hard-ending nouns include
волк 'wolf' and **зуб** 'tooth'.

(iii) End stress in **oblique** cases of **singular** *and* **plural**: гвоздь 'nail'.

	Nom./Acc.	Gen.	Dat.	Instr.	Prep.
Singular	гвоздь	гвозд-я́	гвозд-ю́	гвозд-ём	о гвозд-е́
Plural	гво́зд-и	гвозд-е́й	гвозд-я́м	гвозд-я́ми	о гвозд-я́х

Likewise конь 'steed', уголь 'coal' (gen. sing. **угля́/у́гля**), червь
'worm'.

Note
For all animate nouns acc. = gen. See **47**.

58   First declension: neuter nouns in -o

(1) Declension of **боло́то** 'swamp'.

	Singular	Plural
Nom.	болóт-о	болóт-а
Acc.	болóт-о	болóт-а
Gen.	болóт-а	болóт
Dat.	болóт-у	болóт-ам
Instr.	болóт-ом	болóт-ами
Prep.	о болóт-е	о болóт-ах

Note

(a) Нéбо 'sky', pl. **небесá**, gen. pl. **небéс**, dat. pl. **небесáм**. Likewise **чýдо** 'miracle'.

(b) Сýдно 'ship', pl. **судá, судóв** (cf. сýдно 'chamber-pot', pl. **сýдна, сýден**).

(2) Buffer vowel in the genitive plural.

(i) In the 'zero' genitive plural of many nouns in -**o**, a 'buffer' vowel appears between two final consonants. This may be -**o**- (following **к**):

волокнó 'fibre'   **волóкон**

Similarly окнó 'window', gen. pl. **óкон**; стеклó 'pane of glass', gen. pl. **стёкол**.

(ii) Otherwise the buffer vowel is -**e**-:

бедрó 'hip'   **бёдер**

Others of this type include бревнó 'log', ведрó 'bucket', веслó 'oar', зернó 'grain', кольцó 'ring' (gen. pl. **колéц**), крéсло 'armchair' (gen. pl. **крéсел**), крыльцó 'porch' (gen. pl. **крылéц**), письмó 'letter' (gen. pl. **пúсем**), полотнó 'canvas', пятнó 'stain', ребрó 'rib', ремеслó 'trade' (gen. pl. **ремёсел**), числó 'number', ядрó 'nucleus'.

Note

(a) Vowel change from **e** to **ё** under stress.
(b) Нéдра, недр (pl. only) 'bowels of the earth'.
(c) Яйцó 'egg', pl. я́йца, яи́ц.
(d) Зло 'evil' has only one plural form, genitive plural **зол**: мéньшее из двух **зол** 'the lesser of two evils'.
(e) Nouns in -**ство** have no buffer vowel in the genitive plural: чýвство 'feeling', gen. pl. **чувств**.

(3) The following nouns have nominative plural -**и**: вéко 'eyelid', pl. **вéки, век**; колéно 'knee', pl. **колéни, колéней** (**колéн** in combination with prepositions and comparatives, e.g. вы́ше, нúже колéн 'above, below the knees', до колéн 'to the knees', встать с колéн

'to rise from one's knees', зажа́ть ме́жду коле́н 'to grip between the knees'); о́ко 'eye' (archaic), pl. о́чи, оче́й; плечо́ 'shoulder', pl. пле́чи, плеч; у́хо 'ear', pl. у́ши, уше́й.

Note

Except for о́блако 'cloud', pl. облака́, облако́в, all nouns in -ко have nominative plural -и: блю́дечко 'saucer', pl. блю́дечки, блю́дечек; дре́вко 'shaft', pl. дре́вки, дре́вков; зёрнышко 'small grain', pl. зёрнышки, зёрнышек (likewise пёрышко 'small feather'); колёсико 'small wheel', pl. колёсики, колёсиков (likewise ли́чико 'small face', пле́чико 'small shoulder' – pl. пле́чики also means 'coat-hanger'); озерко́ 'small lake', pl. озерки́, озерко́в; очко́ 'point' (in a game), pl. очки́, очко́в (also 'spectacles'); око́шко 'small window', pl. око́шки, око́шек; у́шко 'small ear', pl. у́шки, у́шек (cf. ушко́ 'eye of a needle', pl. ушки́, ушко́в); я́блоко 'apple', pl. я́блоки, я́блок.

(4) Some nouns in -о have plural -ья: звено́ 'link'.

Plural	Nom./Acc.	Gen.	Dat.	Instr.	Prep.
	звен-ья	звен-ьев	звен-ьям	звен-ьями	о звен-ьях

The following nouns behave similarly:

(i) With initial stress in the plural: крыло́ 'wing', pl. кры́лья, кры́льев; перо́ 'feather'; ши́ло 'awl'.

(ii) With medial stress in the plural: де́рево 'tree', pl. дере́вья, дере́вьев; коле́но 'joint in a pipe' (cf. коле́но 'knee', see (3) above and note that in the meaning 'bend in a river', 'generation' (in a genealogical table), 'part of a dance or song', коле́но has the plural коле́на, коле́н).

(iii) Дно 'bottom' (of a barrel), pl. до́нья, до́ньев.

59   First declension: nouns in -е, -ье, -ё, -ьё

(1) Declension of мо́ре 'sea' (likewise по́ле 'field'):

	Singular	Plural
Nom.	мо́р-е	мор-я́
Acc.	мо́р-е	мор-я́
Gen.	мо́р-я	мор-е́й
Dat.	мо́р-ю	мор-я́м
Instr.	мо́р-ем	мор-я́ми
Prep.	о мо́р-е	о мор-я́х

Note

(a) Nouns in **-це, -ще** replace **я** by **a:** thus блю́дце 'saucer', gen. sing./nom. and acc. pl. **блю́дца**. Similarly кла́дбище 'cemetery' etc.

(b) Nouns in **-ьё** (e.g. бельё 'linen') have instrumental singular **-ьём** and prepositional singular **-ьé**.

(c) Masculine augmentatives in **-ище** have nominative plural **-и:** доми́ще 'large house', pl. **доми́щи, доми́щ** (see **109** (2)).

(2) Nouns in **-e/-ье** and **-ё/-ьё** take a variety of endings in the genitive plural:

(i) **-ев:** боло́тце 'little swamp', **боло́тцев**. Likewise **око́нце** 'small window'.

Note

Some nouns in **-це** have alternative genitive plurals in **-ев** and zero ending: коры́тце 'small trough' (gen. pl. **коры́тцев/коры́тец**). Likewise одея́льце 'small blanket', щу́пальце 'tentacle'.

(ii) **-ей:** мо́ре 'sea', gen. pl. **море́й** (likewise по́ле 'field'); ружьё 'gun', gen. pl. **ру́жей**.

(iii) **-ий:** побере́жье 'coast', gen. pl. **побере́жий**. Likewise варе́нье 'jam', копьё 'spear' (gen. pl. **ко́пий**), ущéлье 'ravine'.

(iv) **-ьев:** верхо́вье 'upper reaches', gen. pl. **верхо́вьев**. Likewise низо́вье 'lower reaches', пла́тье 'dress', подмасте́рье (m.) 'apprentice', у́стье 'river mouth'.

Note

Alternative genitive plurals **верхо́вий** and **низо́вий**.

(v) **Zero ending:** блю́дце 'saucer', gen. pl. **блю́дец**. Likewise зе́ркальце 'small mirror', полоте́нце 'towel', сéрдце 'heart', gen. pl. **серде́ц**, as well as nouns in **-ище/-бище** (кла́дбище 'cemetery', gen. pl. **кла́дбищ**).

Note

Дéревце/деревцó 'small tree' has genitive plural **деревцо́в** or **деревéц; острие́** 'point', gen. pl. **острие́в**.

60   Stress patterns in the plural of neuter nouns

Stress in the plural of many neuter nouns moves as follows:

(1) From the ending on to the stem (**e** changes to **ё**): thus, **окнó** 'window'.

Plural	Nom./Acc.	Gen.	Dat.	Instr.	Prep.
	óкна	óкон	óкнам	óкнами	об óкнах

Similarly ведро́ 'bucket', pl. **вёдра, вёдер**; весло́ 'oar', pl. **вёсла, вёсел**; вино́ 'wine', pl. **ви́на, вин**; гнездо́ 'nest', pl. **гнёзда, гнёзд**; зерно́ 'grain', pl. **зёрна, зёрен**; колесо́ 'wheel', pl. **колёса, колёс**; кольцо́ 'ring', pl. **ко́льца, коле́ц**; копьё 'spear', pl. **ко́пья, ко́пий**; крыльцо́ 'porch', pl. **кры́льца, крыле́ц**; лицо́ 'face', pl. **ли́ца, лиц**; письмо́ 'letter', pl. **пи́сьма, пи́сем**; пятно́ 'stain', pl. **пя́тна, пя́тен**; ружьё 'gun', pl. **ру́жья, ру́жей**; стекло́ 'pane', pl. **стёкла, стёкол**; число́ 'number', pl. **чи́сла, чи́сел**; яйцо́ 'egg', pl. **я́йца, яи́ц**.

(2) From the stem on to the ending: **де́ло** 'matter'.

Plural	Nom./Acc.	Gen.	Dat.	Instr.	Prep.
	дела́	дел	дела́м	дела́ми	о дела́х

Similarly зе́ркало 'mirror', pl. **зеркала́**; ме́сто 'place', pl. **места́**; мо́ре 'sea', pl. **моря́, море́й**; по́ле 'field', pl. **поля́, поле́й**; пра́во 'right', pl. **права́**; се́рдце 'heart', pl. **сердца́, серде́ц**; сло́во 'word', pl. **слова́**; ста́до 'herd', pl. **стада́**; те́ло 'body', pl. **тела́**.

61   Second declension: nouns in -а/-я

(1) Most second-declension nouns are feminine; some are masculine, e.g. **де́душка** 'grandfather', **дя́дя** 'uncle'; others are of common gender, e.g. **пья́ница** 'drunkard', **рази́ня** 'gawper' (see **35**).

(2) Declension of **ка́рта** 'map', **же́нщина** 'woman':

	Singular		Plural	
Nom.	ка́рт-а	же́нщин-а	ка́рт-ы	же́нщин-ы
Acc.	ка́рт-у	же́нщин-у	ка́рт-ы	же́нщин (= gen.)
Gen.	ка́рт-ы	же́нщин-ы	ка́рт	же́нщин
Dat.	ка́рт-е	же́нщин-е	ка́рт-ам	же́нщин-ам
Instr.	ка́рт-ой/-ою	же́нщин-ой/-ою	ка́рт-ами	же́нщин-ами
Prep.	о ка́рт-е	о же́нщин-е	о ка́рт-ах	о же́нщин-ах

Note
(a)   **ы** is replaced by **и** after **г, к, х, ж, ч, ш** or **щ**; ви́лка 'fork', да́ча 'villa', gen. sing./nom. and acc. pl. ви́лки, да́чи (see **16** (1)).
(b)   **о** is replaced by **е** in unstressed position after **ж, ч, ш, щ** or **ц**: у́лица 'street', instr. sing. у́лицей; кры́ша 'roof', instr. sing. кры́шей (see **16** (2)).

(c) Some nouns in **-жа, -ча, -ша** have genitive plural **-ей**: свеча́ 'candle', gen. pl. **свече́й** (but игра́ не сто́ит свеч 'the game is not worth the candle'). Likewise бахча́ 'water melon plantation', левша́ 'left-handed person', ханжа́ 'hypocrite', чу́кча 'Chukchi', ю́ноша 'youth'.

(d) The genitive plural of **мечта́** 'dream' (and of мечта́ние 'reverie') is **мечта́ний**.

(e) The instrumental singular in **-ою** (and **-ею**, see (3)) is the more 'literary' form and is commonly found in poetry.

(3) Declension of **ды́ня** 'melon' and **ня́ня** 'nurse':

	Singular		Plural	
Nom.	ды́н-я	ня́н-я	ды́н-и	ня́н-и
Acc.	ды́н-ю	ня́н-ю	ды́н-и	нянь (= gen.)
Gen.	ды́н-и	ня́н-и	дынь	нянь
Dat.	ды́н-е	ня́н-е	ды́н-ям	ня́н-ям
Instr.	ды́н-ей/-ею	ня́н-ей/-ею	ды́н-ями	ня́н-ями
Prep.	о ды́н-е	о ня́н-е	о ды́н-ях	о ня́н-ях

Note

(a) End-stressed nouns have **-ёй** in the instrumental singular: земля́ 'ground', instr. **землёй**; статья́ 'article', instr. **статьёй**.

(b) *Stem*-stressed nouns in **-ья** have genitive plural **-ий**: го́стья 'female guest', gen. pl. **го́стий**.

(c) *End*-stressed nouns in **-ья́** have genitive plural **-ей**: семья́ 'family', gen. pl. **семе́й**; судья́ 'judge', gen. pl. **суде́й/су́дей**. Similarly до́ля 'share', gen. pl. **доле́й**; дя́дя 'uncle', gen. pl. **дя́дей** (nom. pl. **дядья́**, gen. pl. **дядьёв** are also found); клешня́ 'claw' (of crustacean), gen. pl. **клешне́й**; ноздря́ 'nostril', gen. pl. **ноздре́й**; при́горшня 'handful', gen. pl. **при́горшней/при́горшен**; простыня́ 'sheet', gen. pl. **просты́нь/простыне́й**; ступня́ 'foot', gen. pl. **ступне́й**; тётя 'aunt', gen. pl. **тётей/тёть**.

(d) Nouns in **-ая/-ея** have genitive plural **-ай/-ей**: ста́я 'pack', gen. pl. **стай**; ше́я 'neck', gen. pl. **шей**.

(4) Buffer vowel in the genitive plural.

(i) **-о-** appears between a consonant (see, however, (4) (ii) (a)) and **-к-** (or **-к-** + consonant):

бе́лка 'squirrel'   **бе́лок**

Similarly бу́лка 'roll', gen. pl. **бу́лок**; доска́ 'board, plank', gen. pl. **досо́к**; ку́кла 'doll', gen. pl. **ку́кол**. Note also ку́хня 'kitchen', gen. pl. **ку́хонь**.

(ii) **-e-** appears:

(a) Between **ж, ч, ш** and **-к-**: бáбочка 'butterfly', gen. pl. **бáбочек**; кóшка 'cat', gen. pl. **кóшек**; лóжка 'spoon', gen. pl. **лóжек** etc. (but кишкá 'intestine', gen. pl. **кишóк**).

(b) Between pairs of consonants which do not include **к**:

    соснá 'pine tree'   **сóсен**

Likewise двéрца 'car door', gen. pl. **двéрец**; деснá 'gum', gen. pl. **дёсен**.

(c) In place of a soft sign: дéньги (pl. only) 'money', gen. pl. **дéнег**; свáдьба 'wedding', gen. pl. **свáдеб**; тюрьмá 'prison', gen. pl. **тюрем** (but вéдьма 'witch', gen. pl. **ведьм**, прóсьба 'request', gen. pl. **просьб**).

(d) In place of **-й-** in diphthongs followed by **-к-**: чáйка 'seagull', gen. pl. **чáек** etc. (cf. войнá 'war', gen. pl. **войн**).

(e) Between two final consonants in the genitive plural of many nouns in **-я**: землá 'land', gen. pl. **земéль**; кáпля 'drop', gen. pl. **кáпель**; крóвля 'roof', gen. pl. **крóвель**; пéтля 'loop', gen. pl. **пéтель**; цáпля 'heron', gen. pl. **цáпель**.

Note
Most nouns in consonant + **-ня** have *no* soft sign in the genitive plural: бáшня 'tower', gen. pl. **бáшен**. Similarly вишня 'cherry', жарóвня 'brazier', колокóльня 'belfry', пéсня 'song', сóтня 'hundred', спáльня 'bedroom', черéшня 'cherry tree', читáльня 'reading room'. Note, however, бáрышня 'young lady', gen. pl. **бáрышень**; дерéвня 'village', gen. pl. **деревéнь**.

(iii) **-ё-** appears in the genitive plural of a few nouns: кочергá 'poker', gen. pl. **кочерёг**; серьгá 'ear-ring', gen. pl. **серёг**; сестрá 'sister', gen. pl. **сестёр**.

(iv) Some clusters, many ending in **б, в, л, м, н, п, р**, have *no* buffer vowel in the genitive plural: бóмба 'bomb', gen. pl. **бомб**. Likewise бýква 'letter', волнá 'wave', вы́дра 'otter', зéбра 'zebra', иглá 'needle', игрá 'game', избá 'peasant hut', úскра 'spark', нóрма 'norm', слýжба 'service', ты́ква 'pumpkin', ýрна 'urn', фóрма 'uniform', цúфра 'figure'.

62   Stress patterns in second-declension nouns

Most nouns in stressed **-á/-я́** undergo stress change in declension (nouns in *unstressed* **-а/-я** are immune from stress change).

(1) Stem stress in the plural, e.g. **война́** 'war'.

	Nom.	Acc.	Gen.	Dat.	Instr.	Prep.
Singular	война́	войну́	войны́	войне́	войно́й	о войне́
Plural	**во́йны**	**во́йны**	**войн**	**во́йнам**	**во́йнами**	**о во́йнах**

Similarly волна́ 'wave' (alternative dat., instr., prep. pl. **волна́м, волна́ми, о волна́х**), глава́ 'chapter', заря́ 'dawn' (pl. **зо́ри, зорь**), змея́ 'snake' (pl. **зме́и, змей**), игра́ 'game', красота́ 'beauty' (pl. **красо́ты** 'beauty spots'), овца́ 'sheep' (gen. pl. **ове́ц**), река́ 'river' (acc. sing. **реку́/ре́ку**), сосна́ 'pine', страна́ 'country', струна́ 'string' (of instrument, racket) etc.

Note
е-ё mutation: десна́ 'gum', pl. **дёсны, дёсен**; жена́ 'wife', pl. **жёны, жён**; звезда́ 'star', pl. **звёзды, звёзд**; пчела́ 'bee', pl. **пчёлы, пчёл**; сестра́ 'sister', pl. **сёстры, сестёр**.

(2) Stem stress in accusative singular and nominative/accusative plural, e.g. **рука́** 'hand, arm':

	Nom.	Acc.	Gen.	Dat.	Instr.	Prep.
Singular	рука́	**ру́ку**	руки́	руке́	руко́й	о руке́
Plural	**ру́ки**	**ру́ки**	**рук**	**рука́м**	**рука́ми**	**о рука́х**

Similarly гора́ 'mountain', доска́ 'board' (gen. pl. **досо́к**), нога́ 'foot, leg', щека́ 'cheek' (acc. sing. **щёку/щеку́**, pl. **щёки, щёк, щека́м**), борода́ 'beard' (acc. sing. **бо́роду**, pl. **бо́роды, боро́д, борода́м**), голова́ 'head', полоса́ 'strip' (acc. sing. **по́лосу/полосу́**), сторона́ 'side').

(3) Stem stress in nominative/accusative plural, e.g. **губа́** 'lip':

	Nom.	Acc.	Gen.	Dat.	Instr.	Prep.
Singular	губа́	губу́	губы́	губе́	губо́й	о губе́
Plural	**гу́бы**	**гу́бы**	**губ**	**губа́м**	**губа́ми**	**о губа́х**

Similarly волна́ 'wave' (see also (1) above) and железа́ 'gland' (pl. **же́лезы, желёз, железа́м**).

(4) Stem stress in accusative singular and all plural forms, e.g. **вода́** 'water':

	Nom.	Acc.	Gen.	Dat.	Instr.	Prep.
Singular	вода́	**во́ду**	воды́	воде́	водо́й	о воде́
Plural	**во́ды**	**во́ды**	**вод**	**во́дам**	**во́дами**	**о во́дах**

Similarly спина́ 'back', стена́ 'wall', цена́ 'price'.

(5) Stem stress in nominative/inanimate accusative, dative, instrumental and prepositional plural, e.g. **семья́** 'family':

	Nom.	Acc.	Gen.	Dat.	Instr.	Prep.
Singular	семья́	семью́	семьи́	семье́	семьёй	о семье́
Plural	**се́мьи**	**се́мьи**	семе́й	**се́мьям**	**се́мьями**	**о се́мьях**

Likewise свинья́ 'pig', скамья́ 'bench' (pl. **скамьи́/ска́мьи**), судья́ 'judge' (gen. pl. **суде́й/су́дей**).

(6) Stem stress in accusative singular and nominative, accusative, dative, instrumental and prepositional plural, e.g. **земля́** 'land':

	Nom.	Acc.	Gen.	Dat.	Instr.	Prep.
Singular	земля́	**зе́млю**	земли́	земле́	землёй	о земле́
Plural	**зе́мли**	**зе́мли**	земе́ль	**зе́млям**	**зе́млями**	**о зе́млях**

63   Third declension: soft-sign feminine nouns

(1) Declension of **тетра́дь** 'exercise book' and **свекро́вь** 'mother-in-law' (husband's mother):

	Singular		Plural	
Nom.	тетра́дь	свекро́вь	тетра́д-и	свекро́в-и
Acc.	тетра́дь	свекро́вь	тетра́д-и	свекро́в-ей (= gen.)
Gen.	тетра́д-и	свекро́в-и	тетра́д-ей	свекро́в-ей
Dat.	тетра́д-и	свекро́в-и	тетра́д-ям	свекро́в-ям
Instr.	тетра́дь-ю	свекро́вь-ю	тетра́д-ями	свекро́в-ями
Prep.	о тетра́д-и	о свекро́в-и	о тетра́д-ях	о свекро́в-ях

Note
я is replaced by **а** after **ж, ч, ш, щ**: thus ночь 'night', dat., instr., prep. pl. **ноча́м, ноча́ми, о ноча́х**; likewise вещь 'thing', мышь 'mouse' etc.

(2) Declension of **мать** and **дочь**: мать 'mother' declines in the singular nom./acc. **мать** 'mother', gen./dat. **ма́тери**, instr. **ма́терью**, prep. **о ма́тери**, and in the plural nom. **ма́тери**, acc./gen. **матере́й**, dat. **матеря́м**, instr. **матеря́ми**, prep. **о матеря́х**. Similarly дочь 'daughter' (instr. pl. **дочерьми́**).

(3) The fleeting vowel -**о**-. Genitive, dative and prepositional singular and all plural forms are affected, e.g. вошь 'louse', gen., dat. sing. **вши**,

instr. **во́шью**, prep. **о вши**; pl. **вши**, acc./gen. **вшей**, dat. **вшам**, instr. **вша́ми**, prep. **о вшах**.

Note

(a) Ложь 'lie' is found only in the singular (gen./dat. **лжи**, instr. **ло́жью**, prep. **о лжи**); likewise любо́вь 'love', рожь 'rye'.

(b) As a first name Любо́вь 'Lyubov' has gen./dat. **Любо́ви**, prep. **о Любо́ви**.

(c) Це́рковь 'church' has soft endings in the singular (gen./dat. **це́ркви**, instr. **це́рковью**, prep. **о це́ркви**) and nominative/ accusative and genitive plural (**це́ркви, церкве́й**), but hard endings in the other oblique cases of the plural (**церква́м, церква́ми, о церква́х**).

(4) Stress changes in declension:

(i) Some nouns have prepositional singular **-и́** when governed by the prepositions **в** and **на**:

    дверь 'door'   **на двери́** 'on the door'

Likewise глубь 'depths', горсть 'handful', грязь 'mud' (**в грязи́** 'covered in mud'), кровь 'blood' (**в крови́** 'covered in blood'), мель 'shallows' (**на мели́** 'aground'), печь 'stove', пыль 'dust' (**в пыли́** 'covered in dust'), Русь 'Rus' (**на Руси́** 'in Rus'), связь 'connection' (**в связи́ с** 'in connection with'), сеть 'net', степь 'steppe', Тверь 'Tver' (**в Твери́** 'in Tver'), тень 'shadow', цепь 'chain'.

Note

(a) *Stem* stress is used when these nouns combine with other prepositions (**о две́ри** 'about the door'), or when в and на do *not* denote location (Ему́ отказа́ли **в но́вой две́ри** 'He was refused a new door').

(b) Глушь 'backwoods' and грудь 'chest, breast' have end stress in genitive, dative (**глуши́, груди́**) and prepositional singular (**в глуши́, в груди́**).

(ii) Many nouns have end stress in plural oblique cases, e.g. **сеть** 'net':

Plural	Nom./Acc.	Gen.	Dat.	Instr.	Prep.
	се́ти	сете́й	сетя́м	сетя́ми	о сетя́х

Likewise вещь 'thing', кость 'bone', мышь 'mouse' (acc./gen. pl. **мыше́й**), но́вость 'piece of news', ночь 'night', о́бласть 'oblast, province', о́чередь 'queue', печь 'stove', пло́щадь 'square', ска́терть 'tablecloth', ско́рость 'speed', смерть 'death', соль 'salt', степь 'steppe', тень 'shade', треть 'third', цепь 'chain', часть 'part', че́тверть 'quarter'.

Note

(a) Plural вла́сти 'the authorities', gen. власте́й, dat. властя́м.

(b) Дверь 'door' and ло́шадь 'horse' have alternative instrumental plural дверя́ми/дверьми́ (colloquial), лошадьми́ or лошадя́ми.

64   Declension of neuter nouns in -мя

Declension of и́мя 'name':

	Singular	Plural
Nom./Acc.	и́м-я	имен-а́
Gen.	и́мен-и	имён
Dat.	и́мен-и	имен-а́м
Instr.	и́мен-ем	имен-а́ми
Prep.	об и́мен-и	об имен-а́х

Similarly вре́мя 'time', зна́мя 'banner' (pl. знамёна, знамён), пле́мя 'tribe', се́мя 'seed' (gen. pl. семя́н), стре́мя 'stirrup' and (sing. only) бре́мя 'burden', вы́мя 'udder', пла́мя 'flames' (cf. языки́ пла́мени 'flames, tongues of flame'), те́мя 'temple'.

65   Declension of nouns in -ия/-ие

Declension of ста́нция 'station', зда́ние 'building':

	Singular		Plural	
Nom.	ста́нци-я	зда́ни-е	ста́нци-и	зда́ни-я
Acc.	ста́нци-ю	зда́ни-е	ста́нци-и	зда́ни-я
Gen.	ста́нци-и	зда́ни-я	ста́нций	зда́ний
Dat.	ста́нци-и	зда́ни-ю	ста́нци-ям	зда́ни-ям
Instr.	ста́нци-ей/-ею	зда́ни-ем	ста́нци-ями	зда́ни-ями
Prep.	о ста́нци-и	о зда́ни-и	о ста́нци-ях	о зда́ни-ях

66   The masculine noun путь

Путь 'way' declines as follows:

	Singular	Plural
Nom./Acc.	путь	пут-и́
Gen.	пут-и́	пут-е́й

Dat.	пут-**и́**	пут-**я́м**
Instr.	пут-**ём**	пут-**я́ми**
Prep.	о пут-**и́**	о пут-**я́х**

Note

Despite feminine endings in the genitive, dative and prepositional singular, путь is qualified by masculine adjectives: **Счастли́вого пути́!** 'Bon voyage!'.

67   The neuter noun дитя́

Дитя́ 'child' declines as follows:

Nom./Acc.	дит-**я́**
Gen./Dat.	дитя́т-**и**
Instr.	дитя́т-**ей/-ею**
Prep.	о дитя́т-**и**

Note

Дитя́ is now used only in some figurative expressions, e.g. **дитя́ ве́ка** 'child of the age', and, in some contexts, for emotional effect, e.g. Да он же ещё **дитя́!** 'Why, he's still just a child!' For practical purposes it has been replaced by ребёнок 'child'.

68   Де́ти and лю́ди

Де́ти 'children' (sing. ребёнок or дитя́) and **лю́ди** 'people' (sing. челове́к) decline in the same way:

Nom.	де́т-**и**	лю́д-**и**
Acc./Gen.	дет-**е́й**	люд-**е́й**
Dat.	де́т-**ям**	лю́д-**ям**
Instr.	деть-**ми́**	людь-**ми́**
Prep.	о де́т-**ях**	о лю́д-**ях**

69   Declension of first names

First names ending in a consonant or **-й** (e.g. Ива́н, Никола́й, Ю́рий) decline like first-declension nouns (see **51**), first names in **-а** and **-я** (e.g. О́льга 'Olga', Ната́лья 'Natalya') like second-declension nouns (see **61**). Patronymics (e.g. Ивáнович, Ивáновна) also decline like first- and second-declension nouns respectively.

70   Declension of surnames

(1) Surnames in **-ев, -ёв, -ин, -ов, -ын** decline partly like nouns and partly like adjectives, e.g. Тургéнев 'Turgenev':

	Masculine	Feminine	Plural
Nom.	Тургéнев	Тургéнев-**а**	Тургéнев-**ы**
Acc.	Тургéнев-**а**	Тургéнев-**у**	Тургéнев-**ых**
Gen.	Тургéнев-**а**	Тургéнев-**ой**	Тургéнев-**ых**
Dat.	Тургéнев-**у**	Тургéнев-**ой**	Тургéнев-**ым**
Instr.	Тургéнев-**ым**	Тургéнев-**ой**	Тургéнев-**ыми**
Prep.	о Тургéнев-**е**	о Тургéнев-**ой**	о Тургéнев-**ых**

Note

Foreign names in **-ин** have instrumental singular **-ом**: Чáплин 'Chaplin', instr. **Чáплином**; cf. Гéрцен 'Herzen', instr. **Гéрценом**.

(2) Surnames in **-ский, -ой** etc. decline like adjectives.

(3) Surnames in **-ко, -енко** (e.g. Громы́ко 'Gromyko', Шевчéнко 'Shevchenko') tend not to decline, though in speech they may decline like second-declension nouns in **-а** (Максимéнко, acc. Максимéнку, gen. Максимéнки, dat. Максимéнке, instr. Максимéнкой, prep. о Максимéнке) or (the less-preferred option) like first-declension nouns in **-о**.

(4) Surnames in **-аго, -яго** (e.g. Живáго 'Zhivago'), **-ово** (e.g. Дурновó 'Durnovo'), **-их, -ых** (e.g. Чуткúх 'Chutkikh') and stressed **-кó** (Франкó 'Franko') do not decline:

Никúтин шагáл ря́дом с **Княжкó** (Bondarev)
Nikitin strode along beside Knyazhko

(5) Masculine foreign surnames ending in a consonant (e.g. Шмидт 'Schmidt') decline like nouns of the first declension, but they do *not* decline at all when they refer to a woman: Кáтя перепи́сывается с англичáнкой **Джейн Смит** 'Katya corresponds with the English-woman Jane Smith', cf.

Э́то натолкнýло Мелáнью **Цатиня́н** на мысль написáть пьéсу (*Sputnik*)
This gave Melanya Tsatinyan the idea of writing a play

(6) Foreign surnames ending in **-е, -и, -о, -у** and in stressed **-á** and **-я́** do not decline: Гарибáльди 'Garibaldi', Гёте 'Goethe', Гюгó 'Hugo', Дюмá 'Dumas', Золя́ 'Zola', Шóу 'Shaw'. However, foreign names in

unstressed **-a** and **-я** *do* decline: карти́ны **Го́йи** 'paintings by Goya', пе́сни **Окуджа́вы** 'Okudzhava's songs'. Ва́йда 'Wajda', Куроса́ва 'Kurosawa' etc. also decline. Less-familiar Japanese names such as Тана́ка 'Tanaka' do not normally decline.

71   Declension of place names

(1) Place names ending in a consonant or **-a** (Ки́ев 'Kiev', Москва́ 'Moscow') decline like nouns of the first and second declensions respectively. Hyphenated Russian place names decline in both parts: в Петропа́вловске-Камча́тском 'in Petropavlovsk-Kamchatsky'. Place names in **-ин, -ов, -ын** have instrumental **-ом** (Пу́шкин 'Pushkin', **Пу́шкином**; Росто́в 'Rostov', **Росто́вом**), cf.:

> Держа́л у себя́ до́ма, под **Сара́товом**, мото́рную ло́дку (Trifonov)
> He kept a motor boat at his home near Saratov

(2) Place names in **-ево, -ино, -ово, -ыно** tend *not* to decline (о́коло **Ре́пино** 'near Repino'), especially where the names derive from a proper name (от **Ле́рмонтово** 'from Lermontovo'). The tendency not to decline such names was consolidated by practice in the 1941–45 War, designed to avoid ambiguity in place names such as Пу́шкин 'Pushkin' and Пу́шкино 'Pushkino', which would share declension endings. Despite instances of declension in written styles (e.g. в **Пу́щине** 'in Pushchino' (*Russia Today*)), non-declension remains the recommended norm.

(3) Non-Russian place names in **-е, -и, -о, -у** do not decline, e.g. Ско́пье 'Skopje'; Чи́ли 'Chile'; Брно 'Brno', Ме́хико 'Mexico City'; Баку́ 'Baku'. Бангладе́ш 'Bangladesh' does not decline either: из **Бангладе́ш** 'from Bangladesh'. Та́тры 'the Tatras' declines like a plural noun (gen. Татр). Both nouns in a hyphenated compound decline where a river is involved: во **Фра́нкфурте-на-Ма́йне** 'in Frankfurt-am-Main'. Compare, however, под **Буэ́нос-А́йресом** 'near Buenos-Aires', **в Алма́-Ате́** 'in Alma-Ata' (now also Алматы́), из **Карл-Маркс-Шта́дта** 'from Karl-Marx-Stadt' (now Chemnitz).

72   Apposition in the names of publications, towns etc.

(1) Titles of books, newspapers etc. decline like nouns: в *"Изве́стиях"* 'in *Izvestiya*'; Он чита́л «*Отцо́в и дете́й*» 'He has read *Fathers and*

Sons'. If, however, the genre of the work is mentioned, the title is not declined: в газе́те *"Изве́стия"* 'in the newspaper *Izvestiya*', Он чита́л рома́н «*Отцы́ и де́ти*» 'He has read the novel *Fathers and Sons'*.

(2) In referring to the names of Russian towns, both го́род 'town' and the name decline (в го́роде Москве́ 'in the city of Moscow') except:

(i) When confusion may arise, e.g. in the case of towns in **-ин** and **-ино**, where only the former declines: в го́роде Пу́шкине 'in the town of Pushkin', cf. в го́роде Пу́шкино 'in the town of Pushkino'.

(ii) When a town has a plural name: в го́роде Вели́кие Лу́ки 'in the town of Velikie Luki' (if го́род is omitted, however, the town name is declined: в Вели́ких Лу́ках 'in Velikie Luki').

(iii) When the place name consists of adjective + noun: в го́роде Ни́жний Таги́л 'in the town of Nizhnii Tagil'.

(3) Similar criteria apply to river names: на реке́ Днепре́ 'on the river Dnieper', but на реке́ Се́верный Доне́ц 'on the river Severny Donets'. 'On the Moscow river' may be rendered as на Москве́-реке́/на реке́ Москве́, cf. вниз по Во́лге-реке́/вниз по реке́ Во́лге 'down the river Volga'.

(4) The names of well-known non-Russian towns decline (except for those ending in **-e** etc., see **71** (3)), whether they stand in apposition to го́род or not: в Пари́же 'in Paris', в го́роде Пари́же 'in the city of Paris'. Compare, however, близ го́рода Мэ́нстон 'near the town of Manston' (which is unlikely to be known to Russians and is therefore left undeclined).

(5) With place names other than those of towns and rivers it is normal to decline only the generic term: у горы́ Казбе́к 'by Mount Kazbek', в дере́вне Бе́лкино 'in the village of Belkino', на о́зере Байка́л 'on Lake Baikal', ре́йсы ме́жду порта́ми Оде́сса и Новоросси́йск 'trips between the ports of Odessa and Novorossiisk'.

(6) This also applies to foreign place names: над вулка́ном Э́тна 'above Mount Etna', в гра́фстве Са́ссекс 'in the county of Sussex', на о́строве Дие́го-Гарси́а 'on the island of Diego-Garcia', из по́рта Гды́ня 'from the port of Gdynia', в шта́те Алаба́ма 'in the State of Alabama'. Where the generic term is omitted, however, the place name declines: на о́строве Кипр 'on the island of Cyprus', but на Ки́пре 'on Cyprus'. In a few cases, where the generic term and the place name are of the same gender, both may decline: в пусты́не Саха́ре/Саха́ра 'in the Sahara desert'.

73   Declension of alphabetisms

(1) Only those alphabetisms decline which are masculine and have the form of first-declension nouns ending in a consonant (see **40** (1) (i) (2) (3)):

Долг **ВА́За** бюдже́ту действи́тельно вели́к (*Komsomolskaya pravda*)
The Volga Car Factory's debt to the budget is truly substantial

Риск зарази́ться **СПИ́Дом** вы́ше у наркома́нов (*Sputnik*)
The risk of contracting AIDS is greater in drug addicts

(2) Other alphabetisms are not declined: **ГАИ** [гай] (Госуда́рственная автомоби́льная инспе́кция) 'State Vehicle Inspectorate' (see page 596), **ГЭС** [гэс] (гѝдроэлектроста́нция) 'hydroelectric power station', **НА́ТО** [на́то] 'NATO', **НИИ** [ний] (нау́чно-иссле́довательский институ́т) 'scientific research institute', **ООН** [оон] (Организа́ция Объединённых На́ций) 'UNO', **ОТК** [о-тэ-ка́] (отде́л техни́ческого контро́ля) 'technical control department', **ЦДА** [це-дэ-а́] (Цент-ра́льный дом архите́ктора) 'Central Architects' Club':

– Где ты рабо́таешь? — спра́шиваю.
– В одно́м **НИИ.** (Dovlatov)
'Where do you work?', I ask.
'In a scientific research institute'.

Мо́жно связа́ться с ближа́йшим посто́м **ГАИ́** (*Izvestiya*)
You can contact the nearest traffic police control point

В **НА́СА** пока́ не реши́ли, сто́ит ли соглаша́ться с тре́бованиями законода́телей (*Komsomolskaya pravda*)
NASA has not yet decided if it is worthwhile complying with the requirements of the legislators

Note
(a)   Though **ГЭС** (power station) and **ООН** (UNO) end in a consonant they are of feminine gender and undeclined. Some new *masculine* forms such as **ВИЧ** 'HIV' are also at present undeclined.
(b)   **ЖЭК** [жэк] (жили́щно-эксплуатацио́нная конто́ра) 'housing office', now masculine, is either left undeclined or (in colloquial styles) is declined: в **на́шем ЖЭ́Ке**. Similarly **ДОСААФ** [доса́ф] (Доброво́льное о́бщество соде́йствия а́рмии, авиа́ции и фло́ту) 'Voluntary Association for Co-operation with the Army, Air Force and Navy' and **МИД** [мид] (Министе́рство иностра́нных дел) 'Ministry of Foreign Affairs'.

74   Declension of hyphenated noun co-ordinates

(1) The *first* element in the compound does not decline if it is:

(i) Indeclinable, a recent loan, an abbreviation or a letter of the alphabet: **àльфа**-во́лны 'alpha-waves', **кафе́**-заку́сочная 'snackbar', **конферѐнц**-за́л 'conference hall'.

(ii) Descriptive and qualifies the second element: **национа̀л**-социали́сты 'National Socialists', **шта̀б**-кварти́ра 'headquarters'.

(iii) The first component in a rank or occupation: **генера̀л**-лейтена́нт 'lieutenant-general', **премьѐр**-мини́стр 'prime minister'.

(iv) The first component in a measurement: **килова̀тт**-ча́с 'kilowatt-hour', **во̀льт**-ампе́р 'volt-ampere'.

(2) The *second* element in the compound does not decline if its function is to qualify the first: слова́рь-**ми́нимум** 'minimum vocabulary'.

(3) *Both* components decline, each being a full noun in its own right: автомоби́ль-самосва́л 'tip-up lorry', ваго́н-рестора́н 'restaurant car', дива́н-крова́ть 'divan bed', же́нщина-милиционе́р 'police-woman', заку́сочная-автома́т 'vending machine', инжене́р-строи́тель 'construction engineer', раке́та-носи́тель 'carrier-rocket'. In speech, only the *second* noun may decline in commonly-used compounds: в **ваго́не-рестора́не**/ваго́н-рестора́не 'in the restaurant car', на **дива́не-крова́ти**/дива́н-крова́ти 'on the divan bed'.

Note
In the following, only the *second* element is declined: мàтч-турни́р 'match tournament', плàщ-пала́тка 'groundsheet', я́хт-клу́б 'yacht-club'.

75   Agreement of ряд, большинство́ etc.

(1) **Ряд**

(i) Ряд traditionally combines with a singular predicate, especially in a passive construction:

Допу́щен ряд оши́бок
A number of mistakes have been made

(ii) Ряд may combine with a plural predicate when followed by a dependent **genitive plural**, particularly when the construction involves an **animate** noun and an **active** verb:

Ряд штангѝстов занимáли призовы́е местá
A number of the weight-lifters occupied medal positions

(2) Большинствó also traditionally takes a singular predicate:

(i) In passive constructions: Большинствó пѝсем достáвлено 'Most letters have been delivered'.

(ii) Where it has no post-positive dependent form: Большинствó учáствует в общéственной жѝзни 'Most participate in public life'.

(iii) Where the dependent form is in the genitive singular or is the genitive plural of an **inanimate** noun:

Большинствó населéния пострадáло от наводнéния
Most of the population suffered as a result of the flood

Большинствó телефóнов в гóроде безмóлвствует (Tendryakov)
Most telephones in the town are silent

When, however, большинствó has a dependent form in the genitive plural of an **animate** noun, a **plural** predicate is possible:

Большинствó учáщихся хорошó подготóвлены
Most of the pupils are well prepared

Большинствó родѝтелей прѝняли учáстие
Most parents participated

Note
Other collective nouns of this type behave in similar fashion. Compare

На площáдке перед усáдьбой обы́чно останáвливается мнóжество автóбусов и автомобѝлей
A multitude of buses and cars usually stop on the area in front of the estate

and

Мнóжество людéй поют э́ту пéсню на рáзных языкáх
A great many people sing this song in different languages

Compare also

Часть пѝсем затеря́лась
A number of the letters went missing

Часть учáщихся не явѝлись/не явѝлась
A number of the pupils did not turn up

76   Constructions of the type все повернули го́лову

(1) The singular of the object is regarded as the norm in constructions such as Все поверну́ли **го́лову** 'Everyone turned their head(s)', where identical objects or parts of the body belong to or relate to each member of a group. A plural noun is recommended only when differentiation is essential: Все по́дняли **ру́ку** 'Everyone raised their hand', cf. Все по́дняли **ру́ки** 'Everyone raised their arms'. Otherwise the singular is the preferred form:

Соба́ки бежа́ли, поджа́в **хвост**
The dogs were running along with their **tails** between their legs

Все со свя́занными за **спино́й** рука́ми (Rybakov)
All with their hands tied behind their **backs**

Мама́ша, ба́бушка и па́па в кра́сных носка́х и с таки́м же кра́сным **лицо́м** (Granin)
Mum, Gran and Dad in red socks and with similarly red **faces**

(2) However, there are signs of the alternative use of the *plural* in modern Russian:

Мужики́ слу́шали его́, одобри́тельно кива́я **голова́ми** (Dovlatov)
The peasants listened to him, nodding their heads in approval

Они́ стоя́ли с раскры́тыми **рта́ми** (Kunin)
They stood with their mouths wide open

Мы пожа́ли дру̀г дру́гу **ру́ки** (Rybakov)
We shook hands

Хло́пали дру̀г дру́га по **спи́нам** (Aksenov)
They were slapping each other on the back

Соба́ки с поджа́тыми **хвоста́ми** ле́зли в подворо́тни (Rasputin)
Dogs were slinking into the gateways with their tails between their legs

Вскри́кивали, маха́ли **ша́пками** (Trifonov)
They were screaming, waving their caps

(3) The singular is preferred for words denoting uniform:

В сре́днем ка́тере стоя́ли четы́ре челове́ка в служе́бной полице́йской и тамо́женной **унифо́рме** (Kunin)
In the central launch stood four men in regulation police and customs officer uniforms

(4) A similar alternative use of singular and plural is observed in the case of the noun **жизнь** 'life' (though the singular is more common in Russian, and the plural is used *far* more sparingly than in English). Compare

Я был капита́ном «Кальма́ра» и отвеча́л за их **жизнь** (Gagarin)
I was the captain of the 'Kalmar' and was responsible for their lives

and

Лю́ба, Воло́дя и их това́рищи опери́ровали в полевы́х го́спиталях, мно́гим сохрани́ли **жи́зни** (Rybakov)
Lyuba, Volodya and their comrades operated in the field hospitals and saved many people's lives

Note

With numerals above four, only the genitive plural is possible (see **195**):

Боле́знь, кото́рая уже́ унесла́ почти́ 15 ты́сяч **жи́зней** (*Sputnik*)
A disease which has already claimed almost 15,000 lives

Case Usage

See **401–453** for prepositional usage.

77   The nominative

The nominative is used as follows.

(1) It denotes the subject of an action or state:

Мой брат чита́ет кни́гу
My brother is reading a book

На́ши де́ти дово́льны пода́рками
Our children are pleased with the presents

(2) It may be introduced

(i) by **э́то** 'this is, these are':

Э́то **моя́ жена́**	This is my wife
Э́то **мои́ де́ти**	These are my children

(ii) by **вот** 'here is, here are, there is, there are':

| Вот **мой дом** | There is my house |
| Вот **кни́ги** | Here are the books |

(3) It is used in possessive constructions:

| У меня́ [есть] **кни́га** | I have a book |
| У него́ был **брат** | He had a brother |

(4) It is used in comparative constructions after **чем**:

Я ста́рше, чем **моя́ сестра́**
I am older than my sister

(5) It is used in generalizing constructions after **как**:

в таки́х стра́нах, как **Ниге́рия**
in countries such as Nigeria

Note
The meaning of the above example is 'in countries such as Nigeria **is**'.
Ниге́рия is therefore *not* in apposition to стра́нах. Compare:

Наш заво́д специализи́руется по произво́дству таки́х изде́лий, как **ши́ны** и **колёса**
Our factory specializes in the manufacture of products such as tyres and wheels

(6) It is used in definitions:

Москва́ — **столи́ца** Росси́и Moscow is the capital of Russia

(7) It is used in apposition to various generic terms (see **72**):

Я чита́ю рома́н «**А́нна Каре́нина**»
I am reading the novel *Anna Karenina*

78   The vocative

Vocative meanings are expressed by the nominative: **Ива́н Фёдорович!** 'Ivan Fedorovich!'. Relics of the former vocative case survive only in certain ecclesiastical terms, now used as exclamations: **Бо́же мой!** 'My God!', **Го́споди!** 'Good Lord!'. Some truncated familiar forms are used as vocatives in colloquial Russian: **мам!** 'Mum!', **Нин!** 'Nina!', **Вань!** 'Vanya!', **Коль!** 'Kolya!', **Петь!** 'Pete!' (also **дядь!** 'Uncle!' etc.).

79   The accusative

The accusative case is used as follows.

(1) It denotes the object of a transitive verb:

Он лю́бит **Ма́шу**	He loves Masha
Она́ у́чится води́ть **маши́ну**	She is learning to drive a car

Note

In colloquial Russian the verb may sometimes be 'understood': Бу́дьте добры́ (, попроси́те к телефо́ну) Зо́ю 'Can I speak to Zoya, please'.

(2) It is used in certain impersonal constructions:

Де́вочку рвёт	The girl feels sick
Дом зажгло́ мо́лнией	The house was struck by lightning
Мне жаль (жа́лко) **сестру́**	I feel sorry for my sister (for жаль + genitive, see **80** (8))
Мне бо́льно **ру́ку** (colloquial)	My hand is sore

For other impersonal constructions with the accusative, see **295** (1).

(3) It denotes:

(i) Duration in time:

Всю зи́му бы́ло хо́лодно	It was cold all winter

(ii) Duration in space:

Всю доро́гу они́ шли мо́лча	They walked in silence all the way

(iii) Repetition:

Он э́то говори́л **ты́сячу** раз	He has said that a thousand times
Он боле́ет **ка́ждую весну́**	He is ill every spring

(iv) Cost, weight, measure etc.:

Кни́га сто́ит **до́ллар**	The book costs a dollar
У́голь ве́сит **то́нну**	The coal weighs a ton

Note

(a)   For the use of the accusative after negated transitive verbs, see **87** (4).

(b)   Some verbs which have traditionally governed the genitive may take the *accusative* of animate nouns in colloquial Russian: Он слу́шается **сестру́** 'He obeys his sister', Де́ти боя́лись **мать** 'The children were afraid of their mother', Дожида́лись **А́нну** 'They were waiting for Anna'. See also **88** (1) (ii) (a) and (2) (i).

80   The genitive: possession and relationship

The genitive case is used to denote the following:

(1) Possession:

дом **бра́та**   my brother's house

(2) Relationships:

член **па́ртии**   a member of the party

(3) The whole in relation to the part:

кры́ша **до́ма**   the roof of the house

(4) The agent of an action or process:

выступле́ние **арти́ста**   the artiste's performance

(5) The object of an action or process:

убо́рка **урожа́я**   the gathering in of the harvest

(6) Descriptive attributes:

час **обе́да**   lunch time
бума́га **пе́рвого со́рта**   first-grade paper

(7) The second item in a comparison:

Он моло́же **бра́та**   He is younger than his
                                    brother (see also **182** (1) (ii))

(8) The object of regret (constructions with **жаль**):

Мне жаль **де́нег**   I grudge the money

81   The genitive: quantity

The genitive is used with:

(1) **Ма́ло** 'few', **мно́го** 'much, many', **нема́ло** 'not a little', **немно́го** 'not much, many', **не́сколько** 'a few', **ско́лько** 'how much, many', **сто́лько** 'so much, many':

мно́го **де́нег**	a lot of money
ско́лько **лет?**	how many years?
не́сколько **челове́к**	several people

(2) **Доста́точно** 'enough', **недостава́ть** 'to be insufficient', **скопи́ть** 'to accumulate', **хвата́ть/хвати́ть** 'to be enough': **Вре́мени** хвата́ет 'There is enough time', Ему́ недостаёт **рубля́** 'He is a rouble short', доста́точно **сил** 'enough strength':

> Хва́тит ли им **бензи́на** для ночны́х блужда́ний? (Trifonov)
> Will they have enough petrol for their nocturnal escapades?

(3) Collective nouns:

| ста́до **ове́ц** | a flock of sheep |

(4) Nouns denoting measure:

| литр **молока́** | a litre of milk |

(5) Nouns denoting containers:

| ча́шка **молока́** | a cup of milk |

82   The genitive with adjectives

The following adjectives (and their short forms) govern the genitive: **досто́йный** 'worthy', **лишённый** 'lacking in', **по́лный** 'full', **чу́ждый** 'devoid':

корзи́на, по́лная **я́блок**	a basket full of apples
Он досто́ин **награ́ды**	He is worthy of an award
челове́к, чу́ждый **честолю́бия**	a man devoid of ambition
Он лишён **остроу́мия**	He is lacking in wit

83   The partitive genitive

(1) The genitive is used to denote part of a substance or liquid (Он вы́пил **молока́** 'He drank some milk') or to denote a quantity of objects (Он пое́л **я́год** 'He ate some berries'). The accusative denotes *whole* rather than part: Он вы́пил **молоко́** 'He drank **the** milk'.

(2) The partitive genitive appears only as the *object* of a verb, never as the subject, cf. Она́ налила́ гостя́м **вина́** 'She poured her guests some wine' and На столе́ есть **вино́** 'There is some wine on the table'.

(3) Except for constructions with verbs such as **хотéть/захотéть** 'to want' and **просúть/попросúть** 'to request', where either aspect may be used (Хочý **воды́** 'I want some water', Он прóсит **мёда** 'He asks for some honey'), most partitive constructions involve *perfective* verbs only (Онá принеслá **дров** 'She brought some firewood', Он достáл **дéнег** 'He acquired some money', Он отмéрил **сатúна** 'He measured out some satin'). With many imperfectives the partitive genitive is never used: Он вы́пил **воды́** 'He drank some water' but Он пил **вóду** 'He was drinking some water'; Он съел **хлéба** 'He ate some bread' but Он ел **хлеб** 'He was eating some bread'.

(4) Some perfectives with the quantitative prefix **на-** also take the partitive genitive: наéсться **я́год** 'to eat one's fill of berries', накупúть **книг** 'to buy some books', нарвáть **цветóв** 'to pick some flowers', нарубúть **дров** 'to chop some wood'.

(5) Containers and quantitative words also appear in partitive constructions: лóжка **мёда** 'a spoonful of honey'.

(6) Examples of partitive genitives:

Грúша привёз по её прóсьбе **овощéй** (Trifonov)
Grisha brought some vegetables at her request

Налилá ребя́там **молокá** (Rasputin)
She poured the kids some milk

Дéнег на дорóгу вы́шлю (Shukshin)
I'll send some money for the journey

Я тебé дам **успокóйтельных кáпель** (Rybakov)
I'll give you some tranquillizers

Note
The following are examples of the parallel availability, after verbs, of a relatively new phenomenon, a partitive *accusative:*

Хóчешь, я тебé **чай** принесý (Marinina)
Would you like me to bring you some tea?

"Могý ли я воспóльзоваться вáшим причáлом и купúть **прéсную вóду**?" (Kunin)
'May I use your berth and buy some fresh water?'

Капитáн сел у окнá, заказáл **винó** и шнúцель
The captain sat down by the window, ordered some wine and a schnitzel (Dovlatov)

84   The partitive genitive in -у/-ю

(1) Some masculine nouns, mainly those which denote substances, have genitives in **-а/-я** and in **-у/-ю,** e.g. cáxap 'sugar', **сáxapa/сáxapy**; чай 'tea', **чáя/чáю**. See **53**.

(2) Other nouns with two genitives include бензи́н 'petrol', виногрáд 'grapes', горóх 'peas', кероси́н 'paraffin', кипятóк 'boiling water', коньяќ 'brandy', лук 'onions', мёд 'honey', мел 'chalk', песóк 'sand', суп 'soup', сыр 'cheese', табáк 'tobacco', творóг 'cottage cheese', шёлк 'silk'.

(3) Genitive **-у/-ю** appears only in partitive constructions: нали́ть **чáю** 'to pour some tea', тарéлка **сýпу** 'a plate of soup':

Бáбушка послáла Вóвку пощипáть **лýку** (Belov)
Grandma sent Vovka to pick some onions

Ýтром онá взялá у хозя́ев **кипяткý** (Rybakov)
In the morning she fetched some boiling water from the proprietors

Достáл бутыʹлку **коньякý**
He got out a bottle of brandy

(4) If quantity is *not* implied, **-а/-я** are used: зáпах и цвет **табакá** 'the smell and colour of tobacco', производство **сы́ра** 'the production of cheese', ценá **чáя** 'the price of tea'.

(5) Note that **-а/-я** are also used if the noun denoting the substance or liquid is qualified by an adjective: стакáн **крéпкого чáя** 'a glass of strong tea'.

(6) The use of the partitive genitive in **-у/-ю** is decreasing, and **-а/-я** are now possible in all meanings and styles (чáшка **чáю/чáя** 'a cup of tea'), with the commonest nouns (e.g. сáxap 'sugar', чай 'tea') most likely to be found with a genitive in **-у/-ю**. However, even with such nouns the partitive in **-а/-я** is usually acceptable:

Стою́ в óчереди в кáссу и прики́дываю: килогрáмм **сáxapa**, пáчка **чáя** . . . (*Nedelya*)
I stand in the queue to the cash-desk and calculate: a kilogram of sugar, a packet of tea . . .

(7) Genitive **-у/-ю** is most consistently found in end-stressed diminutives: свари́ть **кофейкý** (from кофеёк) 'to boil some coffee', Хóчешь **чайкý**? (from чаёк) 'Would you like some tea?' (others

include **коньячку́** from коньяќ/коньячо́к 'brandy', **лучку́** from лук/лучо́к 'onions', **сырку́** from сыр/сыро́к 'cheese', **табачку́** from таба́к/табачо́к 'tobacco').

(8) Partitive constructions involving perfective verbs and genitives in **-у/-ю** are also very common: доба́вить **са́хару** 'to add some sugar', завари́ть **ча́ю** 'to make some tea', пое́сть **су́пу** 'to eat some soup', положи́ть **чесноку́** 'to put in some garlic'.

(9) **-у/-ю** are also found with **нет,** with indefinite numerals and with measures and containers: килогра́мм **виногра́ду** 'a kilo of grapes', нет **коньяку́** 'there is no brandy', мно́го **наро́ду** 'many people', па́чка **са́хару** 'a packet of sugar', кусо́к **сы́ру** 'a piece of cheese'; **-а/-я** are also possible in such cases:

> Оста́лось лишь полпа́чки **ча́я** (Povolyaev)
> Only half a packet of tea remained

Only occasionally is the partitive governed by a frequentative *imperfective* verb:

> И́зредка мать набива́ла **творогу́** в ба́ночку (Rasputin)
> Now and again mother would cram some cottage cheese into a little jar

85   Genitive in -y in set phrases

(1) Genitives in **-у** appear in certain idioms and set phrases:

до **заре́зу** ну́жно	very necessary
ни **ра́зу**	not once
ни **слу́ху** ни **ду́ху**	neither sight nor sound
ни **ша́гу** наза́д	not a step back
с **бо́ку** на́ бок	from side to side
с **гла́зу** на́ глаз	tête-à-tête
танцева́ть до **упа́ду**	to dance till one drops
упуска́ть и́з **виду**	to lose sight of

(2) The genitive in **-а/-я** has had very little impact on such phrases, except for **без про́маху/-а** 'unerringly' and **без разбо́ру/-а** 'indiscriminately'.

(3) In some causal expressions **от** combines with **-а/-я** (от го́лода 'from hunger', от испу́га 'from fright', от сме́ха 'with laughter') and **с** with **-у/-ю** (умере́ть **с го́лоду** 'to starve to death', кри́кнуть **с испу́гу**

'to scream with fright', пры́снуть сó **смеху** 'to burst out laughing', умерéть со **стрáху** 'to die of fright'). Some forms in **-у/-ю** appear in spatial expressions: уйти́ и́з **дому** 'to leave home' (cf. уйти́ из **дóма** 'to leave the house'), вы́йти и́з **лесу** 'to emerge from the forest'.

86   Genitive and negative

(1) **Нет** 'there is not', **нé было** 'there was not' and **не бýдет** 'there will not be' combine with the genitive to denote **non-existence** or **non-availability:**

Нет **дéнег**	There is no money
Нé было **врéмени**	There was no time
Не бýдет **войны́**	There will be no war

Note

(a)   Compare frequentative usage in Всё чáще **Ли́ли** не бывáет дóма (Kazakov) 'Lilya is out more and more often'.

(b)   Compare constructions which involve **identification,** where the **nominative** is used: Э́то не **моя́ женá** 'That is not my wife', Э́то нé были **мои́ дéти** 'Those were not my children'.

(c)   Constructions of the type: **Роди́тели** (nominative) не дóма 'The parents are out' (for the normal **Роди́телей** нет дóма) may be used when actual whereabouts are indicated: Они́ не дóма, а **в гостя́х** 'They are not in, but out visiting'.

(2) The genitive is also used in possessive phrases: У меня́ **нет компью́тера** 'I have no computer', У нас **нé было детéй** 'We had no children', У вас **не бýдет проблéм** 'You will not have any problems'.

(3) Other negated verbs denoting non-availability, non-occurrence or non-appearance may be used in this construction: **Лéзвий** не имéется 'There are no blades in stock', **Дéнег** не остáлось 'There was no money left', **Таки́х людéй** не существýет 'Such people do not exist', **Встрéчных маши́н** не попадáлось 'No oncoming vehicles were encountered'.

(4) In some negative constructions a nominative indicates the absence of *specific* objects, a genitive the absence of *all* objects of a particular type, cf. **Докумéнтов** не сохрани́лось 'No documents were preserved' (at all) and **Докумéнты,** о котóрых шла речь, не сохрани́лись 'The documents in question were not preserved'.

(5) The genitive construction is also used after **не ви́дно** 'cannot be seen', **не замéтно** 'cannot be discerned', **не слы́шно** 'cannot be heard':

Из-за дыма **дверей** не ви́дно (Abramov)
You can't see the doors for the smoke

Ни **соба́ки**, ни **голосо́в** не́ было слы́шно (Trifonov)
Neither the dog nor people's voices could be heard

(6) It is also used with **не на́до, не ну́жно** etc.:

Не на́до ни **дров**, ни **угля́** (*Rabotnitsa*)
Neither firewood nor coal is necessary

Note
Compare the use of the *genitive* case in the general statement: **По́мощи**
не ну́жно 'No help is required' and the *nominative* in the specific **Ва́ша**
по́мощь не нужна́ '*Your* help is not required'.

(7) The genitive case is used in negative passive constructions: **Книг** не
выпуска́ется 'No books are issued', **Подтвержде́ния** не полу́чено
'No confirmation has been received'.

(8) It is also used in time expressions:

И **пяти́ мину́т** не прошло́ (Orlov)
Not five minutes had passed

Мы пожени́лись, когда́ мне ещё не испо́лнилось **восемна́дцати**
(*Russia Today*)
We got married when I had not yet **turned 18**

87   The genitive and accusative after negated verbs

(1) Both the genitive and the accusative can be used after a negated
transitive verb:

Он не посеща́л **го́род/го́рода**   He did not visit the town

(2) While in case of doubt it is advisable to use a genitive, there are
situations where one case or the other is preferable.

(3) The **genitive** is preferred:

(i) In generalized statements:

Я не ви́жу **стола́**
I don't see a (i.e. *any*) table

(ii) With compound negatives:

Он никогда́ и никому́ не говори́л **непра́вды** (Trifonov)
He has never told lies to anyone

(iii) With the emphatic negative particle **ни:**

Он не прочита́л **ни одно́й кни́ги**
He has not read a single book

(iv) With abstract nouns: Она́ не скрыва́ет **своего́ раздраже́ния** 'She does not conceal her irritation'. Many set expressions are involved: не игра́ть **ро́ли** 'to play no part', не име́ть **поня́тия** 'to have no idea', не име́ть **пра́ва** 'not to have the right', не име́ть **смы́сла** 'not to have any point', не обраща́ть **внима́ния** 'not to pay any attention', не придава́ть **значе́ния** 'not to attach significance to', не принима́ть **уча́стия** 'not to take part', не производи́ть **впечатле́ния** 'to make no impression', не теря́ть **вре́мени** 'not to waste time'.

(v) With a negative gerund: не скрыва́я свое́й **ра́дости** 'without concealing his joy', не дослу́шав **спо́ра** до конца́ 'without hearing out the argument'.

(vi) With **э́то:** Э́того я не допущу́ 'I won't allow that', and after negated verbs of perception: Он не знал **уро́ка** 'He did not know the lesson', Он не по́нял **вопро́са** 'He did not understand the question', Он не чу́вствовал **бо́ли** 'he did not feel any pain'.

(4) The **accusative** is preferred:

(i) When a specific object or objects are involved:

Я не ви́жу **стол**
I do not see *the* table

Он не получи́л **письмо́**
He did not receive *the* letter (cf. Он не получи́л **письма́** 'He did not receive *a* letter')

(ii) When the object denotes a person:

Он не встре́тил **мою́ сестру́**
He did not meet my sister

(iii) With 'false' negatives such as **едва́ не/чуть не,** 'almost', **не могу́ не** 'I can't help, cannot but':

Он чуть не пропусти́л **трамва́й**
He almost missed the tram

Не могу́ не прости́ть его́ **поведе́ние**
I cannot but forgive his behaviour

(iv) When the noun is qualified by an instrumental predicate:

> Я не счита́ю э́ту **статью́** интере́сной
> I do not consider this article interesting

(v) When a part of the sentence other than the verb is negated:

> Он не **вполне́** усво́ил уро́к
> He has not **completely** assimilated the lesson

> Не **я** приду́мал но́вый поря́док
> It was not **I** who devised the new set up.

(vi) In set phrases: **па́лец** о па́лец не уда́рить 'not to do a stroke of work'.

(5) If none of the above criteria apply, then **either case** is usually possible. Factors which influence choice include:

(i) Word order, the accusative being preferred when the noun precedes the verb (**Иде́ю** она́ не поняла́ 'She did not understand the idea') and the genitive when it follows (Она́ не поняла́ **иде́и** 'She did not understand the idea').

(ii) An accusative is often regarded as the more colloquial alternative: Я не чита́л **вчера́шнюю газе́ту** 'I have not read yesterday's newspaper'.

(iii) Nouns in **-a** and **-я** are more prone to appear in the accusative case after a negated transitive verb than are other nouns.

(iv) When an infinitive appears between the negated verb and the object, the latter usually appears in the accusative:

> Он не хоте́л смотре́ть э́ту **пье́су**
> He did not want to see this play

> Я не уме́ю писа́ть **стихи́**
> I can't write verse

However, the genitive is also possible:

> Вы же никому́ не даёте раскры́ть **рта** (Trifonov)
> Why, you don't give anyone a chance to get a word in edgeways

Note

To avoid ambiguity, it is better to replace, say, Он не чита́ет **кни́ги** either by Он не чита́ет **кни́гу** 'He is not reading the book' or by Он не чита́ет **книг** 'He does not read books' (since it is otherwise not clear whether **кни́ги** is genitive singular or accusative plural).

(6) In cases of doubt it is advisable to use the *genitive* after a negated transitive verb:

Пригну́вшись, что́бы не заде́ть голово́й **потолка́** (Zalygin)
Stooping, so as not to hit his head on the ceiling

Note
Verbs which take a case other than the accusative are not affected by the negative-genitive rule: Он помога́ет бра́ту 'He helps his brother', Он не помога́ет бра́ту 'He does not help his brother'; Он горди́тся свои́м полко́м 'He is proud of his regiment', Он не горди́тся свои́м полко́м 'He is not proud of his regiment'.

88   Verbs that take the genitive

Verbs which govern the genitive case belong to four principal categories:

(1) Verbs of asking, waiting, seeking, achieving etc.:

(i) Verbs that take only the genitive. These include **добива́ться** 'to strive for', **достига́ть** 'to achieve', **жа́ждать** 'to crave for', **жела́ть** 'to desire', **заслу́живать** 'to deserve':

добива́ться	**успе́ха**	to strive for success
достига́ть	**свое́й це́ли**	to achieve one's aim
жа́ждать	**сла́вы**	to crave for glory
жела́ть	**сча́стья**	to desire happiness
заслу́живать	**похвалы́**	to deserve praise

Note
(a) The perfective **заслужи́ть** 'to earn' takes the accusative: заслужи́ть **дове́рие** 'to earn someone's confidence'.

(b) **Жела́ть** 'to wish' is 'understood' in such phrases as **Счастли́вого пути́!** 'Bon voyage!' and **И вам того́ же!** 'The same to you!'.

(ii) Verbs that take the genitive *and* the accusative. Generally speaking, such verbs take the genitive of nouns denoting general and abstract concepts, and the accusative of nouns denoting persons and specific inanimate objects. The verbs include:

(a) **Дожида́ться** 'to wait until'.

Genitive	дожида́ться **побе́ды**	to wait till victory comes
Accusative	дожида́ться **сестру́**	to wait till one's sister comes

(b) **Ждать** 'to wait for'.

Genitive	Жду **ответа**	I am awaiting an answer
	Жду **приказа**	I am awaiting an order
	Жду **решения**	I am awaiting a decision

Ждём **писем** о са́мых интере́сных кду́бах (*Russia Today*)
We are expecting letters about the most interesting clubs

Она́ ждала́ от меня́ **комплиме́нта** (Avdeenko)
She was expecting a compliment from me

Accusative	Жду **сего́дняшнюю**	I am waiting for
	по́чту	today's mail

Сиде́л за столо́м, занима́лся, ждал **жену́** (Grekova)
He sat at the table, worked, waited for his wife

Note

Ждать **авто́бус** No. 5 'to wait for the number 5 bus' (a particular bus), but Жду **авто́буса** 'I am waiting for a bus' (any bus; but Жду **авто́бус** is also possible, especially in spoken Russian).

(c) **Иска́ть** 'to seek, look for'.

Genitive ('to try to achieve')

иска́ть **возмо́жности**	to seek an opportunity
иска́ть **по́мощи**	to seek assistance

Accusative ('to try to find')

иска́ть **упа́вшую иго́лку**	to look for a dropped needle
иска́ть **своё ме́сто** в за́ле	to look for one's place in the hall
иска́ть **пра́вду**	to seek the truth
иска́ть **доро́гу**	to try to find the way

Note

Рабо́та is found in either case (иска́ть **рабо́ты/рабо́ту** 'to look for work'), with the accusative (the more usual form) referring to more specific work.

(d) **Ожида́ть** 'to wait for, expect'.

Genitive	ожида́ть **слу́чая**	to wait for an opportunity
	ожида́ть **авто́буса**	to wait for a bus (cf. **ждать** (b) note)

Втяну́л го́лову в пле́чи, бу́дто ожида́я **уда́ра** со спины́ (Gagarin)
He hunched his shoulders, as if expecting a blow from behind

Accusative   ожида́ть **ма́му**   to wait for, expect Mum

(e) **Проси́ть** 'to ask for'.

Genitive   Прошу́ **по́мощи**   I ask for assistance (also
                                   прошу́ о по́мощи)
              Прошу́ **проще́ния**   I ask forgiveness

See **83** (3) for usage with the partitive genitive.

Accusative   Прошу́ **де́ньги**   I ask for the money (cf.
                                   Прошу́ **де́нег** 'I ask
                                   for **some** money')
              Прошу́ **ма́му**   I ask Mum to open the
              откры́ть окно́   window

(f) **Тре́бовать** 'to demand'.

Genitive   тре́бовать **внима́ния**   to demand attention
              тре́бовать **приба́вки**   to demand an increment
              тре́бовать **книг**   to demand some books
Accusative   тре́бовать **свою́ кни́гу** to demand one's book

(g) **Хоте́ть** 'to want'.

Genitive   Хоти́м **ми́ра**   We want peace

See **83** (3) for usage with the partitive genitive.

Accusative   Хочу́ **бу́лку**   I want a roll

(2) Verbs of fearing, avoiding etc. Such verbs usually take the genitive
of abstract, impersonal and inanimate nouns, but may now govern the
accusative of animate nouns.

(i) **Боя́ться** 'to fear'.

Genitive   боя́ться **темноты́** to be afraid of the dark
              боя́ться **грозы́**   to be afraid of a thunderstorm

Он боя́лся **го́рода**, не хоте́л в него́ (Rasputin)
He was afraid of the town, did not want to go there

Accusative   боя́ться **ба́бушку** to be afraid of grandmother

(ii) Other verbs include дичи́ться 'to be shy of', избега́ть 'to avoid',
опаса́ться 'to fear', остерега́ться 'to beware of', пуга́ться 'to be scared
of', стесня́ться 'to be shy of', сторони́ться 'to shun', стыди́ться 'to be
ashamed of', чужда́ться 'to avoid':

избега́ть **неприя́тностей**   to avoid trouble

избега́ть **тёщу**	to avoid one's mother-in-law
опаса́ться **осложне́ний**	to fear complications
остерега́ться **зара́зы**	to beware of an infection
пуга́ться **гро́ма**	to be scared of thunder
стесня́ться **о́бщества**	to shun society
сторони́ться **недо́брых люде́й**	to shun wicked people
стыди́ться **своего́ ви́да**	to be ashamed of one's appearance
чужда́ться **дурно́й компа́нии**	to avoid bad company

(3) Verbs of depriving etc.

лиша́ть **роди́тельских прав**	to deprive of parental rights
лиша́ться **свобо́ды**	to be deprived of one's freedom

(4) Verbs denoting conformity or non-conformity. These include держа́ться 'to adhere to', ослу́шиваться 'to disobey', приде́рживаться 'to hold to', слу́шаться 'to obey':

держа́ться **мне́ния**	to stick to one's opinion
ослу́шиваться **прика́за**	to disobey an order
приде́рживаться **то́чки зре́ния**	to hold to a point of view
слу́шаться **сове́та**	to heed advice

Note

In colloquial styles the accusative is possible with an animate object: слу́шаться **ма́тери** or **мать** 'to obey one's mother'.

Other verbs that take the genitive include **каса́ться** 'to touch, touch on' and **сто́ить** 'to be worth':

каса́ться **стола́**	to touch the table
каса́ться **вопро́са**	to touch on a question
э́то сто́ит **награ́ды**	that is worth an award

89   The dative as indirect object of a verb

The dative case denotes the indirect object of a verb, i.e. the person for whom an action is performed, the recipient or beneficiary: дава́ть де́ньги **касси́ру** 'to give the money to the cashier', звони́ть **сестре́** на рабо́ту 'to ring one's sister at work', отвеча́ть **сосе́ду** 'to answer a neighbour' (cf. отвеча́ть **на** письмо́ 'to answer a letter'), писа́ть письмо **брату** 'to write a letter to one's brother', платить **другу** 'to pay one's friend', пожимать руку **солдату** 'to shake the soldier's hand', послать деньги **сыну** 'to send money to one's son' (note, however, use of the preposition **к** when the object sent is animate: отправить детей **к родственникам** 'to send the children to stay with relatives'), сказать **отцу** правду 'to tell one's father the truth'.

90   Verbs that take the dative

Verbs which take the dative denote:

(1) Conforming, rendering assistance or other service; conversely, causing a hindrance: аккомпанировать 'to accompany' (music), аплодировать 'to applaud', вредить 'to harm', изменять 'to betray', мешать 'to hinder', напоминать 'to remind', повиноваться 'to obey', позволять 'to allow', покровительствовать 'to patronize', помогать 'to help', препятствовать 'to hinder', противоречить 'to contradict', служить 'to serve', советовать 'to advise', содействовать 'to co-operate', способствовать 'to foster', угождать 'to please'.

Note
(a)   Запрещать 'to forbid' and разрешать 'to permit' take the dative of the person (запрещать/разрешать **солдатам** курить 'to forbid/permit the soldiers to smoke') and the accusative of an action or process (запрещать/разрешать **обгон** 'to forbid/permit overtaking').
(b)   Учить 'to teach' takes the dative of the subject taught: учить детей **музыке** 'to teach the children music'. Учить + accusative means 'to learn': учить **русский язык** 'to learn Russian'.

(2) Attitude: верить 'to believe', грозить 'to threaten', доверять(ся) 'to trust', досаждать 'to annoy', завидовать 'to envy', льстить 'to flatter', мстить 'to take vengeance on' (cf. мстить за + accusative 'to avenge someone'), надоедать 'to bore', подражать 'to imitate', поражаться 'to be amazed at', радоваться 'to rejoice at', сочувствовать 'to sympathize with', удивляться 'to be surprised at'. Note also смеяться, улыбаться **шутке** 'to laugh, smile at a joke' (but смеяться **над** кем-нибудь 'to laugh at someone').

(3) Other meanings: наследовать 'to succeed' (someone), предшествовать 'to precede', принадлежать 'to belong to' (in the meaning of possession; cf. принадлежать **к** 'to belong to' (a group, society etc.)), равняться 'to equal', следовать 'to follow' (advice etc.).

Note

Many verbal and other nouns cognate with the above verbs also take the dative: обуче́ние **ру́сскому языку́** 'the teaching of Russian', подража́ние **ска́зке** 'imitation of a folk tale', по́мощь **же́ртвам** землетрясе́ния 'help for the victims of the earthquake', служе́ние **нау́ке** 'service to science', соде́йствие **фло́ту** 'co-operation with the navy', сочу́вствие **чужо́му го́рю** 'sympathy for others' grief', угро́за **ми́ру** 'a threat to peace'.

91   Adjectives that take the dative

Adjectives (long *and* short forms) which take the dative include:

благода́рный	grateful to
ве́рный	loyal to
знако́мый	known to
изве́стный	well known to
подо́бный	similar to
послу́шный	obedient to
прису́щий	inherent in
рад (short form only)	glad (я рад **гостя́м** 'I am glad to see the guests')
сво́йственный	characteristic of, inherent in

Предусмотри́тельность **сво́йственна** э́тому челове́ку
Prudence is inherent in this person

92   Impersonal constructions using the dative

(1) Most impersonal constructions involving the dative case denote a state of mind, feeling, inclination or attitude:

Ученику́ ве́село, гру́стно, ду́шно, жа́рко, лу́чше, ску́чно, сты́дно, тепло́, удо́бно, хо́лодно, ху́же
The pupil feels cheerful, sad, stifled, hot, better, bored, ashamed, warm, comfortable, cold, worse

(2) Some constructions involve verbs: **Бра́ту** ка́жется, что тепло́ 'My brother thinks it is warm', **Бра́ту** надое́ло рабо́тать 'My brother is bored with working', **Бра́ту** нездоро́вится 'My brother feels off colour', **Бра́ту** нра́вится танцева́ть 'My brother likes dancing', **Бра́ту** прихо́дится мно́го рабо́тать 'My brother is obliged to work hard',

Бра́ту удало́сь доста́ть де́ньги 'My brother managed to get the money', **Бра́ту** хоте́лось уйти́ 'My brother felt like leaving'.

(3) Note also:

(i) Constructions with reflexive verbs that denote disinclination:

> **Сестре́** не поётся, не рабо́тается, не сиди́тся
> My sister does not feel like singing, working, sitting still

(ii) The impersonal predicate **жаль** also combines with the dative:
Отцу́ жаль 'My father feels sorry' (for жаль with accusative see **79** (2) and for жаль with genitive see **80** (8)).

(4) The dative is also used in denoting age: **Сы́ну** (испо́лнилось) 20 лет 'My son is (has turned) 20'.

93   The dative as the logical subject of an infinitive

(1) A noun or pronoun in the dative case may function as the logical subject of an infinitive: Что **де́тям** де́лать? 'What are the children to do?', Не **вам** реша́ть 'It is not for you to decide', **Бра́ту** не́куда идти́ 'My brother has nowhere to go'.

(2) The dative can also be used to express a peremptory command: **Всем сотру́дникам** собра́ться в час! 'All employees meet at one!'

94   The instrumental of function

A noun is placed in the instrumental case to denote that the object it represents is being used to perform a function: мы́ться **горя́чей водо́й** 'to wash with hot water', писа́ть **карандашо́м** 'to write with a pencil', ре́зать **ножо́м** 'to cut with a knife', руби́ть **топоро́м** 'to chop with an axe'.

Note
(a) Analogous use of the instrumental in броса́ть **камня́ми** 'to throw stones' (at a target), говори́ть **гро́мким го́лосом** 'to speak in a loud voice', дыша́ть **кислоро́дом** 'to breathe oxygen', плати́ть **англи́йскими деньга́ми** 'to pay in English money'.
(b) Use of the instrumental of function (e.g. ре́зать **ножо́м** 'to cut with a knife') must be distinguished from c + instrumental ('with' in the meaning 'holding'): он сиде́л **с ножо́м** в руке́ 'he sat with a knife in his hand'.

(c) Корми́ть **ры́бой** 'to feed on (= with) fish', награжда́ть **пре́мией** 'to reward with a bonus', наполня́ть **водо́й** 'to fill with water', снабжа́ть **не́фтью** 'to supply with oil' also belong in the category 'instrumental of function'.

95   The instrumental in constructions denoting movements of the body

The instrumental is used in constructions denoting movements of the body:

(1) Дви́гать **руко́й** 'to move one's arm' (cf. дви́гать **стол** 'to move a table'), кача́ть/кива́ть **голово́й** 'to shake/nod one's head', маха́ть **руко́й** 'to wave one's hand', мига́ть **глаза́ми** 'to blink one's eyes', пожима́ть **плеча́ми** 'to shrug one's shoulders', то́пать **нога́ми** 'to stamp one's feet', щёлкать **языко́м** 'to click one's tongue'.

(2) The construction also applies to objects held with the hand (разма́хивать **па́лкой** 'to brandish a stick', хло́пать **две́рью** 'to slam a door', щёлкать **бичо́м** 'to crack a whip') and to the figurative expressions И **бро́вью** не повёл 'He did not turn a hair', шевели́ть **мозга́ми** 'to use one's brains'.

96   The instrumental in passive constructions

The instrumental is used to denote the agent in a passive construction:

Дом стро́ится **рабо́чими**	The house is being built by workers
Гора́ покры́та **сне́гом**	The mountain is covered with snow
Ве́тром сорва́ло кры́шу	The roof was torn off by the wind

See also **359** and **360** (2) for the use of the instrumental with passive participles.

97   The instrumental in adverbial expressions

The instrumental is used to denote:

(1) The type of route covered in a journey: идти **бéрегом** 'to walk along the shore', éхать **лéсом** 'to ride through the forest', **мóрем** 'by sea', éхать **пóлем** 'to ride through the fields', **сухúм путём** 'overland'. Note also идтú **своéй дорóгой** 'to go one's own way' (fig.).

(2) Time:

(i) Parts of the day: **ýтром, днём, вéчером, нóчью** 'in the morning, daytime, evening, at night' (**глубóкой нóчью** 'at dead of night', **однáжды ýтром** 'one morning', **вечерáми** 'in the evenings', **ночáми** '(at) nights').

Note
Днём may also mean 'in the afternoon' (also rendered as во вторóй половúне дня).

(ii) Seasons of the year: **веснóй, лéтом, óсенью, зимóй** 'in the spring, summer, autumn, winter' (однáжды **зимóй** 'one winter', **пóздней óсенью** 'in late autumn' etc.).

(iii) Others: **цéлыми часáми/днями** 'for hours/days on end'.

(3) The **manner** in which or the **means** by which an action is performed, in terms of:

(i) Position: вверх **дном** 'upside down', вниз **головóй** 'head first', стоять **спинóй** к огню 'to stand with one's back to the fire'.

(ii) Movement: **бегóм** 'at a run', **шáгом** 'at walking pace'.

(iii) Group activity: уéхать **семьёй** 'to leave in a family group', пéние **хóром** 'singing in chorus'.

(iv) Utterance: **другúми словáми** 'in other words', петь **бáсом** 'to sing bass', **шёпотом** 'in a whisper'.

(v) Means of transport: éхать **пóездом**, летéть **самолётом** 'to go by train, by air'.

(vi) Degree of effort: **любóй ценóй** 'at any cost'.

(vii) Quantity: Домá не стрóили **тысячами**, как сейчáс (Rybakov) 'Houses were not built in thousands as they are now'.

(viii) Form, manner: **какúм óбразом?** 'in what way?', Снег пáдает на зéмлю **большúми хлóпьями** (Rasputin) 'The snow falls to earth in large flakes'.

98   Use of the instrumental to denote similarity

The instrumental is also used to express similarity: выть **во́лком** 'to howl like a wolf', умере́ть **геро́ем** 'to die like a hero', шипе́ть **змеёй** 'to hiss like a snake', Снег лежи́т **ковро́м** 'The snow lies like a carpet', лете́ть **стрело́й** 'to fly like an arrow', усы́ **щёточкой** 'toothbrush moustache':

> За кута́рником **тёмной стено́й** выраста́ло чернопе́сье (Abramov)
> Deciduous forest grew up beyond the bushes like a dark wall

99   Verbs that take the instrumental

Verbs that take the instrumental case denote:

(1) **Use** or **control:** владе́ть 'to own, have a command of' (a language), дирижи́ровать 'to conduct' (an orchestra), заве́довать 'to be in charge of', злоупотребля́ть 'to abuse, misuse', кома́ндовать 'to command', облада́ть 'to possess', по́льзоваться 'to use', пра́вить 'to rule', располага́ть 'to have at one's disposal', распоряжа́ться 'to manage', руководи́ть 'to run', управля́ть 'to control'.

(2) **Attitude:** восхища́ться 'to be delighted with', горди́ться 'to be proud of', грози́ть 'to threaten with', дово́льствоваться 'to be satisfied with', дорожи́ть 'to value', интересова́ться 'to be interested in', любова́ться 'to admire' (also на + acc.), наслажда́ться 'to delight in', обходи́ться 'to make do with', пренебрега́ть 'to disregard', увлека́ться 'to be obsessed with', хва́статься 'to boast of', щеголя́ть 'to flaunt'.

(3) **Reciprocal action:** дели́ться 'to share', обме́ниваться 'to exchange'.

(4) **Other meanings:** боле́ть 'to be sick', же́ртвовать 'to sacrifice' (cf. же́ртвовать + acc. 'to donate'), занима́ться 'to busy oneself with', изоби́ловать 'to abound in', ограни́чиваться 'to limit oneself to', отлича́ться 'to be distinguished by', па́хнуть 'to smell of', прославля́ться 'to be renowned for', рискова́ть 'to risk', страда́ть 'to suffer from' (chronically) (cf. страда́ть от 'to suffer from' (a *temporary* ailment)), торгова́ть 'to trade in'.

Note
Participial, verbal and other nouns cognate with many of the above also take the instrumental: владе́ние **до́мом** 'ownership of a house' (but

владе́лец **до́ма** 'house owner'), злоупотребле́ние **вла́стью** 'abuse of power', кома́ндование **а́рмией** 'command of the army', кома́нду- ющий **а́рмией** 'army commander' (but команди́р **диви́зии** 'divisional commander'), руково́дство **па́ртией** 'leadership of the party' (as an action or process, cf. руково́дство **па́ртии** 'the leadership (i.e. 'the leaders') of the party', руководи́тель **гру́ппы** 'leader of the group'), торго́вля **нарко́тиками** 'drugs trade', увлече́ние **матема́тикой** 'obsession with mathematics'.

100   Adjectives that take the instrumental

These include long *and* (where available) short forms: бере́менная (**тре́тьим ребёнком**) 'pregnant' (with her third child), бога́тый 'rich in', больно́й 'sick with', го́рдый 'proud of', дово́льный 'pleased with', изве́стный 'famous for', обя́занный 'obliged':

> **Свои́ми успе́хами** они́ бы́ли обя́заны со́бственному трудолю́бию (Rybakov)
> They owed their success to their own industriousness

101   The instrumental of dimension

The instrumental is used to express dimension: гора́ **высото́й** в 1 000 ме́тров 'a mountain 1,000 m high', река́ **длино́й** в сто киломе́тров 'a river 100 km long', челове́к **ро́стом** в метр во́семьдесят 'a man one metre eighty tall'.

Note

(a)   The preposition **в** may be omitted, especially in technical styles.

(b)   Questions to which these are the notional answers appear in the *genitive*: **како́й высоты́** гора́? 'how high is the mountain?', **како́й длины́** река́? 'how long is the river?', **како́го** он **ро́ста?** 'how tall is he?'

102   The instrumental as predicate

(1) The instrumental is used as predicate to the infinitive, future tense, imperative, conditional and gerund of the verb **быть** 'to be': Я хочу́ быть **врачо́м** 'I want to be a doctor', е́сли бы я был **врачо́м** 'if I were

a doctor', Когда́-нибудь вы бу́дете **старико́м** 'One day you will be an old man', Не будь **тру́сом** 'Don't be a coward', Не бу́дучи **знатоко́м, не могу́ суди́ть** 'Not being a connoisseur I cannot judge'.

Note

The *nominative*, not the instrumental, is used when no part of быть is present: Она́ врач 'She is a doctor'.

(2) In the *past* tense:

(i) The nominative denotes **permanent** state, occupation, nationality etc.: По профе́ссии он был **бота́ник** 'By profession he was a botanist', Она́ была́ **испа́нка** (Granin) 'She was a Spaniard', Смоля́нов был **сара́товец** (Trifonov) 'Smolyanov was a native of Saratov'.

(ii) The instrumental denotes **temporary** status: Во вре́мя войны́ я был **офице́ром** 'During the war I was an officer' (the verb **быть** is sometimes omitted: Я потеря́л роди́телей (когда́ я был/бу́дучи) **ребёнком** 'I lost my parents as a child').

Note

Permanent status may *also* be denoted by the instrumental: Она́ была́ **сестро́й** Полево́го (Propp), 'She was Polevoi's sister', Пу́шкин был **велича́йшим ру́сским поэ́том/велича́йший ру́сский поэ́т** 'Pushkin was the greatest Russian poet'.

(3) Of two nouns (or noun and pronoun) linked by the verb **быть** the more specific appears in the nominative, the more general in the instrumental:

> **Ключо́м** к успе́ху была́ гра́мотность
> The key to success was literacy

> В на́шем до́ме неме́цкий был **тре́тьим языко́м** (Rybakov)
> In our house German was the third language

> **Одно́й** из на́ших гла́вных пробле́м был тра́нспорт
> One of our main problems was transport

Note

The subject may be an infinitive: **Учи́ться** бу́дет его́ це́лью 'His aim will be to study', Пе́рвым её побужде́нием бы́ло **помо́чь** до́чери 'Her first impulse was to help her daughter'.

(4) The rule described in (3) also applies to **явля́ться** 'to be':

> **Основно́й фо́рмой** рабо́ты в шко́ле явля́ется уро́к (*Russia Today*)
> The lesson is the basic form of work in school

(5) An instrumental predicate also appears with verbs such as **запи́сываться** 'to enrol', **рабо́тать** 'to work', **служи́ть** 'to serve':

Записа́лся **доброво́льцем,** да́ли ему́ коня́ (Rybakov)
He signed up as a volunteer, and they gave him a horse

(6) A number of verbs which denote state, appearance or manner also take an instrumental: **вы́глядеть** 'to look', **каза́ться** 'to seem', **называ́ться** 'to be called', **ока́зываться** 'to turn out to be', **остава́ться** 'to remain', **расстава́ться** 'to part', **роди́ться** 'to be born', **состоя́ть** (**чле́ном**) 'to be' (a member), **станови́ться** 'to become', **счита́ться** 'to be considered', **чу́вствовать себя́** 'to feel':

Ещё с войны́ она́ **вдово́й** оста́лась (Shcherbakov)
She had been left a war widow

Он ка́жется **о́пытным инжене́ром**
He seems to be an experienced engineer

Впервы́е в жи́зни я чу́вствую себя́ **преда́телем** (Makarov)
For the first time in my life I feel like a traitor

(7) The instrumental may also be predicate to the object of transitive verbs which denote appointment, naming, considering: Сестру́ зову́т **Та́ней** (alternatively, especially in colloquial Russian, Сестру́ зову́т **Та́ня**) 'My sister is called Tanya', назнача́ть Ивано́ва **председа́телем** 'to appoint Ivanov chairman', Мак счита́ют **снотво́рным сре́дством** 'Poppy is considered to be a soporific':

Он называ́ет Толья́тти «**эксперимента́льной лаборато́рией**» сове́тского градострои́тельства (*Sputnik*)
He calls Togliatti 'an experimental laboratory' in Soviet town planning

Note
Толья́тти 'Togliatti' was renamed Тольяттигра́д 'Togliattigrad' in 1991.

103   Nouns in apposition

When two or more nouns, pronouns or modifiers refer to the same object or person they appear in the same case:

Она́ жила́ в **Москве́, столи́це** Росси́и
She lived in **Moscow, the capital** of Russia

Он знал **моего́ отца́, изве́стного хиру́рга**
He knew **my father, a famous surgeon**

Я чита́ю "*Аргуме́нты и фа́кты*", одну́ из са́мых интере́сных
еженеде́льных газе́т
I am reading *Argumenty i fakty, one* of the most interesting weekly
newspapers

Diminutive and augmentative nouns

104   Meanings and functions of the diminutive

(1) Diminutive suffixes not only denote smallness (**сто́лик** 'a small
table'), but may also express emotional nuances such as affection
(**дя́денька** 'dear uncle'), disparagement (**городи́шко** 'wretched little
town'), irony (**иде́йка** 'a paltry little idea') etc. Depending on context
the same diminutive phrase may convey a caring attitude (Вот тебе́
горя́ченький су́пчик 'Here's some nice hot soup for you' (mother to
child)) or be evidence of affectation.

(2) Diminutives are used mainly in colloquial speech. Many have
acquired independent meanings, e.g. **ру́чка** 'handle', 'pen'.

105   Masculine diminutives

The following diminutive suffixes may be affixed to the stems of
masculine nouns.

(1) **-ец**.

-ец may express an affectionate or positive attitude (**бра́тец** from брат
'brother', **хле́бец** from хлеб 'bread'), or alternatively disparagement
(**анекдо́тец** from анекдо́т 'anecdote').

(2) **-ик**.

(i) **-ик** (*never stressed*) imparts the meaning of smallness to many
masculine nouns: **до́мик** from дом 'house', **ко́врик** 'mat' from ковёр
'carpet'.

(ii) Emotional nuances expressed by **-ик** include affection (**са́дик** from
сад 'garden'), and irony or scorn (**анекдо́тик** from анекдо́т
'anecdote').

(iii) Diminutives with independent meanings include **мо́стик** 'captain's bridge', **но́жик** 'pen-knife' and **сто́лик** 'restaurant table'.

(3) **-ок/-ёк/-ек**.

(i) **-ок/-ёк** (*always stressed*) express affection, irony or disparagement, as well as smallness. Velar consonants undergo mutation:

дружо́к from друг 'friend', **старичо́к** from стари́к 'old man', **пастушо́к** from пасту́х 'shepherd'.

(ii) Other diminutives in **-ок** include **городо́к** from го́род 'town', **лесо́к** from лес 'forest' etc. **Дурачо́к** from дура́к 'fool' and **женишо́к** from жени́х 'fiancé, bridegroom' express irony.

(iii) Nouns in **-ь** and **-й** take the suffix **-ёк: огонёк** from ого́нь 'fire, light' (Нет ли у вас **огонька́**? 'Do you happen to have a light?'), **чаёк** from чай 'tea' (Хоти́те **чайку́**? 'Have some tea?').

(iv) Nouns with independent meanings include **волосо́к** 'filament', **глазо́к** 'peephole', **значо́к** 'badge', **конёк** 'skate', **кружо́к** 'circle, club', **молото́к** 'hammer', **носо́к** 'sock, toe of shoe or stocking', **язычо́к** 'tongue of shoe, clapper of bell'.

Note
(a)   Second-stage diminutives can be formed: друг 'friend', дружо́к, **дружо́чек**.

(b)   Diminutives in unstressed **-ек** include **челове́чек** from челове́к 'person'.

(4)   **-чик**.

(i)   **-чик** (*never stressed*) is affixed mainly to nouns ending in:

(a)   **-л/-ль (автомоби́льчик** from автомоби́ль 'car', **журна́льчик** from журна́л 'journal').

(b)   **-н (карма́нчик** from карма́н 'pocket').

(c)   **-р (забо́рчик** from забо́р 'fence').

(d)   **-й (трамва́йчик** from трамва́й 'tram').

(e)   **-ф (шка́фчик** from шкаф 'cupboard').

(ii) The suffix may also express affection: **дива́нчик** from дива́н 'couch'. Forms with independent meanings include **колоко́льчик** 'bluebell' from ко́локол 'bell'.

(5) Examples of masculine diminutives expressing:

(i) Smallness:

> На корме́ поблёскивал **мото́рчик** (Nagibin)
> In the stern glinted a small engine

(ii) Animosity:

> Я приду́мывал но́вый **вопро́сец** похлёстче (Gagarin)
> I was devising a more scathing question

(iii) Irony:

> А муж счита́ет, что уже́ отве́тил на э́тот вопро́с, наде́в кольцо́ на **па́льчик** свое́й супру́ги
> Whereas the husband thinks he has already answered this question by placing a ring on his wife's dear little finger

(iv) Disparagement:

> **Сыно́к** профе́ссора. Чи́стенький тако́й **пижо́нчик** (Yakhontov)
> A professor's pampered brat. A young fop, pure as the driven snow

106   Feminine diminutives

(1) **-ица**.

(i) The suffix **-ица** bears the stress in diminutives derived from nouns in stressed **-а́, -я́** and in **-ь**: **вещи́ца** from вещь 'thing' (cf. **про́сьбица** from про́сьба 'request').

(ii) Second-stage diminutives in **-ичка** are also formed: вода́ 'water', води́ца, **води́чка** (both have the positive nuance typical of diminutives based on the names of food and drink); сестра́ 'sister', сестри́ца, **сестри́чка** (cf., from Russian folk-tale, **Лиси́чка-Сестри́чка** 'Sister Fox').

(2) **-ка**.

(i) The suffix may denote smallness (**крова́тка** 'cot' from крова́ть 'bed') as well as affection (**до́чка** from дочь 'daughter') or irony (**иде́йка** from иде́я 'idea').

(ii) The stress in diminutives in **-ка** derived from end-stressed nouns falls on the syllable preceding **-ка: голо́вка** from голова́ 'head'. Some diminutives are based on genitive plurals with the vowel **-e-**: пе́сня 'song', gen. pl. пе́сен, dim. **пе́сенка**; семья́ 'family', gen. pl. семе́й, dim. **семе́йка**.

(iii) Velar consonants and **ц** undergo mutation: **кни́жка** from кни́га 'book', **ре́чка** from река́ 'river', **му́шка** from му́ха 'fly', **страни́чка** from страни́ца 'page'.

(iv) The following have independent meanings: **голо́вка** 'head of a nail' (also **боеголо́вка** 'war-head'), **доро́жка** 'path', **ёлка** 'Christmas tree', **кры́шка** 'lid', **маши́нка** 'typewriter', **но́жка** 'leg of chair, table', **пли́тка** 'bar' (of chocolate), **площа́дка** 'stair landing, playground, launch pad', **пти́чка** 'tick', **ру́чка** 'arm of a chair', **се́тка** 'tennis net', **спи́нка** 'back of a chair', **стре́лка** 'clock-hand', **тру́бка** 'telephone receiver, pipe'.

(v) Second-stage diminutives in **-очка** are formed as follows: мину́та 'minute', мину́тка, **мину́точка** (Подожди́те **мину́точку!** 'Wait a sec!').

(vi) Nouns with a double consonant + **-a** form **first-stage** diminutives in **-очка**: звезда́ 'star', **звёздочка** 'small star, asterisk'; ка́рта 'card, map', **ка́рточка** 'greetings card' (but игла́ 'needle', **иго́лка, иго́лочка**).

107   Neuter diminutives

(1) **-ико**.

This suffix is used with very few nouns: **колёсико** from колесо́ 'wheel', **ли́чико** from лицо́ 'face', **пле́чико** from плечо́ 'shoulder' (pl. **пле́чики** also 'coat-hanger').

(2) **-ко**.

Stress is unpredictable in diminutives with this ending, cf. **ведёрко** from ведро́ 'bucket', **озерко́** from о́зеро 'lake'. **К** and **ц** mutate to **ч**: **о́блачко** from о́блако 'cloud', **яи́чко** from яйцо́ 'egg'.

(3) **-цо/це; -ецо**.

The suffixes **-цо/-це** appear after a single consonant, **-ецо** after a double consonant: **зе́ркальце** from зе́ркало 'mirror', **письмецо́** from письмо́ 'letter'. Stress is as in the source noun except for **словцо́** from сло́во 'word' and **де́ревце/деревцо́** from де́рево 'tree'.

108   Other diminutive suffixes

(1) **-ашка** expresses slight disparagement or endearment, depending on context: **мордашка** from мóрда 'mug' (face), **старикашка** from старик 'old man'.

(2) **-ишко** (inanimate)/**-ишка** (animate) express disparagement or irony: **воришка** from вор 'thief', **домишко** from дом 'house':

> У меня дóма **коньячишко** есть (Shukshin)
> I've got a nice little bottle of brandy at home (nuance of affection)

(3) **-онка/-ёнка** express disparagement: **книжóнка** from книга 'book', **лошадёнка** from лóшадь 'horse' (however, **сестрёнка** from сестрá 'sister' denotes affection).

(4) **-ушка/-юшка** and **-енька/-онька** express affection: **дóченька** from дочь 'daughter', **избýшка** from избá 'hut'.

(5) **-ышек, -ышко: кóлышек** 'tent-peg' from кол 'stake', **гóрлышко** 'neck of bottle' from гóрло 'throat', **зёрнышко** from зернó 'grain'.

109   Augmentative suffixes

The suffixes **-ина, -ище** and **-ища** are attached to the stems of nouns to denote largeness. Augmentatives may also express emotive nuances: **идиóтина** 'a blithering idiot'.

(1) **-ина**.

(i) **-ина** is affixed to the stems of masculine and feminine nouns: **зверина** (from зверь) 'an enormous beast', **лáпина** (from лáпа) 'a massive paw'.

(ii) The suffix is stressed if attached to the stem of a noun which has mobile stress in declension (**домина** 'a vast house') and is unstressed if attached to the stem of a noun which has fixed stress in declension (**рыбина** 'a large fish').

(iii) Velar consonants undergo mutation: **дурачина** (from дурáк) 'a great fool', **оплеýшина** (from оплеýха) 'a hefty slap in the face'.

(2) **-ище/-ища**.

(i) These suffixes are far more productive than -ина. **-ище** is affixed to the stems of masculine and neuter nouns, **-ища** to those of feminine nouns: **арбу́зище** (from арбу́з) 'an enormous melon', **бороди́ща** (from борода́) 'a massive beard'.

(ii) Stress position depends on the same principles as those described for -ина: **велика́нище** (from велика́н) (fixed stress in declension) 'an enormous giant', **голоси́ще** (from го́лос) (mobile stress in declension) 'a mighty voice'.

(iii) Velar consonants undergo mutation: **волчи́ще** (from волк) 'a large wolf', **ручи́ща** (from рука́) 'a mighty hand'.

The Pronoun

110 Personal pronouns

(1) The personal pronouns **я** 'I', **ты** 'you' (informal), **он** 'he, it', **она́** 'she, it', **оно́** 'it', **мы** 'we', **вы** 'you' (formal and plural), **они́** 'they' decline as follows:

Nom.		я	ты	он	он-а́	он-о́
Acc./Gen.		мен-я́	теб-я́	его́	её	его́
Dat.		мн-е	теб-е́	ему́	ей	ему́
Instr.		мн-ой	тоб-о́й	им	ей/е́ю	им
Prep.	обо мн-е		о теб-е́	о нём	о ней	о нём

Nom.	м-ы	в-ы	он-и́
Acc./Gen.	н-ас	в-ас	их
Dat.	н-ам	в-ам	им
Instr.	н-а́ми	в-а́ми	и́ми
Prep.	о н-ас	о в-ас	о них

Note

(a) Я and ты have alternative instrumental forms: **мно́ю** and **тобо́ю**, used in verse and in some colloquial registers, are also found in passive constructions (Э́то сде́лано **мно́ю/мной** 'That was done by me').

(b) **Его́**, the accusative/genitive of **он/оно́**, is pronounced [jɪ'vo].

(c) The alternative instrumental form of она́ (е́ю) is preferred to ей in educated speech and is particularly important in passive constructions, avoiding possible confusion with the dative:

Револю́цией перестро́йку мо́жно назва́ть в си́лу радика́льности поста́вленных **е́ю** це́лей (*Izvestiya*)
Restructuring can be called a revolution by virtue of the radical nature of the goals set **by it**

(**Ей** would imply a dative meaning: 'the goals set **for** it'.)

(2) The oblique cases of **он, она́, оно́, они́** take initial **н-** when governed by a preposition: от него́ 'from him', к ней 'to her', с ни́ми 'with them' etc. However, some *compound* prepositions take a third-person pronoun *without* initial **н-**. They include:

(i) A number of derivative prepositions governing the dative: благодаря́ **им** 'thanks to them', ему́ навстре́чу 'to meet him', на зло **ей** 'to spite her'. Others include **вопреки́** 'contrary to', **напереко́р** 'counter to', **подо́бно** 'similar to', **согла́сно** 'in accordance with'.

(ii) Some which take the genitive: **внѐ** 'outside', **в отноше́нии** 'in relation to'. **Внутри̂** 'inside' takes alternative forms with or without **н-**: внутри̂ **их/них** 'inside them'.

Note
When a declined form of the third-person plural pronoun combines with a declined form of **все** 'all', a pronoun with initial **н-** is the norm: смея́ться над все́ми **ни́ми** 'to laugh at all of them'. **У/от неё** 'She has/from her' has an alternative form **у/от ней**, used nowadays mainly in verse.

111   Use of personal instead of possessive pronouns

(1) Personal pronouns are more usual than possessive pronouns in referring to parts of the body, articles of clothing, location etc.: Он пожа́л **мне** ру́ку 'He shook **my** hand', Он пришёл **ко мне** в ко́мнату 'He came to **my** room', Пла́тье у неё всё испа́чкано '**Her** dress is all stained'. The reflexive pronoun (see **117**) is used similarly: Он лёг у себя́ в ко́мнате 'He lay down in **his** room' etc.

(2) Note also the idioms: **мне** пришло́ в го́лову 'it occurred to me' (lit. 'came into **my** head'), Красота́ зда́ния бро́силась **ему́** в глаза́ 'He was struck by the beauty of the building'.

112   Use of the nominative pronoun with э́то

In contrast to English, nominative pronouns are used in such phrases as Э́то **я** 'It's me', Э́то **он** 'It's him', Э́то **мы** 'It's us' etc.

113   The pronoun я

(1) **Я** 'I' combines with first-person singular forms of the present and future of verbs: я **чита́ю** 'I read', я **прочита́ю** 'I shall read', я бу́ду **чита́ть** 'I shall be reading'. The gender of predicative adjectives, of other pronouns and of past verbs depends on the sex of the speaker:

Я дово́лен, я оди́н, я пришёл
I am pleased, I am alone, I have arrived (of a **male** speaker)

Я дово́льна, я одна́, я пришла́
I am pleased, I am alone, I have arrived (of a **female** speaker)

(2) Compare also the oblique cases: Оста́вьте меня́ **одного́** 'Leave me by myself' (of a male), Оста́вьте меня́ **одну́** 'Leave me by myself' (of a female).

Note

(a)   'You and I' is rendered as **мы с ва́ми**, 'he and I' as **мы с ним** etc. (also, in relevant contexts, though less usually, 'you and ourselves', 'he and ourselves').

(b)   **Я** as a noun may be qualified by neuter modifiers: **моё второ́е я** 'my alter ego'.

(c)   **Я** is often omitted in everyday speech (**Начну́** сейча́с! 'I'll begin at once!') and in official applications and announcements (**Прошу́** предоста́вить мне о́тпуск 'I apply to be granted leave'). In spoken Russian, pronouns in general are often omitted, since present and future verb forms alone are sufficient to express person and number (i.e. **пишу́** is first-person singular, **пи́шешь** second-person singular and so on), while past tense forms indicate gender and number. Thus, **Вы писа́ли? Да, я писа́л** 'Did you write?', 'Yes, I wrote' could be rendered as **Вы писа́ли? Да, писа́л** or **Писа́ли? Писа́л**, depending on the degree of familiarity of the speech mode.

114   The pronoun мы

(1) **Мы** 'we' combines with first-person plural forms of the present or future tense of a verb (мы **говори́м** 'we speak'), with plural forms of the past tense (мы **говори́ли** 'we were speaking'), and with plural adjectives and pronouns: Мы **одни́** 'we are alone'.

(2) **Мы** can also be used to refer to the whole of a social or other group, or all society etc.: Я подчёркиваю сло́во «**мы**», и́бо име́ю в виду́ всё о́бщество в це́лом 'I stress the word "we" since I have in mind society as a whole'.

(3) **Мы** also expresses the royal 'we' (**мы**, всеросси́йский импера́тор 'we, Emperor of all the Russias'), the authorial 'we' (**Мы** пришли́ к сле́дующим вы́водам 'We (i.e. I) have come to the following conclusions') and the jocular paternal 'we' used by doctors (Ну, сего́дня **нам** лу́чше? 'Well, are we better today?'). **Мы** may also convey a nuance of mockery (**Мы** улыба́емся! 'So we're smiling!') or contempt (Вида́ли **мы** таки́х! 'We've seen your type before!').

115   The pronouns ты and вы

(1) Ты

(i) **Ты** 'you' (familiar) takes second-person singular forms of the present and future tenses of a verb (ты **говори́шь** 'you speak' etc.). Like я, **ты** is of common gender: Ты **оди́н** 'You are alone' (to a male), Ты **одна́** 'You are alone' (to a female).

(ii) **Ты** is used in addressing a relation, a friend, a colleague of similar age and status, a child, God, nature, oneself, an animal etc. While **ты** is generally acknowledged as the 'familiar' form, older people are likely to restrict its use to a circle of close friends and colleagues, whereas young people are usually quicker to address members of their own age group as **ты**.

(iii) **Ты** may also be used in conveying generalized information or instruction (cf. English 'you'), as in the following guidance for correct breathing in singing: **Ты** набира́ешь по́лную грудь во́здуха, а пото́м ма̀ло-пома́лу выпуска́ешь его́ изо рта 'You fill your lungs with air and then expel it little by little through your mouth'.

(2) Вы

(i) **Вы** is used to address any group of more than one person, or an adult who is not a relation, friend or colleague of similar age and status. When writing to someone, **Вы** is usually spelt with a capital letter.

(ii) **Вы** combines with plural forms of the verb, whether the pronoun represents an individual or a group: вы **чита́ете**, вы **чита́ли** 'you read, were reading'. When reference is to one person, the pronoun combines with the *singular* forms of long adjectives (Вы **тако́й до́брый** (to a male), Вы **така́я до́брая** (to a female) 'You are so kind', Я счита́ю вас **у́мным** (to a male)/**у́мной** (to a female) 'I consider you clever'), but with the *plural* forms of short adjectives and participles: Вы **пра́вы** 'You are right'.

(3) Ты ог вы

Usage may depend on social status, age difference, education and context of situation (e.g. teachers may address each other as **вы** in the presence of pupils or students but as **ты** in their absence). Any transition from **вы** to **ты** is normally initiated by the senior in age or rank. **Вы** is used as a mark of respect to adult strangers, and by academic staff to students and (desirably, though many school teachers prefer to use **ты**) to senior pupils. Subordinates have traditionally used the formal **вы** to their superiors, but have been addressed by them with the familiar **ты**. This practice is still widespread, despite condemnation in official circles of its perpetuation in, for example, the armed forces, the health service and industry.

116 The third-person pronouns (он, она́, оно́, они́)

(1) **Он, она́** may replace nouns denoting persons *or* things of masculine and feminine gender respectively:

Где **брат**?	Вот **он**	Where is my brother?	There he is
Где **стол**?	Вот **он**	Where is the table?	There it is
Где **моя́ сестра́**?	Вот **она́**	Where is my sister?	There she is

Где **кни́га**?	Вот **она́**	Where is the book?	There it is

(2) **Оно́** replaces neuter nouns:

Где **кре́сло**?	Вот **оно́**	Where is the armchair?	There it is

(3) **Они́** replaces plural nouns denoting persons or things:

Где **ма́льчики**?	Вот **они́**	Where are the boys?	There they are
Где **кни́ги**?	Вот **они́**	Where are the books?	There they are
Где **кре́сла**?	Вот **они́**	Where are the armchairs?	There they are

(4) **Они́** may be used when the plural noun it replaces has been mentioned: Что де́лают **маляры́**? **Они́** кра́сят дом 'What are the painters doing?' 'They are painting the house'. In impersonal constructions, however, the third-person plural of the verb is used *without* a pronoun: Здесь **стро́ят** общежи́тие 'They (identity unspecified) are building a hostel here' (or 'A hostel is being built here'). This is in marked contrast with English, in which the pronoun 'they' is used in both personal *and* impersonal constructions. Note also the phrases: Здесь **не ку́рят** 'No smoking', **говоря́т** 'they say, it is said' etc.

(5) Verbs of yearning (**скуча́ть** 'to miss', **тоскова́ть** 'to yearn' etc.) and the verbs **стреля́ть** 'to shoot' and **ударя́ть** 'to strike' take the preposition **по** + the **prepositional** case of first- and second-person pronouns (Скуча́ли по **вас** 'They missed you', Стреля́ли по **нас** 'They were firing at us') and *either* the dative *or* the prepositional of third-person pronouns (Скуча́ли по **нему́**/по **нём** 'He was missed'). Such verbs take по + the *dative* of nouns (e.g. скуча́ть по **му́жу** 'to miss one's husband').

(6) 'He and Sergei/she and Sergei' etc. may be rendered as **они́** с Серге́ем (also, in context, 'they and Sergei').

(7) The instrumental case of a third-person pronoun may be the equivalent of English 'one': Он стал вратарём, потому́ что реши́л **им** стать (Makarov) 'He became a goalkeeper because he had made up his mind to become **one**'.

117   The reflexive pronoun себя́

(1) The reflexive pronoun **себя́** declines as follows:

Nom.	—
Acc./Gen.	себ-**я**
Dat.	себ-**é**
Instr.	соб-**óй**/соб-**óю**
Prep.	о себ-**é**

(2) The reflexive pronoun refers back to the subject of the clause or, more exactly, to the subject or agent of the nearest verb or adjective (it therefore has no nominative case, since it cannot *itself* be a subject). The same form is used for all persons (Онá довóльна **собóй** 'She is pleased with herself', Мы довóльны **собóй** 'We are pleased with ourselves' etc.), there being no differentiation between singular and plural or between the genders.

(3) **Себя** expresses more varied relationships than **-ся, -сь** (see also **285** and **286**), e.g. the indirect object (Онá купи́ла **себé** кни́гу 'She bought herself a book') and government by preposition (Он смóтрит **на себя́** в зéркало 'He looks at himself in the mirror', Они́ разговáривают **мèжду собóй** 'They are talking among themselves').

(4) Считáть **себя́** гéнием means 'to consider oneself a genius', считáться гéнием 'to be considered a genius' (cf. лишáть **себя́** 'to deprive oneself' and лишáться 'to be deprived').

(5) Some verbs combine with **себя́** on a seemingly arbitrary basis: вести́ **себя́** 'to behave', представля́ть **собóй** 'to represent, be', чу́вствовать **себя́** 'to feel'.

(6) Ambiguity may arise when there are two verbs in a sentence: Мать велéла сы́ну **нали́ть** себé чáю (мать is the subject of the sentence, сын is the logical subject of нали́ть). The sentence should be taken to mean 'The mother told her son to pour **himself** some tea', but the following can be used to avoid confusion: Мать велéла, чтóбы сын нали́л себé чáю 'The mother told her son to pour **himself** some tea', cf. Мать велéла, чтòбы сын нали́л **ей** чáю 'The mother told her son to pour **her** some tea'.

(7) Russian is more consistent than English in the use of reflexive pronouns: Он разложи́л перед **собóй** кáрту 'He spread out the map in front of **him**', Онá закры́ла за **собóй** дверь 'She closed the door behind **her**', Возьми́те меня́ с **собóй** 'Take me with **you**'.

(8) The reflexive pronoun appears in a number of set phrases: так себé 'so-so', Он хорóш **собóй** 'He is good-looking', самó **собóй** разумéется 'it goes without saying'.

(9) A reflexive pronoun may combine for emphasis with the emphatic pronoun **сам**: — Я тебя не понимаю. — Я **сам себя** не понимаю! 'I don't understand you'. 'I don't understand myself!' (see **131** (1)).

118   The possessive pronouns мой, твой, наш, ваш

(1) The possessive pronoun **мой** declines as follows:

	Masculine	Feminine	Neuter	Plural
Nom.	мой	мо-**я́**	мо-**ё**	мо-**и́**
Acc.	мой/мо-**его́**	мо-**ю́**	мо-**ё**	мо-**и́**/мо-**и́х**
Gen.	мо-**его́**	мо-**е́й**	мо-**его́**	мо-**и́х**
Dat.	мо-**ему́**	мо-**е́й**	мо-**ему́**	мо-**и́м**
Instr.	мо-**и́м**	мо-**е́й**/-**е́ю**	мо-**и́м**	мо-**и́ми**
Prep.	о мо-**ём**	о мо-**е́й**	о мо-**ём**	о мо-**и́х**

Note

Твой 'your' (familiar) declines like **мой**.

(2) The possessive pronoun **наш** declines as follows:

	Masculine	Feminine	Neuter	Plural
Nom.	наш	на́ш-**а**	на́ш-**е**	на́ш-**и**
Acc.	наш/на́ш-**его**	на́ш-**у**	на́ш-**е**	на́ш-**и**/на́ш-**их**
Gen.	на́ш-**его**	на́ш-**ей**	на́ш-**его**	на́ш-**их**
Dat.	на́ш-**ему**	на́ш-**ей**	на́ш-**ему**	на́ш-**им**
Instr.	на́ш-**им**	на́ш-**ей**/-**ею**	на́ш-**им**	на́ш-**ими**
Prep.	о на́ш-**ем**	о на́ш-**ей**	о на́ш-**ем**	о на́ш-**их**

Note

(a) **Ваш** 'your' declines like **наш**.

(b) Like **мы** and **вы** (see **113** note (a)), **наш** and **ваш** can form compounds with other pronouns or nouns: **ва́ша с па́пой** маши́на 'yours and Dad's car', **наш с тобо́й** дом 'our house' (i.e. yours and mine).

(c) The colloquial phrase **наш брат** means 'people like us': Зна́ю, что нере́дко руга́ют **на́шего бра́та** за рва́чество (*Russia Today*) 'I know that our sort are often cursed for self-seeking'.

(d) Phrases of the type **на́ша** те́ма 'our theme' (i.e. 'the present topic') are used by authors and lecturers (cf. **114** (3)).

(e) The use of possessive instead of personal pronouns is characteristic of casual speech: Он сде́лал бо́льше **моего́** (= бо́льше, чем я) 'He did more than me'.

(f) **Ваш** is spelt with a capital letter in correspondence.

119   The possessive pronouns его́, её, их

Его́ 'his', её 'her', их 'their' are invariable:

его́ сестра́	his sister
её кни́ги	her books
их брат	their brother
Я зна́ю его́ сестру́	I know his sister
Я дово́лен её бра́том	I am pleased with her brother

Note

(a)   **н-** is never affixed to the third-person possessives: cf. письмо́ от **него́** (personal pronoun) 'a letter from him' and письмо́ от **его́** (possessive pronoun) бра́та 'a letter from his brother' (see **110** (2)).

(b)   **Его́** is pronounced [jɪ'vo]. See also **110** (1) note (b).

120   The reflexive possessive pronoun свой, своя́, своё, свои́

(1) The reflexive possessive pronoun **свой** declines like **мой** (see **118** (1)).

(2) Like **себя́**, **свой** refers back to noun and pronoun subjects of any gender and either number (see **117** (2): Я по́мню **свою́** шко́лу 'I remember my school', Ты по́мнишь **свою́** шко́лу 'You remember your school', Де́ти по́мнят **свою́** шко́лу 'The children remember their school'.

(3) In clauses which have a first- or second-person subject, **свой** can be used as an *alternative* to мой, твой, наш and ваш (Я говорю́ о **свое́й/мое́й** рабо́те 'I am talking about my work', Ты продаёшь **свой/твой** дом 'You are selling your house', Мы мо́ем **свою́/на́шу** маши́ну 'We are washing our car'), though **свой** is commoner.

(4) Where there is a third-person subject, however, care must be taken to distinguish between **свой** and the possessive pronouns **его́, её, их** (see **119**), when rendering 'his', 'her', 'their', in order to avoid ambiguity:

Он дово́лен **свои́м** ученико́м
He is pleased with **his** (own) pupil

Он не лю́бит Джо́на, но он дово́лен **его́** ученика́ми
He does not like John, but he is pleased with **his** (John's) pupils

Note that in English 'his' is used in both examples, and context is relied upon to differentiate meaning. Russian **её** 'her' and **их** 'their' are similarly distinguished from свой:

Орлóвы лю́бят **свои́х** детéй
The Orlovs love **their** children

Ивановы поги́бли в катастрóфе, и Орлóвы усынови́ли **их** детéй
The Ivanovs died in an accident and the Orlovs adopted their children

(5) It is important to remember to use the reflexive possessive pronoun even when it is distanced from the subject:

Он, прáвда, никомý не даёт **своегó** áдреса (Trifonov)
It is true that he does not give **his** address to anyone

Он был свидéтелем собы́тий **своегó** врéмени
He was a witness of the events of **his** time

(6) **Свой** cannot qualify the *subject* of a clause in this type of construction:

Он говори́т, что **егó** друг бóлен
He says that **his** friend (subject of new clause) is ill

Врач и **её** помóщник совещáются
The doctor and **her** assistant (joint subjects) are consulting

(7) In a sentence with two verbs, **свой** refers back to the subject of the nearer of the two, cf:

Редáктор попроси́л журнали́ста прочитáть **свою́** статью́
The editor asked the journalist to read his (the journalist's) article

and

Редáктор попроси́л журнали́ста прочитáть **егó** статью́
The editor asked the journalist to read his (the editor's) article

To avoid possible ambiguity, an alternative construction can be used:

Редáктор попроси́л журнали́ста, чтòбы он прочитáл егó статью́
The editor asked the journalist to read his (the editor's) article

Note
When ownership is obvious from the context, Russian usually dispenses with a possessive pronoun: **Я мóю** рýки 'I am washing **my** hands' (it is

clear whose hands are being washed – mine), Он потеря́л **програ́мму** 'He has lost **his** (or 'the') programme'.

Па́рень опуска́ет **ру́ки, го́лову,** закрыва́ет **глаза́** (Rasputin)
The lad lowers his hands, hangs his head, closes his eyes

(8) Свой appears in the *nominative* case in phrases that denote possession: У меня́ **своя́** маши́на 'I have my own car', У нас **свой** дом 'We have our own house' etc. Note: **Своя́** руба́шка бли́же к те́лу 'Charity begins at home', Он у нас **свой** челове́к 'He is one of us'.

121   Declension of the interrogative/relative pronouns

Кто 'who', **что** 'what', **како́й** 'what' (adjective), **кото́рый** 'which' and **чей** 'whose' function as both interrogative and relative pronouns. **Како́й** and **кото́рый** decline like hard-ending adjectives (see **145** and **146** (3) note (b)). **Кто, что** and **чей** decline as follows:

			Masculine	Feminine	Neuter	Plural
Nom.	кт-о	чт-о	чей	чь-я	чь-ё	чь-и
Acc.	к-ого́	чт-о	чей/чь-его́	чь-ю	чь-ё	чь-и/чь-их
Gen.	к-ого́	ч-его́	чь-его́	чь-ей	чь-его́	чь-их
Dat.	к-ому́	ч-ему́	чь-ему́	чь-ей	чь-ему́	чь-им
Instr.	к-ем	ч-ем	чь-им	чь-ей/-е́ю	чь-им	чь-и́ми
Prep.	о к-ом	о ч-ём	о чь-ём	о чь-ей	о чь-ём	о чь-их

122   Кто, что, како́й, кото́рый, чей as interrogative pronouns

(1) Кто

(i) **Кто** 'who' is used in both direct questions (**Кто** э́тот мужчи́на? 'Who is that man?', О **ком** вы говори́те? 'Who are you talking about?') and indirect questions (Он спроси́л, **кому́** вы даёте уро́ки 'He asked whom you give lessons to').

(ii) **Кто** takes a masculine predicate even when only females are involved: Кто **вы́шел** за́муж? 'Who (in a group of women) got married?' However, feminine agreement is possible if the subject contains a reference to a female exponent of an activity: Кто из

лы́жниц пришла́ пе́рвой? 'Which of the skiers (female) came in first?'.

(iii) Russian is consistent in using **кто** for people: **Кто** у вас роди́лся? Ма́льчик и́ли де́вочка? '**What** is it, a boy or a girl?', **Кем** ты хо́чешь быть? '**What** do you want to be?', cf.:

> А **кем** мы ста́нем тепе́рь: друзья́ми и́ли врага́ми? (Gagarin)
> And **what** will we become now, friends or enemies?

(iv) **Кто** may be amplified to **кто тако́й/така́я/таки́е?**: **Кто тако́й** э́тот па́рень? 'Who is this fellow?', **Кто така́я** э́та де́вушка? 'Who is that girl?', **Кто таки́е** э́ти молоды́е лю́ди? 'Who are these young people?', Кто вы **тако́й**? (to a male)/Кто вы **така́я**? (to a female) 'Who are you?'

(2) Что

Что 'what' is used to ask about the identity of a thing or an animal (**Что** э́то — волк и́ли соба́ка? 'What is that, a wolf or a dog?') or the nature of an action (**Что** он де́лает? 'What is he doing?'). **Что** may be expanded to **что тако́е?** (Что э́то **тако́е**? 'What is that?') or be extended by a genitive adjective (Что **но́вого**? 'What's new?', Что же тут **оби́дного**? 'What's so offensive about that?').

(3) Како́й

Како́й means 'What, what kind of?': **Како́й** у него́ го́лос? 'What kind of a voice does he have?', **Каку́ю** кни́гу вы чита́ете? 'What book are you reading?'. **Что за** may be used as a synonym of како́й: Что сего́дня **за** пого́да? (= Кака́я сего́дня пого́да?) 'What is the weather like today?'.

(4) Кото́рый

(i) **Кото́рый?** means 'which?' (in a sequence) and appears in the phrases **Кото́рый** час? 'What's the time?', В **кото́ром** часу́? 'At what time?' (now largely replaced in the speech of young people by Ско́лько вре́мени? and Во ско́лько?). **Кото́рый** can also mean 'umpteenth': **Кото́рый** раз спра́шиваю 'I am asking for the umpteenth time'.

(ii) However, **како́й** is now more commonly used in questions, the answers to which contain an ordinal numeral: **Како́й** ряд? 'Which row?' **Пя́тый** 'Five'.

(5) Чей

Чей means 'whose?': **Чей** э́то дом? 'Whose house is that?', **Чью** да́чу вы покупа́ете? 'Whose country cottage are you buying?'.

123   Кото́рый, како́й, чей, кто and что as relative pronouns

(1) Кото́рый

(i) **Кото́рый** 'who, which' is used with animate and inanimate noun antecedents (кто and что are normally used as relatives to *pronoun* antecedents; see (4) and (5) below).

(ii) **Кото́рый** agrees with its antecedent in gender and number, but its *case* depends on the grammar of the relative clause:

Я познако́мился с молоды́м **челове́ком, за кото́рого** она́ вы́шла за́муж
I made the acquaintance of the young man (whom) she married

Он вошёл в **ко́мнату, кото́рая** находи́лась ря́дом с ку́хней
He went into the room which was next to the kitchen

(iii) The genitive forms **кото́рого** (masculine and neuter), **кото́рой** (feminine), **кото́рых** (plural) mean 'whose', and *follow* the noun:

Вот **студе́нт**, рабо́ту **кото́рого** я проверя́ю
There is the student whose work I am correcting

Про́дали **маши́ну**, владе́льцы **кото́рой** обанкро́тились
They have sold the car whose owners have gone bankrupt

Нельзя́ не жале́ть **дете́й**, роди́тели **кото́рых** поги́бли во вре́мя блока́ды
You cannot but pity the children whose parents perished during the blockade

(2) Како́й

Unlike **кото́рый**, which relates to specific objects and persons, **како́й** relates to things and persons of a particular *type*, cf.:

Вокру́г ви́дишь переме́ны, **каки́е** возмо́жны то́лько здесь
All around you can see changes **of a kind which** are possible only here

and

> Вокру́г ви́дишь переме́ны, **кото́рые** возмо́жны то́лько здесь
> All around you can see changes **which** are possible only here

Compare

> **Тако́е** выраже́ние отча́яния, **како́е** быва́ет у люде́й то́лько перед сме́ртью (Simonov)
> The **kind of** expression of despair **that** people have only at death's door

(3) Чей

The use of **чей** as a relative is a mark of a bookish or poetic style: писа́тель, **чью** кни́гу ты изуча́ешь . . . 'the writer whose book you are studying. . .'. Normal usage is: писа́тель, кни́гу **кото́рого** ты изуча́ешь. . . .

(4) Кто

(i) **Кто** functions as relative pronoun to **тот** (**тот, кто** 'he, the one who'), **те** (**те, кто** 'those who'), **никто́** 'nobody' (**никто́, кто** 'no one who'), **все** 'everybody' (**все, кто** 'everyone who'), **пе́рвый** 'the first' (**пе́рвый, кто** пришёл 'the first to come'), **еди́нственный** 'only' (Он же **еди́нственный, кто** на нас постоя́нно жа́луется 'He is the only one who constantly complains about us').

(ii) **Кто** takes a masculine singular predicate: тот, кто **реши́л** зада́чу 'he who solved the problem'. ('She who' may be rendered as **та** (же́нщина), **кото́рая: Та, кото́рая** полне́е, оде́та с больши́м вку́сом (Zalygin) 'The one who is plumper is dressed with consummate taste'.)

(iii) When, however, there is a *plural* antecedent (**все** or **те**), **кто** may take *either* a singular *or* a plural verb: Все, кто **пришёл/пришли́** на собра́ние, голосова́ли за меня́ 'Everyone who came to the meeting voted for me', cf.:

> Среди́ тех, кто **оста́лся**, был Ива́н Ка́рлович, наш сосе́д (Rybakov)
> Among those who remained was Ivan Karlovich, our neighbour

and

> Те из нас, кто **чита́ли** стихотворе́ние, бы́ли в восто́рге
> Those of us who read the poem were delighted

(iv) **Тот, кто** may be abbreviated to **кто**, with **тот** transferring to the beginning of a separate clause: **Кто** э́то ви́дел, **тот** не забу́дет 'Anyone who has seen that will not forget it'.

(5) Что

(i) **Что** may function as relative pronoun to a full noun (sing. or pl.), e.g.:

> **Дом, что** сто́ит на углу́
> The house that stands on the corner

but **кото́рый** should be regarded as the norm (see (1) (i) above).

(ii) **Что** as a relative pronoun is used mainly with:

(a) **Всё** 'everything':

> Я скажу́ вам **всё, что** зна́ю   I'll tell you all I know

(b) Substantivized adjectives such as **гла́вное** 'the main thing', **пе́рвое** 'the first thing':

> **Пе́рвое, что** броса́ется в глаза́ — àвтовокза́л
> The first thing that strikes you is the bus station

(c) **То** 'that':

> **То, что** он сказа́л, удиви́ло меня́
> **What** (lit. 'that which') he said surprised me

> Случи́лось **то, чего́** ника́к не ожида́л Григо́рий (Sholokhov)
> **Something** happened **that** Grigory had in no way anticipated

> **В том, что** вы говори́те, есть до́ля пра́вды
> There's a measure of truth **in what** you say

> Я не согла́сен **с тем, что** он сказа́л
> I do not agree **with what** he said

Variants of **то, что** thus function as links between clauses:

> Учи́тельницу огорчи́ло **то, что** де́ти не хоте́ли её слу́шать
> The teacher was upset by **the fact that** the children did not want to listen to her

> Мы принима́ем **то, от чего́** вы отказа́лись
> We accept **what** you refused

The construction is particularly important when the verb in the main clause governs an oblique case or prepositional phrase:

Он горди́тся **тем, что** он ру́сский
He is proud **of being** Russian

Начало́сь **с того́, что** Ко́лька о́тнял у меня́ кни́жку (Soloukhin)
It all began **with** Kolka **taking away** my book

То, что may be abbreviated to **что** for special emphasis, **то** transferring to the beginning of a separate clause:

Что нам про́сто ка́жется, **то** на́шим пре́дкам по́том да му́кой доста́лось
What seems simple to us was achieved through the sweat and toil of our ancestors

Что also functions as relative pronoun to a whole clause:

Он не приходи́л на ве́чер, **что** меня́ удиви́ло
He did not come to the party, **which** surprised me (i.e. the fact that he did not come surprised me, *not* any particular noun)

124   Other functions of the interrogative/relative pronouns

(1) **Како́й** can also be used as an exclamation (**Како́й** позо́р! 'What a disgrace!') and, with negatives, can express quantity (**Каки́х** то́лько пода́рков ему́ не накупи́ли! 'And the **presents** they bought him!').

(2) **Кто** appears:

(i) In the phrase **не кто ино́й, как** 'none other than': Э́то был **не кто ино́й**, как мой брат 'It was none other than my brother'.

(ii) In concessive constructions: С **кем** ни говори́, все настро́ены легкомы́сленно 'Whoever you speak to is in a carefree mood'.

(iii) In the meaning 'some . . . others' (also rendered as одни́ . . . други́е): **Кто** за, **кто** про̀тив 'Some are for, others are against'.

(iv) In the reduplicated pronoun **кто-кто**: Кому́-кому́, а ему́-то грех бы́ло не реаги́ровать (Zalygin) 'For him of all people it was sinful not to react'.

(3) **Что** appears:

(i) In the phrase **не что ино́е, как** 'nothing but': Э́то **не что ино́е, как** вымога́тельство 'That is nothing but extortion'.

(ii) In concessive constructions: **Что** бы он ни де́лал, он не забыва́л свои́х друзе́й 'Whatever he did, he never forgot his friends'.

(iii) In quantitative contexts: **Чего́** там то́лько не́ было 'There was everything imaginable there'.

(iv) In the reduplicated pronoun **что-что́**: . . . Уж **что-что́**, а э́то никто́ у неё не отни́мет (Zalygin) 'That of all things no one will take away from her'.

125 Declension of the demonstrative pronouns э́тот, тот, тако́й, сей and э́кий

Тако́й declines like a hard-ending adjective (see **146** (3) note (b)). **Э́тот, тот** and **сей** decline as follows:

	Masculine	Feminine	Neuter	Plural
Nom.	э́тот	э́т-**а**	э́т-**о**	э́т-**и**
Acc.	э́тот/э́т-**ого**	э́т-**у**	э́т-**о**	э́т-**и**/э́т-**их**
Gen.	э́т-**ого**	э́т-**ой**	э́т-**ого**	э́т-**их**
Dat.	э́т-**ому**	э́т-**ой**	э́т-**ому**	э́т-**им**
Instr.	э́т-**им**	э́т-**ой**/**-ою**	э́т-**им**	э́т-**ими**
Prep.	об э́т-**ом**	об э́т-**ой**	об э́т-**ом**	об э́т-**их**

	Masculine	Feminine	Neuter	Plural
Nom.	тот	т-**а**	т-**о**	т-**е**
Acc.	тот/т-**ого́**	т-**у**	т-**о**	т-**е**/т-**ех**
Gen.	т-**ого́**	т-**ой**	т-**ого́**	т-**ех**
Dat.	т-**ому́**	т-**ой**	т-**ому́**	т-**ем**
Instr.	т-**ем**	т-**ой**/т-**о́ю**	т-**ем**	т-**е́ми**
Prep.	о т-**ом**	о т-**ой**	о т-**ом**	о т-**ех**

	Masculine	Feminine	Neuter	Plural
Nom.	сей	си-**я́**	си-**е́**	си-**и́**
Acc.	сей/с-**его́**	си-**ю́**	си-**е́**	си-**и́**/с-**их**
Gen.	с-**его́**	с-**ей**	с-**его́**	с-**их**
Dat.	с-**ему́**	с-**ей**	с-**ему́**	с-**им**
Instr.	с-**им**	с-**ей**/с-**е́ю**	с-**им**	с-**и́ми**
Prep.	о с-**ём**	о с-**ей**	о с-**ём**	о с-**их**

Note

(a) Except for usage in certain set phrases (see **129** (1)), **сей** is regarded as archaic and is used for purposes of irony.

(b) **Э́кий** declines as follows: m. nom. э́кий, acc. э́кий/э́коего, gen. э́коего, dat. э́коему, instr. э́ким, prep. об э́ком; f. nom. э́кая, acc. э́кую, gen. э́кой, dat. э́кой, instr. э́кой/-ою, prep. об э́кой; neut. э́кое, oblique cases as masculine; pl. nom. э́кие, acc. э́кие/ э́ких, gen. э́ких, dat. э́ким, instr. э́кими, prep. об э́ких. It is found mainly in conversational registers.

126   The demonstrative pronouns э́тот and тот

(1) Э́тот/тот

(i) **Э́тот** 'this' refers to something close to hand, **тот** 'that' to something further removed:

Э́то де́рево тако́е же большо́е, как и **то**
This tree is just as big as that one

(ii) **Э́то** is used in the meaning 'this, that is', 'these, those are': Э́то мой дом 'This is my house', Э́то мои́ де́ти 'Those are my children'. Verbs agree with the noun, *not* with э́то: Э́то **бы́ли** мои́ кни́ги 'Those were my books', Э́то **была́** его́ жена́ 'That was his wife'.

Note

Что вы хоти́те **э́тим** сказа́ть? 'What do you mean by **that**?'

(iii) It is necessary to distinguish between

Э́тот дом	This house
Э́та карти́на	This picture
Э́то окно́	This window
Э́ти кни́ги	These books

and

Э́то дом	This **is** a house
Э́то карти́на	This **is** a picture
Э́то окно́	This **is** a window
Э́то кни́ги	These **are** books

(2) Тот

(i) **Тот** is sometimes used where English might use a definite article, especially when the pronoun is part of the antecedent to a relative clause:

Он ча́сто говори́л в **той** холо́дной мане́ре, в како́й на́чал разгово́р с Серпи́линым (Simonov)
He often spoke in **the** cold manner with which he had begun his conversation with Serpilin

Я смотре́л в **ту** сто́рону, отку́да должна́ была́ появи́ться ло́дка
I was looking in **the** direction from which the boat was expected to appear

(ii) **Тот** can also mean, 'he, she, the latter':

О прие́зде бра́тьев Ли́за узна́ла от А́нки. **Та** прибежа́ла к тётке, как то́лько пришла́ телегра́мма (Abramov)
Liza learnt of her brothers' arrival from Anka. **She** (Anka) came running to her aunt as soon as the telegram arrived

Note
The use of **она́** instead of **та** in this example would imply that the first-named (Liza) had come running. **Тот** thus has an important role to play in avoiding ambiguity.

(iii) **Тот** is used as a pronoun antecedent to a relative pronoun:

Арка́дий пожа́л одни́м плечо́м, не **тем, на кото́ром** лежа́ла рука́ Иру́нчика (Zalygin)
Arkady shrugged one shoulder, not **the one on which** Irunchik's arm lay

(iv) **Не тот** means 'the wrong' (cf. непра́вильный 'incorrect'): Он взял **не ту** кни́гу 'He took the wrong book'.

(v) **Тот же** (or **тот же са́мый**) means 'the same':

Гости́ница оказа́лась **той же**, в кото́рой остана́вливались пре́жде (Yakhontov)
The hotel turned out to be **the (same) one** they had stayed in before

Note
(a) **Тот же** can also mean 'just the same as': Ведь не́нависть — **та же** любо́вь, то́лько с обра́тным зна́ком (Zalygin) 'After all hatred is **just the same as** love, but from the reverse side'.
(b) В одно́ и **то же** вре́мя 'at one and the same time'.

(vi) **То** combines with the conjunction **что**:

Она́ привы́кла **к тому́, что** мужчи́ны на неё загля́дываются (Rybakov)
She was used to men feasting their eyes on her

It also appears in many time phrases: в **то** время, как 'while', с **тех** пор 'since then', до **тех** пор 'until then', после **того** как 'after', до **того** как 'before' (see also **466**).

127   Constructions of the type пример тому

Пример, причина and some other abstract nouns combine with the dative of the pronoun **то** (and occasionally **это**):

Примером **тому** является выступление артиста
The artiste's performance is an example of this

Причиной **тому** является его упрямство
His obstinacy is the cause of this

Да и фильм даёт наглядное **тому** свидетельство
And in fact the film bears graphic witness to this

Примеров **этому** можно привести много (*Izvestiya*)
One can quote many examples of this

Note

(a)   These nouns normally combine with the *genitive* of a dependent *noun*: пример **мужества** 'an example of courage', причина **несчастного случая** 'the cause of the accident' (note also the use of the genitive *pronoun* where **причина** is defined by a prepositional phrase: Причина **этого** в демографическом взрыве 'The cause of this is the population explosion').

(b)   The dative reflexive pronoun appears in the expression знать **себе** цену 'to know one's worth'.

128   The demonstrative pronoun такой

(1)   **Такой** 'such' combines with long adjectives: Погода **такая** хорошая (or **так** хороша) 'The weather is so fine'.

(2)   It can have a generalizing meaning: **Таких** марок, **какие** он собирает, очень мало 'There are very few stamps **of the kind that** he collects' (cf. **123** (2) 'какой').

Note

В **таком** случае 'in **that** case', Задам **такой** вопрос 'I shall ask **the following** question', при **таких** обстоятельствах 'in **the** circumstances'.

(3) **Такой же** means 'the same, the same kind': Ты **такой же,** как и все молодые люди твоего возраста 'You're just like all young people of your age'.

Note

Же is absent in the negative: Она не **такая, как** была в детстве 'She's not **the same as** she was in her childhood'.

129   The pronouns сей and экий

(1) **Сей** appears mainly in set phrases: по **сей** день 'to this very day', ни с того ни с **сего** 'for no particular reason', **сию** минуту 'this instant' (Иди сюда **сию** минуту! 'Come here this instant!'), до **сих** пор 'hitherto' etc.

> На **сей** раз в турнире не участвовал наш сильнейший теннисист (*Sputnik*)
> This time round our best tennis player did not take part in the championships

(2) **Экий** 'what a' is a very colloquial form: Экий шалун 'What a rogue' (cf. also этакий: этакая неудача 'such a disaster').

130   Declension of the determinative pronouns сам, самый, весь, всякий, каждый, всяческий

Каждый and **самый** are declined like hard-ending adjectives, **всякий** and **всяческий** like **русский** (see **146** (3)). **Сам** and **весь** decline as follows:

	Masculine	Feminine	Neuter	Plural
Nom.	сам	сам-а	сам-о	сам-и
Acc.	сам/сам-ого	сам-у/сам-оё	сам-о	сам-и/сам-их
Gen.	сам-ого	сам-ой	сам-ого	сам-их
Dat.	сам-ому	сам-ой	сам-ому	сам-им
Instr.	сам-им	сам-ой/-ою	сам-им	сам-ими
Prep.	о сам-ом	о сам-ой	о сам-ом	о сам-их

Note

(a) The accusative feminine **самоё** is the traditional literary form, but **саму́** is now found in all styles. **Самоё,** though obsolescent and 'bookish', is still common with the reflexive pronoun **себя**: уничтожа́ть **самоё себя** 'to destroy oneself'.

(b) Unlike **сам,** the oblique cases of which take *end stress* (**самого́** etc.), **са́мый** is *stem stressed* throughout declension (**са́мого** etc.)

	Masculine	Feminine	Neuter	Plural
Nom.	весь	вс-я	вс-ё	вс-е
Acc.	весь/вс-его́	вс-ю	вс-ё	вс-е/вс-ех
Gen.	вс-его́	вс-ей	вс-его́	вс-ех
Dat.	вс-ему́	вс-ей	вс-ему́	вс-ем
Instr.	вс-ем	вс-ей/-е́ю	вс-ем	вс-е́ми
Prep.	обо вс-ём	обо вс-ей	обо вс-ём	обо вс-ех

131 Сам and са́мый

(1) Сам

(i) **Сам** is an emphatic pronoun: Я **сам** э́то сде́лаю 'I shall do it myself', Она́ **сама́** вста́ла 'She got up by herself'.

(ii) **Сам** may precede or follow a noun: Спроси́те учи́теля **самого́/самого́** учи́теля 'Ask the teacher himself'. Note gender distinction in Я пе́редал письмо́ тебе́ **самому́** 'I passed the letter on to you personally' (to a male), Я пе́редал письмо́ тебе́ **самой** 'I passed the letter on to you personally' (to a female).

(iii) **Сам** can also add emphasis to the reflexive pronoun **себя**: Вы гу́бите **самого́/саму́/сами́х** себя 'You are ruining yourself/yourselves'. It can also qualify *inanimate* nouns:

> **Сам** зако́н заставля́ет алиме́нтщиков идти́ на обма́н (*Nedelya*)
> The law **itself** compels alimony payers to resort to deception

Note

Сам agrees with other pronouns which stand in apposition to it: **Ей** надое́ло **самой** носи́ть бельё в пра́чечную 'She is sick of taking the washing to the laundry **herself.**'

(2) Са́мый

(i) **Са́мый** indicates precise location: Он подошёл к **са́мому** обры́ву 'He went right up to the precipice', в **са́мом** це́нтре го́рода 'in the very centre of the city'. Note also Поезд идёт до **самой** Москвы 'The train goes all the way to Moscow', с **самого** начала 'from the very beginning' (for **самый** in superlative meaning, see also **185**).

(ii) **Тот самый** means 'the very': Он купил **ту самую** книгу, которую вы рекомендовали 'He bought **the very** book you recommended'. **Тот же самый** means 'the same': У нас **те же** (**самые**) интересы 'We have **the same** interests'.

132 Весь, целый, всякий, каждый, любой, всяческий

(1) Весь/целый

Весь means 'all, the whole' etc.: **весь** мир 'the whole world', **Мы** ездили по **всей** стране 'We travelled all over the country', **все** рабочие 'all (the) workers'. **Целый** means 'a whole, whole', cf. Он съел **целое** яблоко 'He ate **a whole** apple' and Он съел **всё** яблоко 'He ate **the whole** apple', Голодали **целые** семьи '**Whole** families starved' and **Все** семьи голодали '**All the** families starved'. **Всё** also means 'everything' (**всё, что** я знаю 'everything I know'), while **все** can mean 'everyone', and takes a *plural* verb or adjective (Все **голосуют** 'Everyone votes'). Note the phrases **все** они, **все** мы etc. 'all of them, all of us'.

(2) Всякий/каждый/любой/всяческий

(i) **Всякий** means 'all kinds of': Он торгует **всякими** товарами 'He trades in all kinds of goods', **Всякое** (adjectival noun) бывает 'All kinds of things happen'. In combination with the preposition **без**, it may be rendered as 'any': без **всякого** сомнения 'without any doubt', без **всякого** труда 'without any trouble'. Note also во **всяком** случае 'in any case, at any rate' (cf. the precautionary на **всякий** случай 'just in case', 'to be on the safe side').

(ii) By comparison with **каждый**, **всякий** expresses *totality* (**всякий** раз 'each and every time', **Всякому** ребёнку нужна ласка 'Every child needs affection'), while **каждый** emphasizes *each one individually* (**каждый** раз 'every time', **Каждый** из учеников получил по книге 'Each of the pupils received a book'). **Каждый** is also used with numerals and with plural-only nouns: **каждые** два дня 'every two days', **каждые** сутки 'every twenty-four hours', **каждые** четверть часа 'every quarter of an hour'.

(iii) **Любо́й** has a strong nuance of *selectivity*: Запиши́ **любо́е** число́ ме́ньше 50 'Write down **any** number less than 50'. Купи́те газе́ту в **любо́м** кио́ске 'Buy the newspaper at any (but not every) kiosk'.

(iv) **Вся́ческий** is a synonym of **вся́кий** in the meaning 'all kinds of'.

133   The negative pronouns никто́, ничто́, никако́й, ниче́й. The negative particle не

(1) **Никто́** 'no one', **ничто́** 'nothing', **никако́й** 'none (whatsoever)', **ниче́й** 'nobody's' decline, respectively, like **кто, что, како́й** and **чей** (see **121**).

(2) The negative particle **не** appears between a negative pronoun and the predicate: Никто́ **не** рабо́тает 'No one works'.

134   Никто́

(1) **Никто́** means 'no one, nobody, not anybody':

Никто́ не пришёл	No one has come
Он **никого́** не лю́бит	He doesn't like anybody
Она́ **никому́** не ве́рит	She doesn't believe anyone
Мы **нике́м** не дово́льны	We are not pleased with anyone

Note

The presence of **нет** or **нельзя́** renders **не** superfluous: Никого́ **нет** 'No one's here', Никому́ **нельзя́** входи́ть 'No one may enter'.

(2) **Никто́** takes a masculine predicate even when reference is exclusively to females (cf. **122** (1) (ii)), unless a feminine noun appears as part of the subject: Никто́ из учени́ц, да́же **Зо́я,** не нашла́сь что сказа́ть 'None of the pupils, **not even Zoya,** could think of anything to say'.

(3) While English reverts to positive after the first negative, e.g. 'No one **ever** says **anything** to **anyone'**, Russian can accumulate negatives: **Никто́ никогда́ ничего́ не** говори́т **никому́.**

(4) In prepositional constructions the prepositions appear between **ни** and the oblique form of **кто:**

Она́ **ни с кем** не игра́ет
She doesn't play with anyone

Он **ни на ком** не собира́ется жени́ться
He doesn't mean to marry anyone

В до́ме **ни у кого́ ни от кого́** нет секре́тов (Rybakov)
No one in the house has any secrets from anyone

(5) 'Hardly anyone' is rendered as **почти́ никто́.**

135 Ничто́

(1) **Ничто́** can act as a subject to adjectives (**Ничто́** не ве́чно 'Nothing is eternal') and to *transitive* verbs (**Ничто́** не интересу́ет его́ 'Nothing interests him'). With intransitive verbs, however, **ничего́** is preferred: С ва́ми **ничего́** не случи́тся 'Nothing will happen to you'.

(2) The same rules of grammatical government and 'accumulation of negatives' apply to **ничто́** as to **никто́** (see **134**):

Он **ничего́ не** де́лает
He does nothing

Я **ниче́м не** дово́лен
I am not satisfied with anything

Никто́ никогда́ ничему́ не ве́рит
No one ever believes anything

Prepositions appear between **ни** and the relevant form of **что:**

Никогда́ и **ни о чём** она́ Никола́я Демья́новича не проси́ла (Trifonov)
She had never asked Nikolay Demyanovich for anything

(3) **Не** is omitted in certain set phrases: уйти́ **ни с чем** 'to come away empty-handed', поги́бнуть **ни за что** 'to die for nothing', Но э́то бы́ло **ни к чему́** сейча́с (Zalygin) 'But this was irrelevant at the moment'.

(4) 'Hardly anything' is rendered as **почти́ ничего́/почти́ ничто́.**

Note the idioms: **Ничего́!** 'Never mind!', Муж у неё **ничего́** 'Her husband is not a bad chap', **ни за что** на све́те 'not for anything in the world', **Ничего́ не** поде́лаешь 'It can't be helped'.

136   Никако́й and ниче́й

(1) **Никако́й** 'none' is used mainly for emphasis: Нет **никако́й** наде́жды 'There is no hope at all', **Никаки́е** угро́зы не мо́гут сломи́ть наш дух 'No threats can break our spirit', Мы **ни перед каки́ми** тру́дностями не остано́вимся 'We shall not baulk at any difficulties'.

(2) **Ниче́й** means 'nobody's':

И де́душка то́же понима́л, что **ничьему́** реше́нию, кро̀ме со́бственного, Ио́сиф не подчини́тся (Rybakov)
And grandfather also realized that Joseph would bow to no one's decision but his own

Вы не де́йствуете **ни в чьих** интере́сах
You are acting in nobody's interest

Note
(a)   Prepositions appear between **ни** and the relevant form of **какой** or **чей.**
(b)   The particle **не** is omitted when **ниче́й** is used predicatively: Э́тот дом ниче́й 'This house isn't anybody's'.

137   The 'potential' negative pronouns не́кого, не́чего

(1) The 'potential' negative, both in English and in Russian, involves a negative + infinitive construction: Не́чего **де́лать** 'There is nothing to do' (cf. Мы **ничего́** не де́лаем 'We are not doing anything').

(2) Only oblique forms of **кто** and **что** appear in the construction (**не́кого, не́кому, не́кем, не́ [о] ком; не́чего, не́чему, не́чем, не́ [о] чем**). (**Не́кто** and **не́что** mean, respectively, 'someone' and 'something'; see **140.**)

The case of the pronoun is determined by the infinitive: thus **писа́ть** (+ instr. case) 'to write with' (**Не́чем** писа́ть 'There is nothing to write with'); **спроси́ть** (+ acc. case) 'to ask' (**Не́кого** спроси́ть 'There is no one to ask').

(3) The construction comprises the following components:

не́ (always stressed) + relevant case of pronoun + infinitive
Не́чем писа́ть   There is nothing to write **with**

Не́кому писа́ть   There is no one to write **to**

(4) There are two variants of the construction:

(i) The impersonal:

Не́чего де́лать   There is nothing to do
Не́кого посла́ть   There is no one to send

(ii) The personal:

Мне не́чего де́лать   I have nothing to do (the logical
                                       subject of an infinitive appears
                                       in the dative, cf. **93** (1))

Не́чего **мне** боя́ться, за ава́рию я не отве́тчик (Tendryakov)
I have nothing to fear, I am not responsible for the accident

Ленингра́д! Тума́н и сы́рость! **Лю́дям** не́чем дыша́ть (Rybakov)
Leningrad! Fog and damp! People have nothing to breathe

(5) In prepositional constructions the preposition appears between **не́**
and the pronoun:

Ему́ **не́ к кому** обрати́ться за по́мощью
He has no one to turn to for aid

Ей **не́ в чем** признава́ться (Rybakov)
She has nothing to confess to

(6) The construction may also be used in the past and future: Мне
не́чем **бы́ло** писа́ть 'I had nothing to write with', Мне не́чем **бу́дет**
писа́ть 'I won't have anything to write with':

Кома́нде **не́ с кем** бы́ло игра́ть (Vanshenkin)
The team had nobody to play against

(7) The *positive* equivalent of the construction involves present **есть**,
past **бы́ло**, future **бу́дет**: **Есть** чем горди́ться 'There is something to
be proud of' (cf. **Не́чем** горди́ться 'There is nothing to be proud of'):

Ребя́т оста́вить **бы́ло** с кем — как раз в э́то вре́мя прибежа́ла
А́нка но́вое пла́тье пока́зывать (Abramov)
There **was** someone to leave the children with — Anka came
running up at that very moment to show her new dress

Note
Idiomatic usage in **Не́чего** (**не́зачем**) обижа́ться 'There's no point in
taking offence', **не́чего** и говори́ть 'needless to say', от **не́чего**

де́лать 'for want of something to do', **Не́ за что** 'Don't mention it'.

(8) In all the above examples, the case of the pronoun is determined by the infinitive: **Кого́** посла́ть? **Не́кого** посла́ть 'Whom to send? There is no one to send'.

However, in phrases of the type 'There is no one to drive the car, look after the children', 'no one' is the logical *subject* of the verb and therefore appears in the dative (see (4) (ii) above):

Не́кому о нём забо́титься (Rybakov)
There is no one to care for him

Поря́док навести́ **не́кому** (Rybakov)
There is no one to establish order

До́ма **не́кому** объясни́ть ма́льчику уро́ки
There is no one at home to explain the homework to the boy

138   The indefinite pronouns кто́-то, кто́-нибудь, кто́-либо; что́-то, что́-нибудь, что́-либо; како́й-то, како́й-нибудь, како́й-либо; че́й-то, че́й-нибудь, че́й-либо

The particles **-то, -нибудь** and **-либо** can be attached to **кто, что, како́й, чей** to form indefinite pronouns (for declension, see **121**; note that they can also be attached to **где, как, куда́, когда́, почему́,** see **395**).

(1) -то

(i) **Кто́-то.**

(a) **Кто́-то** 'someone' denotes one particular person whose identity, however, is unknown to or has been forgotten by the speaker. Since reference is to a definite event, **кто́-то** tends to be confined almost exclusively to the past or present tense (for use with the future, however, see (iv) below): **Кто́-то** стучи́т в дверь 'Someone is knocking on the door' (i.e. a definite person, but the speaker does not know who it is), **Кто́-то** позвони́л из шко́лы 'Someone rang from the school' (again, a definite person, but identity unknown (or possibly forgotten by the person who took the call)), Она́ помога́ла **кому́-то** перейти́ доро́гу 'She was helping someone to cross the road' etc.

(b) **Кто́-то** can also be extended by an adjective: кто́-то **высо́кий** 'someone tall'.

(c) **Кто́-то** takes a masculine predicate even when reference is to a female: Кто́-то звони́л. **Э́то была́ кака́я-то де́вушка** 'Someone rang. It was some girl or other'.

(ii) **Что́-то.**

(a) **Что́-то** 'something' likewise denotes a definite object or thing, details of which are unknown to the speaker: Он **что́-то** сказа́л, но я не расслы́шал, что и́менно 'He said something, but I did not catch exactly what it was', Она́ **что́-то** жуёт 'She is chewing something' (but the speaker does not know what it is), Он **че́м-то** недово́лен 'He is displeased about something', cf.:

> На́дю о **чём-то** спроси́л Михаи́л, она́ **что́-то** отве́тила — всё шёпотом (Rasputin)
> Mikhail asked Nadya about **something,** she gave **some answer or other** — all in a whisper

(b) **Что́-то** can also be extended by a neuter adjective: Он бормота́л что́-то **непоня́тное** 'He was mumbling something incomprehensible'. Note also Э́то сто́ит миллио́н **с че́м-то** 'It costs something over a million roubles'.

(iii) **Како́й-то** and **чей-то.**

(a) **Како́й-то** and **чей-то** are used in similar fashion to кто́-то and что́-то: Он изуча́ет **како́й-то** язы́к 'He is studying some (definite but unspecified) language or other', Она́ проверя́ла **чью́-то** тетра́дь 'She was correcting someone's exercise book'.

(b) **Како́й-то** may sometimes render English 'a': Вас спра́шивала **кака́я-то** де́вушка 'A girl (some girl or other) was asking for you'.

(iv) Forms with -**то** may be used in the future, but only if the identity of the person or thing referred to is already known: Я подарю́ тебе́ **что́-то** ко дню рожде́ния 'I shall give you something for your birthday' (meaning that I have already decided **what** to give. If I still have to make the choice, **что́-нибудь** must be used).

(2) -нибудь

(i) Unlike forms in -**то,** forms in -**нибудь** do not imply a particular person or thing, but someone or something indefinite, or one of an unspecified number, still to be decided or selected:

Я счастли́вее здесь, чем **в како́м-нибудь друго́м ме́сте**
I am happier here than **anywhere else**

The hypothetical nature of forms in **-нибудь** accounts for their usage in **questions,** in the **future,** after **imperatives** and in **conditional** and **subjunctive** constructions:

(a) Questions:

— Ты **в кого́-нибудь** влюби́лся? (Nikolaev)
'Have you fallen in love with **someone**?'

— Ко́ля! **Что́-нибудь** случи́лось? (Yakhontov)
'Kolya! Has **anything** (or **something**) happened?'

(b) Future:

Он приду́мает **како́е-нибудь** неотло́жное де́ло (Koluntsev)
He is bound to think up **some** urgent business **or other**

(c) Imperative:

— Расскажи́те ещё **о чём-нибудь,** — попроси́ла она ободря́юще.
— О чём же?
— О чём хоти́те (Nosov)
'Tell me about **something** else', she asked encouragingly.
'About what, then?'
'About anything you like'

(d) Conditional and subjunctive.

Conditional:

Ра́зве **кто́-нибудь** в э́том слу́чае поступи́л бы ина́че? (Kuleshov)
Do you really think **anyone** would have behaved differently in the circumstances?

Subjunctive:

Он хо́чет, что̀бы **кто́-нибудь** ему́ помо́г
He wants **someone** to help him

(ii) **-нибудь** is also used, irrespective of tense, when reference is to different people or things on different occasions. Thus, Я ча́сто приглаша́ю **кого́-нибудь** сде́лать докла́д, 'I often invite **someone** to give a talk' (different speakers on different occasions), Я всегда́ дарю́ ей **что́-нибудь** ко дню рожде́ния 'I always give her **something** for her birthday' (a different present on each birthday), cf.:

У нас в отде́ле всегда́ **кто́-нибудь** висе́л на телефо́не (Avdeenko)

In our department **someone** (i.e. different people on different occasions) was always on the phone

Чу́дик облада́л одно́й осо́бенностью: с ним постоя́нно **что́-нибудь** случа́лось (Shukshin)
Chudik had a peculiarity: **something** was always happening to him

— Дядь, проведи́те на стадио́н, — проси́л я **како́го-нибудь** до́брого мужчи́ну . . . (Makarov)
'Mister, take me into the stadium with you', I would ask **some** kind man **or other**. . .

Когда́ на́до бы́ло перенести́ из скла́да **что́-нибудь** тяжёлое, то помога́л Кузьма́ (Rasputin)
Whenever **something** heavy had to be moved from the warehouse, Kuzma would help

(iii) **Како́й-нибудь** can also denote:

(a) Approximation:

За **каки́х-нибудь** 70–80 лет на гра́ни исчезнове́ния оказа́лось 600 ви́дов млекопита́ющих (*Selskaya zhizn*)
Over a period of **some** 70–80 years 600 species of mammals have found themselves on the verge of extinction

(b) Inferior quality:

Дам тебе́ не **како́й-нибудь** уче́бник, а хоро́ший
I won't give you just **any old** textbook, but a good one

(3) -либо

Forms in **-либо** are similar in meaning to those in **-нибудь,** but imply an even greater degree of indefiniteness ('anyone, anything you care to name' etc.), functioning sometimes as a 'bookish' alternative to forms in **-нибудь**:

— Коне́чно, ты прав, — сказа́ла она́. — Меня́ть **что́-либо** по́здно (Zalygin)
'You're right, of course', she said, 'It's too late to change **anything whatsoever**'

И происхо́дит э́то . . . без **како́й-либо** волоки́ты (*Nedelya*)
And this happens . . . without **any** red tape **at all**

Ра́зве любо́вь к свое́й кома́нде оскорбля́ет **чьё-либо** досто́инство (Makarov)
Does love for one's team really offend **anyone's** dignity

See also **395** (3).

139   The indefinite pronouns кòе-ктó, кòе-чтó, кòе-какóй

(1) **Кòе-ктó, кòе-чтó** and **кòе-какóй** decline like **кто, что** and **какóй** respectively (see **121** and **146** (3) note (b)). Note that кòе- does *not* decline. Though both **кòе-ктó** and **кòе-чтó** take singular predicates, they have plural meaning (**кòе-ктó** 'one or two people', **кòе-чтó** 'a thing or two'):

Кòе-ктó на Зáпаде задáлся цéлью зáново «переписáть» истóрию вторóй мировóй войны́ (*Russia Today*)
One or two people in the West have set themselves the task of 'rewriting' the history of the Second World War

Нáдо **кòе к комý** забежáть
I need to pop in to see **a couple of people**

Кòе на чтó смотрéли сквòзь пáльцы (Rybakov)
Some things they turned a blind eye to

(2) As the examples show, prepositions appear between **кòе** and the oblique case form. In constructions with **кòе-какóй**, however, prepositions may precede or follow **кòе**:

Он обратúлся ко мне **кòе с какúми** (or **с кòе-какúми**) предложéниями
He approached me with **a number of** proposals

140   Нéкто, нéчто

Нéкто 'someone, a certain' appears only in the nominative (**нéкто** Иванóв 'one Ivanov') and **нéчто** 'something' only in the nominative/accusative. The pronouns are usually qualified, e.g. **нéкто** в бéлых перчáтках 'someone in white gloves', **нéчто** подóбное 'something similar'.

141   Нéкоторый

Нéкоторый declines like a hard adjective. It appears in a number of set phrases (в/до **нéкоторой** стéпени 'to a certain extent', **нéкоторое** врéмя 'a certain time', с **нéкоторого** врéмени 'for some time now'), but usually takes plural form (**нéкоторые** 'some, certain'). By comparison with **не́сколько** it is selective rather than merely quantitative:

У неё в гру́ппе **не́сколько** иностра́нных студе́нтов; **не́которые** из них блестя́щие языкове́ды
There are **a few** foreign students in her group; **some** of them are brilliant linguists

142   Не́кий

(1) The indefinite pronoun **не́кий** declines as follows:

	Masculine	Feminine	Neuter	Plural
Nom.	не́к-**ий**	не́к-**ая**	не́к-**ое**	не́к-**ие**
Acc.	не́к-**ий**/не́к-**оего**	не́к-**ую**	не́к-**ое**	не́к-**ие**/не́к-**оих** or не́к-**их**
Gen.	не́к-**оего**	не́к-**оей**/не́к-**ой**	не́к-**оего**	не́к-**оих**/не́к-**их**
Dat.	не́к-**оему**	не́к-**оей**/не́к-**ой**	не́к-**оему**	не́к-**оим**/не́к-**им**
Instr.	не́к-**оим**/не́к-**им**	не́к-**оей**/не́к-**ой**	не́к-**оим**/не́к-**им**	не́к-**оими**/не́к-**ими**
Prep.	о не́к-**оем**	о не́к-**оей**	о не́к-**оем**	о не́к-**оих**/не́к-**их**

(2) The pronoun's main function is to qualify surnames: **не́кий** Бра́гин 'a certain Bragin'.

(3) The contracted forms **не́ким**, **не́кой**, **не́ких**, **не́кими** are now preferred by many users of the language: У **не́кой** Ивано́вой нет па́спорта 'A certain Ivanova has no passport'. However, the longer forms are still found:

Дом принадлежа́л **не́коему** Кислы́х (Granin)
The house belonged to a certain Kislykh

ссыла́ясь на **не́коего** представи́теля в ОО́Н (*Pravda*)
with reference to a certain representative at the UNO

143   Other parts of speech which can also function as pronouns

Some other parts of speech can also function as pronouns. They include:

(1) **Да́нный** 'present': в **да́нный** моме́нт 'at the present moment'.

(2) **Оди́н:**

(i) 'A (certain)': К вам заходи́л **оди́н** студе́нт 'A student called to see you'.

(ii) 'The same': Они́ учи́лись в **одно́й** шко́ле 'They went to the same school'.

(3) The reciprocal pronoun **друг дру́га** 'each other', the first part of which is invariable, while the second part is governed by the verb or adjective. Only singular forms are involved, never plural:

Они́ лю́бят **дру̀г дру́га** (Uvarova)
They love each other

Они́ сигна́лили **дру̀г дру́гу** фонаря́ми (Aytmatov)
They were signalling to each other with lanterns

Prepositions appear centrally, between **дру̀г** and the declined form:

Они́ се́ли на свои́ крова́ти **дру̀г про̀тив дру́га** (Yakhontov)
They sat down opposite each other on their beds.

This does not apply, however, to some secondary prepositions: **вблизѝ** дру̀г дру́га 'near each other', **благодаря́** дру̀г дру́гу 'thanks to each other', **вопреки́** дру̀г дру́гу 'contrary to each other', **навстре́чу** дру̀г дру́гу 'to meet each other'.

Дру̀г дру́га also functions as a possessive:

Зна́ли о сне́жном челове́ке по расска́зам **дру̀г дру́га** (Povolyaev)
They knew of the yeti from each other's stories.

The Adjective

144 Introduction

(1) Adjectives may be attributive, either preceding the noun (e.g. 'The **black** cat purred') or following it and separated from it by a comma ('A cat, **wet** with the rain, sat on the step'). Adjectives may also be predicative, following the noun and linked to it by a verb: 'The cat **is** **wet**'.

(2) Adjectives also have comparative forms ('My car is **newer** than yours') and superlative forms ('His house is the **oldest** in the street').

(3) Most adjectives in Russian have *two* forms, a long (attributive) form (e.g. **краси́вый, краси́вая, краси́вое, краси́вые** 'beautiful') and a short (predicative) form (e.g. **краси́в, краси́ва, краси́во, краси́вы** 'am, is, are beautiful'). This is also true of comparatives.

Note
Subsequently, 'is, are' are used to designate the short form.

The Long Form of the Adjective

145 The long adjective: hard endings

(1) Most long adjectives in Russian have **hard** endings, that is, the first vowel of the ending is **a**, **o** or **ы**, e.g.

Masculine	Feminine	Neuter	Plural
нóв-**ый**	нóв-**ая**	нóв-**ое**	нóв-**ые** 'new'

(2) Hard-ending adjectives decline as follows:

	Masculine	Feminine	Neuter	Plural
Nom.	нóв-**ый**	нóв-**ая**	нóв-**ое**	нóв-**ые**
Acc.	нóв-**ый**/нóв-**ого**	нóв-**ую**	нóв-**ое**	нóв-**ые**/нóв-**ых**
Gen.	нóв-**ого**	нóв-**ой**	нóв-**ого**	нóв-**ых**
Dat.	нóв-**ому**	нóв-**ой**	нóв-**ому**	нóв-**ым**
Instr.	нóв-**ым**	нóв-**ой**/нóв-**ою**	нóв-**ым**	нóв-**ыми**
Prep.	о нóв-**ом**	о нóв-**ой**	о нóв-**ом**	о нóв-**ых**

Note

(a)   The instrumental feminine form in -**ою** survives mainly in poetry.

(b)   End-stressed adjectives (e.g. **молодóй**) decline like **нóвый** except in the masculine nominative singular and inanimate accusative singular, which have the ending -**óй**.

(c)   -**го** in adjectival endings is pronounced [və] ([vo] under stress).

146   'Mixed' declension

(1) The 'mixed' declension involves adjectives whose final consonant is a velar consonant (**г**, **к** or **х**), a palatal sibilant (**ж**, **ч**, **ш** or **щ**) or **ц**.

(2) Endings are determined by the spelling rules (see **16** (1) and (2)):

(i) **и** replaces **ы** after **г**, **к**, **х**, **ж**, **ч**, **ш** and **щ**;

(ii) unstressed **o** is replaced by **e** after **ж**, **ч**, **ш**, **щ** and **ц**.

(3) Declension of **рýсский** 'Russian':

	Masculine	Feminine	Neuter	Plural
Nom.	рýсск-**ий**	рýсск-**ая**	рýсск-**ое**	рýсск-**ие**
Acc.	рýсск-**ий**/рýсск-**ого**	рýсск-**ую**	рýсск-**ое**	рýсск-**ие**/рýсск-**их**
Gen.	рýсск-**ого**	рýсск-**ой**	рýсск-**ого**	рýсск-**их**
Dat.	рýсск-**ому**	рýсск-**ой**	рýсск-**ому**	рýсск-**им**
Instr.	рýсск-**им**	рýсск-**ой**/-**ою**	рýсск-**им**	рýсск-**ими**
Prep.	о рýсск-**ом**	о рýсск-**ой**	о рýсск-**ом**	о рýсск-**их**

Note

(a)   Adjectives in -**гий** and -**хий** (e.g. **дóлгий** 'long', **тúхий** 'quiet') decline like **рýсский**.

(b) End-stressed adjectives have **-ой** in the masculine nominative singular and inanimate accusative singular, e.g. **другой** 'other', **какой** 'which', **сухой** 'dry'.

(4) Declension of **хороший** 'good':

	Masculine	Feminine	Neuter	Plural
Nom.	хорóш-ий	хорóш-ая	хорóш-ее	хорóш-ие
Acc.	хорóш-ий/-его	хорóш-ую	хорóш-ее	хорóш-ие/хорóш-их
Gen.	хорóш-его	хорóш-ей	хорóш-его	хорóш-их
Dat.	хорóш-ему	хорóш-ей	хорóш-ему	хорóш-им
Instr.	хорóш-им	хорóш-ей/-ею	хорóш-им	хорóш-ими
Prep.	о хорóш-ем	о хорóш-ей	о хорóш-ем	о хорóш-их

Note
(a) Adjectives in **-жий** (e.g. **свéжий** 'fresh'), **-чий** (e.g. **горячий** 'hot') and **-щий** (e.g. **настоящий** 'real') decline like **хороший**.
(b) Adjectives in **-цый** (e.g. **куцый** 'dock-tailed') decline like **хороший** except in the masculine nominative singular and inanimate accusative singular, which end in **-ый**, the masculine and neuter instrumental singular (**куцым**) and the whole of the plural (**куцые, куцых** etc.). See 2 (ii) above.

(5) Declension of **большой** 'big':

	Masculine	Feminine	Neuter	Plural
Nom.	больш-óй	больш-áя	больш-óе	больш-úе
Acc.	больш-óй/-óго	больш-ýю	больш-óе	больш-úе/больш-úх
Gen.	больш-óго	больш-óй	больш-óго	больш-úх
Dat.	больш-óму	больш-óй	больш-óму	больш-úм
Instr.	больш-úм	больш-óй/-óю	больш-úм	больш-úми
Prep.	о больш-óм	о больш-óй	о больш-óм	о больш-úх

Note
Чужой 'someone else's' declines like **большой**.

147   Soft-ending adjectives

(1) Soft-ending adjectives comprise some forty adjectives in **-ний** and the adjective **кáрий** 'hazel' (eye colour).

Declension of **послéдний** 'last':

	Masculine	Feminine	Neuter	Plural
Nom.	после́дн-**ий**	после́дн-**яя**	после́дн-**ее**	после́дн-**ие**
Acc.	после́дн-**ий/-его**	после́дн-**юю**	после́дн-**ее**	после́дн-**ие**/после́дн-**их**
Gen.	после́дн-**его**	после́дн-**ей**	после́дн-**его**	после́дн-**их**
Dat.	после́дн-**ему**	после́дн-**ей**	после́дн-**ему**	после́дн-**им**
Instr.	после́дн-**им**	после́дн-**ей/-ею**	после́дн-**им**	после́дн-**ими**
Prep.	о после́дн-**ем**	о после́дн-**ей**	о после́дн-**ем**	о после́дн-**их**

(2) Adjectives in -**ний** subdivide into those which express:

(i) **Time:** весе́нний 'spring', вече́рний 'evening', всегда́шний 'customary', вчера́шний 'yesterday's', да́вний 'long-standing', давни́шний 'of long standing', дре́вний 'ancient', за́втрашний 'tomorrow's', зи́мний 'winter', ле́тний 'summer', неда́вний 'recent', ны́нешний 'present-day', осе́нний 'autumn', по́здний 'late', пре́жний 'former', прошлого́дний 'last year's', ра́нний 'early', сего́дняшний 'today's', суббо́тний 'Saturday's', тепе́решний 'present-day', тогда́шний 'of that time', у́тренний 'morning'.

(ii) **Location:** бли́жний 'near', ве́рхний 'upper, top', вне́шний 'external', вну́тренний 'internal', да́льний 'far', дома́шний 'domestic', за́дний 'back', зде́шний 'of this place', кра́йний 'extreme', ни́жний 'lower, bottom', пере́дний 'front', сосе́дний 'neighbouring, next', та́мошний 'of that place'.

Note

(a) **Бли́жний** and **да́льний** express relative distance: **бли́жний** у́гол 'the near corner', **да́льний** у́гол 'the far (*not* 'the distant') corner', **Бли́жний** Восто́к 'the Near East', **Да́льний** Восто́к 'the Far East'. Note that the counterpart to **да́льний** ро́дственник 'distant relative' is **ро́дственник** 'relative' or **бли́зкий** ро́дственник 'close relative'.

(b) **После́дний** 'last' and **сре́дний** 'middle' can refer to both time and space.

(c) Some soft endings relate only to compound adjectives: **нового́дний** 'new year' (cf. годово́й 'annual' from год 'year'), **односторо́нний** 'unilateral'.

(iii) **Others:** дочерний 'daughter's, daughterly', заму́жняя 'married' (of a woman), и́скренний 'sincere', ли́шний 'superfluous', поро́жний 'empty', си́ний (dark) 'blue', сыно́вний 'filial'.

148   Formation of adjectives from nouns: the suffixes -н-, -ск- and -ов-/-ев-

(1) Unlike English, in which most nouns can also function as adjectives (e.g. 'steel' (noun) becomes 'steel' (adjective) in '**steel** bridge'), adjectives in Russian derive from nouns mainly through suffixation.

(2) The commonest suffix is **-н-**: thus, **чайный** from чай 'tea' (чайная чашка 'tea cup'), **комнатный** from комната 'room' (комнатная температура 'room temperature'), **местный** from место 'place' (местный наркоз 'local anaesthetic'). **Г, к, х, ц** and **л** undergo mutation before suffix **-н-**:

г : ж	юг 'south'	южный 'southern'
к : ч	река 'river'	речной 'river' (adjective)
х : ш	воздух 'air'	воздушный 'air' (adjective)
ц : ч	улица 'street'	уличный 'street' (adjective)
л : ль	школа 'school'	школьный 'school' (adjective)

(3) The suffix **-ск-** is associated mainly with adjectives derived from the names of:

(i) People, thus : **мужской** 'male', **гражданский** 'civic' etc.

Note
Adjectives from some animate nouns have the suffix **-еск-**, e.g. **человеческий** 'human' from человек 'human'. Adjectives derived from some proper names take the infix **-ов-**: **горьковский** from Горький 'Gorky'.

(ii) Towns, rivers etc. (note also **городской** from город 'town', **сельский** from село 'village'): **донской** from Дон 'the Don', **московский** from Москва 'Moscow'.

Note
(a) Some town names ending in a vowel have adjectives in **-инский**: **алма-атинский** from Алма-Ата 'Alma Ata' (now also Алматы), **бакинский** from Баку 'Baku', **ялтинский** from Ялта 'Yalta' (note also **кубинский** 'Cuban', cf. **кубанский** from Кубань 'the (river) Kuban').
(b) Adjectival stress differs in some cases from noun stress: **астраханский** from Астрахань 'Astrakhan', **новгородский** from Новгород 'Novgorod'.
(c) Consonant mutation occurs in adjectives derived from the names of some towns, rivers, mountain ranges etc.: **волжский** from Волга

'the Volga', **пра́жский** from Пра́га 'Prague', **ри́жский** from Ри́га 'Riga', **ура́льский** from Ура́л 'the Urals'.

(iii) Nationalities and languages: **ру́сский/росси́йский** 'Russian', **по́льский** 'Polish', including more recent formations such as **зимбаб-ви́йский** 'Zimbabwean'. Note that **латви́йский** 'Latvian' refers to the country (e.g. **латви́йское** побере́жье 'the Latvian coastline'), whereas **латы́шский** 'Latvian' refers to the people (e.g. **латы́шский** язы́к 'the Latvian language').

(iv) Organizations: **ду́мский** 'Duma' (adj.), **заводско́й** from заво́д 'factory', **на́товский** from НА́ТО 'NATO' etc.

(v) Months: **октя́брьский** 'October' etc. Note the absence of a soft sign in **янва́рский** 'January' and the infix **-ов-** in **а́вгустовский** 'August', **ма́ртовский** 'March'.

(4) The suffix **-ов-/-ев-** is used to form adjectives from the names of many trees (e.g. **бу́ковый** from бук 'beech'), fruits and vegetables (e.g. **оре́ховый** from оре́х 'nut'), growing areas (e.g. **полево́й** from по́ле 'field'), metals and alloys (e.g. **ци́нковый** from цинк 'zinc'), certain other substances (e.g. **рези́новый** from рези́на 'rubber'), animals (e.g. **слоно́вый** from слон 'elephant'), suits of cards (e.g. **пи́ковый** from пи́ки 'spades'), colours (e.g. **ро́зовый** 'pink' from ро́за 'rose'), the names of some young people (e.g. **подро́стковый/подростко́вый** from подро́сток 'adolescent'), synthetic materials (e.g. **нейло́новый** from нейло́н 'nylon'), nouns in **-инг** (e.g. **ли́зинговый** from ли́зинг 'leasing'), and other nouns (e.g. **звуково́й** from звук 'sound', **ра́ковый** from рак 'cancer' etc.).

149   Adjectival endings with specific meanings

Some adjectival endings have specific meanings. These include:

(1) -ивый, -ливый, -чивый

Adjectives with these endings denote characteristics: **лени́вый** 'lazy', **терпели́вый** 'patient', **разгово́рчивый** 'talkative' etc.

(2) -мый

Adjectives with this ending denote potential qualities (cf. English -ble): **преодоли́мый** 'surmountable', **раствори́мый** 'soluble'. Such adjectives are of participial derivation (see also **344**).

(3) -атый

Adjectives with this ending denote possession of the object denoted by the root noun: **перна́тый** 'feathered', **рога́тый** 'horned'.

(4) -астый

Adjectives with this ending denote possession of a prominent physical feature: **груда́стый** 'busty', **скула́стый** 'high-cheek-boned' etc.

(5) -истый

Adjectives with this ending denote abundance of the feature denoted by the root noun: **тени́стый** 'shady'. They can also denote similarity: **золоти́стый** 'golden' (of colour etc.) (cf. золото́й '(made of) gold').

(6) -чий

Adjectives with this ending denote various states: **вися́чий** 'hanging' (**вися́чий** мост 'suspension bridge'), **сидя́чий** 'sedentary' etc. The adjectives are of participial origin.

150   Nouns with more than one adjective

Nouns with two or more derivative adjectives subdivide as follows:

(1) Different meanings of the same noun are involved. Thus, мир 'world' has the adjective **мирово́й** (мирова́я война́ 'world war'), while мир 'peace' has the adjective **ми́рный** (ми́рный догово́р 'peace treaty').

(2) The adjectival endings express different qualities or properties of a noun. Thus, both **дру́жеский** 'friendly' and **дру́жный** 'concerted, harmonious' derive from друг 'friend', as does the official **дру́жественный** (Переговоры проходи́ли в **дру́жественной** обстано́вке 'The talks were held in a cordial atmosphere').

151   Possessive adjectives

Possessive adjectives fall into two categories:

(1) The type **во́лчий** 'wolf's'.

(i) **Во́лчий** is declined as follows:

	Masculine	Feminine	Neuter	Plural
Nom.	во́лчий	во́лчь-я	во́лчь-е	во́лчь-и
Acc.	во́лчий/во́лчь-его	во́лчь-ю	во́лчь-е	во́лчь-и/-их
Gen.	во́лчь-его	во́лчь-ей	во́лчь-его	во́лчь-их
Dat.	во́лчь-ему	во́лчь-ей	во́лчь-ему	во́лчь-им
Instr.	во́лчь-им	во́лчь-ей/-ею	во́лчь-им	во́лчь-ими
Prep.	о во́лчь-ем	о во́лчь-ей	о во́лчь-ем	о во́лчь-их

(ii) Most adjectives in this category derive from the names of animals, birds, fish etc.: **ли́сий** 'fox's', **ры́бий** 'fish's' and so on. Some derive from the names of human beings. Consonant mutation operates as follows:

г : ж	бог	бо́жий 'god's'
д : ж	медве́дь	медве́жий 'bear's'
к : ч	соба́ка	соба́чий 'dog's'
	охо́тник	охо́тничий 'hunter's'
х : ш	черепа́ха	черепа́ший 'tortoise's'
ц : ч	овца́	ове́чий 'sheep's'
	деви́ца	де́вичий 'maiden' (e.g. де́вичья фами́лия 'maiden name')

(iii) A number of the adjectives appear in set phrases: волк в **ове́чьей** шку́ре 'wolf in sheep's clothing', вид с **пти́чьего** полёта 'bird's eye view'.

Note
Тре́тий 'third' also declines like **во́лчий**.

(2) The type **ма́мин** 'Mum's'.

(i) **Ма́мин** declines as follows, combining adjective and noun endings:

	Masculine	Feminine	Neuter	Plural
Nom.	ма́мин	ма́мин-а	ма́мин-о	ма́мин-ы
Acc.	ма́мин/ма́мин-ого	ма́мин-у	ма́мин-о	ма́мин-ы/-ых
Gen.	ма́мин-ого	ма́мин-ой	ма́мин-ого	ма́мин-ых
Dat.	ма́мин-у	ма́мин-ой	ма́мин-у	ма́мин-ым
Instr.	ма́мин-ым	ма́мин-ой/-ою	ма́мин-ым	ма́мин-ыми
Prep.	о ма́мин-ом	о ма́мин-ой	о ма́мин-ом	о ма́мин-ых

(ii) Possessive adjectives of this type are formed by adding the suffixes **-ин, -нин** or **-ов** to the stems of nouns (ма́ма 'Mum' etc.): **ба́бушкин** 'grandma's', **бра́тнин** 'brother's', **де́дов** 'granddad's', **дя́дин** 'uncle's', **жёнин** 'wife's', **ки́син/ко́шкин** 'pussy's', **ма́мин** 'Mum's', **му́жнин** 'husband's', **ня́нин** 'nanny's', **отцо́в/па́пин** 'Dad's', **се́стрин** 'sister's', **тётин** 'auntie's'. They are used mainly within the family circle:

От **маминых** завтраков он решил бежать (Tendryakov)
He decided to escape from Mum's breakfasts

(iii) They also derive from the familiar forms of first names: **Колин** 'Kolya's':

Я считаю, что **Наташина** мама права (*Rabotnitsa*)
I consider that Natasha's Mum is right

(iv) The endings also appear in phrases deriving from mythology, the Bible etc. (**ахиллесова** пята 'Achilles' heel'), geographical terms (**Берингов** пролив 'Bering Straits'), other phrases (**крокодиловы** слёзы 'crocodile tears') etc.   .

(v) Some forms in **-ин**, mostly denoting animals, have acquired long adjectival endings and decline like **новый: лебединый** 'swan's', **лошадиный** 'horse's' (**лебединая** песня 'swan song', **лошадиная** сила 'horse power').

152   Diminutive adjectives in -енький/-онький

(1) Most diminutive adjectives end in **-енький** (e.g. **новенький** from новый 'new') and (after velar consonants) **-онький** (**высоконький** from высокий, **лёгонький** from лёгкий 'light, easy', **тихонький** from тихий 'quiet'). The stress falls on the syllable preceding **-енький/ -онький**.

(2) Diminutive adjectives may express smallness: **бледненькое** личико 'a pale little face', Алька передёрнула **узенькими** плечами (Koluntsev) 'A spasm convulsed Alka's narrow little shoulders'.

(3) Like diminutive nouns (see **104–108**), diminutive adjectives may also express emotive nuances of sympathy, scorn etc.: **молоденький** студентик 'a nice young student', **глупенький** мальчонка 'a stupid little kid'.

(4) Diminutive endings may also impart a meaning of intensity to an adjective: e.g. **простенький** 'very plain', **чистенький** мальчик 'spotlessly clean little boy', cf.:

Михаил принёс две **холодненькие** бутылки московского пивка (Abramov)
Mikhail brought two **ice-cold** bottles of Moscow beer

153   Diminutive adjectives in -оватый/-еватый

(1) The diminutive suffix **-оват(ый)/-еват(ый)** denotes incompleteness: **дороговáтый** 'rather dear', **кислова́тый** 'rather sour', **синева́тый** 'bluish'.

Note

These diminutives cannot be formed from all adjectives. Thus, they are formed from ста́рый 'old' and глу́пый 'stupid' (старова́тый, глупова́тый), but not from their opposites молодо́й 'young' and у́мный 'clever'.

(2) Such diminutives may acquire an evaluative nuance: **дорогова́тая кварти́ра** 'a rather expensive apartment', **холоднова́тая пого́да** 'weather somewhat on the cold side'.

(3) Maximum colloquial expressiveness is achieved by the addition of **-енький: глухова́тенький** 'somewhat hard of hearing'.

154   Indeclinable adjectives

(1) Most indeclinable adjectives are loan words and *follow* the noun. Some denote colour (e.g. **ха́ки** 'khaki'):

> Два но́вых пла́тья: откры́тое, **беж** . . . и цве́та **бордо́** (Zalygin)
> Two new dresses, an open-necked beige . . . and a deep red

(2) Others denote:

(i) Food and drink:

ко́фе **мо́кко**	mocha coffee
карто́фель **фри**	French fries

(ii) Styles of clothing:

пальто́ **демисезо́н**	spring or autumn coat
брю́ки **клёш**	bell-bottom trousers
ю́бка **ми́ни** (also ми́ни-ю́бка or ми́ни) mini-skirt	
пальто́ **регла́н**	Raglan coat

(iii) Languages (these adjectives *precede* the noun):

ко́ми заи́мствования	Komi loans
урду́ язы́к	Urdu
хи́нди язы́к	Hindi

Compare, however, язы́к **эспера́нто** 'Esperanto'.

(iv) Various other meanings:

вес **бру́тто**	gross weight
вес **не́тто**	net weight
часы́ **пик**	rush hour

Note

Some indeclinable adjectives also function as nouns: **джéрси** 'jersey material', **мáкси** 'maxi clothes'.

155   Attributive use of the long adjective

(1) The long adjective usually precedes the noun and agrees with it in gender, case and number:

	'new house'		'new book'		'new armchair'	
	Masculine		Feminine		Neuter	
Nom.	нóв-**ый**	дом	нóв-**ая**	кни́га	нóв-**ое**	крéсло
Acc.	нóв-**ый**	дом	нóв-**ую**	кни́гу	нóв-**ое**	крéсло
Gen.	нóв-**ого**	дóма	нóв-**ой**	кни́ги	нóв-**ого**	крéсла
Dat.	нóв-**ому**	дóму	нóв-**ой**	кни́ге	нóв-**ому**	крéслу
Instr.	нóв-**ым**	дóмом	нóв-**ой/-ою**	кни́гой	нóв-**ым**	крéслом
Prep.	о нóв-**ом**	дóме	о нóв-**ой**	кни́ге	о нóв-**ом**	крéсле

Plural

Nom.	нóв-**ые**	домá	нóв-**ые**	кни́ги	нóв-**ые**	крéсла
Acc.	нóв-**ые**	домá	нóв-**ые**	кни́ги	нóв-**ые**	крéсла
Gen.	нóв-**ых**	домóв	нóв-**ых**	книг	нóв-**ых**	крéсел
Dat.	нóв-**ым**	домáм	нóв-**ым**	кни́гам	нóв-**ым**	крéслам
Instr.	нóв-**ыми**	домáми	нóв-**ыми**	кни́гами	нóв-**ыми**	крéслами
Prep.	о нóв-**ых**	домáх	о нóв-**ых**	кни́гах	о нóв-**ых**	крéслах

Note

(a) The animate accusative/genitive rule is applied: Знáю **нóвого учи́теля, нóвых учителéй** 'I know the new teacher, the new teachers' (see **47**).

(b) An adjective or pronoun qualifying a masculine animate noun in **-а/-я** takes masculine endings, while the noun takes feminine endings: Я знáю **вáшего дя́дю** 'I know your uncle', дом **вáшего дя́ди** 'your uncle's house', Вéрю **вáшему дя́де** 'I trust your uncle', Я довóлен **вáшим дя́дей** 'I am pleased with your uncle', о **вáшем дя́де** 'about your uncle'.

(2) The long adjective may also follow the noun, separated from it by a comma and agreeing with it in gender, case and number:

Он лежа́л на **траве́, мо́крой** от росы́
He was lying on the grass, (which was) wet with the dew

Note
In certain contexts (e.g. in restaurant menus, with generic nouns) the long attributive adjective may follow the noun: ко́фе **натура́льный** 'real coffee', Тури́зм — де́ло **поле́зное** 'Tourism is a healthy pursuit'.

156   Use of the long adjective with predicative meaning

(1) In predicative position, the long adjective denotes characteristics which are inherent in or completely identified with the noun (cf. the predicative *short* form (see **166–174**)), e.g.

Э́та ко́мната — **больша́я**
This room is **large** (is **a large one**)

(2) When linked to the noun by the past or future tense of the verb **быть**, the long predicative adjective appears:

(i) In the nominative case (the more *colloquial* variant):

Лес был **тёплый** и **споко́йный** (Aksenov)
The forest was warm and serene

И я бу́ду тогда́ **ста́рая, некраси́вая**, в морщи́нках (Kovaleva)
And by that time I shall be old, ugly, wrinkled

(ii) In the instrumental case (more typical of *written* styles):

Перестро́йка была́ **нелёгкой**, но она́ произошла́ (Kovaleva)
Restructuring was not easy, but it occurred

— Бу́ду я когда́-нибудь **бога́тым**? (Rubina)
'Will I ever be rich?'

(3) When linked to the noun by the conditional, subjunctive, infinitive or imperative mood of the verb **быть**, the instrumental case of the adjective is the norm:

Е́сли бы он был **высо́ким**, он поступи́л бы в мили́цию
If he were tall he would join the police

Гла́вное, что́бы э́ти встре́чи бы́ли **регуля́рными**
The main thing is that these meetings should be regular

Э́ти дога́дки мо́гут быть **пра́вильными** или **оши́бочными** (Rybakov)
These conjectures may be right or wrong

Будь всегда́ **ве́жливым**!
Always be polite!

(4) After other verbs which take a predicate (**вы́глядеть** 'to look', **каза́ться** 'to seem', **притворя́ться** 'to pretend', **чу́вствовать** себя́ 'to feel' etc.), the adjective also appears in the instrumental case:

У́лицы вы́глядели **гря́зными**
The streets looked dirty

Мой расчёт оказа́лся **то́чным** (Nikolaev)
My calculation turned out to be accurate

Она́ всегда́ остаётся **споко́йной**
She always stays calm

Я чу́вствовал себя́ перед ним **винова́тым** (Bogomolov)
I felt I owed him an apology

(5) An adjectival complement to intransitive and transitive verbs also appears in the instrumental:

Он на́чал **пе́рвым**
He began first, was the first to begin

Он оста́вил сейф **откры́тым**
He left the safe open

Я никогда́ не ви́дел её **тако́й краси́вой** (Kazakov)
I had never seen her looking so lovely

157   Some uses of singular and plural adjectives

(1) A plural adjective is used to qualify two or more singular nouns if it relates to all the nouns named:

Маргари́та с гро́хотом бро́сила **желе́зные** сово́к и лопа́тку (Rubina)
With a clatter Margarita threw down an iron trowel and spade

Note

A *singular* adjective or pronoun may be used, however, if it is obvious that it relates to all the nouns named. The adjective or pronoun in such circumstances agrees with the first of the nouns: написáть **своιό** фамѝлию, ѝмя и о́тчество 'to write one's surname, first name and patronymic'.

(2) A singular adjective is also used if it relates only to the *first* of the nouns named: **кáменный** дом и гарáж 'a stone house and a garage' (cf. **кáменные** дом и гарáж 'a stone house and (a stone) garage').

(3) Phrases comprising numeral and noun are qualified by a plural adjective: **кáждые** два дня 'every two days'. Adjectives which fulfil an emphatic role (e.g. **дóбрый, пóлный, цéлый**) appear in the genitive plural: **пóлных** три мéсяца 'a full three months', **цéлых** две тарéлки 'two whole plates' (cf. also опоздáл на **цéлых** пòлчасá 'he was a whole half hour late').

(4) Singular adjectives and nouns are used in the following phrases: **в рáзное врéмя** 'at various times', **всякого рóда** 'all kinds of' (**всякого рóда** товáры 'all kinds of goods'), **рáзного рóда** 'of various kinds'.

158   Adjectival nouns

(1) An adjectival noun has the form of an adjective but functions as a noun (**бéлые** 'the Whites').

(2) Most adjectival nouns result from the omission of a word that can be understood from the context, e.g. **столóвая** (кóмната) 'dining room'.

(3) Adjectival nouns decline like adjectives (**в вáнной** (from вáнная) 'in the bathroom'), behave like adjectives when governed by numerals (**два морóженых** 'two ice-creams' (see **194** (2) (v))) and can themselves be qualified by adjectives: **рýсское морóженое** 'Russian ice-cream'.

(4) Most **masculine** adjectival nouns denote people: **рядовóй** 'private soldier', **учёный** 'scientist', **часовóй** 'sentry' etc.

(5) **Feminine** adjectival nouns denote:

(i) Lines: **кривáя** 'curve', **прямáя** 'straight line' (лѝния 'line' understood).

(ii) Rooms and other accommodation: **закусочная** 'snack-bar', **кладовая** 'store-room', **прачечная** 'laundry', **уборная** 'lavatory'.

(6) **Neuter** adjectival nouns denote:

(i) The names of dishes: **первое** 'first course', **сладкое** 'sweet' etc. (блюдо 'dish' understood).

(ii) Time: **прошлое** 'the past', **настоящее** 'the present', **будущее** 'the future' (время 'time' understood).

(iii) Abstracts: **старое и новое** 'the old and the new'.

(iv) Classes of animal: **животное** 'animal', **млекопитающее** 'mammal', **насекомое** 'insect', (существо 'being' understood).

(v) Grammatical terms: **прилагательное** 'adjective', **существительное** 'noun', **числительное** 'numeral' (имя 'noun, nomen' understood).

(7) **Plural** adjectival nouns denote money: **наличные** 'cash', **сверхурочные** 'overtime', **чаевые** 'gratuities' (cf. деньги 'money').

Note
(a) Many adjectival nouns are formed on a seemingly *ad hoc* basis: Она поступила в **архитектурный** (институт) 'She has enrolled at the school of architecture'. Note also **борзая** (собака) 'borzoi', **выходной** (день) 'day off', **сборная** (команда) 'combined team, international team' etc.
(b) Some adjectival nouns function *only* as nouns (**вселенная** 'the universe', **запятая** 'comma', **мостовая** 'roadway'), whereas others function as nouns or adjectives (cf. **рабочий** 'worker' and **рабочий** день 'working day' etc.).

The Short Form of the Adjective

159   Endings of the short form of the adjective

(1) Most adjectives have long forms and short forms (compare, however, **160**).

(2) The short form derives from the long form by the removal of the

whole of the masculine ending and the final vowel of the feminine, neuter and plural endings, e.g. **суро́вый** 'severe':

	Long form	Short form
Masculine	суро́в-**ый**	суро́в
Feminine	суро́в-**ая**	суро́в-**а**
Neuter	суро́в-**ое**	суро́в-**о**
Plural	суро́в-**ые**	суро́в-**ы**

See also **161** on the use of buffer vowels.

160   Adjectives which have long forms only

(1) Some adjectives which denote **inherent characteristics** have long forms only. They include:

(i) Adjectives of colour (except for **си́ний** 'blue').

(ii) Adjectives with the suffix **-ск-**, e.g. **ру́сский** 'Russian'.

Note
Many adjectives in **-ический**, e.g. **драмати́ческий** 'dramatic', have synonyms in **-ичный**, e.g. **драмати́чный**, which *do* have short forms.

(iii) Adjectives in **-ний** (except for **и́скренний** 'sincere' and **си́ний** 'blue').

(iv) Adjectives of time (e.g. **ме́сячный** 'month's') and place (e.g. **ме́стный** 'local').

(v) Adjectives which denote materials or substances: **деревя́нный** 'wooden', **желе́зный** 'iron' etc.

(vi) Possessive adjectives of the type **во́лчий** 'wolf's' (see **151** (1)).

(vii) Ordinal numerals: **пе́рвый** 'first', **второ́й** 'second' etc.

(2) Some adjectives have short forms in certain meanings only. For example, **глухо́й** has short forms in the meaning 'deaf', but not in the meanings 'blank' (**глуха́я** стена́ 'blank wall'), 'remote' (**глуха́я** прови́нция 'remote province') and 'voiceless' (**глухо́й** согла́сный 'voiceless consonant'). **Ви́дный** has a short form in the meaning 'visible' (see **161** (1)) but not in the meaning 'prominent'.

161   The buffer vowels -e-, -o- and -ё- in the masculine short form

A buffer vowel is introduced between two or more final consonants in the *masculine* short form of many adjectives.

(1) The commonest of the buffer vowels is **-e-**:

Long-form masculine		Short forms
ва́жный	'important'	**ва́жен**, важна́, ва́жно, важны́/ва́жны
ви́дный	'visible'	**ви́ден**, видна́, ви́дно, видны́
голо́дный	'hungry'	**го́лоден**, голодна́, го́лодно, голодны́/го́лодны
дли́нный	'long'	**дли́нен**, длинна́, дли́нно, длинны́/дли́нны
слы́шный	'audible'	**слы́шен**, слышна́, слы́шно, слышны́/слы́шны

Compare:

Сейча́с зага́р не **мо́ден** (Koluntsev)
Now a suntan is not fashionable

The buffer vowel **-e-** may replace a soft sign or the semi-consonant **й**:

больно́й	sick	**бо́лен**, больна́, больно́, больны́
дово́льный	pleased	**дово́лен**, дово́льна, дово́льно, дово́льны
споко́йный	calm	**споко́ен**, споко́йна, споко́йно, споко́йны

(2) The buffer vowel **-o-** splits clusters of consonants ending in **к, г**:

до́лгий	long	**до́лог**, долга́, до́лго, до́лги
лёгкий	light, easy	**лёгок**, легка́, легко́, легки́
у́зкий	narrow	**у́зок**, узка́, у́зко, узки́/у́зки

— По мое́й статье́ преде́льный срок доста́точно **до́лог** (Koluntsev)
'The maximum term for my offence is fairly long'

Note
However, **-e-** replaces a *soft sign* in such clusters: го́рький 'bitter', short form **го́рек**. It also appears in unstressed position between **ж, ч, ш** and **к**: тя́жкий 'severe', short form **тя́жек**.

The following adjectives also take **-o-**:

злой	wicked	**зол**, зла, зло, злы
пóлный	full	**пóлон**, полнá, полнó, полны́
смешнóй	funny	**смешóн**, смешнá, смешнó, смешны́

(3) The buffer vowel **-ё-** affects a small number of adjectives:

óстрый	sharp, sharp-witted	**остёр**, острá, острó, остры́
сúльный	strong	**силён**, сильнá, сúльно, сильны́
ýмный	clever	**умён**, умнá, умнó, умны́
хúтрый	cunning	**хитёр**, хитрá, хитрó, хитры́

Note

Some adjectives with a stem ending in more than one consonant do *not* take a buffer vowel in the masculine short form. They include бóдрый 'cheerful' (**бодр**), дóбрый 'kind' (**добр**), гóрдый 'proud' (**горд**), мёртвый 'dead' (**мёртв**), пёстрый 'multicoloured' (**пёстр**).

162   Some special short forms

The following short forms should be specially noted.

(1) Большóй   big   : **велúк, великá, великó, великú.**

(2) Достóйный   worthy   : **достóин, достóйна, достóйно, достóйны.**

(3) Úскренний   sincere   : **úскренен, úскренна, úскренне** (the commoner alternative)/**úскренно, úскренни/úскренны.**

(4) Мáленький   small   : **мал, малá, малó, малы́.**

(5) Сúний   blue   : **синь, синя́, сúне, сúни.**

(6) Солёный   salted   : **сóлон, солонá, сóлоно, солоны́/сóлоны.**

Note

(a) **Рад, рáда, рáдо, рáды** 'glad' has no long form (however, рáдостный means 'glad, joyful': рáдостное собы́тие 'a joyful event').

(b) Каќв, какова́, каково́, каковы́ are used predicatively in the meaning 'what, what kind of' (**Какова́** сме́ртность от ра́ка? 'What is the mortality rate from cancer?') and таќв, такова́, таково́, таковы́ in the meaning 'such' (**Таково́** на́ше мне́ние 'Such is our opinion'). However, **как** and **так** are used to modify short adjectives: Он **так** добр/Она́ **так** добра́ 'He is so kind/She is so kind'.

(c)   For meanings of **вели́к** and **мал**, see **169.**

163   Masculine short forms of adjectives in -енный

(1) The masculine short form of adjectives in unstressed **-енный** ends in **-ен**, e.g. бессмы́сленный 'senseless', short form **бессмы́слен:**

Разгово́р был **бессмы́слен** (Trifonov)
The conversation was senseless

(2) Adjectives in stressed **-е́нный** have masculine short forms in **-е́нен**, e.g. открове́нный 'candid', short form **открове́нен:**

А взгляд его́, пожа́луй, сли́шком **открове́нен** (Koluntsev)
But I suppose his glance is too frank

Note
(a)   Some adjectives in unstressed **-енный** have alternative masculine short forms in **-ен** and **-енен**, e.g. есте́ственный 'natural', **есте́ствен/есте́ственен**, the form in **-ен** usually being preferred.

(b)   Some 'high style' adjectives in **-е́нный** have masculine short forms in **-е́н**, e.g. благослове́нный 'blessed':

Благослове́н ма́стер, дости́гший верши́ны мастерства́
Blessed is the craftsman who has achieved the summit of craftsmanship

164   Stress patterns

(1) Very many adjectival short forms have fixed stem stress throughout:

краси́в краси́ва краси́во краси́вы (is, are) 'beautiful'

(2) Short forms with mobile stress subdivide into the following:

(i) End stress in feminine, neuter and plural:

хоро́ш хороша́ хорошо́ хоро́ши (is, are) 'good'

Similarly **бо́лен** 'ill', **горя́ч** 'hot', **лёгок** 'light, easy', **по́лон** 'full', **смешо́н** 'funny', **тяжёл** 'heavy', **умён** 'clever'.

Note
Some adjectives of this type (e.g. **свеж** 'fresh') have alternative end or stem stress in the plural (**свежи́/све́жи**); others (e.g. **широ́к** 'wide') have alternative end or stem stress in the neuter *and* plural (**широ́ко** or **широко́, широки́/широ́ки**).

(ii) End stress in the feminine:

жив жива́ жи́во жи́вы (is, are) 'alive'

Similarly **цел** 'whole' and, with alternative *end* stress in the plural, **бле́ден** 'pale', **го́лоден** 'hungry', **мил** 'dear', **слы́шен** 'audible', **строг** 'strict'.

(iii) End stress in the feminine and plural:

ви́ден видна́ ви́дно видны́ (is, are) 'visible'

Similarly **силён/си́лен** 'strong'.

165 Divergence in stress between masculine, neuter and plural long and short forms

(1) A handful of adjectives switch from medial or end stress in the long form to initial stress in the masculine, neuter and plural short forms, with end stress in the feminine: весёлый 'merry', **ве́сел, весела́, ве́село, ве́селы**; голо́дный 'hungry', **го́лоден, голодна́, го́лодно, го́лодны/голодны́**; дешёвый 'cheap', **дёшев, дешева́, дёшево, дёшевы**; дорого́й 'dear', **до́рог, дорога́, до́рого, до́роги**; коро́ткий 'short', **ко́роток, коротка́, ко́ротко, ко́ротки/коротки́**; молодо́й 'young', **мо́лод, молода́, мо́лодо, мо́лоды**.

(2) Счастли́вый 'happy' has initial stress in all short forms: **сча́стлив, сча́стлива, сча́стливо, сча́стливы**.

166 The short form: usage. Introductory comments

(1) Both long and short forms may be used predicatively (see **156**).

(2) However, there is usually a distinction in meaning, the long form denoting inherent permanent characteristics (Он **злой** 'He is wicked') and the short form relating to temporary states (Он **голоден** 'He is hungry') or to specific contexts or circumstances (Он **прав** 'He is right' (i.e. about a particular matter)).

(3) Usage depends to a considerable extent on the capacity or incapacity of a particular adjective to denote both permanent and temporary states. Thus, Он **больной** 'He is (chronically) sick' may be contrasted with Он **болен** 'He is (temporarily) ill'. In adjectives, however, where no such distinction is possible, long and short forms are virtually synonymous: Он **умный**/Он **умён** 'He is clever'.

(4) The difference between the two forms of the adjective may be stylistic, the short form reflecting a more 'bookish' style:

Психология личности очень **сложна**
The psychology of the personality is very complex

and the long form being the 'colloquial' variant:

Психология личности очень **сложная**

167   Use of the short form to denote temporary state

While the long form implies *complete identification* of the quality expressed by the adjective with the person or thing it qualifies, the short form indicates a temporary state or condition, cf.

Река **бурная**
The river is a turbulent one (an inherent characteristic)

and

Сегодня река **спокойна**
Today the river is calm (the short form denoting a temporary state)

Similarly Он очень **весёлый, бодрый** 'He is very jolly, cheerful' (i.e. by nature), but Ты был **бодр** и **весел** и шутил всю дорогу (Koluntsev) 'You were cheerful and jolly and joked the whole way', where the short forms refer to a person's mood *on a particular occasion*.

168   Short forms: pairs of opposites

Many short forms comprise pairs of opposites and describe alternative states: hungry/full, healthy/ill etc.:

(1)   **го́лоден, голодна́, го́лодно, голодны́/го́лодны** (is, are) hungry
      сыт, сыта́, сы́то, сы́ты (is, are) full, replete

(2)   **здоро́в, здоро́ва, здоро́во, здоро́вы** (is, are) healthy
      бо́лен, больна́, больно́, больны́ (is, are) sick

Note

(a)   Unlike **здоро́в** and **бо́лен,** which denote *temporary* states, Он
      здоро́вый 'He has a strong constitution' denotes an *inherent*
      characteristic and Он **больно́й** 'He is chronically sick, an invalid'
      denotes a chronic state.

(b)   The colloquial forms **здоро́в, здорова́, здорово́, здоровы́** mean
      'strong, good at': Ему́ удало́сь наконе́ц вы́толкнуть её. — Ну,
      здорова́! (Shukshin) 'He finally managed to shove her out. "Gosh,
      she's strong!"'

(3)   **сча́стлив, сча́стлива, сча́стливо, сча́стливы** (is, are) happy
      несча́стен, несча́стна, несча́стно, несча́стны (is, are) unhappy

(4)   **жив, жива́, жи́во, жи́вы** (is, are) alive
      мёртв, мертва́, мёртво, мёртвы (is, are) dead

Note

Он **живо́й** means 'he is lively' (an *inherent* characteristic).

(5)   **прав, права́, пра́во, пра́вы** (is, are) right
      непра́в, неправа́, непра́во, непра́вы (is, are) wrong

Compare На́ше де́ло **пра́вое** 'Our cause is just'.

Note

Она́ **хоро́шая** 'She is good' but Она́ **хороша́ (собо́й/собо́ю)** 'She is
good-looking'; Он — **плохо́й** 'He is bad' but Он **плох** (здоро́вьем)
'He is poorly'.

169   Adjectives of dimension

The short form of an adjective of dimension relates the dimension to a
particular set of circumstances, while the long form completely
identifies the dimension with the noun it qualifies, cf.

(a)   Э́та ко́мната **больша́я**
      This room is big/a big one

(b)   Эта ко́мната **велика́**
       This room is **too** big (i.e. for a particular purpose)

       Этот пиджа́к **широ́к**
       This jacket is too big (for a particular person)

       Пла́тье ей **мало́**
       The dress is too small for her

Compare Ю́бка **длинна́** 'The skirt is too long', Рукава́ **коротки́** 'The sleeves are too short', Дверь **низка́** 'The door is too low', Костю́м **свобо́ден** 'The suit is too loose-fitting', Сапоги́ **тесны́** 'The boots are too tight', Брю́ки **узки́** 'The trousers are too tight', Но́ша **тяжела́** для ребёнка 'The burden is too heavy for the child' (cf. Но́ша **тяжёлая** 'The burden is a heavy one').

Note
(a)   The idea of excess may be reinforced by the adverb **сли́шком** 'too': Не **сли́шком** ли вы **мо́лоды** для нас? (Rubina) 'Don't you think you are too young for us?'
(b)   The short form of adjectives of dimension can also be used *without* a relative nuance: **Широ́к** круг интере́сов у на́ших чита́телей (*Yunyi naturalist*) 'Our readers' range of interests **is broad**'.

170   Delimitation of meaning by the oblique case of a noun or pronoun

(1) When the meaning of a predicative adjective is 'delimited' by the oblique case of a noun or pronoun, the short form must be used. Compare

       Како́е име́ет значе́ние, **симпати́чен** он **ей** и́ли нет? (Koluntsev)
       What does it matter if she likes him or not?

where the quality denoted by **симпати́чен** is valid only for *her* (**ей**), with

       Он о́чень **симпати́чный**
       He is very good-looking/attractive

where the *long* form denotes an inherent trait.

(2) The short form can be 'delimited' by any of the oblique cases.

(i) Genitive:

Автобус полон **народу**
The bus is full **of people**

Note
Он полный means 'He is over-weight'.

(ii) Dative:

Я **вам** благодарен
I am grateful **to you**

(iii) Instrumental:

Я доволен **вами**
I am pleased **with you**

Этот край богат **нефтью** и **пушниной** (*Sputnik*)
This territory is rich **in oil and furs**

171   Delimitation by a prepositional phrase

(1) The short form is also used when the quality expressed by the adjective is delimited by a **prepositional phrase.** Thus, while either long or short form may be used in

Лекция была **интересная/интересна**
The lecture was interesting

the short form *must* be used in

Лекция была интересна **по форме**
The lecture was interesting in form

since the adjective is 'delimited' by the phrase **по форме.** Compare:

Мы **безоружны** перед мощью современной радиоаппаратуры (*Izvestiya*)
We are powerless in the face of the might of modern radio technology

Раньше она была **равнодушна** к лыжам (Koluntsev)
She used to be indifferent to skiing

(2) Common prepositional phrases include **глух на** (левое ухо) 'deaf in' (the left ear), **готов к** 'ready for', **готов на** + acc. 'ready for' (in the meaning 'desperate'), **добр к** 'kind to', **знаком с** + instr. 'familiar with', **похож на** + acc. 'similar to', **сердит на** + acc. 'angry with',

силён в (математике) 'good at' (mathematics), склонен к 'inclined to', слеп на (правый глаз) 'blind in' (the right eye), согласен на (условия) 'agreeing to' (conditions), согласен с 'in agreement with', способен к 'good at', способен на (обман) 'capable of' (deception), характерен для 'characteristic of', хром на (правую ногу) 'lame in' (the right leg).

Note
Used predicatively, the long forms of some of these adjectives denote inherent characteristics: Она добрая 'She is kind', Он сильный 'He is strong', Он способный 'He is a capable person'.

172   Delimitation by a subordinate clause or an infinitive

The short form predicative is also used when the adjective is delimited:

(1) By a subordinate clause:

Я счастлив, что вас встречаю
I am happy to meet you

(2) By an infinitive, either:

(i) *with* чтобы

Он достаточно умён, чтобы понять, где раскаяние, а где игра
(Koluntsev)
He is intelligent enough to understand where remorse ends and play-acting begins

or:

(ii) *without* чтобы

— Ты не способен понять, чего мне стоило прийти сюда
(Koluntsev)
'You are incapable of understanding what it has cost me to come here'

173   The short form as predicate to infinitives, verbal nouns and nouns with certain qualifiers

The short form is also used as predicate to the following.

(1) Infinitives and verbal nouns:

Пить/Употребле́ние нарко́тиков **вре́дно**
Drinking/Use of drugs is **harmful**

(2) Nouns qualified by **вся́кий/ка́ждый** 'each, every', **како́й?** 'what kind of?', **любо́й** 'any', **тако́й** 'such' etc.:

Любо́й сове́т **поле́зен**
Any advice is useful

Тако́го ро́да комплиме́нты **бессмы́сленны**
Compliments of that kind are meaningless

174   The short form in generalized statements

The short form appears in many generalized sayings, proverbs etc.:

Жизнь **трудна́**	Life is hard
Любо́вь **слепа́**	Love is blind
Мир **те́сен!**	It's a small world!

175   Position of the short form of the adjective

The short form of the adjective normally follows the noun:

Все вели́кие и́стины **просты́**   All great truths are simple

but may, for greater emphasis, precede it (see **484** (1) (i)):

Изве́стна зави́симость доро́жных происше́ствий от во́зраста шофёра
The connection between road accidents and the age of the driver **is well known**

The Comparative Degree of the Adjective

176   The comparative degree. Introductory comments

Most English adjectives have either

a comparative in -er (e.g. '*harder*')

or

a comparative with 'more' (e.g. '*more comfortable*').

By contrast, most Russian adjectives have two comparatives, each with a specific function.

177   The attributive comparative with бо́лее

(1) The attributive form of almost all comparatives comprises бо́лее + long adjective, e.g. **бо́лее краси́вый** дом 'a more beautiful house'.

(2) **Бо́лее** is *invariable*, while the adjective agrees with the noun it qualifies:

(i) In gender and number:

бо́лее	краси́вый	дом	a more beautiful house
бо́лее	краси́вая	де́вушка	a more beautiful girl
бо́лее	краси́вое	де́рево	a more beautiful tree
бо́лее	краси́вые	де́ти	more beautiful children

(ii) In case:

Нет **бо́лее краси́вого са́да**
There is no more beautiful garden

Он подошёл к **бо́лее краси́вой де́вушке**
He went up to the more beautiful girl

(3) Comparatives with **бо́лее** may also be used predicatively:

Перви́чные па̀рторганиза́ции ста́ли **бо́лее кру́пными** (*Pravda*)
The primary party organizations became larger

However, predicative forms in **-ee** or **-e** should be regarded as the norm (see **179–181**).

(4) **Ме́нее** 'less' is used to form a 'reverse' comparative:

Э́то **ме́нее краси́вый** дом   This is a less beautiful house

178   One-word attributive comparatives

Six adjectives have attributive comparatives consisting of one word:

хоро́ший 'good'	**лу́чший** 'better'
плохо́й 'bad'	**ху́дший** 'worse'

ста́рый 'old'	ста́рший 'older, senior'
молодо́й 'young'	мла́дший 'younger, junior'
большо́й 'big'	бо́льший 'bigger'
ма́ленький 'small'	ме́ньший 'smaller'

Note

(a) Ста́рший and мла́дший are used only with animate nouns and collectives, and usually imply seniority and juniority: **мла́дший/ста́рший** сын 'younger/elder son', **мла́дший/ста́рший** класс 'junior/senior class', **мла́дший/ста́рший** лейтена́нт 'junior/senior lieutenant' etc. The context may be amplified to resolve possible ambiguity: ста́рший **по во́зрасту/по служе́бному положе́нию** 'older **in years**/senior **in rank**', мла́дший **по во́зрасту/по до́лжности** 'younger **in years**/junior **in position**'. For inanimate nouns, **бо́лее ста́рый** is used:

На эстра́де стоя́ло ста́рое пиани́но и лежа́ла ещё **бо́лее ста́рая** шта́нга (Kuleshov)
On the stage were an old piano and an even older lifting weight

(b) **Мла́дший** and **ста́рший** can also mean 'youngest' and 'eldest', **лу́чший** and **ху́дший** 'best' and 'worst' (see **185** (3) notes (a) and (b)).

(c) Some forms of **большо́й** 'big' and **бо́льший** 'bigger' are distinguished only by stress: **больша́я** часть 'a large part', **бо́льшая** часть 'the greater part' etc.

179   Predicative comparative forms in -ee

(1) The predicative comparative of most adjectives is formed by adding the ending **-ee** to the stem of the adjective:

краси́в-ее	(is, are) more beautiful
удо́бн-ее	(is, are) more comfortable

(2) Comparatives in **-ee** are invariable, that is, they are used as predicates to nouns of any gender and either number:

сад **краси́вее**	the garden is more beautiful
карти́на **краси́вее**	the picture is more beautiful
де́рево **краси́вее**	the tree is more beautiful

цветы́ **краси́вее**   the flowers are more beautiful

(3) Adjectives which have end-stressed **-á** in the feminine short form have end stress **-ée** in the comparative (see **164** (2)):

нове́е   (is, are) newer

сложне́е   (is, are) more complex

тяжеле́е   (is, are) heavier

Note
Здорове́е, (is, are) 'healthier', despite feminine short form здоро́ва.

(4) An alternative comparative form in **-ей** is confined mainly to conversational styles, verse and the more casual prose styles:

Клу́бы де́лают жизнь свои́х чле́нов **поле́зней** (*Sputnik*)
The clubs make the lives of their members more useful

(5) The following types of adjective either have *no* comparative short forms or have forms which are very rarely used:

(i) Adjectives which denote concepts which cannot be manifested to a greater or lesser degree, e.g. **босо́й** 'barefoot', **бра́тский** 'fraternal', **деревя́нный** 'wooden'.

(ii) Adjectives of colour.

(iii) Some others, e.g. **вне́шний** 'external', **го́рдый** 'proud'.

(6) Some adjectives with no short-form comparative (e.g. **драмати́ческий** 'dramatic') have synonyms which *do* have short forms (**драмати́чнее** 'is, are more dramatic', from драмати́чный).

(7) If an adjective *does* have a short-form comparative, the use of its long form in predicative meaning is regarded as 'bookish' (Э́та кни́га **бо́лее поле́зная** 'The book is more useful' (**поле́знее** is the preferred form)) and may distinguish high style (Показа́тели **бо́лее высо́кие** 'Indices are higher') from neutral style (Дом **вы́ше** 'The house is taller'. See **180**(1)).

180   Comparative short forms in -e

(1) The final consonants of some adjectives undergo mutation in the comparative short form (note, however, that in some adjectives with

suffix **-к-** it is the *preceding* consonant that mutates, e.g. гла́дкий: гла́же). The resultant comparatives end in a single unstressed **-е**:

в : вл	дешёвый	cheap	деше́вле	(is, are) cheaper

(However, но́вый 'new', comparative **нове́е** (is, are) 'newer'.)

г : ж	дорого́й	dear	доро́же	(is, are) dearer
	стро́гий	strict	стро́же	(is, are) stricter
	туго́й	tight	ту́же	(is, are) tighter
д : ж	гла́дкий	smooth	гла́же	(is, are) smoother
	молодо́й	young	моло́же	(is, are) younger
	ре́дкий	rare	ре́же	(is, are) rarer
	твёрдый	hard	твёрже	(is, are) harder

(However, худо́й 'thin', comparative **худе́е** 'is, are thinner'.)

Note
'Is, are younger' is also rendered as **мла́дше**, mainly in a family context: cf. Она́ **мла́дше/моло́же** сестры́ 'She is younger than her sister' and Она́ **моло́же** нача́льника 'She is younger than the boss'.

з : ж	бли́зкий	near	бли́же	(is, are) nearer
	ни́зкий	low	ни́же	(is, are) lower
	у́зкий	narrow	у́же	(is, are) narrower
к : ч	гро́мкий	loud	гро́мче	(is, are) louder
	жа́ркий	hot	жа́рче	(is, are) hotter
	кре́пкий	strong	кре́пче	(is, are) stronger
	лёгкий	light, easy	ле́гче	(is, are) lighter, easier
	ме́лкий	shallow	ме́льче	(is, are) shallower
	мя́гкий	soft	мя́гче	(is, are) softer
	ре́зкий	sharp	ре́зче	(is, are) sharper
с : ш	высо́кий	high	вы́ше	(is, are) higher
ск : щ	пло́ский	flat	пло́ще	(is, are) flatter
ст : щ	густо́й	thick	гу́ще	(is, are) thicker
	просто́й	simple	про́ще	(is, are) simpler
	то́лстый	thick	то́лще	(is, are) thicker
	ча́стый	frequent	ча́ще	(is, are) more frequent
	чи́стый	clean	чи́ще	(is, are) cleaner

т : ч	бога́тый	rich	бога́че	(is, are) richer
	коро́ткий	short	коро́че	(is, are) shorter
	круто́й	steep	кру́че	(is, are) steeper

(However, свято́й 'holy', comparative святе́е 'is, are holier'.)

| х : ш | сухо́й | dry | су́ше | (is, are) drier |
| | ти́хий | quiet | ти́ше | (is, are) quieter |

Note

(a)   Though го́рький 'bitter' has the short-form comparative **го́рче, бо́лее го́рький** (is, are) 'more bitter' is normally used in both attributive and predicative meanings.

(b)   Adjectives which have no short-form comparative or a little-used comparative also form the predicate with **бо́лее : ве́тхий** 'ancient', **го́рдый** 'proud', **зы́бкий** 'shaky', **ли́пкий** 'sticky', **ста́рый** 'old' (of objects) etc.

(2) Irregular short forms include a number which end in **-ше**:

большо́й	big	**бо́льше**	(is, are) bigger
до́лгий	long	**до́льше**	(is, are) longer
ма́ленький	small	**ме́ньше**	(is, are) smaller
ста́рый	old	**ста́рше**	(is, are) older
то́нкий	thin	**то́ньше**	(is, are) thinner
хоро́ший	good	**лу́чше**	(is, are) better

Объём това́рного хле́ба был на 40% **бо́льше**
The volume of marketable grain was 40 per cent greater

Note
Да́льше 'further' and **ра́ньше** 'earlier' are used only as adverbs.

(3) Other irregular short forms end in **-же, -ще, -е** :

глубо́кий	deep	**глу́бже**	(is, are) deeper
плохо́й	bad	**ху́же**	(is, are) worse
по́здний	late	**по́зже**	(is, are) later (also **поздне́е**)
сла́дкий	sweet	**сла́ще**	(is, are) sweeter
широ́кий	wide	**ши́ре**	(is, are) wider

Note
Unlike **поздне́е, по́зже** (here used as an adverb) also has an absolute meaning: Опера́цию ребя́та провели́ то́чно — ска́жет **по́зже** гла́вный геоло́г (*Komsomolskaya pravda*) '"The lads carried out the

operation precisely", the chief geologist was to say later' (i.e. afterwards).

181   The short-form comparative in predicative meaning

The short-form comparative's main function is predicative :

Его голос **громче**
His voice **is louder**

Моя машина была **новее**
My car **was newer**

Её воспоминания будут **интереснее**
Her reminiscences **will be more interesting**

Живые цветы стали ещё **свежее**
The live flowers **became fresher** still

182   Constructions with the comparative

(1) Than

'Than' is rendered in one of the following ways:

(i) By **чем,** preceded by a comma. Both items for comparison must be in the same case:

Я выше, **чем** он
I am taller than he is

У меня более светлые глаза, **чем** у вас
I have lighter eyes than you do

or:

(ii) By the genitive of comparison. This construction is possible only when the first item for comparison is in the *nominative* case:

Я выше **его**
I am taller than he is

Я старше **своей** сестры
I am older than my sister

Note
Only the **чем** construction is possible with attributive adjectives:

Это бо́лее краси́вый дом, **чем** наш
This is a more attractive house than ours

and when the second item for comparison has the form of a third-person possessive pronoun (его́, её, их)

Мой дом краси́вее, **чем** его́
My house is more beautiful than his

(2) Quantification of a difference

A difference is quantified in one of the following ways:

(i) By the preposition **на** + accusative case:

Он ста́рше меня́ **на три го́да**
He is three years older than me

(ii) (Less usually) with an instrumental:

Он **тремя́ года́ми** ста́рше меня́
He is three years older than me

(3) Expression of comparison through a multiple

Comparison may also be expressed through a multiple (constructions with **в** + accusative):

Он **в два ра́за (вдво́е)** ста́рше меня́
He is twice as old as I am

(4) The 'gradational' comparative

Constructions of the type 'the bigger the better' are rendered by **чем** . . ., **тем:**

Чем бо́льше, **тем** лу́чше
The bigger the better

Note
Тем лу́чше 'So much the better'.

(5) The expression of 'much' + comparative

'Much' in combination with a comparative is expressed by **намно́го, гора́здо, куда́** or **мно́го**:

> Его́ рабо́та **намно́го** лу́чше/**гора́здо** лу́чше, чем моя́
> His work is much better than mine

(6) As . . . as possible

'As . . . as possible' is rendered by **как мо́жно** + comparative:

> Купи́ буты́лку **как мо́жно бо́лее дешёвого** вина́
> Buy a bottle of the cheapest wine you can get

Note
This construction, however, is commoner with *adverbs* than with adjectives, in combination with which it can sound somewhat stilted (cf. also use of the *short* form in: Купи́ вина́ **подешёвле** 'Buy some cheaper wine'. See **183** (2).

(7) Repeated comparatives (e.g. 'smaller and smaller')

Repeated comparatives normally combine with **всё**:

> **Всё бли́же и бли́же** роково́й моме́нт (Makarov)
> The fateful moment gets nearer and nearer

Note
Unlike English, Russian may omit the second comparative: всё бли́же 'nearer and nearer'. However, the repetition of the comparative lends greater expressiveness. Cf. **всё бо́льшее** (и бо́льшее) призна́ние 'greater and greater recognition'.

183   The short-form comparative in attributive meaning

(1) In colloquial registers the short-form comparative is sometimes used attributively:

> У тебя́ нет челове́ка **бли́же** (Aksenov)
> There is no person closer to you

(2) This is particularly common with short forms prefixed **по-**:

> Покажи́те пла́тье **подешёвле**
> Show me a slightly cheaper dress

184   Other functions of the short-form comparative

(1) Short-form comparatives can function as introductory words:

Интере́снее говори́ть, чем слу́шать
It is more interesting to speak than to listen

(2) Many short-form comparatives also function as adverbs (see **398**):

Он е́дет **быстре́е**	He is driving faster
Она́ рабо́тает **бо́льше**	She works harder

Вожа́к всё **ни́же и ни́же** опуска́л го́лову к земле́ (Astafev)
The leader of the herd hung his head lower and lower to the ground

Note
In such cases the distinction between comparative adjective and comparative adverb is syntactic only, cf.: Э́та кни́га **интере́снее**, чем та 'This book is **more interesting** (adjective) than that one' and Э́та кни́га напи́сана **интере́снее**, чем та 'This book is written **in a more interesting way** (adverb) than that one'.

(3) Short-form comparatives are also used impersonally: **ве́тренее** 'it is windier', **прохла́днее** 'it is cooler', **светле́е** 'it is lighter', **темне́е** 'it is darker', **тепле́е** 'it is warmer', **холодне́е** 'it is colder'.

Note
Adverbs of the type **бо́лее внима́тельно** 'more attentively' (for standard внима́тельнее) are rarely used.

The Superlative Degree of the Adjective

185   The superlative degree with са́мый

(1) The superlative degree is formed by combining **са́мый** with the positive adjective:

са́мый краси́вый дом	the most beautiful house
са́мая краси́вая маши́на	the most beautiful car
са́мое краси́вое зда́ние	the most beautiful building
са́мые краси́вые де́ти	the most beautiful children

(2) **Са́мый** agrees with the adjective and noun in gender, number and case:

Он провёл пять лет в одно́м из **са́мых краси́вых европе́йских** городо́в
He spent five years in one of the most beautiful European cities

Она́ живёт в **са́мом большо́м** до́ме на на́шей у́лице
She lives in the largest house in our street

(3) **Са́мый** also combines with the comparatives лу́чший and ху́дший:

са́мые лу́чшие пожела́ния
the very best wishes

са́мое ху́дшее, что мо́жно себе́ предста́вить
the worst thing one can imagine

Note
(a) **Лу́чший** and **ху́дший** (see **178** note (b)) also function as superlatives in their own right: **лу́чшая** из же́нщин 'the best of women'; в **ху́дшем** слу́чае 'in the worst case, if the worst comes to the worst'.
(b) **Ста́рший** and **мла́дший** may also function as comparatives or superlatives: **ста́рший** брат 'elder/eldest brother', **мла́дшая** сестра́ 'younger/youngest sister'. Outside the family or other hierarchy, however, 'youngest' and 'oldest' are rendered as **са́мый ста́рый, са́мый молодо́й:**

Ма́слов — кста́ти, **са́мый молодо́й** из полковы́х нача́льников (Bogomolov)
Maslov, incidentally, is the youngest of the regimental commanders
(cf. са́мый **мла́дший** 'the most **junior**')

(c) The phrases **са́мое бо́льшее** 'at most', **са́мое ме́ньшее** 'at the very least': **са́мое бо́льшее** 30 челове́к '30 people at most'.

(4) Superlatives with **са́мый** may also express an extreme manifestation of the quality denoted by the adjective:

Са́мые широ́кие круги́ учёных
The very widest circles of scientists

186　Вы́сший and ни́зший

Вы́сший and **ни́зший** are used mainly in technical and set expressions: **вы́сший/ни́зший балл** 'top/bottom mark', **вы́сший/ни́зший сорт** 'superior/inferior brand', **вы́сшая матема́тика** 'higher mathematics', **вы́сшее учéбное заведéние** 'higher teaching establishment', **в вы́сшей стéпени** 'to the highest degree'.

Note
'Highest' and 'lowest' in the literal sense are rendered as **са́мый высóкий/ни́зкий: са́мый высóкий/ни́зкий** потолóк 'the highest/lowest ceiling'.

187　The superlative in -ейший and -айший

(1) Superlatives in **-ейший** are formed from a limited range of adjectives, mainly with monosyllabic roots: **важнéйший** 'most important', **крупнéйший** 'largest, very large', **малéйший** 'slightest', **новéйший** 'latest, most recent', **сильнéйший** 'strongest', **сложнéйший** 'most complex':

Нет ни **малéйшего** сомнéния
There is not the slightest doubt

Новéйшие достижéния наýки
The latest achievements of science

Чистéйший вздор
The most arrant nonsense

(2) However, a number of superlatives derive from roots of more than one syllable: **вы́годнейший** 'most favourable', **интерéснейший** 'most interesting' etc.

(3) The ending **-айший** is affixed to stems ending in a velar consonant, following mutation of **г** to **ж** (**строжа́йший** from стрóгий 'strict', **дража́йший** from дорогóй 'dear'), **к** to **ч** (**высоча́йший** from высóкий 'high', **кратча́йший** from крáткий 'short', **легча́йший** from лёгкий 'light', **мельча́йший** from мéлкий 'small', **редча́йший** from рéдкий 'rare') and **х** to **ш** (**тиша́йший** from ти́хий 'quiet'). Note also **ближа́йший** 'nearest' from бли́зкий 'near'.

(4) Most superlatives in **-ейший** and **-айший** express an extreme manifestation of the quality denoted by the adjective:

Вернейшее срéдство
A **most reliable** remedy

С пóмощью лáзеров провóдятся **тончáйшие** оперáции (*Russia Today*)
The **most delicate** of operations are carried out with the help of lasers

(5) However, forms in **-ейший** and **-айший** may also be true superlatives:

Ближáйшая останóвка
The nearest stop

Величáйший поэ́т
The greatest poet (or 'A very great poet')

Кратчáйшее расстоя́ние
The shortest distance

Note
Дальнéйший 'further' has comparative, not superlative, meaning.

(6) Forms in **-ейший/-айший** are often characteristic of high style: cf. **глубочáйшие** мы́сли 'the most profound thoughts' and **сáмые глубóкие** сквáжины 'the deepest bore-holes' (neutral style).

188   The superlative with наибóлее

The superlative with **наибóлее** is characteristic of a 'bookish' style. **Наибóлее** is indeclinable and combines mainly with adjectives with roots of more than one syllable (**наибóлее вероя́тный** исхóд 'the most likely outcome', **наибóлее влия́тельный** человéк 'the most influential person', **наибóлее желáтельный** результáт 'the most desirable result') and with a number of adjectives with monosyllabic roots (**наибóлее тóчный** 'the most accurate' etc.).

Note also **наимéнее** 'the least': **наимéнее тóчный** мéтод 'the least accurate method'.

189   Other superlatives

(1) Other superlatives include **наибóльший** 'the greatest', **наивы́сший** 'the highest', **наилу́чший** 'the very best', **наимéньший**

'the smallest'. These forms are characteristic of newspaper style: **наибо́льшая** вы́года 'the greatest benefit', **наилу́чшее** реше́ние 'the best solution', **наиме́ньший** риск 'the smallest risk'.

(2) The prefix пре- is used to form colloquial superlatives of the type **преспоко́йный** 'as cool as a cucumber'.

The Numeral

Cardinal, Collective and Indefinite Numerals

190   The cardinal numeral

The cardinal numerals are as follows:

0	ноль/нуль		
1	оди́н, одна́, одно́; одни́	50	пятьдеся́т
2	два/две	60	шестьдеся́т
3	три	70	се́мьдесят
4	четы́ре	80	во́семьдесят
5	пять	90	девяно́сто
6	шесть	100	сто
7	семь	200	две́сти
8	во́семь	300	три́ста
9	де́вять	400	четы́реста
10	де́сять	500	пятьсо́т
11	оди́ннадцать	600	шестьсо́т
12	двена́дцать	700	семьсо́т
13	трина́дцать	800	восемьсо́т
14	четы́рнадцать	900	девятьсо́т
15	пятна́дцать	1,000	ты́сяча
16	шестна́дцать	2,000	две ты́сячи
17	семна́дцать	5,000	пять ты́сяч
18	восемна́дцать	1,000,000	миллио́н
19	девятна́дцать	2,000,000	два миллио́на

20	два́дцать	5,000,000	пять миллио́нов
30	три́дцать	1,000,000,000	миллиа́рд/биллио́н
40	со́рок	1,000,000,000,000	триллио́н

Note

(a) Each of the numerals 5–20 and 30 ends in a soft sign. The construction of the numerals 11–19 is based on the model **оди́н-на-дцать** 'eleven' (lit. one-on-ten) etc., that of 20 and 30 on the model **два́-дцать** and **три́-дцать** (lit. two tens and three tens), -**дцать** being a contraction of **де́сять** 'ten'. Of the numerals 11–19, only **оди́ннадцать** 'eleven' and **четы́рнадцать** 'fourteen' are *not* stressed on the penultimate **a**.

(b) **Пятьдеся́т** and **шестьдеся́т** have end stress, **се́мьдесят** and **во́семьдесят** initial stress. All four numerals have a soft sign in the middle, but not at the end.

(c) 300–900 subdivide formally into **три́ста** 'three hundred', **четы́реста** 'four hundred' (**три, четы́ре** + gen. sing. of **сто**) and **пятьсо́т** 'five hundred' through to **девятьсо́т** 'nine hundred' (**пять** etc. + gen. pl. of **сто**). The form **две́сти** 'two hundred' is a residue of the dual number.

(d) Compound numerals are formed by placing simple numerals in sequence: **два́дцать четы́ре** 'twenty-four', **шестьсо́т пятьдеся́т два** 'six hundred and fifty-two', **со́рок четы́ре ты́сячи семьсо́т девяно́сто оди́н** 'forty-four thousand seven hundred and ninety-one' etc.

(e) The inversion of numeral and dependent noun indicates approximation: **лет пять** 'about five years'. Prepositions are placed between inverted noun and numeral: **лет через пять** 'in about five years' time'.

191   Declension of cardinal numerals

The cardinal numerals decline as follows.

(1) Ноль/нуль 'nought, zero, nil'

Ноль/нуль declines like a masculine soft-sign noun with end stress in declension (see **57** (2) (ii)).

(2) Оди́н/одна́/одно́/одни́ 'one'

Один/одна́/одно́/одни́ decline like э́тот but with stressed endings, cf. **125:**

	Masculine	Feminine	Neuter	Plural
Nom.	оди́н	одн-а́	одн-о́	одн-и́
Acc.	оди́н/одн-ого́	одн-у́	одн-о́	одн-и́/одн-и́х
Gen.	одн-ого́	одн-о́й	одн-ого́	одн-и́х
Dat.	одн-ому́	одн-о́й	одн-ому́	одн-и́м
Instr.	одн-и́м	одн-о́й/-о́ю	одн-и́м	одн-и́ми
Prep.	об одн-о́м	об одн-о́й	об одн-о́м	об одн-и́х

(3) Полтора́ (m. and n.)/полторы́ (f.) 'one and a half'

There is only one oblique case form: **полу́тора**, the genitive, dative, instrumental and prepositional of полтора́ *and* полторы́.

(4) Два (m. and n.)/две (f.) 'two', три 'three', четы́ре 'four'

Nom.	дв-а/дв-е	тр-и	четы́р-е
Acc.	дв-а, дв-е/дв-ух	тр-и/тр-ёх	четы́р-е/четыр-ёх
Gen.	дв-ух	тр-ёх	четыр-ёх
Dat.	дв-ум	тр-ём	четыр-ём
Instr.	дв-умя́	тр-емя́	четырь-мя́
Prep.	о дв-ух	о тр-ёх	о четыр-ёх

(5) О́ба (m. and n.)/о́бе (f.) 'both'

Nom.	о́б-а	о́б-е
Acc.	о́б-а/обо́-их	о́б-е/обе́-их
Gen.	обо́-их	обе́-их
Dat.	обо́-им	обе́-им
Instr.	обо́-ими	обе́-ими
Prep.	об обо́-их	об обе́-их

Note the phrase де́ти **обо́его** по́ла 'children of both sexes'.

(6) Пять 'five' (declension of numerals ending in a soft sign)

Nom./Acc.	пять	шесть	семь
Gen./Dat.	пят-и́	шест-и́	сем-и́
Instr.	пять-ю́	шесть-ю́	семь-ю́
Prep.	о пят-и́	о шест-и́	о сем-и́
Nom./Acc.	во́семь	два́дцать	
Gen./Dat.	восьм-и́	двадцат-и́	

Instr.	восьм-**ю́**/восемь-**ю́**	двадцать-**ю́**
Prep.	о восьм-**и́**	о двадцат-**и́**

Note

(a) 5–20 and 30 decline like soft-sign feminine nouns, 5–10, 20 and 30 with end stress in declension, 11–19 with medial stress in declension.

(b) Instrumental восьмью́ is characteristic of colloquial styles, восемью́ of written styles.

(7) 50–80

Each of the numerals 50–80 declines like *two* feminine soft-sign nouns. The stress in oblique cases falls on the second syllable:

Nom./Acc.	пятьдеся́т	шестьдеся́т
Gen./Dat.	пяти́десят-**и**	шести́десят-**и**
Instr.	пятью́десять-**ю**	шестью́десять-**ю**
Prep.	о пяти́десят-**и**	о шести́десят-**и**

Nom./Acc.	се́мьдесят	во́семьдесят
Gen./Dat.	семи́десят-**и**	восьми́десят-**и**
Instr.	семью́десять-**ю**	восьмью́десять-**ю**
Prep.	о семи́десят-**и**	о восьми́десят-**и**

(8) Со́рок 'forty', девяно́сто 'ninety', сто 'hundred'

Each of these numerals has one oblique case ending only: -**a**.

Nom./Acc.	со́рок	девяно́ст-**о**	ст-**о**
Gen./Dat./Instr.	сорок-**а́**	девяно́ст-**а**	ст-**а**
Prep.	о сорок-**а́**	о девяно́ст-**а**	о ст-**а**

(9) 200–900

Nom.	две́ст-и	три́ст-**а**	пятьсо́т
Acc.	две́ст-и	три́ст-**а**	пятьсо́т
Gen.	двухсо́т	трёхсо́т	пятисо́т
Dat.	двумст-**а́м**	трёмст-**а́м**	пятист-**а́м**
Instr.	двумя́ст-**а́ми**	тремя́ст-**а́ми**	пятьюст-**а́ми**
Prep.	о двухст-**а́х**	о трёхст-**а́х**	о пятист-**а́х**

(10) **Ты́сяча** 'thousand', **миллио́н** 'million', **миллиа́рд** 'thousand million', **биллио́н** 'billion', **триллио́н** 'trillion'.

Ты́сяча 'thousand' declines like second-declension да́ча 'country cottage', **миллио́н, миллиа́рд, биллио́н** and **триллио́н** like hard-ending masculine nouns of the first declension. However, **ты́сяча** has two forms of the instrumental: **ты́сячью** and **ты́сячей** (see **197** note (a)). The numerals also appear in multiples: две ты́сячи 'two thousand', пять ты́сяч 'five thousand', две́сти пятьдеся́т одна́ ты́сяча '251,000', четы́ре миллио́на 'four million', шестьдеся́т миллио́нов 'sixty million', два́дцать два миллиа́рда 'twenty-two thousand million' and so on.

For declension of compound numerals see **198**.

192 Ноль/нуль. Meanings and usage

(1) **Ноль/нуль** 'nought, zero, nil' governs the genitive case of singular and plural nouns.

(2) The two forms are often stylistically and phraseologically differentiated. Thus:

(i) **Нуль** tends to be used in mathematics, in technical terminology and in indicating temperature:

нуль гра́дусов Це́льсия	zero degrees Celsius
ни́же **нуля́**	below zero

(ii) **Ноль** is used:

(a) In colloquial contexts:

Игра́ ко́нчилась со счётом 5:0 (пять:**ноль**)
The game ended 5:0

Её телефо́н: 231-00-45 (две́сти три́дцать оди́н **ноль ноль** со́рок пять)
Her telephone number is 231 00 45

(Also, in colloquial contexts, ноль **гра́дусов** 'zero degrees'.)

(b) In decimals (see **205** (1)).

(c) In giving precise indications of the time:

шесть **ноль-ноль**
six hundred hours (six o'clock precisely)

(iii) Either numeral may be used to indicate the figure 0, though **нуль** is preferred in technical registers.

(iv) **Нуль** is used in the phrases начинáть с **нуля́** 'to start from scratch' and сводúться к **нулю́** 'to come to nothing', **ноль** in **ноль внимáния** 'no attention whatsoever'. Either is possible in стрúжка под **ноль/нуль** 'a close haircut'.

193   The numeral одúн, однá, однó, однú

(1) The numeral 1 agrees with the noun in gender, number and case:

одúн стол 'one table'   **однó** окнó 'one window'
однá кáрта 'one map'   **однú** часы́ 'one clock'

Он пóднял штáнгу **однóй** рукóй
He lifted the weight with one hand

Note
(a)   The numeral is omitted in some time expressions: час дня 'one o'clock in the afternoon'.
(b)   In counting, **раз** usually replaces **одúн**: Раз . . . два . . . три . . . 'One . . . two . . . three . . .'.
(c)   The animate accusative/genitive rule applies: Вúжу **одногó** мáльчика 'I see one boy'.

(2) The agreement of compound numerals ending in **одúн**, **однá**, **однó** is as follows:

(i) They take a singular noun: сóрок одúн **стул** 'forty-one **chairs**', cf.:

Был день её рождéния, и я принёс **двáдцать однý свечý** (Gagarin)
It was her birthday and I brought twenty-one candles

(ii) They take a singular predicate:

В э́том годý **был задéржан вóсемьдесят одúн нарушúтель** прáвил пожáрной безопáсности в лесý (*Russia Today*)
This year eighty-one people have been arrested for breaches of forest fire safety precautions

В прóшлом годý **погúб 271 человéк** (*Nedelya*)
271 people died last year

21 депутáт **голосовáл** за предложéние
21 delegates voted for the proposal

(iii) Long adjectives and participles also appear in the singular:

Всего́ у Чо́сера два́дцать **оди́н расска́з, изло́женный** просты́м языко́м (Propp)
Chaucer has twenty-one tales in all, told in simple language

(iv) However, *relative pronouns* normally appear in the plural:

Два́дцать оди́н ма́льчик, **кото́рые** бежа́ли по у́лице
Twenty-one boys who were running down the street

(3) The plural form **одни́** is used with plural-only nouns (see **49**): **одни́** са́нки 'one sledge', **одни́** носи́лки 'one stretcher' (also **два́дцать одни́** са́нки, носи́лки 'twenty-one sledges, stretchers').

Note
Compare also the colloquial **одни́** сли́вки 'one cream' (= one portion, packet of cream), heard in shops and buffets.

(4) Other meanings of **оди́н, одна́, одно́, одни́** include:

(i) 'Alone, by oneself': Она́ **одна́** 'She is all by herself', Ему́ ску́чно **одному́** 'He is bored by himself'.

Note
Compare the use of the nominative in Я был **оди́н** 'I was alone' and the use of the instrumental in Я был **одни́м** из его́ друзе́й 'I was one of his friends'.

(ii) 'Only, nothing but': Я **оди́н (одна́)** зна́ю 'Only I know/I alone know':

— Наве́рное, о́стров. Тут **одни́** острова́ (Gagarin)
'It's probably an island. There are nothing but islands here'

(iii) 'A', 'a certain', 'some': У меня́ есть **оди́н** знако́мый, кото́рый роди́лся в Росси́и 'I have a friend who was born in Russia', **Одни́** мои́ знако́мые неда́вно перее́хали в друго́й го́род 'Some of my friends recently moved to another town'.

(iv) 'The same': Мы учи́лись в **одно́й** шко́ле 'We went to the same school'.

(v) **Одни́** . . . **други́е** . . . **тре́тьи** render 'some . . . others . . . others still': **Одни́** молча́т, **други́е** красне́ют, **тре́тьи** возмуща́ются 'Some are silent, others blush, others still get indignant'.

Note

In some cases, potential ambiguity can be resolved only by context: Здесь растёт **одна** ель 'One fir-tree grows here' or 'Only fir-trees grow here'.

See also **143** (2).

194   Полтора́/полторы́; два/две, три, четы́ре; о́ба/о́бе

The numerals **полтора́/полторы́; два/две, три, четы́ре; о́ба/о́бе** take the genitive singular of the noun, when the numerals themselves are in the nominative or inanimate accusative (for usage after *declined* forms of these numerals, see **196**).

(1) **Полтора́** (m. and n.)/**полторы́** (f.) 'one and a half':

полтора́ **часа́**	an hour and a half
полторы́ **мину́ты**	a minute and a half

(i) Other numerals which include a half are expressed as follows: два **с полови́ной** часа́ 'two and a half hours', пять **с полови́ной** часо́в 'five and a half hours' etc.

(ii) Полтора́- also appears in the compound numeral **полтора́ста** '150' (oblique case полу́тораста).

(2) **Два** (m. and n.)/**две** (f.) 'two', **три** 'three', **четы́ре** 'four' (nom. and inan. acc.):

два **ма́льчика**	'two boys'	три **сту́ла**	'three chairs'
два **окна́**	'two windows'	четы́ре **страны́**	'four countries'
две **го́ры**	'two mountains'		

(i) **Ряд** 'row', **час** 'hour', **шаг** 'step', **шар** 'sphere, globe' have *end* stress in the genitive singular after два, три, четы́ре: два **часа́** 'two o'clock', два **шара́** 'two globes', три **ряда́** 'three rows', четы́ре **шага́** 'four steps' (cf. *stem* stress with other forms: о́коло **ча́са** 'about an hour').

(ii) The accusative plural of the noun is used as an alternative to the genitive singular in certain set expressions: отпусти́ть на все четы́ре **сто́роны/сто́роны** 'to give complete freedom of movement'.

(iii) Nouns governed by the numerals **два/две, три, четы́ре** appear in the genitive *plural* if the noun *precedes* the numeral and is linked to it by a form of the verb 'to be' or other copula: **Стака́нов** бы́ло то́лько два (Rasputin) 'There were only two glasses'. Compare usage with 1: **Больни́ц** в го́роде **две**, а **школ** то́лько **одна́** 'There are two hospitals in the town, and only one school'.

(iv) Compound numerals ending in **два/две, три, четы́ре** also take the genitive singular of the noun when the numerals themselves are in the nominative or inanimate accusative case:

со́рок два **дня**	forty-two days
пятьдеся́т две **мину́ты**	fifty-two minutes
сто три **окна́**	one hundred and three windows
девяно́сто четы́ре **челове́ка**	ninety-four people

(v) **Два/две, три, четы́ре** take the *genitive plural* of an adjective qualifying a masculine or neuter noun and the *nominative* plural of an adjective qualifying a feminine noun:

два **больши́х** стака́на/окна́	two large glasses/windows
три **бе́дные** де́вушки	three poor girls

Note

(a) A *genitive* plural adjective is preferred with a feminine noun after 2–4 when there is a stress difference between the genitive singular and nominative plural of the noun (три **высо́ких** горы́ 'three high mountains' (cf. nom. pl. **го́ры**)), when a distributive phrase is governed by the preposition **по** (по три **спе́лых** гру́ши 'three ripe pears each') and in fractions and decimals (see **205** (1)).

(b) Pre-positive adjectives appear in the *nominative* plural: **ка́ждые** три мину́ты 'every three minutes', **после́дние** два дня 'the last two days'. See, however, **157** (3).

(c) Adjectival nouns behave like adjectives after 2–4: два **учёных** 'two scientists', три **гости́ные** 'three living-rooms', четы́ре **живо́тных** 'four animals'. See **158**.

(3) **О́ба** (m. and n.)/**о́бе** (f.) 'both':

(i) **о́ба/о́бе** behave like **два/две** 'two', taking a genitive singular noun and a plural adjective:

о́ба **кру́глых** стола́/окна́	both round tables/windows
о́бе **кру́глые** таре́лки	both round plates

(ii) **о́ба** may also denote a male-female pair: И ста́ли оии́ о́ба смотре́ть дру́г на дру́га . . . Не вы́держала она́ его́ взгля́да (Shcherbakov) 'And they both began looking at each other, . . . she could not withstand his gaze'.

Note

(a) Accusative plural сто́роны is possible as an alternative to genitive singular стороны́ in the phrase в о́бе стороны́/сто́роны: переводи́ть в о́бе стороны́/сто́роны 'to translate both ways'.

(b) Два ряда́ 'two rows' but о́ба ря́да 'both rows'.

---

195   Numerals five and above

The nominative and accusative of the numerals 5-999 take the *genitive plural* of the adjective and noun:

пять **ме́сяцев**	five months
во́семь **часо́в**	eight o'clock, eight hours
пятна́дцать **мину́т**	fifteen minutes
два́дцать **ва́жных пи́сем**	twenty important letters
со́рок пять **дней**	forty-five days
се́мьдесят **школ**	seventy schools
сто семь **грамм/гра́ммов**	one hundred and seven grams
три́ста **просто́рных ко́мнат**	three hundred spacious rooms

Note

(a) See **193** (2) (i) and **194** (2) (iv) for usage after compound numerals ending in 1–4.

(b) 5–999 take the genitive plural **челове́к**, not люде́й: семь **челове́к** 'seven people' (if the noun is qualified by an adjective, however, **люде́й** is preferred: пять незнако́мых **люде́й** (or **лиц** or **челове́к**) 'five unknown people'). Cf. also dat. пяти́ **челове́кам** 'to five people', instr. с пятью́ **челове́ками** 'with five people', etc.

---

196   Agreement of oblique cases of numerals полтора́/полторы́ to 999 with oblique plural forms of nouns

(1) Declined numerals from 1½ to 999 combine with nouns and adjectives in the same case of the *plural*:

(i) Genitive

о̀коло **полу́тора часо́в**	about an hour and a half
бо́льше **трёх дней**	more than three days

В тече́ние **двух–трёх ме́сяцев** по̀сле э́того Лу́жина зва́ли Анто́-шей (Nabokov)

For two or three months after this they called Luzhin Antosha

(ii) Dative

Она́ у́чит **трём языка́м**

She teaches three languages

Он обрати́лся к **четырёмста́м но́вым избира́телям**

He addressed four hundred new voters

(iii) Instrumental

Куда́ она́ могла́ де́ться с **четырьмя́ детьми́**? (Rybakov)

Where could she have got to with four children?

Он обеща́л ограни́читься **десятью́ сигаре́тами** в день (Avdeen-ko)

He promised to limit himself to ten cigarettes a day

(iv) Prepositional

В **двух шага́х** от ка́мня стоя́л челове́к (Gagarin)

At two paces from the stone stood a man

в **пяти́десяти ю́жных города́х**

in fifty southern towns

(2) The **animate accusative/genitive rule** (see **47**) applies to the numerals 2–4 and to 'both', the numeral appearing in the genitive (**двух, трёх, четырёх; обо́их/обе́их**), adjectives and nouns in the genitive *plural*:

Она́ приняла́ на ку́рсы **трёх молоды́х студе́нтов**

She accepted three young students on to the course

Она́ пригласи́ла **четырёх медсестёр**

She invited four nurses

Она́ лю́бит **обо́их бра́тьев** и **обе́их сестёр**

She loves both her brothers and both her sisters

Note

(a)   The animate accusative/genitive rule does *not* apply to *compound* numerals ending in **два/две, три** or **четы́ре**: Она́ приняла́ на курсы **два́дцать три студе́нта** 'She accepted twenty-three students on to the course'.

(b) Application of the animate accusative/genitive rule varies where animals, birds, quasi-animates etc. are concerned: Он пойма́л **двух пти́чек** (or **две пти́чки**) 'He caught two small birds', Он принёс **двух ку́кол** (or **две ку́клы**) 'He brought two dolls' (cf. alternative accusative forms of существо́ 'being': **двух суще́ств** or **два существа́**).

(c) The animate accusative/genitive rule does *not* apply to the numerals 5–999: я встре́тил **пять/со́рок/сто** моряко́в 'I met five/forty/a hundred sailors'.

197 Ты́сяча 'thousand', миллио́н 'million', миллиа́рд 'a thousand million', биллио́н 'billion', триллио́н 'trillion'

Ты́сяча (pronounced ты́ща in colloquial speech), **миллио́н** and **миллиа́рд** etc. take the *genitive plural* of the noun, regardless of their own case (see, however, note (a) below):

ты́сяча **рубле́й**
a thousand roubles

с **тремя́ ты́сячами рубле́й**
with three thousand roubles

забо́титься о **миллио́нах дете́й**
to care for millions of children

Ассигнова́ния равня́ются **семи́ миллиа́рдам до́лларов**
Subsidies amount to seven thousand million dollars

Note

(a) In its capacity as a noun of quantity, **ты́сяча** has instrumental **ты́сячей** + genitive plural (с ты́сячей **друзе́й** 'with a thousand friends'), while in its capacity as a numeral it has instrumental **ты́сячью** + instrumental plural: с **ты́сячью рабо́чими** 'with a thousand workers'. **Ты́сячей** is regarded as the more literary form, **ты́сячью** as the more colloquial. While **ты́сячей** is the preferred instrumental in its function as a noun of quantity, **ты́сячью** is making inroads in this area also. In combination with одно́й, however, **ты́сячей** is always used: с одно́й **ты́сячей** солда́т 'with one thousand soldiers'.

(b) Ты́сяча, миллио́н, миллиа́рд take genitive plural **челове́к**: ты́сяча **челове́к** 'a thousand people'. However, **люде́й** is preferred when qualified by an adjective (ты́сяча **че́стных** люде́й 'a thousand honest people') and with **ты́сячи** 'thousands' (ты́сячи люде́й 'thousands of people') (emphasizing mass rather than precise quantity).

(c)   **Ты́сяча** may be written in figures as '1.000', '1000', or '1 000' (commas are reserved for decimals, see **205** (1)).

(d)   **Ты́сяча** observes feminine singular agreement: Пятьдеся́т одна́ ты́сяча из них **больна́** наркома́нией (*Izvestiya*) 'Fifty-one thousand of them are addicted to drugs'.

198   Declension of compound numerals

(1) In **written** Russian, all parts of a compound numeral are declined, the noun agreeing with the final element of the compound:

К трёмста́м тридцати́ шести́ часа́м приба́вить ещё сто шестьдеся́т четы́ре (Koluntsev)
Add another one hundred and sixty-four hours **to three hundred and thirty-six**

(2) In colloquial speech, however, it is common to decline either:

(i) the **final elements** of the numeral only:

представи́тели **пятьдеся́т одно́й** страны́
representatives of **fifty-one countries** (cf. written norm пяти́десяти одно́й страны́)

с четы́реста **пятью́десятью двумя́ рубля́ми**
with four hundred and fifty-two roubles (cf. written norm с четырьмя́ста́ми . . .)

с шестьсо́т се́мьдесят **семью́ иллюстра́циями**
with six hundred and seventy-seven illustrations (cf. written norm с шестьюста́ми семью́десятью . . .)

or:

(ii) the **first and final** elements only:

с **пятью́ ты́сячами** пятьсо́т се́мьдесят **четырьмя́ рубля́ми**
with five thousand five hundred and seventy-four roubles (cf. written norm с пятью́ ты́сячами пятьюста́ми семью́десятью четырьмя́ рубля́ми)

199   Cardinals as numerical 'labels'

(1) Cardinal numerals are widely used as indeclinable numerical 'labels' in addresses, both with но́мер 'number':

в кварти́ре но́мер **два́дцать семь**
in flat number 27

and without но́мер

Мичу́рина, **два́дцать семь**, кварти́ра **восемна́дцать** (Shukshin)
Flat 18, 27 Michurin Street

Она́ занима́ется у подру́ги в до́ме **четы́рнадцать** (Trifonov)
She is studying at her friend's house at number 14

(2) Cardinal numerals are also used with series of air/spacecraft (Салю́т-4 (**четы́ре**) 'Salyut-4', ТУ-104 (**сто четы́ре**) 'TU-104', ИЛ-62 (**шестьдеся́т два**) 'IL-62'), with the names of major international events, where the cardinal numeral denotes the year of occurrence (Олимпиа́да-88 (**во́семьдесят во́семь**) 'the 1988 Olympics'), with the names of airports (Шереме́тьево-**оди́н** 'Sheremetevo-1'), flight numbers (рейс **сто три́дцать семь** 'flight number 137'), ticket numbers (**два́дцать четы́ре ты́сячи сто се́мьдесят** (ticket number) '24170') and receipt numbers (**семна́дцать два́дцать пять** '1725'). Telephone numbers are read in one group of three digits and two groups of two: **сто пятьдеся́т во́семь двена́дцать ноль четы́ре** (158-12-04).

Note
In other contexts (e.g. the numbers of trains, carriages, seats) the more colloquial **ordinal** is the norm: **восьмо́й** ваго́н 'carriage number 8', три́дцать **пя́тое** ме́сто 'seat number 35', се́мьдесят **второ́й** по́езд 'train number 72'. Compare двадца́тый ряд, середи́на 'row 20, centre', в **пя́той** пала́те 'in ward 5' (rooms are numbered with cardinals or ordinals: ко́мната **пя́тая/пять** 'room 5').

(3) Numerals may be left undeclined in measuring speed: е́хать со ско́ростью **три́дцать** км/ч (киломе́тров в час) 'to travel at a speed of thirty kilometres per hour' (or **тридцати́ киломе́тров в час** or **в три́дцать киломе́тров в час**).

200   Collective numerals

(1) The collective numerals:

(i) Constitute a series from 2 to 10: **двóе** 'two', **трóе** 'three', **чéтверо** 'four', **пя́теро** 'five', **шéстеро** 'six', **сéмеро** 'seven', **вóсьмеро** 'eight', **дéвятеро** 'nine', **дéсятеро** 'ten'. Collectives above **сéмеро** 'seven' are little used now. The collectives decline as follows (**сéмеро, вóсьмеро, дéвятеро, дéсятеро** decline like **шéстеро**):

Nom.	двó-е	трó-е	чéтвер-о
Acc.	двó-е/-и́х	трó-е/-и́х	чéтвер-о/-ы́х
Gen.	дво-и́х	тро-и́х	четвер-ы́х
Dat.	дво-и́м	тро-и́м	четвер-ы́м
Instr.	дво-и́ми	тро-и́ми	четвер-ы́ми
Prep.	о дво-и́х	о тро-и́х	о четвер-ы́х

Nom.	пя́тер-о	шéстер-о
Acc.	пя́тер-о/-ы́х	шéстер-о/-ы́х
Gen.	пятер-ы́х	шестер-ы́х
Dat.	пятер-ы́м	шестер-ы́м
Instr.	пятер-ы́ми	шестер-ы́ми
Prep.	о пятер-ы́х	о шестер-ы́х

(ii) They take the genitive plural of adjectives and nouns when they themselves are in the nominative/inanimate accusative.

(2) Collective numerals are used in four main constructions:

(i) With nouns used only in the plural (see **49**). This applies especially to **двóе** 'two', **трóе** 'three' and **чéтверо** 'four', which, unlike the cardinal numerals **два, три, четы́ре,** govern genitive *plural* forms:

двóе **часóв**	two clocks
трóе **носи́лок**	three stretchers
трóе **похорóн**	three funerals

Через чéтверо **сýток** пóезд бýдет в Москвé (Trifonov)
In four days' time the train will be in Moscow

Above four, collective numerals are the norm with plural-only nouns:

пя́теро санéй	five sledges
шéстеро ворóт	six gates

and cardinals a colloquial variant (пять санéй etc.)

Note

(a)   The collectives can be used with 'paired' objects (e.g. дво́е **лыж** 'two pairs of skis', тро́е **но́жниц** 'three pairs of scissors'), but constructions with **па́ра** 'pair' are preferred: **три па́ры** но́жниц etc.

(b)   Compare also the colloquial **дво́е** сли́вок 'two creams' (= portions, packets of cream), heard in shops and buffets, **дво́е** щей 'two cabbage soups', **тро́е духо́в** 'three types *or* bottles of perfume' etc.

(c)   Collectives cannot appear in compound numerals. Thus, **день,** not **су́тки**, is used in rendering '22 days' (**два́дцать два дня**). Paraphrases with **шту́ка** 'item', **коли́чество** 'quantity' and **па́ра** 'pair' are also found: Про́дано пятьсо́т со́рок три **шту́ки** са́нок or Про́даны са́нки **в коли́честве** пятисо́т сорока́ трёх 'Five hundred and forty-three sledges have been sold', со́рок три **па́ры** сане́й/часо́в '43 sledges/clocks'.

(d)   *Cardinal* numerals, *not* collectives, are used with the *oblique cases* of plural-only nouns: на **четырёх** (not *четверы́х) са́нках 'on four sledges'.

(ii) The collectives can be used with *animate masculine nouns*: дво́е друзе́й (= два дру́га) 'two friends', тро́е ма́льчиков (= три ма́льчика) 'three boys'. As with animate forms in general (see below), the use of the collective numeral emphasizes the cohesiveness of the group, by contrast with the individualizing nature of the cardinals. Usage is particularly common:

(a) With nouns in -а/-я (e.g. мужчи́на, судья́, ю́ноша) (**пя́теро мужчи́н** 'five men', **тро́е суде́й** 'three judges', **дво́е ю́ношей** 'two youths'), including nouns of common gender (**дво́е сиро́т** 'two orphans' (две сироты́ is preferred, however, if both orphans are female)).

(b) With **лю́ди** 'people' and **лицо́** 'person': **тро́е люде́й** 'three people', **пя́теро незнако́мых лиц** 'five strangers'.

(c) With adjectival nouns: **дво́е прохо́жих** 'two passers-by', **тро́е больны́х** 'three patients', **че́тверо знако́мых** 'four acquaintances', **се́меро отдыха́ющих** 'seven holiday-makers'.

Note that either cardinals *or* collectives may be used in oblique cases:

Он вы́грузил в Берёзове **шестеры́х** (or **шесть**) пассажи́ров (Zalygin)
He off-loaded six passengers in Berezovo

The use of collective numerals with *feminine* animate nouns (e.g. че́тверо же́нщин 'four women') is a mark of substandard colloquial Russian, cf. standard **четы́ре же́нщины.**

The collectives are not normally used with nouns denoting high rank: thus **два мини́стра** 'two ministers' rather than дво́е мини́стров; similarly, **два профе́ссора** 'two professors', **четы́ре генера́ла** 'four generals'.

(iii) The collectives are used with **де́ти** 'children': **дво́е дете́й** 'two children', **тро́е дете́й** 'three children', **че́тверо дете́й** 'four children', **пя́теро дете́й** 'five children' (colloquially also два ребёнка 'two children' etc.). The series rarely proceeds beyond **се́меро** 'seven', cf.

Супру́ги Ники́тины, у кото́рых **се́меро** дете́й (*Sputnik*)
The Nikitins, who have seven children

and

Она́ вспомина́ет свою́ мать, у кото́рой бы́ло **де́вять** дете́й (*Russia Today*)
She recalls her mother, who had nine children

In oblique cases, either cardinal or collective numerals may be used, cf.

Мать **четырёх** дете́й . . . (Rybakov)
The mother of four children

and

Пятеры́х дете́й вы́растила (Trifonov)
She raised five children

Note
The collective numerals are also used:

(a) With **ребя́та: пя́теро** ребя́т 'five kids', с пятеры́ми/пятью́ ребя́тами 'with five kids', cf. У него́ пя́теро **ребяти́шек** (Shukshin) 'He has five kiddies'.

(b) With вну́ки 'grandchildren': За столо́м — **че́тверо дете́й и тро́е вну́ков** (Kovaleva) 'At the table are four children and three grandchildren'.

(c) With **близнецы́: тро́е/че́тверо** близнецо́в 'triplets/quadruplets'.

(d) Colloquially, with the young of animals: **тро́е щеня́т/три щенка́** 'three puppies'.

(iv) The collective numerals are also used when an animate noun is absent from the construction: Нас бы́ло **дво́е** 'There were two of us',

Тро́е стоя́ли на углу́ 'Three people were standing on the corner', Э́ти **пя́теро** оста́лись 'These five stayed', Мы **тро́е** протестова́ли 'We three protested', Ко́мната на **трои́х** 'A room for three'. Reference is to:

(a) Groups of males:

Их **ше́стеро** про̀тив на́ших **трои́х** (*Russia Today*)
There are six of them six against our three

(b) Females:

Их **че́тверо;** все они́ машини́стки высо́кого кла́сса
There are four of them; they are all first-class typists

(c) Mixed company:

Нас **че́тверо:** мой прия́тель с де́вушкой, Ли́ля и я (*Kazakov*)
There are four of us: my friend and his girl-friend, Lilya and I

(v) The collectives are also used in some idioms: есть, рабо́тать за **трои́х**, 'to eat, work enough for three' etc., **на свои́х двои́х** (colloquial) 'on foot'.

201   Indefinite numerals

(1) Indefinite numerals include **доста́точно** 'enough', **ма́ло** 'few', **мно́го** 'many, much', **нема́ло** 'not a few', **немно́го** 'not many, a few', **не́сколько** 'several', **ско́лько** 'how many', **сто́лько** 'so many'.

(2) All the indefinite numerals may govern the genitive singular and plural: доста́точно **проду́ктов** 'sufficient provisions', ма́ло **солда́т** 'not many soldiers' мно́го **вре́мени** 'much time', ско́лько **са́хару?** 'how much sugar?', сто́лько **де́нег** 'so much money'.

(3) **Сто́лько** and **ско́лько** often relate to each other, standing in adjacent clauses:

Стара́йтесь дава́ть хомяку́ **сто́лько** ко́рма, **ско́лько** он в состоя́нии съесть (*Yunyi naturalist*)
Try to give the hamster as much food as it is able to eat

(4) **Не́сколько, ско́лько, сто́лько** take genitive plural челове́к (**не́сколько челове́к** 'a few people'), while **ма́ло, мно́го, нема́ло, немно́го** take genitive plural люде́й (**мно́го люде́й** 'many people' etc.).

Note
Ско́лько люде́й is used in emotive contexts: **Ско́лько люде́й**

получи́ли в после́дние го́ды но́вые кварти́ры! 'How many people have received new apartments in recent years!', cf. the matter-of-fact Ско́лько челове́к поги́бло? 'How many people died?'

(5) **Не́сколько** is distinguished from the 'selective' pronoun **не́которые** 'some, certain' (see also **141**). Compare В за́ле сиде́ло **не́сколько пассажи́ров** 'In the hall sat several passengers' and **Не́которые** из них бы́ли недово́льны 'Some of them were dissatisfied'.

(6) **Не́сколько, ско́лько** and **сто́лько** decline like plural adjectives, agreeing with oblique cases of plural nouns:

> Мо́жно одновреме́нно соедини́ться с **не́сколькими абоне́нтами** (*Izvestiya*)
> It is possible to link up with several subscribers simultaneously

(7) **Ма́ло** implies negative quantity (У него́ **ма́ло** де́нег 'He has not got much money'), while **немно́го** can imply negative *or* positive (У него́ **немно́го** де́нег 'He has not got much money' (negative)/ 'He does have a little money' (positive)). Since **ма́ло** does not decline, paraphrase is sometimes necessary: в ре́дких слу́чаях 'in a few cases', с о́чень ма́леньким коли́чеством муки́ 'with very little flour' etc.

(8) **Мно́го** (or **мно́гое**, pl. **мно́гие**) declines both in the singular (**Мно́гое** бы́ло скры́то от меня́ 'Much was concealed from me', Я **мно́гому** научи́лся у него́ 'I learnt a lot from him') and in the plural (**Мно́гие** так ду́мают 'Many people think that', У **мно́гих** рек пра́вый бе́рег вы́ше ле́вого 'The right bank of many rivers is higher than the left').

Note

(a) While **мно́го** means 'a lot' and is often used with passive or static verbs (На собра́нии бы́ло **мно́го** учителе́й 'There were a lot of teachers at the meeting'), **мно́гие** implies 'not all, a considerable proportion', and is more common with verbs which denote action on the part of the subject (**Мно́гие** учителя́ голосова́ли за предложе́ние 'Many teachers voted for the proposal'). **Мно́го** is commoner with inanimate nouns, unless the intention is to individualize, cf. Снесено́ **мно́го** зда́ний 'Many buildings have been demolished' and **Мно́гие дома́** восстано́влены в пре́жнем сти́ле 'Many houses have been restored in their original style', **Мно́гие** берёзы уже́ без ли́стьев 'Many birches are already without leaves'.

(b)   The animate accusative/genitive rule is not normally applied to indefinite numerals: thus, Я встре́тил **не́сколько** (rather than не́скольких) студе́нтов.

202   Agreement of the predicate with a subject which contains a numeral

(1) It is difficult to formulate hard and fast rules for the agreement of a verb predicate with a subject which contains a numeral. In some instances the predicate appears in the *singular*, in others it appears in the *plural*.

(2) Factors which affect choice include word order, with a preference for the *singular* when the verb *precedes* the noun:

Его́ **опереди́ло** не́сколько лы́жников

He was overtaken by several skiers

and for the *plural* when the verb *follows* the noun:

Не́сколько лы́жников **опереди́ли** его́

Several skiers overtook him

(3) **Мно́го** and **ма́ло** almost invariably take a *singular* predicate: Там **бы́ло** ма́ло наро́ду 'There were not many people there', Во вре́мя пожа́ра **поги́бло** мно́го книг 'Many books perished during the fire'.

(4) With cardinal and collective numerals, **не́сколько** 'several' and **ско́лько** 'how much', the choice of a *singular* or *plural* predicate depends on a number of factors. Prime among these is the nature of the verb predicate.

(i) If this denotes state (**быть** 'to be', **существова́ть** 'to exist' etc.), then a *singular* predicate is preferred:

У неё **бы́ло** три бра́та

She had three brothers

Нас **бы́ло** дво́е

There were two of us

Нам **предстои́т** не́сколько тру́дных встреч с роди́телями

We face a number of difficult meetings with parents

(ii) A *singular* is also preferred with verbs which do not denote action on the part of the subject:

> В бою **поги́бло** со́рок солда́т
> Forty soldiers perished in the battle

> Во вре́мя налёта **уби́то** две же́нщины
> Two women were killed during the raid

> **Издаётся** 80 журна́лов
> 80 journals are published

> **Зарегистри́ровано** бо́лее 130 ты́сяч люде́й (*Izvestiya*)
> More than 130,000 people have been registered

in expressions of time

> Ей ско́ро **испо́лнится** два́дцать лет
> She will soon be twenty

> **Прошло́** три го́да
> Three years have passed

> До прихо́да почто́вого авто́буса **остава́лось** часа́ полтора́
> (Abramov)
> About an hour and a half remained to the arrival of the post bus

in expressing approximate quantity

> Кварти́ры **получа́ет** о̀коло трёхсо́т семе́й
> About three hundred families receive apartments

and where a distributive phrase in **по** functions as subject (see also **448**):

> У ка́ждой две́ри **стоя́ло** по солда́ту
> At each door stood a soldier

(iii) A *plural* predicate will be used, however, if the numeral phrase is qualified by a demonstrative or other plural form (Э́ти пять лет **прошли́** незаме́тно 'These five years have passed by imperceptibly', Э́ти три до́ма **про́даны** неда́вно 'These three houses have been sold recently'), or by a relative clause (cf. Со́рок мину́т **истекло́** 'Forty minutes have expired' and Со́рок мину́т, **о кото́рых вы проси́ли, истекли́** 'The forty minutes that you requested have expired').

(iv) A *plural* predicate is also preferred if the verb denotes action on the part of the subject:

> **Вошли́** тро́е в шине́лях
> Three people came in wearing greatcoats

Не́сколько челове́к **ки́нулись** вслед бежа́вшему (Nikitin)
Several people dashed off after the running man

Note also use with fractions and decimals: В движе́нии за сохране́ние национа́льной самобы́тности и охра́ну приро́ды **уча́ствуют** соотве́тственно 3,5 и 3,1 проце́нта (*Komsomolskaya pravda*) '3.5 and 3.1 per cent respectively participate in the movement for the preservation of national identity and nature conservation'. Compare the use of the *plural* of an *active* verb in Сейча́с по̀лго́рода **хо́дят** в таки́х шмо́тках (*Komsomolskaya pravda*) 'Now half the town wears such gear' and the use of the *singular* of a *passive reflexive* verb in По̀лдо́ма **ремонти́руется** 'Half the house is being repaired'.

(v) A *plural* predicate is especially common where attention is drawn to separate activity on the part of individual members of a subject group:

Со́рок демонстра́нтов **разошли́сь**
The forty demonstrators dispersed

Его́ три сестры́ **вы́шли** за́муж
His three sisters got married

Note
This factor may affect even indefinite numerals like **мно́го:** Мно́го фаши́стских самолётов **бомби́ли** испа́нский го́род Ге́рника 'Many Fascist aircraft bombed the Spanish town of Guernica'.

(vi) A *plural* predicate is also used with **о́ба/о́бе:** О́ба сы́на **верну́лись** 'Both sons returned'.

(vii) The *plural* is normal if the predicate is a *short adjective*:

Не́сколько стате́й в э́том сбо́рнике **интере́сны**
Several articles in this collection are interesting

Ordinal Numerals

203   Formation of ordinal numerals

Apart from **пе́рвый** 'first' and **второ́й** 'second', ordinal numerals derive from cardinals (see **190**). They are as follows:

1st	пе́рвый	51st	пятьдеся́т пе́рвый

2nd	второй	60th	шестидеся́тый
3rd	тре́тий	61st	шестьдеся́т пе́рвый
4th	четвёртый	70th	семидеся́тый
5th	пя́тый	71st	се́мьдесят пе́рвый
6th	шесто́й	80th	восьмидеся́тый
7th	седьмо́й	81st	во́семьдесят пе́рвый
8th	восьмо́й	90th	девяно́стый
9th	девя́тый	91st	девяно́сто пе́рвый
10th	деся́тый	100th	со́тый
11th	оди́ннадцатый	200th	двухсо́тый
12th	двена́дцатый	300th	трёхсо́тый
13th	трина́дцатый	400th	четырёхсо́тый
14th	четы́рнадцатый	500th	пятисо́тый
15th	пятна́дцатый	600th	шестисо́тый
16th	шестна́дцатый	700th	семисо́тый
17th	семна́дцатый	800th	восьмисо́тый
18th	восемна́дцатый	900th	девятисо́тый
19th	девятна́дцатый	1000th	ты́сячный
20th	двадца́тый	1001st	ты́сяча пе́рвый
21st	два́дцать пе́рвый	1002nd	ты́сяча второ́й
22nd	два́дцать второ́й	2000th	двухты́сячный
30th	тридца́тый	3000th	трёхты́сячный
31st	три́дцать пе́рвый	5000th	пятиты́сячный
40th	сороково́й	1,000,000th	миллио́нный
41st	со́рок пе́рвый	10,000,000th	десятимиллио́нный
50th	пятидеся́тый		

Note

(a) Ordinal numbers decline like hard adjectives in **-ый/-о́й**, except for **тре́тий** (see **151** (1) note).

(b) **Девя́тый** 'ninth', **деся́тый** 'tenth', **двадца́тый** 'twentieth', **тридца́тый** 'thirtieth' have medial stress, cf. the initially-stressed cardinals from which they derive.

(c) Note the central -**и**- in 50th to 80th: **пятидеся́тый** 'fiftieth' etc.

(d) In abbreviations, the final letter of the ending is used (**1-я** пятиле́тка 'the first five-year plan', **3-й** день 'the third day', **20-е** го́ды 'the twenties'), unless the penultimate letter of the ending is a consonant, in which case the final *two* letters are used (**5-го** ря́да 'of row 5').

(e) In compounds, only the final component has the form of an ordinal and declines: пятьсо́т **четвёртый** биле́т 'the five hundred **and fourth** ticket', в два́дцать **пе́рвом** ряду́ 'in row 21'.

(f)   Roman numerals are used in denoting centuries (в **XX** (двадца́-
       том) ве́ке 'in the 20th century'), Communist Party congresses
       (**XXII** (два́дцать второ́й) съезд 'XXII Congress'), major
       international events (e.g. sessions of the General Assembly of the
       UNO), international congresses (**IX** (девя́тый) Конгре́сс
       МАПРЯ́Л 'the **IX** Congress of MAPRYAL') and monarchs (Пётр
       I (Пе́рвый) 'Peter the First').

204   Ordinal numerals: usage

(1) Like adjectives, ordinal numerals agree in gender, case and number
with the noun they qualify:

в пя́том ряду́   in row five

(2) For use in time expressions see **206.**

(3) Ordinals are used with pages, chapters, TV channels etc.:

уро́к **пятидеся́тый**   lesson **fifty**
на страни́це **семна́дцатой**   on page **seventeen**
в **три́дцать седьмо́й** главе́   in chapter **thirty-seven**
по **второ́й** програ́мме   on channel **two**

and to denote clothes and footwear sizes

ту́фли **три́дцать четвёртого** разме́ра
size **thirty-four** shoes

See also **199** (2) note.

(4) Ordinals cannot be extended by a superlative, as they can in English.
Instead, prepositional phrases with **по** are used:

втора́я река́ **по длине́**   the second **longest** river
тре́тий го́род **по величине́**   the third **largest** town

Special Functions of Numerals

205   Cardinals and ordinals in fractions and decimals

(1) Both cardinals and ordinals are used in **fractions** and **decimals.** In
Russian *commas* are used instead of decimal points:

(i) Fractions

одна́ **пя́тая** (часть or до́ля understood)	one-fifth
две **пя́тых**	two-fifths
пять **восьмы́х**	five-eighths

Note the use of the genitive plural of the ordinal after 2–4 (cf. **194** (2) (v) note (a)).

(ii) Decimals

0,1 (одна́ деся́тая/ноль це́лых и одна́ деся́тая)	0.1 *or* 1/10
0,05 (пять со́тых/ноль це́лых и пять со́тых)	0.05
1,375 (одна́ це́лая и три́ста се́мьдесят пять ты́сячных)	1.375
2,4 (две це́лых и четы́ре деся́тых/два и четы́ре деся́тых)	2.4
57,365 (пятьдеся́т семь це́лых, три́ста шестьдеся́т пять ты́сячных)	57.365

Note

(a)   1, 2 and compounds of 1, 2 take the gender of a following noun: два́дцать **оди́н** и одна́ деся́тая ме́тра '21.1 metres', **две** и четы́ре деся́тых то́нны '2.4 tons'.

(b)   Decimals/fractions are followed by the genitive singular of the noun:

12,5% (двена́дцать и пять деся́тых **проце́нта)**
12.5% (twelve point five per cent)

even if the decimal or fraction is declined:

Су́мма равня́ется пяти́ седьмы́м **насле́дства**
The sum equals five-sevenths of the inheritance

(c)   Треть 'a third', че́тверть 'a quarter' and полови́на 'a half' are commonly used instead of fractions: две **тре́ти**/две **тре́тьих** 'two-thirds', три **че́тверти**/три **четвёртых** 'three-quarters', три с **че́твертью** 'three and a quarter', два **и пять деся́тых** проце́нта/два **с полови́ной** проце́нта 'two and a half per cent'.

(d)   Temperatures are read as follows: три́дцать шесть и шесть '36.6' (normal body temperature).

(2) По̀л- combines with the genitive singular of many nouns to denote half of something: по̀лго́да 'six months', по̀лме́тра 'half a metre', по̀лчаса́ 'half an hour'.

Note

(i) A hyphen separates **пòл-** from the noun component when the latter begins with an **л** or a vowel or has proper-noun status: **пòл-лѝтра** 'half a litre', **пòл-я́блока** 'half an apple', **пòл-Варша́вы** 'half Warsaw'.

(ii) In oblique cases **пòл-** becomes **полу-**, while the noun component declines in the usual way:

Nom./Acc.	пòлчас-á
Gen.	получа́с-а
Dat.	получа́с-у
Instr.	получа́с-ом
Prep.	о получа́с-е

(iii) In colloquial speech, -**у**- is omitted in the declension of some compounds: в **пòл[у]стака́не** воды́ 'in half a glass of water', бóлее **пòл[у]миллиóна** 'more than half a million'. The better-established of these oral forms have found their way into the written language as alternatives to forms with полу-: Ему́ нет и **пòлгóда/полугóда** 'He is not even six months old'. Пòл- also appears in certain set phrases: **на пòлпутѝ** 'half-way', **на пòлста́вки** 'on half-pay', **к пòлпéрвого** 'by half past twelve' etc.

(iv) Compounds in пòл- are qualified by plural adjectives (**пéрвые** пòлчаса́ 'the first half-hour'), while oblique cases are qualified by singular adjectives (пòсле **пéрвого** полугóда 'after the first six months').

(v) **Полу-** is also used as an adjective and noun prefix: **полукру́г** 'semicircle', **полуфина́л** 'semi-final', **получасовóй** 'half-hour' (adjective), **полуша́рие** 'hemisphere'.

206   Telling the time

(1) Numerals are used to answer the questions **котóрый час?/скóлько врéмени?** 'what is the time?' and **в котóром часу́?/во скóлько?** 'at what time?'

(i) On the hour, the question **Котóрый час?/Скóлько врéмени?** 'What is the time?' is answered as

час, два часá, три часá, четы́ре часá, пять часóв
one, two, three, four, five o'clock

up to **двена́дцать часóв** 'twelve o'clock'.

(ii) The 24-hour clock may be used in official contexts: **семнáдцать часóв** 'five p.m.' Otherwise one distinguishes (apart from двенáдцать часóв нóчи 'twelve o'clock at night' and двенáдцать часóв дня 'twelve noon'):

час/два часá/три часá **нóчи**	one/two/three o'clock **in the morning**
четы́ре часá through to одúннадцать часóв **утрá**	four o'clock through to eleven o'clock **in the morning**
час/два часá/три часá/ четы́ре часá/пять часóв **дня**	one/two/three/four/five o'clock **in the afternoon**
шесть часóв through to одúннадцать часóв **вéчера**	six o'clock through to eleven o'clock **in the evening**

Note
(a)   Четы́ре часá **нóчи** 'four a.m.' and пять часóв **вéчера** 'five p.m.' are also found.
(b)   **Пóлдень** 'midday', **пóлночь** 'midnight'.
(c)   Approximation is expressed by the preposition òколо: òколо двух часóв 'about two o'clock', òколо полýночи 'about midnight', òколо девятú вéчера 'about nine p.m.'

(iii) Between the hour and half-hour, the time is rendered as 'five, ten minutes' etc. of the *next* hour (expressed as an ordinal numeral):

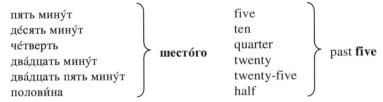

пять минýт			five	
дéсять минýт			ten	
чéтверть		**шестóго**	quarter	past **five**
двáдцать минýт			twenty	
двáдцать пять минýт			twenty-five	
половúна			half	

(Literally, 'five minutes of the sixth', 'ten minutes of the sixth' etc.)

Note
(a)   In spoken Russian **половúна** can be replaced by **пòл-**: **пòлпéрвого** 'half past twelve', **пòлдевя́того** 'half past eight'.
(b)   Минýт may be omitted in multiples of five (**двáдцать пять (минýт)** шестóго 'twenty-five (minutes) past five'); otherwise минýты/минýт must be included (**две минýты** трéтьего 'two minutes past two').
(c)   Ordinal numerals are used to denote unspecified times between hours: **вторóй час** 'between one and two' (usually closer to one

than two), **нача́ло пя́того** 'just after four' (lit. 'the beginning of the fifth') etc.:

Куда́ ж уходи́ть? **Второ́й час.** На метро́ опозда́ла (Trifonov)
'What's the hurry? It's **past one.** You've missed the last train on the Underground'

(iv) After the half-hour the time is rendered as 'without five, ten minutes' etc. one (o'clock), two (o'clock), three (o'clock), the hours being expressed as *cardinal* numerals:

без двадцати́ пяти́ (мину́т)		25 (minutes) to	
без двадцати́ (мину́т)		20 (minutes) to	
без че́тверти	**четы́ре**	quarter to	**four**
без десяти́ (мину́т)		ten (minutes) to	
без пяти́ (мину́т)		five (minutes) to	
без двух мину́т		two minutes to	

(Literally 'without 25 minutes four' etc.)

Note
Neuter agreement in **бы́ло** три часа́/де́сять мину́т пе́рвого/полови́на шесто́го/без пяти́ мину́т три 'it was three o'clock/ten past twelve/half past five/five to three' etc.

(2) **В кото́ром часу́?/во ско́лько?** 'at what time?'

(i) The construction **в** + accusative case is used up to the half-hour:

в час дня	at 1 p.m.
в пять мину́т шесто́го	at five past five

(ii) After the half-hour, however, **в** is omitted:

без че́тверти семь	at quarter to seven
без десяти́ два	at ten to two

It is also omitted when the time phrase is governed by another preposition or a comparative:

Втору́ю то́ню мы зака́нчиваем **о̀коло двух часо́в** но́чи (Nikolaev)
We complete the second haul **at about 2 o'clock** in the morning

Он ложи́лся всегда́ **не по́зже оди́ннадцати** (Yakhontov)
He always went to bed **no later than 11 o'clock**

(iii) **В** + prepositional case is used to denote unspecified times between hours (**в нача́ле** седьмо́го 'at just gone six', **во второ́м часу́** 'between one and two'):

Однако **в одиннадцатом часу** он сам занервничал (Trifonov)
However, **after it had gone ten** he began to get the jitters himself

and for times on the half-hour:

В половине первого (colloquially в пòлпéрвого) нóчи тёща
побежáла на Сóкол, к метрó — встречáть (Trifonov)
At half past midnight mother-in-law rushed off to Sokol to meet
them off the Underground

Note
The time may be given, both colloquially and in official contexts, using
cardinals only: в три пятнáдцать 'at three fifteen', cf.:

Телевизиóнный репортáж по вторóй прогрáмме смотрúте в
семнáдцать часóв двáдцать пять минýт (radio)
Watch TV coverage on channel 2 at 5.25 p.m.

207   Giving the date

(1) The questions **Какóе (бы́ло, бýдет) числó?** 'What is (was, will be)
the date?' are answered by an ordinal numeral in the neuter nominative
and the name of a month in the genitive:

Сегóдня **пéрвое февраля**	Today it is 1 February
Вчерá **бы́ло двáдцать пя́тое мáрта**	Yesterday was 25 March
Скóро бýдет **семнáдцатое ию́ня**	Soon it will be 17 June

(2) The question **Какóго числá?** 'On what date?' is answered by a
genitive:

Междунарóдный жéнский день — **восьмóго мáрта**
International Women's Day is **on 8 March**

(3) The question Какóй год? 'Which year is it?' is answered as follows:
Сейчáс **двухты́сячный год** 'Now it is **the year 2000**' etc.

(4) The question **В какóм годý?** 'in which year?' is answered as
follows:

в ты́сяча девятисóтом годý	in 1900
в ты́сяча девятьсóт пятидеся́том годý	in 1950
в двухты́сячном годý	in the year 2000
в две ты́сячи пятнáдцатом годý	in 2015

Note
(a) Only the final component of the numeral declines (see **203** note
(e)).

(b) If any detail other than the year itself is added, the year appears in the genitive case:

в ма́е ты́сяча девятьсо́т девяно́сто **восьмо́го го́да** in May **1998**

в воскресе́нье тре́тьего сентября́ ты́сяча девятьсо́т три́дцать **девя́того го́да**
on Sunday 3 September 1939

(c) Plural forms may be involved: **В 1957–1963 года́х** во всех респу́бликах появи́лись зако́ны об охра́не приро́ды (*Izvestiya*) **'Over the period 1957–1963** laws on nature conservation appeared in all republics'.

(d) Note the use of **г.** (singular) and **гг.** (plural) in abbreviations: **в 1995 г.** 'in 1995', **в 1957–1963 гг.** 'in 1957–63'.

(e) In denoting decades, **в** is used with the accusative *or* prepositional case: **В пятидеся́тые го́ды/пятидеся́тых года́х XX ве́ка** 'In the 1950s'. Compare: В 90-х года́х в Япо́нии плани́руют вы́пустить но́вую семью́ компью́теров (*Nedelya*) 'The Japanese are planning to manufacture a new family of computers **in the 90s**' (see also **429** (2) (ii) note (c)).

208 Age

(1) The question **Ско́лько вам (ему́, ей** etc.) **лет?** 'How old are you (is he, she etc.)?' is answered as follows:

Ему́ **два́дцать оди́н год**	He is twenty-one
Ей **со́рок два го́да**	She is forty-two
Мне **восемна́дцать лет**	I am eighteen

Ребёнку ещё **нет двух лет** (ещё не испо́лнилось два го́да/двух лет)
The child is not yet two (has not had its second birthday)

The numeral may be used alone in more relaxed speech: **Мне** два́дцать пять (лет) 'I am 25'. Note also the following:

«На́шей Ле́ночке **четвёртый год**» (*Russia Today*)
'Our Lenochka is **in her fourth year**'

Га́лке **шёл 17-й год** (Rasputin)
Galka was **in her seventeenth year**

Ему́ **ужé за со́рок** or Ему́ **40 с чём-то**
He is **in his forties**

Ей ещё **нет двадцати́**
She is in her **late teens**

(2) To answer the question **В како́м во́зрасте?/Ско́льких лет?** 'At what age?' it is possible to use **в** + accusative:

Он у́мер **в се́мьдесят лет**   He died at the age of 70

Alternatively, a genitive construction may be used:

Он у́мер **(в во́зрасте) семи́десяти лет**
He died at the age of 70

209   Quantitative nouns

Quantitative nouns include:

(1) The series **едини́ца** 'one', **дво́йка** 'two', **тро́йка** 'three', **четвёрка** 'four', **пятёрка** 'five', **шестёрка** 'six', **семёрка** 'seven', **восьмёрка** 'eight', **девя́тка** 'nine', **деся́тка** 'ten'. Their functions are as follows:

(i) The first five of the nouns figure in the five-point marking scale: **едини́ца** 'fail', **дво́йка** 'two' (unsatisfactory), **тро́йка** 'three' (satisfactory), **четвёрка** 'four' (good), **пятёрка** 'five' (very good). Colloquially, cardinal numerals can also be used: **учи́ться на пять** 'to get very good marks'.

(ii) The series can denote playing cards **(семёрка бубён, пик** 'seven of diamonds, spades', **деся́тка черве́й, треф** 'ten of hearts, clubs') as well as the numbers of buses etc. (Он прие́хал **на девя́тке** 'He arrived on the no. 9').

(iii) They also denote various other groups or objects consisting of several units: **тро́йка** 'sleigh drawn by three horses', 'three-piece suit', 'three-man commission'; **четвёрка** 'a rowing four'; **пятёрка** 'group of five persons' etc.

(2) The series **пято́к** 'a five', **деся́ток** 'a ten' (also **полтора́ деся́тка** 'fifteen', **два деся́тка** 'a score'), **со́тня** 'a hundred' (**не́сколько со́тен** 'several hundreds'): **пято́к** яи́ц 'five eggs', **деся́ток** сигаре́т 'ten cigarettes', **деся́тки** люде́й 'dozens of people', продава́ть я́йца **со́тнями** 'to sell eggs in hundreds' etc.

210   Numerals in arithmetic

Numerals are used in operating the four arithmetical processes (**четы́ре арифмети́ческих де́йствия**):

(1) Multiplication (Умноже́ние).

оди́ножды три —	три	once three is three
два́жды три —	шесть	two threes are six
три́жды три —	де́вять	three threes are nine
четы́режды три —	двена́дцать	four threes are twelve
пя́тью три —	пятна́дцать	five threes are fifteen
ше́стью три —	восемна́дцать	six threes are eighteen
во́семью три —	два́дцать четы́ре	eight threes are twenty-four etc.

Note
Stress in пя́тью, ше́стью etc. differs from the normal end stress of the instrumental пятью́, шестью́.

(2) Division (деле́ние):

два́дцать во́семь (раздели́ть) на четы́ре — бу́дет семь
twenty-eight divided by four is seven

(3) Addition (Сложе́ние):

к пяти́ приба́вить два — бу́дет семь
сложи́ть пять с двумя́ — бу́дет семь   } five plus two is seven
пять плюс два — бу́дет семь
пять да два — семь

(4) Subtraction (Вычита́ние):

(вы́честь) два из пяти́ — бу́дет три   } five minus two is three
пять ми́нус два — бу́дет три

Note
Два **в квадра́те** — четы́ре 'The square of two is four', Два **в ку́бе** — во́семь 'Two cubed is eight', **Ко́рень квадра́тный** из четырёх — два 'The square root of four is two'.

211   Numerals in compound nouns and adjectives

(1) With the exception of 1, 90, 100 and 1000 (see (2) below), numeral components of compound nouns and adjectives appear in the *genitive* case of the cardinal:

двухле́тний	two year old
пятиле́тка	five-year plan
сорокапя́тка (colloquial)	forty-five (gramophone record)
двадцатипятимину́тная па́уза	a 25-minute break

Note

A number of more abstract or technical terms take **дву-/тре-/четверо-** instead of **двух-/трёх-/четырёх-**: **двусло́жный** 'disyllabic', **двусторо́нний** 'bilateral', **двуязы́чный** 'bilingual' (note also **двою́родный** брат 'cousin'); **тре**уго́льник 'triangle'; **четверо**но́гий 'quadruped'.

(2) 1, 90, 100 and 1000 assume the forms **одно-, девяносто-, сто-** and **тысяче-** in compound nouns and numerals:

одноэта́жный дом	single-storey house
девяно̀стомину́тная игра́	a ninety-minute game
сто̀метро́вка	hundred metres race
стопятѝдесятиле́тие	one hundred and fiftieth anniversary
тысячеле́тие	millennium

The Verb

Conjugation

212 Infinitive-preterite stem and present-future stem

(1) Each Russian verb has:

(i) An *infinitive (infinitive-preterite) stem*, from which the past tense, the future imperfective, past participles and most perfective gerunds are formed.

(ii) A *present-future stem*, from which the present tense, the future perfective, the imperative, present participles, imperfective gerunds and some perfective gerunds are formed.

In some verbs the two stems coincide, in others they differ.

(2) The present-future stem of a verb is derived by removing the last two letters of the third-person plural of the verb:

Infinitive	Third-person plural	Present–future stem
понима́ть 'to understand'	**понима́-ют**	**понима́-**
говори́ть 'to say'	**говор-я́т**	**говор-**
сказа́ть 'to tell'	**ска́ж-ут**	**ска́ж-**

213 The conjugation of the verb

Each Russian verb conjugates in accordance with one of two patterns: the first (or **-е-**) conjugation and the second (or **-и-/-я-**) conjugation. The following endings are added to the present-future stems of verbs:

First-conjugation endings	Second-conjugation endings
-ю	**-ю**
-ешь	**-ишь**
-ет	**-ит**
-ем	**-им**
-ете	**-ите**
-ют	**-ят**

Note

(a) In first-conjugation verbs **у** replaces **ю** after a consonant (except after **л** and **р** in certain verbs, for example, verbs in **-оть, слать** 'to send' and **стлать** 'to spread').

(b) **ё** replaces **е** under stress.

(c) **у** and **а** replace **ю** and **я** respectively after **ж, ч, ш** or **щ** (see **16** (1)).

214 The first conjugation

(1) The first conjugation contains:

(i) Most verbs in **-ать/-ять**.

(ii) Many verbs in **-еть**.

(iii) All verbs with a monosyllabic infinitive in **-ить, почи́ть**, compounds of **-шибить**.

(iv) All verbs in **-оть, -уть, -ыть, -сть, -зть, -ти, -чь**.

(2) First-conjugation verbs subdivide into:

(i) Those with stems ending in **vowels**.

(ii) Those with stems ending in **consonants**.

215 First-conjugation verbs with stems ending in a vowel

First-conjugation verbs with vowel stems comprise most verbs of the first conjugation in **-ать/-ять** (including all verbs in **-авать, -евать, -ивать, -овать, -увать, -ывать**), many in **-еть** and some in **-ить, -уть, -ыть**.

(1) Verbs in -ать/-ять

знать	**гуля́ть**
'to know'	'to stroll'
я зна́-**ю**	гуля́-**ю**
ты зна́-**ешь**	гуля́-**ешь**
он зна́-**ет**	гуля́-**ет**
мы зна́-**ем**	гуля́-**ем**
вы зна́-**ете**	гуля́-**ете**
они́ зна́-**ют**	гуля́-**ют**

Note

(a) Most vowel stems in **-ать/-ять** conjugate like **знать** and **гуля́ть**. See, however, verbs in **-ава́ть** and **-овать/-евать** ((2) and (3) below) and note that *stem*-stressed verbs in **-ять** lose **я** in conjugation (**се́ять** 'to sow': я се́ю, ты се́ешь), except for **ка́шлять** 'to cough': я ка́шляю, ты ка́шляешь.

(b) **Смея́ться** 'to laugh' conjugates смею́сь, смеёшься, смеётся, смеёмся, смеётесь, смею́тся.

(2) Verbs in -ава́ть

дава́ть
'to give'

я да-**ю́**	
ты да-**ёшь**	
он да-**ёт**	
мы да-**ём**	
вы да-**ёте**	
они́ да-**ю́т**	

Note
Compounds of **дава́ть, -знава́ть** (e.g. **узнава́ть** 'to recognize') and **-става́ть** (e.g. **встава́ть** 'to get up') conjugate like **дава́ть**.

(3) Verbs in -овать/-евать

голосова́ть	кова́ть	плева́ть
'to vote'	'to forge'	'to spit'
я голосу́-ю	ку-ю́	плю-ю́
ты голосу́-ешь	ку-ёшь	плю-ёшь
он голосу́-ет	ку-ёт	плю-ёт
мы голосу́-ем	ку-ём	плю-ём
вы голосу́-ете	ку-ёте	плю-ёте
они́ голосу́-ют	ку-ю́т	плю-ю́т

Note

(a) All verbs in **-овать** with more than two syllables conjugate like **голосова́ть** (some are stem stressed, e.g. **тре́бовать** 'to demand', тре́бую, тре́буешь).

(b) Note the conjugation of the following:

воева́ть 'to wage war'	вою́ю, вою́ешь
горева́ть 'to grieve'	горю́ю, горю́ешь
жева́ть 'to chew'	жую́, жуёшь
клева́ть 'to peck'	клюю́, клюёшь
снова́ть 'to dart'	сную́, снуёшь
сова́ть 'to thrust'	сую́, суёшь

(c) **Застрева́ть** 'to get stuck', **затева́ть** 'to undertake', **здоро́ваться** 'to greet', **зева́ть** 'to yawn', **подозрева́ть** 'to suspect', **преодолева́ть** 'to overcome' and secondary imperfectives in **-дева́ть, -пева́ть, -спева́ть** conjugate like **знать.**

(4) Verbs in -еть

красне́ть
'to blush'

я красне́-ю
ты красне́-ешь
он красне́-ет
мы красне́-ем
вы красне́-ете
они́ красне́-ют

Note

(a) Verbs in **-еть** which are derived from adjectives (e.g. **худе́ть** 'to slim' from **худо́й** 'slim') and nouns (e.g. **сироте́ть** 'to be orphaned' from **сирота́** 'an orphan') conjugate like **красне́ть,** as do **владе́ть** 'to own', **греть** 'to heat', **жале́ть** 'to pity', **зреть** 'to ripen', **име́ть** 'to have', **млеть** 'to grow numb', **преодоле́ть** 'to overcome', **сметь** 'to dare', **спеть** 'to ripen', **тлеть** 'to decay', **уме́ть** 'to know how to'.

(b) **Петь** 'to sing' conjugates пою, поёшь, поёт, поём, поёте, поют.

(5) Verbs in -ить

бить	**брить**	**гнить**
'to strike'	'to shave'	'to rot'
я бь-**ю**	бре́-**ю**	гни-**ю́**
ты бь-**ёшь**	бре́-**ешь**	гни-**ёшь**
он бь-**ёт**	бре́-**ет**	гни-**ёт**
мы бь-**ём**	бре́-**ем**	гни-**ём**
вы бь-**ёте**	бре́-**ете**	гни-**ёте**
они́ бь-**ют**	бре́-**ют**	гни-**ю́т**

Note

(a) **Вить** 'to weave', **лить** 'to pour', **пить** 'to drink' and **шить** 'to sew' conjugate like бить (with 'zero vowel' in the present-future stem).

(b) **Почи́ть** 'to rest' conjugates like гнить, but with stress on -**и́**-: почи́ю, почи́ешь.

(6) Verbs in -ыть

мыть
'to wash'

я мо́-**ю**	мы мо́-**ем**
ты мо́-**ешь**	вы мо́-**ете**
он мо́-**ет**	они́ мо́-**ют**

Similarly **выть** 'to howl', **крыть** 'to roof', **ныть** 'to gnaw' and **рыть** 'to dig'.

(7) Verbs in -уть

Дуть 'to blow': ду́ю, ду́ешь, ду́ет, ду́ем, ду́ете, ду́ют. Likewise **обу́ть** 'to put shoes on someone' and **разу́ть** 'to take shoes off someone'.

216 First-conjugation verbs with consonant stems I

(1) Present-future and infinitive stems coincide

(i) Verbs in **-ать**, e.g. **ждать** 'to wait':

я жд-**у**
ты жд-**ёшь**

он жд-**ёт**
мы жд-**ём**
вы жд-**ёте**
они́ жд-**ут**

Similarly:

врать 'to lie'	вру, врёшь
жа́ждать 'to thirst for'	жа́жду, жа́ждешь
жрать 'to devour'	жру, жрёшь
ора́ть 'to yell'	ору́, орёшь
рвать 'to tear'	рву, рвёшь
ржать 'to neigh'	ржу, ржёшь
соса́ть 'to suck'	сосу́, сосёшь
стона́ть 'to groan'	стону́, сто́нешь
ткать 'to weave'	тку, ткёшь

Note

The absence of velar/sibilant mutation in the conjugation of **ткать** is abnormal, cf. mutation in **лгать** 'to lie': лгу, лжёшь, лжёт, лжём, лжёте, лгут.

(ii) Verbs in **-(н)уть**:

гнуть 'to bend'   гну, гнёшь

Likewise all other verbs in **-нуть** (some with stem stress (**мёрзнуть** 'to freeze': мёрзну, мёрзнешь) and a few with mobile stress, see **219** (3)(iv).

(iii) Verbs in **-оть**:

коло́ть 'to chop'   колю́, ко́лешь, ко́лют

Likewise all other verbs in **-оть**: **боро́ться** 'to struggle', **моло́ть** 'to grind' (мелю́, ме́лешь), **поло́ть** 'to weed', **поро́ть** 'to rip'.

(2) Present-future stem and infinitive stem differ

(i) Through the presence of a mobile vowel in conjugation:

брать 'to take'	беру́, берёшь (likewise **драть** 'to flay')
звать 'to call'	зову́, зовёшь
стлать 'to spread'	стелю́, сте́лешь, сте́лют

(ii) **-в-** appears in conjugation:

жить 'to live'	живу́, живёшь
плыть 'to swim'	плыву́, плывёшь (likewise **слыть** 'to have the reputation of being')

(iii) -д- appears in conjugation:

быть 'to be'	бу́ду, бу́дешь
е́хать 'to travel'	е́ду, е́дешь

(iv) **-м-** or **-н-** appears in conjugation:

взять 'to take'	возьму́, возьмёшь
деть 'to put'	де́ну, де́нешь
жать 'to press'	жму, жмёшь
жать 'to reap'	жну, жнёшь
застря́ть 'to get stuck'	застря́ну, застря́нешь
мять 'to crumple'	мну, мнёшь
нача́ть 'to begin'	начну́, начнёшь
поня́ть 'to understand'	пойму́, поймёшь
распя́ть 'to crucify'	распну́, распнёшь
сня́ть 'to take off'	сниму́, сни́мешь
стать 'to become'	ста́ну, ста́нешь
стыть 'to go cold'	сты́ну, сты́нешь

Note

Compounds of **-нять** with prefixes ending in a vowel (except for **приня́ть** 'to accept': приму́, при́мешь) conjugate like **поня́ть** 'to understand'; those with prefixes ending in a consonant conjugate like **снять** 'to take off'.

(v) Mobile vowel lost in conjugation (verbs in **-ереть**):

тере́ть 'to rub'	тру, трёшь (likewise compounds of -мереть, -переть)

(vi) Others (**реве́ть, слать** and compounds of **-шибить**)

ошиби́ться 'to err'	ошибу́сь, ошибёшься
реве́ть 'to roar'	реву́, ревёшь
слать 'to send'	шлю, шлёшь, шлют

217 First-conjugation verbs with consonant stems II: verbs in -ать with consonant mutation throughout conjugation

(1) Verbs of this type:

(i) Undergo consonant mutation throughout conjugation.

(ii) Switch stress from the ending to the *stem* after the first-person singular, except for:

(a) **Алка́ть** 'to crave', **колеба́ться** 'to hesitate', **колыха́ть** 'to sway', which have stem stress *throughout* conjugation.

(b) Verbs with stem stress in the infinitive, e.g. **ма́зать** 'to daub'.

(2) The following consonant mutations operate:

д : ж	т : ч	т : щ	з : ж	с : ш
глода́ть	шепта́ть	клевета́ть	вяза́ть	писа́ть
'to gnaw'	'to whisper'	'to slander'	'to tie'	'to write'
я глож-у́	шепч-у́	клевещ-у́	вяж-у́	пиш-у́
ты гло́ж-ешь	ше́пч-ешь	клеве́щ-ешь	вя́ж-ешь	пи́ш-ешь
он гло́ж-ет	ше́пч-ет	клеве́щ-ет	вя́ж-ет	пи́ш-ет
мы гло́ж-ем	ше́пч-ем	клеве́щ-ем	вя́ж-ем	пи́ш-ем
вы гло́ж-ете	ше́пч-ете	клеве́щ-ете	вя́ж-ете	пи́ш-ете
они́ гло́ж-ут	ше́пч-ут	клеве́щ-ут	вя́ж-ут	пи́ш-ут

г : ж	к : ч	х : ш	ск : щ	б : бл/м : мл/ п : пл
дви́гать	пла́кать	маха́ть	иска́ть	дрема́ть
'to move'	'to weep'	'to wave'	'to seek'	'to doze'
я дви́ж-у	пла́ч-у	маш-у́	ищ-у́	дремл-ю́
ты дви́ж-ешь	пла́ч-ешь	ма́ш-ешь	и́щ-ешь	дре́мл-ешь
он дви́ж-ет	пла́ч-ет	ма́ш-ет	и́щ-ет	дре́мл-ет
мы дви́ж-ем	пла́ч-ем	ма́ш-ем	и́щ-ем	дре́мл-ем
вы дви́ж-ете	пла́ч-ете	ма́ш-ете	и́щ-ете	дре́мл-ете
они́ дви́ж-ут	пла́ч-ут	ма́ш-ут	и́щ-ут	дре́мл-ют

Note

(a) Дви́гать 'to move' conjugates дви́жу, дви́жешь in figurative meanings (Им **дви́жет** самолю́бие 'He is motivated by self-esteem') and in technical contexts (Пружи́на **дви́жет** механи́зм 'A spring activates the mechanism'), but дви́гаю, дви́гаешь in literal meaning (Он **дви́гает** ме́бель 'He moves the furniture'). Note also the distinction between По́езд **дви́гается** 'The train moves off' and По́езд **дви́жется** 'The train is in motion'.

(b) Other verbs of this type include **алка́ть** 'to crave' (а́лчу, а́лчешь), **бормота́ть** 'to murmur' (бормочу́, бормо́чешь), **бры́згать** 'to spray, sprinkle' (бры́зжу, бры́зжешь in intransitive meanings (Фонта́н **бры́зжет** 'The fountain plays'); бры́згаю, бры́згаешь in transitive meanings (Он **бры́згает** во́лосы духа́ми 'He sprays his hair with perfume'), **грохота́ть** 'to rumble' (грохочу́, грохо́чет), **каза́ться** 'to seem' (кажу́сь, ка́жешься) (likewise compounds of -**каза́ть**), **ка́пать** 'to drip' (ка́плю, ка́плешь; also ка́паю, -аешь), **клокота́ть** 'to gurgle' (клоко́чет), **колеба́ться** (коле́блюсь, коле́блешься) 'to hesitate', **колыха́ть** 'to sway' (колы́шу, колы́шешь), **лепета́ть** 'to babble' (лепечу́, лепе́чешь), **лиза́ть** 'to lick' (лижу́, ли́жешь), **ма́зать** 'to daub' (ма́жу, ма́жешь), **мета́ть** 'to throw' (мечу́, ме́чешь), **мурлы́кать** 'to purr' (мурлы́чу, мурлы́чешь; also мурлы́каю, -аешь), **паха́ть** 'to plough' (пашу́, па́шешь), **плеска́ть** 'to splash' (плещу́, пле́щешь), **пляса́ть** 'to dance' (пляшу́, пля́шешь), **полоска́ть** 'to rinse' (полощу́, поло́щешь), **пря́тать** 'to hide' (пря́чу, пря́чешь), **ре́зать** 'to cut' (ре́жу, ре́жешь), **ропта́ть** 'to grumble' (ропщу́, ро́пщешь), **ры́скать** 'to rove' (ры́щу, ры́щешь), **скака́ть** 'to gallop' (скачу́, ска́чешь), **скрежета́ть** 'to grind' (скрежещу́, скреж́ещешь), **сы́пать** 'to sprinkle' (сы́плю, сы́плешь), **теса́ть** 'to hew' (тешу́, те́шешь), **топта́ть** 'to trample' (топчу́, то́пчешь), **трепа́ть** 'to tousle' (треплю́, тре́плешь), **трепета́ть** 'to tremble' (трепещу́, трепе́щешь), **ты́кать** 'to prod' (ты́чу, ты́чешь), **хлопота́ть** 'to busy oneself' (хлопочу́, хлопо́чешь), **чеса́ть** 'to scratch' (чешу́, че́шешь), **щебета́ть** 'to twitter' (щебечу́, щебе́чешь), **щекота́ть** 'to tickle' (щекочу́, щеко́чешь), **щипа́ть** 'to pinch' (щиплю́, щи́плешь).

218 First-conjugation verbs with consonant stems III: verbs in -ти, -сть/-зть, -чь

(1) Verbs in -ти

Verbs in -**ти** subdivide in accordance with the following stem consonants:

-б-	-д-	-з-
грести́	**идти́**	**везти́**
'to row'	'to go'	'to convey'
я греб-**у́**	ид-**у́**	вез-**у́**
ты греб-**ёшь**	ид-**ёшь**	вез-**ёшь**
он греб-**ёт**	ид-**ёт**	вез-**ёт**
мы греб-**ём**	ид-**ём**	вез-**ём**
вы греб-**ёте**	ид-**ёте**	вез-**ёте**
они́ греб-**у́т**	ид-**у́т**	вез-**у́т**

-с-	-т-	-ст-
нести́	**мести́**	**расти́**
'to carry'	'to sweep'	'to grow'
нес-у́	мет-у́	раст-у́
нес-ёшь	мет-ёшь	раст-ёшь
нес-ёт	мет-ёт	раст-ёт
нес-ём	мет-ём	раст-ём
нес-ёте	мет-ёте	раст-ёте
нес-у́т	мет-у́т	раст-у́т

Other verbs include:

блюсти́ 'to conserve'	блюду́, блюдёшь
брести́ 'to wander'	бреду́, бредёшь
вести́ 'to lead'	веду́, ведёшь
обрести́ 'to acquire'	обрету́, обретёшь
пасти́ 'to tend'	пасу́, пасёшь
плести́ 'to plait'	плету́, плетёшь
ползти́ 'to crawl'	ползу́, ползёшь
скрести́ 'to scour, claw'	скребу́, скребёшь
трясти́ 'to shake'	трясу́, трясёшь
цвести́ 'to flower'	цвету́, цветёшь

(2) Verbs in -сть/-зть

Verbs in **-сть/-зть** subdivide in accordance with the following stem consonants:

-д-	-н-	-т-	-з-
класть	**клясть**	**честь**	**лезть**
'to place'	'to curse'	'to consider'	'to climb'
я клад-у́	клян-у́	чт-у	ле́з-у
ты клад-ёшь	клян-ёшь	чт-ёшь	ле́з-ешь
он клад-ёт	клян-ёт	чт-ёт	ле́з-ет
мы клад-ём	клян-ём	чт-ём	ле́з-ем
вы клад-ёте	клян-ёте	чт-ёте	ле́з-ете
они́ клад-у́т	клян-у́т	чт-ут	ле́з-ут

Other verbs include the following:

грызть 'to gnaw'	грызу́, грызёшь
красть 'to steal'	краду́, крадёшь
пасть 'to fall'	паду́, падёшь
сесть 'to sit down'	ся́ду, ся́дешь

Note

Честь 'to consider' is now obsolete as an independent verb, but appears as a component of compound prefixed verbs such as учéсть 'to take into account'.

(3) Verbs in -чь

Verbs in -чь subdivide into г-stems (with mutation to **ж** before **е/ё**) and к-stems (with mutation to **ч** before **е/ё**).

-г-	**-к-**
берéчь	**печь**
'to look after'	'to bake'
я берег-**ý**	пек-**ý**
ты береж-**ёшь**	печ-**ёшь**
он береж-**ёт**	печ-**ёт**
мы береж-**ём**	печ-**ём**
вы береж-**ёте**	печ-**ёте**
они́ берег-**ýт**	пек-**ýт**

Other verbs include the following:

влечь 'to pull, draw'	влекý, влечёшь, влекýт
жечь 'to burn'	жгу, жжёшь, жгут
лечь 'to lie down'	ля́гу, ля́жешь, ля́гут
мочь 'to be able'	могý, мóжешь, мóгут
напря́чь 'to strain'	напрягý, напряжёшь, напрягýт (similarly other compounds of -**пря́чь**)
пренебрéчь 'to disdain'	пренебрегý, пренебрежёшь, пренебрегýт
сечь 'to cut'	секý, сечёшь, секýт
стричь 'to cut' (hair)	стригý, стрижёшь, стригýт
течь 'to flow'	течёт, текýт

Note

Дости́чь (= дости́гнуть) 'to achieve': дости́гну, дости́гнешь. Both infinitives are standard forms. Дости́чь has a colloquial nuance and is commoner in the press; дости́гнуть is regarded as more 'bookish'.

219 Mobile stress in the conjugation of first-conjugation verbs

(1) Stress change in the conjugation of verbs of more than one syllable

usually involves a shift of stress from the *ending* in the first-person singular to the *stem* in the other forms of the present tense or future perfective: **я пишу́** 'I write', **ты пи́шешь** 'you write'; **я приму́** 'I shall accept', **ты при́мешь** 'you will accept' etc.

(2) Verbs with stem-stressed infinitives (e.g. **пря́тать** 'to hide') are not subject to stress change in conjugation.

(3) Stress change takes place in the conjugation of the following types of first-conjugation verbs with *consonant* stems:

(i) Verbs in **-ать** with end stress in the infinitive and consonant mutation throughout conjugation (see **217**). Note that **алка́ть, колеба́ть[ся]** and **колыха́ть** take stem stress *throughout* conjugation.

(ii) **Стлать** 'to spread' (see **216** (2) (i)) and **стона́ть** 'to groan' (see **216** (1) (i)).

(iii) Verbs in **-оть** (see **216**) (1) (iii)).

(iv) Compounds of **-гляну́ть**, e.g. **загляну́ть** 'to peep in' (загляну́, загля́нешь), **обману́ть** 'to deceive', **тону́ть** 'to drown', **тяну́ть** 'to pull' (see **216** (1) (ii)).

(v) **Приня́ть** 'to accept' and compounds of **-нять** with prefixes ending in a consonant (see **216** (2) (iv) note).

(vi) **Мочь** 'to be able' (see **218** (3)).

220 Second conjugation: present-future stems

(1) The present-future stems of verbs in the second conjugation end in a *consonant* (with very few exceptions, which include **бо-я́ться** 'to fear', **сто́-ить** 'to cost', **сто-я́ть** 'to stand', **стро́-ить** 'to build').

(2) Second-conjugation verbs include:

(i) All verbs in **-ить** (except for those with monosyllabic infinitives (see **215** (5), **216** (2) (ii)), **почи́ть** 'to rest' and compounds of **-шибить** (see **216** (2) (vi)).

(ii) Many verbs in **-еть**.

(iii) Some verbs in **-ать**.

(iv) Two verbs in **-ять: боя́ться** 'to fear', **стоя́ть** 'to stand'.

221 Present-future endings in the second conjugation

Second-conjugation verbs conjugate as follows:

Verbs in -ить говори́ть 'to speak'	Verbs in -еть смотре́ть 'to look'	Verbs in -ать стуча́ть 'to knock'	Verbs in -ять стоя́ть 'to stand'
я говор-ю́	смотр-ю́	стуч-у́	сто-ю́
ты говор-и́шь	смо́тр-ишь	стуч-и́шь	сто-и́шь
он говор-и́т	смо́тр-ит	стуч-и́т	сто-и́т
мы говор-и́м	смо́тр-им	стуч-и́м	сто-и́м
вы говор-и́те	смо́тр-ите	стуч-и́те	сто-и́те
они́ говор-я́т	смо́тр-ят	стуч-а́т	сто-я́т

(1) **ю** is replaced by **у** and **я** by **а** after **ж, ч, ш** or **щ** (see **16** (1)).

(2) Second-conjugation verbs in -**еть** include many verbs which denote sounds, and some others: **верте́ть** 'to spin' (верчу́, ве́ртишь), **ви́деть** 'to see' (ви́жу, ви́дишь), **висе́ть** 'to hang' (вишу́, виси́шь), **гляде́ть** 'to glance' (гляжу́, гляди́шь), **горе́ть** 'to burn' (горю́, гори́шь), **греме́ть** 'to thunder' (гремлю́, греми́шь), **гуде́ть** 'to buzz' (гуди́т), **звене́ть** 'to ring' (звеню́, звени́шь), **кипе́ть** 'to boil' (киплю́, кипи́шь), **лете́ть** 'to fly' (лечу́, лети́шь), **свисте́ть** 'to whistle' (свищу́, свисти́шь), **сиде́ть** 'to sit' (сижу́, сиди́шь), **скрипе́ть** 'to creak' (скриплю́, скрипи́шь), **смотре́ть** 'to look' (смотрю́, смо́тришь), **терпе́ть** 'to endure' (терплю́, те́рпишь), **храпе́ть** 'to snore' (храплю́, храпи́шь), **хрипе́ть** 'to wheeze' (хриплю́, хрипи́шь), **шипе́ть** 'to hiss' (шиплю́, шипи́шь), **шуме́ть** 'to make a noise' (шумлю́, шуми́шь). For consonant changes see **222** and for stress changes see **223**.

(3) Second-conjugation verbs in -**ать** include:

(i) Many verbs associated with sound, with stems ending in **ж, ч, ш** or **щ: бренча́ть** 'to strum' (бренчу́, бренчи́шь); likewise **визжа́ть** 'to scream, squeal', **ворча́ть** 'to growl', **дребезжа́ть** 'to jingle' (third person only), **жужжа́ть** 'to buzz', **звуча́ть** 'to sound' (third person only), **крича́ть** 'to shout', **молча́ть** 'to be silent', **мыча́ть** 'to moo, bellow', **пища́ть** 'to squeak', **рыча́ть** 'to roar', **слы́шать** 'to hear', **стуча́ть** 'to knock', **треща́ть** 'to crackle'.

(ii) A number of other verbs: **гнать** 'to drive' (гоню́, го́нишь), **держа́ть** 'to hold' (держу́, де́ржишь), **дрожа́ть** 'to tremble' (дрожу́, дрожи́шь), **дыша́ть** 'to breathe' (дышу́, ды́шишь), **лежа́ть** 'to lie' (лежу́, лежи́шь), **спать** 'to sleep' (сплю, спишь).

(4) **Боя́ться** 'to fear' conjugates бою́сь, бои́шься.

222 Consonant change in the conjugation of second-conjugation verbs

A consistent feature of the second conjugation is the mutation of the consonant in the first-person singular of the present tense and future perfective of verbs in **-ить** and **-еть**. This is regular for all second-conjugation verbs with stems ending in **-б-, -в-, -д-, -з-, -с-, -т-, -ф-** (verbs in **-ить** only), **-м-, -п-** and **-ст-** (verbs in **-ить** *and* **-еть**).

б : бл **люби́ть** 'to love'	**в : вл** **ста́вить** 'to stand'	**д : ж** **гла́дить** 'to iron'	**з : ж** **ла́зить** 'to climb'
я люблю́	ста́влю	гла́жу	ла́жу
ты лю́бишь	ста́вишь	гла́дишь	ла́зишь
он лю́бит	ста́вит	гла́дит	ла́зит
мы лю́бим	ста́вим	гла́дим	ла́зим
вы лю́бите	ста́вите	гла́дите	ла́зите
они́ лю́бят	ста́вят	гла́дят	ла́зят

с : ш **проси́ть** 'to ask'	**т : ч** **плати́ть** 'to pay'	**ф : фл** **графи́ть** 'to rule' (paper)
я прошу́	плачу́	графлю́
ты про́сишь . . .	пла́тишь . . .	графи́шь . . .

м : мл		**п : пл**	
корми́ть 'to feed'	**шуме́ть** 'to make a noise'	**топи́ть** 'to heat'	**храпе́ть** 'to snore'
я кормлю́	шумлю́	топлю́	храплю́
ты ко́рмишь . . .	шуми́шь . . .	то́пишь . . .	храпи́шь . . .

ст : щ	
мстить 'to avenge'	**свисте́ть** 'to whistle'
мщу	свищу́
мсти́шь . . .	свисти́шь . . .

Note

The mutation **т : щ** affects only certain perfective verbs (e.g. **прекра-ти́ть** 'to cease' (прекращу́, прекрати́шь).

For other verbs affected by consonant changes see **221** (2) and **223** (3) (i), (ii).

223 Stress change in the second conjugation

(1) Many second-conjugation verbs with end-stressed infinitives shift stress from the ending in the first-person singular to the stem in the rest of the conjugation, e.g. **кури́ть** 'to smoke' (курю́, ку́ришь, ку́рит). Verbs with *stem*-stressed infinitives (e.g. **ве́рить** 'to believe') do not undergo stress change in conjugation.

(2) Verbs in **-ить, -еть** and **-ать** which undergo stress change in conjugation include the following types:

вари́ть 'to boil'	**смотре́ть** 'to look'	**держа́ть** 'to hold'
я варю́	смотрю́	держу́
ты ва́ришь	смо́тришь	де́ржишь
он ва́рит	смо́трит	де́ржит
мы ва́рим	смо́трим	де́ржим
вы ва́рите	смо́трите	де́ржите
они́ ва́рят	смо́трят	де́ржат

(3) Other verbs which undergo stress change include the following (those which also undergo *consonant* change (see **222**) are indicated with an asterisk):

(i) Verbs in **-ить**:

*броди́ть	'to wander'	дружи́ть	'to be friends'
*буди́ть	'to awaken'	души́ть	'to stifle'
*води́ть	'to lead'	жени́ться	'to marry'
*вози́ть	'to convey'	*заблуди́ться	'to get lost'
вскочи́ть	'to jump up'	*кати́ть	'to roll'
*гаси́ть	'to cancel'	клони́ть	'to incline'
*грузи́ть	'to load'	*колоти́ть	'to hammer'
*дави́ть	'to press, crush'	*копи́ть	'to accumulate'
дари́ть	'to present'	*корми́ть	'to feed'
дели́ть	'to share'	*коси́ть	'to scythe'
дразни́ть	'to tease'	*крести́ть	'to christen'

*купи́ть	'to buy'	*серди́ть	'to anger'
*лепи́ть	'to mould, sculpt'	служи́ть	'to serve'
лечи́ть	'to give treatment'	compounds of *-станови́ть	
*лови́ть	'to catch'	*ступи́ть	'to step'
compounds of -ложи́ть 'to lay'		*суди́ть	'to judge'
*люби́ть	'to like'	суши́ть	'to dry'
мани́ть	'to entice'	тащи́ть	'to drag'
compounds of -мени́ть 'to change'		*топи́ть	'to heat'
моли́ть	'to pray'	*торопи́ть	'to hasten'
*молоти́ть	'to thresh'	точи́ть	'to sharpen'
мочи́ть	'to wet'	*труди́ться	'to labour'
*носи́ть	'to carry'	туши́ть	'to extinguish'
пили́ть	'to saw'	урони́ть	'to drop'
*плати́ть	'to pay'	учи́ть	'to teach'
получи́ть	'to receive'	хвали́ть	'to praise'
провали́ться	'to fail'	*ходи́ть	'to go, walk'
*проглоти́ть	'to swallow'	хорони́ть	'to bury'
*проси́ть	'to request'	цени́ть	'to value'
*простуди́ться	'to catch cold'	*черти́ть	'to draw'
*пусти́ть	'to let go'	*шути́ть	'to joke'
*руби́ть	'to chop'	*яви́ть	'to display'
*свети́ть	'to shine'		

Note

Коси́ть 'to squint' has fixed end stress in conjugation.

Some verbs have alternative stress in conjugation:

до́ит or дои́т	'milks'
зу́брит or зубри́т	'swots'
кро́шит or кроши́т	'crumbles'
кру́жит or кружи́т	'circles'
по́ит or пои́т	'waters'

(ii) Verbs in -еть:

*верте́ть 'to spin'	я верчу́	ты ве́ртишь
смотре́ть 'to look'	я смотрю́	ты смо́тришь
*терпе́ть 'to endure'	я терплю́	ты те́рпишь

(iii) Verbs in -ать:

гнать 'to drive'	я гоню́	ты го́нишь
держа́ть 'to hold'	я держу́	ты де́ржишь
дыша́ть 'to breathe'	я дышу́	ты ды́шишь

224 Irregular verbs

A number of verbs conform to none of the above patterns, or combine elements of both conjugations. They include

бежа́ть	есть	хоте́ть	дать
'to run'	'to eat'	'to want'	'to give'
я бегу́	ем	хочу́	дам
ты бежи́шь	ешь	хо́чешь	дашь
он бежи́т	ест	хо́чет	даст
мы бежи́м	еди́м	хоти́м	дади́м
вы бежи́те	еди́те	хоти́те	дади́те
они́ бегу́т	едя́т	хотя́т	даду́т

as well as **чтить** 'to honour' (чту, чтишь, чтит, чтим, чти́те, чтут/чтят).

225   Deficiencies in the conjugation of certain verbs

(1) The following verbs have no first-person singular: **затми́ть** 'to eclipse', **очути́ться** 'to find oneself', **победи́ть** 'to win', **убеди́ть** 'to convince', **чуди́ть** 'to behave eccentrically'. However, paraphrases can be used: **могу́ очути́ться** 'I may find myself', **я смогу́ победи́ть** 'I shall win', **мне уда́стся его́ убеди́ть** 'I shall convince him', **я не ду́маю чуди́ть** 'I have no intention of behaving eccentrically'. A paraphrase (e.g. **говорю́ де́рзости**) is also required for the first-person singular of **дерзи́ть** 'to be impertinent' (since **держу́**, as the first-person singular of **держа́ть** 'to hold', is not available).

(2) Some doubt remains about the first-person singular of **пылесо́сить** (colloquial) 'to hoover'; **пылесо́шу** is recorded, but the paraphrase **убира́ю пылесо́сом** 'I hoover' is often preferred.

(3) Some verbs have no first- or second-person singular or plural. They include **звуча́ть** 'to sound', **зна́чить** 'to mean' ('I mean', 'you mean' etc. are rendered as **хочу́ сказа́ть, хо́чешь сказа́ть**), **означа́ть** 'to signify', **течь** 'to flow'.

(4) The first and second persons of some other verbs (e.g. **горе́ть** 'to burn', **кипе́ть** 'to boil') appear in figurative meanings only: **горю́** жела́нием уе́хать 'I am burning with a desire to leave', **киплю́** негодова́нием 'I am boiling with indignation'.

(5) **Ку́шать** 'to eat' should not be used in the first-person singular or plural, while in the second-person singular and plural it can sound cloying, and the third-person forms are addressed mainly to children. 'To eat' is best rendered by the verb **есть** (see **224**), except in the imperative, where **ку́шай!, ку́шайте!** are preferred. (Note, however, a mother's strict instruction to her child: **Ешь** всё по поря́дку! 'Eat everything in the right order!' See **229** (2).)

(6) **Слыха́ть** 'to hear' is used only in the infinitive and past tense (there are, however, no such restrictions on **слы́шать** 'to hear').

(7) **Мочь** 'to be able' and **хоте́ть** 'to want' are not normally found in the imperfective future. Instead, the perfectives **смочь, захоте́ть** are used, or, in the case of **мочь,** the paraphrase **быть в состоя́нии** 'to be capable of'.

226 The verb 'to be'

(1) The verb **быть** 'to be' has no present tense in Russian:

Я ру́сский	I am Russian
Э́то мой муж	This is my husband

(2) A dash may be used for emphasis:

Я ру́сский, а он — нет	I am Russian and he is not

A dash also appears in definitions:

Москва́ — столи́ца России	Moscow is the capital of Russia

(3) 'It is' has no equivalent in many impersonal expressions:

Интере́сно слушать ра́дио	It is interesting to listen to the radio
Темне́ет	It is getting dark
Хо́лодно	It is cold

(4) The declarative **'there is/are'** either has no equivalent in Russian or may be rendered by a dash:

На стене́ — карти́на	There is a picture on the wall

Alternatively, На стене́ **есть** карти́на. See (5).

(5) **Есть,** a relic of a former verb conjugation, may be used for emphasis. **Есть** is particularly common:

(i) In questions (and positive answers to questions):

> — Папиро́сы **есть**?
> — **Есть!**
> 'Are there any cigarettes?'
> 'Yes, there are'

(ii) In contexts where the verb is heavily emphasized:

> — Кем же ты хо́чешь быть?
> — Кем **есть** — рядовы́м матро́сом
> 'What do you want to be, then?'
> 'What **I am,** an ordinary rating'

> — Ну́жно справедли́вое реше́ние
> — На́ше реше́ние **и есть** справедли́вое
> 'We need an equitable solution'
> 'Our solution **is** equitable'

> Зако́н **есть** зако́н
> The law is the law

(iii) When 'to be' means 'to exist':

> **Есть** таки́е лю́ди, кото́рые не лю́бят икры́
> There are people who do not like caviar

(iv) **Есть** is also found in definitions:

> Пряма́я ли́ния **есть** кратча́йшее расстоя́ние мѐжду двумя́ то́чками
> A straight line is the shortest distance between two points

(6) In the press and other official contexts the verb **явля́ться** 'to be' also appears in definitions (for case usage see **102** (3) and (4)):

> Це́лью перегово́ров **явля́ется** подписа́ние догово́ра
> The aim of the talks is the signing of a treaty

> Равнопра́вие **явля́ется** осно́вой на́шего о́бщества
> Equality is the basis of our society

(7) To point something out, **вот** is used, the equivalent of English 'here is, are; there is, are':

> **Вот** моя́ тетра́дь
> Here is/there is my exercise book

(8) A more specific verb is often used as an equivalent of 'to be':

> **Наступа́ет** па́уза   There **is** a pause

Раздаю́тся аплодисме́нты	There **is** applause
сиде́ть в тюрьме́	**to be** in prison
служи́ть в а́рмии	**to be** in the army
состоя́ть чле́ном	**to be** a member
стоя́ть на я́коре	**to be** at anchor
Простира́ются леса́	There **are** forests
учи́ться в университе́те	**to be** at university

(9) **Быва́ть** denotes repetition or frequency:

Я ча́сто **быва́ю** в Москве́
I am often in Moscow

В на́шем рестора́не **быва́ют** грибы́
You can sometimes get mushrooms in our restaurant

227 Formation of the imperative

(1) The *familiar* imperative is used in issuing commands to persons one normally addresses as **ты** (see **115**). The *formal* imperative, which is used in addressing people whom one would normally address as **вы** (see **115**), is made by adding **-те** to the familiar imperative.

(2) The familiar imperative is formed from imperfective and perfective verbs by adding **-й**, **-и** or **-ь** to the present-future stem (see **212**).

(i) Imperative in -й

The letter **-й(те)** is added to present-future stems ending in a vowel.

Infinitive	Third-person plural	Stem	Imperative
петь	**по-ю́т**	**по-**	**по́й(те)**
постро́ить	**постро́-ят**	**постро́-**	**постро́й(те)**
рабо́тать	**рабо́та-ют**	**рабо́та-**	**рабо́тай(те)**

Note
(a) The imperatives of **дава́ть** 'to give' and compounds of **-дава́ть**, **-знава́ть** and **-става́ть** are as follows: **дава́й(те)** 'give', **встава́й(те)** 'get up', etc.
(b) **Бить** 'to hit' has the imperative **бей(те)**; **вить** 'to weave', **лить** 'to pour', **пить** 'to drink', **шить** 'to sew' form their imperatives in the same way.
(c) Perfective compounds in **-éхать** (e.g. **прие́хать**) have the same

imperative as imperfective compounds in **-езжа́ть** (e.g. **приезжа́ть**): **приезжа́й(те)!** 'come!'

(ii) Imperative in -и

The letter **-и(те)** is added to the present-future stem of verbs with *final* or *mobile* stress in conjugation and with a present-future stem ending in a *consonant*.

(a) Final stress throughout conjugation:

Infinitive	Third-person plural	Stem	Imperative
вести́	**вед-у́т**	**вед-**	**веди́(те)**
взять	**возь-му́т**	**возьм-**	**возьми́(те)**
говори́ть	**говор-я́т**	**говор-**	**говори́(те)**

(b) Mobile stress in conjugation:

держа́ть	**де́рж-ат**	**де́рж-**	**держи́(те)**
получи́ть	**полу́ч-ат**	**полу́ч-**	**получи́(те)**
шепта́ть	**ше́пч-ут**	**ше́пч-**	**шепчи́(те)**

(iii) Imperative in -ь

A soft sign is added to the present-future stem of verbs which are *stem-stressed throughout conjugation* and whose present-future stem ends in a *single* consonant.

ве́рить	**ве́р-ят**	**ве́р-**	**верь(те)**
зажа́рить	**зажа́р-ят**	**зажа́р-**	**зажа́рь(те)**
ма́зать	**ма́ж-ут**	**ма́ж-**	**мажь(те)**
пла́кать	**пла́ч-ут**	**пла́ч-**	**плачь(те)**
поста́вить	**поста́в-ят**	**поста́в-**	**поста́вь(те)**

Note

(a) Apart from many stem-stressed second-conjugation verbs (**знако́мить** 'to acquaint' (imper. **знако́мь**), **мно́жить** 'to multiply' (imper. **мно́жь**) etc.), this category contains a number of first-conjugation verbs with consonant stems and stress on the stem throughout conjugation: **быть** 'to be' (imper. **будь**), **деть** 'to put' (imper. **день**), **лезть** 'to climb' (imper. **лезь**), **ма́зать** 'to daub' (imper. **мажь**), **пря́тать** 'to hide' (imper. **прячь**), **ре́зать** 'to cut' (imper. **режь**), **сесть** 'to sit down' (imper. **сядь**), **стать** 'to stand' (imper. **стань**). Note **лечь** 'to lie down', imper. **ляг** — a soft sign may not appear after a velar consonant.

(b) Stem-stressed **по́мнить** 'to remember' has imperative **по́мни,** since the stem ends in *two* consonants.

(c) The third-person imperative is expressed by the particle **пусть** and the third-person singular or plural of the present tense or perfective future: пусть (она́) пи́шет 'let her write', пусть (они́) приду́т 'let them come'.

228 Stress in the imperative

With the exception of a number of monosyllabic imperatives, where the stress necessarily falls on the single syllable (**жди!** 'wait!', **пой!** 'sing!', не **сме́йся!** 'don't laugh!'), stress in the imperative falls on the same syllable as in the first-person singular.

Infinitive	First-person singular	Imperative
гнать	**гоню́**	**гони́!**
дыша́ть	**дышу́**	**дыши́!**
звать	**зову́**	**зови́!**
писа́ть	**пишу́**	**пиши́!**
получи́ть	**получу́**	**получи́!**
сказа́ть	**скажу́**	**скажи́!**
смотре́ть	**смотрю́**	**смотри́!**

229 Verbs with no imperative or a little-used imperative

(1) **Ви́деть** 'to see' and **слы́шать** 'to hear' do not have imperatives. However, **слу́шай!** 'listen!' and **смотри́!** 'look!' are commonly used.

(2) **Есть** 'to eat' has the imperative **ешь!** However, it is usually replaced by the imperative of **ку́шать,** since the latter has a courteous nuance absent in the rather familiar **ешь!** (see **225** (5)).

230 Formation of the past tense

(1) The past tense of verbs with infinitives in **-ть** and **-сть** is formed by replacing **-ть** or **-сть** by **-л** to give the masculine past:

кури́ть	**он кури́л**	'he was smoking'
писа́ть	**он писа́л**	'he was writing'
сказа́ть	**он сказа́л**	'he said'

упа́сть	**он упа́л**	'he fell'
покрасне́ть	**он покрасне́л**	'he blushed'

(2) The feminine, neuter and plural are formed by adding **-a, -o** and **-и** respectively to the masculine:

он писа́л/упа́л	(masculine)
она́ писа́л**а**/упа́л**а**	(feminine)
оно́ писа́л**о**/упа́л**о**	(neuter)
мы, вы, они́ писа́л**и**/упа́л**и**	(plural)

(3) The past agrees with the subject of the verb in *number* (singular or plural) and *gender* (masculine, feminine or neuter):

я **писа́л**	I was writing (male subject)
я **писа́ла**	I was writing (female subject)
ты **писа́л**	you were writing (male subject)
ты **писа́ла**	you were writing (female subject)
он **писа́л**	he was writing
она́ **писа́ла**	she was writing
оно́ **писа́ло**	it was writing
мы, вы, они́ **писа́ли**	we, you, they were writing

Note

Уче́сть 'to take into account', past учёл, учла́, учло́, учли́ (similarly other compounds of -честь).

231 Verbs with no -л in the masculine past tense

Some types of verb have no **-л** in the masculine past tense.

(1) Verbs in -ереть

тере́ть 'to rub': **тёр** тёрла тёрло тёрли

Similarly **запере́ть** 'to lock' (он за́пер/она́ заперла́/они́ за́перли 'he/she/they locked'), **умере́ть** 'to die' (он у́мер/она́ умерла́/они́ у́мерли 'he/she/they died').

(2) Verbs in **-ну-**

The suffix **-ну-** is optional in the masculine past of *imperfective* stem-stressed verbs which indicate a change in state:

га́снуть 'to be extinguished': **гас/га́снул** га́сла га́сло га́сли

Similarly:

вя́знуть	'to stick fast'	**кре́пнуть**	'to get stronger'
ги́бнуть	'to perish'	**ме́ркнуть**	'to grow dim'
гло́хнуть	'to go deaf'	**па́хнуть**	'to smell'
до́хнуть	'to die' (of animals)	**сле́пнуть**	'to go blind'
ки́снуть	'to turn sour'	**со́хнуть**	'to become dry'

Note

(a) Some imperfectives in **-нуть** are now often replaced by secondary imperfectives:

га́снуть	**погаса́ть**	'to be extinguished'
ги́бнуть	**погиба́ть**	'to perish'
мёрзнуть	**замерза́ть**	'to freeze'
со́хнуть	**просыха́ть**	'to become dry'
ту́хнуть	**потуха́ть**	'to be extinguished'

(b) Stem-stressed *perfective* verbs in **-нуть** which indicate a change in state (**замёрзнуть** 'to freeze', **привы́кнуть** 'to get used to' etc.) do *not* have optional **-ну-** in the masculine past: он **замёрз**, **привы́к** etc.

(c) Verbs in **-ну-** which denote instantaneous actions (e.g. **пры́гнуть** 'to jump') retain the suffix in all past forms: он **пры́гнул** 'he jumped'.

(3) Verbs in **-ти**

Verbs in **-ти** (except for those with present-future stems in **-д** and **-т**, e.g. **вести́** 'to lead', past **вёл**, **вела́**, **вело́**, **вели́**; **мести́** 'to sweep', past **мёл**, **мела́**, **мело́**, **мели́**).

б-stems	**з**-stems	**с**-stems	**ст**-stems
грести́	**везти́**	**нести́**	**расти́**
'to row'	'to convey'	'to carry'	'to grow'
грёб	**вёз**	**нёс**	**рос**
гребла́	**везла́**	**несла́**	**росла́**
гребло́	**везло́**	**несло́**	**росло́**
гребли́	**везли́**	**несли́**	**росли́**

Note

Пасти́ 'to tend, graze' (past **пас**, **пасла́**), **ползти́** 'to crawl' (**полз**, **ползла́**), **скрести́** 'to scour, claw' (**скрёб**, **скребла́**), трясти́ 'to shake' (**тряс**, **трясла́**).

(4) Verbs in **-зть**

These include **грызть** 'to gnaw' (past грыз, гры́зла, гры́зло, гры́зли) and **лезть** 'to climb'.

(5) Verbs in -чь

г-stems	к-stems
бере́чь	**печь**
'to look after'	'to bake'
берёг	**пёк**
берегла́	**пекла́**
берегло́	**пекло́**
берегли́	**пекли́**

The past of other verbs in -**чь** is as follows:

влечь 'to pull, draw'	влёк, влекла́, влекло́, влекли́
дости́чь 'to achieve'	дости́г, дости́гла, дости́гло, дости́гли
жечь 'to burn'	жёг, жгла, жгло, жгли
лечь 'to lie down'	лёг, легла́, легло́, легли́
мочь 'to be able'	мог, могла́, могло́, могли́
напря́чь 'to strain'	напря́г, напрягла́, напрягло́, напрягли́
пренебре́чь 'to disdain'	пренебрёг, -брегла́, -брегло́, -брегли́
сечь 'to cut'	сёк, секла́, секло́, секли́
стере́чь 'to guard'	стерёг, стерегла́, стерегло́, стерегли́
стричь 'to cut' (hair)	стриг, стри́гла, стри́гло, стри́гли
течь 'to flow'	тёк, текла́, текло́, текли́

(6) Compounds of -шибить

Perfective compounds of -**шибить** (e.g. **ушиби́ть** 'to bruise') have past tense -шиб, -ши́бла, -ши́бло, -ши́бли.

232 Mobile stress in the past tense of verbs

Most past-tense forms from verbs in -**ть** have the same stress as the infinitive. There are, however, a number of verbs which have:

(1) End stress in the feminine past

Most of them are monosyllabic verbs and their prefixed derivatives:

(i) Unprefixed verbs

быть 'to be': был **была** бы́ло бы́ли

Similarly **брать/взять** 'to take', **вить** 'to twine', **гнать** 'to drive', **дать** 'to give', **драть** 'to flay', **ждать** 'to wait', **жить** 'to live', **звать** 'to call', **лить** 'to pour', **пить** 'to drink', **плыть** 'to swim', **рвать** 'to tear', **слыть** 'to have the reputation of being', **спать** 'to sleep', **ткать** 'to weave'.

Note
(a) **Дать** 'to give' has alternative neuter stress да́ло or дало́.
(b) **Не** is stressed when combined with the masculine, neuter and plural past forms of **быть** (**не́** был, не была́, **не́** было, **не́** были) and *may* be stressed when combined with the masculine, neuter and plural forms of the verbs **жить** and **дать**: не́ жил, не жила́, не́ жило, не́ жили *or* не жи́л, не жила́, не жи́ло, не жи́ли; не́ дал, не дала́, не́ дало, не́ дали *or* не да́л, не дала́, не да́ло, не да́ли.

(ii) Prefixed verbs

(a) **Собра́ть** 'to collect': собра́л, **собрала́**, собра́ло, собра́ли.

Similarly **взорва́ть** 'to blow up', **добы́ть** 'to acquire', **избра́ть** 'to elect', **разда́ть** 'to distribute', **сдать** 'to surrender', **снять** 'to take off', **убра́ть** 'to clear away' etc.

(b) **Заня́ть** 'to occupy': за́нял, **заняла́**, за́няло, за́няли.

Similarly **запере́ть** 'to lock' (за́пер, заперла́), **нача́ть** 'to begin', **отпере́ть** 'to unlock', **подня́ть** 'to pick up', **поня́ть** 'to understand', **приня́ть** 'to accept', **умере́ть** 'to die' (у́мер, умерла́) etc.

Note
Зада́ть 'to set' has alternative stem and prefix stress in the masculine, neuter and plural past: за́дал, задала́, за́дало, за́дали, *or* зада́л, задала́, зада́ло, зада́ли. Similarly **нали́ть** 'to pour', **обня́ть** 'to embrace', **отда́ть** 'to give back', **подня́ть** 'to raise', **поли́ть** 'to water', **прода́ть** 'to sell', **прожи́ть** 'to live, spend' (a certain time), **созда́ть** 'to create' etc. **Переда́ть** 'to hand over' has the past forms пе́редал, передала́, пе́редало, пе́редали.

(2) End stress in the feminine, neuter and plural

This affects:

(i) A number of reflexive verbs, e.g.

собра́ться 'to assemble':   собра́лся, **собрала́сь**, **собрало́сь**, **собрали́сь**

Similarly **бра́ться/взя́ться** 'to get down to', **дожда́ться** 'to wait until', **оторва́ться** 'to be torn away from', **созда́ться** 'to be created', **уда́ться** 'to succeed' (план уда́лся 'the plan succeeded', мне удало́сь 'I succeeded').

(ii) All verbs in -**ти**:

блюсти́ 'to conserve'	блюл, блюла́, блюло́, блюли́
брести́ 'to wander'	брёл, брела́, брело́, брели́
везти́ 'to convey'	вёз, везла́, везло́, везли́
вести́ 'to lead'	вёл, вела́, вело́, вели́
грести́ 'to row'	грёб, гребла́, гребло́, гребли́
идти́ 'to go'	шёл, шла, шло, шли
мести́ 'to sweep'	мёл, мела́, мело́, мели́
нести́ 'to carry'	нёс, несла́, несло́, несли́
обрести́ 'to acquire'	обрёл, обрела́, обрело́, обрели́
пасти́ 'to tend'	пас, пасла́, пасло́, пасли́
плести́ 'to weave'	плёл, плела́, плело́, плели́
ползти́ 'to crawl'	полз, ползла́, ползло́, ползли́
расти́ 'to grow'	рос, росла́, росло́, росли́
скрести́ 'to scour'	скрёб, скребла́, скребло́, скребли́
трясти́ 'to shake'	тряс, трясла́, трясло́, трясли́
цвести́ 'to flower'	цвёл, цвела́, цвело́, цвели́

(iii) Most verbs in -**чь** (see **231** (5)).

(3) Reflexive endings stressed throughout

нача́ться 'to begin': **начался́, начала́сь, начало́сь, начали́сь**

Similarly **заня́ться** 'to occupy oneself' (with alternative masculine заня́лся).

233   Formation of the future (imperfective and perfective)

(1) The imperfective future

The compound future (imperfective) consists of the relevant form of the future tense of **быть** and the imperfective infinitive:

я **бу́ду** отдыха́ть	I shall rest
ты **бу́дешь** отдыха́ть	you will rest
он, она́, оно́ **бу́дет** отдыха́ть	he, she, it will rest
мы **бу́дем** отдыха́ть	we shall rest

| вы **бу́дете** отдыха́ть | you will rest |
| они́ **бу́дут** отдыха́ть | they will rest |

Note

(a) **Бу́ду** is also used as a future in its own right: Ле́том он **бу́дет** в Санкт-Петербу́рге 'In the summer he will be in St Petersburg'.

(b) In some contexts it implies suspicion (Вы кто **бу́дете**? 'Who might you be?'), approximation (Ему́ **бу́дет** 50 лет 'He must be about 50') and is used in arithmetic (ше́стью шесть **бу́дет** 36 'six sixes are 36' (see **210**)).

(2) The perfective future

The perfective future is expressed by conjugating a perfective verb. The same endings are used as those used with imperfective verbs in rendering the present tense:

я **пишу́**	(impf.)	письмо́	'I am writing a letter'
я **напишу́**	(pf.)	письмо́	'I shall write a letter'
она́ **чита́ет**	(impf.)	статью́	'she is reading the article'
она́ **прочита́ет**	(pf.)	статью́	'she will read the article'

See **215–223** for conjugation patterns, **238–253** for the formation of aspects and **263–268** for differentiation of imperfective and perfective usage in the future.

234 The buffer vowel -o- in conjugation

In many verbs the vowel -o- appears between a prefix ending in a consonant and a verb form which begins with two or more consonants or with a consonant + soft sign. This may affect:

(1) *All* perfective forms:

Infinitive	Past	Future	Imperative
совра́ть 'to lie'	совра́л	совру́	соври́(те)
отосла́ть 'to send away'	отосла́л	отошлю́	отошли́(те)

(2) The **future, imperative** and **feminine, neuter** and **plural past:**

сжечь 'to burn'	сжёг	сожгу́	сожги́(те)
	сожгла́		
	сожгло́		
	сожгли́		

(3) The **infinitive** and **past tense** only:

разобра́ть	'to discern'	разобра́л	разберу́	разбери́(те)
отозва́ть	'to recall'	отозва́л	отзову́	отзови́(те)
разогна́ть	'to disperse'	разогна́л	разгоню́	разгони́(те)

(4) The **future** and **imperative** only:

сжать	'to compress'	сжал	сожму́	сожми́(те)
отпере́ть	'to unlock'	о́тпер	отопру́	отопри́(те)

(5) The **future** only (compounds of -бить, -вить, -лить, -пить, -шить):

разби́ть	'to smash'	разби́л	разобью́	разбе́й(те)
сшить	'to sew'	сшил	сошью́	сшей(те)

Aspect

235 The aspect. Introductory comments

(1) The Russian verb system is dominated by the concept of **aspect.**

(2) Most Russian verbs have *two* aspects, an **imperfective** and a **perfective,** formally differentiated in one of the following ways:

(i) By prefixation: imperfective писа́ть/perfective **на**писа́ть.

(ii) By internal modification: imperfective забы**ва́**ть/perfective забы́ть 'to forget'; imperfective пу**ска́**ть/perfective пу**сти́**ть 'to let go'.

(iii) By derivation from entirely different roots: imperfective **говори́ть**/perfective **сказа́ть** 'to say'.

(iv) In a few instances, by stress: imperfective **насыпа́ть**/perfective **насы́пать** 'to pour'; imperfective **среза́ть**/perfective **сре́зать** 'to cut down'.

Note
Where aspect is differentiated by stress, the imperfectives are conjugated like **знать** and the perfectives like first-conjugation verbs with consonant stems (type II; see **217**).

(3) *Both* aspects are used in the past and future, the imperative and the infinitive. However, only the *imperfective* is used in the present tense.

(4) Most verbs thus have five finite forms, e.g. imperfective **пить**/perfective **вы́пить** 'to drink':

	Past	Present	Future
Impf.	я пил	я пью	я бу́ду пить
Pf.	я вы́пил	—	я вы́пью

(5) The fundamental distinction between the aspects is that the **imperfective:**

(i) focuses on **an action in progress.**

> Он **пил/пьёт/бу́дет пить** молоко́
> He **was, is, will be drinking** milk

(ii) denotes **frequency** of occurrence:

> Он ча́сто **пил, пьёт, бу́дет пить** молоко́
> He often **drank, drinks, will drink** milk

The **perfective,** by contrast, emphasizes **successful completion and result:**

> Я **вы́пил** молоко́   **I have drunk** the milk
> Я **вы́пью** молоко́   **I shall drink** the milk

(Note, as a *result*, there is, will be no milk left.)

Note
The perfective past can render *both* perfect *and* pluperfect tenses. Thus, Он написа́л письмо́ can mean, in context, either '**He has** written a letter' or '**He had** written a letter'.

(6) The aspects may also distinguish attempted action (imperfective) from successfully completed action (perfective). Compare

> Он **угова́ривал** (impf.) меня́ оста́ться
> He **tried to persuade** me to stay

> Он **уговори́л** (pf.) меня́ оста́ться
> He **persuaded** me to stay

Note
Aspectival usage is dealt with in **255–283.**

236 Verbs with one aspect only

(1) While most verbs have two aspects, some have an imperfective only:

госпо́дствовать	'to dominate'
зави́сеть	'to depend'
изоби́ловать	'to abound'
наблюда́ть	'to observe'
находи́ться	'to be situated'
нужда́ться	'to need'
отрица́ть	'to deny'
повинова́ться	'to obey'
подлежа́ть	'to be subject to'
полага́ть	'to assume'
предви́деть	'to foresee'
предстоя́ть	'to be imminent'
предчу́вствовать	'to have a premonition'
преоблада́ть	'to prevail'
пресле́довать	'to persecute'
принадлежа́ть	'to belong'
противоре́чить	'to contradict'
содержа́ть	'to contain'
состоя́ть	'to consist'
сочу́вствовать	'to sympathize'
сто́ить	'to cost'
уча́ствовать	'to participate'

Note

Утвержда́ть has no perfective in the meaning 'to affirm' but has perfective **утверди́ть** in the meaning 'to fix, establish'.

(2) Other verbs are perfective only (many though not all of these denote precipitate action):

воспря́нуть	'to cheer up'
встрепену́ться	'to start' (with surprise)
гря́нуть	'to burst out, ring out'
очути́ться	'to find oneself'
пона́добиться	'to be needed, come in handy'
хлы́нуть	'to gush'

237 Bi-aspectual verbs

(1) Some verbs are bi-aspectual, that is, imperfective and perfective are represented by one verb form (though some also have alternative

imperfectives: **образова́ть** (imperfective and perfective) 'to form', alternative imperfective **образо́вывать**). There are many bi-aspectuals in **-овать** and **-изировать.** (Some of these have alternative perfectives, e.g. biaspectual финанси́ровать 'to finance', pf. also профинанси́-ровать, similarly инструкти́ровать/проинструкти́ровать 'to brief', координи́ровать/скоординировать' to coordinate', реставри́ровать/отреставри́ровать 'to restore'.)

(2) Among the commonest bi-aspectuals are **атакова́ть** 'to attack', **веле́ть** 'to order, bid', **возде́йствовать** 'to have an effect on', **гармонизи́ровать** 'to harmonize', **жени́ться** 'to marry' (of a man marrying a woman – the perfective **пожени́ться** is used only when both partners are joint subjects of the verb: Они́ пожени́лись 'They got married'), **испо́льзовать** 'to use', **иссле́довать** 'to research', **казни́ть** 'to execute', **коллективизи́ровать** 'to collectivize', **конфискова́ть** 'to confiscate', **крести́ть** 'to christen' (alternative perfective **окрести́ть), минова́ть** 'to pass by', **насле́довать** 'to inherit' (alternative perfective **унасле́довать), обеща́ть** 'to promise' (alternative perfective **пообеща́ть), обору́довать** 'to equip', **ра́нить** 'to wound', **роди́ться** 'to be born' (alternative imperfective **рожда́ться), сочета́ть** 'to combine'.

(3) Thus, for example, **иссле́дую** can mean both 'I research' and 'I shall/will research'. Ambiguity may be resolved by contrastive adverbs, as follows:

Положе́ние **постепе́нно** стабилизи́руется
The situation is gradually stabilizing

Положе́ние **ско́ро** стабилизи́руется
The situation will soon stabilize

Note
Imperfective **бежа́ть** 'to run' is also perfective in the meaning 'to escape'; imperfective **приве́тствовать** 'to greet' is also perfective in the past tense; in the past tense, bi-aspectual **организова́ть** 'to organize' (imperfective also **организо́вывать**) is perfective only.

238 Formation of the aspects

Most pairs of verbal aspects arise in one of the following ways:

(1) Through the addition of a **prefix** to the imperfective to make the perfective:

чита́ть (impf.)   **про**чита́ть (pf.)   'to read'

(2) Through **internal modification** involving:

(i) The insertion of a syllable into the stem infinitive:

завязáть (pf.)   завя́зывать (impf.)   'to tie'

сосредотóчить (pf.)   сосредотóчивать (impf.) 'to concentrate'

разби́ть (pf.)   разбивáть (impf.)   'to smash'

(ii) A change in conjugation, an *imperfective* first-conjugation verb in **-а-/-я-** being paired with a *perfective* second-conjugation verb in **-и-/-е-:**

бросáть (impf.)   брóсить (pf.)   'to throw'
загорáть (impf.)   загорéть (pf.)   'to acquire a
                                              tan'

239 Formation of the perfective by prefixation

(1) An imperfective verb may become perfective through the addition of a **prefix:**

писáть (impf.)   написáть (pf.)   'to write'

(2) The conjugation of a perfective verb gives it **future** meaning:

Я напишу́ э́то письмó
I shall write this letter (= get it written)

(3) While the choice of perfective prefixes appears in most cases to be arbitrary, some prefixes are associated with particular meanings; for example, **на-** is associated with verbs of printing, writing and drawing (**напечáтать, написáть, нарисовáть**), **у-** with verbs of perception (**уви́деть, узнáть, услы́шать**), and so on.

(4) All common prefixes (except for **в-** and **до-**) participate in the process of perfectivization:

Imperfective	Perfective	
кипяти́ть	**вс**кипяти́ть	to boil
учи́ть	**вы́**учить	to learn
плати́ть	**за**плати́ть	to pay
купáть	**ис**купáть	to bathe
писáть	**на**писáть	to write
сиротéть	**о**сиротéть	to be orphaned
редакти́ровать	**от**редакти́ровать	to edit
ночевáть	**пере**ночевáть	to spend the night
смотрéть	**по**смотрéть	to look

ждать	**подо**ждáть	to wait
грозúть	**при**грозúть	to threaten
читáть	**про**читáть	to read
будúть	**раз**будúть	to awaken
петь	**с**петь	to sing
вúдеть	**у**вúдеть	to see

240   Functions of the perfective prefixes

(1) The perfective prefixes tend to be semantically neutral, that is, they change the *aspect* of a verb but *not* its meaning. Thus, both **будúть** and **разбудúть** mean 'to awaken', but **будúть** describes the progress of the action, without any reference to result, whereas the perfective **разбудúть** stresses the result:

Я егó **будúл, будúл** и, наконéц, **разбудúл**
I tried and tried to wake him, and finally woke him

(2) The *imperfective* verb describes:

(i) A past, present or future action in progress:

Он **учúл** урóк/**ýчит** урóк/**бýдет учúть** урóк
He **was learning/is learning/will be learning** the lesson

(ii) Repeated actions:

Онá **платúла/плáтит/бýдет платúть** регулярно
She **paid/pays/will pay** regularly

(3) The *perfective* focuses on the *completion* of a single action in the past or future. Usually, a result is implied:

Онá **написáла** письмó
She has written a letter (it is ready to send)

Онá **прочитáла** кнúгу
She has read the book (now *you* can read it, or it can be returned to the library)

Онá **заплáтит** за электрúчество
She will pay the electricity (the account will be settled)

(4) Often the perfective denotes the *culmination of a process*:

Онá **приготóвила** ýжин   She cooked dinner

In this example the culmination of the action, expressed by the perfective **пригото́вила,** will have been preceded by a process of indeterminate length (она́ **гото́вила** у́жин 'she **was cooking** dinner'), the completion of which is denoted by the perfective.

241 Semantic differentiation of aspects

In some verbs it is possible to detect at least a minor measure of semantic differentiation between imperfective and perfective. Thus, the imperfective past of **ви́деть** 'to see' contains a nuance ('to associate with')

> Я **ви́дел** его́ вчера́   I saw him yesterday

which the perfective **уви́деть** contains in the future, but *not* in the past. Compare

> Я **уви́дел** его́ вчера́
> I caught sight of him (but *not* 'saw, associated with him') yesterday

and

> Я **уви́жу** его́ за́втра
> I shall see him (i.e. 'meet, associate with him') tomorrow

> Я **уви́жу** его́, как то́лько он войдёт
> I shall catch sight of him as soon as he comes in

242 Submeanings of perfectives

Apart from the resultative meaning (see **240** (3)), the perfective has a number of submeanings.

(1) **The inceptive**, denoting the beginning of an action. This meaning is often conveyed by the prefix **за-**:

заболе́ть	to fall ill
заговори́ть	to start speaking
закури́ть	to light up
замолча́ть	to fall silent
запе́ть	to burst into song
запла́кать	to burst into tears
засмея́ться	to burst out laughing
зацвести́	to blossom

Note

(a) Only some of these verbs have imperfectives: **заболева́ть, заку́ривать, запева́ть, зацвета́ть.** Where a verb has no imperfective, a paraphrase may be possible: **залива́ться сме́хом** 'to burst out laughing', **облива́ться слеза́ми** 'to burst into tears'.

(b) The meaning of inception also adheres to the perfective aspects of unidirectional verbs of motion (он **пошёл** 'he set out') (see also **326**) and to the perfectives **полюби́ть, понра́виться:** Вы лю́бите литерату́ру? Да, я **полюби́л** её ещё в шко́ле (Vasilenko) 'Do you like literature?' 'Yes, **I took a liking to it** when still at school'. Compare Вам **понра́вится** фильм 'You **will like** the film'.

(c) Inception can also be expressed by the prefixes **вз-/вс-** and **раз/рас-:** **вс**треве́житься 'to get alarmed', **рас**серди́ться 'to get angry'.

(2) The **instantaneous** or **semelfactive** submeaning:

Он **услы́шал** мой го́лос
He heard, caught the sound of my voice

Note

Instantaneous meanings are often expressed by perfectives with the suffix **-ну-:**

Он **чи́ркнул** спи́чкой   He struck a match

Other semelfactives include **кри́кнуть** 'to shout', **махну́ть** 'to wave', **плю́нуть** 'to spit' etc.

(3) The submeaning of **limited duration** (prefix **по-**):

поговори́ть	to have a chat
посиде́ть	to sit for a while
поспа́ть	to have a nap

Note

(a) **По-** can impart the meaning of limited duration to verbs which form their 'neutral' perfectives with other prefixes:

написа́ть (neutral pf.)	**пописа́ть** 'to write for a while'
прочита́ть (neutral pf.)	**почитать** 'to read for a while'

(b) See **249** for imperfective submeanings.

243 Formation of verbal aspects by internal modification

Many aspectival pairs are created as the result of internal modification, in particular through suffixation. This may involve:

(1) The insertion of a syllable into a perfective infinitive to form the imperfective. This is the commonest method of forming aspectival pairs:

переписа́ть (pf.)   перепи́сывать (impf.)   'to copy'

(2) The pairing of a first-conjugation imperfective in **-а-/-я-** with a second-conjugation perfective in **-и-/-е-**: impf. позволя́ть/pf. позво́лить 'to allow'; impf. реша́ть/pf. реши́ть 'to decide'; impf. загора́ть/pf. загоре́ть 'to acquire a tan'.

244 The formation of imperfectives from prefixed first-conjugation verbs

(1) This occurs when a prefix other than the 'neutral' perfective prefix is added to an imperfective first-conjugation verb, changing not only its *aspect* but also its *meaning*.

(2) Thus, the neutral perfective of писа́ть 'to write' (changing its aspect only, *not* its meaning) is **написа́ть**. But other prefixes may combine with писа́ть, changing aspect **and** meaning:

записа́ть	to note down
переписа́ть	to copy
подписа́ть	to sign

and so on, each newly formed verb being a perfective *with a new meaning*.

(3) Imperfectives of such verbs are formed by inserting the suffix **-ыв-** before the final syllable of the infinitive, with stress falling on to the syllable preceding the suffix. In this way new sets of aspectival pairs are established:

записа́ть (pf.)   запи́сывать (impf.)   'to note down'
подписа́ть (pf.)   подпи́сывать (impf.)   'to sign'

(4) This method of forming 'secondary imperfectives' from compounds of first-conjugation verbs is an important word-formatory device which is used with many verbs, e.g.

вяза́ть 'to tie'   →   связа́ть (neutral pf.) 'to tie'
        ↓
развяза́ть (pf. with new   →   развя́зывать (impf.) 'to untie'
meaning: 'to untie')

(5) Of two adjacent vowels in a compound perfective, the second is replaced by **-ива-** in the imperfective: pf. оттáять 'to thaw out' impf. оттáивать (there are exceptions, e.g. pf. затéять 'to undertake', impf. затевáть).

245 Vowel mutation in secondary imperfective verbs

(1) The vowel **e** becomes **ё** under stress in the secondary imperfective, thus (based on root verb **чесáть** 'to scratch'):

причесáться (pf.)/причёсываться (impf.) 'to comb one's hair'

Similarly,

завоевáть (pf.)/завоёвывать (impf.) 'to conquer'

(2) In similar circumstances, **o** becomes **a** in the secondary imperfective:

зарабóтать (pf.)/зарабáтывать (impf.) 'to earn'
раскопáть (pf.)/раскáпывать (impf.) 'to excavate'

Note
The **o : a** mutation does *not* affect verbs in -овать: pf. образовáть 'to form', impf. образóвывать.

246 Secondary imperfectives based on second-conjugation verbs

(1) A process similar to that described in **244** is used to form secondary imperfectives from second-conjugation verbs, but with the following differences:

(i) The suffix **-ив-** is used instead of **-ыв-**.

(ii) Consonant mutation operates, e.g. **с : ш** in

крáсить (impf.)   →   окрáсить (neutral pf.) 'to paint'
      ↓
перекрáсить (pf. with   →   перекрáшивать (impf.
new meaning 'to repaint')   'to repaint')

Note that **o** mutates to **a** in stressed position:

рассмотрéть (pf.)/рассмáтривать (impf.) 'to scrutinize'

приговорúть (pf.)/приговáривать (impf.) 'to sentence'

Similarly pf. заподо́зрить 'to suspect', impf. заподя́зривать; pf. зако́нчить 'to conclude', impf. зака́нчивать; pf. оспо́рить 'to dispute', impf. оспа́ривать; подгото́вить 'to prepare, train', impf. подготя́вливать; pf. приспосо́бить 'to adapt', impf. приспоса́бливать.

Note

(a) In some secondary imperfectives, **o** and **a** are stylistically differentiated, **o** being characteristic of literary style, **a** of a more conversational style: thus pf. сосредото́чить 'to concentrate'/impf. сосредото́чивать or сосредота́чивать. Similarly, pf. обусло́вить, 'to condition', impf. обусло́вливать/обусла́вливать.

(b) Some imperfectives retain **o**: pf. опоро́чить 'to discredit', impf. опоро́чивать; pf. отсро́чить 'to defer', impf. отсро́чивать; pf. подыто́жить, 'to sum up', impf. подыто́живать; pf. приуро́чить 'to time', impf. приуро́чивать; pf. уполномо́чить 'to authorize', impf. уполномо́чивать; pf. упро́чить 'to consolidate', impf. упро́чивать.

(2) Of two adjacent vowels in a compound perfective, the second is replaced by **-ива-** in the imperfective. The mutation **o : a** operates (pf. успоко́ить 'to reassure', impf. успока́ивать):

pf. прикле́ить 'to stick to'   impf. прикле́**ива**ть
pf. устро́ить 'to arrange'   impf. устра́**ива**ть

247 Consonant mutation in secondary imperfectives based on second-conjugation verbs

Standard consonant mutations are observed in deriving secondary imperfectives from second-conjugation perfective verbs.

б : бл	приспосо́бить 'to adapt'	impf. приспоса́**бл**ивать
в : вл	вы́здороветь 'to recover'	impf. выздора́**вл**ивать
д : ж	проследи́ть 'to track'	impf. просле́**ж**ивать
з : ж	заморо́зить 'to freeze'	impf. замора́**ж**ивать
м : мл	вскорми́ть 'to rear'	impf. вска́р**мл**ивать
п : пл	затопи́ть 'to heat'	impf. зата́**пл**ивать
с : ш	взве́сить 'to weigh'	impf. взве́**ш**ивать
ст : щ	вы́растить 'to grow'	impf. выра́**щ**ивать
т : ч	оплати́ть 'to pay'	impf. опла́**ч**ивать

Note

(a) Absence of mutation in pf. захвати́ть 'to seize', impf. захва́тывать, pf. проглоти́ть 'to swallow', impf. прогла́тывать, pf. сбро́сить 'to drop, throw down', impf. сбра́сывать.

(b) 'Reverse mutation' (**ч : к**) in pf. вы́скочить 'to jump out', impf. выска́кивать, pf. перекрича́ть 'to shout down', impf. перекри́кивать.

248 Secondary imperfectives based on monosyllabic verbs

(1) Secondary imperfectives derive from the compound prefixed perfectives of many monosyllabic verbs by the insertion of the suffix **-ва-** after the root vowel of the perfective. Thus:

бить (impf)   → поби́ть (neutral pf.) 'to hit'
  ↓
заби́ть (pf. with new meaning → забива́ть (impf.) 'to score'
'to score')

Similarly,

pf. зажи́ть 'to heal'	impf. зажива́ть
pf. наде́ть 'to put on'	impf. надева́ть
pf. нали́ть 'to pour'	impf. налива́ть
pf. откры́ть 'to open'	impf. открыва́ть

Note

The initial consonant of the syllable inserted into compounds of monosyllabic verbs in the formation of secondary imperfectives is often identical with that which appears in the first-person singular of the conjugation of the stem verb.

Perfective	Imperfective	First-person singular of stem verb
заже́чь 'to ignite'	зажига́ть	жгу (from жечь 'to burn')
пересе́чь 'to intersect'	пересека́ть	секу́ (from сечь 'to cut')
сгрести́ 'to rake together'	сгреба́ть	гребу́ (from грести́ 'to row')
сжать 'to compress'	сжима́ть	жму (from жать 'to squeeze')
уче́сть 'to take into consideration'	учи́тывать	чту (from честь 'to consider')

Note also pf. разъе́сть 'to corrode', impf. разъеда́ть (cf. **-д-** in, for example, еда́ 'food').

(2) The suffix **-ы-** or **-и-** is inserted between two initial consonants in the stem verb to form the imperfective:

pf. вы́звать 'to call out, cause'   impf. вызыва́ть
pf. вы́рвать 'to tear out'   impf. вырыва́ть
pf. отосла́ть 'to send away'   impf. отсыла́ть
pf. собра́ть 'to collect'   impf. собира́ть

249   Submeanings of some prefixed imperfectives

Some imperfective verbs with the prefixes **пере-, по-** or **при-** have the following submeanings, as distinct from the standard imperfective meanings of duration and frequency:

(1) Reflexives with the prefix **пере-** denote joint action (mostly imperfective only): **перепи́сываться** 'to correspond', **пересту́киваться** 'to communicate by knocking', **перешёптываться** 'to exchange whispers'.

Note
Some verbs of this type have perfectives: **перегля́дываться** (impf.)/**перегляну́ться** (pf.) 'to exchange glances', **переми́гиваться** (impf.)/**перемигну́ться** (pf.) 'to wink at each other'.

(2) Verbs in **по-** with the iterative ending **-ивать/-ывать** denote the intermittent performance of a short-lived action, e.g. **посви́стывать** 'to whistle every now and again'. The mutations **е:ё** and **о:а** operate: **поблёскивать** 'to glint' (cf. блесте́ть 'to shine'), **посма́тривать** 'to steal glances at' (cf. смотре́ть 'to look'). Compare

Голова́ у меня́ **поба́ливает**
I keep getting headaches

Шпиль **поблёскивает** на со́лнце
The spire glints in the sun

Ма́слов флегмати́чно **позёвывал** (Yakhontov)
Maslov kept yawning in a phlegmatic sort of way

Бе́режно, **поста́нывая** и **покря́хтывая,** он опуска́ется вниз (Rasputin)
He descends cautiously, groaning and wheezing intermittently

Note
(a) Verbs in this category have no perfective.
(b) Other verbs of this type include **погла́живать** from гла́дить 'to stroke', **подёргивать** from дёргать 'to tug', **пока́шливать** from ка́шлять 'to cough', **пома́ргивать** from морга́ть 'to blink',

поси́живать from сиде́ть 'to sit', посту́кивать from стуча́ть 'to knock', почи́тывать from чита́ть 'to read'.

(3) Verbs in при- with the suffix -ва- or -ива-/-ыва- may denote actions accompanying other actions: припева́ть 'to sing along', припля́сывать 'to skip up and down', прито́пывать 'to stamp one's feet' (e.g. in time to music).

Note
Verbs in this category have no perfectives.

250 The differentiation of aspects by conjugation

(1) Many aspectival pairs consist of a first-conjugation imperfective in -ать/-ять and a second-conjugation perfective in -ить (or -еть). This affects:

(i) A number of unprefixed verbs (imperfectives first):

броса́ть	бро́сить	'to throw'
конча́ть	ко́нчить	'to finish'
лиша́ть	лиши́ть	'to deprive'
реша́ть	реши́ть	'to decide, resolve'

(ii) More especially, prefixed verbs:

включа́ть	включи́ть	'to switch on'
выполня́ть	вы́полнить	'to fulfil'
выступа́ть	вы́ступить	'to appear, perform'
загора́ть	загоре́ть	'to get sun-tanned'

Note
Покупа́ть, купи́ть 'to buy' (prefixed imperfective/**un**prefixed perfective).

(2) In many pairs the imperfective has *end* stress and the perfective *stem* stress: доверя́ть, дове́рить 'to trust'; измеря́ть, изме́рить 'to measure'; наруша́ть, нару́шить 'to disrupt'; позволя́ть, позво́лить 'to allow'; улучша́ть, улу́чшить 'to improve' etc.

(3) The usual consonant mutations apply to many verbs of this type:

б : бл	pf. употреби́ть 'to use'	impf. употребля́ть
в : вл	pf. оста́вить 'to leave'	impf. оставля́ть
д : ж	pf. заряди́ть 'to load'	impf. заряжа́ть
д : жд	pf. награди́ть 'to reward'	impf. награжда́ть

з : ж	pf. отрази́ть 'to reflect'	impf. отража́ть
п : пл	pf. прикрепи́ть 'to attach, fasten'	impf. прикрепля́ть
с : ш	pf. пригласи́ть 'to invite'	impf. приглаша́ть
ст : ск	pf. пусти́ть 'to let go'	impf. пуска́ть
ст : щ	pf. угости́ть 'to treat'	impf. угоща́ть
т : ч	pf. заме́тить 'to notice'	impf. замеча́ть
т : щ	pf. запрети́ть 'to ban'	impf. запреща́ть

Note

(a) Double perfectivization (imperfective first) in **ве́шать, пове́сить** 'to hang', **куса́ть, укуси́ть** 'to bite', **роня́ть, урони́ть** 'to drop', **сажа́ть, посади́ть** 'to seat' and **стреля́ть, вы́стрелить** 'to shoot'.

(b) Some prefixed derivatives of **меня́ть** 'to change' are imperfective, with a perfective in **-менить: заменя́ть/замени́ть** 'to replace', **изменя́ть/измени́ть** 'to alter', **отменя́ть/отмени́ть** 'to cancel'. Others acquire perfective meaning, with an imperfective in **-менивать: обме́нивать/обменя́ть** 'to exchange', **разме́нивать/ разменя́ть** 'to change' (money to smaller denominations).

251 Aspectival pairs with different roots

The verbs in some aspectival pairs derive from different roots. These include (imperfective first) the following:

бить	уда́рить	'to strike'
брать	взять	'to take'
говори́ть	сказа́ть	'to say'
класть	положи́ть	'to put, place'
лови́ть	пойма́ть	'to catch'

252 Verbs which are reflexive in the imperfective aspect only

Some verbs are reflexive in the imperfective aspect only. These include:

(1) Some verbs of sitting, lying and standing:

ложи́ться	лечь	to lie down
переса́живаться	пересе́сть	to change seats, trains etc.
приса́живаться	присе́сть	to sit down for a while
сади́ться	сесть	to sit down
станови́ться	стать	to (go and) stand

(2) **Ло́паться/ло́пнуть** 'to burst, snap' and **ру́шиться/ру́хнуть** 'to collapse'.

253 Compounds of -ложить

Some perfective compounds of **-ложить** have imperfectives in **-кладывать,** while others have imperfectives in **-лагать.** Those with imperfectives in **-кладывать** have a more literal meaning (**прокла́дывать,** проложи́ть доро́гу 'to lay a road'); those with imperfectives in **-лагать** are more abstract (**предлага́ть,** предложи́ть 'to propose'). The distinction is well marked in verbs which have both types of imperfective, with differing meanings: **вкла́дывать,** вложи́ть письмо́ в конве́рт 'to place a letter into an envelope', **влага́ть,** вложи́ть ду́шу во что́-нибудь 'to put one's heart into something'.

254 Meanings of verbal prefixes

Prefixes are important elements in Russian word formation. As many as sixteen prefixes may be attached to certain root verbs, each prefix imparting a different meaning: thus **вяза́ть** 'to tie', **завяза́ть** 'to knot', **отвяза́ть от** 'to untie from', **привяза́ть к** 'to tie to' and so on. Most prefixes are associated with particular prepositions, as follows.

Prefix	Preposition		Meaning
в-	**в**	+ acc.	into
вы-	**из**	+ gen.	out of
до-	**до**	+ gen.	as far as
за-	**за**	+ acc.	behind
из-	**из**	+ gen.	out of
на-	**на**	+ acc.	on to
от-	**от**	+ gen.	detaching
пере-	**через**	+ acc.	across
под-	**к**	+ dat.	approach
	под	+ acc.	under
при-	**к**	+ dat.	attaching
с-	**с**	+ gen.	down from
	с	+ instr.	together with

Note
(a) Prefixed verbs in some meanings also have non-prepositional government, or government through other prepositions.

(b) Prefixes also impart meanings to parts of speech other than verbs: cf. **перелётный** 'migratory', **приложе́ние** 'supplement', **съезд** 'congress' etc. See also **28**.

(c) Some prefixes have alternative spellings (**вз-/вс-**; **из-/ис-**; **раз-/рас-**), **вс-**, **ис-** and **рас-** combining with stems which begin with unvoiced consonants (**к, п, с, т, ф, х, ц, ч, ш, щ**), **вз-**, **из-** and **раз-** combining with other stems.

(d) Compare also prefixes with verbs of motion (see **331**).

(e) Imperfectives are listed first in aspectival pairs.

(1) В(о)-

(i) Direction into:

включа́ть/включи́ть в спи́сок   to include in a list
вме́шиваться/вмеша́ться в спор   to interfere in an argument

(ii) Movement upwards (mainly with verbs of motion, e.g. **влеза́ть/влезть** на де́рево 'to climb a tree'):

встава́ть/встать из-за стола́   to get up from a table

(2) Вз(о)-/вс-; воз-/вос-

(i) Movement upwards:

взбира́ться/взобра́ться на́ гору   to climb a hill

(ii) Disruption:

взрыва́ть/взорва́ть мост   to blow up a bridge

(3) Вы-

(i) Movement out of:

вырыва́ть/вы́рвать страни́цу из дневника́
to tear a page out of a diary

(ii) Achievement through the action of the root verb:

выпра́шивать/вы́просить о́тпуск
to get leave on request

(iii) Exhaustiveness of action (reflexive verbs):

выска́зываться/вы́сказаться
to have one's say

высыпа́ться/вы́спаться
to have a good sleep

Note
As a perfective prefix, **вы-** is always stressed; as an imperfective prefix it is stressed only in **вы́глядеть** 'to look'.

(4) До-

(i) Completion of action already begun:

дожива́ть/дожи́ть до ста́рости
to live to a ripe old age

допи́сывать/дописа́ть письмо́
to finish writing a letter

(ii) Achievement of hard-won result:

догова́риваться/договори́ться
to come to an agreement

дозва́ниваться/дозвони́ться (к) дру́гу
to get through to one's friend

(5) За-

(i) Movement behind:

закла́дывать/заложи́ть ру́ки за́ спину
to put one's hands behind one's back

(ii) Process covering an area:

заса́живать/засади́ть сад дере́вьями
to plant a garden with trees

(iii) Absorption in an action (often detrimental (reflexives)):

заси́живаться/засиде́ться в гостя́х
to outstay one's welcome

зачи́тываться/зачита́ться
to get absorbed in reading

(iv) Acquisition:

завоёвывать/завоева́ть   to conquer
зараба́тывать/зарабо́тать   to earn
захва́тывать/захвати́ть   to seize

(v) Fastening, securing:

завя́зывать/завяза́ть га́лстук	to fasten a tie
закрыва́ть/закры́ть	to close
застёгивать/застегну́ть пальто́	to fasten a coat

(vi) To spoil by excess:

зака́рмливать/закорми́ть щенка́	to overfeed a puppy

(6) Из(о)-/ис-

(i) Extraction, selection:

избира́ть/избра́ть	to elect
исключа́ть/исключи́ть	to exclude, expel

(ii) Action affecting whole area:

изорва́ть (pf. only) руба́шку	to tear a shirt all over

(7) На-

(i) Action directed on to:

нажима́ть/нажа́ть (на) кно́пку
to press a button

накле́ивать/накле́ить ма́рку на конве́рт
to stick a stamp on an envelope

(ii) Action performed to point of satisfaction:

наеда́ться/нае́сться	to eat one's fill
насмотре́ться (pf. only)	to have a good look

(iii) Quantity, accumulation:

наруба́ть/наруби́ть дров	to chop some firewood
нарва́ть (pf. only) **цвето́в**	to pick some flowers

(8) Над(о)-

(i) Superimposition:

надстра́ивать/надстро́ить эта́ж
to add a storey

(ii) Detaching part of surface:

надкýсывать/надкуси́ть гру́шу
to take a bite out of a pear

(9) Недо- (opposite of 13 (v)).

Shortfall:

недооце́нивать/ недооцени́ть
to underrate

недоса́ливать/ недосоли́ть ка́шу
not to put enough salt in the porridge

(10)О-/об-/обо-

(i) Action affecting many:

опра́шивать/опроси́ть студе́нтов
to canvas student opinion

(ii) Detailed comprehensive action:

обсужда́ть/обсуди́ть	to discuss
осма́тривать/осмотре́ть	to examine

(iii) Action directed over whole area:

окле́ивать/окле́ить сте́ны обо́ями	to wall-paper
окружа́ть/окружи́ть	to surround

(iv) Error:

огова́риваться/оговори́ться	to make a slip of the tongue
ошиба́ться/ошиби́ться	to make a mistake

(v) Endowment with/acquisition of a quality or state:

облегча́ть/облегчи́ть	to lighten, relieve
оглуша́ть/оглуши́ть	to deafen

Note
In some verbs the prefix appears only in the perfective: **вдове́ть/овдове́ть** 'to be widowed', **сле́пнуть/осле́пнуть** 'to go blind'.

(vi) Outdoing:

обгоня́ть/обогна́ть   to overtake
обы́грывать/обыгра́ть to outplay

(vii) Deception:

обма́нывать/обману́ть to deceive
обсчи́тывать/обсчита́ть to short-change a customer
покупа́теля

(11) Обез-/обес-

Deprival (bookish styles):

обесце́нивать/обесце́нить to devalue

(12) От(о)-

(i) Moving, receding a certain distance:

отстава́ть/отста́ть от други́х
to lag behind the others

отступа́ть/отступи́ть
to retreat, digress

(ii) Detachment:

отруба́ть/отруби́ть ве́тку от де́рева
to lop a branch off a tree

отрыва́ть/оторва́ть листо́к
to tear off a sheet

(iii) Reversal of action:

отвыка́ть/отвы́кнуть от куре́ния
to get out of the habit of smoking

отменя́ть/отмени́ть
to cancel

(13) Пере-

(i) Movement across:

перепры́гивать/перепры́гнуть (через) кана́ву
to jump across a ditch

переставля́ть/переста́вить ме́бель
to move furniture round

(ii) Redoing:

перекра́шивать/перекра́сить
to repaint

переодева́ться/переоде́ться
to change one's clothes

(iii) Division:

перепи́ливать/перепили́ть
to saw through

(iv) Action affecting many objects:

пересма́тривать/пересмотре́ть все фи́льмы
to see all the films

(v) Excess:

перегружа́ть/перегрузи́ть маши́ну
to overload a vehicle

(vi) Reciprocal action:

перепи́сываться (impf. only)
to correspond

(vii) Outdoing:

перекри́кивать/перекрича́ть толпу́
to shout down a crowd

(14) Под(о)-

(i) Movement or position under:

подкла́дывать/подложи́ть поду́шку под го́лову
to place a pillow under one's head

подпи́сывать/подписа́ть
to sign

(ii) Approach:

пододвига́ть/пододви́нуть стул к стене́
to move a chair up to the wall

(iii) Addition of substance or material:

подсыпа́ть/подсы́пать са́хару в чай
to add some sugar to one's tea

(iv) Furtive, underhand action:

подде́лывать/подде́лать
to forge, counterfeit

подслу́шивать/подслу́шать
to eavesdrop

(v) Supplementary action:

подви́нчивать/подвинти́ть кран немно́го
to tighten up a tap

(15) Пре- (mainly in bookish styles)

(i) Transformation:

преобразо́вывать/ преобразова́ть
to transform

(ii) Termination:

прекраща́ть/прекрати́ть
to curtail

(iii) Excess:

преувели́чивать/ преувели́чить
to exaggerate

превыша́ть/превы́сить
to exceed

(16) Пред(о)-

Anticipation:

предви́деть (impf. only)
to foresee

предполага́ть/предположи́ть
to presume

предупрежда́ть/предупреди́ть
to warn, prevent

(17) При-

(i) Approach, arrival:

приближа́ться/прибли́зиться
to approach

приземля́ться/приземли́ться
to land

(ii) Attachment:

привя́зывать/привяза́ть соба́ку к де́реву
to tie a dog to a tree

прикрепля́ть/прикрепи́ть фотогра́фию к бла́нку
to attach, pin a photograph to a form

(iii) Addition:

прибавля́ть/приба́вить
to add

припи́сывать/приписа́ть не́сколько строк
to add a few lines

(iv) Limited action:

привстава́ть/привста́ть
to half rise

приоткрыва́ть/приоткры́ть дверь
to open a door slightly

(v) Accustoming:

привыка́ть/привы́кнуть к дисципли́не
to get used to discipline

(18) Про-

(i) Through, past:

пропуска́ть/пропусти́ть
to miss, let past

просма́тривать/просмотре́ть
to look through

(ii) Harmful error:

пролива́ть/проли́ть	to spill
просыпа́ть/проспа́ть	to oversleep, sleep in

(19) Раз(о)-/рас-

(i) Separation, dispersal, disintegration, distribution:

раздвига́ть/раздви́нуть занаве́ски
to part the curtains

размеща́ть/размести́ть раке́ты
to deploy missiles

распи́ливать/распили́ть ствол
to saw up a tree trunk

(ii) Reversal of an action:

развя́зывать/развяза́ть	to untie
раздева́ться/разде́ться	to get undressed
разду́мывать/разду́мать	to change one's mind

(20) С(о)-

(i) Removal:

сверга́ть/све́ргнуть самодержа́вие
to overthrow an autocracy

снима́ть/снять пальто́
to take off one's coat

(ii) Descent:

спуска́ться/спусти́ться на морско́е дно
to descend to the sea bed

(iii) Joining:

скрепля́ть/скрепи́ть	to staple together
скла́дывать/сложи́ть	to fold

(iv) Joint feeling or action:

сочу́вствовать (impf. only)	to sympathize

(21) У-

(i) Removal:

удаля́ть/удали́ть о́пухоль	to remove a tumour

(ii) Imparting a quality:

улучша́ть/улу́чшить	to improve
упроща́ть/упрости́ть	to simplify

255 The imperfective and perfective aspects

See also **235**.

(1) The imperfective

(i) The imperfective may describe an action:

(a) In progress:

> Он за́втракал (impf.)   He was having breakfast

(b) Progressing towards the completion of a goal, represented by a perfective:

> Он до́лго **вспомина́л** (impf.) мою́ фами́лию, и наконе́ц **вспо́мнил** (pf.) её
> He took a long time to recall my name, and finally he **did** recall it

(ii) Imperfectives may describe a number of actions occurring simultaneously or in an indeterminate order:

> Говори́ли (impf.) мы сра́зу, **перебива́ли** (impf.) дру́г дру́га, **смея́лись** (impf.) (Shukshin)
> We were all speaking at once, interrupting each other, laughing

Note

(a) The imperfective here does not *move* events, but describes actions as they *develop*, focusing on *circumstances* rather than completion. The imperfective therefore tends to be associated with conjunctions which imply development or continuity of action: **по ме́ре того́ как** 'in proportion as', **чем . . . тем**, 'the . . . the' (with comparatives), **в то вре́мя как/пока́** 'while' etc. Compare

> **В то вре́мя пока́** он **собира́лся** (impf.), я **успе́ла** (pf.) **убра́ть** (pf.) всю посу́ду в шкаф
> While he was getting ready I managed to clear all the crockery away into the cupboard

> Here the completed action ('I managed to clear all the crockery away into the cupboard' (pf.)) is set against the background of an action in progress ('while he was getting ready' (impf.)).

(b) In the following example two processes are seen developing in parallel and are therefore rendered by imperfectives:

И чем бо́льше Коси́хин его́ **слу́шал** (impf.), тем грустне́е ему́
станови́лось (impf.) (Yakhontov)
And the more Kosikhin listened to him, the sadder he became

(iii) The idea of continuity of action can be reinforced by an adverb
which either:

(a) Emphasizes action in progress:

Он расска́зывал (impf.) **подро́бно**
He related his story in detail

or:

(b) Denotes the passage of time, thus underlining the durative meaning:

Он чита́л (impf.) «*Войну́ и мир*» **три часа́**
He read *War and Peace* for three hours

Attention here is drawn to the *time* involved in the action, *not* its
completion or result; hence the use of the *imperfective* aspect.

Note
For frequentative meanings see **256** (2) (ii), **257** (3), **266**, **269** (2), **274**,
276 (2) (i).

(2) The perfective aspect

(i) Unlike the imperfective, the perfective emphasizes **result**:

Он **дал** (pf.) ученика́м по уче́бнику
He **gave** each pupil a textbook (as a result, they have a copy, can
prepare their homework, take a full part in the class work etc.)

(ii) The perfective **moves** events, advances the action step by step,
unlike the imperfective, which describes an action in progress:

Воше́дший **снял** (pf. 1) плащ, **сел** (pf. 2) за стол и **по́днял** (pf. 3)
дневни́к
The man who had come in **removed** his coat, **sat down** at the table
and **picked up** the diary

Here emphasis is laid on the completion in sequence of a series of
actions: perfective 1 is completed before perfective 2 takes place,
perfective 2 is completed before perfective 3 takes place, and so on,
each perfective moving events a stage further.

(iii) Verbs of different aspect may coexist in the same sentence, the imperfectives **describing the scene** and the perfectives **advancing the action**:

> Она́ **сняла́** (pf.) пальто́, стоя́ла (impf.) спино́й ко мне и **шелесте́ла** (impf.) бума́гами (Kazakov)
> She took off her coat and stood with her back to me, rustling the papers

(iv) An imperfective describing an action in progress can be succeeded by a perfective which denotes successful completion of that action:

> Он до́лго **догоня́л** (impf.) меня́ и, наконе́ц, **догна́л** (pf.)
> He chased me for a long time and finally caught me up

This exemplifies the comparison which has been made between the use of imperfectives and the filming of a scene, and between the use of some perfectives and a **snapshot**.

(v) The perfective tends to combine with conjunctions which imply the completion or the suddenness of an action (**до того́ как** 'before', **как то́лько** 'as soon as', **по́сле того́ как** 'after' etc.), and with adverbs which imply immediacy or unexpectedness (**внеза́пно** 'suddenly', **сра́зу** 'immediately', **чуть не** 'almost, within an ace of' etc.).

(vi) Unlike the imperfective past, which is totally rooted in past time, the perfective may have implications for the present. This occurs when a **present state** results from a past perfective action or process (the so-called 'pure perfect'):

Я **забы́л** (pf.)	I have forgotten, I **forget**
Он **опозда́л** (pf.)	He **is late** (but has arrived; cf. Он опа́здывает (impf.) 'He is late' (and has not yet arrived))
Я **привы́к** к э́тому (pf.)	I **am used** to this
Он **у́мер** (pf.)	He **is dead** (has died)

256 Aspect in the present tense

(1) The present tense has only one form, the imperfective.

(2) The present tense is used:

(i) To denote actions in progress:

> Сейча́с я **пишу́** письмо́
> At the moment I am writing a letter

(ii) To denote habitual actions:

По воскресéньям он **лóвит** рыбу в рекé
On Sundays he fishes in the river

(iii) To make general statements:

Земля́ **враща́ется** вокрýг Сóлнца
The Earth revolves around the Sun

(iv) To denote capabilities and qualities:

Зóлото не **ржа́веет**
Gold does not tarnish

Note
Except for verbs of motion (see **315–325**), the present tense does not distinguish durative from habitual actions, thus: Я **готóвлю** ýжин 'I **am preparing/prepare** supper'

(v) To express intention to perform an action in the not too distant future. The verb involved is often a simple or compound verb of motion in the first-person singular or plural:

Сегóдня вéчером **идý** в кинó
I am going to the cinema this evening

Бýдушей зимóй **уезжа́ем** за грани́цу
We are going abroad next winter

Note
Other verbs found in this meaning include **возвраща́ться** 'to return', **встреча́ть** 'to meet', **начина́ть** 'to begin' etc.

(vi) As a 'historic present'. The use of the present tense with past meaning brings the action more graphically before the mind's eye of the reader or listener. It is a device commonly found in literary works and is much more widely used in Russian than in English:

Приходи́л он к нам ча́сто. **Сиди́т**, быва́ло, и **расска́зывает**
He would often come to see us. He **would sit** and **tell** us stories

(vii) To describe an action or state that *began* in the past and *continues* into the present (the 'continuous present'):

Я **рабóтаю** здесь с прóшлого гóда
I **have been working/have worked** here since last year

Note

The use of the past tense in such contexts would be rendered by an English pluperfect: Она́ **была́** за́мужем уже́ 10 лет 'She **had been** married for ten years'.

(viii) In reported speech (see also **265**).

(a) In reporting a statement, the same tense is used as in direct speech. Thus the statement Я **люблю́** её 'I love her' is reported as:

Я сказа́л, что **люблю́** её
I said I loved her

or

Он сказа́л, что **лю́бит** её
He said he loved her

(b) This contrasts with English, where a past tense in the main clause ('he said') generates a past tense in the subordinate clause: 'He said he *loved* her'. To use a past tense here in Russian would imply that the direct statement had contained a past tense. Thus, Он сказа́л, что **люби́л** её means 'He said he **had loved** her/**used to love** her'.

(c) The construction extends to reported knowing, asking, hoping etc., and can be introduced by **ду́мать** 'to think', **знать** 'to know', **наде́яться** 'to hope', **обеща́ть** 'to promise', **спроси́ть** 'to ask' etc.:

Ей каза́лось, что ма́льчик **спит**
She thought the child **was asleep**

Он писа́л, что **прово́дит** ле́то в Волгогра́де
He wrote that he **was spending** the summer in Volgograd

(d) The same principles of tense sequence apply, though *less rigidly*, to verbs of perception, cf. use of the *present* tense in

Шу́рка слы́шал, как в темноте́ **бе́гает** ёж (Vasilev)
Shurka heard a hedgehog running about in the dark

and the *past* tense in

Слы́шно бы́ло, как **мурлы́кал** Ку́стик (Belov)
You could hear Kustik purring

Бы́ло ви́дно, что он не **боя́лся** холо́дной воды́ (Fadeev)
It was obvious that he was not afraid of cold water

In such contexts, the present tense is said to be more 'vivid' than the past.

257 Aspect in the past tense

(1) The durative meaning

(i) Past durative meanings, that is, descriptions of actions as they develop, are invariably rendered by the **imperfective** aspect:

> Мы **составля́ли** (impf.) телегра́мму в Москву́
> We **were composing** a telegram to send to Moscow

(ii) Passage of time may be indicated by an appropriate adverb or adverbial phrase:

> **Че́тверть ве́ка** он собира́л (impf.) всё, что относи́лось (impf.) к исто́рии кра́я (Granin)
> He spent **a quarter of a century** collecting everything that related to the history of the area

(2) Endeavour contrasted with successful completion

(i) An action in progress (impf.) can be contrasted with its successful completion (pf.):

> Мы до́лго **реша́ли** (impf.) зада́чу — и наконе́ц **реши́ли** (pf.) её
> We **spent a long time solving** the task and finally **solved it**

(ii) The imperfective denotes an *attempt* which may either:

(a) Fail:

> Он **убежда́л** (impf.) меня́, что без согла́сия роди́телей мы всё равно́ не смо́жем быть сча́стливы (*Russia Today*)
> He **tried to convince me** that we could not be happy anyway without our parents' consent

(b) Succeed, achievement being expressed by a perfective:

> Я **пробива́лся** (impf.) к нему́ ро́вно неде́лю и наконе́ц **проби́лся** (pf.)
> I spent exactly a week **trying to force my way** into his office, and finally **succeeded in doing so**

(iii) Some aspectival pairs consist of *imperfectives* which denote attempt to achieve and *perfectives* which denote successful achievement:

Imperfective   Perfective

добива́ться 'to try to achieve' **доби́ться** 'to achieve'

доказывать	'to contend'	**доказать**	'to prove'
ловить	'to try to catch'	**поймать**	'to catch'
решать	'to tackle'	**решить**	'to solve'
сдавать	'to take' (an examination)	**сдать**	'to pass' (an examination)
уверять	'to try to assure'	**уверить**	'to assure'
уговаривать	'to try to persuade'	**уговорить**	'to persuade'

(3) Repeated actions in the past

(i) Repeated actions are normally expressed by the **imperfective**:

Он **звонил** (impf.) нам по вечерам
He used to ring us in the evenings

Бывало is sometimes added to emphasize repetition:

Он, **бывало**, звонил (impf.) нам по вечерам
He was in the habit of ringing us in the evenings

(ii) Frequency may also be stressed by an adverb or adverbial phrase of time: **всегда** 'always', **иногда** 'sometimes', **никогда** 'never', **раз в неделю** 'once a week', **часто** 'often':

Потом он **чаще всего**, не разогревая, съедал (impf.) оставленный матерью обед (Vanshenkin)
Then, **more often than not**, he would eat the lunch left by his mother, without heating it up

Note
Secondary imperfectives (here, **съедать**) are often preferred to *primary* imperfectives (cf. **есть** 'to eat') in frequentative constructions, in view of the durative connotations which adhere to primaries, cf. Он **сидел** (primary impf.) над статьёй не менее трёх часов 'He **pored** over the article for no less than three hours', a reference to one durative action, and Он **просиживал** (secondary impf.) над статьёй не менее трёх часов 'He **would pore** over the article for not less than three hours at a time', a reference to a **series** of actions.

(iii) When reference is made to the **number of times** an action occurs:

(a) The **imperfective** is preferred when the actions are repeated at irregular and spaced-out intervals:

Три раза они **покидали** (impf.) борт станции и **выходили** (impf.) в открытый космос (*Russia Today*)
Three times they left the space station and walked in space

Не́сколько раз я **прогоня́л** (impf.) его́. Он **сади́лся** (impf.) в отдале́нии, немно́го **пережида́л** (impf.) и сно́ва **бежа́л** (impf.) за мной (Kazakov)
Several times I chased him away. He would sit down at a distance, bide his time and run after me again

(b) The **perfective** is preferred when a series of identical actions, repeated in swift succession, can be interpreted as **components of one multiple action:**

Вы́лез (pf.) из-под кры́ши кру́пный воробе́й, **чири́кнул** (pf.) **два́жды** и улете́л (pf.) (Belov)
A large sparrow emerged from under the eaves, **chirped twice** and flew off

Прибли́зившись к нему́, она́ доста́ла (pf.) из су́мочки пистоле́т и **три ра́за вы́стрелила** (pf.) в упо́р
Approaching him she took a pistol from her bag and **fired three times** at point-blank range

Note
The imperfective is preferred for verbs of *beginning*, however, even when a number of actions occur in swift succession:

Он **начина́л** (impf.) письмо́ **раз двена́дцать**, рвал (impf.) листы́, изне́рвничался (pf.), испсихова́лся (pf.) (Shukshin)
He began the letter about a dozen times, kept tearing up the sheets, got all hot and bothered, almost blew a fuse

258 Use of the imperfective past to express a 'statement of fact'

— Вы **звони́ли** (impf.) ему́?	'Have you rung him?'
— Да, **звони́л** (impf.)	'Yes, I have'
— Я где́-то **ви́дел** (impf.) вас	'I have seen you somewhere'
— Вы **чита́ли** (impf.) «*Цеме́нт*»?	'Have you read *Cement*?'
— Да, **чита́л** (impf.)	'Yes, I have'

(1) The imperfective is used in the above examples to denote an action in isolation, with no emphasis on its completion or non-completion, the circumstances in which it occurred, or other detail. The statements and responses show that a phone call has been made, that two people have met before, that *Cement* is one of the books read by a particular person. These are bald statements of fact, with no fleshing-out of the context

and no stress on the achievement of a result. This 'submeaning' of the imperfective is known as **констатáция фáкта** 'statement of fact'. It is particularly common in the past tense and is usually set in the vaguest of contexts:

— Э́тот человéк вам знакóм?
'Do you know that man?'
— Да, я однáжды **встречáл** (impf.) егó
'Yes, I met him once'

(2) The 'statement of fact' is common:

(i) In the imprecise context of an interrogative or in a situation where, for example, a check is being made to see whether a particular action has been carried out:

Вы **провéтривали** (impf.) кóмнату?
Have you aired the room?

(ii) In enquiring about someone's whereabouts:

Вы не **вúдели** (impf.) Лéну?
Have you seen Lena?

(iii) In delivering a reminder:

Но ведь я **говорúл** (impf.) вам об э́том!
But I told you about this!

(3) As the context is firmed up, however, or a result emphasized, the perfective comes into contention. Compare:

(i) Use of the *imperfective* in:

Я **писáл** (impf.) ей	I wrote to her
Я **расскáзывал** (impf.) вам об э́том	I told you about that
Я **звонúл** (impf.) емý	I have rung him
Мы ужé **встречáлись** (impf.)	We have already met
Я **читáл** (impf.) «*Чапáева*» в шкóле	I read *Chapaev* at school

(ii) Use of the *perfective* as the context is filled in:

Я написáл (pf.) ей **письмó**
I wrote her **a letter**

Я **тóлько что** сказáл (pf.) вам об э́том
I have **only just** told you about this

Я позвонúл (pf.) емý, **чтóбы напóмнить емý** о вéчере
I rang him to **remind him about the party**

Я встре́тил (pf.) его́ **в про́шлом году́ на Чёрном мо́ре**
I met him **last year on the Black Sea**

(4) It will be clear from the above examples that the imperfective is preferred where a fact is placed in a contextual vacuum, and that the perfective is preferred when the context is filled in, in terms of **what** action was carried out, **when, where** or **for what purpose**, or if the result or completion of an action is stressed. Thus, the question — Вы **прочита́ли** (pf.) «*Накану́не*»? can be rendered as 'Have you **finished** *On the Eve*?' — completion of the action is important since, say, the person asking the question is waiting to read the novel. The answer to this question might be **Прочита́л** (pf.), возьми́те, пожа́луйста 'Yes, I have; here you are'. The perfective would also be used if someone had been *told* to read the novel: Вы **прочита́ли** (pf.) «*Накану́не*»? '**Did you read** *On the Eve*?' (i.e. as you were told to).

259 Use of the imperfective past to denote an action and its reverse

(1) The imperfective past may be used to denote an action and its reverse:

Она́ **брала́** (impf.) кни́гу в библиоте́ке
She had a book out of the library (*and has now returned it*)

Similarly, **открыва́л** (impf.) can mean 'opened **and closed again**':

У меня́ в ко́мнате так хо́лодно сего́дня. Наве́рное, кто́-то **открыва́л** (impf.) здесь **окно́**
It is so cold in my room today. Someone has probably **had the window open** in here

The implication of this example is that the window has been opened but is now shut again. By contrast, Кто́-то **откры́л** (pf.) окно́ means that the window is still open 'Someone has opened the window', or refers to the single act of opening 'Someone opened the window'.

(2) Other imperfective past forms of this type include:

включа́л	'switched on' (and off again)
встава́л	'got up' (and sat or lay down again)
выключа́л	'switched off' (and on again)
дава́л	'gave' (and received back again)
закрыва́л	'closed' (and opened again)
клал	'put down' (and took up again)

ложи́лся	'lay down' (and got up again)
надева́л	'put on' (and took off again)
поднима́лся	'ascended' (and came down again)
спуска́лся	'descended' (and went up again):

Он **встава́л** (impf.) но́чью
He got up in the night (and went back to bed again)

Ребёнок **просыпа́лся** (impf.), но сейча́с он опя́ть спит
The child woke up, but now he is asleep again

(3) In fact, the imperfective past of *any* verb denoting an action which has an opposite action may be used in this way:

Оди́н из них **по́днял** (pf.) ру́ку. Их ли́ца понра́вились мне, и я остановился. Тот, кто **поднима́л** (impf.) ру́ку, просу́нул в маши́ну сму́глое лицо́ (Strugatskys)
One of them **raised his arm.** I liked the look of them and stopped. The one who **had raised his arm** thrust a dark-skinned face through the car window

Here, the perfective denotes a *one-way* action (**по́днял** ру́ку 'raised his arm') and the imperfective a *two-way* action, the action and its reverse (**поднима́л** ру́ку 'raised his arm **and lowered it again**').

260 Aspectival usage when emphasis is on the identity of the person performing the action

(1) If we examine the examples

| Кто мыл (impf.) посу́ду? | Who washed the dishes? |
| Кто убира́л (impf.) ко́мнату? | Who tidied the room? |

then it is clear that the washing up has been done and the room tidied. Emphasis centres *not* on the *action*, but on the identity of the person who *performed* it. In such circumstances the *imperfective* is preferred:

Та́ня, э́то ты **разбира́ла** (impf.) кни́ги в шкафу́?
Tanya, was it you who sorted the books in the cupboard?

Use of the imperfective may also imply that something (usually untoward) happened while the action was being carried out (e.g. papers were mislaid).

Вы не зна́ете, кто **открыва́л** (impf.) окно́? На подоко́ннике лежа́ли мои́ бума́ги.

Do you know who opened the window? My papers were lying on the window-sill.

(2) The *perfective* is preferred, however:

(i) When the **quality** of the action is stressed:

Кто **так хорошо́** убра́л (pf.) кни́ги в шкаф?
Who made such a good job of tidying the books into the cupboard?

or when the result is specially emphasized:

В ко́мнате так чи́сто. Интере́сно, кто **убра́л** (pf) её?
The room is beautifully clean. I wonder who tidied it?

(ii) When the verb denotes 'discovery':

Кто **изобрёл** (pf.) ра́дио?
Who invented radio?

Кто **откры́л** (pf.) Аме́рику?
Who discovered America?

Кто **нашёл** (pf.) ключи́?
Who found the keys?

(iii) When the action involved is not deliberate or has an untoward result:

Кто **разби́л** (pf.) ча́шку?
Who broke the cup?

(3) The imperfective is also used when attention is directed to the **place** or **time** of an action rather than to the action itself:

Где вы **покупа́ли** (impf.) «Вечёрку»?
Where did you buy the evening paper?

— Я показа́л (pf.) ему́ чертёж
'I showed him the blueprint'
— Когда́ ты **пока́зывал** (impf.)?
'When did you show it to him?'

In these examples the questioner is interested in the place and time of the actions, **not** in their completion, which is in any case clear from the context (as in the first example) or explicitly stated (as in the second).

261   Use of the imperfective past to denote a forthcoming event

The imperfective past is used to indicate that an action was due to take place:

Поезд **отходи́л** (impf.) в пять часо́в
The train **was due to leave** at five o'clock

Он мно́го рабо́тал, потому́ что в воскресе́нье **выступа́л** (impf.) перед большо́й аудито́рией
He worked hard, because on Sunday he **was to appear** in front of a large audience

262   Negated verbs in the past

(1) Both aspects may be used to indicate non-performance of an action in the past, but while the negative imperfective indicates that the action **did not take place at all,** the negative perfective indicates that it took place but **was not successful,** thus:

Он не **реша́л** (impf.) зада́чу
He **did not** do the sum (perhaps because he was off school)

Он не **реши́л** (pf.) зада́чу
He **could not** do the sum (he tried but failed)

(2) The aspects may similarly be used to distinguish an action which has not yet begun (impf.) from one which has begun but is not yet completed (pf.):

Я ещё не **чита́л** (impf.) э́ту статью́
I haven't **read** this article yet

Я ещё не **прочита́л** (pf.) э́ту статью́
I haven't **finished** this article yet

(3) The imperfective past is also used to negate a statement or supposition expressed by a perfective:

— Почему́ вы ушли́ из ци́рка, почему́ вас **уво́лили**? (pf.)
— Меня́ не **увольня́ли** (impf.), я ушла́ сама́ (*Ogonek*)
'Why did you leave the circus, why were you dismissed?'
'I was not dismissed, I left of my own accord'

(4) The imperfective past is also used to denote the continuation of a

negative state:

> Он до́лго **не соглаша́лся** со мной (impf.)
> He **took a long time to agree** with me

(5) The **perfective** past is used when an expected event did not take place:

> Меня́ никто́ не **встре́тил** (pf.)
> No one met me (despite, for example, a promise or understanding that someone would)

Compare Меня́ никто́ не **встреча́л** (impf.), 'No one met me' — a simple statement of fact with no implication that the reverse was expected.

> Мы не **посмотре́ли** (pf.) фильм
> We **didn't see** the film (though, for example, it is just the kind of film we might have been expected to see)

Compare Мы не **смотре́ли** (impf.) фильм 'We **haven't seen** the film'.

(6) The perfective past is also used when an expected or desired result has not yet materialized:

> Он ещё не **пришёл** (pf.)
> He has not arrived yet.

263   Aspect in the future

(1) The imperfective future focuses on the progress of an action, while the perfective future stresses expected result or successful attainment. Compare the two future forms, the first imperfective and the second perfective, in the following example:

> **Бу́ду чита́ть** (impf.) статью́, наде́юсь, что **прочита́ю** (pf.)
> I shall **read/be reading** the article and hope I shall **get it finished**

(2) The imperfective is used when emphasis is placed on the way in which an action is carried out, *not* on its result or successful implementation:

> Как бы **бу́дете отправля́ть** (impf.) кни́ги, просто́й или заказно́й бандеро́лью?
> How will you be sending the books, as ordinary printed matter or registered?

(3) A perfective future may refer to a completed action within the framework of an action in progress, e.g.

Когда́ я **бу́ду проходи́ть** (impf.) ми́мо апте́ки, **куплю́** (pf.) табле́тки от ка́шля
When I pass the chemist's I shall buy some cough drops

Note
(a)   Perfectives often appear in sequence, each perfective advancing the action a stage further: Я **свяжу́сь** (pf.) со свои́ми друзья́ми, всё **узна́ю** (pf.), и **позвоню́** (pf.) (Soloukhin) 'I shall contact my friends, get all the facts and give you a ring'.
(b)   A negated perfective future may be used to denote the impossibility of an action: Раскалённое желе́зо го́лой руко́й **не возьмёшь** 'You cannot take hold of red-hot iron with your bare hands'.

264   The 'logical' future

Unlike English, where the future tense is not used after conjunctions such as 'after', 'as soon as', 'before', 'until', 'when' etc., Russian uses an imperfective or perfective future to express future meaning in such contexts:

Когда́ вы **бу́дете ремонти́ровать** (impf.) маши́ну, не забу́дьте (pf.) поменя́ть све́чи
When you **are overhauling** the car, don't forget to change the plugs

Как то́лько он **придёт** (pf.), поста́вим (pf.) ча́йник
As soon as he **arrives** we shall put the kettle on

265   The future in reported speech

An imperfective or perfective future in **direct** speech

— В э́том году́ я не **бу́ду отдыха́ть**
'This year I won't be having a holiday'

— Я **приду́**, е́сли успе́ю
'I shall come if I have time'

is expressed as a future in **reported** speech:

Он сказа́л, что в э́том году́ не **бу́дет отдыха́ть**
He said he **wouldn't** be having a holiday this year

Она́ обеща́ла, что **придёт,** е́сли **успе́ет**
She promised she **would** come if she **had** time

Compare **256** (2) (viii).

266   Use of the future to express repeated actions

(1) Repeated actions in the future are usually expressed using the imperfective aspect:

Ле́том я **бу́ду** регуля́рно **загора́ть** (impf.)
In summer I shall sun-bathe regularly

(2) A perfective future may be used to stress the sequential nature of actions:

Когда́ пито́мцы **окре́пнут** (pf.), их выпуска́ют (impf.) в тайгу́ (*Sputnik*)
When our small charges (baby sable) **grow strong enough** they are released into the taiga

The use of two imperfectives in this example would imply that the actions occur simultaneously, that the sable are released while they are still in the process of growing strong. The perfective (**окре́пнут**) shows that the actions are sequential: first the sable get strong, then they are released. Compare

У меня́ был кро́хотный но́мер с телеви́зором, кото́рый **включа́лся** (impf.), когда́ в автома́т **опу́стишь** (pf.) сто ие́н (Granin)
I had a tiny room with a television set which switched on when one inserted one hundred yen

In this example, too, the perfective (**опу́стишь**) indicates that the actions are sequential (first the money is inserted, then the set switches on), *not* simultaneous.

(3) The 'historic perfective future' may be used for graphic effect in past frequentative contexts, in literary and other written styles, to denote repeated quick movements:

Она́ то **вздохнёт** (pf.), то **о́хнет** (pf.)
She would now sigh, now moan

Быва́ло serves to stress the past frequentative nature of the action:

Быва́ло, он загля́нет (pf.) к нам
He was in the habit of looking in to see us

(4) The perfective future can also appear in frequentative contexts in combination with temporal adverbs such as **всегда́** 'always':

Он вам **всегда́** помо́жет (pf.)
He will always give you a hand

Note
The meaning of the perfective future in such contexts is 'potential' rather than frequentative, since its use does not imply a repeated action (cf. genuine repetition in Ка́ждый день она́ **бу́дет** ему́ **помога́ть** (impf.) 'She will help him every day'), but rather constant readiness to perform an action if the need should arise, the element of repetition being expressed in terms of one typical action.

267   The perfective future in warnings

In colloquial Russian the first-person singular of the perfective future may be used to express a warning:

Я тебе́ **поспо́рю!** (pf.)
I'll give you argue!

Я тебе́ **погуля́ю!** (pf.)
I'll give you gallivanting around!

268   Aspect in questions

(1) Questions about intended actions are more often than not couched in the imperfective:

Что вы **бу́дете де́лать**? (impf.)
What are you going to do?

Что вы **бу́дете зака́зывать**? (impf.)
What are you going to order?

Вы **бу́дете пить** (impf.) чай йли ко́фе?
Will you have tea or coffee?

unless special emphasis is laid on successful completion:

Вы **найдёте** (pf.) э́тот дом?
Will you find the house?

(2) Answers, however, can be in either aspect, depending on the context:

Я бу́ду дочи́тывать (impf.) кни́гу/**дочита́ю** (pf.) кни́гу
I shall be finishing off the book/shall **get** the book **finished**

Я бу́ду пить (impf.) ко́фе/**вы́пью** (pf.) ча́шечку ко́фе
I shall have coffee/**have** a small cup of coffee

Compare

— Ла́дно, я уйду́. А ты что **бу́дешь де́лать** (impf.)?
— **Уложу́** (pf.) Светла́нку спать, а пото́м **бу́ду реве́ть** (impf.) (Zalygin)
'All right, I'll leave. And what are you going to do?'
'I shall put Svetlanka to bed and then cry my eyes out'

(3) The answer to the question Что вы бу́дете зака́зывать? 'What are you going to order?' is likely to be perfective, however, since the *result* of the action is of particular importance (the diner will presumably get the dish he or she orders):

Я возьму́ (pf.) бульо́н
I will have clear soup

Note

In colloquial Russian *negative* forms of the verb are frequently used in making requests: Вы на сле́дующей **не схо́дите**? (impf.) 'Are you getting off at the next stop?' Quite often the perfective future is used: Вы не **ска́жете** (pf.), ско́лько сейча́с вре́мени? 'You couldn't tell me the time, could you?'; Вы не **разреши́те** (pf.) позвони́ть от вас? 'Would you mind if I used your phone?'

269   Some uses of the imperfective imperative

The imperfective imperative is used to express:

(1) General injunctions:

Береги́те (impf.) приро́ду!
Conserve nature!

(2) Frequentative instructions:

Всегда́ относи́ (impf.) кни́ги в срок
Always return your books on time

(3) Instructions to continue an action:

Пиши́те (impf.) да́льше!
Carry on writing!

270   Use of the imperative in the context of a single action

(1) The **perfective** imperative is used to order the implementation of a single action:

Закро́йте (pf.) окно́!
Shut the window!

Note
The addition of the particle **-ка** adds a nuance of familiarity to the command: Запиши́-**ка**! (pf.) 'Do jot it down!'

(2) The negated **imperfective** imperative is used to **forbid** an action:

Не **закрыва́йте** (impf.) окно́!   **Don't shut** the window!

(3) Both aspects can appear in one sentence, the imperfective forbidding and the perfective ordering an action:

Е́сли всё же что́-то загоре́лось, **не теря́йтесь** (impf.), **постара́йтесь** (pf.) сохрани́ть хладнокро́вие (*Rabotnitsa*)
If something really has caught fire, **don't panic, try** to retain your composure

(4) If a perfective imperative has been ineffectual, then an imperfective may be used to impart a sense of urgency:

Запиши́ (pf.) мой телефо́н. . . . **Запи́сывай** (impf.), пожа́луйста, я о́чень тороплю́сь!
Make a note of my telephone number. . . . **Would you mind writing it down**, please, I am in a terrible hurry!

271   Use of the imperative to exhort and invite

(1) The imperfective imperative is also used:

(i) In exhortations:

— **Встава́й** (impf.), сказа́ла она́   'Do get up', she said

(ii) In expressing wishes:

Поправля́йтесь! (impf.)   Get well soon!

(iii) In conveying an invitation, in social or other conventional situations:

Проходи́те (impf.), пожа́луйста!
Pass down the aircraft, please! (air-hostess to passengers)

Бери́те! (impf.)	Take one/some!
Клади́те (impf.) са́хар!	Have some sugar!
Раздева́йтесь!(impf.)	Take off your hat and coat!
Сади́тесь! (impf.)	Sit down!
Снима́йте (impf.) пальто́!	Take off your coat!

(2) In a more formal or professional relationship, however, the **perfective** may be preferred:

Ню́ра, **сними́** (pf.) с больно́го пижа́му, хладнокро́вно сказа́ла Ве́ра Ива́новна (Aksenov)
'Nyura, remove the patient's pyjamas', said Vera Ivanovna coolly (doctor to nurse)

«Я тебе́ покажу́ фанта́зию! **Сядь** (pf.) как сле́дует!» (Trifonov)
'I'll give you imagination! Sit properly!' (mother to child)

Note

(a)   The first-person plural of an imperfective or perfective verb may also be used to express wishes or appeals: **бу́дем наде́яться** (impf.), что 'let's hope that', **Попро́буем** (pf.) 'Let's have a go'. The addition of **дава́й/дава́йте** lends emphasis: **Дава́йте** бу́дем чита́ть (impf.) Пу́шкина! 'Let's read Pushkin!', **Дава́й** сыгра́ем! (pf.) 'Let's have a game!'

(b)   The negative optative is usually expressed by an imperfective: Не **бу́дем зажига́ть** (impf.) све́та, ла́дно? — сказа́ла она́ (Kazakov) '"Do you mind if we leave the light off?" she said', **Не бу́дем преувели́чивать** (impf.) 'Let's not exaggerate', Дава́йте **не бу́дем спо́рить** (impf.) 'Let's not argue'.

272   A command arising naturally from context

The imperfective imperative is preferred when an instruction is the expected norm in particular circumstances. For example, a student at an examination knows the procedure: he selects a slip of paper with a question on it, prepares his answer and is invited to speak. The examiner's instructions are therefore expressed in the imperfective:

Бери́те (impf.) биле́т! **Отвеча́йте!** (impf.)
Take a slip! Answer!

Similarly, standard recommendations and requests from a shop assistant will be in the imperfective:

Плати́те (impf.) в ка́ссу!   Pay at the cash-desk!

while non-predictable statements will be in the perfective:

Возьми́те (pf.) э́ту ко́фточку! Она́ вам идёт
Take this blouse! It suits you

273   Negative commands/warnings

(1) A negative command usually appears in the imperfective aspect (see **270** (2)). When the imperative implies a **warning**, however, rather than a command, tempered with a nuance of apprehension that the action might occur inadvertently, then the **perfective** is preferred:

Не заболе́й! (pf.)	Mind you don't fall ill!
Не поскользни́сь! (pf.)	Mind you don't slip!
Не проле́й (pf.) молоко́!	Mind you don't spill the milk!
Не простуди́сь! (pf.)	Mind you don't catch a cold!
Не урони́те (pf.) ва́зу!	Mind you don't drop the vase!

Note

(a)   These commands forbid actions which would not normally be performed deliberately, but might occur inadvertently or as the result of carelessness. It is in these circumstances that the negative perfective imperative is used, sometimes combined with смотри́(те)! 'mind!':

Смотри́, не забу́дь! (pf.)	Mind you don't forget!
Смотри́, не обре́жься! (pf.)	Mind you don't cut yourself!
Смотри́, не опозда́й! (pf.)	Mind you're not late!
Смотри́, не упади́! (pf.)	Mind you don't fall!

(b)   Other perfective verbs whose negative imperatives may be used to express warnings include **испа́чкаться** 'to get dirty', **опроки́нуть** 'to overturn, capsize', **потеря́ться** 'to get lost', **промахну́ться** 'to miss the target', **проспа́ть** 'to oversleep'. Compare «Умоля́ю, девчо́нки, **не зарази́тесь** (pf.), бу́дьте осторо́жнее!» (*Rabotnitsa*) 'I implore you, girls, don't get infected, be more careful!' Из сосе́дней ко́мнаты, где шуме́ли го́сти, тётя проси́ла: "Ра́ди Бо́га, **не потеря́й** ничего́!" (Nabokov) 'From the next room, where the guests were making a din, my aunt could be heard asking: "For heaven's sake, don't lose anything!"'

(2) The imperfective is used, however, when reference is to a protracted period rather than a single occurrence:

> Смотри́ **не забыва́й** (impf.) нас!
> Mind you don't forget us!

274   Use of the perfective imperative with repeated actions

While a repeated action is usually associated with an imperfective imperative (See **269** (2).), the perfective is used when reference is made to the number of times an action is repeated in swift succession (cf. **257** (3) (iii) (b)):

> Прослу́шайте (pf.) плёнку **два ра́за/не́сколько раз**
> Listen to the tape twice/several times

275   Use of the future and the infinitive to express peremptory commands

(1) Future perfectives may be used to express categorical commands:

> **Пойдёшь** к ма́ме, **возьмёшь** у неё ключи́ от шка́фа и **принесёшь** посу́ду
> You will go to mother, get the keys of the cupboard from her and bring the crockery

(2) A strict imperative may also be rendered by use of the infinitive:

> **Сиде́ть** сми́рно!   Sit quietly!

276   Aspect in the infinitive. Introductory comments

(1) The perfective infinitive is used to denote the completion of a single action:

> Мне на́до **позвони́ть** (pf.) домо́й
> I need to ring home

(2) The imperfective infinitive denotes:

(i) A repeated action:

> Их на́до **корми́ть** (impf.) три ра́за в день
> They have to be fed three times a day

(ii) A continuous action:

> Помогли́ ей **воспи́тывать** (impf.) де́вочку
> They helped her to bring up the little girl

(3) An imperfective infinitive may simply name an action, with no implication of result or completion, while the perfective stresses intention to achieve a result. Compare

> Мне сего́дня ну́жно **разбира́ть** (impf.) кни́ги
> I must **spend some time sorting out** the books today

and

> Мне сего́дня ну́жно **разобра́ть** (pf.) кни́ги
> I must **get the books sorted out** today

277   Use of the infinitive to denote habitual actions

(1) The imperfective infinitive combines with verbs and other forms that imply habitual processes, tendencies, preferences etc.:

> Ры́бка **научи́лась** открыва́ть (impf.) холоди́льник (*Yunyi naturalist*)
> Rybka (an otter) learned how to open the fridge

> Я **привы́к** встава́ть (impf.) ра́но   I am used to rising early
> Он **уме́ет** рисова́ть (impf.)   He knows how to draw

(2) Other words that combine with an imperfective infinitive include **надое́сть** 'to be bored with', **отвы́кнуть** 'to get out of the habit of', **предпочита́ть** 'to prefer', **привы́чка** 'habit', **разучи́ться** 'to forget how to' (Я **разучи́лся** игра́ть (impf.) на пиани́но 'I have forgotten how to play the piano').

(3) Though **люби́ть** 'to like' almost invariably combines with the imperfective infinitive, the perfective is possible in the meaning of 'intermittent repetition'. Compare

> Он лю́бит **отдыха́ть** (impf.) в саду́
> He likes to relax in the garden

Он лю́бит **отдохну́ть** (pf.) в саду́
He likes relaxing in the garden now and then

Note

Боя́ться 'to fear' is used with the perfective infinitive when it expresses apprehension that something might happen inadvertently: Бою́сь **заблуди́ться** 'I am afraid of getting lost'. In the case of deliberate actions, use of aspect depends on context, cf.: Бою́сь **купа́ться** (impf.) в о́зере 'I am scared of bathing in the lake' and Бою́сь **призна́ться** (pf.) 'I am afraid to confess'.

(4) The perfective infinitive also appears in a frequentative context when the element of frequency relates to another word in the sentence, and *not* to the infinitive. Thus, in

Я всегда́ рад **помо́чь** (pf.) тебе́
I am always glad to help you

the meaning of frequency expressed by **всегда́** 'always' is 'absorbed' by the adjective **рад** 'glad'. The construction: adverb of frequency + adjective or verb + *perfective* infinitive reflects standard practice:

Вы всегда́ мо́жете (impf.) **взять** (pf.) у меня́ слова́рь
You can always get a dictionary from me

Иногда́ мне удава́лось (impf.) **подста́вить** (pf.) ему́ но́жку (Granin)
Sometimes I succeeded in tripping him up

Его́ неоднокра́тно пыта́лись (impf.) **отпугну́ть** (pf.) (*Izvestiya*)
Several times they had tried to scare it (a tiger) off

278 Use of the imperfective infinitive after verbs of beginning, continuing and concluding

The imperfective infinitive is mandatory after:

(1) Verbs of beginning:

начина́ть/нача́ть	to begin
принима́ться/приня́ться	to get down to
стать (pf. only)	to begin

Они́ приняли́сь **выдвига́ть** (impf.) я́щики (Nagibin)
They set to work pulling out the drawers

(2) Verbs of continuing:

продолжа́ть   to continue

Он продолжа́л **укла́дываться** (impf.)
He continued packing

Note
Perfective **продо́лжить** usually takes a direct object, *not* an infinitive:
продо́лжить прове́рку 'to continue the check'.

(3) Verbs of concluding:

броса́ть/бро́сить	'to give up'
конча́ть/ко́нчить	'to finish'
перестава́ть/переста́ть	'to cease'
прекраща́ть/прекрати́ть	'to desist'

Ли́дия Миха́йловна переста́ла **приглаша́ть** (impf.) меня́ за стол
(Rasputin)
Lidia Mikhailovna stopped inviting me for meals

279   Inadvisable and advisable actions

(1) The imperfective infinitive combines with adverbs, impersonal
expressions and other words which imply the inadvisability or deny the
necessity of an action: **бесполе́зно** 'it's useless', **вре́дно** 'it is
harmful', **доста́точно** 'that's enough', **зачем?** 'why?', **не на́до** 'you
should not', **не ну́жно** 'it is not necessary', **не сле́дует** 'you ought not
to', **не сто́ит** 'there is no point in', **не́чего** 'there is no point', **смешно́**
'it is ridiculous', **сты́дно** 'it is disgraceful':

Да и заче́м **меня́ть** (impf.) ку́зов? (*Sputnik*)
And anyway, why change the bodywork?

Не ну́жно **вызыва́ть** (impf.) врача́
There is no need to call the doctor

В ка́ждый дом **заходи́ть** (impf.) нет смы́сла (Rasputin)
There's no point in calling into every house

Нехорошо́ **обижа́ть** (impf.) старика́ (Nagibin)
It's not nice to hurt an old man's feelings

Note
Не до́лжен combines with the imperfective infinitive to denote
inadvisability (Вы не должны́ **подава́ть** (impf.) заявле́ние 'You
shouldn't apply') and with the perfective infinitive to denote

supposition (Он не до́лжен **опозда́ть** (pf.) 'He is not likely to be late') (see also **313** (1)).

(2) **Perfective** infinitives may be used to denote advisability:

Не сле́дует ли **посла́ть** (pf.) поздравле́ние?
Don't you think we should send our congratulations?

Почему́ не **спроси́ть**? (pf.)   Why not ask?

(3) **Нельзя́** combines with the imperfective infinitive in the meaning of inadmissibility and the perfective in the meaning of impossibility:

Нельзя́ **входи́ть** (impf.)
You can't go in (i.e. it is forbidden)

Нельзя́ **войти́** (pf.)
You can't get in (because, for example, the door is locked)

280   A request to perform/not to perform an action

(1) A **perfective** infinitive is used after a verb denoting a request or intention to perform a single completed action:

Она́ попроси́ла меня́ **уйти́** (pf.)   She asked me to leave
Он обеща́л **помо́чь** (pf.) мне   He promised to help me

Other verbs denoting request or intention include реша́ть/реши́ть 'to decide', сове́товать/посове́товать 'to advise', убежда́ть/убеди́ть 'to convince', угова́ривать/уговори́ть 'to persuade'.

(2) An **imperfective** infinitive is used, however, if **не** appears between the verb and the infinitive:

Она́ реши́ла **не уходи́ть** (impf.)
She decided not to go away

Он обеща́л **не приглаша́ть** (impf.) Та́ню на ве́чер
He promised not to invite Tanya to the party

Note

(a)   A negated **perfective** infinitive in such contexts expresses, not a request or undertaking to abstain from certain actions, but apprehension that an undesired action might inadvertently take place: Стара́юсь не **сде́лать** (pf.) оши́бок 'I am trying not to make any mistakes'.

(b) Verbs such as **отговáривать/отоворúть** 'to dissuade' and **раздýмывать/раздýмать** 'to change one's mind' contain a built-in negative meaning and combine with an imperfective infinitive:

Он отговорúл меня **спрáшивать** (impf.)
He dissuaded me from asking

Он раздýмал **éхать** (impf.)
He changed his mind about going (decided not to go)

281   Use of the infinitive after не хочý

(1) Infinitives of either aspect are used after **не хочý** 'I don't want to', **нет желáния** 'I have no wish to', **я не дýмаю** 'I do not mean to', the imperfective being preferred after a categorical negative:

Я и не дýмал **откáзываться** (impf.)
I didn't dream of refusing

Note
The imperfective infinitive is virtually compulsory after the impersonal reflexive **не хотéться**: Домóй **уходúть** (impf.) не хóчется (Abramov) 'We don't feel like going home'.

(2) The use of a *perfective* infinitive after **не хочý** etc. may denote that an action *has* taken place, but *unintentionally*:

Я не хотéл его **обúдеть** (pf.)
I did not mean to offend him

282   Use of the infinitive with порá

(1) In the meaning 'it is time to', **порá** combines with the **imperfective** infinitive:

Порá **начинáть** (impf.)   It is time to begin

(2) In the meaning 'it is necessary to' it combines with the **perfective** infinitive:

Но ведь порá **понять** (pf.), что чýда не бýдет (*Nedelya*)
It is high time we realized that there isn't going to be any miracle

283   Use of infinitives after verbs of motion

(1) The imperfective infinitive is used after verbs of motion to describe actions involving processes:

> Со́ня пошла́ **ста́вить** (impf.) ча́йник (Grekova)
> Sonya went to put on the kettle

> Она́ ведёт ребёнка в поликли́нику **проверя́ть** (impf.) зре́ние
> She is taking the child to the polyclinic to have his eyes tested

(2) If, however, result is emphasized rather than process, then the perfective is preferred:

> Пошёл **почини́ть** (pf.) часы́
> He has gone to get the clock mended

Reflexive Verbs

284   Reflexive verbs: conjugation

In conjugating a reflexive verb, the ending -**ся** is affixed to verb forms ending in a consonant or the semi-consonant -**й**, and to all active participles; -**сь** is affixed to forms ending in a vowel. The reflexive verb is thus conjugated as follows:

мы́ться	**верну́ться**
'to wash'	'to return'
я мо́юсь	верну́сь
ты мо́ешься	вернёшься
он мо́ется	вернётся
мы мо́емся	вернёмся
вы мо́етесь	вернётесь
они́ мо́ются	верну́тся

Past tense

мы́лся, мы́лась	верну́лся, верну́лась
мы́лось, мы́лись	верну́лось, верну́лись

Imperative

мо́йся, мо́йтесь	верни́сь, верни́тесь

For active participles, see **340** (2) and **342** (2).

285   The 'true' reflexive

(1) The number of 'true' reflexives, in which the agent 'turns the action back' upon himself or herself, is relatively small. The category contains a number of verbs which relate to personal grooming:

бри́ться/по-	to shave (oneself)
гото́виться/при-	to get ready, prepare oneself
гримирова́ться/за-	to put on make-up
завива́ться/зави́ться	to have one's hair waved
кра́ситься/вы́-, по-	to dye one's hair
кра́ситься/на-	to make up one's face
купа́ться/вы́-, ис-	to bathe (oneself)
мы́ться/по-, вы́-	to wash (oneself)
обува́ться/обу́ться	to put on one's shoes
одева́ться/оде́ться	to dress oneself
переодева́ться/переоде́ться	to change (one's clothes)
причёсываться/причеса́ться	to do one's hair, have one's hair done
пу́дриться/на-, по-	to powder one's face
раздева́ться/разде́ться	to get undressed
разува́ться/разу́ться	to take off one's shoes
умыва́ться/умы́ться	to wash one's hands and face

(2) Other 'true' reflexives include the following:

(i) **Броса́ться/бро́ситься** 'to rush', **защища́ться/защити́ться** 'to defend oneself', **поднима́ться/подня́ться** 'to ascend', **прислоня́ться/прислони́ться** 'to lean', **спуска́ться/спусти́ться** 'to descend'.

(ii) A number of verbs which are reflexive only in the **imperfective:**

ложи́ться/лечь	to lie down
переса́живаться/пересе́сть	to change places, trains etc.
сади́ться/сесть	to sit down
станови́ться/стать	to (go and) stand

Note
Уса́живаться/усе́сться 'to settle down' is reflexive in both aspects.

286   Semi-reflexive verbs

Semi-reflexive verbs describe an action which the agent performs **for** rather than to himself or herself: **запаса́ться/запасти́сь** 'to stock up with', **укла́дываться/уложи́ться** 'to pack' etc.

287   Intransitive reflexives

A reflexive ending may transform a transitive into an intransitive verb. Compare transitive **возвраща́ть**

Он возвраща́ет кни́гу в библиоте́ку
He returns the book to the library

with intransitive **возвраща́ться** in

Он **возвраща́ется** домо́й
He returns home

Other examples include:

Земля́ **враща́ется**	The Earth rotates
Колесо́ **ве́ртится**	The wheel spins
Война́ **конча́ется/ ко́нчилась**	The war ends/ended
Стул **лома́ется/слома́лся**	The chair breaks/broke
Дом **нахо́дится** на берегу́	The house is situated on the shore
Фильм **начина́ется/ начался́**	The film begins/began
Уро́к **продолжа́ется**	The lesson continues
Боле́знь **распростра- ня́ется/распространи- лась**	The disease is spreading/spread
Положе́ние **улучша́ется/ улу́чшилось**	The situation improves/ improved

Note
(a) All the verbs in the above list can be used transitively without the reflexive endings: Учи́тель **враща́ет** гло́бус 'The teacher rotates the globe' etc.

(b) While English uses many verbs both transitively *and* intransitively ('She *grows* tulips'/'Tulips *grow*'; 'She *stops* the bus'/'The bus *stops*'), Russian always distinguishes transitive from intransitive, either by using different verbs (Она́ **выра́щивает** тюльпа́ны/ Тюльпа́ны **расту́т**) or by affixing a reflexive ending to convert a transitive into an intransitive verb (Она́ **остана́вливает** авто́бус/Авто́бус **остана́вливается**).

288   Reflexive verbs with passive meaning

(1) Reflexive suffixes impart **passive** meaning to many imperfective transitive verbs. There is usually a third-person subject:

Как э́то **де́лается**?
How is that done?

Сона́та **исполня́ется** (орке́стром)
The sonata is performed (by an orchestra)

(2) The possibility of indicating the **agent** of an action (usually in the form of an instrumental) distinguishes the passive from the intransitive construction. Compare:

Passive:

Кни́ги **возвраща́ются** в библиоте́ку **ученика́ми**
The books **are returned** to the library **by the pupils**

Intransitive:

Они́ **возвраща́ются** домо́й
They return home

Likewise, Колёса дви́жутся **водо́й** 'The wheels are moved by water power' (passive), Толпа́ дви́жется по у́лице 'The crowd moves down the street' (intransitive).

Note
In general, only **imperfective** verbs function as reflexive passives: Прое́кт **обсужда́лся** мини́страми 'The project was being discussed by the ministers', Как **пи́шется** э́то сло́во? 'How is this word spelt?' The **perfective** passive is normally rendered by a participle (see **359** (3)).

289   Reciprocal meanings

(1) A small number of reflexives denote reciprocal or joint action:

Они́ ча́сто **встреча́ются**	They often meet
Мы **собира́емся**	We gather
Ско́ро **уви́димся**	We shall see each other soon

(2) Others include:

дели́ться/по-	to share
здоро́ваться/по-	to say hello

мири́ться/по-, при-	to make it up
обнима́ться/обня́ться	to embrace
объединя́ться/объедини́ться	to amalgamate
проща́ться/прости́ться	to say goodbye
сове́товаться/по-	to take advice
совеща́ться (impf. only)	to consult
срабо́таться (pf. only)	to achieve a working relationship
усла́вливаться/усло́виться	to agree
целова́ться/по-	to kiss

(3) **С** + instrumental may combine with such verbs:

Дели́ться **с ке́м-нибудь** куско́м хле́ба
To share a crust of bread with someone

Совеща́ться **со специали́стами**
To consult experts

in which case the **subject** of the verb may be singular

Я здоро́ваюсь/проща́юсь с ним
I say hello/goodbye to him

or plural

Мы срабо́тались с ни́ми
We developed a good working relationship with them

In the absence of **с** + instrumental, however, the subject is always plural:

Друзья́ обняли́сь	The friends embraced
Враги́ помири́лись	The enemies made it up

(4) Some reciprocal reflexives denote conflict and dispute:

Он со все́ми **брани́тся**	He quarrels with everyone

Other verbs include: **би́ться** 'to fight', **боро́ться/по-** 'to struggle', **руга́ться/по-** 'to abuse one another', **ссо́риться/по-** 'to quarrel'.

(5) Reflexive verbs of motion with the prefixes **раз-** and **с-** (**разбега́ться/разбежа́ться** 'to disperse', **слета́ться/слете́ться** 'to congregate' (of birds) etc.) also express joint action (see **331**).

Note
See **143** (3) (constructions with **дру̀г дру́га** 'each other').

290   Reflexive verbs which express feelings and attitudes

A number of reflexive verbs express or reflect feelings and attitudes. They may be subdivided into:

(1) Those which appear only as reflexives: **боя́ться** + gen. 'to fear', **горди́ться** + instr. 'to be proud of', **любова́ться/по-** + instr./**на** + acc. 'to admire', **наде́яться на** + acc. 'to hope for, rely on', **наслажда́ться** + instr. 'to revel in', **нра́виться/по-** + dat. 'to please', **опаса́ться** + gen. 'to fear', **распла́каться** (pf. only) 'to burst into tears', **рассмея́ться** (pf. only) 'to burst out laughing', **смея́ться/за-** + dat./**над** + instr. 'to laugh', **сомнева́ться/усомни́ться в** + prep. 'to doubt', **улыба́ться/улыбну́ться** 'to smile'.

(2) Those which, shorn of their reflexive endings, can be used as transitive verbs in their own right: **беспоко́иться/по-** 'to worry', **весели́ться/по-** 'to enjoy oneself', **волнова́ться/вз-** 'to get excited', **восхища́ться/восхити́ться** + instr. 'to be delighted', **печа́литься/о-** 'to grieve' **признава́ться/призна́ться в** + prep. 'to confess to', **пуга́ться/ис-** + gen. 'to be frightened', **ра́доваться/об-** + dat. 'to rejoice', **расстра́иваться/расстро́иться** 'to get distraught, upset', **серди́ться/рас- на** + acc. 'to get angry', **удивля́ться/удиви́ться** + dat. 'to be surprised'. Compare

    Э́то меня́ **беспоко́ит**   That concerns me

and

    Я **беспоко́юсь**   I am worried

291   Intense or purposeful action

The following reflexive verbs denote intense or purposeful action: **доби́ва́ться/доби́ться** + gen. 'to achieve', **принима́ться/приня́ться за** + acc. 'to tackle', **проси́ться/по-** 'to apply', **пыта́ться/по-** 'to attempt', **стара́ться/по-** 'to try', **стреми́ться** (impf. only) 'to strive', **стуча́ться/по-** 'to knock' (hoping to be admitted), **труди́ться/по-** 'to labour'.

292   Reflexive verbs that emphasize thoroughness

(1) A number of reflexive verbs, mostly prefixed **вы-**, **до-** or **на-**,

emphasize thorough completion of an action: **высыпа́ться/вы́спаться** 'to have a good sleep', **доу́чиваться/доучи́ться** 'to complete one's studies', **наеда́ться/нае́сться** 'to eat one's fill', **напива́ться/напи́ться** 'to slake one's thirst/get drunk', **насмотре́ться** (pf. only) 'to look one's fill' etc.

(2) Reflexive verbs in **за-** denote absorption in an activity: **заду́мываться/заду́маться** 'to be lost in thought', **засма́триваться/засмотре́ться** 'to be absorbed in looking at something' etc.

293   Reflexive verbs that denote potential to perform an action

Some reflexives denote that the subject has the potential to perform some, usually harmful, action:

Коро́вы **бода́ются**	Cows butt
Крапи́ва **жжётся**	Nettles sting
Соба́ки **куса́ются**	Dogs bite
Ко́шки **цара́паются**	Cats scratch

Impersonal Constructions

294   Use of impersonal constructions to denote natural processes

(1) The third-person singulars of some verbs denote climatic or other natural processes:

Вечере́ет	Evening is drawing in
Моро́зит	Frost is in the air
Света́ет	Dawn is breaking
Сквози́т	There is a draught
Смерка́ется ра́но	It gets dark early
Темне́ет	It is getting dark

(2) In the past tense, the neuter is used:

Вечере́ло	Evening was drawing in

295   Impersonal constructions with an animate accusative or dative

Impersonal verbs may denote physical state, inclination or urge, the person affected appearing:

(1) In the accusative case:

Петра́ **зноби́т**	Petr feels shivery
Меня́ ко сну **кло́нит**	I feel drowsy
Ната́шу **лихора́дит**	Natasha feels feverish
Больно́го **рвёт**	The patient vomits (Его́ **вы́рвало** 'He threw up')
Ма́шу **тошни́т**	Masha feels sick (Ма́шу **стошни́ло** 'Masha vomited')
Нас **тяну́ло** дру̀г к дру́гу (Gagarin)	We felt drawn to each other

Меня́ **зуди́ло** посмотре́ть, как они́ отнесу́тся к моему́ появле́нию (Rasputin)
I was itching to see how they would react to my appearance

(2) In the dative case (with a reflexive verb):

Мне **нездоро́вится**	I am feeling off colour
Ей не **рабо́тается**	She doesn't feel like working
Ему́ не **спи́тся**	He doesn't feel sleepy
Мне **хо́чется** пить	I feel thirsty

Про́бовал чита́ть, **не чита́лось,** лёг на крова́ть, кури́л (Trifonov)
He tried to read but **wasn't in the mood for reading,** lay down on the bed, smoked

296   Impersonal constructions involving an external force

(1) In some impersonal constructions the object of a verb (usually in the neuter past tense) appears in the **accusative** and its inanimate agent, often a natural phenomenon or external force, in the **instrumental**:

Да́чу **зажгло́ мо́лнией**	The country cottage was struck by lightning
Подва́л **за́лило водо́й**	The cellar was flooded
Избу́ **занесло́ сне́гом**	The hut was snow-bound
Его́ **уби́ло электри́чеством**	He was electrocuted

| Труп **унесло́ реко́й** | The body was carried away by the river |
| **Засы́пало песко́м** сква́жины (Trifonov) | The bore-holes got clogged with sand |

Note

(a) The agent of the action is not always indicated: Вчера́ на стро́йке **задави́ло** челове́ка 'A man was run over at the building-site yesterday', Ло́дку **кача́ло** 'The boat was pitching and tossing', За́ борт **смы́ло** судово́го по́вара (Gagarin) 'The ship's cook was washed overboard'.

(b) An alternative construction is also possible, with the natural or other phenomenon in the nominative, as the subject of the action: Его́ **уби́ла мо́лния** 'He was struck by lightning'.

(2) The incidents in this type of construction are **accidental.** Compare:

(i) Use of the third-person **plural** for **intentional** occurrences:

Его́ **уби́ли** в рукопа́шном бою́
He was killed in hand-to-hand fighting

(ii) Use of the third-person neuter **singular** for **accidental** occurrences:

Его́ **уби́ло** в перестре́лке   He was killed in a skirmish

297   Expression of other meanings (chance, sufficiency etc.)

Some impersonal constructions are concerned with chance, success, sufficiency/insufficiency, the person affected appearing in the **dative:**

(1) The verb denotes chance, luck, success:

Мне **везёт** в ка́рты
I am lucky at cards

Мне **повезло́**
I am in luck, have been lucky

Ученику́ **удало́сь** реши́ть зада́чу
The pupil succeeded in solving the problem

Отцу́ **довело́сь** побыва́ть на собра́нии
My father had occasion to attend a meeting

Note also **Вы́шло** ина́че 'It turned out differently', where no personal involvement is expressed, and Что **случи́лось/произошло́**? 'What has happened?', where the person affected may appear in a prepositional phrase: Что случи́лось **с ним**? 'What has happened to him?' (cf. У вас что́-то **с телефо́ном** 'Something's wrong with your telephone').

(2) The verb denotes sufficiency/insufficiency, the quantifiable item appearing in the **genitive** case:

Бра́ту **недостаёт о́пыта**	My brother lacks experience
Ему́ всегда́ **не хвата́ет де́нег**	He is always short of money
Хва́тит бензи́ну	There will be enough petrol

Note
Э́того нам ещё не **хвата́ло**! 'That's the last straw!'.

298   Constructions with the second-person singular

(1) Impersonal meanings can be expressed using the second-person singular of a verb (the equivalent of English 'one' or 'you'):

Ко всему́ **привыка́ешь**
You/one can get used to anything

Там не **уви́дишь** на́ших фи́льмов, не **прочтёшь** на́ших книг (*Russia Today*)
You won't see our films or read our books there (in the West)

(2) The second-person singular pronoun may be added for emphasis:

И то́лько при усло́вии, е́сли **ты** бу́дешь кури́ть и пить — **ты** бу́дешь по́льзоваться успе́хом. Е́сли же **ты** не накра́шена и не ра́дуешься пло́ским шу́точкам, ми́мо **тебя́** прохо́дят, как ми́мо пусто́го ме́ста (*Russia Today*)
And you'll only get anywhere if you smoke and drink. But if you don't wear make-up or laugh at their pathetic jokes, they'll cut you dead

299   Constructions with the third-person plural

(1) The third-person plural is used (*without a pronoun*) to denote action taken by 'the authorities' or other third parties:

Говоря́т, что . . .	They say that . . .
Меня́ **задержа́ли**	I was arrested
Его́ **наградили**	He was decorated

Про́сят не кури́ть   You are requested not to smoke

Note

Как тебя́ **зову́т?** 'What is your name?'

(2) Use of the plural may be purely conventional, as in the following examples, in which the subject of the action could be interpreted as singular:

Тебя́ **ждут**
Someone is/Some people are waiting for you

Вас **про́сят** к телефо́ну
You are wanted on the phone

Тебя́ **спра́шивают**
Someone's asking for you

Note

The following example draws a clear distinction between the second-person singular, which identifies with the **individual,** and the third-person plural, which identifies with **authority**:

Са́мое ужа́сное во всех шко́лах, так э́то то, что **сиди́шь** и **трясёшься,** что **тебя́ спро́сят,** и **поста́вят,** наприме́р, тро́йку и́ли дво́йку (*Russia Today*)
The worst thing in any school is sitting there trembling at the prospect of being asked a question and getting a bare pass or a fail

The Passive Voice

300   The passive voice. Introductory comments

(1) In a passive construction, the *natural object* of an action becomes the *grammatical subject*. Compare English:

(i) 'They hate *him*' (active construction, with '*him*' the natural object of the verb).

(ii) '*He* is hated by them' (passive construction in which '*he*' has become the grammatical subject while remaining the natural object).

(2) Russian expresses passive meaning through reflexive verbs, the third-person plural, participles (see **359** and **360** (2)) and word order (see **478** (2) (i)).

301 The passive expressed by imperfective reflexive verbs

(1) The passive may be expressed by an imperfective reflexive verb:

Здесь **ловились** (impf.) селёдка и редкая рыба — кутум (Lebedev)

Herring and a rare species, the kutum, **were fished for** here

(2) The agent of the action may be represented by an **instrumental**

Смета составляется **бухгалтером**
The estimate is being prepared **by an accountant**

or omitted

По радио **передавалась** новая пьеса
A new play **was being broadcast** on the radio

Обувь снималась у входа в храм (Granin)
Footwear was removed at the entrance to the temple

Note

A reflexive verb with an animate subject is often either a 'true' reflexive (Он **моется** 'He is having a wash' (not *'He is being washed', which should be rendered as Его моют)) or denotes joint action (Пассажиры **собираются** 'The passengers congregate'). However, reflexive passives with animate subjects appear in examples such as Герои **награждаются** государством 'Heroes **are rewarded** by the state'.

302 Passive meaning expressed by third-person plural verbs

The use of a third-person plural instead of a reflexive passive emphasizes the involvement of a human agent. Compare use of the reflexive in

Магазин **открывается**   The shop opens

with the third-person plural, with its emphasis on human agency:

И вдруг он слышит, что **дверь открывают**. Но это ещё не парень, это проводница (Rasputin)
And suddenly he hears the door **being opened**. But it's not the boy back yet, it's the guard

303   Perfective reflexives with passive meaning

Perfective passives are normally expressed by a participle (see **359** and **360** (2) (ii)). However, passives may also be expressed by perfective reflexives that denote:

(1) Covering:

> Верши́ны **покры́лись** сне́гом
> The peaks became covered in snow

Note
This sentence describes an *action*. Compare the use of a participle to describe a *state*: Верши́ны **покры́ты** сне́гом 'The peaks **are covered** in snow'.

(2) Filling:

> Таз **напо́лнился** водо́й
> The basin filled with water

(3) Illuminating:

> Поля́ **освети́лись** по́здним со́лнцем
> The fields were illuminated by the late sun

(4) Others, for example 'replacing', 'creating', 'breaking':

> Её пре́жняя ра́дость **смени́лась** чу́вством кра́йнего раздраже́ния
> Her former joy yielded to a feeling of extreme irritation

> **Создало́сь** сло́жное положе́ние
> A complex situation developed

> **Разби́лся** стул
> A chair got smashed

Note
Animate instrumentals are excluded from such constructions. They are possible only with a passive participle (see **359**), cf.:

> Кружо́к **созда́лся/был со́здан**
> The club was set up

> Кружо́к **был со́здан** (but not *созда́лся) **ученика́ми**
> The club was set up by the **pupils**

The Conditional and Subjunctive Moods

304   The conditional mood. Introductory comments

(1) If we compare the sentences

(i) If he *wakes* his wife she *will be* angry

(ii) If he *woke* his wife she *would be* angry

then it is clear that the situation described in (i) *may* occur, while the situation described in (ii) is *hypothetical*. The implication of statements of type (ii) is that the opposite situation obtains, e.g.

If I *knew* (the implication is that I do *not* know), I *would tell* you

(2) In the above examples, (i) is rendered in Russian by a verb in the future

Если он **разбудит** жену, она рассердится

while the two examples under (ii) are rendered by the **conditional mood**:

Если бы он **разбудил** жену, она **рассердилась бы**
Если бы я знал, я **сказал бы** вам

305   Formation of the conditional

A conditional construction comprises:

(i) A conditional clause (**если бы** + past tense of the verb).

(ii) A main clause (past tense of the verb + **бы**):

Если бы отец **был жив**, он **порадовался бы** успехам сына
If father **were** alive he **would rejoice** at his son's success

Note
(a) Alternatively, the main clause may precede the conditional:

Я пошёл бы, если бы меня **пригласили**
I **would go if** they **invited** me

(b) Conditionals can also have **pluperfect** meanings. Thus, the sentence under (a) could also be rendered as '**I would have gone if** they **had invited** me'.

(c) In the main clause, **бы** may precede the verb:

Я **бы помóг** вам, éсли бы вы меня́ попроси́ли
I would help you if you asked me (or **I would have helped** you if you had asked me)

(d) The conjunction **то** 'then' may introduce a main clause that follows the conditional clause:

Éсли бы онá роди́лáсь в нáше врéмя, **то** стáла бы арти́сткой, и́ли ди́ктором, и́ли стюардéссой (*Russia Today*)
If she had been born in our time **then** she would have become a performer, or an announcer, or an air hostess

(e) Sometimes the **éсли** clause is omitted. The implication of such statements is 'this is what I would do if I had my way', as in the following example:

Я **бы запрети́л** шкóльникам появля́ться в общéственных местáх в какóй-либо инóй одéжде, крòме шкóльной фóрмы (*Rabotnitsa*)
I would ban school-children from appearing in public places other than in school uniform

(f) The conditional is used with either aspect, but is commoner with the perfective.

306 Use of (1) the imperative and (2) the preposition без to express conditional meanings

(1) The **singular imperative** may be used colloquially with conditional meaning:

Доведи́сь мне (= éсли бы мне **довелóсь**) встрéтиться с ним рáньше, всё **бы́ло бы** инáче
If I had chanced to meet him earlier everything would have been different

Note
The singular imperative can also replace **éсли** + future tense:

Разгори́сь (= Éсли разгори́тся) áтомный пожáр — и окáжутся бессмы́сленными уси́лия людéй дóброй вóли (Lebedev)
If an atomic holocaust **breaks out,** the efforts of people of goodwill will be pointless

(2) A prepositional phrase with **без** 'without' may also have conditional meaning:

Без Лю́бы (= Éсли бы не Лю́ба), я бы не получи́л вы́сшего образова́ния (Rybakov)
Had it not been for Lyuba I would not have received a higher education

307   Use of the particle бы to express desire

(1) The past tense + **бы** can be used to express desire on the part of the subject:

За́втра я с удово́льствием **пошёл бы** в теа́тр
I would very much **like to go** to the theatre tomorrow

(2) The phrase **хоте́л бы** 'I would like to' is commonly used in this meaning:

Я **хоте́л бы** пойти́ в кино́
I **would like** to go to the cinema

Note
(a)   Note the expression of desire in constructions of the type **Скоре́й бы пришло́** ле́то! 'Roll on summer!', **Пое́хать бы** домо́й! 'Oh, to go home!'
(b)   Past tense + **бы** is also used to express a mild injunction: **Помогли́ бы** ей 'You might give her a hand'. This is much less peremptory than the imperative: **Помоги́те** ей! 'Help her!'

308   Use of the subjunctive to express wish or desire

(1) In translating the sentences

  (i) **I want to vote**
  (ii) **I want you to vote**

the infinitive in (i), in which the subject is the **same** for both verbs, is rendered by a Russian **infinitive**

Я хочу́ **голосова́ть**

while the infinitive in (ii), in which the subjects of the two verbs are **different**

I want
you to vote

is rendered in Russian by a **subjunctive** (**чтòбы** + past tense):

> **Я хочу́, чтòбы** вы голосова́ли

Compare

> Он **не хо́чет, чтòбы** я танцева́л с Тама́рой (Nikolaev)
> He **does not want me to dance** with Tamara

Note
Чтòбы is *never* used with the present or future tense, only with the *past*.

(2) Other words denoting desirability or undesirability may also appear in the main clause: **ва́жно** 'it is important', **жела́тельно** 'it is desirable', **за то** 'in favour of', **лу́чше** 'it is better', **наста́ивать/ настоя́ть** 'to insist', **прòтив того́** 'against', **тре́бовать/по-** 'to demand':

> **Гла́вное,** чтòбы спорт служи́л де́лу ми́ра (Kuleshov)
> **The main thing** is that sport should serve the cause of peace

> Он **настоя́л (на том), чтòбы** я подписа́лся
> He **insisted** I sign

> Я не **прòтив того́, чтòбы** он брал на себя́ часть хлопо́т на ку́хне (*Russia Today*)
> **I do not object to his taking on** some of the kitchen chores

> Никто́ не **тре́бует,** чтòбы де́вушка сиде́ла одна́ взаперти́ (*Rabotnitsa*)
> No one **demands** that a girl should remain locked up in seclusion

Note
(a) Desirability may also be implied by constructions with **сказа́ть** 'to tell' (Мне мой приёмный оте́ц **сказа́л, чтòб я запо́мнил** ме́сто, где ру́кописи зако́паны (*Izvestiya*) 'My foster father **told me to remember** where the manuscripts are buried', **Скажи́те** ва́шему Ви́тьке, чтобы он **за мной не ходи́л** (Rasputin) '**Tell your Vitka to stop following me around**') and **предупреди́ть** 'to warn' (**Я предупреди́л** его, чтòбы он **не уходи́л** 'I warned him **not to go away**').

(b) The idiomatic use of **чтòбы** + past tense to issue a warning: **Чтòбы** я э́того бо́льше **не слы́шал!** 'Don't ever let me hear you say that again!'

(c) In colloquial contexts, **хоте́ть** may combine with a future verb: Хоти́те, я вам **скажу́** 'Would you like me to tell you?'

309   The subjunctive of purposeful endeavour

(1) If we compare

(i) Я хочу́, что̀бы он пришёл
I want him to come

(ii) Я добива́юсь того́, что̀бы он пришёл
I am trying to get him to come

then the wish that he should come, expressed in (i) by the verb **хочу́**, finds its counterpart in (ii) in purposeful endeavour (**добива́юсь**) to achieve the desired aim.

(2) Other words involved in this type of construction include **де́лать всё, что̀бы** 'to do everything to ensure that', **забо́титься о том, что̀бы** 'to take care that', **следи́ть за тем, что̀бы** 'to see to it that', **смотре́ть, что̀бы** 'to mind that', **стреми́ться к тому́, что̀бы** 'to strive':

Забо́титься о то́м, что̀бы вы не проспа́ли, бу́дет ЭВМ телефо́нной ста́нции (*Izvestiya*)
The computer at the telephone exchange **will see to it that** you do not sleep in

Смотри́, что̀б Куту́зов тебя́ не пойма́л (Yakhontov)
Mind Kutuzov doesn't catch you

Note
Добива́ться/доби́ться is used with the *subjunctive* to denote intent to achieve a purpose (Мы **добива́емся того́, что̀бы** она́ согласи́лась 'We are trying to get her to agree') and with the *indicative* to denote achievement (В конце́ концо́в председа́тель **доби́лся того́, что** она́ согласи́лась (Rasputin) 'The chairman eventually got her to agree').

310   Purpose clauses

A purpose clause describes an action which is taken with the aim of achieving a desired result. The result clause is introduced:

(1) By **что̀бы + infinitive** if both clauses have the **same** subject:

Он встал, **что̀бы откры́ть окно́**
He got up **in order to open the window**

Я позвоню́ бра́ту, **что́бы напо́мнить** ему́ о ве́чере
I shall ring my brother **in order to remind him of the party**

(2) By **что́бы** + the **past tense** (the **subjunctive of purpose**) if the two clauses have **different** subjects:

Он встал, **что́бы она́ могла́ сесть**
He got up **so that she could sit down**

Я позвоню́ бра́ту, **что́бы он знал**, что я прие́хал
I shall ring my brother, **so that he knows** I have arrived

Челове́к снял лы́жи, **что́бы они́ не меша́ли** ему́ ползти́ (Nagibin)
The man removed his skis, **so that they should not prevent him** from crawling

311   The expression of hypothesis

(1) If we compare the sentences

(i) I have not met *the man who swam the Channel*
(ii) I have never met *a man who has not heard of Leo Tolstoy*

then it is clear that (i) refers to *an actual person* (the man who swam the Channel), while (ii) is dealing with *a hypothetical situation* (an imaginary person who has not heard of Leo Tolstoy).

(i) is expressed in Russian using the **indicative**:

Я не встреча́л челове́ка, **кото́рый переплы́л** Ла-Ма́нш
I have not met the man who swam the Channel

(ii) is expressed using the **subjunctive of hypothesis** (past tense + **бы**):

Я не встреча́л челове́ка, **кото́рый бы не слыха́л** о Толсто́м
I have never met a man who has not heard of Tolstoy

Compare

Нет о́трасли промы́шленности, для кото́рой освое́ние косми́ческого простра́нства **не оказа́лось бы** поле́зным (*Izvestiya*)
There is no industry which **has not benefited** from the conquest of space

(2) A similar distinction is made in constructions with **слу́чай** between:

(i) Incidents which *did* occur, where the indicative is used:

Ско́лько у нас бы́ло **слу́чаев, когда́ снима́ли** с маши́н стёкла (*Literaturnaya gazeta*)
There have been umpteen **cases of** car wind-screens **being removed**

(ii) Incidents which did *not* occur, where the subjunctive is used:

Не́ было слу́чая, **что̀бы он заблуди́лся** (Kazakov)
There was not a single instance **of his getting lost**

(3) The same principle applies to constructions with verbs of perception and statement: **ви́деть** 'to see', **заме́тить** 'to notice', **по́мнить** 'to remember', **сказа́ть** 'to say', **слы́шать** 'to hear' etc.

(i) The indicative is used to refer to an actual occurrence:

Ви́жу, **как они́ игра́ют** в футбо́л
I see **them playing** football

(ii) The subjunctive indicates that the subject did not witness or recall the incident and may doubt whether it in fact occurred:

Не по́мню, **что̀бы она́** хоть раз **взяла́** ко́рку хле́ба (Rasputin)
I do not recall **her** even once **taking** a crust of bread

Я не заме́тил, **что̀бы он упа́л в о́бморок**
I did not notice **him fainting**

Use of the indicative here would constitute an acknowledgement that the incident occurred — but that the subject did not witness it:

Я не заме́тил, **что он упа́л в о́бморок**
I did not notice **that he had fainted**

Note

(a)   Hypotheses may also be introduced by the phrase **не то, что̀бы**,

И он **не то что̀бы был** недово́лен жи́знью, счита́л себя́ неуда́чником (Tendryakov)
It is not that he was dissatisfied with life, he just considered himself unlucky

or by negated verbs which imply an unreal situation:

Дня ведь не проходи́ло, **что̀бы она́ не похвали́ла** неве́стку (Zalygin)
Never a day passed **without her praising** her daughter-in-law

(b)   **Боя́ться** 'to fear' combines either with the indicative (Бою́сь, **что он прова́лится** 'I am afraid he will fail', Бою́сь, **что он не** придёт 'I am afraid he won't come') or a subjunctive (note 'illogical' negative): Бою́сь, **что́бы он не провали́лся** 'I am afraid he may fail'.

312   Concessive constructions

(1) The particle **бы** also appears in concessive constructions (English 'whoever', 'whatever' etc.):

кто/что/как/где/куда́/како́й/ско́лько + бы + ни + past tense

Чего́ бы э́то мне ни сто́ило, на каки́е бы же́ртвы **ни пришло́сь** пойти́ — а своего́ добью́сь (*Rabotnitsa*)
Whatever it costs, whatever sacrifices I may be called upon to make, I shall achieve my goal

Я ви́дел, что черепа́хам пло́хо в нево́ле, **ка́к бы я ни стара́лся** хорошо́ за ни́ми уха́живать (*Yunyi naturalist*)
I saw that the tortoises were ill at ease in captivity, **however much I might try** to look after them properly

(2) **Бы** may be omitted, in reference to an actual incident:

Ско́лько Но́сов **ни тряс** приёмник, го́лос ди́ктора не зазвуча́л вновь (*Povolyaev*)
However much Nosov **shook** the receiver, the announcer's voice remained silent

Как я ни боро́лся за её здоро́вье, всё напра́сно (*Yunyi naturalist*)
No matter how much I fought to restore her to health, it was all in vain

(3) The future may be used to denote that all instances are covered:

Каку́ю газе́ту **ни откро́ешь** — всю́ду разгово́р о же́нщине (*Russia Today*)
Whichever paper you open, the talk is only of women

Note the set phrases

во что бы то ни ста́ло	at any cost
как бы то ни́ было	however that might be
как э́то ни парадокса́льно	paradoxical as it may seem
как э́то ни стра́нно	strange as it may seem

Лы́жник **во что бы то ни ста́ло** хоте́л продолжа́ть свой
мучи́тельный путь (Nagibin)
The skier was determined to continue his agonizing journey **come
what may**

Constructions Expressing Obligation, Necessity, Possibility or Potential

313   The expression of obligation and necessity

Obligation and necessity can be expressed in the following ways:

(1) До́лжен + infinitive

(i) **До́лжен, должна́, должно́, должны́** have the endings of short-form adjectives and agree with the subject in gender and number:

я, ты, он **до́лжен**	'I, you, he must' (masculine subject)
я, ты, она́ **должна́**	'I, you, she must' (feminine subject)
оно́ **должно́**	'it must'
мы, вы, они́ **должны́**	'we, you, they must'

(ii) They also combine with past and future forms of **быть**:

я, ты, он до́лжен **был**	'I, you, he had to' (masculine subject)
я, ты, она́ должна́ **была́**	'I, you, she had to' (feminine subject)
оно́ должно́ **бы́ло**	'it had to'
мы, вы, они́ должны́ **бы́ли**	'we, you, they had to'

я до́лжен/должна́ **бу́ду**	'I shall have to'
ты до́лжен/должна́ **бу́дешь**	'you will have to'
он до́лжен **бу́дет**	'he will have to'
она́ должна́ **бу́дет**	'she will have to'
оно́ должно́ **бу́дет**	'it will have to'
мы должны́ **бу́дем**	'we shall have to'
вы должны́ **бу́дете**	'you will have to'
они́ должны́ **бу́дут**	'they will have to'

(iii) **До́лжен** expresses moral necessity:

Ка́ждый челове́к **до́лжен** труди́ться
Every person must work

(iv) It is also used to express other modal concepts, the equivalents of 'should', 'ought to', 'is supposed to', 'is due to' etc.:

Це́ны **должны́** быть ги́бкими (*Literaturnaya gazeta*)
Prices **should** be flexible

В разли́чных стра́нах ми́ра храня́тся великоле́пные па́мятники культу́ре, и мы **должны́** знать о них (*Nedelya*)
Splendid monuments to culture are preserved in various countries of the world, and we **ought to** know about them

Пыта́юсь буты́лки из-под минера́льной воды́ сдать, а пункт хоть и **до́лжен** рабо́тать, но не рабо́тает (*Nedelya*)
I try to hand in some empty mineral-water bottles, but the collection point is not working, though it **is supposed to** be

По́езд **до́лжен** прийти́ в час дня
The train is **due** in at 1 p.m.

Note
(a) Past and future usage:

Сейча́с Мансу́ров **до́лжен был** подойти́ к ней, обня́ть её (Zalygin)
Now Mansurov **should have** come up to her and embraced her

Она́ **должна́ бу́дет** помо́чь ма́тери
She **will have to** help her mother

(b) The use of **должно́ быть**, in parenthesis, to denote supposition:
Она́, **должно́ быть**, заболе́ла 'She must have fallen ill'; Он, **должно́ быть**, не по́нял 'He can't have understood'.

(2) Ну́жно, на́до

(i) **Ну́жно, на́до** refer to necessity:

Ему́ **ну́жно/на́до бы́ло** преждевре́менно уйти́ на пе́нсию по сла́бости здоро́вья
He **had to** retire early due to ill health

(ii) They can also express the meaning 'ought to':

Больно́му **на́до бы́ло** сде́лать перелива́ние кро́ви
The patient **ought to have** had a blood transfusion

(iii) Compare **не ну́жно** 'it is not necessary' and **не на́до** 'one should not':

Не ну́жно запира́ть дверь
It is **not necessary** to lock the door

Не на́до запира́ть дверь
You **should not** lock the door

(3) Сто́ит, сле́дует, прийти́сь, вы́нужден, обя́зан

(i) **Сто́ит** refers to recommended action:

Сто́ит посмотре́ть э́тот фильм
It is worth seeing this film

(ii) **Сле́дует** is more categorical:

Не сле́дует так поступа́ть
One shouldn't behave like that

(iii) **Прийти́сь** implies reluctant acceptance of necessity:

Ему́ **пришло́сь** бежа́ть всю доро́гу
He had to run all the way

(iv) **Вы́нужден** means 'forced', **обя́зан** means 'obliged':

Пило́т **был вы́нужден** посади́ть самолёт в пусты́не
The pilot was forced to land the aircraft in the desert

Врач **обя́зана** помо́чь больно́му
The doctor is obliged to help the patient

314   The expression of possibility or potential

Possibility or potential may be expressed in the following ways:

(1) Мочь, смочь 'to be able'

Я могу́/смогу́ приня́ть ва́ше приглаше́ние
I can/shall be able to accept your invitation

Note
(a)   A distinction is made between **мочь** 'to be (physically) able' and
       уме́ть 'to be able, know how to'. Compare Я **уме́ю** пла́вать 'I
       can/know how to swim' and Сего́дня я не **могу́** пла́вать: у меня́
       рука́ боли́т 'I can't swim today: I have a sore arm'.
(b)   The imperfective future of **мочь** is rarely, if ever, used. Instead,
       the future of **быть в состоя́нии** + the infinitive is preferred (see
       225 (7)).

(c) **Мочь** can also be the equivalent of English 'may', 'might', 'could have', 'might have':

Мне **мо́гут** возрази́ть: лу́чше по кооперати́вной цене́, чем вообще́ отсу́тствие това́ра в магази́не (*Literaturnaya gazeta*)
People **may** object: better at the co-operative price, than the unavailability of the product in the shops

В ка́ссе **мо́гут** быть биле́ты
There **might be** tickets at the box-office

Как он **мог** отве́тить ина́че?
What other answer **could he have** given?

Éсли она́ реши́лась на э́то, зна́чит, **могла́** реши́ться и на друго́е (Zalygin)
If she made this decision, she **might** equally well **have** made a different decision

(2) Мо́жно/нельзя́, (не)возмо́жно

(i) **Мо́жно** and **нельзя́** can denote:

(a) Permission/prohibition:

— **Мо́жно** сюда́ сесть?
— Нет, **нельзя́**
'May I sit here?'
'No, you may not'

Note
Нельзя́ ли is used to express a very polite request: **Нельзя́ ли** сюда́ сесть? 'Please, may I sit here?' (cf. 'neutral' **Мо́жно ли?**). Conversely, it may express irritation: **Нельзя́ ли** поти́ше?! 'Couldn't you be a little quieter?!'

(b) Possibility/impossibility:

Кислоро́д **мо́жно** получи́ть из воды́
Oxygen can be extracted from water

Нельзя́ согласи́ться с ним
One cannot agree with him

Note
(a) **Мо́жно** is often used with interrogative words: На како́м авто́бусе **мо́жно** дое́хать до це́нтра? 'Which bus do I take for the city centre?'

(b) See **279** (3) for the aspect of the infinitive with **нельзя.** Note that the imperfective infinitive may be used with **нельзя** in the meaning of impossibility in a **frequentative** context: **Нельзя** мыть маши́ну ка́ждый день 'It is impossible to wash the car every day'.

(ii) **Возмо́жно/невозмо́жно** denote only possibility or impossibility (*not* permission/prohibition):

Возмо́жно/мо́жно поста́вить то́чный диа́гноз
It is possible to make a precise diagnosis

Невозмо́жно/нельзя́ реши́ть э́ту зада́чу
It is impossible to solve this problem

Verbs of Motion

315   Unidirectional and multidirectional verbs of motion

Each of fourteen types of motion are represented in Russian by two **imperfective** verbs.

(1) One denotes **movement in one direction** (unidirectional verbs):

| Я **иду́** на заво́д | **I am on my way** to the factory |
| Я **шёл** на заво́д | **I was on my way** to the factory |

(2) The other denotes **movement in more than one direction, movement in general, habitual action, return journeys** (multidirectional verbs):

Ка́ждый день он **хо́дит** в шко́лу
He **goes** to school every day

Она́ **хо́дит** по ко́мнате
She **is walking up and down** the room

Он **хо́дит** с па́лкой
He **walks** with a stick

Она́ **ходи́ла** в кино́
She **went** to the cinema

316   Conjugation of verbs of motion

The fourteen pairs of imperfective non-prefixed verbs are conjugated as follows (unidirectional first):

(1)	**идти́**	иду́, идёшь, идёт, идём, идёте, иду́т	'to go,
	ходи́ть	хожу́, хо́дишь, хо́дит etc.	walk'
(2)	**éхать**	éду, éдешь, éдет, éдем, éдете, éдут	'to travel,
	éздить	éзжу, éздишь, éздит etc.	ride'
(3)	**бежа́ть**	бегу́, бежи́шь, бежи́т, бежи́м, бежи́те, бегу́т	'to run'
	бéгать	бéгаю, бéгаешь, бéгает etc.	
(4)	**летéть**	лечу́, лети́шь, лети́т etc.	'to fly'
	летáть	летáю, летáешь, летáет etc.	
(5)	**плыть**	плыву́, плывёшь, плывёт etc.	'to swim,
	плáвать	плáваю, плáваешь, плáвает etc.	float'
(6)	**нести́**	несу́, несёшь, несёт etc.	'to carry'
	носи́ть	ношу́, но́сишь, но́сит etc.	
(7)	**вести́**	веду́, ведёшь, ведёт etc.	'to lead'
	води́ть	вожу́, во́дишь, во́дит etc.	
(8)	**везти́**	везу́, везёшь, везёт etc.	'to convey,
	вози́ть	вожу́, во́зишь, во́зит etc.	transport'
(9)	**лезть**	лéзу, лéзешь, лéзет etc.	'to climb'
	лáзить	лáжу, лáзишь, лáзит etc.	
(10)	**ползти́**	ползу́, ползёшь, ползёт etc.	'to crawl'
	пóлзать	пóлзаю, пóлзаешь, пóлзает etc.	
(11)	**тащи́ть**	тащу́, тáщишь, тáщит etc.	'to drag'
	таскáть	таскáю, таскáешь, таскáет etc.	
(12)	**гнать**	гоню́, гóнишь, гóнит etc.	'to drive,
	гоня́ть	гоня́ю, гоня́ешь, гоня́ет etc.	chase'
(13)	**кати́ть**	качу́, кáтишь, кáтит etc.	'to roll'
	катáть	катáю, катáешь, катáет etc.	
(14)	**брести́**	бреду́, бредёшь, бредёт etc.	'to wander'
	броди́ть	брожу́, брóдишь, брóдит etc.	

Note

There are grounds for excluding **брести́/броди́ть** from the series, since the two verbs differ somewhat in meaning: **брести́** 'to walk along slowly, with difficulty', **броди́ть** 'to wander aimlessly'. **Броди́ть** differs from other multidirectional verbs in that it cannot denote motion towards a destination. However, the two verbs have traditionally been treated as verbs of motion, and are accordingly dealt with in this section.

317   Imperatives of verbs of motion

Imperatives of verbs of motion are formed according to the rules formulated in **227**:

беги́!	run!
веди́!	lead!
иди́!	go!
неси́!	carry!

Note

Поезжа́й! 'Go!', the imperative of **пое́хать**, is used for single positive commands (**Поезжа́й** по́ездом! 'Go by train!'), **е́зди!** for frequentative commands and **Не е́зди!** for negative commands (**Не е́зди** авто́бусом! 'Don't go by bus').

318   Past tense of verbs of motion

(1) Verbs of motion in **-ать/-ять/-еть/-ить** have past tense forms in **-л**: **ходи́л, лете́л** etc.

(2) The past tenses of other verbs of motion are as follows:

брести́:	брёл, брела́, брело́, брели́
везти́:	вёз, везла́, везло́, везли́
вести́:	вёл, вела́, вело́, вели́
идти́:	шёл, шла, шло, шли
лезть:	лез, ле́зла, ле́зло, ле́зли
нести́:	нёс, несла́, несло́, несли́

319   'To go': идти́/ходи́ть and е́хать/е́здить

(1) 'To go' on foot is rendered in Russian as **идти́/ходи́ть:**

Она́ **идёт** в шко́лу
She **is going (is walking, is on her way)** to school

Она́ **хо́дит** в шко́лу
She **goes (walks)** to school

(2) 'To go' by some form of transport is rendered as **е́хать/е́здить:**

Она́ **е́дет** в шко́лу
She **is going (is riding, travelling, driving)** to school

Она́ **е́здит** в шко́лу авто́бусом
She **goes (travels)** to school by bus

(3) Thus, 'I am going to town' can be rendered as

Я **иду́** в го́род
'I am going to town' (on foot)

Я **е́ду** в го́род
'I am going to town' (by some form of transport)

Substantial trips normally imply the use of **е́хать/е́здить**: Я е́ду во Фра́нцию 'I am going to France'.

Note

Идти́/ходи́ть is used with trains (По́езд **идёт** 'The train is travelling along'), with ships, as an alternative to **плыть** 'to sail', and with road vehicles, as an alternative to **е́хать** (Маши́на **идёт/е́дет** по доро́ге 'The car **is driving** along the road').

320   Functions of unidirectional verbs of motion

(1) Unidirectional verbs of motion denote movement in one particular direction, usually on one occasion:

Не́которое вре́мя мы **шли** мо́лча (Nikolaev)
For a time we **walked along** in silence

Три дня и три но́чи **нас везли́** в арестáнтском вагóне (Gagarin)
For three days and nights **we were transported** in a convict truck

often with a named destination:

Е́дем в **го́род**
We are driving to **town**

От пьедестáла до **раздевáлки** егó несу́т на рукáх (Khrutsky)
They carry him shoulder-high from the rostrum to the changing-room

(2) The movement is not necessarily in a straight line:

Он шёл **зигзáгами** к дóму
He was **zigzagging** towards the house

but in all instances the verb advances the subject or object along a line of progression:

Он **плыл** прòтив вéтра и был слабéе нас (Nikolaev)
He **was swimming** against the current and was weaker than we were

Шу́рка до́лго **шёл** ле́сом, унося́ ежа́ пода́льше от жилья́ (Vasilev)

Shurka **walked** through the forest for a long while, carrying the hedgehog further and further away from human habitation

(3) The destination or direction of the movement may be:

(i) unspecified, as in the last example,

(ii) specified, as in

К зали́ву шли через па́рк (Yakhontov)
They were walking through the park **towards the bay**

(iii) more generally specified, e.g. in terms of points of the compass:

По́езд шёл **на восто́к**
The train was on its way **east**

Note
The future of unidirectional verbs is far less common than the present and past: Когда́ мы **бу́дем идти́** ми́мо кинотеа́тра, мы ку́пим биле́ты на за́втра 'When we **are passing** the cinema, we shall buy tickets for tomorrow', **Бу́дем вести́** по о́череди 'We shall take it in turns to drive'.

321   Unidirectional verbs in frequentative contexts

(1) Unidirectional verbs usually describe movement in progress on one occasion:

Он **идёт, шёл** в шко́лу   He **is, was going** to school

while habitual actions are usually the province of the multidirectional verb (see **322** (3)).

(2) Unidirectional verbs are, however, used to express repeated actions:

(i) Where **movement in one direction** is particularly stressed:

Я **иду́** на рабо́ту це́лых полчаса́
I **take** a whole half-hour **to get** to work

(Compare Ка́ждый день я **хожу́** на рабо́ту 'Every day I **go** to work' (and back).)

Обы́чно я **иду́** с рабо́ты пешко́м, а на рабо́ту **е́ду** на авто́бусе
I usually **walk home** from work but **go** to work on the bus

Пи́сьма 5–6 дней **иду́т** отсю́да в Росси́ю
Letters **take** 5–6 days **to get** from here to Russia

Note
A unidirectional verb is also used in Ка́ждый день **летя́т** пи́сьма из страны́ в страну́ 'Every day letters **wing their way** from country to country' (since each individual letter progresses *in one direction only*).

Когда́ я **иду́** на рабо́ту, я всегда́ покупа́ю газе́ту
When I **am on my way** to work, I always buy a newspaper

О́сенью журавли́ **летя́т** на юг
In the autumn the cranes **fly** south (*one-way* (*though repeated*) *flight* within the given time-span (о́сенью))

Ка́ждое у́тро в 8.45 **иду́** на авто́бусную остано́вку
Every morning at 8.45 I **walk** to the bus-stop (but not back again!)

(ii) Where reference is to actions or processes occurring **in sequence:**

Ка́ждое у́тро встаю́, за́втракаю и **иду́** на авто́бусную остано́вку
Every morning I get up, have breakfast and **go** to the bus-stop

Ка́ждый год, как то́лько наступа́ет ле́то, я **е́ду** на мо́ре
Every year, as soon as summer comes, I **am off** to the sea-side

(Compare Ка́ждый год **е́зжу** на мо́ре 'Every year I go to the seaside' (and back).)

322   Functions of multidirectional verbs of motion

As their name implies, multidirectional verbs denote **movement in more than one direction.** Meanings may be subdivided as follows:

(1) They denote the action in general, a capacity to perform it, to perform it in a particular way, to know how to perform it, to like performing it and so on:

Я хорошо́ **бе́гаю** на конька́х
I **skate** well

Челове́к **хо́дит** на двух нога́х
Man **walks** upright

Истреби́тели **лета́ют** бы́стро
Fighter-planes **fly** fast

Multidirectional infinitives frequently combine with verbs such as **люби́ть** 'to like', **предпочита́ть** 'to prefer', **уме́ть** 'to know how to', **учи́ться** 'to learn how to' etc.:

Девча́та лю́бят **ходи́ть** в ро́щу за цвета́ми (Nikolaev)
The girls like **going** to the grove for flowers

Он предпочита́ет **ходи́ть** пешко́м, она́ **е́здит** в авто́бусе и́ли в трамва́е (Kovaleva)
He prefers **to walk,** she **goes** by bus or tram

А ты меня́ нау́чишь так **ла́зить?** . . . спроси́л мальчи́шка (Povolyaev)
'And will you teach me **to climb** like that?', asked the boy

Я уме́ю **води́ть** маши́ну
I know how **to drive** a car

(2) They denote movement **in various directions,** up and down, round and round, to and fro, backwards and forwards, and so on:

Всё своё внима́ние сосредото́чил на проти́внике, кото́рый **гоня́лся** за ним по ри́нгу (Salnikov)
He concentrated all his attention on his opponent, who **was chasing him round** the ring

В сара́е **лета́ли** белогру́дые ла́сточки (Belov)
White-breasted swallows **were flying about** in the shed

А стару́хи до по́здней но́чи **по́лзали** по кла́дбищу, втыка́ли обра́тно кресты́ (Rasputin)
And the old women **crawled round** the cemetery until late at night, sticking the crosses back into the ground

Никола́й Ива́нович стал **ходи́ть** по ко́мнате (Proskurin)
Nikolai Ivanovich began to **walk up and down** the room

(3) They denote habitual action, expressed as return journeys:

По воскресе́ньям мы **бу́дем е́здить** за́ город
On Sundays we shall drive into the country

Авто́бусы **ходи́ли** в са́мые да́льние сёла (Rybakov)
The buses **would go** to the most remote villages

Я **хожу́** в це́рковь
I **go** to church

323 Use of the past tense of a multidirectional verb to denote a single return journey

(1) The past tense (but **never** the present or future) of a multidirectional verb can be used to denote a single return journey:

> На про́шлой неде́ле она́ **е́здила** в Ло́ндон
> Last week she **went** to London (and back)

> Она́ неда́вно **вози́ла** дете́й в Нью-Йорк
> Recently she **took** the children to New York (and back)

(Compare Она́ **отвезла́** дете́й в Нью-Йорк 'She took the children to New York' (and returned alone).)

> Не обраща́йте на него́ внима́ния, — говори́т она́ Кузьме́. — Он опя́ть в рестора́н **ходи́л** (Rasputin)
> 'Pay no attention to him', she says to Kuzma. 'He's **been** to the restaurant again'

> Пока́ я **бе́гал** за фо̀тоаппара́том к маши́не, оле́нь ушёл
> By the time I **had run** to the car for my camera the deer had gone

Note
In this example **бе́гал** denotes running to the car *and back*. The use of the unidirectional **бежа́л** would imply that the deer escaped while the subject *was still running* towards the car.

(2) Sentences which refer to a return journey may also report what happened at the point of destination, between the outward and return legs of the trip:

> **Ходи́л** с отцо́м в зоопа́рк и там **ката́лся** на ма́ленькой лоша́дке (Belov)
> I **went** with my father to the zoo, where I **had a ride** on a little horse

Note
This sentence comprises three actions: (a) went to the zoo, (b) rode on a little horse while there (c) came home again, (a) and (c) being represented by the verb **ходи́л**.

(3) The multidirectional verb is also used in interrogative and negative sentences which refer to return trips:

> **Ты ходи́л** в шко́лу сего́дня?
> **Have you been/Did you go** to school today?

> Сего́дня **я не ходи́л** в шко́лу
> **I haven't been/I didn't go** to school today

324 The verbs нести́, носи́ть; вести́, води́ть; везти́, вози́ть

Нести́, носи́ть; вести́, води́ть; везти́, вози́ть may all mean 'to take':

(1) **Нести́, носи́ть** means 'to take (on foot), carry':

Он **несёт** кни́гу в библиоте́ку
He **is taking** the book to the library (on foot)

Она́ **носи́ла** малю́тку по ко́мнате
She **was carrying** the baby up and down the room

(2) **Вести́, води́ть** means 'to take, lead' (persons or animals):

Она́ **вела́** дете́й в шко́лу
She **was taking** the children to school (on foot)

Она́ **води́ла** дете́й в цирк
She **took** the children to the circus

Note
Вести́/води́ть also means 'to drive' (a vehicle).

(3) **Везти́, вози́ть** means 'to take, drive, convey' (in a vehicle):

Авто́бус **во́зит** тури́стов по А́нглии
The bus **is taking** the tourists round England

Она́ **везёт** ребёнка в коля́ске
She **is wheeling** the child in a pram

Note
(a) While **нести́/носи́ть, вести́/води́ть** and **везти́/вози́ть** denote the *specific* purpose of a journey, **брать/взять** 'to take' does not. Compare **Веди́те** дете́й в зооса́д 'Take the children to the zoo' (the specific reason for the outing) and **Возьми́те** меня́ с собо́й 'Take me with you' (the person addressed is going anyway).
(b) A similar principle distinguishes **нести́/носи́ть** from **везти́/вози́ть** in contexts which involve travelling. Thus, a passenger in a train who is taking a picture to an exhibition may say — **Везу́** карти́ну на вы́ставку в Москву́, while of the briefcase he happens to be carrying he will say — **Несу́** портфе́ль, since it is *not* the object of his journey to transport the briefcase, which is simply an item of personal equipment.

325   Translation of 'to drive'

The verb 'to drive' can be rendered as follows:

(1) **Éхать/éздить** 'to drive, travel':

> Я **éду** в го́род
> I **am driving** to town

(2) **Везти́/вози́ть** 'to drive, convey, transport':

> Я **вёз** бага́ж на ста́нцию
> I **was taking** (driving) the luggage to the station

(3) **Вести́/води́ть** 'to drive' (a vehicle):

> Я учу́сь **води́ть** маши́ну
> I am learning **to drive**

Note
Гнать/гоня́ть ста́до 'to drive' (a herd).

326   Perfectives of unidirectional verbs

(1) The perfective infinitives of unidirectional verbs are formed with the prefix **по-**:

идти́/**пойти́**	'to go'	éхать/**по-**	'to travel'
лете́ть/**по-**	'to fly'	бежа́ть/**по-**	'to run' etc.

Note
Only **идти́** undergoes modification (to **-йти**) in the formation of the perfective.

(2) The perfectives of unidirectional verbs denote the beginning of movement, setting off for a destination etc.:

> Он **пошёл** на по́чту
> He **has gone** to the post office

(Compare Он **ходи́л** на по́чту 'He went/has been to the post office' (implying a return journey).)

> Она́ **поéхала** за грани́цу
> She **has gone** abroad

(Compare Она́ **éздила** за грани́цу 'She went/has been abroad' (and has returned).)

Он **понёс** книгу в библиотеку
He **has taken** the book to the library (and is not back yet)

Note

(a) English '**went**' can refer to one-way journeys ('He **went** to China last week'), rendered by the perfective of a unidirectional verb:

На прошлой неделе он **поехал** в Китай

or to return trips ('**I went** on holiday to France last year'), rendered by a Russian multidirectional verb:

В прошлом году я **ездил** на каникулы во Францию

(b) Note the contrast between durative **шёл** and perfective **пошёл** in the following example: Он круто повернулся и **пошёл** навстречу противнику, который **шёл** на него уже без улыбки (Salnikov) 'He turned sharply and **set off** towards his opponent, who **was bearing down** on him, no longer with a smile on his face'.

(3) The future of unidirectional perfectives can be used independently (Я **пойду** с тобой 'I will go with you') or with the future perfective of another verb:

— **Пойду покурю**, — говорю я (Kazakov)
'I'll go and have a smoke', I say

(4) The unidirectional perfective may indicate a new phase of an action already in progress (e.g. a change in tempo):

Они шли медленно, потом **пошли** быстрее
They were walking along slowly, then **quickened their pace**

Пловец почувствовал усталость и **поплыл** медленнее
The swimmer felt tired and **began to swim** more slowly

(5) An English phrase may translate a unidirectional perfective:

Мы оттолкнулись от бакена и **поплыли** к берегу (Nikolaev)
We pushed off from the buoy and **struck out** for the shore

Он шёл по берегу, но **побежал**, увидев меня
He was walking along the shore but **broke into a run** on catching sight of me

327   Special meanings of пойти

Пойти can mean:

(1) 'To start walking' of a toddler:

Он **пошёл** с десяти ме́сяцев
He **started walking** at ten months

(2) 'To start school' of an infant:

Ми́ша в э́том году́ **пошёл** в шко́лу
Misha **started** school this year

Note also the 'illogical' use of the past in Я **пошёл!** 'I'm off!',
Пое́хали! Let's go!' etc.

328   Не пошёл and не ходи́л

(1) **Не ходи́л** denotes that a journey did not take place:

Вчера́ мы никуда́ **не ходи́ли**
We didn't go anywhere yesterday

(2) **Не пошёл** implies an intention unfulfilled:

Вчера́ мы никуда́ **не пошли́**
We didn't go anywhere yesterday (though we had planned to)

329   Perfectives of multidirectional verbs

(1) The perfectives of multidirectional verbs are also formed with the
prefix **по-**:

ходи́ть/**по-**   'to walk'   е́здить/**по-**   'to travel' etc.

(2) They denote an action of short duration in the past or future:

Он **полета́л** над го́родом и опусти́лся
He **circled** the town **for a while** and then landed

Оста́лось два ра́унда. **Походи́** немно́го, пото́м укро́йся
полоте́нцем и сиди́ здесь, жди меня́ (Salnikov)
There are two rounds left. **Walk around for a bit**, then wrap
yourself in a towel, sit here and wait for me

330   Figurative and idiomatic uses of verbs of motion

Verbs of motion have a number of figurative or idiomatic meanings. In most cases only one of a pair (either the unidirectional or the multidirectional) can be used in a particular figurative sense: the usual differential criteria between unidirectional and multidirectional do *not* apply when the verbs are used figuratively.

(1) Only **unidirectional** verbs can be used in the following:

(i) **Идёт** война́, уро́к, фильм
A war, a lesson, a film **is on**

Э́та шля́па вам **идёт**
This hat **suits** you

Страна́ **идёт** к социали́зму
The country is **moving** towards socialism

Идти́ про̀тив во́ли большинства́
To go against the will of the majority

Идёт дождь, снег
It is raining, snowing

Иду́т часы́
The clock **is going**

Note
Часы́ **хо́дят** is possible in certain contexts: Часы́ **давно́** не хо́дят 'The clock has not gone **for a long time**'.

(ii)	**вести́** войну́	**to wage** war
	вести́ дневни́к	**to keep** a diary
	вести́ перепи́ску	**to carry on** a correspondence
	Доро́га **ведёт** в лес	The road **leads** to the forest
	Ложь к добру́ **не ведёт**	No good **can come of** lying
(iii)	**нести́** отве́тственность	**to bear** the responsibility
	нести́ поте́ри	**to bear** losses
	нести́ наказа́ние	**to undergo** punishment
(iv)	А́кции **летя́т** вниз	Shares **are plummeting**
	Вре́мя **лети́т**	Time **flies**
(v)	**лезть** в дра́ку	**to get into** a brawl
(vi)	Ему́ **везёт/повезло́**	He **is lucky/is in luck**

> **Повезло́**, что отыска́ли льди́ну толщино́й 47 см. (Lebedev)
> **We were lucky** enough to find an ice-floe 47 cm thick

(vii) Дни **бегу́т**; Кровь **бежи́т** The days **fly past**; Blood **flows**

(viii) Тролле́йбус **ползёт**, как черепа́ха
The trolley-bus **is crawling along** at a snail's pace

(2) Only **multidirectional** verbs are used in the following:

(i)   **носи́ть** зва́ние, и́мя   **to bear** a title, a name
    носи́ть отпеча́ток   **to bear** the imprint
    носи́ть оде́жду   **to wear** clothes (habitually: cf. Он
                        но́сит шля́пу 'He wears a hat' and
                        Он **в шля́пе** 'He is wearing a hat')

(ii)   **води́ть** за́ нос   **to lead** up the garden path

(iii) **хо́дит** слух/**хо́дят** слу́хи
rumour **has it**/rumours **are rife** (also, though less commonly, **иду́т** слу́хи)

(iv)   **ката́ться** на конька́х   **to skate**
    ката́ться на велосипе́де **to go** for a cycle ride
    ката́ться на ло́дке   **to go** for a row

331 Compound verbs of motion

(1) All simple verbs of motion combine with up to fifteen different prefixes to form compound aspectival pairs, multidirectional verbs forming the basis of the imperfectives and unidirectional verbs the basis of the perfectives (see **332** for modified verb stems).

(2) These prefixed imperfective/perfective aspectival pairs lack the unidirectional/multidirectional dichotomy of the simple verbs.

(3) Most compound verbs of motion are intransitive and are linked to the following noun by a preposition (see (4)).

(4) Prefixed compounds of **-ходи́ть/-йти́**, for example, are as follows:

Imperfective	Perfective	Preposition	Meaning
входи́ть	войти́	в + acc.	to enter
всходи́ть	взойти́	на + acc.	to go up on to
выходи́ть	вы́йти	из + gen.	to go out of
доходи́ть	дойти́	до + gen.	to go as far as
заходи́ть	зайти́	к + dat.	to call on someone

заходи́ть	зайти́	в/на + acc.	to call in at a place
		в + acc.	to go a long way into
находи́ть	найти́	+ acc.	to find
обходи́ть	обойти́	вокру̀г + gen.	to go round
		+ acc.	to inspect/avoid
отходи́ть	отойти́	от + gen.	to move away from
переходи́ть	перейти́	через + acc.	to cross
		+ acc.	
подходи́ть	подойти́	к + dat.	to go up to
приходи́ть	прийти́	к + dat.	to come to see a person
		в/на + acc.	to come to/arrive at a place
проходи́ть	пройти́	мѝмо + gen.	to pass
		+ acc.	to cover (a distance)
расходи́ться	разойти́сь	по + dat	to disperse to (separate destinations)
сходи́ть	сойти́	с + gen.	to come down from, step off
сходи́ться	сойти́сь	с + instr.	to come together with
уходи́ть	уйти́	от + gen.	to leave a person
		из/с + gen	to leave a place

Note

(a) Alternative usage may be determined by context: Она́ вы́шла в коридо́р/на у́лицу 'She came out **into** the corridor/**on to** the street', Он ушёл **на рабо́ту** 'He left **for** work', Они́ пришли́ **от дире́ктора** 'They have come **from** the manager', Она́ сошла́ **на перро́н** 'She got down **on to** the platform' etc.

(b) The choice of preposition with **заходи́ть/зайти́** and **приходи́ть/ прийти́** depends on the type of location involved: Он пришёл **в шко́лу/на заво́д** 'He arrived **at the school/factory**' (cf. Он ушёл **из шко́лы/с рабо́ты** 'He left **school/work**'). See **408** and **412**.

(c) Some compounds in **на-** take **на** + acc.: **нае́хать на де́рево** 'to run into a tree'.

(d) Prefix and prepositional usage is similar to but not identical with usage with other verbs (see **254**).

332   Stems of compound verbs of motion

Prefixes are added to the following stems to make imperfective and perfective compounds. Stems which differ in form from the simple verbs of motion (for meanings, see **316**) are in **bold** type:

Imperfective	Perfective
-ходи́ть	**-йти́**
-езжа́ть	-е́хать

-бега́ть	-бежа́ть
-лета́ть	-лете́ть
-леза́ть	-лезть
-плыва́ть	-плыть
-ползáть	-ползти́
-носи́ть	-нести́
-води́ть	-вести́
-вози́ть	-везти́
-та́скивать	-тащи́ть
-гоня́ть	-гнать
-ка́тывать	-кати́ть
-бреда́ть	-брести́

Note

The stems **-бега́ть** and **-ползáть** differ from the simple verbs of motion **бе́гать** 'to run' and **по́лзать** 'to crawl' only in stress.

333   Spelling rules in the formation of compound verbs of motion

(1) For **вз-/-вс-**, **раз-/рас-**, see **16** (4).

(2) The vowel '**o**' is inserted between a consonant and **-йти**:

войти́ (impf. **входи́ть**)   to enter (future **войду́**; past **вошёл**)

Likewise **взойти́** 'to ascend', **обойти́** 'to go round', **отойти́** 'to move away from', **подойти́** 'to go up to', **разойти́сь** 'to disperse', **сойти́** 'to descend', **сойти́сь** 'to come together'.

(3) A hard sign is inserted between a prefix ending in a consonant and all forms based on the infinitive stems **-езжа́ть/-éхать**:

въезжа́ть, въéхать   to drive in etc.

334   Prefixed verbs of motion

The following examples illustrate the use of compound verbs of motion (for examples with **-ходи́ть/-йти́** see **331** (4)):

(1) **К** подно́жью раке́ты **подъезжа́ет** авто́бус (*Russia Today*)
   A bus **draws up to** the base of the rocket

(2) Дети **выбегают из** моря на пляж (Muraveva)
The children **run out of** the sea on to the beach

(3) Их объединяет одна общая цель – они должны **доплыть до берега** (*Russia Today*)
They are united by a common aim – they must **reach** the shore

(4) Кононов **отполз** в угол палатки (Belov)
Kononov **crawled off** into the corner of the tent

(5) Мяч **залетел на** крышу
The ball **sailed away on to** the roof

(6) Она **перелезла через** забор
She **climbed over** the fence

(7) **Разбредались по** влажному лесу (Vanshenkin)
They **were wandering off through** the damp forest

(8) Мяч **перекатился через** линию
The ball **rolled over** the line

(9) **Вытащили** лётчика **из** горящего самолёта
They **dragged** the pilot **out** of the burning aircraft

(10) Моторы их катеров сверхмощные, рыбинспекторам не **догнать** (*Izvestiya*)
The engines of their launches are high-powered, the fisheries inspectors haven't a hope of **catching up with** them

(11) **Перенёс** телефон **на** тахту (Avdeenko)
He **carried** the telephone **over** to the divan

(12) — Вот, матроса тебе **привёл**, — сказал Кутузов (Yakhontov)
'Look, I have **brought** you a sailor', said Kutuzov

(13) Кутузов сообщил: яхты уже **привезли** (Yakhontov)
Kutuzov reported that the yachts **had** already **been delivered**

335   Use of the imperfective past of a compound verb of motion to denote an action and its reverse

(1) The past tense of the imperfective aspect of a compound verb of motion can denote the action and its reverse (see also **259**): Он **приходил** 'He came' (and has now gone away again), Он **уезжал** 'He went away' (and has now returned).

(2) The prefixes most frequently involved are **в-/вы-**, **за-**, **под-**, **при-/у-**:

Ка́к-то она́ **приводи́ла** свои́х дете́й на рентге́н (Aksenov)
She **had** once **brought** her children for an X-ray

Каки́е краси́вые цветы́! Кто́-то, **должно́ быть**, **входи́л** в ко́мнату без меня́
What beautiful flowers! Someone **must have been** into the room when I was out

Же́нщина, кото́рая то́лько что **подходи́ла к** кио́ску за газе́той, изве́стная актри́са
The woman who **has just been up to** the kiosk for a newspaper is a famous actress

336   Figurative and idiomatic uses of compound verbs of motion

Many compound verbs of motion have figurative or idiomatic meanings. The following list contains only a representative sample:

(1) Compounds in -ходи́ть, -йти́

входи́ть/войти́ в мо́ду	to come into fashion
выходи́ть/вы́йти из стро́я	to break down
доходи́ть/дойти́ до слёз	to be reduced to tears
заходи́ть/зайти́ сли́шком далеко́	to go too far
переходи́ть/перейти́ к друго́й те́ме	to switch to a different topic
подходи́ть/подойти́	to be suitable
приходи́ть/прийти́ в го́лову (кому́-нибудь)	to occur (to someone)
проходи́ть/пройти́	to pass (e.g. вре́мя, боль прохо́дит 'time, pain passes')
расходи́ться/разойти́сь во мне́ниях	not to see eye to eye
сходи́ть/сойти́ с ума́	to go mad
сходи́ться/сойти́сь во мне́ниях	to see eye to eye

(2) Compounds in -води́ть, -вести́

вводи́ть/ввести́ в обраще́ние	to bring into circulation

выводи́ть/вы́вести из терпе́ния	to exasperate
доводи́ть/довести́ до конца́	to put the finishing touches to
заводи́ть/завести́ часы́	to wind up a watch
наводи́ть/навести́ спра́вки	to make enquiries
отводи́ть/отвести́ ду́шу	to unburden one's soul
переводи́ть/перевести́	to translate
подводи́ть/подвести́ дру́га	to let a friend down
приводи́ть/привести́ к	to lead to
проводи́ть/провести́ вре́мя	to spend time
разводи́ть/развести́	to breed (livestock)
разводи́ться/развести́сь	to get divorced
своди́ть/свести́ к ми́нимуму	to reduce to a minimum

(3) Compounds in -носи́ть, -нести́

вноси́ть/внести́ вклад	to make a contribution
выноси́ть/вы́нести пригово́р	to pass sentence
доноси́ть/донести́ на + acc.	to denounce
заноси́ть/занести́	to record, register
наноси́ть/нанести́ пораже́ние	to inflict a defeat
переноси́ть/перенести́ зи́му	to survive the winter
приноси́ть/принести́ по́льзу	to bring benefit

337   Perfectives in c- based on multidirectional verbs

(1) Multidirectional verbs combine with the prefix **c-** to form perfectives: **сбе́гать, сходи́ть, съе́здить** etc. They do not have imperfectives.

(2) Such verbs denote the performance of an action and its result, usually within a limited period of time:

Ни́кон **сходи́л** (pf.) за дрова́ми, затопи́л ма́ленькую пе́чку (Abramov)
Nikon **went to fetch** some firewood and lit the small stove

Note
Compounds with **c-** are preferred to the simple unprefixed multidirectional verb (e.g. он ходи́л, он е́здил):

(a) where sequential actions are involved:

Съе́здил (pf.) за кни́гами и **сел** занима́ться
He **went to fetch** the books and sat down to study

(b) where a time element is involved:

Он **сходи́л** (pf.) за газе́той **за 10 мину́т**
He **took 10 minutes to fetch** the newspaper

(3) Unlike the simple unprefixed multidirectional verb, which can describe single return journeys in the past tense only (see **323**), perfectives in **c-** can also express this meaning in the future, the infinitive and the imperative:

Да и ле́гче, пожа́луй, **на Луну́ слета́ть** (pf.), чем приду́мать тако́й вездехо́д (Abramov)
I do believe it would be easier **to fly to the Moon and back** than devise a cross-country vehicle like that

Сходи́ (pf.) к Ма́йе и переда́й ей, что́бы она́ подошла́ за́втра по́сле игры́ к газе́тному кио́ску (Trifonov)
Pop over to Maya's and tell her to come to the newspaper kiosk after the game tomorrow

Note
It is important to distinguish perfectives **сходи́ть, слета́ть, сбе́гать** from imperfectives **сходи́ть**/perfective **сойти́** 'to go down', **слета́ть**/perfective **слете́ть** 'to fly down' and **сбега́ть**/perfective **сбежа́ть** 'to run down'.

338 Perfectives in за-, из- and на- based on multidirectional verbs

За-, **из-** and **на-** also combine with multidirectional verbs to form compound perfectives (such verbs do not have imperfectives):

(1) За- (in the meaning 'beginning of an action')

Он в волне́нии **заходи́л** (pf.) по ко́мнате
He **began walking about** the room in agitation

(2) Из- (in the meaning 'to cover the whole area')

Он **изъе́здил** (pf.) всю страну́
He **has travelled the length and breadth** of the country

Он **избе́гал** (pf.) весь сад
He **covered every inch** of the garden

(3) На- (in the meaning of time or distance covered)

Э́тот шофёр **нае́здил** (pf.) 100 000 км.
This driver **has clocked** 100,000 km.

Лётчик **налета́л** (pf.) 1000 часо́в
The pilot **has clocked** 1,000 hours

Note
It is important to distinguish perfective **заходи́ть** from imperfective
заходи́ть/perfective **зайти́** 'to drop in' and perfective **избе́гать** from
imperfective **избега́ть**/perfective **избежа́ть** 'to avoid'.

Participles

339   Participles. Introductory comments

There are five verbal participles in Russian. The active participles, the
imperfective passive and the long-form perfective passive decline like
long adjectives and agree in case, gender and number with the nouns
they qualify, while the short-form perfective passive functions like a
short adjective:

the present active	**чита́ющий**	'who is reading'
the past active (imperfective)	**чита́вший**	'who was reading'
the past active (perfective)	**прочита́вший**	'who read'
the imperfective passive	**чита́емый**	'which is read'
the perfective passive (short form)	**прочи́тан**	'has been read'
the perfective passive (long form)	**прочи́танный**	'which has been read'

Note
The participles are confined mainly to written styles, except for those
used as adjectives and nouns and the perfective passive short form.

340   Present active participle. Formation

(1) The present active participle is formed by replacing the final -**т** of
the third-person plural of the present tense by the endings -**щий** (m.),
-**щая** (f.), -**щее** (n.), -**щие** (pl.):

бегу́т	бегу́щий	-ая	-ее	-ие	'who is, are running'
крича́т	крича́щий	-ая	-ее	-ие	'who is, are shouting'
танцу́ют	танцу́ющий	-ая	-ее	-ие	'who is, are dancing'
чита́ют	чита́ющий	-ая	-ее	-ие	'who is, are reading'

(2) In the case of reflexive verbs, **-ся** is used throughout:

| смею́тся | смею́щий**ся** | -ая**ся** | -ее**ся** | -ие**ся** | 'who is, are laughing' |

341   Stress in the present active participle

(1) The stress in present active participles formed from **first-conjugation** verbs is usually as in the third-person plural:

понима́ть	понима́ют	**понима́ющий**	'who understands'
тону́ть	то́нут	**то́нущий**	'who drowns/is drowning'
иска́ть	и́щут	**и́щущий**	'who looks for/is looking for'
течь	теку́т	**теку́щий**	'which flows/is flowing'

Note
There are a few exceptions to this rule, e.g. **могу́щий** from мо́гут, third-person plural of мочь 'to be able'.

(2) The stress in participles from **second-conjugation** verbs is usually the same as that of the **infinitive**:

буди́ть	бу́дят	**будя́щий**	'who wakes, is waking'
води́ть	во́дят	**водя́щий**	'who leads'
кати́ть	ка́тят	**катя́щий**	'who is rolling'

(3) However, a number of participles from second-conjugation verbs have the same stress as the third-person plural: **ды́шащий** from дыша́ть 'to breathe', **ле́чащий** from лечи́ть 'to treat' (medically), **лю́бящий** from люби́ть 'to love', **ру́бящий** from руби́ть 'to chop', **су́шащий** from суши́ть 'to dry', **те́рпящий** from терпе́ть 'to endure', **ту́шащий** from туши́ть 'to extinguish'.

(4) A number of participles have alternative stress: **ва́рящий/варя́щий** from вари́ть 'to boil', **го́нящий/гоня́щий** from гнать 'to drive', **де́лящий/деля́щий** from дели́ть 'to share', **су́дящий/судя́щий** from суди́ть 'to judge', **у́чащий/уча́щий** from учи́ть 'to teach', **хва́лящий/хваля́щий** from хвали́ть 'to praise', **шу́тящий/шутя́щий** from шути́ть 'to joke'.

342   The past active participle. Formation

(1) The past active participle is formed from imperfective and perfective verbs by replacing the -л of the masculine past tense by -вший (m.), -вшая (f.), -вшее (n.), -вшие (pl.):

писа́л	писа́вший	-вшая	-вшее	-вшие	'who was, were writing'
написа́л	написа́вший	-вшая	-вшее	-вшие	'who wrote'

(2) In reflexive verbs, the suffix -ся is used throughout:

     смея́вшийся   'who laughed, was laughing'

(3) If the masculine past does not end in -л, the endings -ший, -шая, -шее, -шие are added to it to make the participle:

замёрз	замёрзший	-шая	-шее	-шие	'who, which froze'
привы́к	привы́кший	-шая	-шее	-шие	'who got used to'
у́мер	уме́рший	-шая	-шее	-шие	'who died'

Note

(a)   Unprefixed verbs with the suffix -ну-, e.g. га́снуть 'to go out' (past гас/га́снул), ги́бнуть 'to perish', па́хнуть 'to smell', and the prefixed verb исче́знуть 'to disappear' (past исче́з) form the past participle with the suffix -вш-: га́снувший, ги́бнувший, исче́знувший, па́хнувший.

(b)   Дости́гнуть 'to achieve' (past дости́г) has alternative participles: дости́гший/дости́гнувший. Likewise compounds of -вергнуть, e.g. подве́ргший/подве́ргнувший from подве́ргнуть 'to subject' (past подве́рг) and вто́ргшийся/вто́ргнувшийся from вто́ргнуться 'to invade' (past вто́ргся). Воскре́сший from воскре́снуть 'to rise again' (past воскре́с) is commoner than воскре́снувший.

(4) Verbs in -ти with a present-future stem in -т- or -д- have participles based on stems ending in these consonants:

идти́, past шёл	ше́дший	-шая	-шее	-шие	'who was, were going'
вести́, past вёл	ве́дший	-шая	-шее	-шие	'who was, were leading'
цвести́, past цвёл	цве́тший	-шая	-шее	-шие	'which was, were blooming'

Note

Произойти́ 'to occur' has alternative participles происше́дший and произоше́дший.

343   Stress in the past active participle

Stress is as in the masculine past, with the exception of **уме́рший** 'who died' (cf. past **у́мер**).

344   The imperfective passive participle. Formation

(1) The imperfective passive participle is formed by adding adjectival endings to the first-person plural of an imperfective **transitive** verb:

First-person plural	Participle				
лю́бим	**люби́мый**	-ая	-ое	-ые	'who, which is, are loved'
це́ним	**цени́мый**	-ая	-ое	-ые	'who, which is, are valued'
чита́ем	**чита́емый**	-ая	-ое	-ые	'which is, are read'

(2) Many unprefixed transitive verbs (e.g. **жева́ть** 'to chew', **копа́ть** 'to dig') do not form the participle. However, participles can be made from most prefixed transitive secondary imperfectives and verbs in **-овать**:

испы́тываемый	-ая	-ое	-ые	'which is, are (being) tested'
сжига́емый	-ая	-ое	-ые	'which is, are (being) burnt'
тре́буемый	-ая	-ое	-ые	'which is, are (being) demanded'
устра́иваемый	-ая	-ое	-ые	'which is, are (being) arranged'

(3) Participles from transitive verbs in -ава́ть are as follows: **дава́емый** 'which is given/being given', **признава́емый** 'which is acknowledged' etc.

Note

(a) The participle is also formed from a limited number of **intransitive** or **semi-transitive** verbs. Some of these take the dative: **предше́ствовать** 'to precede' (**предше́ствуемый**), **угрожа́ть** 'to threaten' (**угрожа́емый**). Others take the instrumental: **кома́ндовать** 'to command' (**кома́ндуемый**), **пренебрега́ть** 'to scorn, take no heed of' (**пренебрега́емый**), **руководи́ть** 'to run' (**руководи́мый**), **управля́ть** 'to manage, guide' (**управля́-**

емый). The series also includes **обита́емый** 'inhabited' (from intransitive **обита́ть**).

(b) Among verbs in **-ти**, only **вести́** 'to lead' (**ведо́мый** (**ведо́мый** самолёт 'wing-man' (in an aircraft formation))) and **нести́** 'to carry' (**несо́мый**) form imperfective passive participles (see **346** (2)).

345   Stress in the imperfective passive participle

Stress in imperfective passive participles derived from **first-conjugation** verbs is as in the first-person plural: **испо́льзуемый** 'which is used'. In participles derived from **second-conjugation** verbs the stress falls on **-и-**: **гони́мый** 'which is driven', from **гнать** 'to drive' (except for verbs with stem stress throughout: **слы́шимый** from **слы́шать** 'to hear').

346   Verbs which have no imperfective passive participle

Many verbs have no imperfective passive participle. These include the following:

(1) Verbs in **-ереть**, **-зть**, **-оть**, **-сть**, **-уть**, **-чь**.

(2) Verbs in **-ти** (except for **вести́** 'to lead' and **нести́** 'to carry' (see **344** (3) note (b)).

(3) Very many monosyllabic verbs, including **бить** 'to strike', **брать** 'to take', **брить** 'to shave', **есть** 'to eat', **жать** 'to press', **ждать** 'to wait for', **звать** 'to call', **знать** 'to know', **лить** 'to pour', **мыть** 'to wash', **петь** 'to sing', **пить** 'to drink', **рвать** 'to tear', **ткать** 'to weave', **шить** 'to sew'.

(4) First-conjugation consonant-stem verbs of the type **вяза́ть** 'to tie', **писа́ть** 'to write', **пря́тать** 'to hide'. However, **иска́ть** 'to seek' has the participle **иско́мый** (**иско́мая** величина́ 'unknown quantity') and **колеба́ть** 'to shake' has **коле́блемый** 'which is being shaken'. See **217**.

(5) Many second-conjugation verbs: **благодари́ть** 'to thank', **буди́ть** 'to awaken', **гла́дить** 'to iron', **гото́вить** 'to prepare', **держа́ть** 'to hold', **жа́рить** 'to fry', **корми́ть** 'to feed', **кра́сить** 'to paint', **лечи́ть** 'to treat' (medically), **находи́ть** 'to find', **плати́ть** 'to pay', **по́ртить**

'to spoil', **руби́ть** 'to chop', **смотре́ть** 'to watch', **ста́вить** 'to stand', **стро́ить** 'to build', **суши́ть** 'to dry', **тра́тить** 'to spend', **туши́ть** 'to extinguish', **учи́ть** 'to teach, learn', **чи́стить** 'to clean'.

347 Formation of passive participles from secondary imperfectives whose primaries have no participle

Most imperfective passive participles derive from prefixed verbs. They include synonyms or cognates of a number of unprefixed verbs which have no participle (see **346**). Thus, the verb **есть** 'to eat' has no participle, whereas its synonym, the secondary imperfective **съеда́ть**, *does* have a participle: **съеда́емый** 'which is eaten'. Compare

жева́ть	= разжёвывать	**разжёвываемый**	'which is chewed'
жечь	= сжига́ть	**сжига́емый**	'which is burnt'
пить	= выпива́ть	**выпива́емый**	'which is drunk'
плати́ть	= опла́чивать	**опла́чиваемый**	'who is paid'
тере́ть	= растира́ть	**растира́емый**	'which is rubbed'

348 The perfective passive participle. Introductory comments

(1) The perfective passive participle has a **short** (predicative) form and a **long** (attributive) form. It is derived only from verbs which are (i) *perfective* and (ii) *transitive*.

(2) Most perfective passive participles contain the suffix -**н**-/-**ен**-, while a minority contain the suffix -**т**-.

349 Formation (infinitives in -ать/-ять)

(1) The masculine short form of the participle derives from infinitives in -**ать** and -**ять** (except for a number of monosyllabic roots, see **357** (5)) by replacing -**ть** by -**н**, to give endings -**ан**/-**ян**. The syllable immediately preceding -**ан**, -**ян** bears the stress:

задержа́ть	**заде́ржан**	'has been arrested'
избра́ть	**и́збран**	'has been elected'
написа́ть	**напи́сан**	'has been written'

Note

The perfective prefix **вы́**- is always stressed: **вы́игран** 'has been won'.

(2) -**е**- is liable to mutate to -**ё**- under stress:

| завоева́ть | **завоёван** | 'has been conquered' |
| причеса́ть | **причёсан** | 'has had his hair done' |

(3) The feminine, neuter and plural forms are derived from the masculine by the addition of -**а**, -**о**, -**ы**:

| напи́сан | напи́сан**а** | напи́сан**о** | напи́сан**ы** |
| заде́ржан | заде́ржан**а** | заде́ржан**о** | заде́ржан**ы** |

350 Stress in the participles from дать and its compounds

(1) The short forms of the perfective passive participle of the verb **дать** 'to give' have end stress in the feminine, neuter and plural:

дан   дана́   дано́   даны́

Им дана́ власть
Authority has been given to them

Similarly **сдать** 'to hand over'.

(2) The short forms of other compounds of **дать** (e.g. **изда́ть** 'to publish') have prefix stress except in the end-stressed feminine (where prefix stress is, however, also allowable):

и́здан   издана́   и́здано   и́зданы   'has, have been published'

Similarly **отда́ть** 'to return', **переда́ть** 'to convey' (**пе́редан, передана́**), **пода́ть** 'to serve', **прида́ть** 'to impart', **прода́ть** 'to sell', **разда́ть** 'to distribute' (**ро́здан, раздана́, ро́здано, ро́зданы**), **созда́ть** 'to create'.

351 Formation of the long-form (attributive) participle from verbs in -ать/-ять

Long-form participles are made from verbs in -**ать**/-**ять** by adding -**ный**, -**ная**, -**ное**, -**ные** to the masculine short form:

Masculine	Feminine	Neuter	Plural
напи́сан	**напи́санный**	**напи́санная**	**напи́санное**	**напи́санные**
				'written'

352 Formation of the short-form participle from second-conjugation verbs in -ить/-еть

The masculine short form of the participle is derived from second-conjugation infinitives in **-ить/-еть** by replacing the infinitive ending by **-ен** or **-ён**:

(1) **-ен**

(i) Verbs with **fixed stem stress** or **mobile stress** in conjugation take the ending **-ен**.

(a) Fixed stem stress in conjugation: **запо́лнить** 'to fill in', **прове́рить** 'to check':

Бланк **запо́лнен**	The form has been filled in
Счёт **прове́рен**	The account has been checked

(b) Mobile stress in conjugation: **осмотре́ть** 'to examine' (**осмотрю́, осмо́тришь**), **получи́ть** 'to receive' (**получу́, полу́чишь**):

Больно́й **осмо́трен**	The patient has been examined
Докла́д **полу́чен**	The report has been received

(ii) The feminine, neuter and plural forms derive from the masculine by the addition of **-а**, **-о** and **-ы**: запо́лнен, запо́лнен**а**, запо́лнен**о**, запо́лнен**ы**.

> Анке́та **запо́лнена**   The questionnaire **has been completed**

Note
Принуждён from **прину́дить** 'to compel'.

(2) **-ён**

(i) Verbs with **fixed end stress** in conjugation take the masculine short-form ending **-ён**: **реши́ть** 'to decide' (**решу́, реши́шь**), **включи́ть** 'to switch' (**включу́, включи́шь**):

Вопро́с **решён**	The question has been decided
Телеви́зор **включён**	The TV has been switched on/is on

(ii) The feminine, neuter and plural endings are **end stressed**: решён, решен**а́**, решен**о́**, решен**ы́**:

Пробле́ма **решена́**	The problem has been solved

Note

A few verbs with *mobile* stress in conjugation take *end* stress in the participle:

изменить: изменён -ена́ -ено́ -ены́   'has, have been changed'

Likewise **осуждён** from осудить 'to condemn', **оценён** from оценить 'to estimate', **разделён** from разделить 'to divide', **склонён** from склонить 'to incline' (cf. **склонен, склонна** (adjective) 'is inclined').

353 Consonant mutation in participles from second-conjugation infinitives in -ить/-еть

The following consonant changes operate in the formation of perfective passive participles from second-conjugation verbs in -ить/-еть (for stress rules see **352**):

б : бл	срубить	срублен	has been felled
	употребить	употреблён	has been used
в : вл	доставить	доставлен	has been delivered
	удивить	удивлён	is surprised

Note
Dual mutation in умерщвлён from умертвить 'to mortify'.

м : мл	офо́рмить	офо́рмлен	has been designed
п : пл	купить	куплен	has been bought
	прикрепить	прикреплён	is pinned to
ф : фл	разграфить	разграфлён	is ruled (with lines)
д : ж	зарядить	заря́жен/заряжён	is loaded
	обидеть	обижен	is offended

Note
The participle from **увидеть** 'to see' is **увиден**.

д : жд	освободить	освобождён	has been liberated

Note
-жд- also appears in the imperfective infinitive (**освобожда́ть**) and the verbal noun (**освобожде́ние** 'liberation'). Other verbs which undergo this mutation are mainly abstract and, like **освободи́ть**, have fixed end stress in conjugation: **подтверди́ть** 'to confirm', **убеди́ть** 'to convince' etc.

| з : ж | загру́зи́ть | загру́жен/загружён | is laden |
| | изобрази́ть | изображён | is depicted |

Note

The mutation does not operate in some participles: **вонзён** from вонзи́ть 'to plunge', **пронзён** from пронзи́ть 'to transfix'.

| с : ш | пригласи́ть | приглашён | has been invited |
| | скоси́ть | ско́шен | has been mown |

Note

One or two participles do not undergo mutation: **обезле́сен** from обезле́сить 'to deforest'.

ст : щ	запусти́ть	запу́щен	has been launched
	прости́ть	прощён	has been forgiven
т : ч	оплати́ть	опла́чен	has been paid, settled
т : щ	сократи́ть	сокращён	has been curtailed

Note

-**щ**- also appears in the first-person singular (**сокращу́**), the imperfective infinitive (**сокраща́ть**) and the verbal noun (**сокраще́ние** 'curtailment'). Other verbs of this type, mainly abstract and with fixed end stress in conjugation, include **запрети́ть** 'to ban'.

354 Formation of the long-form (attributive) participle from second-conjugation verbs in -ить/-еть

Long-form participles from second-conjugation verbs in -**ить**/-**еть** are derived by adding -**ный**, -**ная**, -**ное**, -**ные** to the masculine short form:

Masculine	Feminine	Neuter	Plural	
запо́лненный	запо́лненная	запо́лненное	запо́лненные	'completed'
включённый	включённая	включённое	включённые	'switched on'

355 Formation of perfective passive participles (short form) from verbs in -ти, -чь, -зть, -сть

The masculine short form of perfective passive participles from verbs in -**ти**, -**зть**, -**сть** and -**чь** is derived by replacing the final -**т** of the third-person singular of the conjugation of the verb by -**н**:

Infinitive		Third-person singular	Participle			
перевести́	to translate	переведёт	**переведён**	-ена́	-ено́	-ены́
подмести́	to sweep	подметёт	**подметён**	-ена́	-ено́	-ены́
спасти́	to save	спасёт	**спасён**	-ена́	-ено́	-ены́
испе́чь	to bake	испечёт	**испечён**	-ена́	-ено́	-ены́
обже́чь	to scorch	обожжёт	**обожжён**	-ена́	-ено́	-ены́
разгры́зть	to gnaw	разгрызёт	**разгры́зен**	-ена	-ено	-ены
укра́сть	to steal	украдёт	**укра́ден**	-ена	-ено	-ены

Note

(a) The participles from найти́ 'to find' and пройти́ 'to cover' (a distance) are, respectively, **на́йден** and **про́йден**.

(b) Дости́чь 'to achieve' has no participle. However, a participle is formed from its synonym дости́гнуть: **дости́гнут**. See **357** (2).

(c) Stem stress in participles from some verbs in -зть/-сть.

(d) For participles formed from compounds of -клясть, see **357** (5) note (a).

(e) Съесть 'to eat' has the participle **съе́ден**.

356   Long-form participles from verbs in -ти, -чь, зть, -сть

The long form of participles from verbs in -**ти**, -**чь**, -**зть** and -**сть** is made by adding -**ный**, -**ная**, -**ное**, -**ные** to the short-form masculine, e.g. **переведён**:

Masculine	Feminine	Neuter	Plural
переведённый	**переведённая**	**переведённое**	**переведённые** 'translated'

357   Perfective passive participles in -т

The masculine short form of the participle of certain categories of verb is made by removing the soft sign of the infinitive: **откры́ть** 'to open', participle **откры́т**. The feminine, neuter and plural forms derive from the masculine by the addition of the endings -**а**, -**о**, -**ы**. The following types of verb are involved:

(1) Verbs in -**оть** (note stress change in participle):

смоло́ть 'to grind'   **смо́лот, -а, -о, -ы**

(2) Verbs in **-уть** (note stress change in participle):

протяну́ть 'to stretch out'   **протя́нут, -а, -о, -ы**

Note

е is liable to mutate to **ё** under stress: заверну́ть 'to wrap', **завёрнут**; застегну́ть 'to fasten', **застёгнут**.

(3) Verbs in **-ыть**:

забы́ть 'to forget'   **забы́т, -а, -о, -ы**

(4) Compounds of **бить, вить, лить, пить, шить**:

вы́шить 'to embroider'   **вы́шит, -а, -о, -ы**
разби́ть 'to smash'   **разби́т, -а, -о, -ы**

Note

(a) Зали́ть 'to flood': **за́лит, залита́, за́лито, за́литы** (likewise **проли́ть** 'to spill': **про́лит** etc.).

(b) Разви́ть 'to develop': **ра́звит/разви́т, развита́, ра́звито/ разви́то, ра́звиты/разви́ты**

(5) Verbs which introduce '**н**' or '**м**' in conjugation (**взять** 'to take', compounds of **деть** 'to put', **жать** 'to press', **клясть** 'to curse' and **-нять, нача́ть** 'to begin', **распя́ть** 'to crucify'):

Infinitive		First-person singular	Participle
взять	'to take'	возьму́	**взят, -а́, -о, -ы**
заня́ть	'to occupy'	займу́	**за́нят, -а́, -о, -ы**
нача́ть	'to begin'	начну́	**на́чат -а́, -о, -ы**
оде́ть	'to dress'	оде́ну	**оде́т, -а, -о, -ы**
распя́ть	'to crucify'	распну́	**распя́т, -а, -о, -ы**
сжать	'to compress'	сожму́	**сжат, -а, -о, -ы**
сжать	'to reap'	сожну́	**сжат, -а, -о, -ы**
смять	'to crumple'	сомну́	**смят, -а, -о, -ы**

Note

(a) Прокля́сть 'to curse', first-person singular прокляну́, participle **про́клят, -а́, -о, -ы**. Compare *stem* stress in the adjective **прокля́тый** 'wretched'.

(b) Participles from all compounds of **-нять** have the same stress pattern as **за́нят** (except **снят, снята́, сня́то, сня́ты** from **снять** 'to take off').

(6) Verbs in **-ереть** (note loss of second **-е-** in formation of participle):

| запере́ть | 'to lock' | за́перт, -а́, -о, -ы |
| стере́ть | 'to erase' | стёрт, -а, -о, -ы |

(7) Others:

вы́брить	'to shave'	вы́брит, -а, -о, -ы
спеть	'to sing'	спет, -а, -о, -ы
прожи́ть	'to spend' (time)	про́жит, прожита́, про́жито, про́житы

358   The long form of participles in -т

The long-form participle is formed by adding full adjectival endings to the masculine short form in -т, e.g. **оде́т**:

| Masculine | Feminine | Neuter | Plural | |
| **оде́тый** | **оде́тая** | **оде́тое** | **оде́тые** | 'dressed' |

Note

Compare the participles **ра́звитый** (ско́рость, **ра́звитая** теплово́зом 'speed developed by a diesel locomotive') and **разви́тый** (**разви́тая** пружи́на 'uncoiled spring'), and the adjective **развито́й** (**развита́я** промы́шленность 'highly-developed industry').

359   Functions of short-form participles

(1) Only passive participles have short forms. Active participles have long forms only.

(2) The short form of the imperfective passive participle is rarely used:

Э́тот писа́тель все́ми **люби́м, уважа́ем**
This writer is loved and respected by everyone

A reflexive verb or third-person plural is preferred instead:

Прое́кты **финанси́руются** госуда́рством
Projects are financed by the state

Э́того писа́теля **лю́бят и уважа́ют**
This writer is loved and respected

(3) The short form of the **perfective** passive participle is very much used. It functions as predicate to the noun, with which it agrees in gender and number, and denotes:

(i) The completion of an action:

Война́ **объя́влена**	War has been declared
Флаг **по́днят**	The flag has been hoisted
Письмо́ **подпи́сано**	The letter has been signed

(ii) The existence of a state:

| Дверь **заперта́** | The door is locked |
| Телеви́зор **включён** | The television is on |

Note

(a) The participle may precede or follow the noun:

Укрощены́ не́которые опа́сные боле́зни (*Russia Today*)
Certain dangerous diseases **have been curbed**

О́стров **превращён** в зака́зник (Lebedev)
The island **has been converted** into a nature reserve

(b) It may also combine with forms of the verb **быть**:

Он то́лько что **был разбу́жен** гро́мким го́лосом Солоу́хи
(Povolyaev)
He **had** just been **awakened** by Soloukha's loud voice

(Likewise Он **бу́дет разбу́жен** 'He will be awakened', Он **был бы**
разбу́жен 'He would be/would have been awakened', Рабо́ты должны́
быть напеча́таны 'The essays have to be typed'.)

(c) The agent of the action may be rendered by an instrumental:

Письмо́ подпи́сано **мини́стром**
The letter is signed by a minister

360   Functions of long-form participles

Long-form participles, both active and passive, replace relative clauses
beginning with **кото́рый** 'who', 'which'.

(1) Active participles

Active participles relate to and qualify nouns which are the subject of an
action or state. A comma appears between the noun and the following
participle which qualifies it.

(i) The **present** active participle denotes an action which is
simultaneous with the action or state denoted by the main verb:

Вы́ставки, **расска́зывающие** о предупрежде́нии несча́стных
слу́чаев, всегда́ вызыва́ют большо́й интере́с
Exhibitions **which describe** accident prevention always arouse great
interest

Note
The main verb may denote present *or* past action: **Я ви́дел/ви́жу**
соба́ку, бегу́щую по бе́регу 'I saw/see a dog running along the shore'.

(ii) The **imperfective past** active participle denotes an action
simultaneous with the action of a main verb in the *past tense*:

Же́нщина, **продава́вшая** я́блоки, подошла́ к прохо́жему
The woman **who was selling** apples approached a passer-by

(iii) The **perfective past** active participle denotes an action completed
prior to the action of the main verb:

Медве́дя прогна́л рабо́чий, **прибежа́вший** на бе́рег с
заря́женным ружьём
The bear was chased off by a worker **who had come running** on to
the shore with a loaded gun

(2) Passive participles

Passive participles relate to and qualify nouns which are the natural
object of the action denoted by the participle.

(i) The **imperfective** passive denotes an action which is simultaneous
with the action of the main verb. The main verb may be in the present,
past or future tense of either aspect. A *comma* appears between the noun
and the participle which qualifies it:

Он писа́л статью́	о **предме́те,**	
Он написа́л статью́	о **предме́те,**	**изуча́емом** все́ми
Он пи́шет статью́	о **предме́те,**	учениками
Он бу́дет писа́ть статью́	о **предме́те,**	
Он напи́шет статью́	о **предме́те,**	

('He was writing/wrote/is writing/will be writing/will write an article
about a subject **studied** by all pupils'.)

Note
The meaning expressed by the participle may be durative:

програ́мма, **передава́емая** по ра́дио
a programme **being broadcast** on the radio

or habitual:

> пе́сни, **люби́мые** наро́дом
> songs **loved** by the people

(ii) The **perfective** passive participle denotes an action completed prior to the action of the main verb. A *comma* appears between the noun and the following participle which qualifies it:

> Пересма́тривается програ́мма, **одо́бренная** мини́страми
> A programme **approved** by the ministers is being revised

> В прода́жу поступи́ла ма́рка, **вы́пущенная** в Финля́ндии
> A stamp **issued** in Finland has gone on sale

361   Agreement of long-form participle and noun

(1) The long-form participle agrees with the noun it qualifies in gender, number and case. It differs in this respect from the relative pronoun **кото́рый**, which agrees with the noun in gender and number but *not* in case (the case of **кото́рый** being determined by the function it fulfils in the relative clause it introduces. See **123** (1) (ii).).

(i) Present active participle

> Я зна́ю **ма́льчика, пи́шущего** письмо́
> I know **the boy (who is) writing** the letter

(ii) Past active participle

> Я помога́ю **ученика́м, провали́вшимся** на экза́мене
> I am helping **the pupils who failed** the examination

(iii) Imperfective passive participle

> Э́то — **де́вочка, люби́мая** все́ми
> That is **the girl liked** by everyone

(iv) Perfective passive

> Он пи́шет статью́ о **ю́ношах, нака́занных** за хулига́нство
> He is writing an article about **the youths punished** for hooliganism

(2) Long participles may *precede* the noun:

(i) If the participle is the noun's only qualifier and functions as an adjective:

> **спя́щий** ребёнок   a sleeping child

замёрзшее óзеро   a frozen lake
Развáлины **разбомблённых**   The ruins of bombed towns
    городóв (Granin)

Note

In some cases the participle may be qualified by an adverb:

хорошó оплáчиваемые рабóчие
well-paid workers

вновь вы́шедший ромáн
a novel which has been republished

(ii) A pronoun or noun may appear between the participle and the noun it qualifies:

спасённые **им** дéвочки   the girls rescued **by him**

(iii) It is also possible, especially in literary and journalistic styles, for circumstantial detail to appear between the participle and the noun:

Сошéдшие **с пóезда** немнóгие пассажи́ры разошли́сь (Nosov)
The few passengers who had alighted **from the train** dispersed

передавáемые **по телеви́зору** прогнóзы погóды
weather forecasts transmitted **on TV**

Дви́гался конвéйер уви́денных **в рáзное врéмя** людéй (Gagarin)
A panorama of people he had seen **at various times** passed before him

362   Participial synonymy

(1) The imperfective passive participle may be synonymous with the present active participle of the corresponding reflexive verb:

словá, **употребля́емые/употребля́ющиеся** в рéчи
the words **used** in a speech

(2) The active participle is used if the verb (e.g. **стрóить** 'to build') has no passive participle:

стрóящееся здáние   a building **under construction**

(3) A 'true' reflexive cannot be used with passive meaning, however. Thus, одевáющийся can only mean 'who is dressing' (but not *'who is being dressed').

(4) Where both types of participle are available, the passive participle is used when the *agent* is named:

> слова́, **употребля́емые** (not *употребля́ющиеся) ора́тором
> в публи́чной ре́чи
> words **used** by an orator in a public speech

363   Participles as adjectives and nouns

Many participles are also used as adjectives or nouns.

(1) Present active

(i) Adjectives:

блестя́щий	brilliant
веду́щий	leading
выдаю́щийся	outstanding
далеко́ иду́щий	far-reaching
подходя́щий	suitable
сле́дующий	next, following
соотве́тствующий	appropriate
теку́щий	current

(ii) Nouns:

куря́щий	smoker
начина́ющий	beginner
непью́щий	tee-totaller
трудя́щийся	worker
уча́щийся	pupil, student

(2) Past active

(i) Adjective:

бы́вший	former

(ii) Nouns:

пострада́вший	a casualty
сумасше́дший	a madman
уме́рший	the deceased
уцеле́вший	a survivor

(3) Imperfective passive

вообража́емый	imaginary
люби́мый	favourite
терпи́мый	tolerable
уважа́емый	respected

Note

Many have negative prefixes, cf. English equivalents in -ble:

невыноси́мый	unbearable
незабыва́емый	unforgettable
необходи́мый	indispensable

A number derive from perfective stems

незамени́мый	irreplaceable
(не)излечи́мый	(in)curable
неоспори́мый	indisputable
непобеди́мый	invincible
(не)совмести́мый	(in)compatible

or intransitive verbs

незави́симый	independent

A few are used as nouns:

обвиня́емый	the accused
содержи́мое	contents (of a receptacle)

(4) Perfective passive

заключённый	convict

364   Participial adjectives

(1) A number of long adjectives of participial origin differ from long-form participles:

(i) In having no prefix.

(ii) In having one -**н**- instead of two:

варёное яйцо́	a boiled egg
жа́реная карто́шка	fried potatoes
кра́шеный пол	a painted floor

(не)пи́саный зако́н   a(n) (un)written law
сушёные фру́кты   dried fruit

Note

(a) Adjectives based on second-conjugation verbs in **-ить** with mobile
     stress in conjugation tend to have suffix **-ён-**.

(b) If circumstantial detail is added, *participles* must be used:
     ра́ненный в но́гу солда́т 'a soldier wounded in the leg' (cf.
     ра́неный солда́т 'wounded soldier'), **сва́ренное** в кастрю́льке
     яйцо́ 'an egg boiled in a saucepan' (cf. варёное яйцо́ 'boiled
     egg').

(2) Some of the adjectives have the suffix **-т-**:

кры́тый ры́нок   covered market
небри́тое лицо́   unshaven face

К обе́ду мы яви́лись в **мя́той** оде́жде (Nikolaev)
We appeared for lunch in crumpled clothing

(3) Others function as adjectival nouns: **кра́деное** 'stolen goods'.

365 Distinction between short-form adjectives and short-form participles

Certain short adjectives differ from short-form participles in having the
suffix **-нн-** in their feminine, neuter and plural forms by contrast with
-н- in the participle:

озабо́чен, озабо́ченна, озабо́ченно, озабо́ченны (adjective)
озабо́чен, озабо́чена, озабо́чено, озабо́чены (participle)

Compare

Глаза́ его́ бы́ли **озабо́ченны** (adj.)
His eyes were troubled

and

Она́ была́ **озабо́чена** (part.) отъе́здом ма́тери
She was upset by her mother's departure

Likewise Его́ речь была́ **сде́ржанна** (adj.) 'His speech was restrained',
but Вода́ была́ **сде́ржана** (part.) плоти́ной 'The water was contained
by a dam'. A similar distinction is made between **образо́ван, -a, -o, -ы**
'has been formed' (part.) and **образо́ван, -нна, -нно, -нны** 'educated'
(adj.), **ограни́чен, -a, -o, -ы** 'limited' (part.) and **ограни́чен, -нна,**

-нно, -нны 'hide-bound' (adj.), **рассе́ян**, **-а**, **-о**, **-ы** 'dispersed' (part.) and **рассе́ян**, **-нна**, **-нно**, **-нны** 'absent-minded' (adj.).

366   Impersonal function of short-form participles

(1) The neuter short forms of the perfective passive participles of certain verbs can be used impersonally:

— Здесь **за́нято**?	Is this place occupied?
За всё **запла́чено**	Everything has been paid for
В ваго́не бы́ло битко́м **наби́то**	The carriage was packed
В за́ле **наку́рено**	The hall is smoke-filled
Ку́шать **по́дано**	Dinner is served
С доски́ **стёрто**	The board has been cleaned
С ве́чера не **у́брано** бы́ло со стола́ (Rasputin)	The table had not been cleared since the previous evening
Вам **отка́зано** в про́сьбе	Your request has been refused

(2) Imperfective participles of this type are found in colloquial speech (mainly in the negative):

Давно́ **не то́плено**
The heating has not been on for a long time

Compare Пол **не мыт** 'The floor has not been washed', Бельё **не гла́жено** 'The washing has not been ironed'.

Note
Impersonal usage in **Прика́зано** оста́ться 'We have been instructed to stay', Кому́ э́то **ска́зано**? 'How many times do I have to tell you?', and the phrase **Ска́зано** — **сде́лано** 'No sooner said than done'.

Gerunds

367   The gerund. Introductory comments

(1) Gerunds (or 'verbal adverbs') are *indeclinable* forms of the verb that substitute for co-ordinate or adverbial clauses in 'and', 'when', 'since', 'by', 'without' etc.

(2) Gerunds, like active participles, have English equivalents in '-ing', but participles are adjectival in form, agree in gender, case and number with the noun they qualify and replace relative clauses in **кото́рый** (see **360**), while gerunds are invariable. Compare the use of the *participle* in

> the **weeping** boy (= the boy **who is weeping**): **пла́чущий** ма́льчик

with the use of the *gerund* in

> he sits **weeping** (= **and weeps**): он сиди́т, **пла́ча**

(3) There are imperfective and perfective gerunds.

368   Formation of the imperfective gerund

Most imperfective gerunds are formed by adding **-я** (**-а** after **ж, ч, ш** or **щ**) to the present-tense stem of the verb (see **212**):

говоря́т	говор-	**говоря́**	'speaking'
ды́шат	дыш-	**дыша́**	'breathing'
несу́т	нес-	**неся́**	'carrying'
пла́чут	плач-	**пла́ча**	'weeping'
тре́буют	требу-	**тре́буя**	'demanding'
чита́ют	чита-	**чита́я**	'reading'

Note

(a) **Дава́ть** and compounds, compounds of **-знава́ть**, **-става́ть** form gerunds as follows: **встава́я** 'rising', **дава́я** 'giving':

> — Извини́те, у меня́ дела́, — сказа́л Неша́тов, **встава́я** со сту́ла (Grekova)
> 'Excuse me, I have something to attend to', said Neshatov, **getting up** from his chair

(b) The gerund from **маха́ть** 'to wave' has alternative forms: **маха́я** and **маша́**. Similarly **бры́згать**, **бры́зжа** 'playing' (of a fountain), **бры́згая** 'sprinkling' (water on ironing etc.). **Ка́пать** 'to drip' has **ка́пая**, **сы́пать** 'to strew' has **сы́пля**.

(c) Быть has the gerund **бу́дучи** 'being':

> Он прие́хал в Ло́ндон давно́, ещё **бу́дучи** солда́том
> He arrived in London long ago **when he was** still a soldier

(d) **Е́дучи** from е́хать 'to travel' is sometimes found in poetic or folk speech; **припева́ючи** is used in the phrase жить **припева́ючи** 'to live in clover'.

(e) Imperfective gerunds from reflexive verbs take the ending -сь: жа́луясь from жа́ловаться 'to complain'.

369 Stress in the imperfective gerund

Stress in the gerund is normally as in the first-person singular:

голосова́ть	'to vote'	голосу́ю	'I vote'	**голосу́я**	'voting'
держа́ть	'to hold'	держу́	'I hold'	**держа́**	'holding'
кури́ть	'to smoke'	курю́	'I smoke'	**куря́**	'smoking'
смотре́ть	'to look'	смотрю́	'I look'	**смотря́**	'looking'
шепта́ть	'to whisper'	шепчу́	'I whisper'	**шепча́**	'whispering'

Note
Гля́дя 'looking', **лёжа** 'lying', **си́дя** 'sitting' and **сто́я** 'standing' have *stem* stress despite *end* stress in conjugation: Бараба́нов, **сто́я** на одно́м коле́не, дошнуро́вывал бу́тсы (Vanshenkin) 'Barabanov was kneeling to finish lacing his boots'.

370 Verbs with no imperfective gerund

Many verbs have no imperfective gerund. These include the following:

(1) **Бежа́ть** 'to run', **бить** 'to strike', **вить** 'to twine', **врать** 'to lie', **гнить** 'to rot', **драть** 'to flay', **есть** 'to eat', **éхать** 'to travel' (see, however, **368** note (d)), **жа́ждать** 'to hunger for', **жать** 'to press', **ждать** 'to wait', **лгать** 'to lie', **лезть** 'to climb', **лить** 'to pour', **мять** 'to crumple', **петь** 'to sing', **пить** 'to drink', **рвать** 'to tear', **слать** 'to send', **стона́ть** 'to groan', **ткать** 'to weave', **хоте́ть** 'to want', **шить** 'to sew'.

Note
Gerunds from some other verbs are rarely used: **беря́** from брать 'to take', **гоня́** from гнать 'to drive', **зовя́** from звать 'to call', **плывя́** from плыть 'to swim'. **Нося́** from носи́ть 'to carry' and **ходя́** from ходи́ть 'to go' are rarely found; cf., however, compound **принося́** 'bringing' etc.

(2) First-conjugation consonant-stem verbs with **с:ш**, **з:ж** mutation (e.g. **писа́ть** 'to write', **ре́зать** 'to cut', see **217** (2)).

(3) Verbs in -**чь**.

(4) Verbs in **-ереть**.

(5) Verbs with the suffix **-ну-** (**га́снуть** 'to go out' etc.).

371   Compensation for the lack of an imperfective gerund

(1) If a primary verb has no imperfective gerund it is often possible to form one from its synonym. Thus, **мочь** 'to be able' has no gerund, but **быть в состоя́нии** 'to be capable of' does: **бу́дучи в состоя́нии** 'being able to'. Likewise, **хоте́ть** 'to want' has no gerund, but **жела́ть** 'to wish' does (**жела́я** 'wishing, wanting'):

Жела́я скоре́е уе́хать, он торопи́лся зако́нчить рабо́ту
Wishing to get away as soon as possible he hastened to finish his work

(2) Other primaries with no gerund have a synonymous secondary imperfective from which a gerund may be formed:

Primary verb	Secondary imperfective	Gerund	
есть	съеда́ть	**съеда́я**	'eating'
е́хать	проезжа́ть	**проезжа́я**	'travelling'
ждать	ожида́ть	**ожида́я**	'waiting'
жечь	сжига́ть	**сжига́я**	'burning'
петь	распева́ть	**распева́я**	'singing'
пить	выпива́ть	**выпива́я**	'drinking'
рвать	разрыва́ть	**разрыва́я**	'tearing up'
слать	посыла́ть	**посыла́я**	'sending'
тере́ть	вытира́ть	**вытира́я**	'wiping'

Ко́стя Пимурзя́ весь извёлся, **ожида́я** нас (Nikolaev)
Kostya Pimurzya suffered agonies waiting for us

372   The perfective gerund: formation (verbs in -ть, -сть (д-stems))

(1) The perfective gerund is formed from verbs in **-ть** by replacing the perfective infinitive ending by **-в**:

написа́в	having written
постро́ив	having built

промо́кнув   having got soaked

(2) Likewise gerunds from verbs in -**сть** (д-stems only: **присе́сть** 'to sit down for a while', **укра́сть** 'to steal', **упа́сть** 'to fall'):

присе́в   having sat down for a while

373   Reflexive perfective gerunds

Reflexive perfective gerunds have the ending -**вшись**:

верну́вшись   having returned
умы́вшись   having washed

Note

Опершись from **опере́ться** 'to lean on' (cf. figurative usage: **опе́рвшись** на инициати́ву масс 'relying on the initiative of the masses'); similarly **вто́ргшись** 'having invaded' from вто́ргнуться, **вы́тершись** 'having dried oneself', **заперши́сь** 'having locked oneself in'.

374   Perfective gerunds with alternative forms in -я/-а

(1) Some perfective gerunds have alternative forms in -**в** and -**я/-а**, the forms in -**в** generally being preferred in written styles:

заме́тив/заме́тя   having noticed
уви́дев/уви́дя   having seen

(2) The forms in -**я-/-а** are common with reflexive verbs: **возвратя́сь/ возврати́вшись (верну́вшись)** 'having returned', **встре́тясь/встре́- тившись** 'having met', **прищу́рясь/прищу́рившись** 'screwing up one's eyes':

Я ждал, **прислоня́сь** к стене́ (Granin)
I waited, **leaning** against a wall

375   Gerunds from perfective verbs in -ти and -сть

Gerunds from most perfective verbs in -**ти** and (except for д-stems, see **372**) -**сть** are formed by replacing the final two letters of the third-person plural of the verb by -**я**:

пройд-у́т	**пройд-я́**	'having passed'
сойд-у́т	**сойд-я́**	'having descended'

Likewise **изобретя́** 'having invented' from изобрести́, **подметя́** 'having swept' from подмести́, **принеся́** 'having brought' from принести́, **разбредя́сь** 'having wandered off in different directions' from разбрести́сь (cf. also **учтя́** 'having taken into consideration' from уче́сть):

> **Принеся́** самова́р и завари́в чай, Да́рья наконе́ц заговори́ла (Rasputin)
> **Having brought in** the samovar and made the tea Darya finally began to speak

Note

Compounds of грести́, пасти́, расти́ and цвести́ have perfective gerunds in -ши: **вы́росши** 'having grown up' from вы́расти, **расцве́тши** 'having blossomed' from расцвести́, **сгрёбши** 'having raked together' from сгрести́, **спа́сши** 'having saved' from спасти́.

376   Gerunds from perfective verbs in -чь and -зть

Gerunds from perfective verbs in -**чь** and -**зть** are formed by adding -**ши** to the masculine past tense of the verb: **вы́лезши** 'having climbed out' from вы́лезть, **испёкши** 'having baked' from испе́чь, **сжёгши** 'having burnt' from сжечь.

377   Functions of the gerunds

Gerunds replace co-ordinate clauses or adverbial clauses of time, manner, cause, condition etc. They are found mainly in written Russian, co-ordinate or adverbial clauses (English equivalents enclosed in parentheses in the following examples) being preferred in speech.

(1) Imperfective gerunds

The imperfective gerund denotes an action which is simultaneous to the action of the main verb. Either the two actions run in parallel or one interrupts the other. The following meanings are conveyed by the gerund:

> Он сиди́т, **чита́я**
> He sits **reading** (= and reads)

Он бежи́т, тяжело́ **дыша́**
He is running along, **breathing** (= and breathes) heavily.

Чита́я, запи́сываю незнако́мые слова́
When reading (= when I read) I make a note of words I do not know

Поднима́ясь по ле́стнице, она́ упа́ла
While going up (= when/while/as she was going up) the stairs, she fell

Занима́ясь аэро́бикой, укрепл́ю здоро́вье
By doing aerobics (= if I do) I shall improve my fitness

Боя́сь грозы́, я поспеши́л домо́й
Fearing (= since I feared) a thunderstorm I hurried home

Я шёл, **не встреча́я** ни души́
I walked along **without meeting** (= and did not meet) a soul

(2) Perfective gerunds

(i) The perfective gerund describes an action which is completed prior to the action denoted by the main verb:

Написа́в письмо́, он лёг спать
Having written (= when, after he had written) the letter he went to bed

Не поня́в вопро́са, она́ растеря́лась
Not having understood (= since she had not understood) the question she got confused

Примени́в но́вый ме́тод, брига́да смо́жет перевы́полнить но́рму
By using (= if it uses) the new method, the work-team will be able to over-fulfil its norm

(ii) The perfective gerund may also denote a state resulting from the completion of an action:

Он сиде́л, **вы́тянув** но́ги
He sat, **stretching out** (= having stretched out) his legs

Note
Care must be taken to resolve English ambiguity in rendering verb forms in -ing. Compare

Stepping (= **as** she was stepping) off the pavement she tripped and fell

Сходя́ (imperfective gerund) с тротуа́ра, она́ споткну́лась и упа́ла and

> **Stepping** (= **having** stepped) off the pavement she crossed the road
> **Сойдя́** (perfective gerund) с тротуа́ра, она́ перешла́ доро́гу

378   Special features of constructions with gerunds

Certain features are characteristic of constructions with gerunds:

(1) The subject of the gerund and the subject of the main clause are the same:

> **Верну́вшись** домо́й, **он поста́вил** самова́р
> Having returned home he put on the samovar

> **Возвраща́ясь** домо́й, **я попа́л** под дождь
> While returning home I got caught in the rain

Note

(a)   In this example the main clause could *not* be replaced by the synonymous Меня́ засти́г дождь 'I got caught in the rain', since this would involve a change in subject.

(b)   The gerund is not normally used in conjunction with an impersonal phrase; thus one should write *not* *Подходя́ к ле́су, мне ста́ло хо́лодно, but Когда́ я подходи́л к ле́су, мне ста́ло хо́лодно 'As I approached the forest I felt cold'. Impersonal constructions involving *infinitives* may, however, sometimes combine with gerunds: Выполня́я э́то упражне́ние, **мо́жно по́льзоваться** словарём 'When doing this exercise you may use a dictionary'. (Note, however, that an alternative rendering: Выполня́я э́то упражне́ние, обраща́йтесь к словарю́ 'When doing this exercise, consult the dictionary' observes the principle of identity of subject in both clauses.)

(c)   A gerund should be avoided when the subject of the main clause appears in a passive construction, since in such cases the *grammatical* subject of the main clause is not the *logical* subject. Thus По́сле того́ как он переле́з (rather than Переле́зши) че́рез забо́р, он был заде́ржан сторожа́ми 'Having climbed over the fence, he was detained by guards'.

(2) A comma separates the main clause from the clause in which the gerund appears:

Он **говори́л, стара́ясь** сохраня́ть хладнокро́вие
He spoke, trying to retain his composure

Прочита́в письмо́, он **спря́тал** его́ в я́щик
Having read the letter he hid it in a drawer

(3) The verb in the main clause may be in any tense and either aspect:

Возвраща́ясь с заво́да, я **встреча́л/встре́тил/встреча́ю/бу́ду** (ча́сто) **встреча́ть/встре́чу** И́ру
When returning from the factory **I used to meet/met/meet/will (often) meet/will meet** Ira

Верну́вшись домо́й, он **ста́вил/поста́вил/ста́вит/бу́дет ста́вить/ поста́вит самова́р**
Returning home, **he used to put on/put on/puts on/will put on the samovar**

Compare

Он **просыпа́лся** по утра́м и, **откры́в** фо́рточку, **начина́л** в ри́тме разма́хивать рука́ми (Trofimov)
He **would wake up** in the morning and, **opening** the casement window, **begin** rhythmically to swing his arms

Note
The use of the perfective gerund **откры́в** shows that the actions of opening the window and swinging the arms were sequential (imperfective **открыва́я** would suggest that they were simultaneous).

379   Reversal of the sequence of actions expressed by main verb and gerund

Occasionally the action denoted by the verb in the main clause *precedes* that denoted by the gerund:

Он вы́шел, **хло́пнув**   He went out, slamming the door
две́рью

This construction should *not*, however, be regarded as the norm.

380   Gerunds as other parts of speech

Some gerunds or former gerunds also function as other parts of speech, in particular prepositions and adverbs.

(1) **Imperfective:**

благодаря	thanks to (+ dat.; cf. **благодаря** as gerund + acc.)
исключа́я	excluding, except for
кра́дучись	stealthily
мо́лча	silently
не счита́я	not counting
не теря́я вре́мени	without delay
су́дя по	judging by (cf. gerund **судя́**)

Note

(a) Some phrases are compounded with the gerund **говоря́**: **открове́нно говоря́** 'frankly speaking', **стро́го говоря́** 'strictly speaking', **не говоря́ уже́** 'let alone, to say nothing of' etc.:

О́бщество предоставля́ет им библиоте́ки, музе́и, **не говоря́ уже́** о теа́трах и кино́ (Kovaleva)
Society puts at their disposal libraries and museums, to say nothing of theatres and cinemas

(b) Other phrases include отвеча́ть не **заду́мываясь** 'to answer without hesitation', говори́ть **заика́ясь** 'to stammer', не **поклада́я** рук 'tirelessly', не **спеша́** 'unhurriedly', **не́хотя** 'reluctantly'.

(2) **Perfective** (mainly in set phrases involving gerunds in -я/-а; see **374**):

слу́шать **рази́ня** рот	to listen open-mouthed
сказа́ть **положа́** ру́ку на́ сердце	to say hand on heart
рабо́тать **спустя́** рукава́	to work in a slipshod fashion
согласи́ться **скрепя́** се́рдце	to agree reluctantly
сиде́ть **сложа́** ру́ки	to sit twiddling one's thumbs

Note also the preposition **спустя́**: неде́лю **спустя́** 'a week later'. See **439** (2)(i).

The Adverb

381 Introductory comments

(1) Adverbs are indeclinable forms that modify verbs ('he writes *well*'), adjectives ('*surprisingly* good'), other adverbs ('*extremely* quickly') or nouns ('reading *aloud*').

(2) They answer questions such as **'where?', 'when?', 'how?', 'why?', 'for what purpose?', 'to what extent?'**

(3) A feature of Russian adverbs is that they all derive from other parts of speech (though in the case of most primary adverbs (так 'thus', там 'there', тогда́ 'then' etc.) the principle of their formation is no longer clear).

(4) The most productive types of adverb are those which derive from **adjectives.** They also derive from **nouns, verbs, numerals** and **pronouns.**

382 Adverbs derived from adjectives

(1) Adverbs in -о/-е

(i) Most adverbs derived from descriptive adjectives are identical with the neuter adjectival short form in **-о/-е** (see **159, 161, 164**):

Long adjective	Adverb
высо́кий 'high'	высоко́ 'high up'

гла́дкий 'smooth'	гла́дко 'smoothly'
краси́вый 'beautiful'	краси́во 'beautifully'
вне́шний 'external'	вне́шне 'externally'
и́скренний 'sincere'	и́скренне 'sincerely'
кра́йний 'extreme'	кра́йне 'extremely'

(ii) In some cases, however, there is a difference in stress, cf. больно́ (neuter short adjective) 'is sick' and бо́льно (adverb) 'painfully, it hurts'; мало́ (neuter short adjective) 'too small' and ма́ло (adverb) 'not much'.

Note

(a) Soft-ending adjectives да́вний 'long-standing', по́здний 'late' and ра́нний 'early' have hard-ending adverbs давно́ 'long ago', по́здно 'late, it is (too) late', ра́но 'early, it is (too) early'. Note that whereas ра́нний has double н, ра́но has only one.

(b) Adverbs in -о/-е also derive from participles: неожи́данно 'unexpectedly' from неожи́данный, угрожа́юще 'threateningly' from угрожа́ющий.

(2)   Adverbs based on по- + dative singular of the adjective

Adverbs of manner of the type **по-** + the dative masculine/neuter singular of the adjective derive from adjectives in **-ый/-ий/-о́й** which have no adverb in **-о/-е** (e.g. друго́й 'different', но́вый 'new', пре́жний 'former'):

по-друго́му	in a different way
по-настоя́щему	in a proper fashion
по-но́вому	in a new way
по-пре́жнему	as before
по-ра́зному	in various ways

(3) Adverbs in -и

(i) Adverbs from adjectives in **-ский/-цкий** (mostly adverbs of **manner**) take the ending **-и**: thus бра́тски 'fraternally', дура́цки 'foolishly, in a foolish way', логи́чески 'logically' etc.

(ii) Those with animate connotations, including all which denote nationality, may take the prefix **по-**: ко́фе по-туре́цки 'coffee Turkish style', по-ле́нински 'after the style of Lenin', по-ру́сски 'in Russian, in the Russian style'.

(iii) In some contexts, prefixed and unprefixed variants are synonymous: бра́тски/по-бра́тски похло́пать по плечу́ 'to slap on the shoulder in a brotherly fashion', **герóйски/по-герóйски** вестú себя́ 'to behave in a heroic way', **дéтски/по-дéтски** довéрчивый 'as trusting as a child':

> В Нóвый год осóбенно сердéчно и **по-дрýжески/дрýжески** мы вспоминáем сóтни имён знакóмых людéй
> At New Year we recall, in a particularly cordial and friendly way, the names of hundreds of acquaintances

(iv) In most cases, however, choice is dictated by usage: **дрýжески** подмигнýть 'to wink in a friendly manner', **звéрски** голóдный 'ravenously hungry', **по-дéтски** обúделся 'he took childish offence'.

Note
(a)   While forms with **по-** answer the implied question **подóбно комý/чемý**? 'similar to whom/what?', forms without **по-** answer the questions **как/какúм óбразом**? 'how/in what way?'
(b)   Adverbs in **-ически** cannot combine with **по-**.

(4) Adverbs in -ьи

Adverbs from adjectives of the type **вóлчий** 'wolf's' (see **151** (1)) take the ending **-ьи**, and are prefixed **по-**: Он **по-медвéжьи** неуклю́ж 'He is as clumsy as a bear', Он **по-собáчьи** прéдан своемý хозя́ину 'He displays a dog-like devotion to his master'.

(5) Adverbs based on preposition + the oblique case of an adjective

(i) Most adverbs of this type consist of a preposition + the fossilized oblique case of a short adjective, run together to form a single word (e.g. **с** + old genitive *прáва = **спрáва** 'on, from the right'). The adverbs denote variously location, time, manner and extent:

вскóре	soon
(раздевáться) **догола́**	(to strip oneself) naked
(вытирáть) **дóсуха**	(to rub) dry
издалека́	from a distance
слéва	on, from the left
снóва	again

(ii) A smaller number of adverbs consist of the preposition **в** + the feminine accusative of a long adjective:

вплотнýю	right up close to
вручнýю	by hand
(летéть) **вслепýю**	(to fly) blind

383   Adverbs derived from nouns

(1) Adverbs based on the oblique cases of nouns

(i) Many adverbs have the form of the **instrumental singular** of a noun. The adverbs denote location or manner:

верхо́м	on horseback
да́ром	free, for nothing
ря́дом	next door, adjacent
шёпотом	in a whisper

Note

(a) End stress in the adverb **круго́м** 'around' and stem stress in the instrumental of the noun **круг (кру́гом)** and in the phrase голова́ идёт **кру́гом** 'my head is spinning'.

(b) Some adverbs derive from no-longer extant nouns: **о́птом** 'wholesale', **о́щупью** 'gropingly', **пешко́м** 'on foot', **укра́дкой** 'furtively'.

(c) Instrumentals are also used to denote the time of day and the season of the year (see **97** (2) (i), (ii)).

(ii) Other adverbs derived from nouns include **вчера́** 'yesterday' (also **позавчера́** 'the day before yesterday'), **до́ма** 'at home', **домо́й** 'home(wards)', **за́втра** 'tomorrow' (also **послеза́втра** 'the day after tomorrow'), **о́чень** 'very, very much' (Я **о́чень** люблю́ моро́женое 'I am very fond of ice-cream'), **сего́дня** 'today'.

(2) Adverbs based on preposition-noun phrases

(i) The preposition appears as a separate word in some phrases (**в прида́чу** 'into the bargain', **на днях** 'the other day', **на ходу́** 'while on the move'), but in most cases preposition and noun are run together. The prepositions **в, на, по** + dative, **с** + genitive are particularly common in this type of formation. All oblique cases are represented:

(a) Accusative:

вслух	aloud
наоборо́т	on the contrary

(b) Genitive:

и́здали	from afar
све́рху	from above

(c) Dative:

кста́ти	apropos
поблизости	in the vicinity

(d) Instrumental:

сли́шком	too

(e) Prepositional:

вме́сте	together

(ii) Some adverbs appear in pairs, one denoting location and the other destination or goal:

вдали́/вдаль	in/into the distance
внизу́/вниз	downstairs (location/direction)
внутри́/внутрь	inside (location/direction)
впереди́/вперёд	in front/forwards
за грани́цей/за грани́цу	abroad (location/direction)
наверху́/наве́рх	upstairs (location/direction)

Note

Compare **за́мужем за** + instrumental 'married to' and **выходи́ть/ вы́йти за́муж за** + accusative 'to get married' (of a woman).

(iii) Some prepositional phrases involve *two* nouns:

бóк ó бок	cheek by jowl
вре́мя от вре́мени	from time to time
лицо́м к лицу́	face to face

384   Adverbs derived from verbs

Some adverbs are based on imperfective gerunds (see also **380** (1)):

кра́дучись	stealthily
не́хотя	reluctantly

Others are based on perfective gerunds, often as part of an adverbial phrase:

сломя́ го́лову	at breakneck speed

See also **380** (2).

385   Adverbs derived from numerals

Adverbs derived from numerals include the series

вдвоём/втроём/вчетвером. . .
two/three/four together. . .

во-пе́рвых/во-вторы́х/в-тре́тьих. . .
in the first/second/third place . . .

одна́жды/два́жды/три́жды. . .
once/twice/thrice. . .

as well as **впервы́е** 'for the first time', **наедине́** 'in private, alone (with)', and the phrase **оди́н на оди́н** 'tête-à-tête'.

386   Adverbs derived from pronouns

A number of adverbs are based on:

(i) The demonstrative pronouns **э́тот** 'this', **тот** 'that', **сей** 'this':

зате́м	afterwards
пото́м	then, afterwards
поэ́тому	for that reason, therefore
сейча́с	now
с тех пор/до тех пор/до сих пор	since then/until then/hitherto

Note

(a) **Пото́м** and **зате́м** are synonymous in referring to sequential actions, though **пото́м** is commoner: Куплю́ биле́т, **пото́м/зате́м** зайду́ к прия́телю 'I shall buy a ticket, **then** call on a friend'. **Пото́м** is also used in the meaning 'afterwards, in a little while': Я сде́лаю э́то **пото́м** 'I'll do that later'. In colloquial registers it can be governed by a preposition (отложи́ть **на пото́м** 'to put off until afterwards') and can also be used colloquially in the meaning 'besides': Не хочу́ я е́хать, **а пото́м** у меня́ и вре́мени нет 'I don't want to go, and besides I don't have any time'. **Зате́м** can also denote purpose: Поговори́м, ведь я **зате́м** и пришёл 'Let's talk, after all that's the reason I have come', Я пришёл (**зате́м**), что́бы поговори́ть 'I have come (in order) to have a chat'.

(b) **Тепе́рь** 'now' is more limited in meaning and usage than **сейча́с**, which can refer to the past and future, as well as to the present: О чём они́ говори́ли **сейча́с**? 'What were they talking about **just now**?', Я бу́ду с ва́ми **сейча́с** 'I'll be with you **in a minute**', Что вы де́лаете **сейча́с/тепе́рь**? 'What are you doing **now**?'

(ii) The pronoun **что** 'what': **заче́м**? 'for what purpose?', **почему́**? 'why?' Compare

Заче́м включи́ли свет? — Что̀бы мо́жно бы́ло чита́ть
Why have you switched on the light? So as to be able to read (purpose)

and

Почему́ включи́ли свет? — Уже́ темно́
Why have you switched on the light? Because it's dark (cause)

(iii) The possessive pronouns **мой, твой, свой, наш, ваш**:

по-мо́ему/по-тво́ему	in my opinion/in your opinion (familiar)
по-на́шему/по-ва́шему	in our opinion/in your opinion (formal)

Note
(a)   The difference in stress between **по-мо́ему, по-тво́ему**, and the dative case of the possessive pronouns (**моему́, твоему́**).
(b)   'In his/her/their opinion' are rendered as **по его́/её/их мне́нию**.
(c)   **По-сво́ему** means 'in one's own way': Он всё де́лает **по-сво́ему** 'He does everything in his own way'.

(iv) **Весь** 'all':

везде́/всю́ду; отовсю́ду	everywhere; from everywhere
весьма́	extremely
совсе́м	quite

Note
Compare Э́то **не совсе́м** пра́вда 'That's **not quite** true' and Э́то **совсе́м не** пра́вда 'That's **not at all** true'.

387   Primary spatial adverbs

(1) **Где** 'where', **здесь** 'here' and **там** 'there' denote location:

Где вы рабо́таете?	Where do you work?
Я рабо́таю **здесь**; Он рабо́тает **там**	I work here; He works there

Note

Тут 'here' is more colloquial than **здесь** and can also have a temporal meaning, e.g. **Тут** расска́зчик замолча́л 'Here the narrator fell silent'.

(2) **Куда́** 'where' (to), **сюда́** 'here' and **туда́** 'there' indicate direction:

Куда́ вы идёте?	Where are you going?
Иди́те **сюда́**!	Come here!
Туда́ идёт авто́бус но́мер пять	The number 5 bus goes there

(3) **Отку́да** 'from where', **отсю́да** 'from here' and **отту́да** 'from there' indicate withdrawal:

Отку́да он пришёл?	Where has he come from?

Note

Отку́да вы зна́ете? '**How** do you know?'

388   Primary adverbs of time

(1) Тогда́ 'then'

Тогда́ 'then, at that time' must be differentiated from **пото́м/зате́м** 'then, afterwards'. Compare

Тогда́ я жил на се́вере
I lived in the north **then**/at that time

and

Снача́ла ду́май, **пото́м** говори́
First think, **then** speak

(2) Когда́/как 'when/as'

(i) **Когда́** or **в то вре́мя как** are preferred to **как** in rendering 'as' (= 'when') in clauses of time:

Когда́/в то вре́мя как я шёл по доро́ге, я встре́тил ста́рого знако́мого
As I was walking down the road I met an old acquaintance

(ii) However, **как** is used with verbs of perception (**ви́деть** 'to see', **слу́шать** 'to listen', **слы́шать** 'to hear', **смотре́ть** 'to watch'):

Смо́трим, **как** де́ти игра́ют
We watch the children playing

Я слу́шаю, **как** она́ поёт
I listen to her singing

(iii) **Ждать** 'to wait' and **люби́ть** 'to like' govern object clauses introduced by **когда́**:

Жду, **когда́** вы ко́нчите
I am waiting for you to finish

Люблю́, **когда́** ты поёшь наро́дные пе́сни
I like you to sing folk songs

Note
For constructions with **слу́чай** 'case' see **311** (2).

(3) Как/как вдруг 'when suddenly/than'

(i) **Как** (or **как вдруг**) is used to introduce a sudden or unexpected action, often interrupting another action:

Я как раз гла́дил брю́ки, **как вдруг** пога́с свет
I was just ironing my trousers **when suddenly** the light went out

(ii) The main clause in such constructions is often introduced by a negative:

Не прошёл он и десяти́ шаго́в, **как** разда́лся вы́стрел
He had not taken ten paces **when** a shot rang out

(iii) Frequently the verb (**не**) **успе́ть** or the conjunction **едва́** is involved in such constructions:

Не (or **Едва́**) успе́л я нажа́ть кно́пку, **как** дверь распахну́лась
I had not had time (had hardly had time) to press the button when the door flew open

Едва́ я вы́шел на у́лицу, **как** пошёл си́льный дождь
Hardly had I gone out on to the street **than** it began raining heavily

Note
See also **466–467** for further examples of adverbial clauses of time.

389   Уже́, уже́ не

(1) **Уже́** 'already' is far commoner in Russian than 'already' in English, which often has no equivalent in indicating the early implementation or completion of an action:

Он пришёл **ужé** вчерá
He arrived yesterday/as early as yesterday

(2) **Ужé** is particularly important in clarifying tense sequence:

Демонстрáнты **ужé** разбежáлись, когдá приéхала операти́вная маши́на
The demonstrators **had already** dispersed when the squad car arrived

Note

Without **ужé** the above sentence means 'The demonstrators dispersed **when** the squad car arrived'.

(3) **Ужé не** (or **бóльше не**) means 'no longer, not any more': Он **ужé не/бóльше не** рабóтает здесь 'He doesn't work here any more'.

Note

Ужé нет replaces **ужé не** in the absence of a predicate: Он рабóтает здесь? **Ужé нет** 'Does he work here? Not any more'.

390   Ещё, ещё не

(1) **Ещё** 'still/yet', **ещё не** 'not yet' can be used with temporal meaning:

Ребёнок **ещё** (or **всё ещё**) спит
The child is still asleep

Ещё дéвочкой онá лиши́лась мáтери
She lost her mother when she was only a little girl

Онá **ещё не** пришлá
She hasn't arrived yet

Note

Ещё нет replaces **ещё не** in the absence of a predicate: Онá пришлá? **Ещё нет** 'Has she arrived?' 'Not yet'.

(2) **Ещё** can also mean 'additional', compare:

Дай **ещё** чáшку чáю
Give me another (= an additional) cup of tea

and

Дай **другýю** чáшку
Give me another (= a different) cup

(3) It can also be synonymous with **ужé** in a temporal context:

Он уéхал **ещё/ужé** на прóшлой недéле
He left last week

Note

(a) The use of **ещё** with comparatives, as an adverb of degree: **ещё** лýчше 'still/even better'.

(b) **Ещё раз** 'once more', referring to a repeated action (but not a repeated state): Я позвоню́ **ещё раз** 'I'll ring again'. Compare **снóва**, which may denote resumption rather than repetition: Пòсле болéзни он **снóва** стал ходи́ть в кинó 'After his illness he has begun going to the cinema again'. **Опя́ть** may be used as a synonym of **снóва** (**Снóва/опя́ть** пошёл дождь 'It began raining again'), but may also have emotional overtones, sometimes expressing irritation (**Опя́ть** пóезд опáздывает! 'The train is late again!').

391   The temporal adverbs дóлго, давнó and недáвно

(1) **Дóлго** denotes a definite but unspecified period of time:

Он **дóлго** одевáется
He takes a long time to dress

(2) **Давнó** 'for a long time' (it also means 'a long time ago') implies an unfinished action or process:

Он **давнó** рабóтает здесь
He has been working here for a long time (and still is)

Он **давнó** жил там
He **had** been living there for a long time

Note

(a)   Cf. **256** (2) (vii).

(b)   Cf. tense usage in *negative* contexts: Я давнó не **курю́** 'I haven't smoked for some time' (have given it up) and Я давнó не **кури́л** 'I haven't smoked for some time' (but may do so again).

(3)   **Недáвно** refers to a recent event

Он ýмер **недáвно**
He died **recently**

while (**в/за**) **послéднее врéмя** 'recently, of late' refers to a process or state extending over a period of time. Absence of a preposition represents more colloquial usage:

> **После́днее вре́мя** не́ было дождя́
> There hasn't been any rain **recently**

392   Primary adverbs of manner and extent

(1) **Как** and **так** may denote:

(i) Manner:

Вот **как** на́до писа́ть!	That's **how** to write!
На́до вести́ себя́ **так**	You should behave **like that**

Note

(a) **Как** also combines with the verb **люби́ть** 'to like' in expressing manner: Люблю́, **как** ты гото́вишь еду́ 'I like the way you cook'.

(b) **Не так** may mean 'wrongly': Вы **не так** меня́ете про́бку 'You're not changing the fuse the right way' (cf. непра́вильно 'incorrectly').

(ii) Degree or extent:

Как хорошо́ она́ игра́ет!	How well she plays!
Я **так** мно́го ходи́л, что уста́л	I have walked so much that I am tired

(2) In comparisons, the particle **же** usually follows **так:**

> Он **так же** умён, **как** я   He is just as clever as I am

but this does not occur in a negative comparison

> Он **не так** умён, **как** я   He is not as clever as I am

When two qualities relate to the same person, the particle **и** is used for emphasis:

> Он **так же** умён, **как и** добр   He is as clever as he is kind

(3) **Как**? is used as the equivalent of English 'what?' in establishing personal and other details:

> **Как** твоё и́мя?/твоё о́тчество?/твоя́ фами́лия?
> What is your first name?/your patronymic?/your surname?

Как тебя́ зову́т?
What is your name?

Как ваш а́дрес?
What is your address?

Note also the phrase **Как** э́то по-ру́сски? 'What is the Russian for that?'

393   Interrelating adverbs

Interrelating adverbs

там, где
туда́, куда́
туда́, отку́да
тогда́, когда́
так, как etc.

may be used when no specific referent of place, time or manner is named:

Я рабо́таю **там, где** он рабо́тал ра́ньше
I work **where** (lit. '**there, where**') he used to work

По́мню, как побежа́ли мы **туда́, куда́** нас вела́ густа́я толпа́ люде́й (Grekova)
I recall how we ran **to where** a dense crowd of people led us

Люба́я рабо́та то́лько **тогда́** увлека́ет, **когда́** ты в ней уже́ каки́е-то та́йны откры́л (Yunyi naturalist)
A job only becomes absorbing **when** you have discovered some of its secrets

Он поступи́л **так, как** я ему́ веле́л
He acted **as** I told him to

394   То́же, та́кже

(1) Both **то́же** and **та́кже** mean 'also, as well, too'. **То́же** may be regarded as the more colloquial variant, **та́кже** as the more official:

Он **то́же/та́кже** пое́дет   He will go **too**
Мы **то́же/та́кже** согла́сны   We **also** agree

Note

(a) **То́же/та́кже не** means 'not . . . either': Он **то́же/та́кже** не пое́дет 'He won't go **either**'.

(b) See **472** (9) for **то́же** as a particle.

(2) **То́же** is preferred in contexts which express identification with an action, state or attribute already referred to:

Вы за́няты? Я **то́же**
Are you busy? **So am I**

— Я о́чень хочу́ пойти́ на конце́рт
'I am very keen to go to the concert'
— Она́ **то́же** хо́чет пойти́
'She wants to go **too**'

У стены́ стоя́л бе́лый стол и четы́ре сту́ла, **то́же** бе́лых
A white table and four chairs, **also** white, stood by the wall

(3) **Та́кже** is preferred when providing additional or supplementary information (in the meaning **кро́ме того́, ещё и** 'apart from that, in addition'):

Я на́чал, кро́ме книг, чита́ть **та́кже** и журна́льные статьи́
I began to read magazine articles **as well as** books

Он о́чень хитёр, не ху́же бра́та; но он **та́кже** о́чень тала́нтлив
He is very cunning, no less so than his brother; but he is **also** very talented

Существу́ют **та́кже** стереоти́пы маскули́нности и фемини́нности (*Nedelya*)
There **also** exist stereotypes of masculinity and femininity

(4) **Та́кже** is particularly common with the conjunction **а:**

Речь шла в основно́м о проблéмах двусторóнних отношéний, **а та́кже** о положéнии в Ливáне
It was basically a question of problems of bilateral relations, **and also** the situation in the Lebanon

Note

А never combines with **то́же**.

(5) Compare the contrasting usage of **то́же** and **та́кже** in the following:

Он **то́же** вы́разил гото́вность помо́чь
He **also** expressed his willingness to help (emulating **someone else's** willingness to help)

Он **та́кже** вы́разил гото́вность помо́чь
He **also** expressed his willingness to help (in addition to **other
action** he had agreed to take)

395   Indefinite adverbs (adverbs in -то, -нибудь, -либо and кòе-)

Adverbs in -**то**, -**нибудь** and -**либо** are adverbial counterparts to the indefinite pronouns (see **138**). They include:

где́-то	somewhere	**где́-нибудь**	somewhere, anywhere
куда́-то	somewhere (direction)	**куда́-нибудь**	somewhere, anywhere (direction)
ка́к-то	somehow	**ка́к-нибудь**	somehow, anyhow
когда́-то	once, at one time	**когда́-нибудь**	at any time, ever
почему́-то	for some reason	**почему́-нибудь**	for some, any reason

All the adverbs can also combine with -**либо**. **Кòе-** combines with **где, как, когда́** and **куда́**.

(1) Adverbs in -то

Где́-то/куда́-то denote a particular but unidentified place, **когда́-то** a particular but unidentified time, **почему́-то** a particular but unidentified cause. The adverbs relate predominantly to the past or present tense:

Вор пря́чется **где́-то** поблизости
The thief is hiding **somewhere** nearby

Он **ка́к-то** спра́вился с зада́чей
Somehow he coped with the task

— Э́то мой друг, игра́ли **когда́-то** в футбо́л (Vanshenkin)
'That is my friend, we used to play football **at one time**'

Тре́тий пассажи́р то́же есть, но, ви́дно, **куда́-то** вы́шел (Rasputin)
There is a third passenger too, but he must have gone out **somewhere**

Он **почему́-то** недово́лен на́шим реше́нием
For some reason he is displeased with our decision

(2) Adverbs in -нибудь

Adverbs in -**нибудь** are used:

(i) In **questions**:

> Вы **когда́-нибудь** отдыха́ли на Чёрном мо́ре?
> Have you **ever** holidayed on the Black Sea?

(ii) In the **future**, implying a choice still to be made:

> Через го́дик **куда́-нибудь** переберу́сь: в Ха́рьков, Ки́ев, Днепропетро́вск (Rybakov)
> In a year or so I shall move **somewhere**: to Kharkov, Kiev, Dnepropetrovsk

(iii) After **imperatives**:

> Загляни́ ко мне **когда́-нибудь**
> Pop in to see me **some time**

(iv) In referring to **different** circumstances on different occasions, irrespective of tense:

> По воскресе́ньям мы всегда́ е́здим **куда́-нибудь** на маши́не
> We always go for a drive somewhere on Sundays (different places on different occasions)

(v) In contexts where the adverb implies inferior quality:

> Я стал коммуни́стом. И не **где́-нибудь**, а в Средизе́мном мо́ре (*Russia Today*)
> I have become a Communist. And not **any old where**, but in the Mediterranean

(3) Adverbs in -либо

Adverbs in -**либо** express an even greater degree of indefiniteness than adverbs in -**нибудь**. They denote 'anywhere' (at any place you like to name), 'ever' (at any time you like to name) etc.:

> Э́то была́ сильне́йшая кома́нда, кото́рая **когда́-либо** выи́грывала чемпиона́ты ми́ра (*Sputnik*)
> It was the strongest team that had **ever** won world championships

(4) Adverbs in ко̀е-

(i) **Ко̀е-где́** means 'in various places':

> **Ко̀е-где́** в на́шем го́роде проводи́лись демонстра́ции
> Demonstrations were held **at various localities** in our town

(ii) **Ко̀е-ка́к** means 'with great difficulty'

Мы **кòе-кáк** добралѝсь домóй
Somehow we struggled home

or 'carelessly'

Рабóта сдéлана **кòе-кáк**
The work has been done **any old how**

Note
Кòе-когдá means 'occasionally', **кòе-кудá** 'to a particular place'.

396 The negative adverbs нигдé, никудá, ниоткýда, никогдá, никáк, нискóлько

(1) Negative adverbs are formed by affixing **ни-** to the adverbs **где** 'where', **как** 'how', **когдá** 'when', **кудá** 'where to', **откýда** 'from where', **скóлько** 'how much':

нигдé	'nowhere'	**никудá**	'nowhere' (direction)
никáк	'in no way'	**ниоткýда**	'from nowhere'
никогдá	'never'	**нискóлько**	'not at all'

Note
'Hardly ever' is rendered as **почтѝ никогдá**, 'hardly anywhere' as **почтѝ нигдé** etc.

(2) Like negative pronouns (see **133**), negative adverbs combine with the particles **не/нет**:

Он **нигдé не** рабóтает	He does not work anywhere
Он **никудá не** идёт	He isn't going anywhere
Ниоткýда нет пѝсем	There are no letters from anywhere
Онá **никогдá не** лжёт	She never tells lies
Онá **никáк не** реагѝровала	She did not react at all
Я **нискóлько не** обѝделся	I wasn't at all offended

Note
Нельзя́ also combines directly with a negative adverb: **Никáк нельзя́** согласѝться с ним 'One can in no way agree with him'.

(3) It is possible to accumulate negatives within one sentence:

Никтó никогдá никудá не éздит
No one ever goes anywhere

Дéти **никогдá ничегó не** узнáют о них (Zalygin)
The children will never learn anything about them

Note

Ни ра́зу 'not once' and **не раз** 'more than once'. Compare:

> Он **ни ра́зу** не прибра́л в ко́мнате у А́ндерсена (Paustovsky)
> **Not once** did he tidy Andersen's room

and

> О недоста́тках **не раз** уже́ писа́лось
> These shortcomings have been written about **more than once**

397 The negative adverbs не́где, не́куда, не́когда, не́откуда, не́зачем

(1) Like the 'potential' negative pronouns (see **137**), the 'potential' negative adverbs appear in infinitive constructions: (**Нам**) **не́где** жить 'There is nowhere (for us) to live'. The series comprises

не́где	'there is nowhere to'
не́зачем	'there is no point'
не́когда	'there is no time to'
не́куда	'there is nowhere to' (direction)
не́откуда	'there is no place from where'

Note

Не́когда can also mean 'once, at one time'.

(2) There are two variants of the construction:

(i) The **impersonal:**

> Утере́ться бы́ло не́чем, переоде́ться **не́где** (Vanshenkin)
> There was nothing to dry oneself on and nowhere to change

> Копа́ть моги́лу бы́ло **не́когда** и **не́зачем** (Rybakov)
> There was no time to dig a grave and no point in doing so

(ii) The **personal**, with the logical subject appearing in the dative case (see **93**):

Ему́ не́где рабо́тать	He has nowhere to work
Ей не́когда бы́ло разгова́ривать	She had no time to converse
Нам не́куда бу́дет е́хать	We shall have nowhere to go

Note

As with the 'potential' negative pronouns, there is a positive counter-part to this construction involving **есть** (present tense), **было** (past) and **будет** (future), e.g.

Е́сть/бы́ло/бу́дет куда́ пойти́
There is/was/will be somewhere to go

398   Comparative adverbs

(1) The comparatives of adverbs in **-о/-е** are identical with short-form comparative adjectives (see **179** and **180**):

Всё сильне́е и глу́бже осознаём духо́вное родство́ с други́ми наро́дами (Kostomarov)
We are **more and more intensively** and **profoundly** conscious of our spiritual kinship with other nations

Note

Adverbs with more than two syllables have an alternative comparative in **бо́лее: вы́годнее/бо́лее вы́годно** 'more beneficially', cf. **ме́нее вы́годно** 'less beneficially'. The form with **бо́лее** is the *norm* for comparatives of adverbs other than those in **-о/-е: бо́лее логи́чески** 'more logically' (cf. **ме́нее лочи́чески** 'less logically').

(2) Comparative adverbs appear in the same types of construction as comparative adjectives (see **182**), i.e. constructions:

(i) With **чем** 'than':

Но сильне́й, **чем** заво́д, люби́л Пётр Телепнёв свой сад (Trifonov)
But Petr Telepnev loved his garden more **than** the factory

(ii) With the **genitive**:

Тре́нер ча́ще **други́х слов** употребля́ет сло́во «рабо́та» (Salnikov)
The trainer uses the word 'work' more often **than other words**

(iii) With **гора́здо** 'much' (also **мно́го, намно́го, куда́**):

Он верну́лся домо́й **гора́здо** по́зже
He returned home **much** later

(iv) With **чем** . . . **тем** 'the . . . the':

Чем бо́льше я отдыха́л от футбо́ла, **тем** сильне́е хоте́лось игра́ть
The more I rested from football **the** more I wanted to play

(v) With the prefix **по-** 'a little':

Но́чью капита́н **поту́же** затя́гивался ремнём (Gagarin)
At night the captain would tighten his belt **a little**

(vi) With instrumental or **на** + accusative in quantifying a difference:

Я верну́лся **на пять мину́т/пятью́ мину́тами** ра́ньше, чем ожида́л
I arrived **five minutes** earlier than I had expected

(vii) With **как мо́жно** 'as . . . as possible':

Мы е́хали **как мо́жно** ме́дленнее
We were driving **as** slowly **as possible**

399   Variant forms of some comparative adverbs

Some comparative adverbs have variant forms:

(1) Бо́льше/бо́лее 'more'; ме́ньше/ме́нее 'less'

(i) These may be differentiated stylistically, the comparatives in -**ше** belonging to the 'neutral' register and those in -**ee** to a more 'bookish' style (**бо́льше/бо́лее тридцати́** 'more than thirty').

(ii) Only **бо́льше/ме́ньше** are used to denote extent or degree: Он лю́бит дочь **бо́льше** (*not* бо́лее), чем сы́на 'He loves his daughter more than (he loves) his son'.

(iii) **Бо́лее** and **ме́нее** are mainly used in the formation of long comparative adjectives and adverbs (see **177** and **398** (1) note), and in a number of set phrases: **бо́лее и́ли ме́нее** 'more or less', **бо́лее того́** 'furthermore' etc.

(2) Да́льше/да́лее 'further'

Apart from its spatial meaning, **да́льше** 'further' also implies subsequent action (А **да́льше** что случи́лось? 'And what happened next?') or encouragement (Ну — **да́льше!** 'Well, go on!'). **Да́лее** is limited mainly to the phrase **и так да́лее (и т.д.)** 'and so on'.

400   The superlative adverb

(1) A superlative adverb consists of a comparative adverb in -**e** or -**ee** + **всего** (for **internal** comparison) or **всех** (for **external** comparison):

> Я работаю лучше **всего** вечером
> I work best of all in the evening (i.e. compared with other times)

> Я работаю лучше **всех** вечером
> I work best in the evening (i.e. compared with other people)

Compare

> Мы все старели, Ада Ефимовна — **меньше всех** (Grekova)
> We were all ageing, Ada Efimovna **least of all** (= **less than anyone**)

(2) **Наиболее** can also be used in the formation of superlative adverbs (**наиболее свободно** 'most freely, fluently' (cf. **наименее свободно** 'least fluently'), and this is the *norm* with adverbs which do not end in -**о/-е**, e.g. **наиболее логически** 'most logically'.

The Preposition

401   Introductory comments

(1) A preposition is a part of speech which expresses the relationship of one word to another: коло́дец **без** воды́ 'a well without water', добр **к** де́тям 'kind to children', пры́гнуть **через** забо́р 'to jump over the fence'.

(2) Each Russian preposition governs a noun or pronoun in an oblique case. Some prepositions govern two or even three cases.

(3) Prepositions may be subdivided as follows:

(i) Primary: **в** 'in', **до** 'as far as', **на** 'on' etc.

(ii) Adverbial: **бли́з** 'near', **вдо́ль** 'along' etc.

(iii) Prepositions derived from nouns (e.g. **в по́льзу** 'in favour of', **насчёт** 'on account of') and from verbs (**благодаря́** 'thanks to' etc.).

402   Primary prepositions and cases

The primaries (central meanings only) can be arranged in a grid, as follows.

Preposition	Acc.	Gen.	Dat.	Instr.	Prep.
(1) **без**		'without'			
(2) **в**	'into'				'in'

Preposition	Acc.	Gen.	Dat.	Instr.	Prep.
(3) **для**		'for'			
(4) **до**		'as far as'			
(5) **за**	'behind' (motion)			'behind'	
(6) **из**		'out of'			
(7) **из-за**		'from behind'			
(8) **из-под**		'from under'			
(9) **к**			'towards'		
(10) **крòме**		'except for'			
(11) **мèжду**				'between'	
(12) **на**	'on to'				'on'
(13) **над**				'above'	
(14) **о**	'against'				'about'
(15) **от**		'from'			
(16) **перед**				'in front of'	
(17) **по**	'up to'		'along'		'after'
(18) **под**	'under' (motion)			'under'	
(19) **при**					'in the presence of'
(20) **про**	'about'				
(21) **ра́ди**		'for the sake of'			
(22) **с**	'approximately'	'down from'		'with'	
(23) **у**		'at'			
(24) **через**	'across'				

Note

(a) Though not strictly speaking primary prepositions, **из-за** and **из-под** are usually included in the series.

(b) See **419** (1) (i) *Note* for **мèжду** + *genitive* case.

(c) **о** is written as **об** before words beginning with **а, э, и, о** or **у** (e.g. **об А́нглии** 'about England') and as **обо** in combinations such as **обо всём** 'about everything' and **обо мне** 'about me'.

403   Repetition of prepositions

The repetition of prepositions is optional, compare:

В Москве́ и не́которых други́х города́х . . . (*Izvestiya*)
In Moscow and certain other cities . . .

and

Он был **в** пижа́ме и **в** дома́шних ту́флях (Zalygin)
He was wearing pyjamas and slippers

except where two or more items governed by the same preposition appear in different clauses, when repetition is mandatory:

Я наде́ялся не то́лько **на** неё, **но** и **на** него́
I relied not only on her, but also on him

404   The buffer vowel -o

Primary prepositions which end in a consonant acquire a final -**o** when followed by certain clusters of consonants. These subdivide as follows:

(1) Clusters which affect many prepositions:

(i) **Вр-** (mainly вре́мя 'time'): во вре́мя 'during', ко вре́мени 'by the time', со вре́мени 'since the time'.

(ii) **Вс-** (mainly declined forms of весь 'all'): во всём 'in everything', изо всех сил 'with all one's might' (but из всех мои́х друзе́й 'of all my friends'), обо всём 'about everything', со всех концо́в 'from all parts' (над, перед, от are not affected).

(iii) **Вт-** (mainly вто́рник 'Tuesday' and второ́й 'second'): во вто́рник 'on Tuesday', ко вто́рнику 'by Tuesday', со вто́рника 'since Tuesday'; во второ́м 'in the second', со второ́го 'since the second'.

(iv) **Дн-** (mainly oblique cases of день 'day' and дно 'bottom'): ко дню 'for the day', со/с днём 'with the day', со дня 'since the day', изо дня в день 'daily, constantly'; ко дну 'to the bottom'.

(v) **Мн-** (mainly oblique cases of я 'I' and мно́гое/мно́гие 'many'): во мне 'in me', ко мне 'to me', надо мной 'above me', передо мной 'in front of me', подо мной 'below me', со мной 'with me', обо мне 'about me'; во мно́гом 'in many ways', со мно́гими 'with many people' (*but* из мно́гих 'of many people', от мно́гих 'from many people').

(2) Clusters that affect only certain prepositions; the cluster often repeats the final consonant of the preposition or its unvoiced/voiced/mutated counterpart: во Владивосто́ке 'in Vladivostok', во МХА́Те 'in the Moscow Art Theatre', во Пско́ве 'in Pskov', во фло́те 'in the navy', во Фра́нции 'in France'; со зло́сти 'out of malice', со ско́ростью 'at a speed', со среды́ 'since Wednesday', со ста́нции 'from the station', со стены́ 'from the wall', со стола́ 'from the table', со шта́том 'with a staff'; подо льдом 'under the ice', etc.

Note
Also во Вьетна́ме 'in Vietnam', во дворе́ 'in the yard', во избежа́ние 'in avoidance of', во и́мя 'in the name of', во ско́лько? 'at what time?' and clusters in monosyllabic oblique case forms whose nominatives contain a fleeting vowel: во рту 'in the mouth' (from рот 'mouth'), со лба 'from the forehead' (from лоб 'forehead'), со льдом 'with ice' (from лёд 'ice').

405   Stress in primary prepositions

(1) Prepositions are usually unstressed; however, some primaries, in particular **за, на, по, под** and, to a lesser extent, **до, из** and **о/об**, take the stress when combined with certain nouns and numerals. Many such combinations are characteristic of colloquial registers.

(2) The types of noun involved include parts of the body (e.g. голова́ 'head'), geographical features (бе́рег 'shore'), other locations (го́род 'town'), time words (год 'year') and some others (вид 'view'). All nouns and numerals involved are monosyllables or have *initial* stress in the declined form.

(3) The commonest case involved is the accusative, but others are also found.

(4) Among the commonest combinations are the following:

(i) **До** + genitive: до́ дому 'as far as home', (с утра́) до́ ночи (from morning) 'till night', до́ смерти (испуга́лся) (was scared) 'to death'.

(ii) **За** + accusative: за́ борт 'overboard' (direction), за́ волосы 'by the hair', за́ год 'in a year', за́ голову 'by the head', за́ город 'into the country', зá гору 'beyond the mountain' (direction), зá два (гóда), две (недéли), три (гóда), пять, шесть, семь, восемь, девять, десять, сто (лет) 'in two (years/weeks), three, five, six, seven, eight, nine, ten, a hundred' (years), зá день 'in a day', зá зиму 'during the winter', зá кóсу/кóсы 'by the plait/plaits', зá лето 'during the summer', зá море 'beyond the sea' (direction), зá нóгу/нóги 'by the leg/legs', зá нос 'by the nose', зá ночь 'during the night', зá плечи 'by the shoulders', зá полночь 'beyond midnight', зá реку 'beyond the river' (direction), зá руку/руки 'by the hand/hands', зá спину 'behind the back' (direction), (держáться) зá стену (to hold) 'on to the wall', зá угол 'round the corner' (direction), зá ухо/уши 'by the ear/ears', (ущипнýть) зá щеку (to pinch) 'on the cheek'.

Note
Alternative noun/numeral stress is found in за вóлосы, гóлову, два/две, три, пять, шесть, семь, вóсемь, дéвять, дéсять, сто, лéто, мóре, плéчи.

(iii) **За** + instrumental: зá городом 'in the country' (cf. за гóродом 'beyond the town'), зá морем (ог за мóрем) 'overseas', зá ухом 'behind the ear'.

(iv) **Из** + genitive: и́з виду 'from sight', и́з дому 'out of the house' (one's own house, cf. из дóма 'out of someone else's house', e.g. из дóма Сáши 'from Sasha's house'), и́з лесу 'from the forest' (also из лéса), и́з носу 'from the nose' (also из нóса).

(v) **На** + accusative: нá берег 'on to the shore', нá бок 'on to one's side', нá борт 'on board' (direction), (спустúть) нá воду (to launch) 'on to the water' (cf. смотрéть на вóду/нá воду 'to look at the water'), нá год 'for a year', нá голову 'on to the head', нá гору 'onto the hill', нá два (numerals behave as with за + accusative (see (ii) above)), нá день 'for a day', нá дом 'to the premises' (but смотрéть на дом 'to look at the house'), нá зиму 'for the winter', нá лето 'for the summer', нá море 'to the sea', нá нóгу/нóги 'on to the leg/legs, foot/feet', нá нос 'on to the nose', нá ночь 'for the night', нá пол 'on to the floor', нá реку 'to the river', нá руку 'onto the hand'/нá руки 'into the arms', нá спину 'on to the back', нá стену 'on to the wall', (шептáть) нá ухо (to whisper) 'into the ear' (cf. нацепúть на у́хо 'to attach to the ear').

Note
The following take alternative noun/numeral stress: на бéрег, гóлову, два (and other numerals), лéто, мóре, рéку, стéну.

(vi) **На** + prepositional: нá море/на мóре 'on the sea, at the seaside'.

(vii) **О/об** + accusative: (бóк) ó бок '(side) by side', óб пол/об пóл 'against the floor', (рукá) óб руку (hand) 'in hand'.

(viii) **По** + accusative: пó два/две, двóе, три, трóе, стó 'two, three, a hundred each' (with alternative numeral stress: по двá 'two each' etc.).

(ix) **По** + dative: пó лесу/по лéсу 'through the forest', пó морю/по мóрю 'over the sea', пó полю/по пóлю 'over the field'.

(x) **Под** + accusative: пóд воду/под вóду 'under the water' (direction), пóд гору 'downhill', пóд ноги 'under one's feet' (direction), пóд руку/руки 'by the arm/arms'.

(xi) **Под** + instrumental: пóд боком/под бóком 'close at hand'.

(xii) **Прú** смерти 'at death's door'.

Note
Alternative stress is possible in many literal contexts, while idioms retain prepositional stress: лезть нá стену/на стéну 'to climb up on to the wall', but лезть нá стену (fig.) 'to go berserk'. Compare положá рýку нá сердце 'hand on heart' and жáловаться на сéрдце 'to complain of heart trouble'.

406   Adverbial prepositions

Adverbial prepositions take the following forms.

(1) One-word prepositions (all + genitive unless otherwise indicated): блúз 'near', вблизú 'close to', вглубь 'into the depths of', вдóль 'along', взамéн 'in exchange for', вмéсто 'instead of', внè 'outside', внутрú 'inside' (location), внýтрь 'inside' (direction), вòзле 'close to', вокрýг 'around', вопрекú + dative 'contrary to', впередú 'in front of', врòде 'like', мùмо 'past', навстрéчу + dative 'towards', наканýне 'on the eve of', наперекóр + dative 'counter to', напрóтив 'opposite', òколо 'near', относúтельно 'with regard to', пòдле 'by the side of', подóбно + dative 'similar to', позадú 'behind', поперёк 'across, athwart', пòсле 'after', посредú 'in the midst of', прòтив 'opposite', свèрх 'above', свы́ше 'more than', сзàди 'behind', сквòзь + accusative 'through', соглáсно + dative 'according to', средú 'among'.

(2) Compounds involving a primary preposition: вблизú от 'close to', вдалú от 'far from', вмéсте с + instrumental 'together with', вплóть до 'right up to', вслед за + instrumental 'after', независимо от

'irrespective of', рядом с + instrumental 'next to', согласно с + instrumental 'in accordance with'.

407   Prepositions derived from nouns and verbs

(1) Compound prepositions derived from nouns comprise:

(i) One-word prepositions (all + genitive): порядка 'of the order of', посредством 'by means of', путём 'by dint of'.

(ii) Those that combine with one primary preposition (all + genitive): в виде 'in the form of', ввиду 'in view of', в интересах 'in the interests of', в качестве 'in the capacity of', в направлении 'in the direction of', во время 'during', в пользу 'in favour of', в продолжение 'in the course of', в результате 'as a result of', в силу 'on the strength of', вследствие 'in consequence of', в сторону 'in the direction of', в течение 'during the course of', в ходе 'during the course of', в целях 'for the purpose of', за счёт 'at the expense of', на протяжении 'during', с целью 'with the object of'.

(iii) Those that combine with two primaries: в зависимости от 'depending on', в отличие от 'unlike', в связи с + instrumental 'in connection with', по направлению к 'in the direction of', по отношению к 'in relation to', по сравнению с + instrumental 'by comparison with'.

(2) Most prepositions derived from verbs are based on gerunds: благодаря + dative 'thanks to', включая + accusative 'including', начиная с + genitive 'beginning with', несмотря на + accusative 'despite', не считая + genitive 'not counting', спустя + accusative 'after', судя по + dative 'judging by'. See also **380**.

Note
Спустя may follow or precede the noun: две недели **спустя/спустя** две недели 'two weeks later'.

Spatial Prepositions

408   В and на + prepositional/accusative, из/с + genitive

(1) В/на + prepositional

(i) The central meaning of **в** + prepositional is 'in, inside':

Игру́шки **в я́щике**   The toys are **in the drawer**

(ii) The central meaning of **на** + prepositional is 'on, on top of':

Кни́ги **на по́лке**   The books are **on the shelf**

(2) В/на + accusative

В and **на** + accusative are used to denote, respectively, direction **into** or **on to**:

Я кладу́ игру́шки **в я́щик**   I put the toys **in(to) the drawer**
Я ста́влю кни́ги **на по́лку**   I stand the books **on(to) the shelf**

(3) Из/с + genitive

Из 'out of' and **с** 'down from' + genitive denote withdrawal. They are the 'opposites', respectively, of **в** and **на**:

Я вынима́ю игру́шки **из**   I take the toys **out of the**
   я́щика   **drawer**
Я беру́ кни́ги **с по́лки**   I take the books **off the shelf**

Note

(a)   The oppositions **в/из** and **на/с** are consistently observed, though there are exceptions: Я лежу́ **в посте́ли** 'I am lying in bed' but Я встаю́ **с посте́ли** 'I get out of bed' (**из посте́ли** is used with verbs prefixed **вы-**: Он **вы́скочил из посте́ли** 'He leapt out of bed'). For other exceptions, see **411** (2).

(b)   Nouns which normally combine with **из**, e.g. **из го́рода** 'from the town', combine with **с** when qualified by **весь**: **со всего́ го́рода** 'from all over the town' (the meaning is 'from the whole area' not 'from inside', cf. **со всех концо́в** 'from all parts', **со всех сторо́н** 'from all sides').

(c)   **В** also combines with the prepositional case of nouns denoting articles of clothing etc.: Он **в боти́нках** 'He is wearing shoes', Она́ **в бе́лом пла́тье** 'She is wearing a white dress', Он **в очка́х** 'He is wearing glasses' (cf. **носи́ть** 'to wear habitually').

(d)   **В** and **на** + accusative are used after nouns such as **биле́т** and **дверь**: **биле́т в теа́тр/на о́перу/на по́езд** 'a theatre/opera/train ticket', **дверь в ко́мнату** 'the door to the room'. Compare **вид на мо́ре** 'a view of the sea'.

409 The use of в and на with geographical terminology and the names of organizations, buildings and parts of buildings

With certain categories of noun the distinction between **в** and **на** is not always clear cut.

(1) Countries

(i) **В** is used for almost all countries: **в Великобритáнии** 'in Great Britain', **в Россúи** 'in Russia'.

(ii) **На** is used with some states which are also islands: **на Кýбе** 'in Cuba'. Note also **на рóдине** 'in the homeland', **на Русú** 'in Rus' (but **в дрéвней Русú** 'in ancient Rus') and **на чужбúне** 'in a foreign land'.

(2) Republics and other territories in the former USSR

(i) The names of former Soviet Republics and other major territories take **в**: **в Армéнии** 'in Armenia', **в Сибúри** 'in Siberia'.

(ii) Note **на (в) Украúне** 'in Ukraine' (but **в Зáпадной Украúне** 'in Western Ukraine') and the use of **на** with areas ending in -**щина**: **на Днепрóвщине** 'in the area of the Dnieper'.

(3) Natural features and climatic zones

(i) **В Áрктике** 'in the Arctic', **в пустýне** 'in the desert', **в степú** 'in the steppe', **в тайгé** 'in the taiga'.

(ii) **На возвы́шенности** 'in the highlands', **на лугý** 'in a meadow', **на нúзменности** 'in the lowlands', **на пóлюсе** 'at the Pole', **на полянé** 'in a glade', **на прóсеке** 'in a forest cutting', **на равнúне** 'in the plain', **на целинé** 'in the virgin soil'.

(4) Mountain ranges

(i) **В** is used with plural **гóры** 'mountains' (**в горáх** 'in the mountains') and with ranges that have plural names: **в Áльпах** 'in the Alps', **в Áндах** 'in the Andes', **в Карпáтах** 'in the Carpathians' etc. (Exceptions include **на Балкáнах** 'in the Balkans' and **на Воробьёвых горáх** 'on the Sparrow Hills'.)

(ii) **На** is used with ranges that have singular names: **на Алтáе/ Кавкáзе/Памúре/Урáле** 'in the Altai/Caucasus/Pamirs/Urals'. (**Тянь-Шáнь** 'Tien-Shan' is used with either **в** or **на**: **в/на Тянь-Шáне**.)

Note

В replaces **на** when the noun is qualified by an adjective: **в Восто́чном Пами́ре** 'in the Eastern Pamirs' (except for Кавка́з Caucasus': **на Восто́чном Кавка́зе** 'in the Eastern Caucasus').

(5) Islands, archipelagoes, peninsulas

(i) **На** is the norm: **на Аля́ске** 'in Alaska', **на Гава́йях** 'in Hawaii', **на Ки́пре** 'in Cyprus', **на Ко́рсике** 'in Corsica', **на Кри́те** 'on Crete', **на Ма́льте** 'in Malta', **на Таймы́ре** 'on the Taimyr peninsula', **на Я́ве** 'in Java'.

(ii) However, **в** is used in **в Крыму́** 'in the Crimea' and with islands ending in -**ия**: **в Гренла́ндии** 'in Greenland', **в Сарди́нии** 'in Sardinia', **в Сици́лии** 'in Sicily' (cf. **на о́строве** Сарди́ния/ Сици́лия 'on the island of Sardinia, Sicily' etc).

(6) Points of the compass

На is used with points of the compass: **на восто́ке/за́паде/ю́ге/ се́вере** 'in the east/west/south/north', **на ю̀го-восто́ке/сѐверо-за́паде** 'in the south-east/north-west'. Political **на За́паде** 'in the West' (i.e. 'in Western countries') is distinguished from geographical **на за́паде** 'in the west'. Compare **на Бли́жнем/Да́льнем Восто́ке** 'in the Near/Far East'.

(7) Towns

(i) Town names, many parts of towns and most regions of Moscow combine with **в**: **в Москве́** 'in Moscow'; **в переу́лке** 'in a side-street', **в при́городе** 'in a suburb'; **в Оста́нкино** 'in Ostankino', **в Черёмушках** 'in Cheremushki'.

(ii) **На** is used as follows:

(a) **На окра́ине** 'in the outskirts', **на пло́щади** 'in the square', **на у́лице** 'in the street' (**в** is possible only when narrowness is emphasized: **в у́зких у́лицах** 'in the narrow streets'). Note **в/на скве́ре** 'in the small public garden'.

(b) With some Moscow regions: **на Арба́те** 'in the Arbat', **на Пре́сне** 'in Presnya', **на Со́коле** 'in Sokol'.

(8) Buildings (and parts of buildings), areas and workplaces

(i) Most names of buildings and organizations take **в**: **в аптéке** 'at the chemist's shop', **в аэропортý** 'at the airport', **в колхóзе** 'at the collective farm', **в цúрке** 'at the circus', **в шкóле** 'at the school' etc.

(ii) Combinations with **на** relate especially to areas historically associated with open spaces or complexes of buildings rather than single structures. Thus, both **пóчта** 'post office' and **стáнция** 'station' take **на** by association with the pre-Revolutionary **почтóвая стáнция** 'relay station', an area with stables, administrative offices and sleeping accommodation, where travellers could obtain fresh horses. Combinations with **на** include the following:

(a) **На аэродрóме** 'at the aerodrome', **на бáзе** 'at the base', **на вокзáле** 'at the main station', **на вы́ставке** 'at the exhibition', **на дáче** 'at the country cottage', **на завóде** 'at the plant', **на пóчте** 'at the post office', **на почтáмте** 'at the main post office', **на предприя́тии** 'at the enterprise', **на ры́нке** 'at the market', **на склáде** 'at the warehouse', **на спортúвной площáдке** 'at the sports ground', **на стадиóне** 'at the stadium', **на стáнции** 'at the station', **на стройтельстве/стрóйке** 'at the building site', **на фáбрике** 'at the factory', **на фéрме** 'at the farm', **на я́рмарке** 'at the trade fair'.

(b) Certain parts of buildings and organizations: **на балкóне** 'on (theatr. 'in') the balcony', **на галёрке** 'in the gallery' (theatr.), **на кáфедре** 'in the (university) department', **на факультéте** 'in the faculty', **на чердакé** 'in the attic', **на я́русе** 'in the circle' (theatr.).

Note

В дóме 'in the house', but **на домý** 'on the premises, at home': Он зарабáтывает и **на домý** 'He earns extra money at home' (cf. Закáз достáвлен **нá дом** 'The order has been delivered to the door'). Compare also **в теáтре** 'in the theatre' and Рабóтаю **на теáтре/рáдио/телевúдении** 'I work in the theatre/in radio/on TV' (professional parlance).

(9) Miscellaneous

На дéреве 'in a tree', **на кормé** 'in the stern', **на носý** 'in the prow', **на рéйде** 'in the roads' (of a harbour), **на сковородé** 'in a frying-pan'.

410   Nouns which may be used with в and на, but with different meanings

Many nouns may be used with either **в** or **на**, with negligible difference in meaning: **в/на кварти́ре** 'in the flat', **в/на коню́шне** 'in the stable', **в/на ку́хне** 'in the kitchen', **в/на фло́те** 'in the navy' etc.

Other nouns combine with в and на, but with a *difference* in meaning.

(1) Авто́бус (and other vehicles)

(i) **В авто́бусе** 'in the bus' is used if there is emphasis on the vehicle as a scene of activity: Уро́ки я вы́учила **в авто́бусе/в по́езде/в метро́** 'I did my homework in the bus/the train/on the underground'.

(ii) **На** is preferred when emphasis is on travel (though either preposition *may* be used): две остано́вки **на метро́** до Арба́та 'two stops on the underground to the Arbat'. Only **на** is possible with the names of ships: **на парохо́де** 'on the steamer'. Public transport vehicles may appear in the instrumental case, as an alternative to a prepositional construction: дое́хать **трамва́ем** 'to get there by tram', доста́вить груз **самолётом/парохо́дом** 'to deliver a load by aircraft/by steamer'. However, this does not apply to **велосипе́д** 'bicycle', **ло́дка** 'boat', **метро́** 'underground', **мотоци́кл** 'motorcycle', **такси́** 'taxi', which appear only with prepositions (е́хать **на велосипе́де/на такси́** 'to ride a bicycle/go by taxi' etc.).

(2) Во́здух

(i) **В во́здухе** means 'up in the air, pervading the air': Самолёт **в во́здухе** 'The aircraft is up in the air', **В во́здухе** пови́с за́пах табака́ 'The smell of tobacco hung in the air'.

(ii) **На во́здухе** means 'out in the open air': **на** све́жем/откры́том **во́здухе** 'in the fresh/the open air'. Compare the use of **на** in other outdoor contexts: Зна́мя колы́шется **на ветру́** 'The flag flutters in the breeze', сиде́ть **на со́лнце** 'to sit in the sun' etc.

(3) Высота́/глубина́

(i) **В** is used in the absence of quantification: **в прозра́чной высоте́** 'in the translucent heights', **в морско́й глубине́/в океа́нских глуби́нах** 'in the ocean depths'. Note also **в глубине́** за́ла 'at the back of the hall', **в глубине́** ле́са 'in the depths of the forest', **в глубине́** са́да 'at the bottom of the garden'.

(ii) **На** is used when quantification is stated or implied: **на высоте́** двух киломе́тров/**на** э́той **высоте́** 'at a height of two kilometres/at this height', **на глубине́** трёх сантиме́тров 'at a depth of three centimetres'.

(4) Глаза́

(i) **В** is used in contexts of emotion or opinion: выраже́ние страда́ния **в глаза́х** 'an expression of suffering in the eyes', Каки́м болва́ном я вы́глядел **в её глаза́х** 'What an idiot I appeared in her eyes'.

(ii) **На** denotes:

(a) 'On the surface': Конта́ктные ли́нзы остаю́тся **на глаза́х** ме́сяцами 'Contact lenses stay in the eyes for months on end'.

(b) 'Swiftly/in the presence of': Города́ рожда́ются **на на́ших глаза́х** 'Towns spring up before our very eyes'.

Note
Either preposition may be used in the context of tears: **В/на глаза́х** показа́лись слёзы 'Tears appeared in her eyes'.

(5) Гора́

В го́ру means 'uphill': идти́ **в го́ру** 'to go uphill'. **На́ гору** refers to a specific hill or mountain: забра́ться **на́ гору** 'to climb a mountain'.

Note the mining term **на-гора́** 'to the surface'.

(6) Двор

(i) **Во дворе́** 'in the yard' refers to an area surrounded by houses or a fence: **Во дворе́** бы́ло две покры́шки 'There were two tyre covers in the yard'.

(ii) **На дворе́** denotes:

(a) A specific kind of yard: **на ко́нном дворе́** 'in the stable yard'.

(b) 'Outside': **На дворе́** зима́ 'It is winter outside'.

(7) Ме́сто

(i) **В ме́сте** is used to denote:

(a) Part of a whole: Кни́га по́рвана **в одно́м ме́сте** 'The book is torn in one place'.

(b) A three-dimensional area: **в тёмном ме́сте** 'in a dark place'.

(c) 'Together': всё собра́ть **в одно́м ме́сте** 'to collect everything in one place'.

(d) 'The same': Мы всегда́ встреча́лись **в одно́м ме́сте** 'We always met in the same place'.

(e) A locality: **в чудесном месте** 'in a delightful spot'.

Note

В is also used in certain adjectival combinations: **в другом месте** 'somewhere else', **в разных местах** 'in various places'.

(ii) **На месте** is used to denote:

(a) 'The proper place': Все вещи **на месте** 'Everything is in its proper place'.

(b) Immobility: стоять **на месте** 'to stand still'.

(c) Possession: Я сижу **на твоём месте** 'I am sitting in your place'.

(d) Former whereabouts: Деньги лежат **на прежнем месте** 'The money is lying where it was'.

(e) Replacement: **На месте** пустырей выросли жилые кварталы 'Blocks of flats have sprung up in place of waste ground'.

(f) Flat areas: **на ровном месте** 'on a level stretch of ground'.

(g) Preferred conduct: **на вашем месте** 'if I were you'.

(h) Scale of priorities: **На втором месте** — жилищные условия 'Housing conditions are in second place'.

Note

На местах 'in the provinces': Первый тур проводится **на местах** 'The first round is being held in the provinces'.

(8) Море

(i) **В море** denotes:

(a) Activity or location beneath the surface: Эти рыбы водятся **в Чёрном море** 'These fish are found in the Black Sea'.

(b) Out at sea, on a voyage etc.: Корабль уже давно **в море** 'The ship has been under way for some time'; compare also **в открытом море** 'in the open sea'.

(ii) **На море** denotes activity or location on the surface of the sea (приключения на суше и **на море** 'adventures on land and sea') or on the seashore (Ялта находится **на Чёрном море** 'Yalta is on the Black Sea').

(9) Небо

Either preposition is used to denote the location of natural phenomena (огро́мное со́лнце **в/на чи́стом не́бе** 'an enormous sun in the clear sky'), while **в** is preferred for birds, aircraft, sounds etc. (Ва́ря уви́дела **в не́бе** два вертолёта 'Varya saw two helicopters in the sky', **В не́бе** послы́шался ро́кот 'A low rumble was heard in the sky').

(10) Окно́

(i) **В окне́** means 'visible at the window': **В окне́** показа́лась его́ голова́ 'His head appeared at the window'.

(ii) **На окне́** means 'on the window/the window-sill': **На окне́** стоя́ли цветы́ 'There were flowers on the window-sill'. Note also **На о́кнах** ро́зовые занаве́ски 'There are pink curtains at the windows'.

(11) По́ле

(i) **В по́ле** means 'out in the fields': В дере́вне пу́сто, все **в по́ле** 'The village is deserted, everyone is out in the fields'.

(ii) **На по́ле** denotes a specific area or plot: **На по́ле** стоя́л тра́ктор 'In the field stood a tractor', **На поля́х** рабо́тали лю́ди 'People were working in the fields', **на карто́фельном по́ле** 'in a potato field', **на по́ле бо́я** 'on the battle field', **на лётном по́ле** 'on the flying field', **на футбо́льном по́ле** 'on the football field'.

Note
На поля́х also means 'in the margin'.

(12) Разве́дка

В разве́дке refers to military intelligence, **на разве́дке** to prospecting: Он рабо́тает **на разве́дке** не́фти 'He works in oil prospecting'.

(13) Рука́/ру́ки

(i) **В руке́/рука́х** means 'in the hand/hands': У Арсе́ния **в рука́х** аво́ська 'Arseny is holding a string-bag'.

(ii) **На руке́/рука́х** means 'in the arm(s)': **На одно́й руке́** у неё ребёнок 'She has a child in one arm', Она́ подошла́ с Ви́тькой **на рука́х** 'She came up with Vitka in her arms'.

Note
Кни́га **на рука́х** 'The (library) book is out', У него́ семья́ **на рука́х** 'He has a family to support'.

(14) Свет

(i) **В свете** means 'in the light/bathed in light': **В жёлтом свете** фонарей толпились девушки 'The girls crowded in the yellow light of the lanterns'. Note also figurative usage: **в свете** новых открытий 'in the light of recent discoveries'.

(ii) **На свете** means 'in the world': Сколько видов слонов **на свете**? 'How many species of elephant are there in the world?'. **На свету** is used when something is examined: Она осматривала одежду **на свету** 'She was examining the clothes in the light'.

(15) Село

В селе means 'in a village', **на селе** 'in country areas': роль интеллигенции **на селе** 'the intelligentsia's role in country areas'.

(16) Середина

В or **на** are used to denote the centre of an area: Трактор **в/на середине** поля 'The tractor is in the middle of the field'. **В середине** denotes enclosure, 'in between': **в середине** толпы 'in the middle of a crowd'.

(17) Студия

В is used for an artist's studio, and for radio and recording studios (**в радиостудии/в студии** звукозаписи), whereas **на** is used with film studios (фильм дублирован **на киностудии** 'The film has been dubbed at the film studio').

(18) Суд

В суде means 'in the court-room': **В суде** сегодня многолюдно 'The court-room is crowded today'; **в/на суде** 'at the trial'.

(19) Ухо

На ухо is the norm: шепнуть **на ухо** 'to whisper in someone's ear'. **В ухо** may be used to emphasize directed sound: шепнуть прямо **в ухо** 'to whisper directly into someone's ear'.

(20) Шахта

В шахте means 'down the mine', **на шахте** 'at the mine/colliery'.

411   Special uses of c + genitive

(1) The nouns enumerated in **410** combine with:

(i) **В/на** + accusative to denote direction:

Шахтёр спусти́лся **в ша́хту**
The miner went down the mine

Она́ подхвати́ла ребёнка **на́ руки**
She gathered the child up in her arms

(ii) **Из/с** + genitive to denote withdrawal:

Моне́та вы́пала **из её рук**
The coin fell from her hands

Он упа́л **с большо́й высоты́**
He fell from a great height

(2) Some nouns combine only with **c** + genitive to denote withdrawal, even where location is expressed by **в** + prepositional: cf.

Самолёт **в во́здухе**
The aircraft is in the air

Самолёт **c** (*not* из!) во́здуха заме́тил те́рпящих бе́дствие
The aircraft spotted the victims of the disaster from the air

Compare also

с горы́	downhill
со двора́	from the yard
с мо́ря	from the sea
с не́ба	from the sky
с по́ля/поле́й	from the field/fields

412   Uses of в and на when the dependent noun denotes an activity, event

(1) **На** combines with the prepositional of nouns which denote activities or events: **на войне́** 'at the war', **на конце́рте** 'at a concert', **на ма́тче** 'at a match', **на рабо́те** 'at work', **на сва́дьбе** 'at a wedding', **на собра́нии** 'at a meeting', **на уро́ке** 'at the lesson'.

(2) **На** + accusative/**с** + genitive denote, respectively, movement towards and withdrawal from these activities, thus

Иду́ **на рабо́ту**	I am going to work
Иду́ домо́й **с рабо́ты**	I am going home from work

Note
В combines with nouns that denote a performance (a) if the performer is the subject of the verb (петь **в о́пере** 'to sing in an opera') and (b) in references to the *content* of a work (**В э́той о́пере** мно́го краси́вых а́рий 'There are many beautiful arias in this opera').

413   В and на: extension of the spatial meanings

A number of meanings of **в** and **на** can be regarded as extensions of the spatial meanings.

(1) **В** + prepositional

(i) 'Covered in':

Па́льцы у меня́ **в цара́пинах**
My fingers are covered in scratches

(ii) Distance:

В киломе́тре от ГЭС — большо́е о́зеро
A large lake is situated a kilometre from the power station

Он живёт **в пяти́ мину́тах ходьбы́** от ста́нции
He lives five minutes' walk from the station

Note
'At what distance?' is rendered as **на како́м расстоя́нии**? (See **415** (2) for **за** + accusative in the meaning of distance.)

(iii) A group to which the subject belongs:

Он **в гостя́х**	He is on a visit
остава́ться **в живы́х**	to survive

Note
The idea of plurality in phrases of this type is often an abstraction, since **в гостя́х**, for example, can be used even if the subject is the only guest (cf. also идти́ **в го́сти** 'to go visiting').

(iv) Various physical states:

в её прису́тствии	in her presence (cf. в её **отсу́тствие** 'in her absence')
в пути́	*en route*
в хоро́шем состоя́нии	in good condition

(v) Various mental states:

Он **в восто́рге**	He is delighted
Она́ **в хоро́шем настрое́нии**	She is in a good mood

Note

The phrase **в са́мом де́ле** implies confirmation (Он говори́т, что он кита́ец, и **в са́мом де́ле** он кита́ец 'He says he is Chinese, and he **really is** Chinese'), while **на са́мом де́ле** implies contrast (на вид таки́е ми́лые, а **на са́мом де́ле** злы́е 'seemingly so nice, but **in fact** spiteful').

(2) На + prepositional

На + prepositional is used in a number of phrases:

ката́ться **на конька́х**	to skate
ходи́ть **на лы́жах**	to ski
рука́ **на пе́ревязи**	an arm in a sling

including some which denote state:

на во́ле/свобо́де	at liberty
быть **на пе́нсии**	to be on a pension, retired
на второ́й/тре́тьей ско́рости	in second, third gear
на ра́нней ста́дии	at an early stage

Prepositions that Denote the Position of an Object in Relation to Another Object (Behind, in Front of, Below, on Top of etc.), or Movement to or from that Position

414   За + instrumental/accusative, из-за + genitive

(1) За + instrumental

(i) **За** + instrumental means 'behind, on the other side of, beyond' etc.:

за до́мом	behind the house
за мосто́м	on the other side of the bridge
за реко́й	beyond the river

Note

Сза́ди and **позади́** + genitive are synonymous with **за** + instrumental in the meaning 'behind': **сза́ди, позади́** до́ма 'behind the house'. **Сза́ди меня́** 'behind me' lacks the idea of close proximity that adheres to **за мной**.

(ii) The following phrases are particularly common:

за бо́ртом	overboard
за́ городом	in the suburbs, in the country
за грани́цей	abroad
за две́рью	behind, outside the door
за окно́м	outside the window (from the inside), inside the window (from the outside)
за рулём	at the wheel
за столо́м	at the table (also **за обе́дом** 'at lunch' etc.)
за угло́м	round the corner

Note also **за́мужем** 'married' (of a woman): Она́ **за́мужем** за ру́сским 'She is married to a Russian'.

(2) За + accusative

За + accusative is used to denote movement to these positions:

пое́хать	за́ город	to drive out of town
е́хать	за грани́цу	to go abroad
спря́таться	за дверь	to hide behind the door
сесть	за стол	to sit down at the table
зайти́	за́ угол	to go round the corner

Note also **за́муж**: Она́ вы́шла **за́муж** за актёра 'She married an actor'.

(3) Из-за + genitive

Из-за + genitive denotes withdrawal from these positions:

Он верну́лся	из-за грани́цы	He returned from abroad
Она́ вста́ла	из-за стола́	She got up from the table
Они́ показа́лись	из-за угла́	They appeared round the corner

415   За + instrumental/accusative: extension of the spatial meanings

Other spatial meanings of **за** are as follows:

(1) За + instrumental

(i) Sequence:

> Самолёты взлетéли **одúн за другúм**
> The aircraft took off one after the other

(ii) An object followed or pursued:

гнáться	**за мячóм**	to chase the ball
охóтиться	**за тúгром**	to hunt a tiger (for the zoo, cf. охóтиться **на** тúгра 'to hunt (to kill) a tiger')
слéдовать	**за экскурсовóдом**	to follow the guide

(iii) Occupation with an activity:

> проводúть вéчер **за игрóй** to spend the evening playing

(2) За + accusative

За + accusative may denote distance from a point:

> **За пять** километрóв отсю́да сегóдня свáдьба
> There is a wedding today five kilometres from here

Note
В пятú километрáх could also be used here (see **413** (1) (ii)), but only **за** is possible:

(a) When movement to a goal is implied:

> бежáть **за вóсемь километрóв** домóй
> to run eight kilometres home

(b) When **за** combines with **до** to distinguish two spatial points:

> **За** пятьсóт мéтров **до** фúниша подтянýлся англичáнин
> Five hundred metres from the finish the Englishman rallied

(c) When distance is expressed in terms of **дверь** 'door', **дом** 'house', **квартáл** 'block':

За два до́ма до э́того угла́ в 20-е го́ды бы́ло общежи́тие (Panova)
There was a hostel two doors down from this corner in the 1920s

416 Перед + instrumental, впереди́ + genitive

(1) **Перед** means 'in front of':

перед до́мом	in front of the house

Note

(a) Unlike **за, перед** cannot take the accusative to denote movement
to a position, cf. Он пове́сил пальто́ **за дверь** 'He hung the coat
behind the door', but Он поста́вил ми́ску **перед собо́й** 'He put
the bowl in front of him'.

(b) Note figurative usage: **Перед на́ми** больша́я зада́ча 'A major task
faces us'.

(2) **Впереди́** + genitive 'in front of, ahead of' is usually associated with
animate nouns or moving objects: éхать **впереди́ авто́буса** 'to drive
ahead of the bus'. Unlike **перед**, it does not imply closeness: Де́ти
бежа́ли **далеко́ впереди́ взро́слых** 'The children were running far
ahead of the adults'.

417 Под + instrumental/accusative, из-под + genitive

(1) Под + instrumental

(i) The central meaning of **под** is 'under':

пла́вать **под водо́й**	to swim under water
стоя́ть **под мосто́м**	to stand under the bridge
под мы́шкой	under one's arm
по́ле **под ро́жью**	a field under rye

Note the phrases

под но́сом, под руко́й	near by, close at hand
под горо́й	at the bottom of the hill
под дождём	in the rain
под потолко́м	from the ceiling (Ла́мпы вися́т **под** **потолко́м** 'The lamps hang from the ceiling')

(ii) **Под** also denotes proximity to towns:

бои́ **под Москво́й**   the battles near Moscow

(iii) **Под угло́м** means 'at an angle':

У́лица выходи́ла **под угло́м** к трамва́йной остано́вке
The street went off at an angle to the tram stop

(iv) **Под** is also used figuratively: **под аре́стом, влия́нием, давле́нием, контро́лем, угро́зой** 'under arrest, the influence, pressure, control, threat', cf.:

Экспериме́нты прово́дятся **под руково́дством** учёных
The experiments are carried out under the guidance of scientists

Note
Что вы понима́ете **под э́тим** сло́вом? 'What do you understand **by** this word?'

(2) Под + accusative

Под + the accusative denotes:

(i) Movement to a position underneath something:

Они́ се́ли **под де́рево**   They sat down under a tree
Он спря́тал ру́ки **под стол**   He hid his hands under the table

Compare also the phrases

спуска́ться **по́д гору** (= **с горы́**)   to go downhill
Она́ попа́ла **под дождь**   She got caught in the rain
обрабо́тать по́де **под пшени́цу**   to put a field under wheat

(ii) Movement to a position near (a town):

Мы перее́хали **под Санкт-   We moved to near St
   Петербу́рг**   Petersburg

(iii) Transfer to a state:

ста́вить **под угро́зу**   to place under threat

(3) Из-под + genitive

(i) **Из-под** means 'from underneath, from near' (a town):

Он вы́лез **из-под стола́**	He climbed out from under the table
Он верну́лся **из-под Росто́ва**	He has returned from near Rostov

(ii) It is also used figuratively:

Маши́на вы́шла **из-под контро́ля**	The car went out of control
Она́ вы́шла **из-под его́ влия́ния**	She escaped from his influence

418   Над + instrumental, пове́рх + genitive

(1) **Над** means 'over, above':

над голово́й
overhead

Самолёт лети́т **над го́родом**
The aircraft is flying over the town

над у́ровнем мо́ря
above sea level

Note

(a)   Unlike **под** (see **417** (2)(i)), **над** does *not* take the accusative to denote movement to a position: Пове́сили ла́мпу **над столо́м** 'They hung the lamp over the table'.

(b)   **Над** is also used figuratively: побе́да **над фаши́змом** 'victory over Fascism', рабо́тать **над рома́ном** 'to work on a novel', сжа́литься **над сирото́й** 'to take pity on an orphan', смея́ться **над дурако́м** 'to laugh at a fool', суд **над Э́йхманом** 'the trial of Eichmann'.

(2) **Пове́рх** means 'over, over the top of, on top of': смотре́ть **пове́рх очко́в** 'to look over the top of one's spectacles', Он наде́л сви́тер **пове́рх руба́шки** 'He put his sweater on over his shirt'.

419   Мѐжду + instrumental, средѝ, посредѝ, напро́тив, про̀тив, вдо̀ль, внѐ, внутрѝ, вну̀трь, вокру̀г, мѝмо + genitive

(1) Мѐжду/средѝ

(i) **Мѐжду** means 'between'

мѐжду магазѝном и дорóгой
between the shop and the road

Мѐжду домáми есть забóр
There is a fence between the houses

мѐжду нáми
between you and me

Note

Мѐжду governs the instrumental singular and the instrumental or (less frequently) *genitive* plural (**мѐжду дерéвьями/дерéвьев** 'between the trees'); the genitive is found mainly in poetic speech and idiomatic phrases (**мѐжду двух огнéй** 'between the devil and the deep blue sea', читáть **мѐжду строк** 'to read between the lines').

(ii) **Средѝ/посредѝ** means 'in the middle' (of an area):

Средѝ/посредѝ пóля стоя́ло нéсколько кустóв
In the middle of the field stood several bushes

Note

Средѝ (but *not* посредѝ) can also mean 'among, surrounded by':

Средѝ дерéвьев стои́т дом A house stands among the trees

(2) Напрóтив/прòтив

Напрóтив/прòтив mean 'opposite', combining with verbs of state *and* movement:

Я живу́ **напрóтив/прòтив завóда**
I live opposite the factory

Крéсло постáвлю **напрóтив/прòтив** телеви́зора
I shall put the chair opposite the TV set

Note

Прòтив (but not **напрóтив**) also has the meaning 'against, opposed to': идти́ **прòтив вéтра** 'to walk into the wind', плыть **прòтив течéния** 'to swim against the current', **прòтив часовóй стрéлки** 'anti-clockwise'.

(3) Вдòль, внѐ, внутрѝ, внỳтрь, вокрỳг, мѝмо

(i) **Вдòль** means 'along, alongside':

идти́ **вдо́ль шоссе́**
to walk alongside the highway (cf. е́хать **по** шоссе́ 'to drive **along** the highway')

Вдо́ль забо́ра поса́жены дере́вья
Trees are planted along(side) the fence

Note
See also **424** (1) (d) for **вдоль** in the meaning 'along the surface of'.

(ii) **Внѐ** means 'outside':

Часть дня он прово́дит **внѐ до́ма**
He spends part of the day outside the house

Note
Figurative usage: **внѐ опа́сности, о́череди** 'out of danger, out of turn'.

(iii) **Внутрѝ** and its directional counterpart **внутрь** mean 'inside':

внутрѝ го́рода	inside the town
проника́ть **внутрь** помеще́ния	to penetrate inside the building

(iv) **Вокру̀г** means 'round':

Земля́ враща́ется **вокру̀г** свое́й о́си	the Earth rotates round its axis
Они́ сиде́ли **вокру̀г стола́**	They sat round the table

(v) **Мѝмо** means 'past':

идти́ **мѝмо до́ма**	to go past the house

Prepositions that Denote Spatial Closeness to an Object, Movement Towards or Away from an Object, or Distance from an Object

420   У + genitive, к + dative, от + genitive

(1) У + genitive case

(i) The central meaning of **у** + genitive is 'at, by, near' an object:

останови́ться **у са́мой** две́ри	to stop right by the door
сиде́ть **у окна́**	to sit by the window

Note

(a)   For prepositions denoting proximity to a *person*, see **421**.

(b)   Figurative usage: быть **у власти** 'to be in power'.

(ii) **У** also means 'at the house of, with, at' (the doctor's etc.):

> Она́ отдыха́ет **у сестры́** в дере́вне
> She is relaxing at her sister's place in the country

> Сего́дня Са́ша был **у врача́**
> Today Sasha was at the doctor's

> **у нас**
> at our place, in our country

(2) К + dative case

(i) **К** is used in the meaning 'towards' (a place), 'to see' (a person):

Я побежа́л **к вы́ходу**	I ran towards the exit
Она́ идёт **к го́роду**	She is going towards the town (cf. идти́ **по направле́нию к го́роду, в направле́нии** го́рода/к го́роду 'to walk in the direction of the town')
Он пошёл **к врачу́**	He has gone to see the doctor

Note

(a)   Он пришёл **к власти** 'He came to power', путь **к сча́стью** 'the path to happiness'.

(b)   Идти́ **навстре́чу дру́гу** 'to go to meet a friend', and figurative usage: идти́ **навстре́чу всем опа́сностям** 'to face up to all kinds of dangers'.

(ii) **К** can also denote bodily attitude:

Я стоя́л бо́ком **к мосту́**	I stood sideways on to the bridge
Он сиде́л спино́й **ко мне**	He sat with his back to me

(3) От + genitive case

The central meaning of **от** is 'away from':

Он шёл **от реки́**	He was walking away from the river (cf. Он шёл **со стороны́** реки́ 'He was walking from the direction of the river')
Она́ ушла́ **от му́жа**	She left her husband

421   Близ, бли́зко от, во́зле, недалеко́ от, неподалёку от, о́коло, по́дле + genitive; бли́зко к, бли́же к + dative; ря́дом с + instrumental

Of these prepositions, по́дле 'beside' is rarely used, while **близ, во́зле** and **о́коло** 'near, close to' are commonly used to denote proximity to a person or an object:

близ/во́зле/о́коло до́ма   near the house

Note

(a) **Во́зле** may imply *greater* proximity: Он живёт **во́зле нас** 'He lives very near us'. Additional emphasis may be imparted by the pronoun **са́мый**: во́зле **са́мого ле́са** 'hard by the forest'.

(b) **О́коло** 'near' expresses a greater degree of proximity than **недалеко́ от** 'not far from'. **Неподалёку** is more colloquial than **недалеко́**.

(c) **Бли́зко от** 'close to' is used to denote passage at close quarters, as well as close location: Пти́ца пролете́ла **бли́зко от него́** 'The bird flew past very close to him'.

(d) **Ря́дом с** means 'next to, next door to': Дом **ря́дом с** па́рком 'The house is next to the park'.

(e) **Бли́зко/бли́же к** denote direction towards: Он подошёл **бли́зко/бли́же к до́му** 'He went up close/closer to the house'.

(f) For **под** + instrumental/accusative and **из-под** + genitive in meaning of proximity see **417** (1) (ii), (2) (ii), (3) (i).

422   При + prepositional

При + prepositional:

(i) combines with the following nouns in the meaning of proximity: **вход/въезд** 'entrance', **вы́ход** 'exit', **доро́га** 'road':

Да́ча стоя́ла **при доро́ге**
The country cottage stood at the roadside

пове́сить объявле́ние **при вхо́де**
to hang a notice at the entrance

поста́вить часовы́х **при въе́зде** в тунне́ль
to post sentries at the entrance to the tunnel

(ii) combines with the names of the sites of battles: би́тва **при Сталингра́де** 'the battle of Stalingrad' (cf. бой **за Великобрита́нию** 'the Battle of Britain').

(iii) denotes attachment: **При университе́те** есть поликли́ника 'There is a polyclinic attached to the university', пра́чечная **при общежи́тии** 'a laundry attached to the residence'.

423   Вдали́ от, далеко́ от, пода́льше от + genitive

Both **вдали́ от** and **далеко́ от** mean 'far from': **вдали́/далеко́ от родно́го го́рода** 'far from one's home town'. However, **вдали́ от** never denotes movement: Он отошёл **далеко́ от** (but not вдали́ от) дере́вни 'He moved far away from the village'. (**(По)да́льше от,** however, is used in such contexts: Сел **пода́льше от** окна́ 'He sat down a little further away from the window'.)

See also **413** (1) (ii) and **415** (2) (**в** + prepositional, **за** + accusative, **на** + prepositional in the meaning of distance).

Prepositions that Denote Along, Across, Through a Spatial Area

424   По + dative; через, сквозь + accusative; поперёк, вглубь, вдоль + genitive

(1) **По** means 'over the surface/along/up/down' etc.:

идти́ **по бе́регу**
to walk along the shore

плыть вверх **по тече́нию**
to sail upstream

Ка́пли дождя́ стека́ют **по стеклу́**
Raindrops stream down the pane

По коридо́ру мать прошла́ на ку́хню
Mother proceeded down the corridor to the kitchen

Note

(a)   Movement may be in more than one direction: ката́ться **по кру́гу** 'to skate in a circle', Меня́ вози́ли **по всей Болга́рии** 'I was driven all over Bulgaria'.

(b) The distinction between **идти́** по у́лице 'to walk down the street' and **ходи́ть** по у́лице 'to walk up and down the street' (see also **320** and **322** (2)).

(c) **По** may also denote location at or movement to various points in space: Пе́репись населе́ния провели́ **по всем населённым пу́нктам** 'The census was carried out throughout all populated areas', Весь день я ходи́л **по магази́нам** 'I spent all day walking round the shops'.

(d) In combination with **доро́га** 'road', **у́лица** 'street' and nouns that denote other lines of progress (**бе́рег** 'shore', **опу́шка** 'outskirts' etc.), **по** + dative is synonymous with the instrumental or **вдоль** + genitive: идти́ **по бе́регу/бе́регом/вдоль бе́рега**.

(e) Either **по** or **через** may be used to denote movement across an inhabited area: прое́хать **по всей Москве́/через всю Москву́** 'to travel right across Moscow' (**через** implies crossing and emerging from the other side of the city).

(2) The central meaning of **через** is 'through', 'across', 'from one side to the other' (often with a verb prefixed **пере-: перебежа́ть** через доро́гу 'to run across the road'), 'over', 'via':

В шко́лу мы ходи́ли **через лес**
We used to go to school through the forest

Он переле́з **через забо́р**
He climbed over the fence

е́хать в Ки́ев **через Москву́**
to travel to Kiev via Moscow

мост **через ре́ку**
a bridge over the river

Note

(a) **Через** implies a direction or destination and therefore does not combine with verbs such as **броди́ть** 'to roam', **гуля́ть** 'to stroll', **по** + dative being preferred: мы гуля́ли **по́ лесу** 'we were strolling through the forest'.

(b) **Через** in the meaning 'across' is not normally repeated within a sentence, thus: Маши́ны переезжа́ют **через ре́ку, по краси́вому мосту́** 'The cars drive across the river over a handsome bridge'

(cf., used in isolation, synonymous идти **через мост** and идти **по мосту** 'to walk across a bridge')

(c)   **Через** may also denote:

(i)   A spatial interval: **Через два дóма** живёт её дочь 'Her daughter lives two doors down', Килóметров **через пять** нашли скалу 'Some five kilometres on they found the rock'.

(ii)   A recurrent interval: **через прáвильные промежутки** 'at regular intervals', спотыкáться **через кáждые два шагá** 'to stumble at every two paces', печáтать **через стрóчку** 'to type double-spaced'.

(iii)   An intermediary: разговáривать **через перевóдчика** 'to converse through an interpreter'.

(3) **Сквозь** implies difficulty of accomplishment, resistance etc.:

смотрéть **сквозь щель**
to peer through a crack

Сквозь крышу протекáла водá
Water was leaking through the roof

пробирáться **сквозь толпу**
to push one's way through
the crowd

Note

(a)   **Через** in such contexts implies less resistance in passing through: Лучи сóлнца проникáли **сквозь/через** листву 'The rays of the sun were penetrating/passing through the foliage'.

(b)   Only **сквозь** (*not* через) is possible with a noun that denotes a climatic feature: Сóлнце пробивáлось **сквозь метéль/тумáн/тучу** 'The sun was forcing its way through the snow storm/mist/cloud'.

(c)   Figurative usage: смотрéть **сквозь пáльцы** на чтó-нибудь 'to turn a blind eye to something'.

(4) **Поперёк** means 'transversely across, athwart, crosswise':

лечь **поперёк постéли**
to lie across the bed

Грузовик стоя́л **поперёк дорóги** и тормозил движéние
The lorry was blocking the road, impeding the traffic

(5) **Вглубь** means 'deep into':

вглубь лесóв   into the heart of the forest вглубь материка́   inland

Prepositions that Denote Spatial Limit

425   До + genitive, по + accusative

(1) **До** + genitive means 'as far as': Автобус идёт то́лько **до Арба́та** 'The bus only goes as far as the Arbat'.

(2) **По** + accusative denotes the limit of an action or process, up to and including a point in space represented by:

(i) A part of the body:

> обнажённая **по ло́коть** рука́
> an arm bared to the elbow

> Он вошёл в во́ду **по по́яс**
> He waded into the water up to his waist

(ii) Other spatial points:

> дома́, **по о́кна** занесённые сне́гом
> houses buried up to the windows in snow

Note the idioms за́нят **по го́рло** 'up to one's eyes in work', сыт **по го́рло** 'fed up to the back teeth', влюбля́ться **по́ уши** 'to fall madly in love', **по́ уши** в долга́х 'up to the ears in debt'.

Temporal Prepositions

426   Telling the time

The question **В кото́ром часу́?/Во ско́лько?** 'At what time?' is answered as follows:

(1) By **в** + accusative on the hour and up to the half-hour:

в час/два часа́. . .	at one o'clock/two o'clock. . .
в пять мину́т шесто́го	at five past five
в по́лдень/в по́лночь	at midday/midnight

(2) By **в** + prepositional on the half-hour:

в полови́не пе́рвого	at half past twelve (colloquially **в по̀лпе́рвого**)

(3) By **без** + genitive after the half-hour:

без пяти́ пять	at five to five

Note

(a) **В** + prepositional and **о̀коло** are used to denote approximate time: **в восьмо́м часу́** 'between seven and eight', **в нача́ле девя́того** 'just after eight', **о̀коло двух часо́в** 'at about two o'clock'.

(b) In colloquial Russian, prepositions may be juxtaposed: До како́го ча́са вы рабо́тате сего́дня? **До без** че́тверти во́семь 'What time do you work until today?' 'Until a quarter to eight'.

(c) **В** + accusative is usual in phrases with **миг/мгнове́ние (в после́дний миг/в после́днее мгнове́ние** 'at the last instant'), **мину́та (в после́днюю мину́ту** 'at the last minute', **в после́дние мину́ты** 'in the final minutes'), **моме́нт (в после́дний моме́нт** 'at the last moment') and **час (в по́здний час** 'at a late hour').

(d) However, **на** + prepositional is used in sporting contexts: **На шесто́й мину́те** по́льская кома́нда откры́ла счёт 'The Polish team opened the score in the sixth minute', **на пе́рвых/после́дних мину́тах** ма́тча 'in the opening, closing minutes of the match'. Compare similar usage in chess: Па́ртия заверши́лась **на 16-м ходу́** 'The game finished at the 16th move'.

See **206** for a detailed account of how to tell the time.

427 Days

(1) **В** combines with the accusative of **день** and the days of the week:

в како́й день/в каки́е дни?	on what day/on what days?
в понеде́льник, во вто́рник	on Monday, on Tuesday
в сре́ду, в четве́рг, в пя́тницу	on Wednesday, Thursday, Friday
в суббо́ту, в воскресе́нье	on Saturday, Sunday
в э́тот, про́шлый, бу́дущий понеде́льник	this, last, next Monday

(2) While **в** is used with days qualified by **пе́рвый (в пе́рвый день/в пе́рвые су́тки** 'on the first day'), **на** + accusative is used with ordinal numerals above **пе́рвый (на тре́тий день/тре́тьи су́тки** 'on the third day', **на второ́й день** по̀сле отъе́зда 'on the second day after

leaving'), and with **другóй, слéдующий: на другóй/слéдующий** день 'on the next day' (cf. **в другóй день** 'on **another** day').

(3) **По** combines with the dative plural to denote recurrent points in time: **по средáм** 'on Wednesdays', **по суббóтам ýтром** 'on Saturday mornings'.

Note

(a)   **День** itself is used in this meaning only in certain phrases: **по чётным/нечётным дням** 'on even/odd days' etc.

(b)   An alternative construction with **в** + accusative plural is possible in certain combinations: **по бýдням/в бýдни** 'on weekdays', **по выходны́м дням/в выходны́е дни** 'on days off', **по прáздникам/в прáздники** 'on holidays'. In some expressions only **в** + accusative is possible: **в обы́чные дни** 'on normal days'.

(c)   **По** + dative plural also indicates temporal continuity: **по цéлым часáм/дням** 'for hours/days on end' (also **цéлыми дня́ми/часáми**).

428   Parts of a day

(1) Nouns that denote part of a day (**ýтро** 'morning' etc.) usually appear in the instrumental: **ýтром** 'in the morning' etc. (but **пять часóв утрá** 'five o'clock in the morning'; see **97** (2) (i)) and **206** (1) (ii).

(2) However, **в** + accusative is used with nouns denoting parts of a day which are qualified by pronouns or adjectives (including **пéрвый** 'first'): **в пéрвый/послéдний вéчер** 'on the first/the last evening', **в ту ночь** 'that night', **в э́то воскрéсное ýтро** 'on that Sunday morning'.

(3) When nouns which denote part of a day are qualified by **другóй/слéдующий** or ordinals above **пéрвый**, however, they combine with **на** + accusative: **на слéдующий вéчер/слéдующую ночь/другóе ýтро/трéтье ýтро** 'on the next evening/the next night/the next morning/the third morning'.

(4) **По** + dative plural denotes recurrent points in time: по **вечерáм/ночáм/утрáм** 'in the evenings/at nights/in the mornings'; **по ночáм** он не спит 'he doesn't sleep at nights'.

Note

В сýмерки/сýмерках 'at dusk', but **на восхóде** 'at sunrise', **на закáте** 'at sunset', **на зарé/рассвéте** 'at dawn'.

429   Weeks, months, years and centuries

(1) **На** combines with the prepositional of **неде́ля** 'week':

на э́той, про́шлой, бу́дущей неде́ле	this, last, next week

(2) **В** combines with the prepositional of:

(i) **Ме́сяц** 'month' and the names of calendar months:

в январе́, феврале́ ма́рте . . .	in January, February, March . . .
в э́том, про́шлом, бу́дущем ме́сяце	this, last, next month

Note

(a) All names of months are masculine and are spelt with a small letter. The six months from **сентя́брь** 'September' through to **февра́ль** 'February' take end stress in declension: **в сентябре́** 'in September' etc. The other six, from **март** to **а́вгуст**, have fixed stress in declension.

(b) 'This March, last April, next December' are rendered as **в ма́рте э́того го́да, в апре́ле про́шлого го́да, в декабре́ бу́дущего го́да**.

(c) The use of **на** + prepositional in contexts relating to pregnancy: Он оста́вил её **на седьмо́м ме́сяце** бере́менности 'He abandoned her in the seventh month of her pregnancy'.

(d) The use of consecutive dates in ночь **с 11-го на 12-е января́** 'the night of 11 January'.

(ii) **Год** 'year':

в э́том, про́шлом, бу́дущем году́	this, last, next year
в ты́сяча девятьсо́т девяно́сто восьмо́м году́	in 1998
в двухты́сячном году́	in the year 2000

Note

(a) **В сле́дующем году́** is also used, especially with a reference point in the past: **В сле́дующем году́** овладе́ли ча́стью Финля́ндии 'In the following year they captured part of Finland'.

(b) The prepositional case is also used with years in the plural: **в 1920–1921 годах** 'in 1920–1921'.

(c) With decades, the accusative is preferred for processes extending over a period: **В 1960-е годы** здесь продавались русские книги 'Russian books were sold here in the 1960s'. The prepositional is preferred for an event occurring at a point within a decade: Магазин закрылся **в 1970-х годах** 'The shop closed in the 1970s'.

(iii) **Век/столетие** 'century' and **тысячелетие** 'millennium':

в этом, прошлом, будущем веке/столетии	this, last, next century
в XX (двадцатом) веке	in the twentieth century
в третьем тысячелетии	in the third millennium

Note

(a) When qualified by modifiers other than **этот, прошлый, будущий, в** combines with the accusative of **неделя, месяц, год**: **в первую, последнюю неделю** 'in the first, the last week', **в первые недели** осени 'in the first weeks of autumn', **в первый месяц** курса 'in the first month of the course', **в первый/последний год** войны 'in the first/last year of the war', **в год** рождения 'in the year of my birth', **в послевоенные годы** 'in the post-war years'. (This also applies to the seasons, cf. **осенью, зимой** 'in the autumn, winter' but **в ту осень** 'that autumn', **в трудную зиму** 'in a difficult winter'.)

(b) With ordinal numerals above **первый, на** + accusative is the norm: **на четвёртый месяц** 'in the fourth month', **на вторую неделю** 'in the second week', **на четвёртый год** 'in the fourth year' (but **на четвёртом году** перестройки 'in the fourth year of restructuring', where reference is to a stage in a process).

430 General time words

В governs the accusative case of nouns which denote time in general or an indefinite period of time (**век** 'age', **время** 'time', **эпоха** 'epoch' etc.):

в а́томный век/сре́дние века́	in the atomic age/the middle ages
в ми́рное вре́мя	in peace time
во времена́ Петра́ I	during the time of Peter I
в пери́од социали́зма	under socialism
в зи́мнюю по́ру	in winter time
в зи́мний сезо́н	in the winter season (also в зи́мнем сезо́не)
в старину́	in the old days
в тече́ние	during the course of
в на́шу эпо́ху	in our era

Note

(a) **Во вре́мя** is used with activities/events (**во вре́мя уро́ка** 'during the lesson'), but *not* with words of time. **В тече́ние** can be used with either, thus: Репорта́жи бу́дем передава́ть **в тече́ние** всей конфере́нции 'We shall be transmitting reports **throughout** the whole conference', **в тече́ние** сле́дующих не́скольких неде́ль 'during the next few weeks'.

(b) **Во времена́** is used for the distant past: **во времена́** крепостно́го пра́ва 'during serfdom', **во времена́** Шекспи́ра (= при Шекспи́ре/при жи́зни Шекспи́ра) 'in Shakespeare's time' (see **442** (2) for **при** in temporal meaning). **Во времена́** is preferred to **при** when the events are distant in time *and* (from a Russian viewpoint) location. Compare Росси́я европеизи́ровалась **при Петре́ Пе́рвом/во времена́ Петра́ Пе́рвого** 'Russia was Europeanized in the reign of Peter the First' (an event distant in time) and **Во времена́ Петра́ Пе́рвого** А́нглия была́ вели́кой морско́й держа́вой 'Britain was a great naval power during the time of Peter the First' (a historical fact distant in time *and* location).

(c) **В хо́де** is common in scientific and journalistic literature, combining with a noun that denotes a process: **в хо́де обсужде́ния (= в проце́ссе обсужде́ния/при обсужде́нии)** 'during the discussion'.

(d) **За** + accusative denotes the period during which an event occurs or events occur: Он встреча́л **за э́то вре́мя** не бо́лее 60 други́х автомоби́лей 'During this period he encountered no more than 60 other cars'.

(e) **На протяже́нии** is used with longish periods of time: **на протяже́нии не́скольких веко́в** 'over the course of several centuries'.

431   Nouns that denote stages in a process

B is used in temporal meaning with the prepositional case of:

(1) The nouns **про́шлое** 'past', **настоя́щее** 'present', **бу́дущее** 'future':

> **в про́шлом, настоя́щем, бу́дущем**   in the past, present, future

(2) The nouns **коне́ц** 'end', **нача́ло** 'beginning', **середи́на** 'middle':

> **в нача́ле, середи́не, конце́**   at the beginning, in the middle, at the end

Note the phrase **в конце́ концо́в** 'eventually/in the end'.

(3) Nouns that denote stages in life:

> **в младе́нчестве, де́тстве**   in babyhood, childhood
> **в мо́лодости, ста́рости**   in youth, old age
> **в глубо́кой ста́рости**   at a ripe old age (but **на ста́рости лет** 'in old age')

Note

(a) **В во́зрасте** 'at an age': Приуча́ться к ко́фе **в её во́зрасте** нежела́тельно 'It is undesirable to get used to drinking coffee at her age'. 'At my age' may be rendered as **в моём во́зрасте/в мои́ го́ды**. 'At the age of seven' is expressed as follows: **в во́зрасте семи́ лет/в семиле́тнем во́зрасте/в семь лет/семи́ лет**.

(b) Use of **на** in Он **на 76-м году́** потеря́л зре́ние 'He lost his sight in his 76th year', **на 6-м деся́тке** 'in one's fifties', **на моём веку́** 'in my lifetime'.

(4) Nouns that denote a stage in an activity or event:

> **в антра́кте, в переры́ве**   in the interval, at break-time
> **в тре́тьем пери́оде**   in the third period (ice-hockey)
> **во второ́м та́йме**   in the second half
> **в после́днем ту́ре соревнова́ния**   in the final round of a competition

432   The weather

B + accusative is used to describe the weather:

в плоху́ю пого́ду
in bad weather

Самолёты **в тума́н** прико́ваны к земле́
In fog the aircraft are grounded

Note

Во вре́мя can also be used in more general meanings (**во вре́мя метéли** 'during the snowstorm'), cf. **в** + accusative with its implications of time and circumstance (**В метéль** они́ сби́лись с пути́ 'They lost their way in the snowstorm'). Nouns such as **жара́** 'heat', **пого́да** 'weather', **хо́лод** 'cold' combine only with **в** + accusative.

433 Festivals

The names of some festivals combine with **в** or **на** + accusative: **в/на Но́вый год** 'at New Year'. **В** is commoner (**в Пра́здник** Побе́ды 'at the Victory Festival', **в нового́дний пра́здник** 'at the new year festival', **в ма́йские пра́здники** 'at the May festivities'), but **на** persists with religious festivals (**на Па́сху** 'at Easter', **на Рождество́** 'at Christmas').

The Use of Prepositions to Denote Action in Relation to Various Time Limits

434   The use of c + genitive, до + genitive/по + accusative to denote terminal points in time

(1) **C** + genitive denotes 'since/from' a point in time:

C суббо́ты мы вме́сте	We have been together **since Saturday**
с да́вних пор	**since time immemorial**
с тех пор	**since then**

(Начина́я) **с апре́ля** Ве́нгрия перейдёт на ле́тнее вре́мя
(With effect) from April Hungary will switch to summer time

Note

Со вре́мени, со дня, с моме́нта etc. combine with nouns that denote the names of activities or events:

Два десятилéтия прошлó **со врéмени побéды**
Two decades have passed **since the victory**

со дня новосéлья
since the house-warming

с момéнта получéния вáшего письмá
since receipt of your letter

Note also **со времён: со времён Ивáна Ш** 'since the time of Ivan III'.

(2) **До** means 'until':

ждать **до вéчера**	to wait until evening
Я бýду здесь (вплóть) **до пяти часóв**	I shall be here (right up) until five o'clock
до сих пор	up till now, hitherto

Note
'Not until' is rendered by **тóлько** 'only': **тóлько** пòсле полýночи 'not until after midnight'.

(3) **По** + accusative means 'up to and including': **по шестóе** мáя (or **до** шестóго мáя **включи́тельно**) 'up to and including 6 May'.

С and **до/по** denote the terminal limits of an action:

Он отдыхáет **с 26 мáрта до пéрвого апрéля**
He is on holiday from 26 March to 1 April (reporting back on 1 April)

Он отдыхáет **с 26 мáрта по пéрвое апрéля**
He is on holiday from 26 March to 1 April inclusive (reporting back on 2 April)

Note the phrases **со дня́ нá день** 'any day now', **с минýты на минýту** 'any minute now', **с чáсу на чáс** 'any time now'.

435   Use of к + dative and под + accusative to denote temporal approach

(1) **К** + dative means 'by':

к концý недéли	by the end of the week
к понедéльнику	by Monday

(2) **Под** + accusative denotes:

(i) 'Towards, approaching' a time, in combination with **вéчер** 'evening', **воскресéнье** 'Sunday', **прáздник** 'festival', **стáрость** 'old age', **ýтро** 'morning' etc.:

Он вернýлся **под вéчер**	He returned towards evening
под конéц сентября́	towards the end of September
Я встал **под ýтро**	I got up in the early hours

(ii) 'On the eve of' a holiday or festival (a synonym of **наканýне** + genitive):

под Нóвый год	on New Year's Eve

436   Use of в/за + accusative to denote the time taken to complete an action

Both **в** and **за** + accusative denote the time taken to complete an action:

Смéна паровóзов была́ произведена́ **в двé–три минýты** (Bek)
The switch of locomotives was carried out in 2–3 minutes

Он окрáсил кýхню **за четы́ре дня**
He painted the kitchen in four days

Note

(a) If the *duration* of an action is emphasized, *not* its completion, the accusative is used *without* a preposition: Он читáл ромáн **четы́ре часá** 'He read the novel for four hours'. Compare Он прочитáл ромáн **за/в четы́ре дня** 'He read the novel **in** four days'.

(b) **За** is sometimes preferred to **в** in order to avoid possible ambiguity: Он состáвил доклáд **за три часá** 'He compiled the report in three hours' (**в три часá** could mean 'at three o'clock').

(c) **За** is also usually preferred when the time appears excessive in relation to the task: В элèктросвáрке **и за полгóда** не разберёшься! (Kochetov) 'You won't get the hang of arc-welding even in six months!'.

(d) **В** appears in the phrases: **в два счёта** 'in two shakes', **в мгновéние óка** 'in the twinkling of an eye', **в счи́танные минýты** 'in a few brief minutes'.

437   Use of в + accusative to denote the period during which an action occurs a stated number of times

В combines with the accusative of a time word to denote the period during which an action occurs a stated number of times:

Он éздит на Кýбу **4 рáза**   He goes to Cuba 4 times a year
в год

438   Use of на + accusative to denote the time for which something has been arranged

На + accusative denotes the time for which an event has been arranged:

Собрáние назнáчено **на седьмóе мáрта**
The meeting has been arranged for 7 March

Отложи́ть **на бýдущую недéлю**
To postpone to next week

Note
(a)   Other verbs which appear in the construction include **заказáть (на срéду)** 'to order' (for Wednesday), **перенести́ (на четвéрг)** 'to carry over' (till Thursday).
(b)   The elliptical construction **На деся́тое** билéтов ужé нет 'There are no tickets left for the tenth'.

439   Use of prepositions to denote sequence in time (before, after etc.)

(1) Prepositions denoting precedence in time

(i) **До** means (any time) 'before':

до войны́   before the war

(ii) **До** also combines with **за** + accusative where one event precedes another by a stated time interval:

Провéрили мотóры **за час до вы́лета**
They checked the engines an hour before take-off

Note also the adverb **задо́лго: задо́лго до войны́** 'long before the war'.

(iii) **Перед** means '*just* before':

перед сном	before going to bed
переоде́ться **перед у́жином**	to change for (just before) dinner

Note

(a)   The noun can be qualified by **са́мый: перед са́мым отъе́здом** 'just prior to departure'.

(b)   The comparative **ра́ньше** is restricted to usage with animate nouns and nouns that denote deadlines: Он пришёл **ра́ньше меня́, ра́ньше вре́мени** 'He arrived before me, ahead of time'.

(iv) **Наза́д** + accusative 'ago' is now more commonly used than the pronoun + adverb formation **тому́ наза́д**: неде́лю (тому́) **наза́д** 'a week ago'.

(2) Prepositions denoting subsequent action

(i) **По́сле, через**

По́сле means 'after' an event (**по́сле заня́тий** 'after lessons'), while **через** is used with words of **time** to denote 'after the expiry of/in/later', with reference to the past, present or future:

Начнём **через час**	We shall begin in an hour's time
Мы на́чали **через час**	We began an hour later

Note

(a)   The preposition must not be separated from its noun: **ме́нее, чем через час** 'in less than an hour's time' (or 'less than an hour later').

(b)   **По истече́нии** 'on expiry of' is synonymous with **через** in this meaning. Compare **спустя́**, which combines mainly with past tense verbs: Он у́мер **спустя́ ме́сяц/ме́сяц спустя́** 'He died a month later'.

(c)   **По́сле** replaces **через** when the time word is extended by a genitive: **через год** 'after a year', but **по́сле** го́да разлу́ки 'after a year's separation'.

Both **через** *and* **по́сле** are used in constructions which denote the temporal relationship of sequential events:

Через во́семь дней по́сле Рождества́ на́ши на́чали наступле́ние
Our lads went on the offensive eight days after Christmas

Note
(a) **Через** is *optional* in such contexts (cf. **за . . . до** (1) (ii) above, where **за** is *compulsory*).
(b) **Спустя́** may replace **через** in such constructions: **спустя́ 8 дней/8 дней спустя́** по́сле Рождества́.

Через is also used to denote a recurrent temporal interval:

Парохо́д остана́вливается здесь **через раз**
The steamer stops here every other time

Авто́бусы хо́дят **через ка́ждые де́сять мину́т**
The buses run every ten minutes

(ii) По + prepositional

По + prepositional is synonymous with **по́сле** in official and scientific styles, in combination with verbal and some other abstract nouns:

по возвраще́нии (= **по́сле возвраще́ния**) домо́й
on returning home
по оконча́нии университе́та
on graduating
по получе́нии письма́   on receipt of the letter
по прие́зде   on arrival
по его́ сме́рти   on his death

(iii) За + instrumental

За + instrumental denotes sequence in time:

год за го́дом, день за днём year after year, day after day

(iv) В + accusative

В + ordinal numeral + **раз** defines an event's place in a series:

Она́ голосу́ет **в пе́рвый раз**
She is voting for the first time

(v) На + accusative

На + accusative is used to denote the time subsequent to the **completion** of an action:

Он **на́ год** пое́хал за грани́цу
He has gone abroad for a year

Она́ пря́тала **на ле́то** зи́мние ве́щи
She would put her winter things away for the summer

Он встал с посте́ли **на 5 мину́т**
He got out of bed for 5 minutes

Note

(a) The accusative *without* a preposition denotes the time spent *performing* an action. Compare:

Он шёл в шко́лу **10 мину́т**
He took 10 minutes to get to school

and

Он выключа́ет свет **на** 10 мину́т
He puts the light out for 10 minutes

where the 10 minutes *follow the completion* of the action of putting out the light, and the result (darkness) is effective throughout that time.

(b) The accusative without a preposition is therefore used with durative verbs (**Я три неде́ли отдыха́л** в Я́лте 'I holidayed in Yalta for three weeks' (time and action coincide)), while **на** + accusative is used with verbs that denote completed actions (Пья́ниц **сажа́ют в ка́меру на́ ночь** 'Drunks are put in a cell for the night' (the time is subsequent to the completion of the action)).

Note also the adverb **надо́лго**: Она́ уе́хала **надо́лго** 'She went away for a long time'.

440   Temporal prepositional phrases as attributes to nouns: за + accusative, от + genitive

(1) **За** + accusative is used to denote a journal publication date:

«*Мета́лл*» **за апре́ль**   the journal *Metall* for this April
э́того го́да

(2) **От** + genitive denotes the date of a document:

письмо́ **от пе́рвого а́вгуста**   a letter of 1 August

441   Positioning an event within a time span: среди́ + genitive, мѐжду + instrumental

Среди́ denotes 'in the middle of': **среди́ но́чи** 'in the middle of the night' (note also **средь бе́ла дня** 'in broad daylight'). **Мѐжду** positions an event between two other events: **мѐжду двумя́ во́йнами** 'between two wars', он отдыха́л **мѐжду обе́дом и у́жином** 'he relaxed between lunch and dinner'.

442   Coincidence in time: при + prepositional

При is used in a number of contexts denoting coincidence in time:

(1) 'In the presence of':

при свиде́телях   in the presence of witnesses

(2) 'In the (life-)time of', 'during' (see **430** note (b)):

при жи́зни А́ни   in Anya's lifetime
при Ста́лине   in Stalin's time, under Stalin

(3) It governs:

(i) The nouns **вид, звук, мысль, сло́во/слова́**:

при ви́де Петро́ва (= **когда́** я уви́дел Петро́ва)
at the sight of Petrov (= **when** I saw Petrov)

при зву́ке звонка́
at the sound of the bell

Он содрогну́лся **при одно́й мы́сли** о пораже́нии
He shuddered at the mere thought of defeat

При э́тих слова́х она́ побледне́ла
She grew pale at these words

(ii) Nouns that denote a source of light:

Он чита́л **при све́те ла́мпы/при ла́мпе**
He was reading by the light of a lamp

(iii) The noun **возмо́жность** 'opportunity':

при ка́ждой/пе́рвой возмо́жности
at every/the first opportunity

(iv) Nouns denoting various types of state or circumstance:

при таки́х обстоя́тельствах
in the circumstances

при температу́ре три́дцать гра́дусов
at a temperature of thirty degrees

(v) Verbal and some other abstract nouns:

При взлёте у́ровень шу́мов достига́л 112 децибе́л
On (= during) take-off engine noise reached 112 decibels

При перево́зке ме́бели бы́ло разби́то не́сколько сту́льев
Several chairs were broken during the move

(vi) Nouns that denote a social order:

при социали́зме	under socialism
при сове́тской вла́сти	under Soviet power
при э́том режи́ме	under this regime

Note
При́ смерти 'at death's door'.

Other Meanings

443   Prepositions with causal meaning

The following prepositions are used to denote the cause of an action or state:

(1) Из-за + genitive/благодаря́ + dative

Из-за and **благодаря́** are used when the cause of an action is *external* to the subject, **из-за** being preferred when the outcome is unfavourable and **благодаря́** when it is favourable:

По́езд опозда́л **из-за тума́на**
The train was late because of the fog

Я провали́лся **из-за тебя́**
I failed because of you

Благодаря́ вам я вы́жил
Thanks to you I survived

Note

The distinction between **из-за** and **благодаря** is sometimes blurred, **благодаря** being used on occasion as a synonym of **из-за**, in particular when the outcome is neutral from the subject's point of view.

(2) От + genitive in the meaning 'physical cause'

Phrases with **от** + genitive denote the physical cause of a state or process:

доро́га, мо́края **от дождя́**	a road wet with rain
боль **от ожо́га**	pain from a burn
Он у́мер **от ра́ка**	He died of cancer

(3) От/из + genitive in the meaning 'emotional cause'

Both **от** and **из** combine with nouns of feeling which provoke a reaction on the part of the subject:

(i) Phrases with **от** imply an **involuntary or spontaneous reaction:**

Он запла́кал **от ра́дости**	He wept **with joy**
Она́ дрожи́т **от стра́ха**	She is trembling **with fear**
Он покрасне́л **от стыда́**	He blushed **with shame**

(ii) Phrases with **из** denote that the feeling experienced motivates a **deliberate action** on the part of the subject:

уби́йство **из ре́вности**	murder **motivated by jealousy**
Он солга́л **из стра́ха**	He lied **out of fear**
Он отказа́лся **из** **упря́мства**	He refused **out of obstinacy**

(4) От/с + genitive

(i) **С** + genitive expresses causal meanings similar to those expressed by **от**. Often the prepositions are interchangeable when the dependent noun denotes:

(a) A feeling: пла́кать **от стра́ха/со стра́ха/со стра́ху** 'to weep with fear'.

(b) A physical sensation or state: умере́ть **от го́лода/с го́лоду** 'to starve to death'.

Note

In such examples the phrases in **c** incline towards the *colloquial*.

(ii) **C** + genitive is common in figurative usage: умира́ть **со ску́ки/со́ сме́ху** 'to die of boredom/laughing'.

(iii) It also appears in certain set expressions:

уста́ть **с доро́ги**	to get tired from the journey
с непривы́чки	due to lack of practice
ни с того́ ни с сего́	for no particular reason

(5) По + dative

Phrases with **по** + dative case express causal meaning:

(i) When the dependent noun itself is causal (**причи́на** 'cause' etc.):

По како́му по́воду вы об э́том вспо́мнили?	What made you think of that?
по како́й причи́не?	for what reason?
по фина́нсовым соображе́ниям	for financial considerations

(ii) When the dependent noun denotes handicaps or drawbacks associated with:

(a) Ill-health:

по боле́зни
due to sickness

По сла́бости здоро́вья он почти́ не покида́ет го́рода
Because of poor health he hardly leaves the town

(b) Age or inexperience:

Сын **по мо́лодости** не понима́ет её
Her son does not understand her because of his youth

Нигде́ уже́ не рабо́тал **по ста́рости**
He had stopped working altogether due to old age

(c) Negative character traits:

Ма́льчик э́то сде́лал **по глу́пости**
The boy did this out of stupidity

Note

Из-за would be used, however, if there was a change in subject:

Из-за его́ глу́пости пострада́ли его́ друзья́
His friends suffered because of his stupidity

(d) Error, ignorance:

По вине́ води́теля происхо́дит 8 из 10 ава́рий	Eight out of ten road accidents are caused by driver error
по оши́бке, недосмо́тру	by mistake, due to an oversight

Note also брак **по расчёту** 'marriage of convenience'.

(6) За + instrumental

(i) The spatial origins of the causal meanings of **за** + instrumental are evident in examples such as **За стено́й** не ви́дно 'You can see nothing for the wall' (lit. 'behind the wall').

(ii) **За** also combines with nouns that denote:

(a) Absence:

Лаборато́рия не рабо́тает **за неиме́нием** лабора́нта
The laboratory is not functioning for want of a laboratory assistant

Его́ оправда́ли **за отсу́тствием** ули́к
He was acquitted for lack of evidence

(b) Worthlessness:

бро́сить **за него́дностью**
to discard as worthless

Про́дали **за нена́добностью**
It was sold as surplus to requirements

Note also the compound causal prepositions **в результа́те** 'as a result of' and **всле́дствие** 'in consequence of'. Both take the genitive case.

444 Prepositions that denote the object of feelings and attitudes

(1) К + dative

К is used to denote the object of many feelings and attitudes:

Она́ **ве́жлива**	**ко** всем	She is **polite**	**to** everyone
Он **добр**	**к** живо́тным	He is **kind**	**to** animals
интере́с	**к** этимоло́гии	**interest**	**in** etymology
любо́вь	**к** ро́дине	**love**	**for** the homeland
относи́ться	**к**	**to relate to, to**	**treat** (someone)
презре́ние	**к** врагу́	**scorn**	**for** an enemy

Note

C + instrumental is used in certain combinations: Ла́ра **ве́жлива со все́ми** 'Lara is polite to everyone' (cf. ве́жлива ко всем, above), **Я** была́ с **ва́ми груба́** 'I was rude to you', Суд был **строг с** подсуди́-мыми 'The court was hard on the defendants'. Compare **обраща́ться с** + instrumental 'to treat'.

(2) На + accusative

На + accusative denotes the object of anger and similar emotions:

Он **негодова́л**	**на** неё	He was indignant	with her
Я **оби́делся**	**на** его́ слова́	I took offence	at his words
Он **серди́т/зол**	**на** меня́	He is angry	with me
Я **таи́ла**	**на** неё мно́го	I nursed many	
	оби́д	grudges	against her

(3) Перед + instrumental

Phrases with **перед** denote the object of feelings of guilt, duty, responsibility, fear, embarrassment, ingratiation, defiance etc.:

Я **винова́т**	**перед** ва́ми	I owe you an apology
долг	**перед** ро́диной	duty to the homeland
заи́скивать	**перед** нача́льником	to ingratiate oneself with the boss
Он **извини́лся**	**перед** ни́ми	He apologized to them
Отвеча́ю	**перед** роди́телями	I am responsible to the parents
страх	**перед** сме́ртью	fear of death
Ему́ **сты́дно**	**перед** сами́м собо́й	He is ashamed of himself

(4) По + dative

Phrases in **по** + dative denote the object of yearning, grieving etc.:

скуча́ть	**по** де́тям	to miss the children
тоска́	**по** ро́дине	homesickness
Она́ **в тра́уре**	**по** му́жу	She is in mourning for her husband

(First- and second-person pronouns appear in the *prepositional* case after such verbs: скуча́ли **по нас, вас** 'they missed us, you'. Third-person pronouns appear in the dative or prepositional.)

Note

The compound prepositions **в отноше́нии** + genitive, **по отноше́нию к**: щепети́льный **в отноше́нии** свои́х обя́занностей/**по отноше́нию к** свои́м обя́занностям 'punctilious **with respect to** his obligations'.

445   Prepositions that denote extent

Some prepositions denote extent in its various forms: the dimensions of an object, quantitative difference and so on.

(1) B + accusative

B + accusative is used to quantify a dimension:

(i) In terms of objects:

кабели толщиной **в руку**   cables the thickness of one's arm

(ii) In terms of conventional units of measurement:

река глубиной	**в три метра**	a river	three metres deep
гора высотой	**в тысячу метров**	a mountain	1,000 metres high
площадь шириной	**в пятьдесят метров**	a square	50 metres wide

Note
(a)   The dimension word appears in the instrumental in such constructions, but questions about dimension are posed in the genitive: **Какого он роста?** 'How tall is he?'
(b)   The dimension word can be omitted altogether where it is obvious which dimension is meant: турбина (мощностью) **в двести тысяч киловатт** 'a 200,000-kilowatt turbine', места (стоимостью) **в семьдесят рублей** '70-rouble seats'.
(c)   Conversely, **в** may be omitted where the dimension word is retained, especially in journalistic, colloquial and technical styles: гора высотой **(в) пять тысяч метров** 'a mountain 5,000 metres high'.

B + accusative is also used in comparative constructions with **раз**:

Его дом **в три раза** больше моего
His house is three times bigger than mine

(2) B + prepositional

(i) **B** governs the prepositional of nouns that denote extent, scale etc.:

в крупном масштабе   on a large scale
в какой-то мере   in some measure

Природа изучена **в такой степени**, что неожиданности вряд ли возможны

Nature has been studied to such a degree that surprises are hardly possible

(ii) In some constructions with **сте́пень, в** and **до** are synonymous: **в/до не́которой сте́пени** 'to a certain extent', **в/до тако́й сте́пени** 'to such a degree', but **в** is preferred in the lower and comparative ranges: **в ма́лой сте́пени** 'to a small extent', **в бо́льшей сте́пени** 'to a greater extent', **в ра́зной сте́пени** 'to varying degrees'.

(3) До + genitive

(i) The central meaning of **до** is 'limit' or 'extent':

роди́тели, име́ющие **челове́к дете́й**	**до пяти́**	parents having up to five children
наку́риваться	**до тошноты́**	to smoke to the point of nausea
доводи́ть	**до слёз**	to reduce to tears

Note also the set expressions

Он промо́к **ни́тки**	**до косте́й/до после́дней**	He got soaked to the skin
Он эго́ист	**до мо́зга косте́й**	He is an egoist to the core
вы́пить всё	**до после́дней ка́пли**	to drain to the last drop
танцева́ть	**до упа́ду**	to dance till you drop

(ii) **До** also combines with **сте́пень** (see (2) (ii) above).

(4) За + accusative

The preposition is used in constructions that denote excess:

Моро́з уже́	**за три́дцать**	There are already over thirty degrees of frost
Бы́ло	**за́ полночь**	It was past midnight
Ему́	**за со́рок**	He is over forty
Давле́ние перевали́ло атмосфе́р	**за́ сто**	The pressure exceeded 100 atmospheres

(5) На + accusative

На + accusative case denotes quantification:

(i) With comparatives (see also **182** (2) (i)):

| Он **на три го́да** ста́рше меня́ | He is three years older than me |

(ii) In terms of:

(a) Percentages and fractions:

| Земля́ **на три че́тверти** океа́н | The Earth is three-quarters ocean |
| выполня́ть но́рму **на сто пять** проце́нтов | to fulfil one's norm by 105% |

(b) Ratio/distribution:

На ка́ждые три кварти́ры должно́ быть два телефо́на
There should be two telephones to every three apartments

(c) Monetary value:

| штрафова́ть **на 500 рубле́й** | to fine 500 roubles |
| **на 300** (рубле́й) ма́рок | 300 roubles' worth of stamps |

(d) Scholastic achievement:

| учи́ться **на кру́глые пятёрки** | to get straight As |

(e) Projection through space:

бег	**на ты́сячу ме́тров**	1,000 metres race
Сосна́ простира́ется **на полтора́ста киломе́тров**		The pines extend for 150 kilometres
Кричи́т	**на весь двор**	He shouts so loud as to be heard over the whole yard

(6) О̀коло + genitive

О̀коло denotes approximation:

о̀коло ме́тра	about a metre
о̀коло ча́са	about an hour
о̀коло двух неде́ль	about two weeks

Note
Unlike **с** + accusative (see (8)), **о̀коло** combines only with nouns that denote units of measurement.

(7) Поря́дка + genitive

Поря́дка + genitive denotes approximate numerical quantity:

Це́ны **поря́дка двадцати́–тридцати́ до́лларов**
Prices of the order of 20–30 dollars

До ближа́йшей дере́вни **поря́дка пяти́десяти киломе́тров**
(*Moskovskii komsomolets*)
It is about fifty kilometres to the nearest village

(8) С + accusative

С + accusative expresses many types of approximation (cf. (6)):

Он про́жил там	**с ме́сяц**	He spent about a month there
Он ро́стом	**с сестру́**	He is about the same height as his sister
ми́на величино́й	**с таре́лку**	a mine about the size of a plate

446   Prepositions that denote purpose

Many prepositional phrases denote the purpose for which an action is performed or for which an object is designed:

(1) В + accusative

В + accusative appears in a number of phrases which denote the purpose of an action:

Он вы́ступил	**в защи́ту** свои́х прав	He spoke up in defence of his rights
Я по́днял о́бе руки́	**в знак** примире́ния	I raised both arms as a token of reconciliation
Посади́ли де́рево	**в па́мять** о па́вших во́инах	They planted a tree in memory of soldiers who fell in battle
Устро́или приём	**в честь** отца́	They arranged a reception in honour of father

(2) Для + genitive 'meant for/designed for'

па́пка	**для бума́г**	a file for documents
общежи́тие	**для студе́нтов**	a residence for students

Note

(a)   **Для** can also govern a verbal noun: Учёные собрали́сь **для**

обсужде́ния ря́да вопро́сов (= что́бы обсуди́ть ряд вопро́сов) 'The scientists gathered for a discussion of a number of questions'.

(b)   The set phrases **для ве́рности** 'just to make sure', **для ви́да** 'for the sake of appearances', **для разнообра́зия** 'for a change'.

(3) За + accusative

За + accusative denotes the object of struggle, competition etc.:

боро́ться	**за** незави́симость	to struggle for independence
соревнова́ться урожа́и	**за** высо́кие	to compete for high-yield harvests

(4) За + instrumental in the meaning 'for/to fetch'

идти́	**за водо́й**	to go	for water
Я зашёл	**за свои́м дру́гом**	I called	for my friend
о́чередь	**за хле́бом**	a queue	for bread

Note usage in abstract contexts: Он обрати́лся ко мне **за сове́том/по́мощью** 'He turned to me for advice/help'.

(5) На + accusative

На + accusative denotes:

(i) A profession aspired to (constructions with **учи́ться**):

учи́ться на инжене́ра   to study to be an engineer

(ii) A quality, the presence/evaluation of which is the object of testing:

испы́тывать но́вый шлем **на про́чность**
to test a new helmet for strength

(iii) The purpose of a precautionary measure (constructions with **слу́чай**):

Она́ взяла́ с собо́й зо́нтик **на слу́чай дождя́**
She took an umbrella with her in case of rain

Note
На вся́кий слу́чай 'just in case/to be on the safe side':

Спусти́лся в овра́г, **на вся́кий слу́чай** с ножо́м в руке́ (Aitmatov)
He descended into the gully with a knife in his hand, just to be on the safe side

(6) O + prepositional

O + prepositional can denote the purpose of a request or plea:

крик, призы́в о по́мощи	a cry, an appeal for help
про́сьба о деньга́х	a request for money

(7) По + dative (constructions with **де́ло/дела́** 'business')

Éду в го́род **по де́лу/дела́м** I am going to town on business

(8) Под + accusative

Под + accusative denotes the function for which an area is designated:

Да́ли зе́млю **под огоро́ды**
They allocated land for market gardens

ко́мнаты, отведённые **под музе́й**
rooms ear-marked for a museum

Note also **в интере́сах** 'in the interests of' and **в це́лях** 'for the purpose of' (both + genitive): **в це́лях** повыше́ния производи́-тельности труда́ 'for the purpose of increasing labour productivity' (cf. **с це́лью** 'with the aim of', which normally combines with a verbal noun or an infinitive).

447   Concessive meanings expressed by prepositions

(1) **Несмотря́ на** + accusative 'despite' is the commonest of the concessive prepositions:

Несмотря́ на плоху́ю пого́ду, они́ игра́ли в те́ннис
Despite the bad weather, they played tennis

(2) **Вопреки́** + dative 'contrary to', **невзира́я на** + accusative 'despite, regardless of', **напереко́р** + dative 'in defiance of' relate to more official styles: **вопреки́ прика́зу** 'contrary to orders'.

(3) **При** may also be used with concessive meaning, especially in combination with **весь** 'all':

При всём своём тала́нте он не годи́тся в мини́стры
For all his talent he is not cut out to be a minister

При всём жела́нии не могу́ вам помо́чь
Much as I would like to I cannot help you

448　По + dative/accusative in distributive meaning

In distributive meanings **по** combines:

(1) With the dative of singular nouns:

> Он дал ученика́м **по уче́бнику**
> He gave the pupils a book each

> В 25% семе́й бы́ло **по одному́ ребёнку**
> 25% of families had one child each

(2) With the accusative of two, three and four (also 200, 300 and 400):

> Мы вы́пили **по две ча́шки** We drank two cups each

(3) With the dative *or* accusative of other numerals, the dependent noun appearing in the *genitive plural*:

> Нам да́ли **по пяти́/по пять тетра́дей**
> They gave us five exercise books each

Note
The accusative, formerly confined mainly to colloquial styles, is now freely used in written styles also:

> За стола́ми сиде́ло **по де́сять студе́нтов**
> At each of the tables sat ten students

> Рабо́тают **по семь часо́в** в день
> They work seven hours a day

> Трои́м из них бы́ло **по трина́дцать** (Marinina)
> Three of them were thirteen years old

(4) Indefinite numerals are found in either case:

> Э́ти слова́ име́ют **по не́сколько/не́скольку** значе́ний
> These words have several meanings each

Note
A distributive phrase in **по** may function as:

(a) The subject

> По о́бе стороны́ пара́дной име́лось **по балко́ну**
> There was a balcony at either side of the main entrance

(b) The object:

Сжима́л в ка́ждой руке́ **по пистоле́ту**
He gripped a pistol in each hand

(c) A temporal expression:

Остана́вливаются два по́езда в су́тки, ка́ждый **стои́т по три мину́ты**
Two trains a day stop here, each for three minutes at a time

(d) An attribute:

Четы́ре биле́та **по два́дцать рубле́й**
Four tickets at twenty roubles each

Note the colloquial phrase **По чём**? 'how much?' (each): По чём я́блоки? 'How much are apples?' (each).

Other Important Meanings Expressed by Prepositions

449   Prepositions that take the accusative

(1) **В**

В + accusative denotes:

(i) The target of throwing, knocking, shooting etc. (see also **451** (2) (iv)):

Он бро́сил	**в меня́** поду́шку	He threw a pillow	**at me**
Он вы́стрелил	**в цель**	He fired	**at the target**
Он ра́нен	**в го́лову**	He is wounded	**in the head**
стуча́ть	**в дверь**	to knock	**on/at the door**
Он уда́рил меня́	**в че́люсть**	He punched me	**on the jaw**

(ii) A game (constructions with **игра́ть**; see also **453** (2) (i)):

игра́ть **в футбо́л/пря́тки**   to play football/hide and seek

(iii) The object of belief/infatuation:

ве́рить **в социали́зм**   to believe in socialism
Он влюби́лся **в медсестру́**   He fell in love with a nurse

(iv) An object looked/shouted into or through:

Он **в бино́кль** рассма́тривает ре́ку
He examines the river through binoculars

смотре́ть на себя́	**в зе́ркало**	to look at oneself in the mirror
смотре́ть	**в окно́**	to look out of the window
кри́кнуть	**в мегафо́н**	to shout through a megaphone

(v) A professional or other group (note that what appears to be the nominative plural in these constructions is historically an *accusative*):

Он не годи́тся	**в музыка́нты**	He is not cut out to be a musician
идти́	**в го́сти**	to go visiting
произвести́	**в офице́ры**	to commission

Note that the idea of plurality is lost in many such expressions: Он годи́тся ей в отцы́ 'He is old enough to be her father'.

(2) За

Constructions with **за** involve:

(i) Thanking, paying, rewarding, punishing for:

меда́ль	**за отва́гу**	a medal	**for bravery**
Его́ наказа́ли	**за оши́бку**	He was punished	**for the mistake**
Она́ пла́тит ему́	**за молоко́**	She pays him	**for the milk**
продава́ть	**за 1000 рубле́й**	to sell	**for 1,000 roubles**
спаси́бо	**за сове́т**	thanks	**for the advice**

(ii) Identifying, evaluating as:

Он вы́дал себя́ **за специали́ста**
He passed himself off **as an expert**

Принима́ли её **за мою́ де́вушку**
They took her **for my girl friend**

Он слывёт **за знатока́**
He passes **for a connoisseur**

(iii) Seizing, holding, leading by:

Я взял И́нку **за́ руку**	I took Inka **by the hand**
Он схвати́лся **за́ голову**	He clutched **his head**

(iv) Feelings experienced on behalf of someone else:

Она́ бои́тся **за меня́**	She is afraid **for me**
Я рад **за тебя́**	I am glad **for you**

(v) The meaning 'in favour of':

Я голосова́л **за вас**	I voted for you
пить **за здоро́вье** отца́	to drink to father's health

Note

Что за in the meaning **како́й** does not affect the case of the dependent noun: Что за **му́ка**! 'What torment!', Что э́то за **друзья́**? 'What kind of friends are those?', Что за **кни́гу** она́ купи́ла? 'What kind of book did she buy?'

(3) На

(i) **На** has many literal and figurative meanings which denote various forms of direction, allocation, expenditure etc.:

жа́ловаться на пита́ние	to complain about the food
зака́з на пла́тье	an order for a dress
лес на постро́йку	timber for building
мо́да/спрос на иностра́нные маши́ны	fashion/demand for foreign cars
наде́яться на успе́х/**на** бра́та	to hope for success/rely on one's brother
обменя́ть кварти́ру **на** да́чу	to exchange a flat for a country cottage
обраща́ть внима́ние на сове́т	to pay attention to advice
ока́зывать давле́ние на кого́-нибудь	to put pressure on someone
охо́титься на во́лка	to hunt a wolf
пра́во на о́тдых	the right to relaxation
производи́ть впечатле́ние на дру́га	to make an impression on a friend
рабо́тать на семью́	to work for one's family
реце́пт на лека́рство	a prescription for medicine
смотре́ть на ка́рту	to look at a map
тра́тить вре́мя на пустяки́/ **де́ньги на** конфе́ты	to spend time on trifles/money on sweets
что на обе́д?	what's for lunch?

(ii) The main verb or adjective may denote resolve:

Он **гото́в на** всё	He is prepared to go to any lengths
идти́ на риск	to take a risk

Note
Гото́в на implies desperate resolve, **гото́в к** only preparedness.

(iii) The main verb, adjective or noun may express reaction:

отвеча́ть на вопро́с	to answer a question
реа́кция на кри́тику	reaction to criticism

(4) О

О + accusative denotes the object of collision, friction, pressure etc.:

Во́лны **разбива́ются о** ри́фы	The waves smash against the reefs
Она́ **споткну́лась о** ка́мень	She tripped over a stone
Он **уда́рился ного́й о** стул	He struck his leg against a chair

(5) Под

Под + accusative implies:

(i) 'Support' for the dependent noun (usually **рука́** or **ру́ки**):

Его́ подде́рживали **по́д руки**
They were supporting him by the arms

Они́ прогу́ливаются **по́д руку**
They are strolling about arm in arm

(ii) 'Accompaniment':

танцева́ть **под орке́стр**	to dance to an orchestra
Она́ се́ла **под бу́рные аплодисме́нты**	She sat down to tumultuous applause

(iii) 'Imitation', 'adaptation to style' etc.:

Он пел **под Шаля́пина**
He sang in imitation of Shalyapin

комо́д **под кра́сное де́рево**
an imitation mahogany sideboard

стри́чься **под ма́льчика**
to have one's hair cut like a boy's

450   Prepositions that take the genitive

(1) Для

Для can have a comparative/relative meaning:

| Тепло́ **для ноября́** | It is warm for November |

(2) Из

Из denotes source:

Э́то я узна́л	**из газе́т**	I learnt that from the papers
Он	**из рабо́чей семьи́**	He is from a working-class family
посу́да	**из гли́ны**	crockery made of clay
Оди́н	**из нас** помо́жет	One of us will help
Со́лнце состои́т	**из водоро́да и ге́лия**	The sun consists of hydrogen and helium

(3) Из-под

Из-под denotes the former content of a container:

| буты́лка **из-под молока́** | a milk bottle/empty milk bottle |

Compare буты́лка **молока́** 'a bottle of milk'.

(4) От

(i) **От** appears in contexts involving protection, evasion, riddance etc.:

возде́рживаться	от голосова́ния	to abstain from voting
защища́ть го́род	от врага́	to defend the town against an enemy
избавля́ться	от привы́чки	to get rid of a habit
Она́ отказа́лась	от обе́да	She refused lunch

(ii) This also applies in curative contexts:

| лека́рство | **от ка́шля** | cough medicine |
| лечи́ть ма́льчика | **от дифтери́та** | to treat the boy for diphtheria |

(5) С

С + genitive is used:

(i) With verbs of beginning:

| Их дру́жба **начала́сь с дра́ки** | Their friendship began with a fight |

(ii) To indicate the spelling of initial letters:

писа́ть сло́во **с большо́й/ма́лой бу́квы**
to spell a word with a capital/a small letter

Note

Через is used with *non*-initial letters: Сло́во 'парашю́т' пи́шется **через ю** 'The word парашю́т is spelt with a ю'.

(iii) To denote 'permission':

Приезжа́йте ещё — то́лько **с разреше́ния роди́телей**
Come again, but with your parents' permission

(6) У

У denotes the person from whom something is bought, borrowed, stolen, from whom lessons are taken, of whom a request is made etc.:

Беру́	**у него́** уро́ки	I take lessons from him
заказа́ть костю́м	**у портно́го**	to order a suit from a tailor
Он занима́ет	**у них** де́ньги	He borrows money from them
Я купи́л дом	**у дя́ди**	I bought the house from my uncle
Я мно́гому научи́лся	**у э́того па́рня**	I learnt a lot from this chap
Я попроси́л	**у него́** ру́чку	I asked him for a pen
Спроси́те доро́гу	**у милиционе́ра**	Ask a policeman the way
У меня́ укра́ли часы́		I had my watch stolen

Note

(a) **От** is used, however, when the subject is a passive recipient (Я получи́л письмо́ **от отца́** 'I received a letter from my father') and **с** + genitive in contexts denoting the exaction of due payment, tax etc. (собира́ть нало́г **с ча́стников** 'to collect tax from private owners', Ско́лько **с меня́**? 'How much do I owe you?').

(b) **Узна́ть** 'to learn, find out' combines with either **от** or **у**, **от** implying passive, **у** active participation: Э́то я узна́л **от неё** 'I heard that from her', Э́то я узна́л **у неё** 'I found that out from her'.

451   Prepositions that take the dative

(1) К

К is used:

(i) To relate a part, component or supplement to the whole:

увертю́ра к «*Пи́ковой да́ме*» the overture to *Queen of Spades*

(ii) With **гото́в** 'ready', **гото́виться** 'to prepare', **гото́вность** 'readiness':

гото́в к труду́ и оборо́не	ready for labour and defence

(iii) With nouns that denote emotional reaction to an event or impression:

к сожале́нию	unfortunately
к сча́стью	fortunately
к моему́ удивле́нию	to my surprise

(2) По

По is used:

(i) With nouns that denote means of communication:

по желе́зной доро́ге	by rail
по (àвиа)по́чте	by (air)mail
по второ́й програ́мме	on channel two
по ра́дио, по телеви́зору/ **телеви́дению** (also **на телеви́дении**)	on the radio, on TV

Разгово́р на э́ту те́му состои́тся **по городско́му ка́бельному телеви́дению** (*Argumenty i fakty*)
A conversation on this subject will take place on municipal cable television

по телефо́ну	on the telephone
по моби́льному	on a mobile
по фа́ксу	by fax

Note:
броди́ть по Интерне́ту 'to surf the Internet', but **в Интерне́те** 'on the Internet', **на Интерне́т-са́йте** 'at a web-site'.

(ii) In the meaning 'according to', 'by' etc.:

по приглаше́нию	by invitation
по про́сьбе	at the request of
по расписа́нию, пла́ну	according to the timetable, the plan
По мои́м часа́м (or на мои́х часа́х) уже́ по́лночь	By my watch it's already midnight

(iii) To denote a criterion for judgment:

Врач су́дит о здоро́вье ребёнка **по цве́ту** его́ лица́
A doctor judges the health of a child by its complexion

(iv) To denote a target, especially a moving or diffuse target (cf. **449** (1) (i)):

| Откры́ли ого́нь | **по врагу́** | They opened fire on the enemy |
| стреля́ть | **по демонстра́нтам** | to fire on the demonstrators |

Compare also **стуча́ть по столу́** 'to bang on the table' and **стуча́ть в дверь** 'to knock at the door' (see **449** (1) (i)).

(v) To define the 'frame of reference' of persons, groups, objects etc.:

инжене́р	**по профе́ссии**	engineer by profession
чемпио́н	**по бо́ксу**	boxing champion
экза́мен	**по исто́рии**	history examination

(vi) With ordinal numerals, to denote position in a scale of dimensions or priorities:

А́фрика — **второ́й по величине́** матери́к
Africa is the second largest continent

452   Prepositions that take the instrumental

(1) За

За links verbs of observation, supervision to their objects:

| Ко́шка наблюда́ла | **за соба́кой** | The cat was observing the dog |
| Он следи́л | **за разви́тием** те́хники | He was following the development of technology |

(2) С

(i) The central meaning of **с** is 'with/together with/accompanied by' etc.:

| ма́льчик | **с у́дочкой в руке́** | a boy with a rod in his hand |
| челове́к | **с краси́вым лицо́м** | a man with a handsome face |

Я согла́сен	**с ва́ми**	I agree with you
Он говори́т	**с акце́нтом**	He speaks with an accent
Она́ слу́шала	**с интере́сом**	She listened with interest
Он реши́л зада́чу	**с трудо́м**	He had difficulty in solving the problem

Note

(a) **Со ско́ростью** 'at a speed': Он е́хал **со ско́ростью** пятьдеся́т киломе́тров в час 'He was driving at a speed of fifty kilometres per hour'.

(b) **Развести́сь с** 'to divorce', **расста́ться с** 'to part with', while denoting separation, retain the meaning of joint involvement.

(c) Nouns and pronouns can be linked by **с**: мы с ва́ми 'you and I', они́ с сестро́й 'he and his sister', оте́ц с ма́терью 'father and mother'. Note also хлеб с ма́слом 'bread and butter'. A plural verb is used if the nouns are of equal status: Оте́ц с ма́терью отказа́лись помо́чь 'Father and mother refused to help'. Otherwise a singular verb is used: Мать с ребёнком пошла́ в больни́цу 'The mother went to the hospital with the child'.

(d) A nuance of purpose: обраща́ться к кому́-нибудь **с про́сьбой** 'to make a request of somebody', Премье́р-мини́стр прие́хал в Герма́нию с **визи́том** 'The prime minister arrived in Germany on a visit'.

(e) See **94** for constructions in which 'with' is rendered by a simple instrumental (писа́ть **карандашо́м** 'to write with a pencil').

(ii) **С** is used with the names of public service vehicles when these are qualified by adjectives:

прие́хать **с ра́нним, с двухчасовы́м** по́ездом
to arrive on the early, the two o'clock train (cf. прие́хать **по́ездом** 'to arrive by train')

453   Prepositions that take the prepositional

(1) В

(i) **В** links verbs, adjectives, nouns denoting 'guilt', 'suspicion', 'confession', 'certainty', 'doubt', 'reproach' to their objects:

Всех шестеры́х **обвиня́ли во взры́ве комендату́ры**
All six were accused of blowing up the commandant's office

Он был аресто́ван **по подозре́нию в кра́же**
He was arrested on suspicion of theft

Он **призна́лся**	**в уби́йстве**	He confessed to the murder
Я **сомнева́юсь**	**в э́том**	I doubt that
Она́ **уве́рена**	**в себе́**	She is sure of herself
Его́ **упрека́ют**	**в ле́ни**	He is reproached with laziness

(ii) The dependent noun may also define the context of forms such as **беда́** 'trouble', **де́ло** 'matter, fact', **причи́на** 'cause' etc.:

Беда́ в том, что он её лю́бит
The trouble is that he loves her

Де́ло в том, что он ненадёжный
The fact is that he is unreliable

(2) На

The dependent noun may denote:

(i) A musical instrument:

игра́ть **на скри́пке**   to play the violin

(ii) A language:

Он говори́т **на трёх языка́х**   He speaks three languages

(3) О

The central meaning of **о** + prepositional is 'concerning', 'about':

ду́мать	**о пла́не**	to think about the plan
зако́н	**о разво́де**	divorce law
напомина́ть кому́-нибудь	**о до́лге**	to remind someone of their duty
мысль	**о сча́стье**	the thought of happiness

Note
Про + accusative is a colloquial synonym of **о** 'about'.

(4) При

При can mean 'in view of', 'thanks to', 'with', 'given':

При тако́м тала́нте он ста́нет знамени́тостью
With talent like that he will become a celebrity

При её обая́нии не ка́ждая же́нщина помеша́ла бы ей блиста́ть
With her charm not every woman would be able to prevent her from standing out

The Conjunction

(1) Conjunctions fulfil a cohesive function in linking words and concepts to create connected speech.

(2) They fall into the following broad categories:

(i) **Co-ordinating conjunctions** link words and clauses of comparable status (bread *and* butter, young *but* experienced etc.). They subdivide into connective, adversative and disjunctive.

(ii) **Subordinating conjunctions** introduce statements that are dependent on the main clause (he said *that* he had no objection; I called the doctor, *because* I felt unwell; I want to play tennis, *if* the weather improves etc.). They subdivide into explanatory, causal, conditional, concessive, comparative and temporal conjunctions, and conjunctions of purpose and result.

Many compound conjunctions, traditionally separated by a comma, can now also be written without: ввиду того (,) что 'in view of the fact that'; до того (,) как 'before'; из-за того (,) что 'because of the fact that'; после того (,) как 'after'; с тех пор (,) как 'since' etc. The use of a comma throws the meaning expressed by the subordinate clause into greater relief.

Co-ordinating Conjunctions

455   Connective conjunctions

(1) **И** 'and'

И links:

(i) Like parts of speech:

Брат **и** сестра́	Brother and sister
Она́ поёт **и** игра́ет	She sings and plays

(ii) Compatible ideas:

Свети́ло со́лнце, **и** бы́ло жа́рко
The sun was shining and it was hot

(2) И . . . и 'both . . . and'

(i) **И . . . и** lend greater emphasis than **и**:

Он **и** спосо́бный, **и** трудолюби́вый
He is both capable and industrious

(ii) The same meaning may be expressed:

(a) Ву **как . . . так и** (a mark of a more literary style):

Таки́е вопро́сы интересу́ют мно́гих специали́стов **как** в Росси́и, **так и** в зарубе́жных стра́нах
Such questions interest many specialists both in Russia and abroad

(b) With still greater emphasis, by **не то́лько . . . но и** (also characteristic of a bookish style): Он говори́т **не то́лько** по-кита́йски, **но и** по-япо́нски 'He speaks not only Chinese but also Japanese'.

(3) Ни . . . ни 'neither . . . nor'

Он не получи́л **ни** пи́сем, **ни** газе́т
He received neither letters nor newspapers

Note
(a)   The second **ни** ('nor') is preceded by a comma.

(b) **Не** is normally required only when there is a single predicate: Ни
он, ни она́ **не игра́ет** (single predicate) на фле́йте 'Neither he nor
she plays the flute'. Compare the absence of **не** in Она́ ни игра́ет,
ни поёт 'She neither plays nor sings' and Он ни ру́сский, ни
поля́к 'He is neither a Russian nor a Pole', where there are two
predicates (**игра́ет/поёт**; **ру́сский/поля́к**). **Не** is retained,
however, in constructions involving the past or future of **быть** 'to
be' (or other copula): Вчера́ **не́ было**/за́втра **не бу́дет** ни
хо́лодно, ни жа́рко 'Yesterday it was not/tomorrow it will neither
be cold nor hot'. Note also usage with **нельзя́**: С ним **нельзя́** ни
хитри́ть, ни шути́ть (Zalygin) 'With him you can neither pretend
nor joke'.

(c) If there are two subjects, the predicate must be compatible with
both: Ни он, ни она́ не **зна́ет** 'Neither he nor she knows' (зна́ет
agrees with он and with она́), but Ни он, ни она́ не **зна́ли**
'Neither he nor she knew', Ни он, ни она́ не **дово́льны** 'Neither
he nor she is pleased', Ни он, ни я не **говори́м** по-по́льски
'Neither he nor I speak Polish'.

456   Adversative conjunctions

(1) A 'and, but, whereas'

The conjunction **а**:

(i) links ideas which contrast without conflicting. The same parts of
speech usually appear on either side of the conjunction:

Он сиди́т,	**а** я стою́	He sits and I stand
Это ко́шка,	**а** это соба́ка	That is a cat and that is a dog

(ii) introduces a positive statement via a preceding negative:

Приро́да **не** храм,	**а** мастерска́я	Nature is not a temple, but a workshop
Он **не** пи́шет,	**а** чита́ет	He is not writing but reading
Кни́га **не** бе́лая,	**а** кра́сная	The book is not white, but red

Note
The order of the clauses may be reversed:

А́страхань, Сара́тов — города́ на Во́лге, **а не** на Дону́
(Vvedenskaya)
Astrakhan and Saratov are towns on the Volga and not on the Don

(iii) introduces a supplementary statement or question:

А где други́е го́сти?   And where are the other guests?

Note the phrase **а вдруг**?: **А вдруг** он не во́время придёт? 'Suppose/What if he doesn't get here in time?'

(iv) introduces parenthetical statements:

Появле́ние зри́телей, **а** их бы́ло челове́к 80, сно́ва мобилизова́ло актёров (Garin)
The appearance of the audience, and they were about 80 in number, again stirred the actors into action

(2) Но 'but'

(i) **Но** links clauses which express incompatible ideas, e.g.

Маши́на ста́рая, **но** хоро́шая
The car is old *but* good (an arguably unexpected combination)

(ii) The conjunction is often close in meaning to **одна́ко** 'however', **несмотря́ на э́то** 'despite this' (note, however, that **одна́ко** can *replace* **но**, while **несмотря́ на э́то** *combines* with it, except when it appears at the beginning of a new sentence):

Ему́ захоте́лось позвони́ть в больни́цу, **но** (= **одна́ко/но несмотря́ на э́то**) он сдержа́л себя́ и позвони́л то́лько у́тром (Panova)
He was tempted to ring the hospital **but** (= despite this) restrained himself and didn't ring until morning

Мы овладе́ли сложне́йшими ме́тодами позна́ния, **но** ещё пло́хо понима́ем други́х люде́й и сами́х себя́ (Kron)
We have mastered the most complex methods of cognition, **yet** still have an imperfect understanding of other people and ourselves

Note
Всё же means 'all the same', **зато́** 'on the other hand':

До́рого, **зато́** хоро́шая вещь
It's expensive, **but then** it is a quality article

(3) И, а and но
Learners sometimes experience difficulty in selecting the appropriate conjunction, especially where **а** and **но** are concerned. The following examples, each of which begins in the same way, illustrate their usage:

(i) **И** introduces additional information:

Он молодо́й **и энерги́чный**
He is young and (he is also) energetic

Она́ лю́бит ко́шек **и соба́к**
She likes cats and (she also likes) dogs

(ii) **А** introduces information which contrasts with but does not conflict with the first statement:

Он молодо́й, **а она́ ста́рая**
He is young, and (= whereas) she is old

Она́ лю́бит ко́шек, **а он лю́бит соба́к**
She likes cats, and he likes dogs

(iii) **Но** introduces information which is in antithesis to the first statement:

Он молодо́й, **но о́пытный**
He is young, but (i.e. despite this, nevertheless) experienced

Она́ лю́бит ко́шек, **но не лю́бит соба́к**
She likes cats, but she does not like dogs

Note

А and **но** sometimes appear in the same context, **но** expressing a stronger antithesis than **а**: Он хо́чет, **а** я не хочу́ 'He wants to, and I don't'; Он хо́чет, **но** я не хочу́ 'He wants to, but I don't'.

457   Disjunctive conjunctions

(1) Йли 'or'

Йли presents alternatives:

Э́то соба́ка **и́ли** волк?   Is that a dog or a wolf?

Note

(a) **Йли** does not normally appear in negative contexts. Thus, 'He doesn't like football or tennis' is rendered as Он не лю́бит **ни** футбо́ла, **ни** те́нниса (or ни футбо́л, ни те́ннис).

(b) 'Or' (= 'or else', 'otherwise') may be rendered as **а то/а не то/ина́че**:

На остано́вках не выходи́те, **а (не) то** загуля́етесь
Don't get out at the stops **or** you'll get lost

(2) Йли . . . и́ли (less commonly ли́бо . . . ли́бо) 'either . . . or'

Йли я пойду́ к нему́, **и́ли** он придёт ко мне
Either I will go to him or he will come to me

Note

As in constructions with **ни . . . ни** 'neither . . . nor' (see **455** (3) note (c)), a compatible predicate must be found for subjects of different gender: Се́мьи, где **появи́лись** и́ли но́вая ма́ма и́ли но́вый па́па (*Semya*) 'Families in which a new mummy or a new daddy has appeared'.

(3) Не то . . . не то 'either . . . or'

Не то . . . **не то** may imply difficulty of identification:

До нас донёсся **не то** стон, **не то** вскрик (Trifonov)
The sound of a groan **or possibly** a scream reached our ears

(4) То . . . то 'now . . . now'

Он **то** красне́ет, **то** бледне́ет
Now he blushes, now he grows pale

(5) То ли . . . то ли 'maybe . . . maybe'

То ли . . . **то ли** implies an element of conjecture:

И ско́лько лет ему́, сказа́ть бы́ло невозмо́жно — **то ли** под три́дцать, **то ли** за со́рок (Trifonov)
And it was impossible to say how old he was - **maybe** getting on for thirty, **maybe** in his forties

Subordinating Conjunctions

458   Explanatory conjunctions

(1) Что 'that'

(i) **Что** is used after verbs of saying, thinking etc.:

> Он сказа́л, **что** он мне помо́жет
> He said (**that**) he would help me

Note

Что should *not* be omitted in such contexts, cf. English: 'I think (that) he's out' and Russian Я ду́маю, **что** его́ нет до́ма.

(ii) (**То**), **что** also renders the English (**preposition +**) '**-ing**':

(a) **Изве́стен** + instrumental:

> Она́ изве́стна **тем, что** переплыла́ проли́в Ла-Ма́нш
> She is famous **for having** swum the Channel

(b) **Наказа́ть за** + accusative 'to punish for':

> Ма́льчика наказа́ли **за то, что** разби́л окно́
> The boy was punished **for breaking** the window

(c) **Нача́ть с** + genitive 'to begin by':

> Она́ начала́ **с того́, что** приве́тствовала госте́й
> She began **by welcoming** the guests

(d) **Обвини́ть в** + prepositional 'to accuse of':

> Его́ обвини́ли **в том, что** он укра́л часы́
> They accused him **of stealing** the watch

(e) **Поздра́вить с** + instrumental 'to congratulate on':

> Я поздра́вил его́ **с тем, что** он сдал экза́мен
> I congratulated him **on passing** the examination

(f) **Привы́кнуть к** 'to get used to':

> Он привы́к **к тому́, что** его́ уважа́ют
> He is accustomed **to being** respected

Note

То, как; то, где; то, когда́ etc. are also possible with some verbs, e.g. **зави́сеть**: э́то зави́сит **от того́, что** он ска́жет/**где** он живёт/**как** он себя́ чу́вствует/**когда́** он ко́нчит, 'it **depends what** he says/**where** he lives/**how** he feels/**when** he finishes'.

(2) Что́бы

Чтòбы + past tense is used after verbs of request, command or warning:

> Скажи́ ему́, **чтòбы** он не уходи́л
> Tell him not to leave

> Она́ предупреди́ла его́, **чтòбы** он не купа́лся в о́зере
> She warned him not to bathe in the lake

> Она́ проси́ла, **чтòбы** все вытира́ли но́ги у две́ри
> She asked that everyone should wipe their feet at the door

> Он приказа́л, **чтòбы** нас пусти́ли во дворе́ц
> He ordered that we should be admitted to the palace

See also **308** (2) note (a).

Note
Проси́ть, по-/прика́зывать, приказа́ть, **чтòбы** are preferred in impersonal constructions. Compare use of the **infinitive** when the verbs take a direct or indirect object: Он попроси́л меня́ **откры́ть** дверь 'He asked me to open the door', Он приказа́л солда́там **стреля́ть** 'He ordered the soldiers to shoot'.

(3) Бу́дто/бу́дто бы 'as if, that', я́кобы 'allegedly, supposedly'

Бу́дто, бу́дто бы, я́кобы question the truth of a statement: Он уверя́ет, **бу́дто** сам ви́дел 'He alleges that he saw it with his own eyes'. Compare:

> Арти́сты, ты́сячный раз игра́я пье́су, де́лают вид, **бу́дто** им неизве́стно — чем ко́нчится (Zalygin)
> Actors performing a play for the thousandth time pretend they do not know how it will end

> Он её убежда́л, **бу́дто бы** её но́вая физионо́мия лу́чше ста́рой (Zalygin)
> He tried to convince her that her new face was better than her old one

> Он утвержда́ет, **я́кобы** прика́з отменён
> He alleges that the order has been rescinded

See **464** (2) (i) for **бу́дто** as a comparative conjunction.

459   Causal conjunctions

(1) Благодаря́ тому́ что

Благодаря́ тому́ что is associated with favourable circumstances (see **443** (1)):

Она́ сдала́ экза́мен **благодаря́ тому́ что** рабо́тала усе́рдно
She passed the examination **thanks to having** worked industriously

(2) Ввиду́ того́ что

Ввиду́ того́, что 'in view of the fact that', like **всле́дствие того́, что** 'in consequence of the fact that' and **в си́лу того́, что** 'on account of the fact that', belongs to official styles:

Ввиду́ того́, что я во вре́мя о́тпуска был бо́лен, прошу́ продли́ть мне о́тпуск
In view of the fact that I was ill while on holiday I request an extension of leave

(3) Из-за того́ что

Из-за того́ что, like **из-за** (see **443** (1)), is often associated with unfavourable circumstances:

Из-за того́ что я в ука́занный срок не верну́л книг в библиоте́ку, у меня́ бы́ли неприя́тности
I got into trouble **for not returning** the library books on time

(4) Оттого́ что

Like **от** (see **443** (3) (i)), **оттого́ что** is associated with involuntary cause:

Бы́ло нело́вко **оттого́, что** его́ заподо́зрили в жела́нии порисова́ться (Granin)
He felt awkward **at being suspected** of wishing to show off

(5) Поско́льку 'as long as'

Поско́льку ты согла́сен, я не бу́ду возража́ть
As long as you agree I won't object

(6) Потому́ что 'because'

Его исключи́ли из кома́нды, **потому́ что** он не прису́тствовал на трениро́вках

He was left out of the team because he had not attended training sessions

Note

(a) A comma separates **потому́** and **что** when the cause is emphasized, usually by the addition of **бу́дто бы** 'as if', **ещё и** 'also', **мо́жет быть** 'perhaps', **то́лько** 'only' etc. (see also **454** (2) (ii)):

ещё и потому́, что	also because
мо́жет быть потому́, что	maybe because
потому́ бу́дто бы, что	seemingly because
то́лько потому́ (or **потому́ то́лько**), **что**	only because

Его́ пригласи́ли **потому́ то́лько, что** он племя́нник режиссёра
They **only** invited him **because** he is the producer's nephew

(b) Emphasis may also be expressed by distancing **потому́** from **что**:

Потому́ бу́дто бы его́ и пригласи́ли, **что** он племя́нник режиссёра
The reason why they seem to have invited him is that he is the producer's nephew

(7) Так как 'because, since'

Америка́нский учёный встре́тился с учёными университе́та, **так как** круг пробле́м, над реше́нием кото́рых они́ рабо́тают, сродни́ те́мам его́ рабо́т
The American scientist met scientists in the university since the problems they are working on are akin to his own areas of interest

Note

(a) **Потому́ что** and **так как** are virtually identical in meaning. However, clauses beginning with **потому́ что** always *follow* the main clause, while clauses in **так как** can precede or follow: Мы уста́ли, **так как** рабо́тали без переры́ва 'We were tired since we had worked without a break' or **Так как** рабо́тали без переры́ва, мы уста́ли 'Since we had worked without a break we were tired'.

(b) **Под предло́гом что/под тем предло́гом что/под предло́гом того́ что** 'on the pretext that' denote pretended cause; **и́бо** 'for' relates mainly to high style or scientific contexts.

460   Conjunctions of purpose

Чтòбы 'in order to/in order that'

See also **309–310**.

(i) **Чтòбы** is used:

(a) With an **infinitive** if the subject of both clauses is the same:

Я взял ведрò, **чтòбы набрáть** в роднике́ воды́ (Kazakov)
I took a bucket **in order to** draw some water from the spring

(b) With the **past tense** if there is a change in subject:

Я дал ей ведрò, **чтòбы онá моглá** набрáть в роднике́ воды́
I gave her the bucket **so that she could** draw water from the spring

(ii) **Для тогò/с тем чтòбы** throw the meaning of purpose into greater relief:

Гру́зы перетáскивались в склáды, . . . **для тогò, чтòбы (с тем, чтòбы)** на товáры не лил дождь (Semushkin)
The freight was dragged over to the warehouses **so that** the merchandise should not get rained on

(iii) **Чтòбы** combines with prepositional phrases and verbs which denote purpose or desire: **добивáться/добúться** + genitive 'to achieve', **забòтиться о** + prepositional 'to be concerned about', **за то** 'in favour of', **настáивать/настоя́ть на** + prepositional 'to insist on', **прòтив тогò** 'against', **стремúться к** 'to strive for':

Мы **добивáемся тогò, чтòбы** все голосовáли на вы́борах
We are trying to get everyone to vote at the election

Я за то (прòтив тогò), чтòбы все учúлись ру́сскому языку́
I am in favour of (against) everyone learning Russian

Госудáрство **забòтится о том, чтòбы** грáждане не голодáли
The state is concerned that its citizens should not go hungry

Он **настáивает (на том), чтòбы** я остáлся ночевáть
He insists I should stay the night

Мы **стремúмся к тому́, чтòбы** кит был объя́влен вúдом, находя́щимся под угрòзой исчезновéния
We are striving to get the whale declared an endangered species

(iv) **Чтòбы** is normally *omitted* after verbs of motion and their equivalents if there is no change in subject: Он пришёл поговорùть 'He came to have a chat'. However, **чтòбы** is *retained* after verbs of motion:

(a) When the action expressed by the **чтòбы** clause represents the purpose expressed by the main clause *but is not subsequent to it in time*:

> Я вы́шел из кòмнаты, **чтòбы** доказàть своё безразлùчие к разговòру
> I left the room in order to show my indifference to the conversation

(b) When the **чтòбы** clause contains a negative subordinate infinitive:

> Я вы́шел из кòмнаты, **чтòбы не разбудùть** ребёнка
> I left the room so as not to awaken the child

(c) When the subordinate infinitive is accompanied by adverbial modifiers:

> Я забрàлся нà гору, **чтòбы оттýда как слèдует** оглядèть окрèстность
> I climbed the hill so as to survey the surrounding district properly

(v) **Вмèсто тогò чтòбы** 'instead of' implies choice of a preferred alternative:

> **Вмèсто тогò, чтòбы** отдыхàть на пля́же, он пошёл на концèрт
> Instead of relaxing on the beach he went to a concert

Note
Чтòбы does not *always* denote purpose:

> Посетùтели уèхали с тем, **чтòбы** через чàс явùться ещё раз
> The visitors left, only **to turn up again** an hour later

461   Conjunctions of result

Так что 'so/so that'

> Он провалùлся, **так что** емý пришлòсь пересдавàть экзàмен
> He failed, so he had to resit the examination

The conjunctions **вслèдствие чегò** 'in consequence of which' and **в результàте чегò** 'as a result of which' are used in official registers.

462   Conditional conjunctions

(1) Если 'if'

Если (бы) is dealt with in **304–305**.

Note also the precautionary **на случай если** 'just in case':

Она́ мне дала́ свой телефо́н, **на случай если** придётся что́-нибудь переда́ть

She gave me her telephone number **just in case** a message needed to be passed on

See also **446** (5) (iii).

(2) Если не 'unless'

Он уйдёт, **если** вы **не** помеша́ете ему́
He'll go away unless you stop him

(3) При усло́вии что 'on condition that'

Она́ вы́йдет за́муж за него́ **при усло́вии, что** он уе́дет из А́нглии
She will marry him on condition that he leaves England

(4) Раз 'if, since, now that'

Раз has passed from conversational into literary style:

Раз дал сло́во, на́до его́ сдержа́ть
Now that he's given his word he should keep it

(5) Ко̀ли/ко̀ль; ко̀ль ско́ро 'if'

Ко̀ли/ко̀ль is a colloquial and obsolescent synonym of **е́сли** (ко̀ли на то пошло́ 'for that matter/if that's the way it is') and is rarely found in written styles. **Ко̀ль ско́ро** may be used in polemic, where it raises the emotional tension:

И уж **ко̀ль ско́ро** лю́ди де́ржат живо́тных, **то** несоверше́нство слу́жбы ветерина́рной по́мощи «бьёт» пре́жде всего́ по владе́льцам (*Semya*)
And since people keep animals, imperfections in the veterinary service hit their owners hardest

(6) Доста́точно (it is) 'sufficient/all it needs'

Доста́точно 'it is sufficient' may acquire a conditional nuance:

> **Доста́точно** бы́ло одно́й из пуль попа́сть в ми́ну, **и** (or **как**) она́ взлете́ла бы на во́здух (Stepanov)
> All it needed was for one of the bullets to hit the mine and it would have exploded

463   Concessive conjunctions

(1) Хотя́/хоть 'although'

> **Хотя́** (= **несмотря́ на то, что**) он тако́й молодо́й, его́ избра́ли депута́том Госуда́рственной Ду́мы
> Although (= 'despite the fact that') he is so young he was elected a member of the State Duma

The main clause may be introduced by **a** 'but', **зато́** 'on the other hand', **но** 'but', **одна́ко** 'however':

> Фёдор **хоть и** нача́льник, **но** всё-таки сосе́д (Zhukhovitsky)
> Although Fedor is the boss, he is a neighbour just the same

(2) Пусть 'even if, albeit'

Пусть (**пуска́й**) is characterized by colloquial or emotive nuances:

> Лю́ди всегда́ бу́дут стреми́ться к верши́нам, **пусть** да́же с ри́ском для жи́зни
> People will always aim for the heights, albeit at risk to their lives

For concessive constructions with **ни** see **312**.

464   Comparative conjunctions

(1) Как 'as, like'

(i) **Как** can be used to introduce a comparison:

> Верши́ны колыха́лись, **как** гре́бни волн
> The summits swayed **like** the crests of waves

(ii) For additional emphasis, **так же как** or **то́чно так же как** is used:

> Их на́до обуча́ть э́тому, **так же как** их у́чат чита́ть и писа́ть
> They have to be taught this, **just as** they are taught to read and write

(2) Бýдто/как бýдто/слóвно/тóчно 'as if'

(i) **Бýдто** introduces statements which are seemingly at variance with reality:

> Вцепи́лся глаза́ми, **бýдто** следи́л за разду́мьями Дрóбышева (Granin)
> He fastened his eyes on him as if he were following Drobyshev's meditations

See **458** (3) for **бýдто** as an explanatory conjunction.

(ii) **Как бýдто (бы)/слóвно/тóчно** are used to compare similar situations:

> Он перецелова́лся со все́ми, **как бýдто** уезжа́л на не́сколько лет
> He exchanged kisses with everyone, as if he were going away for several years

> Усну́ла так, **как бýдто бы** она́ что́-то соверши́ла (Zalygin)
> She fell asleep as if she had accomplished something

> Слу́шать его́ бы́ло тя́гостно, **тóчно** больно́го, кото́рый не жела́ет сознава́ть безнадёжность своего́ положе́ния (Granin)
> It was distressing to listen to him, like listening to a sick person who is reluctant to acknowledge the hopelessness of his situation

465   Temporal conjunctions. Introductory comments

(1) Some English temporal prepositions, e.g. 'before', 'after', 'until', 'since' etc., also function as conjunctions:

Preposition	Conjunction
before dinner	**before** he arrived
after the lesson	**after** the lesson finished
until Thursday	**until** we turned the corner
since May	**since** he left

(2) This does *not* apply, however, to their counterparts in Russian.

(i) The temporal prepositions are dealt with in **434** and **439**:

English	Russian
before dinner	до у́жина, **перед** у́жином
after the lesson	по̀сле уро́ка
until Thursday	**до** четверга́
since May	**с** ма́я

(ii) The equivalent conjunctions are as follows:

before	**до того́ как/пре́жде чем**
just before	**перед тем как**
after	**по̀сле того́ как**
until	**(до тех пор) пока́ . . . не**
since	**с тех пор как**

Note

English conjunctions such as 'when', 'if', 'until', 'as soon as' do not normally combine with the future tense, even when reference is to the future: 'when he *arrives*', 'if he *gets* here in time', 'I'll wait until you *finish/have finished*', 'I'll leave as soon as the clock *strikes* 12' etc. In Russian, however, future *meaning* is expressed by the future of the verb in such contexts: когда́ он **придёт** 'when he arrives', Подожду́, пока́ вы не **ко́нчите** 'I'll wait until you finish'. (See also **264**.)

466 Temporal conjunctions which render 'before', 'after', 'by the time that', 'until', 'since'

(1) До того́ как 'before'

До того́, как мы вам рассказа́ли о Венесуэ́ле, вы, вероя́тно, и не подозрева́ли, что её назва́ние свя́зано с назва́нием Вене́ции (Vvedenskaya)
Before we told you about Venezuela you probably had no idea its name was associated with that of Venice

Note

Задо́лго до того́ как 'long before', **ещё до того́ как** 'even before'.

(2) Перед тем как 'just before'

Она́ зажгла́ све́чи **перед тем как** го́сти се́ли за стол
She lit the candles just before the guests sat down to table

Note

(a) An *infinitive* may be used in the time clause if the subject of both clauses is the same: Она́ наде́ла но́вое пла́тье **перед тем как** спусти́ться на встре́чу с гостя́ми 'She put on a new dress before going down to meet the guests'.

(b) **Перед тем как** retains the meaning of close proximity to the event which is expressed by the preposition **перед** (see **439** (1) (iii)), and can combine with adverbs and adverbial phrases which stress immediacy: **в после́дний моме́нт перед тем как** 'in the final moment before', **как раз перед тем как** 'just before', **непосре́дственно перед тем как** 'immediately before' etc.

(3) Пре́жде чем 'before'

Пре́жде чем is a synonym of **до того́ как** in strictly temporal meanings. However, *only* пре́жде чем may be used in contexts that denote:

(i) Precaution:

Ка́ждый раз пти́цы улета́ют, **пре́жде чем** я успе́ю подойти́ к ним (Aramilev)
Every time the birds fly away before I have time to approach them

(ii) Inexpediency:

Пре́жде чем осужда́ть сосе́да, на́до присмотре́ться к самому́ себе́
Before condemning one's neighbour, one should take a hard look at oneself

(iii) The dependence of the time clause on the main clause:

На́до самому́ что́-то знать, **пре́жде чем** учи́ть други́х
You must know something yourself before teaching others

(4) По̀сле того́ как 'after'

По̀сле того́ как де́ти легли́ спать, она́ поста́вила самова́р
After the children had gone to bed she put on the samovar

Однáжды **пòсле тогó, как** óтчим óчень сúльно егó удáрил, Волóдя дáже обратúлся в милúцию (*Semya*)
Once, after his stepfather had hit him with particular force, Volodya even went to the police

A perfective gerund may be used instead of a conjunction if the subject of the temporal clause is the same as that of the main clause: **Сдав** (= **пòсле тогó как онá сдалá**) приёмные экзáмены, онá поступúла в МГУ́ 'Having passed the entrance examinations she enrolled at Moscow University'.

(5) Покá

Покá means:

(i) 'By the time': **Покá** приéхали пожáрные, плáмя удалóсь потушúть 'By the time the fire brigade arrived the fire had been put out'.

(ii) 'While':

(a) When two actions or processes are running parallel:

 Покá я занимáюсь, дéти игрáют в садý
 While I am studying the children play in the garden

 Покá вы в путú, помещéние прогрéется (*Izvestiya*)
 While you are on your way the building will warm up

(b) When one action or process interrupts another:

 Покá мы собирáлись в дорóгу, стáло темнó
 While we were getting ready for the journey it grew dark

Note
Покá may be replaced by **в то врéмя как** in these meanings. 'While' (= 'whereas') is rendered by **в то врéмя как/тогдá как**: Он за нóвый режúм, **в то врéмя как/тогдá как** я решúтельно прòтив 'He is in favour of the new regime, while I am emphatically against it'. **Покá** is also used in 'opportunist' contexts: Перейдём дорóгу, **покá** машúн нет 'We'll cross the road while it's clear'.

(6) Покá . . . не 'until'

Пока́ . . . **не** can be used with future and past tense forms:

Я подожду́, пока́ он не **вернётся**
I shall wait until he returns

Я подожда́л, пока́ маши́на не **вы́шла** на пло́щадь
I waited until the car came out on to the square

Note
(a) The conventional negative in **пока́** . . . **не**.
(b) Compare Жду, **когда́** вы ко́нчите 'I am waiting for you to finish'.

(7) С тех пор как 'since'

С тех пор как он живёт в но́вом до́ме, мы ни ра́зу не встреча́лись
Since he has been living in his new house, we haven't once met

467   Other conjunctions of time

(1) Когда́ 'when, as, whenever, after'

Когда́ вы ко́нчите, бу́дем чай пить
When (after) you have finished we shall drink tea

Когда́ я возвраща́лся домо́й, я встре́тил своего́ бы́вшего учи́теля
As I was returning home I met my former teacher

(**Ка́ждый   раз**), **когда́** маши́на остана́вливается, ребёнок просыпа́ется
Whenever the car stops the baby wakes up

Note
(a) For English present tense rendered by a Russian future, see **264** and **465** *Note*.
(b) A gerund may be used instead of **когда́** + finite verb if the subject of both clauses is the same: **Возвраща́ясь** домо́й, я встре́тил своего́ бы́вшего учи́теля 'While returning home I met my former teacher'.
(c) **Когда́** is also used with **ждать** and **люби́ть**: Мы жда́ли, **когда́** кто́-нибудь из девча́т поя́вится на доро́ге (Nikolaev) 'We were waiting for one of the girls to appear on the road'; — А твоя́-то, зна́чит, не о́чень лю́бит, **когда́** ты пьёшь? (Rasputin) 'So your old woman isn't very keen on you drinking?'

(d)   Constructions with **слу́чай** 'case':

Иногда́ сообща́ют **о слу́чаях, когда́** води́тели наруша́ют пра́вила из-за того́, что доро́жные зна́ки пло́хо видны́ (*Nedelya*)
Sometimes there are reports of drivers committing an offence because road signs are not easily visible

(2) Как 'as, when'

(i) **Как** 'as, when' is not used independently in temporal meaning, **когда́** being preferred (see above). Alternatively, **как** may be modified to **в то вре́мя как** 'while': **В то вре́мя как** докла́дчик говори́л, я де́лал запи́ски 'While the speaker was giving his talk I made notes'. The addition of **как раз** lends a sense of immediacy: Он ре́зко оберну́лся **как раз в то вре́мя как** она́ откры́ла дверь (German) 'He turned abruptly just as she opened the door'.

(ii) **Как** is also used to denote suddenness/unexpectedness:

(a) A negative verb often appears in the main clause:

Не про́жили и двух лет, **как** получи́ли кварти́ру
They had spent less than two years there **when** they received a flat

in particular **не успе́ть** 'not to have time to, not to manage':

Не успе́л я добра́ться до две́ри, **как** свет пога́с
I hadn't managed to reach the door **when** the light went out

(b) The conjunction **едва́** 'hardly' may also appear in the main clause:

Едва́ мы добрали́сь до ле́са, как пошёл дождь
Hardly had we reached the forest **than** it began raining

(c) **Сто́ит, сто́ило** 'hardly, no sooner than' also appear:

Сто́ило ему́ сверну́ть на просёлочную доро́гу, **как** мото́р загло́х
No sooner had he turned on to a country road **than** the engine cut out

Note
Сто́ит/сто́ило combine only with *perfective* infinitives.

(3) Как вдруг 'when suddenly'

Как вдруг introduces an action which interrupts the action of the main clause:

Он застёгивал воротни́к, **как вдруг** оторвала́сь пу́говица
He was fastening his collar when suddenly a button came off

(4) Как то́лько 'as soon as'

Как то́лько он вернётся, бу́дем проверя́ть рабо́ты
As soon as he returns we shall correct the papers

Как то́лько побли́зости появля́ется враг, пингви́ны выска́кивают из воды́
As soon as an enemy appears in the vicinity the penguins jump out of the water

(5) По ме́ре того́ как 'as, in proportion as'

The conjunction **по ме́ре того́ как** '(in proportion) as' links two actions or processes advancing in parallel ('gradational' meaning):

По ме́ре того́ как поднима́лось со́лнце, день тепле́л (Bunin)
As the sun rose the day was becoming warm

The Particle

468 The particle. Introductory comments

(1) Particles are parts of speech which impart additional semantic nuances to other words, phrases or sentences, in most cases having no independent meanings of their own. Some, however, are polysemantic (see **473**), precise translation often being possible only within a wider context.

(2) Particles are, in the main, a feature of colloquial Russian, where they are used to express a variety of emotions, subjective attitudes and assessments, imbuing individual speech with emotive colour and expressive spontaneity, sometimes in combination with other emotional intensifiers such as diminutives: **Ну, давáйте, мужичкú**, поднúмем за счáстье молодых (Shcherbakov) 'Come on, chaps, let's raise our glasses to the happiness of the young couple'.

(3) The effect of a particle may be varied or intensified by intonation. Thus, for example, Петь **так** петь 'If we're going to sing, let's sing' can, depending on the intonational pattern with which the phrase is uttered, denote an eagerness to sing or a reluctant acceptance of the inevitable.

(4) Some particles are formally identical with conjunctions (e.g. **а, да, же**), others with adverbs (e.g. **ещё, тóлько, ужé**) or pronouns (e.g. **то**). Some are of verbal origin (e.g. **ведь, мол, пусть, хоть**). There is considerable overlap between particles and certain interjections: **Ох уж** эти мне рóдственники! 'Oh, these relations!', **Ну и** морóз! 'Quite a frost!'

469   The position of the particle in the sentence

(1) Some particles always *precede* the word they qualify:

Да здра́вствует мир!	Long live peace!
Ну, пое́хали!	Right, let's go!
Пусть ска́жет	Let him tell us
Что за безобра́зие!	How disgraceful!

(2) Others always *follow* the word they qualify:

Расскажи́ **же**	Come on, tell us all about it
Помолчи́-**ка**	Do be quiet
Ты́ **ли** э́то сде́лал?	Was it you who did that?

Тепе́рь-**то** я по́нял весь у́жас своего́ положе́ния
It was now that I realized the full horror of my situation

(3) Others still may stand at the beginning or in the middle of a sentence (or occasionally at the end of a sentence):

Ведь он ошиба́ется *or* Он **ведь** ошиба́ется
He is wrong, you know

(4) Some, e.g. **так**, may occupy a central position between two forms:

Пить **так** пить, — ти́хо сказа́ла Га́лка (Gagarin)
'If we're drinking, let's drink', said Galka softly

470   The use of particles to impart different nuances of meaning

A phrase such as, for example, Э́то не подлежи́т сомне́нию 'That's not open to doubt', can combine with a number of different particles, each of which imparts to it a different emphasis. Thus:

(1) **Ведь** may be used to introduce a self-evident fact or to issue a gentle reminder:

Ведь э́то не подлежи́т сомне́нию
You know, that's not open to doubt

(2) **Вот** cites the statement as an example:

Вот э́то не подлежи́т сомне́нию
Now this, for instance, is beyond doubt

(3) **Да** implies that the statement can be taken for granted:

Да э́то не подлежи́т сомне́нию
Of course that is beyond doubt

(4) **Же** introduces a more categorical emphasis:

Э́то **же** не подлежи́т сомне́нию
Now that really isn't open to doubt

(5) **-то** indicates that the subject has been referred to before:

Э́то-**то** не подлежи́т сомне́нию
Now there's something that is beyond doubt

(6) **Уж** rules out any possibility of contradiction:

Уж э́то не подлежи́т сомне́нию
That is definitely not open to doubt

471   Some of the principal meanings expressed by particles

Particles are used:

(1) To **point out**:

Вот дом	Here is/There is the house
Дом **вон** там	The house is over yonder

(2) To **define or make more precise**:

Почему́ **и́менно** он протесту́ет?	Why **exactly** is he protesting?
Ро́вно в час	**Exactly** at one
Э́ти боти́нки ему́ **как раз** впо́ру	These shoes are **exactly** the right size for him

(3) To **express approximation**:

Я **почти́** гото́в	I am **almost** ready
Он **едва́ не** помеша́лся	He **almost** went out of his mind
Она́ **чуть не** умерла́ с го́ря	She **very nearly** died of grief

Note
Чуть не/едва́ не combine mainly with verbs.

(4) To **restrict or exclude**:

> **Тóлько óн** смóжет решúть э́ту проблéму
> **Only he** will be able to solve this problem

Note

(a) **Тóлько** immediately precedes the word it qualifies: Он смóжет решúть **тóлько** э́ту проблéму 'He will be able to solve only **this** problem'.

(b) It may also be used idiomatically: А он **тóлько** знáет, что посмéивается 'All he can do is keep sniggering'.

472 Modal functions of particles

Particles also fulfil modal functions:

(1) **Desirability**:

Отдохнýть **бы**!	**Oh for** a rest!
Лишь бы побóльше врéмени	**If only** there were more time

(2) **Command or exhortation**:

Давáй останóвимся!	**Let's** make a halt!

(3) **Confirmation**:

— Ты лю́бишь óперу?	'Do you like opera?'
— **Ещё бы**!	'I'll say!'

(4) **Negation**:

Нет, он **не** читáет кнúгу	**No**, he is **not** reading the book
Нет **ни** минýты врéмени	There's **not** a spare moment

Note

(a) The particle **не** 'not' *precedes* the word it qualifies, thus:

> **Не óн** читáет кнúгу
> **He is not the one** who is reading a book

> **Не кнúгу** он читáет
> **It's not a book** he's reading

(b) If the negated form is *not* a verb, the negative/genitive rule does *not* apply: cf. Я не вúжу столá 'I don't see a table' and Не **стóл** я вúжу 'It's not a table I see'. The negated word in such constructions (here, **стол**) bears the logical stress and is pronounced with rising intonation.

(c) 'Yes' is rendered as **нет** in a positive answer to a negative question: Вы не лю́бите ко́шек? **Нет**, люблю́! 'Don't you like cats?' 'Yes, I do!'

(5) **Interrogative**:

Давно́ **ли** он у́мер?	Is it **long** since he died?
Не **о́н ли** опозда́л?	Wasn't it **he** who was late?
Мно́го ли там бы́ло наро́ду?	Were there a **lot** of people there?
Ра́зве вы не зна́ете?	**Surely** you know?
Неуже́ли он прав?	**Surely** he can't be right?

Note

(a) **Ли** follows the emphasized word, which bears the logical stress. This also applies in reported questions, where **ли** follows the 'operative' element:

Он спроси́л, **зна́ю ли я**	He asked if I knew
Я не по́мню, **хоро́шая ли** э́то кни́га	I don't remember if that is a good book

(b) **Ли** may also express uncertainty (Не оши́бся **ли** он? 'Could he have made a mistake?') and may appear in rhetorical questions (Не сты́дно **ли** тебе́? 'Aren't you ashamed of yourself?').

(c) If **ли** is omitted from a question, the word order is *not* inverted: 'Is he working?' is rendered either as Рабо́тает **ли** он? or Он рабо́тает? (no inversion, and with rising intonation on the stressed syllable).

(d) Both **ра́зве** and **неуже́ли** 'really/surely not' imply doubt in the reliability of a statement, or a conviction that the opposite is true. **Неуже́ли** is much more emphatic than **ра́зве**, and is commoner in spoken Russian. **Ра́зве** can also denote hesitancy: **Ра́зве** в кино́ сходи́ть? '**I wonder if** I should go to the cinema?'

(6) **Direct speech**: the particles **де/де́скать/мол** indicate that direct speech is being quoted:

Пётр снисходи́тельно пожа́л плеча́ми: чего́, **мол**, моро́чить го́лову (Abramov)
Peter shrugged his shoulders in a condescending way, **as if to say**, 'Pull the other one'

(7) **Probability or improbability**:

Ты, **пожа́луй**, прав	You **may well** be right

Вря́д ли он придёт	He's **hardly likely** to come
Едва́ ли мо́жно	One can **hardly** agree with him
согласи́ться с ним	

(8) **Comparison or similarity: бу́дто/как бу́дто/как бы/сло́вно** are used to compare similar events, actions etc.:

Мо́жет быть, пыль пусти́л в глаза́? — Нет, **как бу́дто** и взапра́вду уе́хал (Azhaev)

Maybe he was having us on? No, he **really does seem** to have gone

(9) **Emotional nuances: пря́мо, то́-то, так, уж** render emotional and expressive nuances (enthusiasm, resignation, determination, irony etc.):

Пря́мо стра́шно!	Simply terrifying!
То́-то бы́ли ра́дости!	We were **over the moon**!
Е́хать **так** е́хать!	If we're going, **let's** go!
То́же у́мник нашёлся!	**Some** genius we have here!
Вот они́, рабо́тнички!	**Some** workers!

473   The meanings of individual particles

While some particles convey one meaning only, others are poly-semantic.

(1) **А**

А is used:

(i) In prompting an answer:

Я́блоко дать, **а**?	I'll give you an apple, **shall I**?

(ii) In making a request:

Помоги́ мне немно́жко, **а**?	Give us a hand, **would you?**

(iii) In stating the apparently obvious:

— Что же мне тепе́рь де́лать?	Whatever should I do now?
— **А** о́чень про́сто	**Why**, it's very simple

(iv) In a conversational exchange:

— Ми́тю мо́жно?	'Can I speak to Mitya?'
— **А** он на рабо́те	'**I'm afraid** he's at work'
— **А** когда́ он бу́дет?	'**And** when will he be in?'
— **А** кто его́ спра́шивает?	'**Now**, who is this asking for him?'

(2) Было

Было is used to denote:

(i) The immediate cancellation or reversal of an action:

Пёс по́днял **было** го́лову и сно́ва опусти́л (Abramov)
The hound raised its head and lowered it again

(ii) The reversal or abandonment, often through interruption, of an action or process which has just begun:

«Ско́рая по́мощь» тро́нулась **было** вперёд, но вахтёр вдруг суетли́во замаха́л шофёру, и маши́на останови́лась (Tendryakov)
The ambulance **had begun** to move off, but the porter suddenly began waving to the driver in agitation and the vehicle stopped

(iii) The abandonment of a projected action:

Он по́днял **было** стака́н, но разду́мал
He **was about** to pick up the glass, but changed his mind

Note

(a) The verb in such constructions is almost invariably perfective. The only imperfective forms commonly found are **собира́ться** and **хоте́ть**, which are followed by a *perfective* infinitive: Он собира́лся/хоте́л **было попроси́ть** разреше́ния вы́йти, но испуга́лся 'He was **on the point** of asking permission to go out, but took fright'.

(b) **Было** also combines with perfective participles and gerunds:

У Тихоокеа́нского побере́жья вновь наблюда́ют **исче́знувших было** се́рых кито́в (*Selskaya zhizn*)
Grey whales, which **had been on the verge of extinction**, are again being sighted off the Pacific coast

Останови́вшись было у перекрёстка, шофёр всё-таки пое́хал на кра́сный свет
Having been on the point of stopping at the crossroads, the driver jumped the lights instead

(3) Ведь

Ведь is used:

(i) To explain or justify:

Коне́чно, уме́ю стреля́ть из винто́вки, служи́л **ведь** в а́рмии

Of course I can fire a rifle, **after all** I did do my army service

(ii) To prompt a desired answer:

Ведь ты пойдёшь в магазин?
Now you are going to the shop, **aren't you**?

(iii) To issue a gentle reminder:

Ты **ведь** обещал   You did promise, **you know**

(iv) To administer a mild reproof:

Ведь я просила тебя не   **Now** I did ask you to be quiet
шуметь

(4) Вот

See also **471** (1). **Вот** can be used:

(i) In combination with interrogative words:

Вот где я живу   **That's** where I live
Вот почему он ушёл   **That's** why he left

(ii) For contrast:

С Ваней я дружу, а **вот** с Ниной никак не лажу
I'm friends with Vanya, but I **just** can't get on with Nina

(iii) In warnings:

Вот всем расскажу об этом
Now I'm going to tell everyone about this

(iv) In expressing feelings such as amazement, indignation etc.:

Вот дурак!   **What** an idiot!

(5) Да

Да is used:

(i) In self-exoneration:

Да я молчу!   **But** I am being quiet!

(ii) In consolation:

Да ты не расстраивайся! **Now** don't upset yourself!

(iii) In indefinite answers:

| Да я не зна́ю! | Oh, I don't know! |

(6) Ещё

Ещё is used to express:

(i) Outrage or indignation:

| Ещё учёным называ́ется! | And he calls himself a **scholar**! |

(ii) Emphatic affirmation:

| — Брат игра́ет в ша́хматы? | 'Does your brother play chess?' |
| — Ещё как! | '**I'll say** he does!' |

(iii) Emphatic denial:

— Вы го́лодны?	'Are you hungry?'
— Ещё чего́! Я то́лько	'**Hungry**! I've only just had
что поза́втракала!	breakfast!'

(iv) A warning or threat:

| Ещё уво́лят! | You'll get the sack (**if you don't watch out**)! |

(7) Же

(i) **Же** denotes categorical, insistent affirmation, often stressing the indisputability of a statement:

| Ты **же** обеща́л! | But you promised! |

(ii) When qualifying interrogative words, **же** imparts a peremptory nuance, implying astonishment, indignation, disapproval etc.:

Куда́ **же** ты идёшь?
Where do you think **you're** going?

Кто **же** так поступа́ет?
Now whoever behaves like **that**?

(iii) The particle can also specify precisely a place or time denoted by an adverb or adverbial phrase, e.g. здесь **же** 'at this very spot':

Прие́ду сего́дня **же**   I shall come **straightaway**
Там **же** живёт мой брат   **That's** where my brother lives

Тогда́ **же** бы́ло произнесено́ гла́вное сло́во совреме́нной биоло́гии — ген (*Russia Today*)

It was precisely at **that** point that the most important word in modern biology was uttered — gene

(iv) With demonstrative pronouns **же** conveys meanings of identity or similarity:

Мы идём по **той же** улице
We are walking down **the same** street

Он одет в **такой же** пиджак
He is dressed in the **same kind of** jacket

(v) **Же** imparts an insistent or impatient nuance to imperatives:

Стой **же** спокойно,   Now, **will** you stand still!
наконец!

(vi) The set phrase **надо же**! expresses extreme indignation:

— Это он так написал?! — громко возмутилась Попова. — Нахалюга! **Надо же**! . . . Ну **надо же**! (Shukshin)
'He wrote that?!', shouted Popova indignantly. 'The impudent puppy! **What a nerve! What a confounded nerve!**'

(8) И

(i) **И** may lend emphasis to the word which *follows* it:

Я **и** стараюсь!   I **am** trying!

(ii) It can also mean 'even/also/too/as well':

Он говорит **и** по-китайски   He speaks Chinese **as well**

(iii) In negative statements it means 'either':

И я не знаю   I don't know **either**

(9) -ка

(i) **-ка** may combine with the first-person perfective future of a verb to denote mild resolve:

Пойду-**ка** домой   **I think I might** go home

(ii) It softens the force of an imperative, expressing:

(a) Gentle exhortation:

Дай-**ка** спички, Стас (Gagarin)
'**Do** give me the matches, Stas'

(b) Feelings of admiration, scorn etc.:

Смотри-**ка**, какие книжки он читáет!
Just look what books he is reading!

(iii) Alternatively, it may contain a note of indignant challenge:

Постóй-**ка** под холóдным дýшем!
Just you try standing under a cold shower!

(10) Ну

Ну is used:

(i) In exclamations:

Ну, устáл!	**Am I** tired!
Ну и ну!	**Well, well!**

(ii) In emphasis:

Ну, морóз!	**Quite** a frost!

Note
Sometimes there is an element of sarcasm:

Ну, герóй!	**Some** hero!

(iii) With the perfective future to denote grudging consent:

Ну пойдём, éсли ты так хóчешь!
All right, let's go, if you are so keen!

(iv) To express impatience:

Ну, хвáтит!	That's enough of **that!**

(v) To express a peremptory imperative:

Ну, говори!	**All right**, out with it!

(11) -то

(i) -**то** may be used to express diffidence, a reluctance to be categorical:

— Тут у вас выпить-**то** мóжно?
'Are you allowed to have a **drink** here?'
— Вообщé-**то** не полóжено
'**Actually** it's not normally allowed'

(ii) It is frequently used to refer to something already mentioned:

— Я вчера́ и в магази́не-то не́ был . . . (Shukshin)
'Yesterday I wasn't even **in** the shop . . .'

(iii) It may be the equivalent of English 'I mean':

— Он что, зарегистри́рован как алкого́лик? Королёв-**то**? (Shukshin)
'Is he registered as an alcoholic? Korolev, **I mean**?'

(iv) Emphatic use is common with adverbs:

Тепе́рь-то я по́нял, что́ его беспоко́ит
It was now that I realized what was bothering him

Са́мое стра́шное — плаву́чие ми́ны. **Потому́-то** кру́глые су́тки несу́т ва́хту вперёдсмотря́щие (Gagarin)
The most terrible things are mines. **That's why** the look-outs are on 24-hour watch

(v) The particle may also be used to strengthen a negative:

Э́то не так-**то** про́сто   It's not so simple **at that**

(12) Уж

Уж emphasizes the main emotive content of a statement, ranging from:

(i) Confident assertion:

Уж мно́го лет в э́тих края́х нет ди́ких оле́ней (Astafev)
Now there haven't been any wild deer in these parts for many years

(ii) Resigned acceptance of the inevitable:

— Да **уж** пусть себе́   '**Oh** let them play'
игра́ют

(iii) Reassurance:

Не беспоко́йтесь, **уж** я не   Don't worry, I won't forget!
забу́ду!

(iv) Condescension:

Уж приду́мал!   That's a tall story!

(13) Хоть

Хоть can denote:

(i) A minimum requirement or expectation:

Хоть причешись!   **At least** comb your hair!

(ii) An exemplary meaning:

Взять **хоть** тебя; ты ведь ни разу не пожаловался
Take you, **for example**; now you haven't once complained

(iii) A readiness to oblige, or to indulge a whim:

Поедем **хоть** завтра!   Let's go tomorrow, **for all I
                                         care!**

(iv) Intensity or extreme manifestation (with imperatives):

Работы у него **хоть**   He's **up to his eyes** in work!
отбавляй!

(14) Что

(i) In questions, **что** often emphasizes the preceding noun or pronoun:

А я **что**, возражаю?   I'm not objecting, **am I**?
Ты **что**, с ума сошла?   Are you mad, **or what**?

(ii) The phrase (**ну**) **что** вы! denotes energetic denial:

Ну **что** вы! Я вполне   Now **come off it**! I'm perfectly
здорова!   fit!

474   The aggregation of particles for increased emphasis

(1) Particles may be aggregated to heighten emphasis:

(i) **А ведь/да ведь/но ведь**:

А ведь Александр считался одним из сильнейших игроков
(*Russia Today*)
And yet, you know, Aleksandr was considered to be one of the very
best players

(ii) **А ещё**:

Сам не учился, **а ещё** специалистов критикует!
He hasn't studied himself, **yet has the nerve** to criticize the experts!

(iii) **Бы уж**:

— О господи, — перекрестилась баба, — молчал **бы уж** (Belov)
'Oh, my God', the woman said, crossing herself, 'you **really ought**

to have kept your mouth shut'

(iv) **Вот ещё/вот уж**:

— На́до бы его́ разыска́ть — сказа́л Пётр.
— **Вот ещё**. — нахму́рилась Лёля. — Бо́льше тебе́ де́лать не́чего? (Uvarova)
'I suppose we ought to go looking for him', said Petr.
'**Come off it**', said Lelya with a frown. 'Have you nothing better to do with your time?'

Вот уж не зна́ю.
I haven't the **foggiest**

(v) **Да и/да уж**:

А костёр горе́л-горе́л **да и** спали́л 1 700 гекта́ров ле́са (*Russia Today*)
And the bonfire burnt on and on and **went and** destroyed 1,700 hectares of woodland

Да уж и сама́-**то** хороша́! (Shcherbakov)
She's a fine one to talk!

(vi) **Ещё бы/ещё как**:

Ве́село на душе́! **Ещё бы**: сбыла́сь мечта́ (Sobolev)
I'm overjoyed! **You bet**, my dream has come true

Согласи́тся? **Ещё как согласи́тся**!
Will he agree? **I'll say he will**!

(vii) **Как э́то**:

Оби́дится? **Как э́то оби́дится**!
Take offence? **Not a chance**!

(viii) **Не то чтобы уж**:

А Кла́вдия была́ **не то чтобы уж** краса́вица . . . (Shcherbakov)
And Claudia was **not exactly** what you might call a raving beauty . . .

(ix) **Ну и; ну уж; ну уж и; ну-ка; ну что ж**:

Ну и ба́ба! — бормота́л он (Grekova)
'**What a** woman!', he murmured

Ну уж не сердись, я не хотела тебя обидеть
Come on, don't get angry, I didn't mean to offend you

Ну уж и придумал!
That's a tall story **if you like**!

Ну-ка, попробуй мою походку, — сказал Кондрат (Shukshin)
'**Go on then**, do my walk', said Kondrat

Правда, не стал ни поэтом, ни певцом . . . **Ну что ж**, не всем быть поэтами! (Kazakov)
It's true I became neither a poet nor a singer . . . **Oh well**, not everybody can be a poet!

(x) **Так и**; **так уж**:

Я **так и не** понял   I **simply didn't** understand

Не буду я **так уж** расхваливать эти фильмы (*Russia Today*)
I'm not **exactly** going to give these films rave notices

(xi) **Хоть бы/хотя бы/лишь бы**:

Хоть бы кто-нибудь мимо прошёл . . . (Gagarin)
If only someone passed this way . . .

Она рада была бы любому попутчику, **хотя бы** технику Мишелю (Zalygin)
She would have been glad of any travelling companion, **even if** it was only the technician Michel

(xii) **Что же, что ж**:

Что же ты не целуешь меня? — слабо шепчет она (Kazakov)
'**Why ever** don't you kiss me?', she whispers faintly

(2) Particles may appear separately, at different points in the statement:

(i) **Ведь . . . же**:

Знаменитые спортсмены: боксёр Геннадий Шатков, конько-бежец Борис Стенин — кандидаты наук. Но **ведь** это **же** единицы. Исключение (*Russia Today*)
There are famous sportsmen who have doctorates: the boxer Gennady Shatkov, the skater Boris Stenin. **But you know**, these are isolated exceptions

(ii) **Ведь** . . . **-то**:

Опозда́ем **ведь** на по́езд-**то**
You know, we're **going to go and** miss that train

(iii) **Ну** . . . **же**:

Ну, ну, — серди́то доба́вил он. — Я **же** сказа́л, что иду́ (Proskurin)
'**All right**', he added angrily, 'I said I was coming, **didn't I?**'

— **Ну, обними́тесь же**
– **Come on then**, give each other a hug

(iv) **Уж** . . . **-то**:

Уйдёт. **Уж** о́н-**то** её зна́ет! (Koluntsev)
He'll leave. **After all**, he knows her **if anyone does**!

(3) Feelings such as indignation can generate whole strings of particles:

Ну да ведь и дура́к **же** он!
Well, really, you know, the man is a complete idiot!

(4) The phrase **куда́ там** can appear either with or without **уж**:

Про́бовали её учи́ть программи́рованию — **куда́ там**. Си́нус пу́тала с интегра́лом (Grekova)
They tried to teach her programming. **Some hope.** She confused sines with integrals

— Тепе́рь таки́х мужико́в и нет, как мой стари́к, — говори́т стару́ха.
— **Куда́ уж там**! (Rasputin)
'They don't make them like my old man any more', says the old woman.
'**No way!**'

Word Order

475   Introductory comments

(1) The inflected nature of Russian allows greater flexibility of word order than is possible in English, where only rigid order of words differentiates the meaning of sentences such as 'Ivan loves Masha' and 'Masha loves Ivan'.

(2) In Russian, by contrast, inflexional endings indicate the functions of words irrespective of their position in the sentence. Thus, the feminine noun accusative ending -**y** in **Ма́шу** identifies Masha as the object of the verb both in Ива́н лю́бит **Ма́шу** 'Ivan loves Masha' and **Ма́шу** лю́бит Ива́н 'It is Ivan who loves Masha', the difference between the two sentences being one of emphasis rather than meaning.

(3) Word order in Russian, though flexible, is by no means arbitrary, however; any disruption of the accepted or 'neutral' order throws the displaced elements into sharp relief.

(4) Questions of word order are ideally considered within the wider context of a narrative, since the order of elements in a sentence is often determined by what has gone before (see **476**) (3) (ii)).

476 'New' and 'given' information

(1) 'New' information

Each statement contains *new* information. Except in emotionally charged language, where different criteria apply (see **484**), this *new* information appears at or towards the *end* of a statement in Russian, in contrast with English, where it usually appears at or near the *beginning*. Thus, in the sentence

В Жене́ве состоя́лся   A festival took place in Geneva
фестива́ль

the festival (**фестива́ль**), as the nucleus of the new information, occupies the *final* position, while the verb **состоя́лся** 'took place' is also new but of secondary significance. **В Жене́ве** 'in Geneva', as incidental or '*given*' information (see (2)), appears in *initial* position.

Note

(a)   The reverse order: **Фестива́ль состоя́лся в Жене́ве** answers the question **Где состоя́лся фестива́ль?** '**Where** did the festival take place?' and can be rendered as 'The festival took place in Geneva'.

(b)   In English, nouns which are the subject of *new* information are usually preceded by '*a*': 'There is **a** dog in the garden' (**В саду́ есть соба́ка**). Nouns which are the subject of *given* information are usually preceded by '*the*': '**The** dog is in the garden' (**Соба́ка в саду́**).

(2) 'Given' information

Most statements contain an item or items of '*given*' information, that is, information which is either known or presumed to be known to the reader, has been mentioned before, can be assumed from the context, or is entirely incidental to the event being described. *Given* information is never the point of the utterance. It is often circumstantial, taking the form of an adverb of time, place or manner:

Здесь удо́бно   It's comfortable **here**

5 октября́ в Жене́ве в непринуждённой обстано́вке начали́сь переговоры по разоруже́нию
Disarmament talks began **in a relaxed atmosphere in Geneva on 5 October**

(3) 'Given' and 'new' information

(i) The order 'given' information + 'new' information (with less essential preceding essential new items) is standard in a Russian sentence:

От рефо́рмы цен никто́ не пострада́ет (*Ogonek*)
No one will suffer from the price reform

In this example, price reform (**рефо́рма цен**), as a matter of common knowledge ('*given*' information), occupies initial position, while **никто́ не пострада́ет** 'no one will suffer' is *new* information and appears in final position.

(ii) An utterance must be considered within its overall context. Thus, in the following extracts, the *new* information at the end of each successive sentence becomes the *given* information at the start of the next:

В то вре́мя я жил в ма́леньком се́верном **го́роде. Го́род** стоя́л на берегу́ **реки́. По реке́** плы́ли бе́лые парохо́ды (Kazakov)
At that time I lived in **a small northern town. The town** stood on the bank of **a river. Down the river** sailed white steamers

На пло́щади во́зле решётки стоя́т **столбы́. К столба́м** прикреплены́ желе́зные **табли́чки.** Во́зле э́тих **табли́чек** остана́вливаются авто́бусы (Soloukhin)
On the square close to the railing stand **pillars. To these pillars** are attached iron **plaques.** Buses stop close to **these plaques**

Note
The principle that 'given' information precedes 'new' allows the differentiation of ostensibly synonymous statements such as На столе́ **ва́за** 'There is **a vase** on the table' (answering the question **Что** на столе́? 'What is on the table?') and Ва́за **на столе́** 'The vase is **on the table**' (answering the question **Где** ва́за? 'Where is the vase?').

(iii) Sometimes the relative status of items is implied by context. Thus, in

Я включи́л ра́дио и услы́шал **знако́мую балла́ду. Пе́ла** А́лла Пугачёва
I switched on the radio and heard a **well-known ballad. It was being sung** by Alla Pugacheva

the reference in the first sentence to a well-known ballad (*new* information) determines the status of **пе́ла** 'it was being sung' as *given* information at the start of the second. **А́лла Пугачёва**, as new information, appears in *final* position, since the point of the statement is to establish, not that someone was singing a ballad (that is known from the first sentence), but *who* was singing it.

477   Relative position of subject and verb

The order of the items in an utterance containing a subject and a verb depends on which is *new* information and which is *given*.

(1) Subject + verb

In the following example the subject (**отец**) represents *given* information and precedes the verb (**умер**), which reports *new* information:

Отец умер   Father has died

(2) Verb + subject

The reverse order (verb + subject) is found in the following contexts; in each of them the *new* information is represented by the *noun*, which accordingly occupies *final* position:

(i) Impersonal statements, statements about the weather etc.:

Идёт дождь   It is raining
Дул свежий ветер   A fresh breeze was blowing

(ii) Statements in which the verb denotes existence, non-existence, coming into existence, beginning, continuing, finishing etc.:

Наступила осень   Autumn arrived
Идёт фильм   A film is on

Проходит день, **начинается** другой — ни звука (*Literaturnaya gazeta*)
One day passes, another dawns; not a sound is heard

(iii) Statements in which the verb denotes occurrence, state, process etc.:

Произошёл несчастный   An accident happened
  случай
Родилась дочь   They have had a daughter
У меня болит горло   I have a sore throat
Зазвонил телефон   The phone began to ring

(iv) Constructions which involve the quotation of direct speech:

— Кто такая? — **спросил** он вполголоса (Grekova)
'Who is she?', he asked *sotto voce*

Note

This also applies to statements which indicate a **source of information**:
Как **сообщает ИТА́Р-ТАСС** . . . 'As **ITAR-TASS reports** . . .'.

(v) Questions introduced by an interrogative word:

| Где **живёт ва́ша дочь**? | Where does your daughter live? |
| Когда́ **открыва́ется магази́н**? | When does the shop open? |

Note

(a)   The order interrogative word + subject + predicate is compulsory with a *pronoun* subject (Почему́ **он пришёл**? 'Why has he come?'), but optional with a *noun* subject (Куда́ **лети́т самолёт**/Куда́ **самолёт лети́т**? 'Where is the aircraft flying to?').

(b)   Questions which are *not* introduced by an interrogative word have the same order as a direct statement. Compare Она́ передала́ вам письмо́ '**She passed** the letter to you' and Она́ передала́ вам письмо́? '**Did she pass** the letter to you?' Alternatively, **ли** may appear as second element after the operative word (or words) in the question: Передала́ **ли** она́ вам письмо́? 'Did she pass the letter to you?' Compare **Она́** ли вам передала́ письмо́? 'Was it **she** who passed the letter to you?', **Письмо́** ли она́ вам передала́? 'Was it a **letter** she passed to you?' The order operative word + **ли** is also used in reported questions: Он спроси́л, **передала́** ли она́ вам письмо́ 'He asked if she had passed the letter to you'.

478   Subject, verb, object

(1) Subject + verb + object

The order subject + verb + object is encountered in the vast majority of sentences which contain these three elements:

| **Пётр купи́л кни́гу** | Peter has bought a book |

Note

(a)   A *pronoun* object may precede (or follow) the verb: — Я **вас** не понима́ю, това́рищ генера́л (Grekova) 'I don't understand you, comrade general'; Он **ничего́** не ест 'He isn't eating anything'.

(b)   The order *subject + object noun + verb* places unusual emphasis on the verb (or object noun): Пётр Ната́шу **уважа́ет** 'Peter **respects**

Natasha' (even though he may not, for example, **like** her); Мы **дом** купи́ли 'We have bought a **house**'. This order is found predominantly in spoken Russian.

(c) The order *subject + verb + object* is virtually mandatory when the accusative case of subject noun and object noun is the same as the nominative, since a reversal of the order would change the meaning, cf. Кли́мат меня́ет расти́тельность 'The climate alters vegetation' and Расти́тельность меня́ет кли́мат 'Vegetation alters the climate', Мать лю́бит дочь 'The mother loves her daughter' and Дочь лю́бит мать 'The daughter loves her mother'.

(2) Object + verb + subject:

(i) The order object + verb + subject

Кни́гу купи́л Пётр

in which the subject (**Пётр**) is central to the *new* information, is rendered in English by a passive construction ('The book **was bought** by Peter') or by a construction introduced by 'It is . . .' ('**It is Peter** (and not someone else) who bought the book').

(ii) This order is also common:

(a) With an **inanimate** subject:

Меня́ разбуди́ла **гроза́**
I was awakened by a thunderstorm

А́нну Каре́нину задави́л **по́езд**
Anna Karenina was crushed by a train

(b) In sentences which contain set phrases in which the noun component is **qualified**:

Большо́е значе́ние име́ет уче́бный проце́сс
The teaching process is of great significance

Суще́ственную роль игра́ли профсою́зы
A significant role was played by the unions

(c) In impersonal constructions involving the third-person plural: О́вощи уже́ **выгружа́ют** 'The vegetables are already being unloaded', Вас **про́сят** к телефо́ну 'You are wanted on the phone', Её **зову́т** Ната́лья 'She is called Natalya'.

(3) Object + subject + verb

Other variants in word order depend on the relative weighting of elements in a particular context. Thus, in the example

Э́ту рабо́ту Генера́льный секрета́рь хорошо́ понима́л (*Literatur-naya gazeta*)
This was work the General Secretary understood well

the *subject* (Генера́льный секрета́рь) and *object* (э́ту рабо́ту) are *given* information, while *adverb* + *verb* (хорошо́ понима́л) are *new* information and appear in final position.

479   The position of the adjective

(1) The long (attributive) adjective

(i) An attributive adjective normally precedes the noun it qualifies:

И вот — оди́н из **со́лнечных ию́ньских дней** (Tokareva)
And now it was one of those sunny June days

Note
(a)   See **484** (1) for stylistic variants.
(b)   The attributive adjective may follow the noun in menus, stock lists etc. (ко́фе натура́льный 'real coffee', рома́шка садо́вая 'garden camomile') and where the noun is generic (Еле́на — де́вушка у́мная 'Elena is an intelligent girl').
(c)   The long adjective follows the noun when used in **predicative** meaning: Он о́чень **молодо́й** (or мо́лод) 'he is very young'.

(ii) Contrary to English practice, circumstantial information may be placed in parenthesis between the attributive adjective and the noun:

Они́ жи́ли в большо́м, **с тремя́ этажа́ми и со мно́гими о́кнами**, особняке́
They lived in a large detached house **with three floors and many windows**

(iii) As in English, the adjective may follow the noun, standing in apposition to it and separated from it by a comma:

На на́рах лежа́л полушу́бок, **но́венький**, о́чень **наря́дный** (Bogomolov)
On the bunk lay a sheepskin coat, brand-new, very smart

(2) The short adjective

A short adjective normally follows the noun, as its predicate.

Note
See **484** (1) (i) for stylistic variants and **359** (3) (ii) note (a) for the
position of short-form perfective passive participles.

480   The position of the adverb

As a class which tends to convey *less essential* rather than *new*
information, adverbs more often than not *precede* the verb. The adverb
is usually positioned next to the verb it qualifies; in other positions it is
thrown into sharp relief, since it then normally conveys new, not given,
information and moves towards the end of the statement.

(1) Adverbs and adverbial phrases of time

(i) Adverbs of time usually *precede* the verb:

Он **всегда** ошибается	He always gets it wrong
Он **ещё не** проснулся	He has not woken up yet

Вы **до́лго** жда́ли? — спроси́л Криворучко (Rybakov)
'Did you have long to wait?', asked Krivoruchko

(ii) In descriptions of incidents and events, the adverb of time is usually
in initial position, followed by verb + subject, which jointly convey the
new information:

Вдруг разда́лся вы́стрел (Rybakov)
Suddenly a shot rang out

(iii) However, adverbs and adverbial phrases that convey essential *new*
information appear in *final* position: e.g. the question **Когда́** экипа́жи
соверши́ли пе́рвый совме́стный полёт? '**When** did the crews make
the first joint flight?' can be answered as follows:

Экипа́жи соверши́ли пе́рвый совме́стный полёт **в ию́ле 1975
го́да**
The crews carried out the first joint flight in July 1975

(2) Adverbs and adverbial phrases of place

(i) Adverbs and adverbial phrases of place also normally appear in
initial position as incidental or *given* information, preceding the *new*
information conveyed either by the subject alone or by the verb +

subject:

В го́роде два теа́тра
There are two theatres **in the town**

Из служе́бного зда́ния вы́шел высо́кий вя́лый челове́к (Greko-va)
A tall sluggish-looking man left **the service building**

(ii) However, adverbs of place that report *new* information appear in *final* position: e.g. the question **Где** располо́жена Кра́сная пло́щадь? 'Where is Red Square situated?' can be answered as follows:

Кра́сная пло́щадь располо́жена **в це́нтре Москвы́**
Red Square is situated in the centre of Moscow

(3) Adverbs and adverbial phrases of manner and degree

(i) Adverbs of manner and degree in **-o/-e** usually precede the verb or adjective:

Он **хорошо́** говори́т
He speaks well

— А вы отку́да? — **дружелю́бно** спроси́л Тёткин (Grekova)
'And where are you from?', asked Tetkin amicably

Она́ **и́скренне** ра́да нам
She is genuinely glad to see us

Compare also adverbs of the type по-дру́жески: Он **по-дру́жески** пожа́л мне ру́ку 'He shook my hand in a friendly manner'. However, adverbs of nationality and language normally *follow* the verb: Он понима́ет **по-ру́сски** 'He understands Russian'.

(ii) A number of other adverbs of manner and degree, e.g. **во́все не** 'not at all', **едва́** 'barely', and analogous prepositional phrases also precede the verb, cf.:

Она́ **в спе́шке** забы́ла подня́ть кни́гу
In her haste she forgot to pick up the book

481 Sentences that contain more than one adverb or adverbial phrase

The normal sequence for different types of adverb and adverbial phrase appearing within the same sentence is as follows:

1 adverbs/adverbial phrases of *time*
2 adverbs/adverbial phrases of *place*
3 other types of adverb/adverbial phrase (*manner, cause* etc.):

Среди́ но́чи к пере́днему кра́ю оборо́ны тайко́м подкра́лся солда́т-разве́дчик
In the middle of the night a reconnaissance scout stealthily crept up to the front line

Ка́ждый час в на́шей стране́ от боле́зни се́рдца умира́ет 80 челове́к (*Ogonek*)
Every hour 80 people in our country die of heart disease

Неда́вно в Москве́ проводи́лся кинофестива́ль
A film festival was held recently in Moscow

В Росси́и бы́стро вы́росли города́ и сёла
Towns and villages sprang up quickly in Russia

482 The position of the noun or pronoun in impersonal constructions

The accusative or dative noun or pronoun normally occupies initial position in impersonal expressions, with *new* information in final position:

Бра́та лихора́дит	My brother is feverish
Дом зажгло́	The house caught fire
Та́нюшке во́семь лет	Tanyushka is eight years old
Мне хо́лодно	I feel cold
Ей пришло́сь бежа́ть	She had to run
Нам нельзя́ бы́ло кури́ть	We were not allowed to smoke

Note
The same order applies to constructions with **нра́виться/по-** and with **ну́жен, нужна́, ну́жно, нужны́**: Взро́слым понра́вился фильм 'The adults liked the film', Студе́нту нужны́ де́ньги 'The student needs money'. Reversal of this order throws the noun or pronoun into sharp relief: Фильм понра́вился **взро́слым (, но не де́тям)** 'The **adults** liked the film (, but the **children** didn't)'; Де́ньги нужны́ **мне (, а не ей)** 'I need the money (, and she **doesn't**)'.

483   The position of particles in the sentence

For the position of particles see **469.**

484   Word order in expressive styles

A departure from neutral word order may create an expressive, emotionally charged style which is particularly characteristic of *spoken* Russian. Most parts of speech are involved:

(1) Adjectives

(i) In expressive styles short predicative adjectives may *precede* the noun, while in neutral style they *follow* the noun:

Лёгок вопро́с, **незначи́тельна** фигу́ра студе́нта (Rybakov)
The question is simple, the figure of the student insignificant (cf. neutral word order Вопро́с лёгок, фигу́ра студе́нта незначи́тельна)

(ii) This also applies to short-form participles:

Решён вопро́с о вы́ходе диспе́тчеров на пе́нсию в во́зрасте 55 лет (*Literaturnaya gazeta*)
The question of retirement for air traffic controllers at age 55 has been resolved (cf. neutral order Вопро́с решён)

(iii) Conversely, attributive adjectives may *follow* the noun in expressive styles, whereas in neutral style they precede it:

Техни́ческое оснаще́ние, коне́чно, де́ло **ва́жное** (*Literaturnaya gazeta*)
Technical equipment is, of course, an important matter (cf. neutral word order ва́жное де́ло)

Compare also displacement of the adjective in:

— Да, **комфорта́бельной** э́ту маши́ну не назовёшь (Grekova)
'No, you wouldn't exactly call this vehicle comfortable'

(iv) Another expressive device is to place the verb between the attributive adjective and the noun:

Уда́чная была́ охо́та!   That **was** a successful hunt!

(2) Verb + subject

In expressive styles, *new* information may precede *given*, a reversal of neutral order:

У меня голова́ боли́т
I have a headache (cf. neutral У меня́ боли́т голова́)

Кто звони́л? **Мари́на звони́ла**
Who rang? Marina rang (cf. neutral Звони́ла Мари́на)

(3) Adverbs

(i) The order of adverbs/adverbial phrases may be reversed in expressive styles:

Хо́лодно сего́дня
It is cold today (cf. neutral Сего́дня хо́лодно)

Стально́й зуб сверка́л у него́ во рту (Rybakov)
A steel tooth glittered in his mouth (cf. neutral У него́ во рту сверка́л стально́й зуб)

(ii) Compare also the displacement of adverbs in their function as introductory words:

Смотре́ть э́тот фильм **стра́шно и сты́дно** (*Ekran detyam*)
It is terrible and embarrassing to see this film (cf. neutral Стра́шно и сты́дно смотре́ть э́тот фильм)

(4) Pronouns

The pronoun may *follow* the predicate in expressive styles, often with a concomitant change of emphasis:

— Хоро́шая пе́сня, — сказа́л Марк.
— То́лько **поёте вы́** её пло́хо, заме́тила Со́фья Алекса́ндровна (Rybakov)
'Nice song', said Mark.
'Except that **you** don't sing it very well', remarked Sofia Aleksandrovna (cf. neutral вы пло́хо её поёте)

Что сде́лал **ты́**?
What did **you** do? (cf. neutral Что ты сде́лал?)

GLOSSARY

The glossary contains brief definitions of the most important grammatical terms used in the book. Additional information may be obtained through the subject index.

Acronyms — words formed from the initial letters of other words: **вуз** from **вы́сшее уче́бное заведе́ние** 'higher educational institution' (HEI).

Adjectival nouns — words that have the form of adjectives but function as nouns: **столо́вая** 'dining room'.

Adjectives — parts of speech that qualify or describe a noun or pronoun: **большо́й** дом 'a **large** house' (long, attributive, form), она́ **голодна́** 'she is **hungry**' (short, predicative, form).

Adverbs — parts of speech that modify a verb: он бежа́л **бы́стро** 'he ran **quickly**', an adjective: **неожи́данно** хоро́ший '**unexpectedly** good', or another adverb: **кра́йне** ме́дленно '**extremely** slowly'.

Agent nouns — nouns denoting persons who perform an action: **писа́тель** 'a writer'.

Agreement — convention that (a) adjectives, pronouns and numerals should be in the same *case* as the noun they qualify: они живу́т в **двух больши́х пала́тках** 'they live in two large tents'; (b) adjectives, nouns, pronouns and verbs should share the same *gender*: **ста́рая соба́ка спала́** 'the old dog was asleep', and *number* (singular or plural): **э́тот ма́льчик был** до́ма '**this boy was** at home', **э́ти ма́льчики бы́ли** до́ма '**these boys were** at home'.

Alphabetisms — words comprising initial capital letters which are pronounced as letters of the alphabet: РФ [эр-э́ф] (Росси́йская Федера́ция) 'RF' (Russian Federation) or as words: **ВИЧ** [вич] (ви́рус иммунодефици́та челове́ка) 'HIV'.

Apposition — a situation in which a series of nouns or noun phrases denote the same object or person and thus share the same grammatical case: она́ за́мужем за **мои́м бра́том Ива́ном** 'she is married to **my brother Ivan**'.

Aspect — a grammatical feature of the Russian verb that distinguishes repeated or durative actions (expressed by the **imperfective** aspect: он **пьёт** 'he **drinks**', она́ **писа́ла** 'she **was writing**') from actions that denote initiation (он **запла́кал** 'he **began weeping**'), conclusion or result (она́ **заведёт** часы́ 'she **will wind up** the clock'), or short duration (де́ти **поспа́ли** 'the children **had a nap**').

Attributive adjective — the full (long) form of an adjective, usually appearing before the noun, qualifying it and agreeing with it in gender, case and number: она́ добра́ к **мла́дшему бра́ту** 'she is kind to **her younger brother**', она́ дово́льна **приле́жными ученика́ми** 'she is pleased with the **diligent pupils**'.

Augmentative nouns — suffixed nouns that denote largeness: ры́б-**ина** 'a **large fish**'.

Cardinal numerals — the basic numbers denoting quantity: **оди́н** дом 'one house', **два** карандаша́ '**two** pencils', etc.

Case — the form of a noun, pronoun or adjective that shows its grammatical relationship to other words in the sentence: он смо́трит на **мою́ сестру́** 'he is looking at **my sister**' (accusative case), она́ сиде́ла в **са́мом удо́бном кре́сле** (prepositional/locative case) 'she was sitting in **the most comfortable armchair**', etc.

Collective nouns — nouns that denote a collection or group of beings or things: **скот** 'cattle', **листва́** 'foliage'.

Comparative degree — the second degree of comparison in the series 'positive' (e.g. **у́мный** 'clever'), 'comparative' (e.g. **бо́лее у́мный** 'cleverer') and 'superlative' (e.g. **са́мый у́мный** 'cleverest').

Compound — a word created by joining together two or more other words or forms: **книголю́б** 'book-lover', **виноградосоковыжима́лка** 'grape-juice squeezer'.

Conditionals — verb forms that express conditions or hypotheses: **е́сли бы я знал, я сказа́л бы вам** 'if I **knew**, I **would tell** you'.

Conjunctions — parts of speech that join words, phrases or clauses: соба́ки **и** ко́шки 'dogs **and** cats', молодо́й, **но** о́пытный 'young **but** experienced', го́лоден, **потому́ что** не за́втракал 'hungry **because** he hasn't had breakfast', etc.

Declension — the process of adding endings to the stems of nouns, adjectives, pronouns and numerals to indicate their grammatical relationship to other words in the sentence: цвет кро́в-**и** 'the colour of blood', разошли́сь по ра́зн-**ым** причи́н-**ам** 'separated for various reasons', обе́дал с пять-**ю́** друзь-**я́ми** 'dined with five friends'.

Diminutives — suffixed forms of nouns and adjectives that denote smallness: бле́дн-**енькое** ли́ч-**ико** 'a pale little face'.

Direct object — noun or pronoun that denotes the person or thing affected by the action of a verb: она́ нака́зывает **его́** 'she punishes **him**', он чита́ет **кни́гу** 'he is reading **a book**'.

Fleeting vowels — vowels that interrupt a sequence of consonants but are lost in declension: ры́нок 'market' (genitive ры́нка).

Gender — the classification of words, in accordance with their endings, as masculine (дом 'house', музе́й 'museum' [zero endings]), feminine (маши́н-**а** 'car', неде́л-**я** 'week') or neuter (окн-**о́** 'window', по́л-**е** 'field').

Gerund (verbal adverb) — indeclinable verb form that fulfils an adverbial function, replacing a co-ordinate or adverbial clause: он сиди́т, **чита́я** 'he sits **reading**' (= and reads), **прочита́в** кни́гу, я поста́вил её на по́лку '**having read** (= after I had read) the book I put it on the shelf'.

Imperative — verb form used to express commands: **Слу́шай! 'Listen!'**

Imperfective verb — a verb that denotes a past, present or future action (a) in progress: она́ **вела́** маши́ну 'she **was driving** a car', я **бу́ду отдыха́ть** 'I **will be relaxing**' or (b) repeated: он **звони́т** ей раз в неде́лю 'he **rings** her once a week'.

Impersonal constructions — constructions that have no subject: **хо́лодно** 'it is cold', ему́ **повезло́** 'he is in **luck**', **говоря́т**, что '**it is said** that', etc.

Indefinite numerals — numerals that denote an imprecise quantity: **мно́го** де́нег '**a lot of** money', **не́сколько** челове́к '**a few** people'.

Indefinite pronouns — pronouns that refer to unspecified persons or things: кто́-то 'someone', что́-нибудь 'something, anything'.

Indirect object — person or object indirectly affected by an action, e.g. benefiting from it: он подари́л ку́клу **де́вочке** 'he gave the doll [direct object] **to the little girl** [indirect object]'.

Infinitive — the basic form of a verb: **чита́ть/прочита́ть** 'to read'.

Intransitive verbs — verbs that do not require an object in order to express their meaning: он **лежа́л** на полу́ 'he **was lying** on the floor'.

Modals — forms that denote necessity, possibility or impossibility: он **до́лжен** рабо́тать 'he **must** work', ей **ну́жно** отдыха́ть 'she **needs** to relax', он **не мог** отве́тить на вопро́с 'he **could not** answer the question'.

Mood — the manner in which the action of a verb expresses itself, allowing the action to be judged as real or unreal. Of the four moods, the **indicative** states a fact: он **копа́л** в саду́ 'he **was digging** in the garden', the **imperative** expresses a command: **Сотри́** с доски́! '**Clean the board!**', the **conditional/subjunctive** expresses a state, event or action as possible, conditional or desirable: **скоре́е бы ле́то** 'roll on summer', and the **infinitive** denotes the action of the verb in its most abstract form, without relation to person, time or number: **чита́ть** 'to read'.

Morphology — the study of linguistic forms: the declension of nouns, adjectives, pronouns and numerals, the conjugation of verbs, etc.

Mutation — sound changes caused by adjacent morphemes or words: т:ч in лете́ть 'to fly'/лечу́ 'I am flying'.

Nouns — words that name a person, thing or quality: **оте́ц** 'father', **стол** 'table', **любо́вь** 'love'.

Number — grammatical category that distinguishes whether a noun is singular (**кни́га 'book'**) or plural (**кни́ги 'books').**

Numerals — figures or words used to represent numbers, e.g. **три (3)** 'three'.

Oblique case — any case form of a noun, pronoun or adjective except for the nominative.

Ordinal numerals — numerals that express order or position in a series and are adjectival in form: **тре́тий** уро́к '**the third** lesson'.

Palatalization — the softening of a consonant by raising the centre of the tongue towards the hard palate during pronunciation. A palatalized or soft consonant is indicated by a following soft sign (ь), я, е, и, ё or ю: мать 'mother', пятёрка 'a five', люди 'people'.

Particles — indeclinable words that impart emotive or expressive nuances of meaning to other words, phrases or whole sentences: Что же ты делаешь? 'whatever are you doing?', Уж придумал! 'Now pull the other one!'.

Participles — verb forms that take the form of adjectives and (a) replace relative clauses: Мальчик, пишущий письмо (= который пишет письмо) 'A boy writing a letter (= who is writing a letter'), Дача, построенная соседями (= которую соседи построили) 'A country cottage built by the neighbours' (= which the neighbours built'), or (b) function as predicates: Вопрос решён 'The question has been solved'.

Partitive genitive — a genitive that indicates that only part of a substance is involved in an action or state: она выпила молока 'she drank some milk'.

Passive constructions — constructions in which the grammatical subject is the object of the action: водка делается из картофеля 'vodka is made from potatoes', он был спасён пожарником 'he was saved by a fireman'.

Perfective verb — verb that describes a completed action in the past (она подписала письмо 'she signed the letter') or anticipates its completion in the future (я закрою окно 'I will close the window').

Possessive pronouns — pronouns that denote possession: мой телефон 'my telephone number', её компьютер 'her computer'.

Predicate — that part of a sentence or phrase that conveys information about the subject: отец болен 'father is ill', дети пели песню 'the children were singing a song', мой брат стал солдатом 'my brother became a soldier'.

Prefix — form added to the beginning of a word to create a new word with a different meaning: перечитать 'to reread', спуск 'descent' or a different aspect: написать 'to write'.

Prepositions — words that precede a noun (or pronoun), expressing its relation to another word in the sentence: она из России 'she is from Russia', я разговаривал с гостями 'I was conversing with the guests'.

Pronouns — words used instead of nouns, to avoid repetition: где

Пётр? Вот **он** 'Where is Peter? There **he** is'.

Reflexive constructions — constructions in which subject and object refer to the same person or thing: он **мóется** 'he **washes (himself)'**.

Reflexive pronouns — pronouns that refer to the same person as the subject of the sentence: **он** довóлен **собóй** 'he is pleased with **himself'**, **онá** смóтрит на **себя́** в зéркало 'she looks at **herself** in the mirror'.

Relative pronouns — pronouns that refer back to a preceding noun (the antecedent): дéвочка, **котóрая** сдалá экзáмен 'the girl **who** passed the examination', кни́га, **котóрую** все читáют 'a book **(that)** everyone is reading'.

Root — an irreducible element of language from which other words are formed: **-да-** as in **дать** 'to give', издáтель 'publisher', продáжа 'sale', etc.

Semantics — the study of the meanings of words, morphemes, word groups, etc.

Stem — the root of a word, to which prefixes, suffixes and endings may be added: **-сух-** as in зáсуха 'drought', or the root and its variants: **-зр-** as in зри́тельный 'visual'/**-зер-** as in зéркало 'mirror'/**-зор-** as in обзóр 'survey', etc.

Stump compounds — abbreviations based on the abridged form of one or more words: **драгметáлл** (from **драгоцéнный метáлл**) 'precious metal', **спецхрáн** (from **специáльное храни́лище**) 'special storage area'.

Subject — the person about whom or the thing about which the sentence conveys information: **пóезд** остановúлся '**the train** stopped', **егó сестрá** вышла зáмуж '**his sister** got married', **мы** готóвы '**we** are ready'.

Subjunctive mood — a verb structure that presents a state, event or act as something desired: он хóчет, **чтóбы я голосовáл** 'he wants **me to vote**', or hypothetical: я не пóмню, **чтóбы** он хоть раз **ошúбся** 'I don't remember **him** even once **making a mistake**'.

Suffixes — forms added to the end of a word or stem to create a new word: социал**ú**зм 'social**ism**'.

Superlative degree — *see* Comparative degree

Syntax — the set of rules that determines the grammatical arrangement of words in a sentence to show their relationship to each other (e.g. the relationship of verbs, adjectives and prepositions to the case of the noun they govern: **подражáть** 'to imitate' + dative, **довóлен** 'satisfied' + instrumental, **из** 'from' + genitive, etc.).

Tense — verb form that denotes the time of an action (past, present or future): они́ **вы́играли** 'they **won**', я **слу́шаю** 'I **am listening**', мы **начнём** 'we **will begin**'.

Transitive verbs — verbs which can express their meaning only through government of a direct object: он **снимáет пальтó** 'he **takes off his coat**'.

Transliteration — representation of the spelling of a word using the letters of a different alphabet: **perestroika** (transliteration of перестрóйка 'restructuring'), **Solzhenitsyn** (transliteration of Солжени́цын).

Unvoiced (voiceless) consonants — consonants pronounced without vibration of the vocal cords: **п, к, с, т, ф, ш** and others.

Verbs — parts of speech that denote an action (он **печáтает** 'he **is typing**') or state (онá **жилá** на ю́ге 'she **lived** in the south').

Voiced consonants — consonants pronounced with vibration of the vocal cords: **б, г, з, д, в, ж** and others.

Bibliography

Dictionaries

Russian Monolingual

Chernyshev, V. I. et al. (eds), *Словарь современного русского языка*, 17 vols, Академия наук, Moscow, 1950–65.

Evgen'eva, A. P. et al. (eds), *Словарь русского языка,* 4 vols, 2nd edn, Русский язык, Moscow, 1983.

Levashov, E. A., (ed.), *Новые слова и значения. Словарь-справочник по материалам прессы и литературы 80-х годов.* Дмитрий Буланин, St Petersburg, 1997.

Ozhegov, S. I., Shvedova, N. Yu., *Толковый словарь русского языка,* 4th edn, Азбуковник, Moscow, 1997.

Sklyarevskaya, G. N. (ed.), *Толковый словарь русского языка конца XX века*, Фолио-Пресс, St Petersburg, 1998.

Russian–English/English–Russian

Ozieva, A. et al., *Russian – English, English – Russian Dictionary,* HarperCollins, Glasgow, 1994.

Wheeler, M., Unbegaun, B. and Falla, P., eds, *The Oxford Russian Dictionary. Russian–English, English–Russian*, further rev. edn, Oxford University Press, Oxford, 1986.

Special-purpose

Avanesov, R. I. (ed), *Орфоэпический словарь русского языка,* 3rd edn, Русский язык, Moscow, 1987.

Efremov, T. F. and Kostomarov, V. G., *Словарь грамматических трудностей русского языка,* Русский язык, Moscow, 1986.

Kovalenko, E. G. (ed.), *Новый словарь сокращений русского языка,* ЭТС, Moscow, 1995.

Ledenev, S. D. et al., *Большой словарь русского языка,* Дрофа/ Русский язык, Moscow, 1998.

Lopatin, V. V. et al., *Орфографический словарь русского языка,* 36th edn., Русский язык, Moscow, 1996.

Treshnikov, A. F., principal ed., *Географический энциклопедический словарь,* Советская энциклопедия, Moscow, 1983.

Tsyganenko, G. P., *Словарь служебных морфем русского языка,* Радянська школа, Kiev, 1982.

Zaliznyak, A. A., *Грамматический словарь русского языка,* Русский язык, Moscow, 1977.

Grammars

Miloslavsky, I. G., *Краткая практическая грамматика русского языка,* Русский язык, Moscow, 1987.

Shvedova, N. Yu. and Lopatin, V. V., *Краткая русская грамматика,* 2nd rev. edn, Русский язык, Moscow, 1990.

Shvedova, N. Yu. et al. (eds), *Русская грамматика,* 2 vols, Наука, Moscow, 1982.

Other books on language

Amiantova, E. I. et al., *Сборник упражнений по лексике русского языка,* Русский язык, Moscow, 1989.

Barykina, A. N., Dobrovol'skaya, V. V. and Merzon, S. N., *Изучение глагольных приставок,* Русский язык, Moscow, 1979.

Bel'dyushkin, V. S. et al., *Adverbial Relations in Russian and Their English Equivalents,* Русский язык, Moscow, 1988.

Bivon, R., *Element Order* (Studies in the Modern Russian Language 7),

Cambridge University Press, Cambridge, 1971.

Borras, F. M. and Christian, R. F., *Russian Syntax*, 2nd edn, The Clarendon Press, Oxford, 1979.

Bratus, B. V., *The Formation and Expressive Use of Diminutives* (Studies in the Modern Russian Language 6), Cambridge University Press, Cambridge, 1969.

Comrie, B., Stone, G. and Polinsky, M., *The Russian Language in the 20th Century* (2nd rev. edn of Comrie, B. and Stone, G., *The Russian Language since the Revolution*), Clarendon Press, Oxford, 1996.

Cubberley, P., *Handbook of Russian Affixes*, Slavica Publishers, Columbus, Ohio, 1994.

Dulichenko, A. D., *Русский язык конца XX столетия*, Otto Sagner, Munich, 1994.

Graudina, L. K., *Вопросы нормализации русского языка*, Наука, Moscow, 1980.

Graudina, L. K., Itskovich, V. A. and Katlinskaya, L. P., *Граммати-ческая правильность русской речи*, Наука, Moscow, 1976.

Harrison, W., *Expression of the Passive Voice* (Studies in the Modern Russian Language 4, in one volume with J. Mullen, *Agreement of the Verb-Predicate with a Collective Subject*), Cambridge University Press, Cambridge, 1967.

Kaidalova, A. I. and Kalinina, I. K., *Современная русская орфогра-фия*, Высшая школа, Moscow, 1983.

Karaulov, Yu. N. (ed.), *Русистика сегодня, функционирование в язы-ке: лексика и грамматика*, Наука, Moscow, 1993.

Klepko, V., *A Practical Handbook on Stress in Russian*, Dover Publications, New York, 1977.

Kokhtev, N. N. and Rozental', D. E., *Популярная стилистика русского языка*, Русский язык, Moscow, 1984.

Kostomarov, V. G., *Языковой вкус эпохи*, 3rd, rev. edn, Златоуст, St Petersburg, 1999.

Krylova, O. and Khavronina, S., *Word Order in Russian Sentences*,

Русский язык, Moscow, 1976.

Miloslavsky, I. G., *Зачем нужна грамматика?*, Просвещение, Moscow, 1988.

Murav'eva, L. S., *Verbs of Motion in Russian*, Русский язык, Moscow, 1975.

Mustajoki, A., Heino, H., *Case Selection for the Direct Object in Russian Negative Clauses*, University of Helsinki Press, Helsinki, 1991.

Offord, D., *Using Russian. A Guide to Contemporary Usage*, Cambridge University Press, Cambridge, 1996.

Panov, M. V. (ed.), *Русский язык и советское общество. Социолого-лингвистическое исследование* (monograph comprising four books), Наука, Moscow, 1968.

Rakhmanova, L. and Suzdal'tseva, V. N., *Современный русский язык*, ЧеРо, Moscow, 1997.

Rassudova, O. P., *Aspectual Usage in Modern Russian*, Русский язык, Moscow, 1984.

Rozental', D. E., *А как лучше сказать?*, Просвещение, Moscow, 1979.

Rozental', D. E., *Прописная или строчная?*, Русский язык, Moscow, 1984.

Rozental', D. E., *Управление в русском языке*, Книга, Moscow, 1986.

Ryazanova-Clarke, L. and Wade, T., *The Russian Language Today*, Routledge, London, 1999.

Shapiro, A. B., *Пунктуация*, 2nd edn, Просвещение, Moscow, 1974.

Shaposhnikov, V. N., *Русская речь 90-х. Современная Россия в языковом отображении*, МАЛП, Moscow, 1998

Shilova, K. A. and Usmanova, E. E., *100 диалогов по телефону*, Русский язык, Moscow, 1988.

Skvortsov, L. I. (principal editor), Itskovich, V. A. and Mis'kevich, G. I., *Грамматика и норма*, Наука, Moscow, 1977.

Vakurov, V. N., et al., *Трудности русского языка*, 2 vols., МГУ, Moscow, 1993–4.

Vasilenko, E., Egorova, A. and Lamm, E., *Russian Verb Aspects*, Русский язык, Moscow, 1988.

Vasil'eva, A. N., *Particles in Colloquial Russian*, Progress Publishers, Moscow, undated.

Vinogradov, V. V., *Русский язык*, Высшая школа, Moscow, 1972.

Vsevolodova, M. V. and Parshukova, Z. G., *Способы выражения пространственных отношений*, МГУ, Moscow, 1968.

Wade, T., *The Gender of Soft-Sign Nouns in Russian*, Collets International, London, 1988.

Wade, T., *Prepositions in Modern Russian*, Durham Modern Language Series, 1983.

Ward, D., *Russian Pronunciation*, Oliver and Boyd, Edinburgh and London, 1958.

Ward, D., *The Russian Language Today. System and Anomaly*, Hutchinson, London, 1965.

Zemskaya, E. A., *Словообразование как деятельность*, Наука, Moscow, 1992.

Zemskaya, E.A. (ed.), *Русский язык конца XX столетия (1985–1995)*, Языки русской культуры, Moscow, 1996

Language journals

Russian-language

Вопросы языкознания
Русистика сегодня
Русская речь
Русский язык за рубежом
Русский язык в СНГ
Русский язык в школе
Филологические науки

Others

Journal of Russian Studies
Rusistika
Russistik

Newspapers and magazines

Аргументы и факты
Известия
Итоги
Комсомольская правда
Литературная газета
Московский комсомолец
Московские новости
Неделя
Независимая газета
Огонек
Правда
Работница
Сельская жизнь
Семья
Спутник
Экран детям
Юный натуралист

Wade, T. and White, N., *Russia Today*, 2 vols and glossary, University of Strathclyde, Glasgow, 1985 (press extracts).

Literary and other sources

By individual or joint authors

Abramov, F., *Дом*, Советский писатель, Leningrad, 1980.
Belyakova, E., *В семье растут дети*, Русский язык, Moscow, 1983.
Dovlatov, S., *Заповедник*, Новый Геликон, St Petersburg, 1996.
Dovlatov, S., *Зона*, Новый Геликон, St Petersburg, 1996.

Gagarin, S., *Возвращение в Итаку*, Молодая гвардия, Moscow, 1972.

Granin, D., *Сад камней*, Современник, Moscow, 1972.

Grekova, I., *Пороги*, Советский писатель, Moscow, 1986.

Kazakov, Yu., *Selected Short Stories*, Pergamon, Oxford, 1963.

Koluntsev, F., *Ожидание*, Советский писатель, Moscow, 1969.

Kovaleva, L., *Создана семья . . .*, Лениздат, Leningrad, 1982.

Kunin, V., *Иванов и Рабинович*, Новый Геликон/Интерспект, St Petersburg, 1994.

Marinina, A., *Убийца поневоле*, Вече, Moscow, 1997.

Nabokov, V., *Защита Лужина*, Фолио, Kharkov/АСТ, Moscow, 1997.

Nikolaev, V., *Не один в пути*, Молодая гвардия, Moscow, 1974.

Orlov, V., *Серый парус карбаса*, Знание, Moscow, 1984.

Propp, V., *Русская сказка*, Издательство Ленинградского университета, Leningrad, 1984.

Rasputin, V., *Последний срок. Прощание с Матерой*, Советский писатель, Moscow, 1985.

Rubina, D., '*Завтра, как обычно . . .*', Юность, July 1984, 26–47.

Rybakov, A., *Дети Арбата*, Советский писатель, Moscow, 1987.

Rybakov, A., *Тяжелый песок*, Советский писатель, Moscow, 1979.

Shukshin, V., *Рассказы*, Русский язык, Moscow, 1984.

Strugatsky, A. and Strugatsky, B., *Понедельник начинается в субботу*, Юнацва, Minsk, 1986.

Tendryakov, V., *Находка*, Советская Россия, Moscow, 1966.

Tendryakov, V., *Поденка — век короткий* (and other works), Молодая гвардия, Moscow, 1969.

Tokareva, V., *Повести и рассказы*, Советский писатель, Moscow, 1987.

Trifonov, Yu., *Избранные произведения*, 2 vols, Художественная литература, Moscow, 1978.

Trifonov, Yu., *Утоление жажды*, Профиздат, Moscow, 1979.

Zalygin, S., *Южноамериканский вариант*, Московский рабочий, Moscow, 1987.

Compilations

Lebedev, V. (compiler), *Стратегия освоения*, Молодая гвардия, Moscow, 1986.

Pecheritsa, T. (compiler), *Дороги. Рассказы советских писателей*, Русский язык, Moscow, 1979 (Yu. Kazakov, Yu. Nagibin, K. Paustovsky, P. Proskurin, V. Shukshin etc.).

Povolyaev, V. (compiler), *Московский рассказ*, Московский рабочий, Moscow, 1980 (Yu. Avdeenko, Yu. Kazakov, E. Khrutsky,

A. Kuleshov, A. Makarov, Yu. Nagibin, V. Povolyaev, L. Sal'nikov, Yu. Trifonov, L. Uvarova, K. Vanshenkin, A. Yakhontov etc.).

Smirnov, V. (compiler), *Белый конь*, Русский язык, Moscow, 1985 (F. Abramov, V. Astaf'ev, V. Belov, V. Lebedev, E. Nosov, V. Shcherbakov, V. Shukshin, V. Sobolev, P. Vasil'ev, S. Zalygin etc.).

Zolotavkin, V. (compiler), *Проза 70-х годов*, Русский язык, Moscow, 1985 (F. Abramov, C. Aitmatov, V. Belov, D. Granin, Yu. Kazakov, Yu. Nagibin, V. Shukshin, K. Simonov, V. Soloukhin, V. Tokareva, S. Zalygin etc.).

Note

Some quotations have been taken from standard grammars of the Russian language.

Subject Index

Note: references are to *page* numbers. When English and Russian words appear together in a list, account is taken of the order of letters in both alphabets.

Word Index

The *Word Index* does not include every word that appears in the *Grammar*. It is intended to interact with the *Contents* and the *Subject Index* to facilitate access to all parts of the book. It contains all verbs with a difficult conjugation, all prepositions, conjunctions, particles, verbs and adjectives which take an oblique case, prefixes, many suffixes and other endings, and additional words and forms which illustrate significant grammatical points.

Words which appear in lists are not normally included. Thus, instead of enumerating nouns which have a locative in -ý, only the ending -ý appears in the *Word Index*, as a guide to relevant nouns. This principle is adhered to throughout the *Word Index*.

Many verb forms can be traced through their infinitives, and the forms of many nouns, pronouns, adjectives and numerals through their nominative case.

The Word Index contains references to stress patterns, except for stress in prepositions (for prepositional stress see pages 419–21).

All references are to page numbers.

Note

ГАИ [гай] (Госуда́рственная автомоби́льная инспе́кция) 'State Vehicle Inspectorate' (see pp. 61 and 99) has now been replaced by **ГИБДД** [ги-бэ-дэ-дэ́] (Госуда́рственная инспе́кция безопа́сности доро́жного движе́ния) 'State Road Traffic Safety Inspectorate'

ALSO AVAILABLE FROM BLACKWELL PUBLISHERS:

A Russian Grammar Workbook

by Terence Wade
University of Strathclyde

"An outstanding contribution to Russian studies . . . I am sure it will quickly become an essential handbook for all serious students of Russian in the English-speaking world and beyond."

Dr Margaret Tejerizo, University of Glasgow

"Terence Wade's A Comprehensive Russian Grammar rapidly became a standard text for students after its publication in 1992. The present volume complements the Grammar but can be used either in conjunction with it or independently. Over 230 exercises reflect every grammatical point and include grammatical quizzes and translation texts. The book is well set out with clear, largish print for ease of perusal."

British East-West Journal

Developing on the success of his widely-acclaimed textbook, *A Comprehensive Russian Grammar*, Terence Wade provides a workbook for all English-speaking students of Russian. The *Workbook* can be used either as a companion volume to the reference grammar, or independently. Exercises range from substitution drills and multiple choice to grammatical quizzes and translation exercises, with every important grammatical point illustrated and explored.

A Russian Grammar Workbook offers a structured and stimulating approach to the study of Russian for learners at all levels.

Contents:
Preface; 1. The Noun; 2. The Pronoun; 3. The Adjective; 4. The Numeral; 5. The Verb; 6. The Adverb; 7. The Preposition; 8. The Conjunction; 9. The Particle; 10. Word Order; Key.

246 x 171 mm, 252 pages
0-631-19381-2, paperback, 1995

This book can be bought through your local bookshop, or you can order a copy by calling Marston Book Services on (0)1235 465500 for orders outside the Americas, or by calling (800) 216-2522 (toll-free in North America) if ordering from North or South America.

Or visit our website at www.blackwellpublishers.co.uk